Introduction to Management

Introduction to Management

Functions and Challenges

Edited by
Sarah Birrell Ivory and Emma Macdonald

OXFORD
UNIVERSITY PRESS

Great Clarendon Street, Oxford, OX2 6DP,
United Kingdom

Oxford University Press is a department of the University of Oxford.
It furthers the University's objective of excellence in research, scholarship,
and education by publishing worldwide. Oxford is a registered trade mark of
Oxford University Press in the UK and in certain other countries

Published in the United States of America by Oxford University Press
198 Madison Avenue, New York, NY 10016, United States of America

British Library Cataloguing in Publication Data
Data available

Library of Congress Control Number: 2023946449

ISBN 978-0-19-289351-2

Printed in the UK by
Bell & Bain Ltd., Glasgow

PREFACE

Welcome to *Introduction to Management: Functions and Challenges*. We wrote this text for a number of reasons. The primary one was to inspire students to enjoy the study of management as much as we do. Finding enjoyment in the study of anything is the key to success. It makes the work that is necessary to take on board new ways of thinking not a chore, but, ideally, a joy.

More specifically, we believe passionately in the importance of thinking as a key aspect of learning. By this, we mean that education should be about improving both your thinking skills and your confidence in thinking for yourself. Gaining foundational knowledge is important, but it should be learnt in the service of better and more critical thinking—not instead of that aim.

The study of management, with its many different contexts and challenges, provides a rich and exciting field to introduce, apply, and practise thinking. As we mention in Chapter 1, there is no simple 'how-to' guide to becoming a manager. The study of management is nuanced and complex, and open for debate, discussion, and difference of opinion.

Management is also a vital societal function that affects the world around us. Almost every human on the planet will be subject to, or impacted by, decisions made by a person in management. This is one of the reasons that Part 1 of the book looks not at management per se, but at the context in which management happens. Studying management in isolation would neglect an appreciation for management as a contributor to a thriving society (or, unfortunately, in some instances, to an unstable society).

If we could ask one thing of every student working through this text, it is to keep an open mind to the different ideas, opinions, and world views that you encounter both in this text and in your lectures and tutorials. We learn so much by questioning the world around us, and also by questioning ourselves and the assumptions we bring to our studies.

We wish you much joy as you start this journey of reading and learning about management. We hope you find your studies valuable in understanding the approaches to management that you observe as you move through the world—and inspirational in deciding what kind of manager *you* want to be when faced with the opportunity in your professional or personal life.

GUIDE TO USING THIS BOOK

Introduction to Management is a uniquely accessible and engaging companion to managing in the real world. Placing issues of digital, environmental, and social disruption at the centre stage, it guides you through the varied and complex reality of management with ease, encouraging you to develop your own critical view of this dynamic area. Outlined here are the key features included in the text to help you understand each topic and, importantly, help you to apply this knowledge and translate theory into practice.

OPENING CASE STUDY

Gain real-world insights from the start. Each chapter kicks off with an engaging opening case study, placing you right in the heart of a real-world organization from across the private, public, and third sectors. By connecting theory with real scenarios, you'll be equipped with a practical perspective to apply your knowledge.

RUNNING CASE STUDY

Experience management principles in action. Follow a fictional organization throughout the text with our running case study, and learn how each chapter's concepts come alive in a practical setting.

SPOTLIGHT

Delve deeper into captivating topics. The spotlight features dotted throughout the text delve deeper into key areas, highlighting complexities and nuance, to give you a complete understanding of each topic.

CHAPTER SUMMARY

Consolidate your learning. Chapter summaries offer concise overviews of the key points, distilling each chapter into memorable takeaways.

CLOSING CASE REFLECTION

Reflect on your learning journey. The closing case reflection revisits the opening case study, encouraging you to connect the dots by analysing how what you've learned applies directly to that real-world organization.

REVIEW QUESTIONS

Assess your progress and challenge yourself. The review questions provided at the end of each chapter test your knowledge and encourage analytical thinking. They serve as valuable tools to evaluate your understanding and mastery of the key management concepts.

EXPLORE MORE

Expand your horizons and deepen your knowledge. The 'Explore more' feature offers a curated selection of additional resources. Discover recommended readings, thought-provoking videos, and many more resources that will enrich your understanding of management.

ORGANIZATION CHART FOR IMPERIAL FINE FOODS

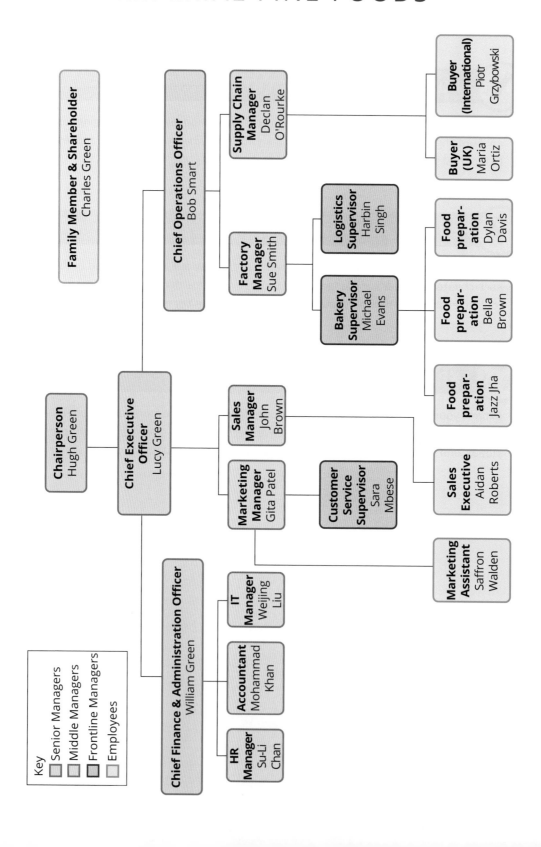

Key
- Senior Managers
- Middle Managers
- Frontline Managers
- Employees

Family Member & Shareholder — Charles Green

Chairperson — Hugh Green

Chief Executive Officer — Lucy Green

Chief Operations Officer — Bob Smart

Chief Finance & Administration Officer — William Green

Supply Chain Manager — Declan O'Rourke

Factory Manager — Sue Smith

Buyer (International) — Piotr Grzybowski

Buyer (UK) — Maria Ortiz

Logistics Supervisor — Harbin Singh

Bakery Supervisor — Michael Evans

Food preparation — Dylan Davis

Food preparation — Bella Brown

Food preparation — Jazz Jha

Sales Manager — John Brown

Marketing Manager — Gita Patel

Customer Service Supervisor — Sara Mbese

Sales Executive — Aidan Roberts

Marketing Assistant — Saffron Walden

IT Manager — Weijing Liu

Accountant — Mohammad Khan

HR Manager — Su-Li Chan

ACKNOWLEDGEMENTS

Sarah Birrell Ivory

First and foremost, thanks are due to every student I have ever taught: I have learned so much from all of you. I would also like to acknowledge all of the academic and professional services staff at the University of Edinburgh, and the Business School in particular, who have supported my passion for effective and engaging teaching. In relation to this textbook, thanks to Todd Bridgman, Stephen Cummings, and Owen Kelly for their contributions, to all the chapter authors, to the practitioners who have contributed their thoughts via video, to our Running case author David Paulson, to my co-author Emma Macdonald, and to our fantastic OUP editor, Anna Galasinska. It has been a pleasure working with all of you on this mammoth task. Finally, thanks to my family, Mark, Lachie, and Amy, who are a constant source of support.

Emma Macdonald

Thank you to the many students and professionals with whom I have spent time in the classroom teaching and learning from at Warwick Business School, Cranfield School of Management, and Strathclyde Business School. Thank you to the organizations who have invited me inside to study and learn from them. It has been a pleasure to work with a team of knowledgeable and thoughtful co-authors on the chapters and case studies in this text. Thank you especially to David Paulson for his insightful storytelling. A massive thank you to my co-editor, Sarah Ivory for her vision and energy and to our OUP editor, Anna Galasinska for being wise and calm. As always, I am indebted to my beautiful family, Brett and Marion.

The publisher

EDITORIAL ADVISORY PANEL

The authors and Oxford University Press would like to thank the many members of the academic community whose generous and insightful feedback helped to shape this text, including those who wished to remain anonymous.

Dr Sunday Adebola, Keele University

Dr Nathalie Benesova, University of Leeds

Dr Gemma Blackledge-Foughali, Queen Margaret University

Dr Minjie Cai, University of Greenwich

Ms Maeve Caraher, Dundalk Institute of Technology

Dr David Cross, Southampton Business School

Professor Wilfred Dolfsma, Wageningen University

Dr Yiorgos Gadanakis, University of Reading

Dr Marianna Koukou, University of Glasgow

Dr Tosin Lagoke, Oxford Brookes University

Dr Iain MacLeod, Robert Gordon University

Dr Natasha Katuta Mwila, De Montfort University

Dr Omid Omidvar, University of Warwick

Dr Stephen Robertson, Edinburgh Napier University

Dr Lubica Strakova, University of Portsmouth

Dr Sarah Warnes, University College London

ABOUT THE AUTHORS

Dr Sarah Birrell Ivory

Sarah is a Senior Lecturer in Climate Change and Business Strategy at the University of Edinburgh Business School. She has four degrees in business and management, and spent almost a decade as a manager prior to moving into academia. While she hails from Australia, she has spent 15 happy, but slightly colder years, living in Edinburgh with her husband, two children, dog, and cat.

Dr Emma K. Macdonald

Emma is Charles Huang Chair in International Business and Director of the Stephen Young Institute at the University of Strathclyde, as well as Visiting Professor at Cranfield School of Management. Her research is on organizations and how they can collaborate with each other and their customers to improve sustainability. With a background in marketing, she has delivered executive and MBA programmes at University of Warwick, Cranfield University and Australian Graduate School of Management. Emma loves walking in the countryside wherever she finds herself in the world.

Dr David Paulson

David is Executive Dean of the Business School at University College Birmingham and a former Professor of Practice in Management at Queen's University Belfast. Previously a leader of international businesses, his research and teaching focus on leadership in small and medium-sized enterprises and family firms. He is a qualified Executive Coach and is passionate about helping entrepreneurs to realize their full potential. He enjoys being outside with his family, especially if it involves mountains or athletics.

Dr Simon Brooks

Simon is an Associate Professor at Swansea University School of Management, where he has held many senior roles including Director of the DBA programme. Moving to academia after a career in the private sector, Simon has worked with many organizations on their strategy and ethics, including the Welsh Assembly and South Wales Police. Simon is happiest when he is on the water, sailing around the Swansea area.

About the authors

Dr Emily Yarrow

Emily is a Senior Lecturer in Management and Organisation, at New-castle University Business School. She is the Degree Programme Director for the MSc Global Human Resource Management, and her work focuses on contemporary understandings of gendered organizational behaviour, women's experiences of organizational life, and the future of work. She is a Senior Fellow of the Higher Education Academy (SFHEA) and Academic Member of the CIPD (MCIPD).

Dr Catherine Berrington

Catherine is a Teaching Fellow in the Organisation and Work group at the University of Warwick. She has a degree in International Business Management and two degrees in Human Resource Management. She teaches HRM to students across a range of Warwick Business School programmes and her research focuses on gender in the HR profession. Catherine's happiest times are spent outdoors, travelling, skiing, and hiking.

Dr Ishbel McWha-Hermann

Ishbel is a Senior Lecturer in International Human Resource Management, at the University of Edinburgh Business School. Her research focuses on social justice at work, with a particular focus on fairness, decent work, and sustainability. She is interested in the role of organizations in addressing poverty and inequality, and how organizational policies and practices can impact well-being and quality of life for workers, their families, organizations, and society. Ishbel is originally from New Zealand, but lives in Scotland, with her German husband and their two children.

Dr Thomas Calvard

Tom is a Senior Lecturer in Human Resource Management, at the University of Edinburgh Business School. He has an undergraduate degree in psychology and postgraduate degrees in organizational psychology, and his research and teaching focus on diversity—in all its many forms—in the workplace. Tom's one-eyed rescue pug, Odin, is the star of his Twitter channel.

Dr Sarah Woolley

Sarah is a Senior Research Fellow at Warwick Business School and has two PhDs—in management and in biochemistry. She previously worked as a Board Director in the UK's National Health Service and continues as a non-executive director on the board of a social housing and care provider. Sarah is happiest when she is exploring new places with Alma, her dog.

Dr Farah Arkadan

Farah is an Assistant Professor in Marketing at the American University in Dubai. She has a PhD from Cranfield and an MA in Luxury Marketing from Istituto Europea di Design in Italy. She researches and teaches about physical and digital customer experience management and previously worked at luxury fashion retailer, Burberry's, headquarters in London. She loves fashion, tech, and travelling.

Dr Anthony Alexander

Anthony is a Senior Lecturer in Operations Management at the University of Sussex Business School. His research focus is on how operations and supply chain management can help deliver sustainable and responsible business. He previously worked in senior roles in engineering consultancy, and the telecoms and media sectors. He is happiest when being productive.

Dr Alexander Glosenberg

Alexander (Alex) Glosenberg is Associate Professor of Entrepreneurship at Loyola Marymount University in Los Angeles. Alex founded his own social enterprise and has worked to train and mentor hundreds of entrepreneurs in six countries around the world. Alex grew to love entrepreneurship and recognize its importance to the world when he served as a United States Peace Corps volunteer in the Republic of South Africa, where he was tasked to assist with community development.

CONTENTS IN BRIEF

CONTENTS IN FULL

Introduction to Management

PART ONE **CONTEXT**

PART TWO **ORGANIZATION**

PART THREE **PEOPLE**

PART FOUR **VALUE CHAIN**

PART ONE

Managing in Context

CHAPTER ONE
Understanding Management

Sarah Birrell Ivory and Emma Macdonald

OPENING CASE STUDY **WHAT A MANAGER LOOKS LIKE**

Indra Nooyi joined PepsiCo in 1994 as Senior Vice President, Strategic Planning, aged 38. In 2006 she took over as CEO—the first time a woman had held the post in PepsiCo. Indeed, she was the first woman of colour, and the first immigrant, to lead any Fortune 50 company (the 50 largest publicly-listed US-based companies).

Born in India, Nooyi was raised a devout Hindu, and grew up in Chennai, in a house with her siblings, parents, and grandparents. She graduated from the Indian Institute of Management in 1976 and with a postgraduate degree from Yale University in 1980 (where she worked as a receptionist to make ends meet).

Showing significant foresight, early in her time at the company before even becoming CEO, Nooyi coined the term 'Performance with a Purpose' as Pepsi's new mantra. This included three pillars of adjusting to meet what she saw as shifting consumer demand for healthier eating, committing to being a good corporate citizen on environmental issues, and focusing on retaining talent at the company, including through paid parental leave for men and women alike.

During her 12 years as CEO, PepsiCo's profit more than doubled from US$2.7 billion to US$6.5 billion annually. She developed a reputation as a strategic long-term thinker and a skilful communicator. She oversaw the sale of Yum! Brands (which included KFC, Taco Bell, and Pizza Hut), and the acquisition of Tropicana, Quaker Oats, and Gatorade, into the PepsiCo family.

Showing her wide range of interests, Nooyi has served on the boards of the International Cricket Council, the Lincoln Centre for the Performing Arts, Tsinghua University School of Economics and Management, and the World Economic Forum, as well as being co-chair of the World Justice Project.

1.1 **Introduction**

Welcome to this text, *Introduction to Management: Functions and Challenges*, and to the start of your journey studying this wide-ranging topic. The activities of management are dynamic and complex, and so studying this topic is challenging. While this may seem daunting, it also makes studying management both liberating and fascinating. Let us explain.

One reason that studying management is challenging is because, unlike other professions, studying management will not make you a manager. Studying law or medicine—and then taking the appropriate professional exams—will make you a lawyer or a doctor. However, there is no specific degree or professional exam that makes you a manager. Indeed, you may already be a manager in a part-time job or community activities. More broadly, you are already managing your time, effort, and relationships within your university and social life. So, if reading a text on management, or even completing a degree does not make you a manager, then what does make you a manager? The answer is that you become a manager when you are given—or create for yourself—a role in which management is required. This means that many different people, with vastly different backgrounds, education, world views, values, ambitions, and interpersonal styles become managers.

The variation among managers links to the second element of studying management to consider. While graduate jobs after university may involve elements of management, it is likely that you will experience *being managed* before you experience *being a manager*. Also, your managers will likely come from among a diverse range of people, and you will need to be prepared for these differences. Your manager may manage you and your colleagues, as well as the processes, projects, or operations you are involved in, very well. They may also manage these things badly.

The final element that makes studying management challenging is that it does not lend itself to a simple, clear, 'how-to' guide, a step-by-step approach, a best-practice formula, or even a set of universally accepted 'dos' and 'don'ts'. This is in part because of the variety of functions, processes, and roles that management comprises, which we will explore in this chapter. It is also because of the different organizations in which management happens, such as business, not-for-profit, and public sector organizations, which we distinguish in Chapter 2. All of these have different purposes, objectives, cultures, values, and constraining factors. Moreover, the current context in which management happens comprises significant social, environmental, digital, and geopolitical complexity and disruption, which we will explore in Chapter 3. This means that there is no one-size-fits-all approach to management, or a simple and fool-proof formula that can be taught in a book, course, or degree programme, that will enable you to become an ideal manager.

So, what is the point of studying management, then? And why have we written this text to support your studies?

The answer is relatively simple. You are not studying management in order to be able to 'do it'. You are studying management to think about it; to understand it; to be able to evaluate whether it is done effectively; to critique when it is not effective and analyse the reasons for this; to appreciate the difficulties associated with managing well; and to prepare yourself for the challenges you will face when you one day take on a management role yourself. This means that the lens that you apply to studying management becomes essential to your success in this endeavour. Moreover, this lens may need to change from how you have studied other topics in the past, as we explain in Section 1.2. But first, let's consider how this text is structured to support you in this Introduction to Management.

1.1.1 **The structure of this text**

While management is a complex and all-encompassing topic, it is useful to provide a more simplistic depiction when first studying it. In Figure 1.1, which mirrors the structure of this text, we depict four interrelated elements important in managing organizations: context, organization, people, and value chain. We start with Part 1—Managing in Context, which positions

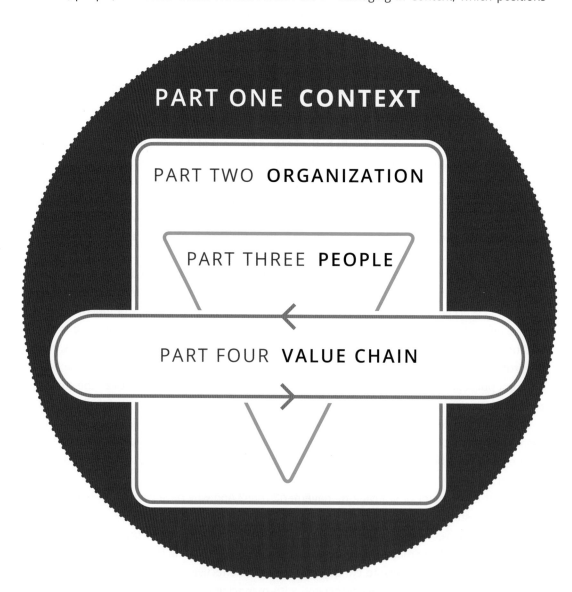

FIGURE 1.1 **Interrelated elements important in managing organizations.**

management in relation to wider contextual factors beyond any specific individual manager or organization. This includes the history and function of management itself as a constantly changing concept, the types of organizations in which management happens and their differing attributes, as well as the changing world in which we live. From this wider view, we then focus in on Part 2—Managing an Organization to explore elements specific to organizations, such as their external environment, their internal environment, and their organizational culture and change management. Part 3—Managing People, takes this focus one step further to consider the key, human element of management. It covers human resource management broadly, as well as specifics such as designing work well, teams, and leading. Finally, Part 4—Managing through the Value Chain examines the breadth of management from supply chain through operations to marketing. Here also we include entrepreneurship, given management's focus on creating something of value.

This delineation of Context—Organization—People—Value Chain provides a useful visual aid to understand how different elements fit together in the broad topic which we call management. However, by virtue of its simplicity, it also misses some obvious links. For example, we explore 'organizational culture' in Managing an Organization (Part 2), despite the pivotal role of Managing People (Part 3), in this topic. Nevertheless, we believe that this depiction will help guide and simplify interrelated elements, as you begin your journey of studying management. In the next section, we return to the idea of the most effective lens for studying management.

1.1.2 A critical thinking lens

Many students approach learning—especially before coming to university—with a 'learn-and-repeat' or 'teach-me-how' lens. This comes from the belief that others have greater knowledge, expertise, or abilities than themselves. It is also a by-product of the typical approach to assessment that we encounter at school, in which assessors are often in search of the 'right' answer. Given what we now understand about management, it is clear that 'learn-and-repeat' or 'teach-me-how' won't be appropriate for the level of complexity and uncertainty associated with management. More importantly, this won't enable a critical analysis of different approaches to managing. Rather, our approach needs to resemble an 'understand, explore, discuss, debate, and come to your own conclusions' journey. This approach describes a critical thinking lens to studying management, which is the lens that we use throughout this text, and is likely one of the reasons it was recommended to you.

Critical thinking is a cognitive (brain) process of actively and carefully evaluating the reasoning and evidence behind knowledge and arguments, and developing defensible knowledge and arguments ourselves (Ivory, 2021). In our view, one of the key reasons to attend university is to become better, more critical thinkers. This idea is explored in great depth in a book written by one of us dedicated to this topic: *Becoming a Critical Thinker: For Your University Studies and Beyond* (Ivory, 2021). The book outlines three aims of critical thinking: Quality of Argument, Strength of Evidence, and Clarity of Communication. At university—and in your graduate professional lives—you will need to be able to develop a high-quality argument about a problem or question you face; to support this with strong, reliable, and rigorous evidence; and to communicate this clearly to all the stakeholders necessary. *Becoming a Critical Thinker* also explains the five tools needed to achieve this aim and how to use them effectively in a university context:

1

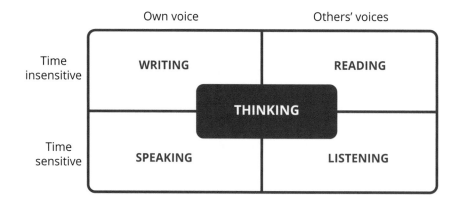

FIGURE 1.2 **The five tools of critical thinking (Ivory, 2021).**

Reading, Writing, Listening, Speaking, and Thinking itself—depicted in Figure 1.2. Importantly, this depiction distinguishes between the time-sensitive nature of each tool (whether it is used 'on the spot' or allows longer reflection) as well as whose voice is involved. The book argues that students need to balance the use of all five tools during their university studies, in order to become critical thinkers.

Used appropriately, these tools help us to make sense of a complex world, appreciate and evaluate the resources and options available to us, consider the purpose of our task and its appropriateness in context, and make decisions about what to do (or not do). The study of management will be more effective if approached with a critical thinking lens, and the practice of management requires such a lens in order to be successful. We will return to these ideas throughout this text.

Now that we have briefly introduced the study of management, its complexity, and the approach we take in this text, let's turn to focus on what management is in more detail.

1.2 What is management?

There is no one generally accepted definition of management. It can mean different things, to different people, in different contexts, and at different times. At an individual level, the idea of management can be applied to managing our time, our career, our mental and emotional state, or our relationships with others. Within a group context, it might apply to managing a sports team, a family (as many parents will tell you), or a social calendar of events. At an organizational level—the focus of our text—management still has many different definitions. It can describe a practice, a process, a function, or a job title or level.

So, perhaps we can ask, who is a manager? Even this seemingly simple question has a quite complex answer. It is difficult to point to a manager in the same way as you can point to practitioners like a doctor, a lawyer, a teacher, or a plumber. Indeed, most people in these jobs (and many others) also undertake a variety of management tasks.

In 1916, Henri Fayol said that 'to manage is to forecast and plan, to organize, to command, to coordinate and to control'. It has been described as a 'social process' (Brech, 1957), and an 'operational process' (Koontz & O'Donnell, 1984). A famous early management scholar, Mary Parker Follett (1868–1933), argued that a defining characteristic of management was the involvement of others: 'The art of getting things done through the efforts of other people' (quoted in Graham, 1995). These previous definitions help us to define **management** as a social and operational process with the aim of bringing people and other resources together in order to get something done. While this may be a useful definition for us to learn, it is also undoubtedly so broad as to include almost anything that happens in an organization. Parts 2, 3, and 4 of this text are an attempt to categorize and define further different aspects of management, so as to be more useful than this broad definition. One approach to understanding management may also be useful: considering management as either a science, a craft, or an art.

> **Management:** a social and operational process with the aim of bringing people and other resources together in order to get something done.

There are different perspectives that we can explore in an attempt to understand management, which are depicted in Figure 1.3. Some views on management present it as a science. In this view, management is achieved by logical and rational decision-making, which takes place within a formal, stable, and structured organization. Based on these assumptions, a set of rational principles or laws of management could be universally applied to achieve the aims of management. Theories are developed which describe and explain management; some popular ones, which we reference in Section 1.4, include scientific management theory, human relations theory, and contingency theory. Approaching management as a science supports the idea that essential skills and competencies for management can be identified, and can therefore be trained in (almost) anyone, in order to make them a manager.

A different perspective sees management as a craft—and as with other artisan crafts (think of carpenters or cheesemakers)—it can be learned only by working with and being apprenticed to a skilled practitioner: observing, understanding, and attempting to emulate what they do.

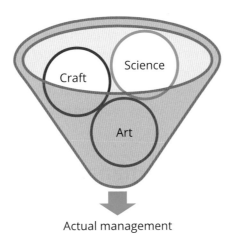

Actual management

FIGURE 1.3 **Perspectives on management.**

1

The 'student' of management must study the 'master', learning to interpret why and how they act, so that once the student is on their own, they can maintain this standard. In this sense, they 'practise' management under the watchful eye of a more senior manager who offers advice, guidance, and reassurance.

Others see management as an art, which relies on intuition, 'gut' feel, and potentially an inspired sense of the possible, rather than an analytical report on the probable. Creativity and imagination are embraced in the art of management, often linked to new ways of seeing things, new ways of doing things, and a willingness to experiment with alternatives to see how they feel. This is particularly portrayed in relation to management in new digital entrepreneurial contexts—for example, new tech start-ups (although the extent to which this portrayal is an accurate reflection of reality is debatable).

This brief review of differing perspectives of management as a science, a craft, or an art begs the question of whether we are talking about nature or nurture when it comes to effective management. That is, is management in someone's genes when they are born, or are they nurtured into the role based on socialization, education, and opportunity? This question becomes even more relevant as we look at the data showing the vast majority of managers of large corporations are still white and male. For example, in Fortune 500 companies (the annual list of the 500 largest US industrial corporations), only 7 per cent of CEO posts are held by women and only 9 per cent are ethnically diverse (Larcker & Tayan, 2020). Indra Nooyi, introduced in the Opening case study of this chapter, stands out as an exception. Throughout this text, many of these issues and more will emerge as we employ a critical thinking lens to understand arguments and seek evidence for why these issues exist. Further, we will discover what obstacles to change exist, and how these can be overcome.

Of course, it is likely that management is a combination of science, craft, and art. While some aspects can be explained and written down, are generalizable to many contexts, and can be trained into individuals, other aspects can only be learned and understood implicitly and through observation. Furthermore, some aspects rely on instinct, creativity, and imagination. This conclusion— that actual management is a combination of science, craft, and art—makes teaching management difficult, understanding management sometimes confusing, and developing a one-off training programme to make someone a 'manager' almost impossible. It is the reason why the critical thinking approach to studying management is essential. This text aims to include elements of all three perspectives in studying management, although it focuses more often on management as a science. This is not because we believe this element is truer or more important—far from it. It is because management as a science is often (although not always) more able to be 'taught'. Conversely, management as a craft or art is something that you as a student of management are better able to develop with experience, observation, and by bravely following your instinct.

1.3 **The emergence of management as a practice**

Many textbooks explore the practice of management by looking into history books. They point, for example, to the challenges associated with building some of the greatest structures ever conceived—such as the pyramids in Egypt, the Great Wall of China, or the less famous Walls of

1

Benin in modern-day Nigeria. They examine the coordination of some of the most significant expeditions, like Magellan's circumnavigation of the world. Or they look to the running of royal courts with rigorous traditions, large palaces, gardens, and land, and different levels of servants, gardeners, footmen, cooks, stable hands, and the like. Some also explore how wars were fought and armies built: finding, training, clothing, feeding, and arming soldiers, not to mention making strategic battle decisions about where and how to deploy them to minimize losses and maximize the chance of victory, and ensure supply lines (of food, weapons, and replacement soldiers) were maintained. Indeed, it has been argued that the oldest management textbook is *The Art of War* by Chinese military strategist Sun Tzu, dated to the fifth century BC, which includes chapters on assessment and planning; weaknesses and strengths; variations and adaptability; and intelligence (i.e. information) and espionage (translations from How, 2003).

In all of these events, projects, expeditions, and households, there were undoubtedly complex organizational, logistical, and engineering challenges which needed to be overcome to achieve success. But was any of this 'management'? This, of course, depends on our definition.

In Section 1.2, we defined management as 'a social and operational process with the aim of bringing people and other resources together in order to get something done'. But how does one assemble a group of people and make them work together to achieve an outcome? If humans were machines, we could simply move them around and push an 'on' button to have them undertake whatever task we want. But humans are not machines: we are thinking creatures with minds of our own and a diversity of experiences and expectations. In the absence of a simple 'on' switch, we need to use other methods to get humans to act and collaborate. History shows us a variety of ways in which societies have organized themselves to get things done, many of which involve some members of society being deprived of resources, rights, and even their liberty. Forcing an individual to undertake a task against their will is known as coercion. Removing their rights as an individual and depriving them of their liberty is known as slavery.

Implicit in our definition of management is the absence of coercion. Cummings et al. (2017) draw on a number of recent authors, as well as those as far back as Adam Smith—an economist in the eighteenth century who wrote on many topics, including morality—to argue that management emerged—in the western world, at least—as a *solution* (both legal and moral) to end the use of control, coercion, and forced labour as a means of getting things done. That is: as a solution to the abolition of slavery and servitude. They suggest that taking this perspective does two things. First, it provides us with a definition of management as being 'about non-coercive ways of achieving progress' (Cummings et al., 2017: 80). However, it also provides us with a starting point for the entire field of management and helps us to use the past (appropriately) to inform both our current understanding, and study, of management. Indeed, it distinguishes the modern practice of 'management' from the examples of building the pyramids and other monumental projects which relied on coercion, oppression, and slavery as a means to achieve spectacular feats of construction.

While this provides a useful 'starting point' for management, it does result in a blinkered study of management as a largely western phenomenon (albeit acknowledging differences between distinct cultures in the western world). This is particularly so with the proliferation of management studied, in a western context, and then developed and disseminated by western Business Schools. However, a recent and important trend has seen many question why so little attention has been paid to approaches to management in Africa, South America, and large

1

parts of Asia. We are seeing calls to decolonize the curriculum within Business Schools and management teaching generally, to embrace a diversity of perspectives. We will attempt to do so in this text by introducing non-western ideas about management where possible. However, we acknowledge that much more could be done to increase both the visibility and study of such ideas, and to include them in texts such as these. This would add breadth, depth, richness, and context to the study and teaching of the field of management.

1.4 **The emergence of management as a discipline of study**

Many texts introducing students to the study of management present a chronological narrative about the different approaches and theories that have come to dominance and then gone out of fashion, over the past century or so. These are necessarily simplified for three reasons. Firstly, so that students who are new to the approach or theory have the greatest chance of understanding it. Secondly, theories need to be condensed due to time and space limitations. Finally, extracting only the key elements allows you to practise applying them (for example, using the exercises associated with the Running case feature throughout this text).

All of these factors mean that theories, frameworks, and ideas may differ from their original and fuller depictions. There is nothing inherently wrong with this—part of the learning process for any discipline is to start with more simplified ideas and approaches. However, we need to take care to address two issues. The first is to ensure that what we learn, although simplified, is still an accurate representation of original research, ideas, and theories. In the field of management, it has been argued that some theories have been distorted or even entirely fabricated to take advantage of the valuable market in providing advice and consulting services to management across organizations (Bridgman & Cummings, 2021). As such, it is particularly important to assess the validity and rigour of the research underlying the theories by adopting a critical thinking lens to the study of management. Secondly, it is important to remember that there is complexity, nuance, and context behind every seemingly simple theory or framework, especially when applying it in practice. As your learning journey progresses, you should strive to understand and integrate such complexity into your management studies and ultimately into your management practice.

Spotlight 1.1 provides such a simplified narrative of the emergence of management as a discipline of study. Read it now, using a critical thinking lens, before reading the paragraphs below which provide a more detailed explanation.

There are a number of issues with histories of management as a discipline of study, such as the one presented in Spotlight 1.1. The key question is around the extent to which these different approaches accurately represented their original proponents' ideas *or* the rigour and validity of the research studies on which the theories are based. The reasons that inaccurate or invalid theories may have become so entrenched in the 'history' of the management discipline are complex, and not all will be explored here (we encourage students interested in this to read Bridgman and Cummings (2021) in the first instance, which is mentioned in the 'Explore more' feature at the end of the chapter, or Cummings et al., 2017 for greater detail). However, we will

SPOTLIGHT 1.1 A 'HISTORY' OF MANAGEMENT AS A DISCIPLINE OF STUDY

Note: use a critical thinking lens when reading this summary, then consider the further explanation provided in the text.

Management as a discipline started with the classical management approach founded by Frederick Taylor in 1911 on the publication of his book, *Principles of Scientific Management*. This approach prioritizes productivity and efficiency above all other aims of management, and assumes managers are best placed to design very specific work processes. Similar to other machinery, workers are expected to act exactly as told without deviation. It treats all the 'inputs' necessary for the process as resources to be managed, allocated, and rationalized, including human resources. To this end, scientific management does not cope well with uncertainty created by a changing context or environment, or the unpredictability and potential emotional aspects of human and team behaviour.

Soon after this, however (as traditional histories would have it), a 'human relations' approach emerged, which refocused attention on the individual human worker and their motivations and subsequent behaviours. This was popularized by Elton Mayo in the 1930s, following the famous Hawthorne studies, which concluded that workers increase productivity when their social needs, such as a sense of belonging and importance, are fulfilled.

By the 1960s, a 'systems' or 'contingency' approach was emerging, which suggested that no one single approach (like scientific management or human relations) was universal, but saw organizations as complex, open systems comprising not only people and machinery, but also processes, technology, and many other elements. Because of this, managers needed to vary their approach, depending on the specific environment and circumstances.

A strategic management approach gained traction from the 1990s onwards, focusing on strategic mission and decisions, aligned organizational culture, effective change management, and optimized stakeholder relations.

Finally, some have recently suggested a new sustainable management approach is emerging, which balances a drive for profit or performance, with questions of social and environmental impact—and wider questions of organizational purpose.

touch on two factors that are important as we take a critical thinking lens to understanding and studying management.

First, there is a recency bias in which there is an assumption that more recent contributions are superior, and earlier contributions represent ideas that are naïve, out-dated, ill-informed, or poorly thought through. Indeed, the emerging sustainable management approach implies that earlier approaches to management were either ignorant of, or actively opposed to, environmental concerns. Only recently—so this narrative goes—have we become more aware of the side effects of unchecked efficiency pursuits characterized by Taylor's scientific management, and have begun to introduce 'new' ideas of sustainability. While this is an attractive and convenient story, as with many things, the reality is more complex. Recent historical studies (Cummings & Bridgman, 2021) point out that while the original *focus* of Taylor's scientific management may have been efficiency, the *purpose* of this was to achieve conservation—what we may now call sustainability—rather than profitability: it was developed to limit the increasing impacts of big business on depleting the natural resources of the USA, and protect these for the future. Subsequent simplifications (and distortions) of scientific management saw this aspect lost, or intentionally excluded (Bridgman & Cummings, 2021).

1

The second issue is one that we will explore in greater detail in Section 1.5: the way in which 'management' has become increasingly synonymous with for-profit business and its focus on increased efficiency and the ultimate aim of economic value. Indeed, this is the perspective that has been taught, explicitly or implicitly, in management courses in Business Schools in particular, for many years (and to this day). As we will point out, what has often been lost is the fact that management happens in many different organizational contexts for whom efficiency and economic gain are not the ultimate aim. Even the for-profit business sector is experiencing a turn towards being more purpose-driven (which itself may not be as new as some make out), as we explore in Chapter 2.

The fact that there is controversy over the history of management, and even over the 'founders' of the discipline and what they really said or believed, may feel frustrating to those new to studying the topic. However, embracing this controversy enables you as a student of management to be more reflective on the topic. It also enables you to consider the fact that how you are managed or are taught to manage, is not necessarily how you *have to be* managed or how *you can choose* to be a manager. This is precisely what makes the study of management both liberating and fascinating.

We can now turn to examine management in greater detail and ask the key questions about its purpose, which are so often neglected.

1.5 **The purpose of management**

Why do we need managers and management? It is very easy to fall into the trap of answering that question with a functional list: what managers do, what roles they undertake or what functions they serve. We will explore many of these in the second half of this chapter. But before we explore these *functional* questions, it is important that we ask a more *fundamental* question, which is much less commonly explored, let alone answered: why do managers exist? That is, what is the purpose of management?

1.5.1 **Management and 'value'**

We can recall our definition of management as a social and operational process with the aim of bringing people and other resources together in order to get something done. This definition implies the purpose of management—of getting something done—is that some form of value is created for someone. **Value** refers to the relative worth of something which is often, but not always, linked to economic worth (Mackay et al., 2020). Managing the production of a musical creates value for the audience (entertainment), the performers (satisfaction and pay), and the production company (reputation and income). All of these things are of 'value' and are achieved in part because of the role of management. Managers of a local government may create value for the community by bringing together expertise to design, build, and operate a new local park and playground facility. Managers of a health care centre may create value for their patients by bringing together GPs, nurses, and administration staff to efficiently and effectively address their health care needs. Managers of a clothes company may create value for their shareholders by designing, sourcing, manufacturing, and selling t-shirts for a profit. This final example is where it could be argued that some management education has gone astray, or at least taken on a very specific focus. Because the concept of management has been strongly linked to for-profit business, many definitions of management focus on economic resources and economic value. For example, the famous strategist, Peter Drucker (1954: 4) described management as 'the systematic organization of economic resources', while organizational theorist Haridimos Tsoukas defined management as 'the maintenance of control of employees in the pursuit of capital accumulation' (Tsoukas, 1994: 294). We see such economic or financial primacy, while common in management texts and education, as problematic for two key reasons.

The first reason is that the assumed purpose of management as creating economic value neglects the many contexts in which management happens outside a for-profit business. In Chapter 2 we categorize different types of organizations into private, public, and third-sector. The latter two sectors include organizations whose purpose is not linked to creating economic value for owners (or for anyone), such as charities, Non-Governmental Organizations (NGOs), and government bodies. In the UK, around 20 per cent of the workforce is employed outside the private sector (Office for National Statistics, 2023) and this percentage increases greatly in other countries. Consequently, if we study management from the perspective of for-profit business and increasing economic value alone, we may miss key differences, challenges, and lessons linked to the public and third sectors of the economy. Moreover, many of these not-for-profit roles are vital to thriving communities, public health, and the stability of society generally. Therefore, it is essential that the study of management is broad enough to incorporate these contexts, be it for a community hospital, an adoption agency, a housing association, an animal welfare charity, an energy utility, or a government department. In these contexts, the purpose of management cannot simply be understood as increasing economic value.

1

The second reason is that the narrow profit-centred view—even of for-profit business—neglects the complex (and, some will argue, changing) purpose of such organizations beyond a sole focus on economic value. Of course, there have always been some for-profit organizations that prioritize societal as well as profit goals. However, even traditional 'for-profit' businesses are increasingly nuanced in their stated aims. As we will explore in Chapter 2, there are emerging trends towards 'purpose-driven' for-profit business, as well as other new shapes of organizations, such as social enterprises or Benefit Corporations (B Corps), which explicitly combine and prioritize social and/or environmental value alongside economic value. The role of for-profit business in addressing environmental and social challenges, highlighted in the United Nations' 17 Sustainable Development Goals (SDGs), is of particular interest. We explore these in Spotlight 3.2. What is clear is that even managers in for-profit businesses are increasingly seeing their purpose as much wider than the creation of economic value alone.

The risk of focusing on economic value at the expense of other valid types of value is that managers—even those not operating in a for-profit context—can become fixated on one aspect of their role, and lose a wider vision of the purpose of their role. We have seen this in recent times with the dominance of efficiency, which we discuss next.

1.5.2 Management and 'efficiency'

As we have argued, the western approach to management that dominates much of the global management profession and management teaching emerged as a non-coercive way of getting things done. This was around the time of the Industrial Revolution, which started in the UK, where mechanization enabled organizations to grow dramatically in size, geographic reach, technology, and breadth. Many texts about management suggest that, in this context, the primary purpose of management is achieving greater efficiency for the organization. Just like the input–output dynamic of the machines that powered the Industrial Revolution, efficiency is about achieving the greatest outputs for the fewest inputs. As such, the role of management emerged at this time to focus on analysing all the resources that go into an organization, and reducing them as much as possible, while maintaining or increasing the outputs (or, at least, the monetary gain from the outputs).

It is clear that this approach to management prioritizes outputs measured in economic value. This is problematic for the many organizations for whom economic value is not the only or primary aim. While organizations in the third and public sectors (as explored in Chapter 2) must carefully manage their finances to ensure survival, such financial management is not the *purpose* of the organization or management. Where efficiency becomes the purpose of management, other possible purposes may fall away. For example, some managers view their roles as social or community leaders, and their purpose as building and fostering strong, supportive, and safe communities within which the organization operates. Other managers see their role as stewards of resources and the environment, whose purpose is to find the least harmful approach to their strategy and operations, protecting required natural resources and environmental services for future generations. Many would consider these perfectly acceptable purposes for management.

Nevertheless, efficiency has become a focus of many approaches to management over the last century. This focus is commonly associated with reductions and savings. Managers are often depicted as continually looking for ways of doing things faster (saving time), with fewer inputs (saving resources), or by negotiating lower prices from suppliers (saving money). This approach of management for efficiency is not wrong per se—a wasteful manager would not be considered a good manager. But when efficiency becomes the sole purpose of management, it is easy to lose sight of something more significant.

Better managers will always have a wider view of the purpose of both their organization and their role, as well as the different types of value they are attempting to create or protect. They will consider what they plan to *do* with the time, resources, or money saved. Managers will also consider the tangible impacts of the efficiency measures. Time and money saved on employee health and safety training may have consequences for workplace accidents and employee absence. Cutting the monitoring of product quality may lead to higher defect rates and customer dissatisfaction. Negotiating hard to reduce the per unit cost of an input may cause your supplier to struggle with their own finances and even go out of business, negatively impacting your supply chain as you search for an alternative. These are instances in which departments become siloed and fail to consider the impacts they can have on other areas. Managers in one department may save costs or time, but this may have unintended implications on another department, and may fail to achieve the purpose of the organization. This issue was the key factor leading to an ambitious management initiative in Cleveland, USA which focused on the joint fundamental purpose of a number of linked organizations, and ways in which managing the interactions of these organizations differently, achieved their own true purpose. See Spotlight 1.2 on the Cleveland model.

SPOTLIGHT 1.2 **THE CLEVELAND MODEL**

In 2008, the managers of a number of large organizations in Cleveland, Ohio (USA) came together to discuss their separate and overlapping purposes. These 'anchor organizations' included teaching hospitals and medical clinics, university campuses, and the municipal government. The anchor organizations realized that finding the lowest cost providers for certain services did not help the problems endemic in their local neighbourhoods, caused largely by a lack of jobs and training opportunities for people living in those communities. Embracing grassroots economic development, the Evergreen Initiative (also called by some 'the Cleveland model') was instead developed as an alternative wealth-building and wealth-sharing model.

As part of this initiative, cooperative businesses, which are owned and operated by their employees, were established to provide goods and services to these anchor organizations, and others. These businesses included Green City Growers, which provides lettuce and other greens; Evergreen Energy Solutions, which provides LED lighting upgrades and solar panels; and Evergreen Cooperative Laundry, which provides industrial laundry services. These (and other) cooperative businesses were located in six low-income neighbourhoods surrounding and serviced by the original anchor organizations. The cooperative businesses have confidence in these large organizations as anchor clients and can focus on business growth to win more contracts and train more local residents.

The purpose of a hospital, university, or local government is—ultimately—the improvement of the lives of those it serves. If we take the definition of who it serves broadly, each of these anchor organizations is achieving their purpose by being involved in this initiative and playing a transformational role in building vibrant local neighbourhoods—as well as buying delicious, locally-grown lettuce. For more information visit the Evergreen Cooperatives website.

1

In reaction to the managerial focus on economic value and efficiency, in recent years a more rounded approach to understanding management has gained traction, led in part by scholars such as Stephen Cummings and Todd Bridgman. This changed perspective does not come about by inventing or offering a new theory of management, but by exploring the origins of existing theory and analysing how it has been used (and potentially distorted) over many years to further the 'efficiency agenda'. This shift in perspective is timely because of the increasing concern about the impacts that organizations and management decisions have had on the environment and society, characterized by environmental crises, community breakdown, and growing levels of inequality. That is, the importance of management in the effective functioning of a thriving society (and in contributing to an unstable and disrupted society) is increasingly recognized. While we examine such disruptions in more detail in Chapter 3, we will briefly discuss the importance of management in the next section.

1.6 **The importance of management**

It is probably fair to say that management has had a greater impact on the modern world than almost any other profession or role. This is in part because of the fact that 'management' happens in every organization, globally, from small businesses to large multinational corporations, national governments, and the United Nations (UN). However, it is also because the implications of how we manage (or are managed) extend well beyond the organization itself. These implications can be seen in obvious and not so obvious ways. Managers are responsible for the policies, processes, and resource allocation decisions which impact their employees, their suppliers and customers, and their wider stakeholders. The consequences of management decisions and practices can be felt at three different levels, which are summarized in Figure 1.4: individual, organizational, and societal.

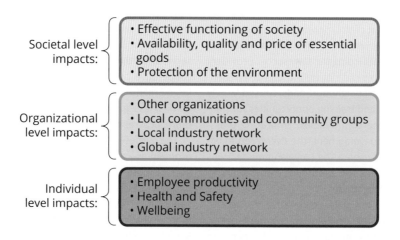

FIGURE 1.4 **Management decisions and examples of their impact on individuals, organizations, and society.**

At an individual level, management contributes to issues such as their own employees' productivity, safety, and well-being. Managers determine whether employees are treated fairly and respectfully, and are able to survive and thrive, both within and outside of the workplace. Management decisions contribute to a safe and supportive work environment (or the opposite), living wage opportunities (or exploitation), human rights protections (or abuses), and individuals' ability to plan for their futures (or live payday-to-payday).

At an organizational level, management contributes to its impact beyond its boundaries, including on other organizations, community groups, and industry networks. In relation to suppliers, managers' decisions impact payment terms and expectations, including conditions of work in their supplier's premises. For instance, modern slavery and exploitation in the supply chains of many well-known brands globally is still a significant issue (Crane et al., 2021).

At a societal level, management contributes to the extent to which society functions effectively. Management practices can help to prevent wealth inequalities by ensuring the availability of jobs with fair remuneration and training, and can build communities that feel supported and thrive. Managers are also responsible for the availability, quality, and price of certain products necessary for a functioning society. For example, during the Covid-19 pandemic, managers of pharmaceutical companies made different decisions about pricing strategies for the vaccines they had developed: some opted to provide vaccines on a not-for-profit basis until the end of the pandemic, while others set relatively high prices affecting the ability of certain nations to buy and provide vaccines for their citizens (Kollewe, 2021). Effective management in public organizations ensures countries, cities, and neighbourhoods thrive, with services such as rubbish collection, transport links, and public amenities like parks. The management of health care determines the extent to which accidents and illnesses can be effectively treated to protect life. These aspects may be less obvious but are no less important roles of management in society. For many years, managers of many different types of organizations have placed little or no value on the natural environment and the benefits that it provides (like clean air, fertile earth for growing crops, or a stable climate). This has contributed to the environmental crises we are seeing today, which we explore in Chapter 3, and which are leading many organizations (including governments) to rethink the value and rights of the natural environment, and the ways in which managers and management should weigh up and consider its importance when making managerial decisions.

These factors—and many more—make management not just a functional or mechanical task or role. Management comprises both explicit and implicit moral, political, philosophical, and ethical elements. These can be linked to an individual's values, and the purpose, expectations, and cultural norms of the organization. This is why studying management is both empowering and fascinating. It requires us to think, to feel, to listen, to empathize, to analyse, and to theorize. It liberates our thinking away from there being 'one right way', to appreciating differing approaches relevant to different contexts. It also reminds us of the importance of management in a functioning, thriving, and stable society.

Throughout this text, we have a running case study which will explore the management of a fictional organization: Imperial Fine Foods. We will see the way in which the managers go about their roles. Turn now to Running case 1.1 to get an introduction to the company you will be studying throughout every chapter in this book.

RUNNING CASE 1.1 **HANDING OVER THE REINS**

Today is Hugh Green's 60th birthday. He has been with his family's business, Imperial Fine Foods Limited, for his entire career. He succeeded his father, James, as CEO on James's own 60th birthday, just as James had succeeded Hugh's grandfather Edward, the founder of the business, on his. And today his daughter Lucy Green will succeed him, becoming Imperial's fourth CEO. Hugh will remain in place as the company's Chairperson, ready to advise, but determined to let Lucy manage the company as she sees fit.

Imperial Fine Foods supplies globally-sourced ingredients, including speciality jarred and tinned produce like sauces and olives, as well as premium fine-leaf tea under its own brand. It also sources and distributes premium cuts of meat and a limited range of vegetable produce from around the UK. Finally, Imperial is most famous for the meat pies (beef, lamb, and chicken) it manufactures and sells under its own brand 'Imperial Pies'. Imperial's customers are other hospitality and retail organizations, including restaurants and cafés, as well as university and school campuses. That is, Imperial is a BtoB (business to business) supplier, not a BtoC (business to consumer) supplier.

Many of Imperial's UK suppliers of meat and produce have been in partnership with Imperial for generations. However, a quarter of Imperial's revenues come from the sale of fine teas to specialist retailers, purchased from a network of suppliers in Asia and Africa with whom a relationship was established many decades ago by Imperial's founder.

Imperial has grown over time, so that there are now 30 people in the office and over 100 in the food preparation factory and distribution warehouse. Though some employees are the second or third generation of their own family to work at Imperial, the annual staff photos in the company boardroom reflect the changes in the composition of the city's population over the decades.

Imperial is still a family-owned business. Hugh and his children still own over half of the shares, but the remainder are owned by a number of their relatives. Although Hugh is proud of their common heritage, he finds some of his relatives' attitudes are very different from his own. These people don't contribute to the running of the company but are often vocal and critical about the way it is run. Some of them just want more profits, so they can earn higher dividends each year. 'This isn't a charity, Hugh,' his cousin Charles Green said publicly at the last shareholders' Annual General Meeting. These unhelpful shareholder demands are a pressure he could do without, and he is sorry to pass them on to Lucy.

While Hugh was brought up to understand that it's important to pay the bills and to invest wisely, he and his wife and children have always viewed the company as a community, rather than as a purely commercial enterprise. He is conscious of growing public concern with environmental matters. Additionally, the pandemic that first hit the business in 2020 caused disruption in many areas and has raised all sorts of questions. He wonders whether, if he were not retiring, he would have had to make some significant changes to the company's approach.

Though he feels some trepidation about the handover and Imperial's long-term prospects, Hugh has confidence in Lucy's commercial sense and managerial potential. He is pleased that she seems to share most of his values. Like him, she does not see the sole purpose of the company as making profit for its own sake. But her background is different from his. Hugh started in the company straight from school, but Lucy went to university to study ecology, then went to work for Fairtrade Food, an NGO in Tanzania, eventually working for several years as a manager in their marketing division. Hugh was delighted when she said she wanted to come back and work in the family business, and he is proud of the work she has done as its commercial director since she joined. But he's a little concerned about Lucy's recent personal decision to shift her diet towards mostly vegetarian and vegan meals: after all, Imperial has built its reputation on supplying the finest traditional meat products.

Questions for reflection

1. Considering Figure 1.4, what specific impacts could decisions by Imperial's management have at the individual, the organization, and the societal level?

2. What 'value' is provided by Imperial? To whom? What is the role of Imperial's managers in providing that value?

3. In your view, will Lucy Green approach management as a science, a craft, or an art (Figure 1.3)? Why do you think this?

In the first half of this chapter we explored the definition of management, where it emerged from, and why—for many reasons—it is a complex topic to study. Having developed this foundational understanding of the concept, in the second half of this chapter we explore in greater depth the different functions, processes, roles, and levels of management.

1.7 Management: Functions and processes

There are many different ways in which we can think about and categorize what management is and what managers do. One common method is to distinguish between management functions and management processes. This can help us get a sense of 'who' is a manager, as well as 'what' managers do.

1.7.1 Management functions

Management functions are the ways in which managers are grouped within an organization into departments that focus on specific tasks. For example, **Human Resources** is a management function in many organizations, focused on hiring and developing employees (explored in Chapter 7). Different organizations will have different management functions, depending on their industry. These can change over time in terms of both the existence of the function and its seniority. For example, even just 20 years ago, few retail businesses would have had a digital manager, such as a CTO (Chief Technology Officer). Yet now it is almost a standard, given the popularity of online shopping. Indeed, CSOs (chief sustainability officers) are becoming very common across all industries and organization types, as sustainability is identified as a key societal—and so organizational—issue. Some other common management functions (in addition to human resources) include:

- **Marketing**, which focuses on customers and is responsible for the design, development, promotion, and sale of goods and services.
- **Operations**, which is responsible for the production of goods and/or the delivery of services.
- **Finance**, which is responsible for the monetary inflow and outflow in the organization, as well as debt and borrowing, and reporting on these aspects.
- **Digital**, which is responsible for all technological aspects, likely to include hardware and software, as well as data storage and security.

As you progress through this text you will get much more detail on many of the functions of management.

1.7.2 Management processes

As distinct from functions, management *processes* are the activities that managers use in order to bring people and other resources together to get things done (recall our definition of management). There are many different management processes and it would be

1

impossible to identify and explore all of them. As such, here we identify some of the most common and universal processes that are likely to exist within all organizations and be practised by all managers. We can group processes based on whether they are forward-looking, day-to-day, looking to the past, or exist throughout this spectrum. Management processes include the following:

- Forward-looking: developing **strategy** linked to the mission of the organization and **planning** to determine how that strategy can be achieved. Additionally, **budgeting** is a process essential to determining the financial implications and viability of such plans.

- Day-to-day: **organizing** resources, activities, and tasks so that the strategy and plans are implemented, or **motivating** employees and other key stakeholders whose roles are essential for daily operations and projects.

- Looking to the past: **monitoring** what has occurred in the past to determine whether the plans were implemented smoothly, and, if not, how to react. **Reporting** on different aspects of outputs, outcomes, or performance in order to inform future strategy, planning, or organizing.

- **Decision-making** throughout the spectrum of forward-looking and looking to the past as well as day-to-day. For example, deciding on the goals that the strategy should achieve, determining how and where resources should be allocated, and evaluating what past performance or behaviour is relevant for further consideration.

Table 1.1 depicts management functions and processes in the form of a matrix. While most managers in the various functions will spend time and effort on all management processes, some processes will be more relevant for specific functions. For example, Human Resources managers are likely to spend a significant amount of time organizing and motivating, but will have to undertake all of the other processes at some point. By contrast, Finance managers are likely to spend a significant amount of time on budgeting, monitoring, and reporting.

TABLE 1.1 **Management functions and management processes**

		Management Processes						
		Forward-looking		Day-to-day		Past		Throughout
		Strategy/ Planning	Budgeting	Organizing	Motivating	Monitoring	Reporting	Decision-making
Management Functions	Human Resources							
	Marketing							
	Operations							
	Finance							
	Digital							

1.8 **Management: Roles**

An alternative to a functions and processes view is one which focuses on management's roles, drawing on managerial characteristics. Henry Mintzberg has spent many years studying management and has written a number of influential articles and books. He has been particularly interested in moving away from the theory of management (what managers are said to do) to the empirical reality of management (what managers spend their time actually doing). His research in this area led him to report on the roles of management. He identified 10 management roles ('organized sets of behaviours') which he clustered into three groups, illustrated in Figure 1.5 (Mintzberg, 1973). These groups are interpersonal roles, informational roles, and decisional roles.

Despite presenting these 10 different roles separately, it is worth noting that Mintzberg reported that the wide variety of roles and tasks managers undertake are characterized by their pace, interruptions, brevity, and fragmented activity. That is, he dispelled any notions that managers sit in an office working on one task or role for hours at a time. Rather, they are likely to be simultaneously juggling different responsibilities, are likely to have their work interrupted, and

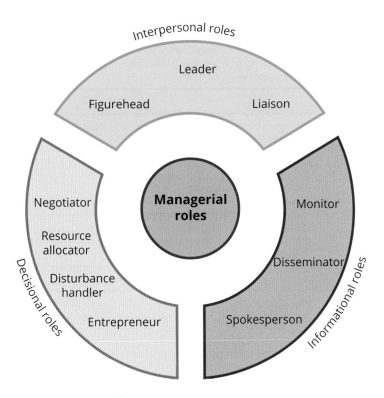

FIGURE 1.5 **Management roles.** Credit: Reprinted by permission of Harvard Business Review. Excerpt/ Exhibit. From 'The Manager's Job: Folklore and Fact' by Henry Mintzberg, March–April 1990. Copyright © 1990 by Harvard Business Publishing; all rights reserved.

may be expected to complete some tasks very quickly and move on to the next. While we can neatly categorize management roles and study them one at a time, managing in the real world is much less orderly and less certain, again emphasizing the importance of a critical thinking lens in both studying and undertaking management. Such a lens helps a manager develop reasoned arguments based on the evidence available immediately (which may not be the best evidence) in order to make fast decisions, before moving quickly to consider the next issue. We will now examine each of Mintzberg's 10 roles in more detail, summarizing these in Table 1.2.

TABLE 1.2 **Mintzberg's 10 management roles**

Interpersonal Roles	
Figurehead	Managers have formal authority over their project, function, or organization and so hold a symbolic position and role, which might include legalities such as signing legal documents, or niceties, such as welcoming guests or partners.
Leader	Managers bring together the needs of the entire organization or project, and the individuals and teams within it by informing, motivating, or guiding others to perform the activities expected of them.
Liaison	Managers facilitate relationships internally within the organization either vertically (between senior, middle, and junior levels) or horizontally (for example across different senior managers), as well as externally with key stakeholders outside the organization, such as suppliers, clients, regulators, or communities.
Informational Roles	
Monitor	Managers continuously seek information about the performance of their task, project, function, or organization.
Disseminator	Managers regularly transmit information to others within the organization, ensuring it is specific, relevant, and appropriate to the individual or team receiving the information.
Spokesperson	Managers transmit information outside the organizations, acting as spokesperson to those who need to be informed, such as the general public, regulators or governments, or stakeholders such as shareholders or suppliers.
Decisional Roles	
Entrepreneur	Managers recognize the need to initiate change, identify opportunities, design change, and drive transformation and action.
Disturbance Handler	Managers react to unforeseen events that cause disruptions to plans, deciding how to overcome these challenges.
Resource Allocator	Managers have a strong grasp of the resources available to them, and determine how to allocate these in the best combination to different tasks, projects, or teams, in order to achieve their aims.
Negotiator	Managers negotiate with key parties who may be internal or external to gain resources, overcome challenges, or even to develop relationships.

1.8.1 **Interpersonal roles**

One group of roles identified by Mintzberg is interpersonal roles, which reflect the relationships managers make and maintain with others. Mintzberg characterized interpersonal roles into three categories: figurehead, leader, or liaison:

- The figurehead role stems from the manager's authority and may be symbolic, but can also have legal components.
- The leader role focuses on the manager bringing together the needs of the organization or specific project, and motivating relevant staff and stakeholders.
- The liaison role is focused on the relationships that the manager develops with those both inside and outside the organization.

This categorization of management roles points to the human nature of both management and organizing more generally. While it is undoubtedly true that in recent years there has been a turn towards more technology-driven aspects of management, there are still many human aspects to the role. Ultimately, organizations all exist with some human aspect to them, and very often exist to address a need, want, or demand of humans.

1.8.2 **Informational roles**

Another group of roles Mintzberg identified are informational roles, which deal with the enormous amount of information that managers need to collect and disseminate in different ways. He identified the monitor, the disseminator, and the spokesperson roles. The monitor role is linked to the collection of information—often continuously—about the teams, projects, or tasks for which the managers are responsible. The information may include:

- informal feedback from team members;
- formal feedback from staff surveys;
- data on operational performance of assets;
- customer satisfaction results;
- sales figures; or
- reports on project impact.

Once managers have collected such information through the monitoring role, they take on a disseminator role internally, ensuring that others have the relevant information they need to complete their own roles, jobs, or tasks. The spokesperson role is more externally facing, ensuring those outside the organization have the information they need. While the spokesperson role may seem similar to the interpersonal liaison role, the latter focuses on relationship development with external parties, while the former focuses on information communication. Remember also that managers undertake multiple roles simultaneously. As such, when a manager interacts with an external party—such as a client—they may both be developing the relationship (the liaison role) as well as communicating key information relevant to the service that the organization is providing (the spokesperson role).

1

1.8.3 **Decisional roles**

Finally, managers have decisional roles, which Mintzberg argued is a crucial part of management. He divides the different roles in this group based on the different types of decisions they need to make: entrepreneur, disturbance handler, resource allocator, and negotiator.

- The entrepreneurial role focuses on proactively initiating change to a task, project, or whole organization. Distinct from 'an entrepreneur' who starts a business, being entrepreneurial is something that anyone can display, even within a large established organization (see Chapter 13).

- The disturbance handler role, on the contrary, is reactionary and requires managers to deal with an unexpected issue beyond their control. As we will see in Chapter 3, managers need to draw on this role to react to unexpected issues and disruptions.

- The resource allocator role is the one most commonly thought of in relation to management: deciding how to allocate resources such as people, equipment, time, managerial effort, and finances to achieve the aims of the project or organization.

- Finally, in the negotiator role, the manager has to interact with others, accept trade-offs, and hold firm on certain issues in order to secure the resources, time, supplies, or other assets necessary to achieve the aims of the project or organization.

There is a link between these final two roles: the negotiator role recognizes the fact that the resource allocator role is not as simple as it may seem. Rarely does a manager have access to all the resources required: the perfect staff or staffing levels, all the money they need, or the ideal equipment. More likely they must negotiate trade-offs and then allocate the resources they have been able to accumulate accordingly. Table 1.2 provides a summary of Mintzberg's 10 management roles.

This slightly chaotic depiction of management roles is worth keeping in mind as you move through this text and take time to study, reflect on, and apply the theories of management you are learning. Study and reflection are exactly what you should be doing as a student of management, but bear in mind that practising managers often have a more hectic and less calm environment that can limit time for reflection and analysis.

1.9 **Management: Levels**

Another way of thinking about management is in relation to the different levels of the organization that managers inhabit. Indeed, we often divide organizations into senior management and middle management, and distinguish these levels from employees. In large organizations, as hierarchies grow, there is probably a group of junior management as well. These individuals are sometimes called 'front line' managers, as they are dealing directly with the key tasks or functions of the organization. We will now explore these three different levels of management to understand what distinguishes them, starting with the front line.

1.9.1 **Front line managers**

Front line managers direct the day-to-day activities and operations of a specific task or project, often implementing operational plans developed by middle managers. While they may be more junior in the hierarchy, they frequently hold the ultimate power and responsibility for achieving objectives or completing tasks: that is, they are often the most important manager in determining the success of a project, and the management and treatment of employees. They may have direct and daily responsibility for a specific asset like a piece of machinery or a website, and have very clear objectives and a short-term time frame.

Front line managers need to assess the concerns and issues linked to their project or area, such as those raised by the employees who report to them. They then determine what they can act on themselves, and what they should escalate to a more senior manager. Such escalation may be needed if solving the issue requires action from outside their area of responsibility or control. This might be either because it is linked to a wider or longer-term issue that should be considered strategically, or because it requires an investment of resources beyond the front line manager's sign-off. If we picture an organization like an office building, a front line manager will be sitting in one room, with a specific group of people, all with their heads down, focused on their task or project.

Recent trends have seen flatter organizational structures with fewer levels of hierarchy. As such, the role of front line managers has been expanding and they have taken on some of the responsibilities of the shrinking middle management layer.

1

1.9.2 **Middle managers**

Middle managers hold more responsibility for a wider range of different tasks or projects. They usually manage more people, and organize across whole units, departments, functions, or locations. Middle managers often implement the strategic plans which are developed by senior managers. They will likely spend less time on reactive day-to-day issues, typically getting involved only in those issues that their front line managers escalate. Instead, they will focus on the coordination and organization of various tasks and projects. If we picture an organization like an office building, a middle manager will be walking up and down a corridor monitoring the tasks and projects being completed in different rooms and ensuring they are available to intervene when issues emerge or in order to improve coordination between different rooms.

Large organizations may have several layers of middle management, although the trend is for this to reduce, both because of the role of automation in organizing and co-ordinating tasks, as well as the delegation of more management responsibility to front line managers.

1.9.3 **Senior managers**

Senior managers have overall responsibility for the organization. A group of senior managers is often called the 'C-suite', referring to having 'Chief' in their job title: Chief Executive Officer (CEO), Chief Financial Officer (CFO), or Chief Sustainability Officer (CSO), for example. The most senior manager may be called the CEO, but also may be the Managing Director, the Chairperson (Chair), or the President. Senior managers are primarily focused on setting the mission and purpose of the organization, and developing the future-looking strategy (rather than daily operations), drawing what they need from the internal and external environments in order to inform that strategy. As such, their view will not only be inward-looking but also external-looking—sometimes called horizon scanning. If we picture an organization like an office building, a senior manager is in the foyer, with a view down all the corridors to their middle managers to stay apprised of what is happening internally, as well as regularly turning to look out the front doors to see what is happening externally.

Much of senior managers' time will also be spent as the figurehead or 'voice' of the organization, communicating with both internal and external stakeholders. This role links to recent trends which have seen the most senior manager of some especially large organizations becoming the brand or face of the organization both to the entire staff body, and more publicly in the media. For example, Apple became synonymous with Steve Jobs and Facebook with Mark Zuckerberg. Other recent trends have seen questions raised over the level of remuneration of senior management, especially in comparison to workforce remuneration.

Table 1.3 provides a summary of the different levels of management we have discussed in this section. While all three levels of management are likely to exist in larger, traditional organizations, many smaller, newer, or more innovative organizations adopt very different structures. These might employ matrix structures (where employees report to multiple managers in an attempt to keep communications open and prevent silos), have a much flatter hierarchy with fewer layers of management, or have innovative approaches to task management, often

TABLE 1.3 **Levels of management**

Level of management	Focused on	Temporal perspective	Recent trends
Front line	Specific task or project	Short-term	Increasing responsibilities and roles.
Middle	Multiple tasks and projects and how they fit together	Short- to medium-term	Decreasing in number, due to increased delegation and role of technology in undertaking monitoring and coordination roles.
Senior	All tasks and projects, as well as the external environment and the future	Medium- to long-term; becoming longer-term as firms become more 'purpose-driven'	Increasingly the face of the organization. Questions raised over remuneration levels.

utilizing agile decision-making, communications, and tracking technology. We will see some of these examples throughout this text.

Let's return to Imperial Fine Foods, our fictional organization, and get a sense of its management roles, processes, and levels, as well as the people who occupy these roles and the issues they face in Running case 1.2.

RUNNING CASE 1.2 **MANAGING IMPERIAL**

Lucy has now been CEO of Imperial for three months. She was apprehensive when she started; she knew it wouldn't be easy to succeed her father. He'd been in the job for as long as she could remember, and he'd always seemed so calm and in control. In practice, everything has turned out to be much more difficult than she had anticipated. On most days since she took over from Hugh, Lucy has felt anything but calm and in control. She tries not to show it to the staff, but there's just so much to worry about! Hugh had warned her that business had got tougher over the last few years, and she knew before she took over from him that Imperial was making less profit each year despite everyone's efforts.

Now she is living with the problems every day. Changing regulations and staff shortages have made running the factory much more challenging. Brexit has made Imperial's relationships with its European customers and suppliers much less straightforward than they were in the past. And though

Hugh was rather sceptical when she told him that she had decided to eat less meat, eating habits are definitely changing throughout their customer base. The trouble is, Lucy realizes, Imperial's product range isn't keeping pace with these changes.

Although Imperial is a much smaller company than Fairtrade Food, where she used to work, Lucy finds it harder than she expected to manage the organization. The finance and HR staff report to her younger brother William Green, the Chief Financial Officer (CFO). The Factory Manager and Supply Chain Manager report to Bob Smart, Chief Operating Officer (COO), who is her father's age and has always been considered a great asset to the business. Even though she trusts both William and Bob, Lucy still feels she has to know what they are doing every day.

Lucy decided when she became CEO that she would retain direct control of the commercial part of the business, which means that John Brown, the Sales Manager, and Gita Patel, the Marketing

(Continued)

Manager, both report directly to her. So, on top of getting updates from William and Bob on their parts of the business, she also has to work closely with John and Gita. She feels she must also be sure that all the company's front line managers, the people responsible for managing the employees and their work in the factory and warehouse, are happy and effective. On top of that, in his handover to her, Hugh emphasized that Imperial's compliance with laws and regulations is now her legal responsibility, and that she should also take a special personal interest in the company's major suppliers and customers to continue to build good relationships. There just never seem to be enough hours in the day.

Questions for reflection:

1. Considering the management processes listed in the columns of Table 1.1, which do you think would dominate the daily activities of Lucy, William, and Bob, respectively?

2. Which of Mintzberg's roles (Figure 1.5) can you identify in what you know of Lucy's experience as a manager so far?

3. Should Lucy be taking a special interest in whether the front line managers are happy and effective? Provide an argument for and against this and determine which argument you think is more convincing.

1.10 **Conclusion**

We opened this chapter by exploring why the study of management can be daunting but also liberating and fascinating. Throughout, we demonstrated why managing does not lend itself to 'how-to' or 'step-by-step' guides, but is instead context-dependent—varying depending on expectations, the type of organization, and its purpose, as well as the individual who is managing. We defined management as a social and operational process with the aim of bringing people and other resources together in order to get something done. We explored management as a science, craft, or art, and looked at more granular aspects of what managers *do*, including functions (like human resources), processes (like planning), and the roles they take on (like interpersonal roles). We introduced more complexity when exploring the purpose of management, linked to issues such as the end of coercion and a focus on efficiency, especially in a western context. Finally, we undertook a brief journey on the history of management as it is typically taught. However, here again we moved away from simply accepting this, in order to question arguments and query the evidence around the suggestions that 'better' management has emerged in more recent years. As we come to the end of the first chapter of this text we hope you are keen to understand more, explore more, think more, discuss and debate more, and come to your own conclusions as you study management.

CHAPTER SUMMARY

○ Management can be defined as a social and operational process with the aim of bringing people and other resources together in order to get something done.

○ Studying management is complex as it is context-specific and requires a critical thinking lens.

○ We can say that management emerged following the end of coercion as a means of getting things done, and has strong links to issues of 'value' and 'efficiency'.

○ Manager's decisions, behaviours, and attitudes have impacts at the level of the individual, the organization, as well as wider society.

○ Management can be classified based on functions or processes, different roles (interpersonal, informational, and decisional), or different levels (front line, middle, and senior).

CLOSING CASE REFLECTION

What a manager looks like

Reflecting on our opening case study, we can imagine the balancing act that Indra Nooyi must have faced as a manager. During her career, Nooyi has undertaken all of the different management processes we identified in this chapter, although probably focusing more on strategy and planning, during her tenure as CEO, and budgeting, monitoring, and reporting, during her time as CFO. The key decisional roles would have been particularly prominent in her choices as regards the sale and acquisition of different brands, based on her view of the company's pathway to success. Such strategic decisions were subject to significant scrutiny by shareholders and the public. Nooyi was also globally recognized for her interpersonal strengths, her compassion, and as a skilled communicator.

However, as well as a manager, Indra Nooyi is also a human. Her autobiography, *My Life in Full* (2021), focuses in particular on work–life balance, where she admits that there were many times when she felt she fell short as a mother (Nooyi has two daughters). She also publicly shares the credit for her success with her husband, Raj, noting, 'the truth is, there is no such thing as balancing work and family. It's a constant juggling act. And many times, it's the people around us—like our life partners—who make this juggling possible' (Johnson, 2023).

REVIEW QUESTIONS

1. Why is studying management challenging?

2. How does this chapter define management? What else might you expect to see in a definition of management? Why?

3. What is the link between management and the end of coercion as a means of getting things done?

4. Why is a simplified history of management unlikely to reflect reality?

5. Considering Table 1.1, what are examples of some management processes that you can map onto a management function, such as human resources?

1

EXPLORE MORE

- **WATCH** Elizabeth Lyle talk about 'How to Break Bad Management Habits Before They Reach the Next Generation of Leaders', by searching for 'Elizabeth Lyle' on the TED Talks website.

- **READ** a blog from US-based executive coaching company Jody Michael Associates which explores the truths no one tells you when you become a manager, and consider whether you agree or disagree with the author's views. Search for 'Becoming a Manager: What No One Tells You' on Google.

- **READ** the text from Todd Bridgman and Stephen Cummings called *A Very Short, Fairly Interesting and Reasonably Cheap Book about Management Theory* (published in 2021 by Sage). It provides a fascinating insight into the history of management theory. You can also watch extracts of this book by searching for its title on YouTube.

- **READ** the autobiography of Indra Nooyi, *My Life in Full: Work, Family, and Our Future* (2021), to understand her background as well as her life as a manager.

- **WATCH** Indra Nooyi talk about 'Truths from the Top' at the 2019 Women in the World Summit, interviewed by Margaret Brennan, CBS News, in a session about the lessons she learnt during her time as one of the world's most successful female CEOs. Search for 'Indra Nooyi truths from the top' on YouTube.

CHAPTER TWO
Exploring Organizations

Sarah Birrell Ivory and Emma Macdonald

OPENING CASE STUDY **WHO ARE OUR FIREFIGHTERS?**

Most cities and towns have firefighting services, often run by governments, charged with protecting communities from fire and other dangers. However, these services have been provided by different types of organizations in the past, and still today.

In the late eighteenth century, fire services were often provided by businesses: it was part of the service offered by insurance companies to their customers. However, this left uninsured buildings to burn. As such, some citizens organized volunteer fire services, with equipment funded by charities.

Governments, recognizing the benefit to entire communities of putting out fires in their early stages, began organizing and funding fire services from the early nineteenth century onwards. The Singapore Fire Brigade was officially formed in 1888, equipped with horse-drawn steam fire engines (Remember Singapore, 2014). In Nigeria's capital, the first fire service began in 1901 as a police department—the Lagos Police Fire Brigade (Simwa, 2019). Both are examples of government-funded services, and this is the most common model globally.

However, fire services are not universally provided by governments, as seen in Copenhagen, Denmark. In 1906, Sophus Falck established Falcks Redningskorps (Falck Rescue Corps) after witnessing the disorganized firefighting attempts at the Great Christiansborg Palace. Starting as a family-owned business, Falck's original motto was to always assist, irrespective of ability to pay. As such, we might call this a social enterprise. Today, Falcks Redningskorps provides 65 per cent of fire services, and 85 per cent of ambulance services in Denmark, often entering into contracts with governments.

Context can be important when considering the management of fire services. In the Australian state of Victoria, the government funds two different fire services: the metropolitan/town fire brigades with a permanent, professional body of firefighters, and the Country Fire Authority (CFA) with 55,000 volunteer firefighters who fight bushfires during the summer months. While both are government funded, the CFA has specific management challenges, more like a charity, as they are reliant on firefighters who volunteer their services because of a sense of duty and goodwill.

2.1 **Introduction**

There are many contexts in which management happens, including parents managing family members' activities and commitments, or students managing time, deadlines, and social pursuits. However, in this text we are focused on managing organizations. As such, an essential precursor to exploring different management theories, practices, or approaches (as we do in Parts 2, 3, and 4) is understanding key aspects of the organizations in which management happens. **Organizations** are defined as a collective of people, working together, with a particular purpose, typically comprising structures, hierarchies, legal contracts, employees, strategies, and plans. All organizations require some form of management, even though they vary greatly based on a wide range of factors. While all organizations have commonalities, a management practice or approach in one type of organization may be less effective, or may even result in failure, in a different type of organization. Moreover, there are several areas of disagreement, contention, and ongoing debate about what organizations do, why they exist, whom they serve, and how they are run and are held to account. Giving consideration to these topics at the start of your journey in studying management will enable you to continuously come back to these ideas and to better apply the critical thinking lens we encouraged you to adopt in Section 1.1.2.

2.2 **Categorizing organizations**

While there are many different ways to categorize organizations, in this chapter we will explore them based on the sector within which they operate: the **private sector**, the **public sector**, and the **third sector**.

It is important to think critically about the distinctions between organizations in different sectors for a number of reasons. Firstly, despite management being commonly associated with business (in the private sector), many graduates of management programmes, and even business degrees, do not work in the private sector for their entire career, or at all. Seeing management as a universal skill across many different sectors and contexts broadens the view of graduates as to what opportunities lie ahead. Secondly, organizations from different sectors are increasingly working together on specific projects, programmes, or contracts. Moreover, some organizations from different sectors may compete for such projects or contracts. Being able to think critically about the similarities and differences between management in these different sectors will be useful in your future roles working together with, or working competitively against, an organization in a different sector. Finally, there are very few hard or permanent distinctions between the organizations in these different sectors. Indeed, throughout this chapter we will learn about organizations starting in one sector and becoming more similar to, or entirely changing into, a different sector. Being able to think about management in many different (and changing) contexts is essential to be able to perform well, irrespective of the sectors you end up working in.

We will now briefly introduce the three different sectors, before examining each in greater detail.

2.2.1 **Private sector organizations**

An organization in the private sector is often called a commercial organization or a business: we will use the latter term throughout this text. A **business** is an organization engaged in some form of trade: the production, distribution, and sale of goods or services for profit. **Profit** can be defined as the difference between how much is earned in a trade as compared to how much the trade costs the seller. A trade such as this is called a business transaction, although such transactions can happen in other sectors, such as a charity shop in the third sector selling goods. A business can be as small as a mechanic working alone and fixing cars in a garage, or as large as Unilever, a global corporation which comprises 150,000 people, 400 different brand names, and operates in 190 countries.

While defining a business in this way is accurate, it also obscures an issue that has come to prominence in understanding 'business': the role of profit. While all businesses incorporate some focus on profit, the extent of this is debated. We will return to this issue of the focus on profit in Section 2.3, as well as the purpose shift we are seeing in Section 2.6.3.

2.2.2 **Public sector organizations**

Public sector organizations are sometimes called governmental organizations. They are typically wholly or largely owned (and often run) by government. Public sector organizations include local or municipal councils, national governments, as well as the departments and services that they run, including the military, police, and education organizations.

Public sector organizations exist to provide **public goods**, which are broadly defined as goods or services that benefit all members of society, usually provided without cost to users. This might include paved roads, or education. In the study of economics, public goods are more precisely defined as those which are non-excludable (people can't be stopped from accessing or using them) and non-rivalrous (the consumption by one person does not reduce availability to others) (Gillespie, 2023). While there are some public goods that are universally accepted, different countries have differing ideological, cultural, political, and other reasons which determine what is—and what is not—a public good. For example, a minimum standard of health care is typically a public good in most countries, provided through hospitals funded by government. However, how far this extends—and what further care is provided without cost to patients— varies greatly between different countries.

Public goods are provided because it is generally accepted that there are some services that people should be able to access irrespective of their ability to pay, and because the provision of such services contributes to a stable society. An example of this is the public education system. Ensuring every child, irrespective of their ability to pay, has access to primary and secondary education is recognized in most countries as a basic human right, and a benefit to the individual who undertakes that education. However, having an educated society does not just benefit the individual. It also ensures that organizations have a pool of skilled labour to comprise their

2

workforce, it decreases crime and reliance on government benefits as individuals can support themselves through employment, and it ensures that citizens can make informed choices when voting in elections. As such, it makes more sense for governments to provide education as a public good. However, it has not always been this way. In many countries, children's education was originally provided by religious organizations or charities, which are part of the third sector which we will now outline.

2.2.3 Third sector organizations

Third sector organizations are sometimes called non-profit organizations, not-for-profit organizations (NFPs), or non-governmental organizations (NGOs), or referred to as the voluntary or civic sector. The third sector is, in some ways, a catch-all category for organizations which are neither private nor public sector. It exists to fill the gap between private and public sector service provision. It includes charities, activist organizations, community clubs, trade unions, and industry bodies. Such organizations can be very small and local—such as a food bank operating in a local neighbourhood, like the Edinburgh Food Project—or large, international, NFPs with complex global operations—such as the Red Cross/Red Crescent, the world's largest humanitarian network.

Third sector organizations exist and thrive all over the world and make a substantial contribution to people's health and well-being—as well as to animals, habitats, the environment, and cultural or historical artefacts. These organizations exist because humans care, want to come together to help, and have a passion to protect what is important to them and what they believe in. Those involved in third sector organizations are often motivated by something they believe in, or something they enjoy and want to promote. This makes the management of the third sector different to that of the public or private sector, as we will see throughout this chapter.

Despite outlining the differences between these three sectors, and the organizations within them, being able to determine which sector an organization belongs to is more complicated than it first seems. Moreover, organizations doing the same or a very similar thing, might all be part of different sectors. Spotlight 2.1 on the UK water industry shows an example of how the same service (water provision) within one country can be run by organizations from all three different sectors.

While we have described the three sectors here separately, in reality there are overlaps between sectors. That is, there are organizations that do not fit neatly within just one sector but hold characteristics of two sectors. Figure 2.1 depicts the three sectors and the overlaps between them. Organizations that exist in the overlap between the private and third sector are often called hybrid organizations and are examined in more detail in Section 2.6.3. Organizations which exist in the overlap between the public and third sector often include educational institutions, such as public universities, who are funded (or part-funded) by government and subject to government oversight, but are explicitly free from government control or intervention.

We now move on to explore each of the three sectors in much more detail, starting with the private sector.

SPOTLIGHT 2.1 **THE UK WATER INDUSTRY**

The UK water industry demonstrates how, within just one country (albeit with the devolved nations of Scotland, Wales, and Northern Ireland), organizations doing exactly the same thing can belong to different sectors.

Scottish Water was established by the Scottish Government in 2002 and operates across Scotland. As such, it is a *public sector organization*—more specifically, a non-departmental public body. This means that while the Scottish Government sets objectives and appoints the Chair and non-executive members of the board, it then allows Scottish Water to make its own operating and strategic decisions, subject to specific regulators including the Scottish Environment Protection Agency. Any financial surplus ('profit') generated is either reinvested back into the organization, used to reduce customer bills, or returned to government. The Board of Directors (appointed by the government) makes these decisions.

Wessex Water operates in the south west of England, including Bristol and Bournemouth. Since 2002 it has been owned by a Malaysian-based company which owns utilities across the world. As such, it is a *private sector organization*. Wessex Water is run by a board of executive and non-executive

directors, appointed by the owners, who are subject to UK regulators including the Environment Agency. Any profit generated is either reinvested back into the business, used to reduce customer bills, or returned to the owners. The Board of Directors (appointed by the owners) makes these decisions.

Dwy Cymru (Welsh Water) operates in Wales, and part of west England. It does not have shareholders (similar to Scottish Water) but is also independent of government (similar to Wessex Water). As such, it is a *third sector organization*. Sixty-three members represent the customers of Dwy Cymru (additional members can be added in accordance with the membership policy). They appoint an independent Board of Directors, who are subject to UK regulators including the Environment Agency on some issues, and the Welsh government on other issues. Any financial surplus ('profit') is either reinvested back into the organization or used to reduce customer bills. The Board of Directors (appointed by members) makes these decisions.

This discussion of UK water provision demonstrates how exactly the same service (provision of water) can be provided by organizations from the public, private, or third sector.

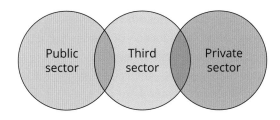

FIGURE 2.1 **Organizations operating in each sector, and sector overlaps.**

2.3 **Private sector organizations: Businesses**

As we have already explored, the private sector comprises business organizations that are involved in business transactions which include some element of profit. We now examine how such organizations emerged, focusing initially on the first business transactions.

2.3.1 **The emergence of businesses**

The first 'business' transactions were forms of bartering—an exchange or trade in which no cash or money is involved. I might trade six eggs from my chickens for a jug of milk from your cow. Bartering is less common today, but does still exist in more informal agreements, such as a bricklayer building a new wall for a colleague who is a plumber, in exchange for the colleague fixing the plumbing in the bricklayer's home. Moreover, online platforms—such as Craigslist and Facebook Marketplace—are increasingly facilitating a resurgence in bartering.

Bartering is based on *direct exchange* (of eggs for milk; of a wall for plumbing) with the owners of each product or service negotiating directly with each other. This means that each owner can take into account any factors they care about in their negotiations and ultimate decision. If I am unhappy with the way you treat your cow, I can factor that into my decision to sell you my eggs. Or I could pay a different farmer more (say eight eggs) for milk from a better-treated cow. Of course, bartering requires that you have what I want—and that I have what you want.

The invention that changed these first business transactions was money. While money has a long and complex history, we can think of it as metal coins, printed notes, or an electronic or digital account, which are all representations of underlying value. The invention of money created a system which facilitated *indirect exchange* with a standardized means of valuing goods and services. This new system, in turn, led to more complex and ambitious business transactions, and supported the geographic breadth of trade—after all, there is only so far you can travel with six eggs before they break or go bad.

Despite the potential that money provided for more ambitious trade, until the twentieth century, most businesses were still owned, financed, and run by small family groups operating from a single location and selling to customers in the local area. They may have aimed to make a profit to support the family and grow the business, but this element of profit had not yet come to define them. The Industrial Revolution, however, led to a number of changes which contributed to the birth of the for-profit business that many will recognize today.

The Industrial Revolution began in the UK in the mid-eighteenth century, but spread to Europe and then further afield in the nineteenth century. It saw a shift from an agricultural-based economy to one based on the production of goods, typically in large factories built in urban areas. While the impacts of the Industrial Revolution fill entire textbooks, we will identify some factors which impacted management—then and now. We will then explore further implications of the Industrial Revolution in Chapter 3.

Until the Industrial Revolution, the energy that created power to produce goods and services was small-scale. This energy included three main sources:

- animal, such as teams of oxen to plough fields;
- natural—or, as we know it, 'renewable'—powering individual water wheels or windmills, for example, to grind wheat into flour; and
- human, either through coerced labour (see the discussion of slavery in Section 1.3) or through skilled artisan workers, such as bakers turning flour into bread by hand.

One driver of the Industrial Revolution was alternative sources of energy derived from fossil fuels (including coal, petroleum, and natural gas). This facilitated new inventions, such as the internal combustion engine. Work previously requiring animal, natural, or human energy could be completed more quickly and efficiently by machines powered by fossil fuel energy. For example, tractors could achieve more than teams of oxen, and factories could house machinery to undertake production processes at scale, such as grinding wheat. This usage of fossil fuels, in turn, reduced the value of skilled artisan workers as their products could be replicated at a lower cost and higher scale in factories. The workforce dynamics therefore shifted to accommodate the new methods of production, with more people needing to be located where factories were being concentrated, typically in cities, to undertake the unskilled, routinized tasks that were integrated with new machinery. Integrating human work with machinery efficiently was a complex task and required more oversight from management processes to ensure that human activity was used effectively and that raw materials were properly processed through each step, to result in products that could be sold.

Until this point, most businesses were established, operated, and expanded with funds from the owner or their family. The use of money to facilitate trade and fossil fuels to power centralized factories (as well as many other factors) shifted the economy towards larger businesses with greater ambition: producing more of their primary product, diversifying to produce other products, operating in more than one location, and selling their products further afield (including beyond national borders). Increased size and ambition called for more funding to build factories, employ many workers, and pay for raw materials: potentially all before the business was in a position to sell any actual products. As such, increasingly, businesses sought funding from a number of different individuals who received a share of ownership in return. That is, they became shareholders.

The increasing number of shareholders contributed to another important shift. Previously businesses were run by their owners. But with the emergence of shareholders, a new profession emerged: a manager appointed by the shareholders to run the business and act in their interests. While the emergence of managers may sound like a simple and obvious development, as we will see throughout this text, this change has contributed to a number of significant issues, debates, and unexpected impacts. But first, having explored how businesses emerged, let's look at how we can categorize them.

2

2.3.2 **Classifying businesses**

Businesses are organizations involved in some form of trade for profit. Within this broad description there are a number of different ways to categorize businesses, all of which can help inform different elements of management. Here we will briefly explore three different ways of categorizing business: by their size, by their offering (e.g. product or service), or by the type of ownership.

Size

Classifying businesses by size may seem simple; however, there are different ways to assess size. A common approach is to categorize businesses by number of employees, divided into four groups: micro, small, medium, and large. Figure 2.2 indicates the number of employees typically associated with each category, although definitions can vary across different governments and other institutions that report on such factors. However, we can also categorize size by a business' revenue (how much they earn), or by their market capitalization (the value of their shares). In 2021, the largest business globally by employees was the US-based retailer Walmart, which employed 2.3 million people (CompaniesMarketCap, 2023). It was also the largest business by revenue, earning over US$600 billion (Statista, 2022a). The largest business by market capitalization (the value of the shares issued) was Apple, valued at around US$2.64 trillion (Statista, 2022b).

Offering (product or service)

Businesses may be classified based on whether they are focused on products (making or selling goods) or services (creating or selling advice, expertise, solutions, experiences, etc.).

We can think of a good as something tangible which results in ownership, and a service as something intangible which typically involves use or experience, but does not result in ownership.

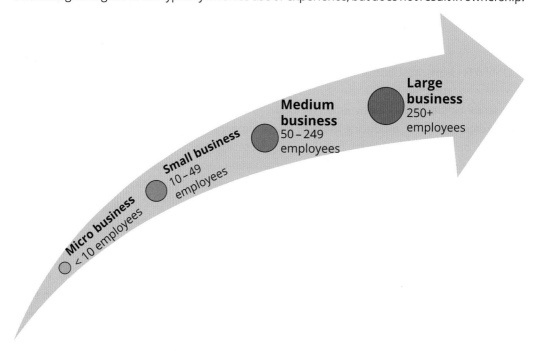

FIGURE 2.2 **Business categories by size.**

FIGURE 2.3 **The product–service continuum.**

For example, historically automobile companies produced a product (a car) that they sold to a customer (transferring ownership). Conversely, public transport companies provided a service to a customer (a bus journey). Given the emergence of the 'sharing economy' and a focus on more efficient use of resources, we are increasingly seeing a shift towards a service-based economy, even in areas traditionally dominated by product sales. In the car industry for example, car leasing and car clubs are growing significantly, in which customers get access to the benefits of owning a car for a period of time, without ever actually owning it.

We can think of products and services on a continuum, as depicted in Figure 2.3. Some businesses may focus only a product (potatoes) or only on a service (education). However, others may offer a combination, such as a restaurant which offers a product (a meal) as well as a service (the delivery of the meal, and the experience of the dining environment).

Ownership structure

In addition to size and offering, a useful way of classifying businesses is based on their ownership structure. This is because it can have significant implications for management, as we will see throughout this chapter. Ownership structures are grounded in legal frameworks, which have differing implications for the rights and responsibilities of owners and managers of the business. While there are many different ownership structures, we will present just three here: sole traders, partnerships, and limited companies. However, in order to distinguish between them and understand the implications for management, we first need to outline the concept of 'liability'.

Liability refers to the extent to which an individual person who owns part of a business can be held legally responsible for it, including in relation to its debts. Liability can take two forms: unlimited and limited. An ownership structure with **unlimited liability** means that the owner (or owners) can be held personally responsible for the business. In extreme situations, such as bankruptcy where the business has unpaid debts or fines, owners with unlimited liability are legally obliged to meet these costs. If they cannot do so from their own personal finances, they may be forced to sell other assets such as their car or house. **Limited liability**, however, means that the owner (or owners) cannot be held personally responsible for the business. In the case of bankruptcy comprising unpaid debts or fines, the owners may lose the value of their shares, but they are not legally obliged to cover any additional costs. As such, their 'liability' for the business is 'limited' to the value of their shareholding. Now that we understand liability, we can explore the most common types of ownership structures.

A **sole trader** is the simplest ownership structure in which the business is owned by one person. Common sole traders include gardeners, hairdressers, electricians, or bookkeepers who work for themselves with no or few employees. Though advantageous in terms of the simple structure, the disadvantage is that the sole trader personally takes all the risk associated with the business, including unlimited liability for its debts, and can find it difficult to get additional investment to grow their business.

TABLE 2.1 **Business ownership structures**

Ownership structure	Number of owners	Liability	Example
Sole trader	One	Unlimited	An independent bicycle repairer
Partnership	Two+	Usually unlimited, but can be made limited	Ernst & Young (EY)—professional services firm
Limited company	Only restricted by the number of shares issued	Limited	Tesco PLC—supermarket

A **partnership** is a group of at least two individuals who co-own their business. Common partnerships include dental, medical, or law practices. Partnerships require a legal contract which outlines how much money each invested and what role each partner plays. Similar to sole traders, partners have unlimited liability, although there are legal mechanisms to create a limited partnership which addresses this issue of liability, which are especially common as the number of partners grows.

Finally, a common ownership structure is a **limited company** which issues a certain number of shares (sometimes called 'stocks'). These can often be identified by acronyms following their names such as PLC (public limited company—not to be confused with public sector), LLC (limited liability company), or Pty Ltd (proprietary limited). Shares are bought by individuals or other companies, who become shareholders. The only restriction on the number of shareholders is the number of shares that have been issued. Shareholders have limited liability for the business. Sometimes shares are traded publicly on one of the 60 major stock exchanges globally, such as the FTSE in London or the New York Stock Exchange. However, shares can also be held privately and not listed on a stock exchange. Limited companies are run by a Board of Directors, appointed by the shareholders. Table 2.1 illustrates the different ownership structures and their associated liability.

2.3.3 Management challenges in businesses

This text is dedicated to understanding, and overcoming, the challenges of management across all types of organizations. However, here we will touch on some challenges of managing businesses specifically. That said, management challenges can be very different in different types of businesses. Referring back to classifications of business, the size and offering can be a factor in this. The management challenges for an accounting business with just five employees operating locally will be different than those of a bike manufacturing firm with 5,000 employees selling products globally. However, here we focus on common challenges associated with managing a business.

Consider first the three statements about the purpose of business:

A: Businesses exist to make a profit, and do so by producing goods and services.

B: Businesses exist to produce goods and services, and in doing so make a profit.

C: Businesses exist to support a thriving society, by producing goods and services, and in doing so make a profit.

These statements vary based on the purpose of the business or the reason for its existence: for the profit itself, for the production of goods and services, or to support a thriving society. When asking this in our teaching and executive education, there is often much division over which statement best reflects people's views. Moreover, many believe so strongly in one specific statement, that they cannot believe others support different statements.

What we can conclude is that this fundamental question about why business exists, and its relationship to profit, is contested. This is not necessarily a problem—people can have different views on this, and, indeed, different businesses can exist for different reasons, or can balance a number of reasons, such as social enterprises, which we discuss in Section 2.6.3. However, it does become an issue when different stakeholders of a business have differing views, which can present a significant challenge for the managers. This is particularly the case when owners or shareholders hold a specific view, which is linked to the challenge of governance.

Governance and ownership

Governance refers to the system by which an organization is controlled and held to account for the actions and decisions of management. As such, it is often linked to the complex relationship between owners and managers. In owner-operated businesses such as sole traders or partnerships, the owners also run the business. As such, there is an alignment between the owner's view of the purpose of the business and the manager's view: because they are the same person (or people). However, in relation to a limited company which comprises many shareholders, a Board of Directors led by a Chair is appointed to oversee the governance of the business, and a manager, often called a Chief Executive Officer (CEO) or a Managing Director, is appointed to run it.

While this may sound straightforward, many businesses have complex shareholding structures. This creates two challenges for managers in relation to shareholders: one of distance and another of diversity of interests. Even if (and we will challenge this shortly) a CEO is aiming to make decisions in the interests of shareholders, how does the CEO know what these interests are? Moreover, what if different shareholders have different interests?

Most CEOs will have visibility of their largest shareholders and particularly those who own shares in their business directly. However, there may be a significant number of smaller shareholders, as well as those who invest indirectly, through investment fund managers. Figure 2.4 provides a simplified view of the distance that emerges between shareholders and managers.

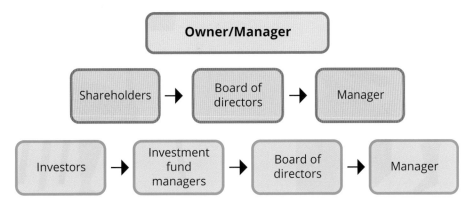

FIGURE 2.4 **Distance between owners (shareholders/investors) and the manager of a business.**

2

This distance, among other factors, has led Boards of Directors and their appointed CEOs to focus on what is typically a common interest of most shareholders: to increase the value of their shareholding in part by increasing profit. However, as we have indicated, shareholders may have many different interests, ethics, ambitions, and principles. As such, a CEO must attempt to understand and navigate these interests. This becomes particularly challenging when shareholders have competing interests—for example, when some shareholders expect a business to maximize short-term profit at any costs, and other shareholders expect more attention to long-term value through innovative products or services, to ethics or principles, or to the contribution to a thriving society.

This difference between an owner-operator business and a shareholder business can be understood by considering the managers depicted in Figure 2.5: Duncan MacLean and Dianne Patel.

In 1722, Duncan is a blacksmith who owns and runs his own metal forge in a village in rural Scotland. He is well known in his region for making swords. A man unknown to Duncan walks into his forge and wants to order 500 swords. Duncan has to decide whether to accept this order. In 2022, Dianne is the CEO of a defence manufacturing firm based in Paris. A buyer unknown to the business wants to order 500 rocket grenade launchers. Dianne has to decide whether to accept this order.

In this scenario, Duncan is an owner-operator, meaning he is both the owner and the manager of his business. As such, Duncan can take into account (or ignore) any factors he chooses to when making his decision. This might include:

- his own financial interests and those of his family;
- his concern for the safety of his family and fellow villagers;
- his political allegiances (this was a turbulent time in Scotland);
- his supply of raw materials for such an order; or simply
- the fact that he promised his neighbour he would make horseshoes.

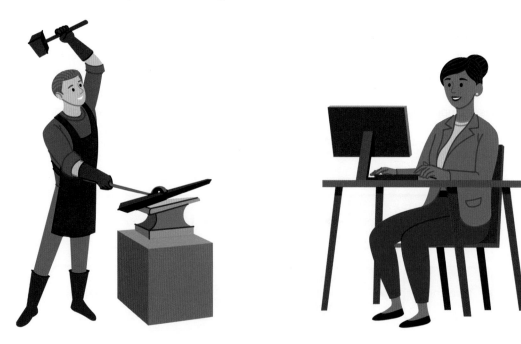

FIGURE 2.5 **Example managers: Duncan MacLean, 1772, and Dianne Patel, 2022.**

Ultimately, Duncan may have some, all, or none of these reasons, linked to his desires, interests, ethics, ambitions, and principles. But, importantly, he does not need to *justify* his ultimate decision to anyone other than himself.

Dianne is in a more complex position. She has been appointed as CEO by the Board of Directors to make decisions. In whose interests does she make these decisions? A simplistic answer is that she makes decisions in the interests of her shareholders. However, as we have already pointed out, she may not know who all her ultimate shareholders actually are, and even the major shareholders may have a number of competing views and opinions. However, there is a further issue which creates a significant challenge for any business, but in particular for a complex shareholder-owned business like the one Dianne leads: how does she balance the interests of *all* of her different stakeholders?

Balancing shareholders and stakeholders

All organizations—across all sectors—have many different stakeholders. The stakeholders of an organization include any individuals, groups, communities, other organizations, or entities like the natural environment who have a direct or indirect stake or interest in the operations of the organization. We explore stakeholders in much greater detail in Section 4.6.1. Figure 2.6 provides a depiction of a number of different stakeholders that an organization might need to consider.

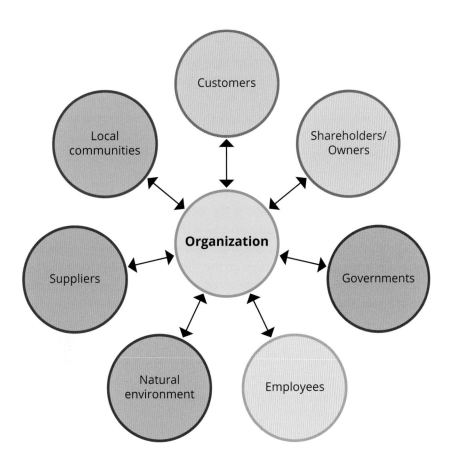

FIGURE 2.6 **Stakeholders of an organization.**

2

Not all organizations will have all of the stakeholders listed, and different organizations will prioritize the interests of different stakeholders. The ways in which managers choose to behave and the decisions they make have implications for all of these different stakeholders, and indeed for society more widely. This is where a specific management challenge for businesses—especially shareholder-owned businesses—occurs: in balancing the interests of shareholders versus other stakeholders.

There has been a trend in business which has focused on shareholder primacy: prioritizing profits and shareholder returns over other stakeholder interests (Stout, 2012). For example, cutting your workforce and reducing remaining employees' pay to save on salary costs, changing to lower-cost suppliers and bargaining hard to reduce input costs, or attracting new customers who your competitors do not want to do business with. None of these decisions is wrong—and management may have sound reasons to support them. However, they may also weaken the longer-term success of the business—for example, because the remaining employees become overworked and stressed, because the new supplier's inputs are of inferior quality, or because the relationship with the new customer risks the reputation of the business.

Acclaimed Cornell Law Professor Lynn Stout's book on this issue is titled *The Shareholder Value Myth: How Putting Shareholders First Harms Investors, Corporations and the Public*. Note especially her subtitle: she provides arguments and evidence that putting shareholders first harms *shareholders themselves* (which she terms 'investors') in part because it has longer-term implications for the stability and strength of relationships with the other important stakeholders of the business. We encourage you to read this book if you are interested in these ideas—you can find the full reference in the 'Explore more' feature at the end of the chapter.

Returning to Dianne's situation described earlier, consider the stakeholders she might need to balance, and the implications her decision to sell her product to this new buyer might have for them. If the order will delay delivery to an existing and valued customer, what might their response be? If there are concerns about the intentions of this buyer and what they plan to do with such weapons, how might existing employees react to the business selling this product to them? What are the wider implications for society—and for the safety of communities potentially far from Dianne's Paris headquarters—if these weapons fall into the hands of a less trusted organization? What will be the impact on the reputation of the business? While profit-maximizing shareholders might focus on the short-term returns from such a profitable sale, other shareholders might be more interested in the long-term strength of the company by only associating with reputable buyers, or be concerned about the ethical implications of the decision.

We can link these challenges back to the statements proposed at the start of Section 2.3.3. Is the ultimate purpose of this business to make profit, to produce goods, or to support a stable and thriving society? Moreover, who gets to decide on this purpose? Dianne as the current CEO? The Board of Directors? The shareholders? We will return to this issue in Section 2.6.3 focused on the purpose shift of business.

Then, having examined the private sector in detail, which comprises business organizations, we will explore public sector organizations.

Refer now to Running case 2.1 to see how Imperial is being impacted by these differing views.

RUNNING CASE 2.1 **THE ULTIMATE QUESTION**

Lucy's brother, William Green has worked at Imperial Fine Foods since he qualified as an accountant after studying Economics at university. Last year he became the company's CFO, reporting to Lucy. While he believes in the values of Imperial, he is concerned to see costs rising, especially in the factory. Unless Imperial can sell more products at higher prices, things will get very difficult. 'We can't go on like we've always done, Lucy,' he told her recently, 'We're going to have to get the costs down, and if that means being tougher on staff costs and negotiating lower prices with all our suppliers, that's what we'll have to do'.

Lucy understands the challenges. However, she believes they need to think more holistically about the problems they face. Her experience tells her that cutting costs and raising prices may only work in the short term. For the long term, she's cautious about the impact of more aggressive negotiations on supplier relationships, and nervous about creating unhappy Imperial employees.

Lucy often finds herself wondering why the business exists. Is its purpose only to make money for its shareholders by selling as many food products as possible? Or are Lucy and everyone else there to serve all stakeholders, including Imperial's workers, its customers, and its suppliers' workers? However, even to meet the needs of these multiple stakeholders, Lucy realizes, she will still have to work out how to address profit issues. But if they decide on a course of action which harms Imperial's purpose, would that be worth it? This thought leads her to ask two key questions that she is not sure anyone has ever asked—or answered: what is the purpose of Imperial Fine Foods? And who gets to decide the answer to that question?

Questions for reflection

1. Imagine what Lucy would say if asked about the purpose of Imperial Fine Foods. Would it be different if her brother, William, or their father, Hugh, were asked?

2. Who gets to decide on the purpose of Imperial? Consider cousin Charles Green introduced in Chapter 1. Should he get a say in the purpose? Why? Why not?

3. Why is profit important, irrespective of what 'purpose' is decided?

2.4 **Public sector organizations**

Public sector organizations are typically owned and operated by local, regional, or national governments, and provide public goods which are available to all users, irrespective of their ability to pay. While the departments of the government itself are public sector organizations, determining what other organizations are part of the public, private, or third sector in different countries can be difficult, and can change over time. The public sector often (but not always) includes services in the following areas:

- health, including hospitals;
- emergency responses, such as police, fire, and ambulance services;
- military and defence forces;
- postal;
- infrastructure, such as road building and maintenance;

2

- public transport;
- waste and recycling;
- social and welfare;
- legal and judiciary; and
- education.

2.4.1 **The emergence of the public sector**

Public sector organizations have been around for thousands of years, in the form of actual governing bodies, like village councils and national governments. However, many services which are commonly part of the public sector today, have their origins in other sectors. For example, many hospitals were originally established in the third sector by charities relying on donations, such as the Hospital for the Sick Poor established in 1729 in Edinburgh, Scotland. Moreover, the Opening case study examined the changes in the provision of firefighting services between all three sectors.

As we can see, the boundary between public, private, and third sectors has changed over time, remains changeable, and may depend on the geographic context. Moreover, the size and reach of the public sector in most countries grows and shrinks in cycles. This can happen for a number of reasons including:

- changes in values and social norms, where societies determine which services should be universally available, irrespective of an individual's ability to pay;
- the state of the nation's economy, which may require different levels of public sector intervention to support the production of goods and services for a thriving society;
- differing ideologies (beliefs or ideals, often relating to political theories and policies) about the size and role of government in the private affairs of individuals; and
- potential external threats to nations, such as war or disease, impacting the status quo.

In general, across many western economies in particular we have seen a shrinking public sector. We will explore these trends in greater detail in Section 2.6.1.

2.4.2 **Classifying public sector organizations**

Public sector organizations can take many different forms, but the key distinguishing factor between them is the level of control or influence from government. We can classify three different types of public sector organizations, from most to least government control and influence: the government itself, non-departmental public bodies, and public enterprises.

Government

The government itself is a complex organization whose role is to run a country or region, creating a stable and thriving life for its citizens. Governments can exist at different levels. Most countries will have a national government and local governments for smaller regions (also called local councils or municipal government). Many countries will also have a middle level of government, with specific powers delegated to them by the national government or the constitution. For example: in the UK there are devolved governments for Scotland, Wales, and Northern Ireland; the US, Brazil, Nigeria, and India have state governments for each of their states; South Africa, Argentina, and Canada have provincial governments for each of their provinces; China has 34 different divisions comprising provinces, autonomous regions, municipalities, and special administrative regions; while Switzerland is made up of 26 cantons.

Governments at all levels establish different departments that focus on specific aspects of society, the environment, or the economy. National governments will typically have a treasury department (responsible for collecting revenue, government budgets and spending, and managing national finances); a defence department (responsible for managing the military and national borders); and a diplomatic service (responsible for international relations and negotiations with other country's governments). Depending on the country, the education department and the health department might be part of the national government or part of a regional or devolved government. Departments responsible for waste collection and recycling are typically part of local government. Each of these departments is its own organization, comprising significant budgets and staff, with its managers responsible for delivering the relevant services, objectives, and outcomes.

Non-departmental body

A second type of public sector organization is a **non-departmental public body**. While these types of organizations exist in most countries, this specific label is most commonly found in the UK. Moreover, even in the UK there are other labels such as the acronym 'Quango', which stands for QUasi (meaning 'semi') Autonomous Non-Governmental Organization. Irrespective of label, these organizations are established by a government for the delivery of a service, but are not directly run by government within their departments. However, as the government makes all the senior appointments and provides funding, the organizations are within their direct control and influence, especially in relation to objective-setting and strategic direction. In the UK, examples of non-departmental public bodies include the Environment Agency, regulators including Ofcom (regulating communication) and Ofsted (regulating education), or cultural organizations such as national galleries and museums.

Public enterprise

A third type of public sector organization is a **public enterprise**. A public enterprise is created in legislation by national governments to oversee certain aspects of the economy or society and is funded by government. However, due to the nature of what it does, it is more independent from government. The Bank of England is a public enterprise which acts as the UK's central bank. While it is owned entirely by the government, it is not a government department, but rather has full independence in many matters, including setting monetary policy to ensure national financial stability.

Figure 2.7 illustrates the relationship between the three types of public sector organizations and the degree of influence that government has over them.

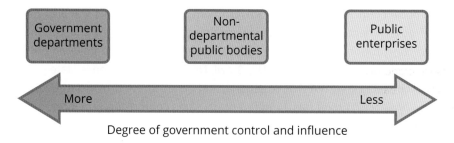

FIGURE 2.7 **Public sector organizations and their relationship to the government.**

2.4.3 **Management challenges in the public sector**

In relation to management, there are many similarities between the public and private sectors: both sectors need to be designed and managed well, organizations need to be structured in a way that supports the goods or services provision, and staffed by people who are managed and motivated effectively. This is why some private sector management theory can be applied in public sector contexts. However, there are some management challenges specific to the public sector.

Politicized contexts

Public sector organizations are funded by governments that use taxes, levies, or duties contributed by their citizens or businesses, or by government borrowing. There are also often complex fund transfers between levels of government—for example, between national governments and local councils. As such, managers of public sector organizations operate in highly politicized environments and can be subject to very close oversight by elected executives, governmental bodies, the media, and interest groups, which can require extensive management time and effort. Public sector managers are also aware of being subject to the ideologies of the ruling government, which may change every few years, or even between elections when ministers responsible for their area can be replaced unexpectedly.

Users instead of customers

Another difference relates to the concept of customers versus users. In a business, the aim is to attract customers, persuade them to pay a specific price for your offering, and satisfy them enough that they recommend you to others or return to you next time. Public services do not exist to 'attract' customers—they exist to provide a service to users. However, because resources are scarce (public sector managers often have limited budgets), managers often need to determine eligibility criteria for their services (who 'needs' it most). Moreover, in some cases, service users have no choice but to return to the same provider next time. The motivation of the manager is not the return of the customer, but the delivery of the values the service upholds. Indeed, attracting more service users in the public sector may mean more work, sometimes for little or no extra gain depending on how budgets are structured.

Measurement issues and bureaucracy

Managers in the public sector are often responsible for the creation or protection of public value: democratic process, safety, health, welfare, or education, for example. Defining 'success' in these areas can be very challenging, making it difficult to set specific objectives for an organization. Even if such objectives can be set, measurement of actual performance can also be difficult. This may in part contribute to the perception of public sector managers as bureaucratic, inefficient, and ineffective (Almquist et al., 2013)—it can be difficult to demonstrate results. In part in response to this, there has been a 'marketization' and 'accountingization' (Osborne, 2010) or 'tick box mentality' (Lapsley, 2009) in public sector management. That is, some argue there has been a disproportionate focus on measurability—of service provision, outcomes, or 'values'—at the expense of the actual public value.

Having explored public sector organizations and management in this sector, we now turn to the final section: the third sector.

2.5 Third sector organizations

The third sector got this title because the public sector was traditionally known as the first sector and the private sector as the second sector. Over time, these labels have faded; however, the title of 'third' sector remains popular. The third sector has also been called the non-profit sector, not-for-profit, voluntary sector, the independent sector, and the civic or social sector, or referred to as NGOs.

In some ways, the third sector is an all-encompassing term for any organization which does not fit neatly into the other two sectors. As such, it includes a very diverse range of organizations with a range of purposes. In 2020 in the UK, in the voluntary sector alone (which comprises many but not all third sector organizations), there were 163,000 organizations, 16.3 million people volunteered their time at least once, and it comprised a paid workforce of almost 1 million people—having grown by 3 per cent compared to the previous year (the private sector declined by 2 per cent over the same time period, according to the National Council for Voluntary Organisations (NCVO, 2021)).

Generally, third sector organizations:

- are independent of government;
- exist primarily to further their specific values or cause; and
- reinvest any money they earn in their organization, rather than returning such funds to owners.

This final point is important. Often these organizations are called 'non-profit' or 'not-for-profit'. This is misleading. Many third sector organizations *do* earn money from activities such as charity shop sales or membership fees. Indeed, that is how they survive financially. However, these profits—often called 'financial surpluses' to provide some distinction from 'profit' (recall the reference to 'financial surplus' in Spotlight 2.1)—are used to further the aims of the

2

organization, rather than being returned to owners or the government. As such, these organizations are sometimes referred to as not-for-*personal*-profit organizations, to help make the financial motives of the organizations clearer.

2.5.1 The emergence of the third sector

Third sector organizations have been in existence for as long as civilization, although they would not have been called this. They have often emerged in times of great upheaval, such as wars or political instability. Early forms of third sector organizations included groups of people helping others in need, or attempting to change the policy or actions of a governing party or leader. There is evidence of what we would now call third sector organizations in early Egyptian civilizations, in ancient India, among early Jewish communities, in Islamic society, and in the Roman empire (Hudson & Rogan, 2009). These organizations included: groups set up to establish hospitals; hardship funds for those needing to get back on their feet, or to support the sick, infirm, or poor; digging of wells for communities to access water; as well as those aiming to influence policies and practices of governments, emperors, and kings to make them more supportive of those in need.

2.5.2 Classifying third sector organizations

Due to the range of organizations that comprise the third sector, it is difficult to pinpoint similarities. Some will be involved in fundraising, while others will provide goods or services to those they are aiming to help. Some will provide direct support or advice to their members or target audience, while others will focus on achieving long-term and systemic change to society generally, or to relevant local, national, or international policies. To narrow this variety down and provide a succinct overview of the third sector, we will outline four main types of organization: charities, clubs and associations, trade and professional bodies, and political parties or pressure groups, as summarized in Figure 2.8.

Charities

A charity is an organization that aims to help society or nature in some way. They may do so by providing support to a specific group of people, with goods such as food or clothes, or through protection of the environment, or a specific animal species. Sometimes charities make use

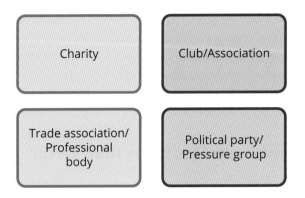

FIGURE 2.8 **Classifying third sector organizations.**

of volunteers, which is why this is often called the voluntary sector. However, it is important not to be dismissive of the complex management issues that charities face in terms of their operations, managing people, achieving their purpose, staying financially viable, and growing to meet demand. Indeed, charities often have additional complexity when compared with private sector organizations, given they need to involve and serve a wider range of influential stakeholders, including customers, donors, funders, volunteers, and beneficiaries, all of whom may have strong opinions about the charity's activities, but few of whom managers have direct control over.

Clubs or associations

A club or association exists for the enjoyment and service of members. They are typically focused on an interest or hobby, such as a tennis club. Some are small, informal organizations such as a knitting circle, while others are larger, with membership fees covering the costs of operations. In fact, they can be very large and complex, such as the Marylebone Cricket Club, with a number of paid staff. Some organizations which start as a club or association, grow in size and complexity, and convert into business organizations in the private sector.

Trade associations or professional bodies

Trade associations or professional bodies exist to protect and promote the interests of a particular occupational group or type of business. They can be very influential in ensuring that their members have a coordinated voice—for example, in relation to negotiating with business owners or managers, or influencing government policy or international treaties. Some organizations in this group also provide accreditation for those wanting to enter the profession that they serve. Trade unions also fit within this category, acting as a membership body and protecting the interests of their members, typically focused on one or two industries or trades.

Political parties and pressure groups

Political parties and pressure groups are also in the third sector. Political parties are not to be confused with governments—which are in the public sector. The political parties themselves aim to persuade people to agree with their beliefs, manifesto, and views on how the public sector should be run, and ultimately to convince the public to vote for their representatives.

2

Pressure groups include lobby groups (groups that aim to persuade or influence government officials or other influential organizations) and activist organizations who are typically aiming to change the belief systems or behaviours of governments, or society at large. For example, Extinction Rebellion is a pressure group established to bring the danger of the climate crisis to the attention of the general public using disruptive tactics. The key distinction between political parties and pressure groups is that the latter are not aiming to be voted into government.

2.5.3 Management challenges in the third sector

Many of the management challenges facing third sector organizations are similar to other sectors, including finding, managing, and motivating staff, as well as prudent financial management, and decision-making about future plans and growth. However, the third sector also faces a number of specific management challenges, some of which we explore here.

Adopting management approaches

One key challenge in the third sector is even just the idea of adopting 'management tools and approaches'. Given the historical dominance of the pursuit of economic value and efficiency, which we explored in Section 1.5, some leaders and organizations in the third sector have avoided the field of 'management'. Either they felt management approaches and frameworks were simply not relevant or useful to them given they were not profit-focused, or they felt such approaches were actively contrary to their values and beliefs. Making a charity 'more business-like' by improving efficiency and not wasting resources sounds like a good idea. However, this may also negatively affect the charity if it places a monetary value on things that do not suit such monetization, such as educational attainment, or because it alienates the volunteers who are dedicated to the cause. In more recent years this has been changing, in particular as a subfield of third sector management is now a well-established area, which has more carefully and appropriately introduced specific elements of the field of management to the third sector.

Complex accountability and governance

Managers in the third sector must also be accountable to funding bodies, individual donors, staff, volunteers, and of course to their service users and beneficiaries. These groups may all have a strong claim to influence the strategic direction of the organization, and yet all may have very different visions. As such, third sector managers have a difficult balancing act and may be required to adhere to a complex structure of formal governing bodies, user-groups, funder-groups, committees, and the like. Managers are often expected to consult widely and fairly throughout this entire complex structure before acting, especially if decisions are very important, or are taking the organization in a new direction.

Identifying and measuring objectives

Another challenge emerges because many of the objectives and outcomes which are the focus of third sector organizations are difficult or even impossible to measure. Even if measurement is possible, it can be difficult to attribute these outcomes directly to the intervention of the organization. Moreover, the benefit or outcome might lie in what the organization prevents, rather than what it creates. A charity that works to regenerate a disadvantaged town may contribute to the prevention of crime, to avoid unemployment, alleviation of poverty, or prevention of health issues in local community members. A number of these factors may be challenging to measure, may have a long-term time horizon, and may result in benefits that accrue to others. This includes cost and resource savings which may accrue to the police service which has less crime to investigate, the health service which has less illness to treat, or the government with reduced benefit payments. Managers of the charity may struggle to directly attribute their decisions and projects to these outcomes.

Voluntarism

Voluntarism is an essential ingredient in much of the third sector. This includes voluntary governing boards, volunteers involved in operations, or voluntary donations to the organization. As such, third sector managers need to hold this coalition of voluntary interests together carefully, despite having no formal power or control over these individuals. Indeed, sometimes volunteers may mean well, but underperform and need to be managed by other means. Moreover, because of the voluntary commitment people give, they may expect to have their views listened to, and to see the common values flow throughout all aspects of the organization. A perceived failure of the organization to uphold its values can lead to lengthy debate, suspicion from key organizational members (including volunteers) and a well-intentioned passionate defence of those values, which may make the management of other aspects of the organization more complex. It is also worth noting that not all those who work with third sector organizations do so out of altruism: some may have more self-serving motives such as recognition, esteem, status, accessing powerful contacts, or gaining influence over the organization.

Returning to Imperial, we can explore Lucy's impressions of management challenges she recalls from her time working for the NGO, Fairtrade Food, in Running case 2.2.

RUNNING CASE 2.2 MANAGING IN THE THIRD SECTOR

During her years working at Fairtrade Food in Tanzania, Lucy's job was to ensure that the food they produced and sold was labelled appropriately and marketed effectively. As an NGO, any increases in profit margins and increased sales they generated would lead to more returns that could be distributed to farmers and their communities. Lucy was involved in long discussions about the NGO's purpose and how it should best balance its responsibilities to various stakeholders. A key stakeholder group was clearly the farmers whose food the organization sold to supermarkets in Europe. Another key stakeholder group was the European supermarkets who sometimes had suggestions or expectations about the features and delivery of Fairtrade Food's products. Some of these expectations appeared to be consistent with the purpose of Fairtrade Food, including that products are bought at a price that allows a profit, in turn guaranteeing returns to farmers. But demands from some supermarkets, she felt, were unfairly biased in favour of the supermarket's profits without benefiting their key stakeholder group. Still, she reasoned, maximizing profits which were then shared with many stakeholders including her own organization and their farmers was better than maximizing profits for shareholders, wasn't it?

She also recognized a third key stakeholder group included donors to Fairtrade Food. These donors sometimes visited their offices and farms, wanting to see what their contributions were paying for. They sought to be reassured that their donations were being ethically and effectively spent on

(Continued)

2

projects, such as education and health care for the farming communities with which they worked.

As well as reflecting on the key stakeholders, Lucy recalls two particular managers in her time at Fairtrade Food who appeared to have different approaches to their roles, and the NGO's engagement with stakeholders. The first manager spent an enormous amount of time talking to many different stakeholders. He would be on the farm talking to farmers and their families, he would have meetings with local government officials and take them to lunch, and take donors on tours of key projects and sites. He would attend every community event put on by the local schools and cultural centres. She admired the relationships he developed and his constant focus on putting their needs ahead of his own, or sometimes even the NGO. 'We exist for them', he used to say. Unfortunately, there were a number of operational, budgeting, and reporting issues under his management.

Lucy's next manager came from a business background. On joining the NGO, she focused on planning, budgeting, and reporting, and ensuring the processes were streamlined and efficient. In doing so, Lucy believes she alienated a number of community members, local officials, and even donors, who didn't feel like she cared about their needs or their contributions to the NGO. Even though Lucy saw some improvements in how the NGO was run-

ning, she had to admit that she herself wasn't as inspired by her new manager because it all felt like a business. Her new manager said 'our success financially will benefit the community more than our kindness'. Lucy got the point, but she wasn't sure she agreed with it. When her father hinted that his 60th birthday and impending retirement were only a few years away, she felt much more inclined to head home than she might have under her previous manager.

Questions for reflection

1. Why do you think Lucy's first manager focused so much on developing relationships in his role? Was he right to do this or not? Provide your reasons.

2. Imagine Lucy's second manager conducted an exit interview—an interview which takes place after someone has resigned and gives them the opportunity to provide feedback to the organization. What should Lucy say about her reasons for leaving? What feedback should she give this manager?

3. Compare the types of management challenges Lucy faces in her role at Imperial with those faced by her managers at Fairtrade Food. What are the similarities? What are the differences?

Having explored the private, public, and third sectors in detail, we will now turn to examine the overlaps, shifts, and key trends which have implications for managing organizations.

2.6 Shifts within and between sectors

We have already acknowledged that determining whether an organization is private, public, or third sector can be more complicated than it first seems. Knowing the industry of the organization can help, but not always. Recall also Spotlight 2.1 regarding the UK water industry, or the fire services in the Opening case study. Most retail companies are private sector, but third sector organizations have retail outlets, such as charity shops that sell goods. Moreover, some organizations—and indeed entire industries—can change sector over time, or between different countries or contexts. In the final section of this chapter, we will consider some recent trends in these shifts within and between sectors in order to deepen our understanding.

2.6.1 **The shrinking public sector**

Over the past 50 years, in particular in western economies, we have witnessed a shrinking of the public sector. This has been associated with growth in both the third and private sectors. The reasons for this are complex. One factor is that the public sector of many nations impacted by World War 2 (WW2) had expanded considerably in order to support the rebuilding effort (Flynn, 2016). For example, immediately following WW2 the UK government owned and ran automobile and aircraft manufacturing, shipbuilding, airports, coal-mining, and steel-making, as well as oil, gas, and electricity extraction, production, and distribution. Workers in all of these organizations were public sector workers. Over the decades since then, many rounds of privatization have happened, as the government has sold these organizations to the private sector, allowing them to run independently of government. There are many reasons for this, including ideological views on the appropriate size of government, practical reasons given the complexity of running organizations and the expertise required to do so, as well as economic reasons given the significant funds that can be raised by selling organizations to the private sector. The debates around the advantages and disadvantages of privatization fill entire textbooks and are studied in politics and public policy disciplines, so we will not explore them here. However, it is enough to conclude that there has been a trend towards privatization.

Moreover, even where public sector organizations have not been privatized entirely, governments have made other decisions that have blurred the boundaries between sectors. For example, governments may ask organizations in the third and private sectors to bid for contracts for the delivery of public goods. In other cases, public sector organizations have entered joint ventures with either private or third sector organizations to leverage their differing strengths.

Despite this trend towards a shrinking public sector, we have also seen examples of the reverse happening. For example, during the global financial crisis in 2007–08 a number of large, private sector banks were in such serious financial difficulty—yet were so integral to the stability of their country's economy—that governments 'bailed them out' (provided the funding to ensure their survival often in return for a significant shareholding), ultimately shifting them from the private, back towards the public sector. The book by Andrew Ross Sorkin, *Too Big to Fail* (2009), and the subsequent movie chronicle this fascinating period.

Given some of the significant global disruptions which are explored in Chapter 3, it is worth considering the potential implications for further growth or shrinkage of the public sector in countries around the world.

2.6.2 **The growing third sector**

A further trend we are seeing is a growing third sector in many countries. There is debate over whether a large third sector is a good or bad reflection on a nation. Some argue that the indicator of a healthy country is the presence and impact of a thriving third sector. Others agree with the importance of a strong third sector, but suggest it is reflective of a society needing to help itself due to the failings of the public and private sectors. For example, in relation to public sector failure, many modern governments are supposedly founded on a welfare state which supports and protects its most vulnerable citizens, ensuring they have the means to survive and thrive. Some

2

argue that government failure in this regard is why so many third sector organizations are needed to help those not being helped by the welfare state. The opposing argument, of course, is that the extensive government funding of the third sector is evidence of the government providing this support, just through third sector organizations, rather than directly through the public sector.

There is also a suggestion that the priorities and management of the private sector have contributed to the growing need for a strong third sector. Some argue that the private sector has contributed to unequal wealth in society, for example, by paying executives very high salaries while reducing the pay of workers, or abolishing jobs altogether either through automation or offshoring. Circumstances such as these may contribute to the growing demands on the third sector as more people live in poverty. Additionally, where the provision of a product or service is not deemed profitable enough, a private sector organization may choose to exit that market. It may fall to third sector organizations to fill this gap.

Conversely, we will now explore a third shift that is seeing a resurgence of purpose over the sole focus on profit in the private sector.

2.6.3 **The private sector's purpose shift**

Recall Section 2.3.3 with three different statements about why business exists. The progression of these three statements mirrors a shift we are increasingly seeing: the purpose shift. Previously we have seen business focus on profit—and shareholder returns—as their stated reason for existence. However, there has been a resurgence of interest in purpose-driven businesses which balance the priorities and needs of *multiple stakeholders*. The word 'resurgence' is important here: such businesses have existed in the past and, indeed, many commentators suggest the dominance of maximizing profit and shareholder returns is very recent indeed, emerging just 40 years ago (Stout, 2012).

Evidence of this trend can be found in the influential US-based Business Roundtable—an association of CEOs of the US's leading companies—who redefined their statement on the purpose of the corporation. Previously, they publicly stated that corporations exist principally to serve the interest of shareholders: that is, shareholder primacy. However, in 2019 they redefined this purpose to commit their businesses to act for the benefit of all stakeholders—including customers, employees, suppliers, and communities (Business Roundtable, 2019).

This purpose shift reflects an acknowledgement that the focus on profit and shareholder primacy can result in significant negative externalities. An **externality** is an indirect cost or benefit incurred by a third party due to the actions of another. The purpose shift is attempting to question the appropriateness of profit which is earned while contributing to negative externalities for society—for example when a business burns fossil fuels contributing to climate change, or destroys a forest and river system on which local villagers rely.

The extent to which a business is genuine about its commitment to a purpose shift is debated. Some suggest that it is **impact-washing**: a new form of greenwashing which refers to organizations that make commitments to being green, but whose actions do not reflect such commitment. Again, this is a situation in which careful analysis of the claims, actions, and impacts of an organization needs to be considered, using our lens of critical thinking and looking at the arguments and evidence to support our conclusion.

In part because of potential questions over motives, and also because of their genuine commitments to the purpose shift, a number of businesses are making public and often legal moves into the overlap between the private and third sectors. Organizations which exist in this overlap are often called hybrid organizations (Battilana and Dorado, 2010). They combine an explicit social or environmental motive with a business model. We can distinguish between different types of hybrid organizations based on whether they are more similar to a third sector organization or more similar to a private sector (albeit within the overlap).

Those more similar to a third sector organization typically focus on their social or environmental purpose, with profit being used largely to achieve their greater purpose. Such organizations often include social enterprises, cooperatives, or mutual organizations. Those more similar to private sector organizations typically balance their social or environmental purpose with their profit aims. Such organizations are often termed purpose-driven businesses. Purpose-driven businesses may be established by entrepreneurs in this way, such as the shoe brand Toms, established in 2006, which championed a 'one for one' model, in which they deliver a free pair of shoes to a child in need for every pair of shoes they sell. They may also be well-established businesses that are increasingly embracing their sense of purpose. The Brazil-based steel corporation Gerdau which has 28,000 employees announced significant shifts towards a purpose-driven model in 2019 (Marquis, 2021). A number of countries are increasingly offering a dedicated legal framework for businesses choosing to operate in this way. Spotlight 2.2 introduces the Benefit Corporation (B Corps) movement for one such innovation which began in the US and has spread globally. Both Toms and Gerdau have become Certified B Corp.

SPOTLIGHT 2.2 **B CORPS MOVEMENT**

We began in 2006 with the idea that a different kind of economy was not only possible, but necessary—and that business could lead the way towards a new, stakeholder-driven model (B Lab, 2023).

The 'B Corps' movement is an international network of businesses that hold themselves to account to contribute (via their own business model) to a collective vision of an inclusive, equitable, and regenerative economy. Starting as the B Lab, a group of like-minded people decided to establish a way of certifying businesses that voluntarily meet the highest standards of social and environmental performance, accountability, and transparency—that
(Continued)

2

is, those who were genuinely adopting a purpose-driven agenda for their business.

B Lab (who provides the B Corps certification) is an NFP (so is firmly in the third sector) funded by donations from charities and philanthropy, as well as an annual fee paid by businesses who become Certified B-Corporations.

Research (Kim & Schifeling, 2016) suggests that businesses are motivated to become B Corps to ensure their genuine purpose-driven credentials stand out in the midst of the greenwash (especially from larger companies), allowing consumers to sort through the marketing hype, as well as to be part of a movement towards a new economy with a new set of rules which redefines the way people perceive success in the business world. Interestingly, these research results link to the way in which B Corps describes themselves: as businesses which are the best *for* the world, not just the best *in* the world.

To achieve certification, businesses are scored across areas of societal and environmental impact as well as governance transparency. Importantly, they need to agree to be legally bound to consider the needs of all stakeholders—workers, communities, customers, suppliers, and the environment—not just shareholders. This avoids any expectations of shareholder primacy which, as we have argued in this chapter, can impact the long-term interests of the company (and therefore of the shareholders themselves).

Certified B Corps can be sole traders, partnerships, or limited companies with shareholders. In the case of the latter, these can be privately held, or listed publicly on stock exchanges, as is the case with Lemonade Insurance.

Famous B Corps include Patagonia, Ben & Jerry's and Seventh Generation (both owned by Unilever), and Natura & Co based in Brazil. As of 2022, there are almost 5,000 Certified B-Corporations in more than 70 countries and across 150 industries, including consumer goods, hospitality, food, agriculture, consulting, banking, and finance.

2.7 Conclusion

Before we can explore management, we need to understand the implications of the different types of organizations in which management happens. Categorizing organizations into three different sectors: private, public, and third sector, helps to start to consider these implications. The private sector typically comprises businesses that engage in business transactions with some form of profit motive. Indeed, much of the study of management has focused on business organizations. However, this chapter has reminded us of just how much of our daily lives is impacted by management of both the public and third sectors. Moreover, in this chapter we also considered the blurred boundary between each sector, as well as the shifts and changes that continually occur. The aim of this chapter was to provide a more comprehensive understanding of the complex context in which management happens and where managers have to undertake their roles. In doing so, we hope it has left you with an appreciation for the many different and sometimes competing expectations placed on managers. Turning now to Chapter 3, we examine the disruption and uncertainty which further complicate the management and the role of managers across all sectors.

 CHAPTER SUMMARY

○ Organizations can be categorized into private sector (businesses), public sector (those related to governments in some way), and third sector (charities or other groups with a societal or environmental purpose).

- Private sector organizations—which we call businesses—can be classified by size, offering, or ownership structure, and in relation to the latter can face complexities surrounding governance, and balancing the needs and expectations of shareholders and other stakeholders.

- Public sector organizations are either run by or closely linked to governments, and so face politicized contexts as well as needing to serve users or the wider public, rather than customers in a more traditional sense.

- Third sector organizations face challenges in adopting management approaches, added complexity in accountability and governance as well as in measuring objectives, and with issues related to voluntarism.

- Recent trends have seen a shrinking public sector, a growing third sector, and a purpose shift in the private sector.

CLOSING CASE REFLECTION

Who are our firefighters?

In the Opening case study, we learned about insurance companies providing firefighting services to their customers. In this case, fire services were provided by the private sector for profit. Indeed, some companies were known to negotiate a substantial fee with an uninsured building owner while standing on the pavement watching their property being destroyed by fire.

Falcks Redningskorps, the Danish-founded fire service, has gone through many different forms of ownership over the years. At one point it was a limited company listed on a stock exchange, and therefore would fit within the private sector, albeit with a purpose-driven mission, so arguably sitting in the overlap between the private and third sectors. However, today Falck is owned by two NFP foundations. As such, arguably, Falck is currently a third sector organization.

The Australian CFA is facing an uncertain future, given Australia's Black Summer in 2019–20, which burnt over 10 million hectares of bush—almost the size of Germany (Rumpff et al., 2023). Because the fire season lasted an unprecedented five months, and with climate change expected to make such megafires more likely, there are increasing questions about just how long the volunteer CFA firefighters can be absent from their day jobs without payment for their services.

REVIEW QUESTIONS

1. What are the three sectors and how can we distinguish them?
2. In what ways are there overlaps between sectors and why do these change over time?
3. In relation to the private sector, why is there a debate about distinctions between shareholders versus stakeholders and what have been some of the tangible implications of this?

4. In relation to the public sector, why is management in this sector different to the private sector? Provide multiple reasons.

5. In relation to the third sector, why do volunteering aspects create challenges for management?

EXPLORE MORE

READ this acclaimed book by Cornell Law Professor Lynn Stout: *The Shareholder Value Myth: How Putting Shareholders First Harms Investors, Corporations, and the Public* (Berrett-Koehler Publications, 2012), which provides important insight into the balance between shareholders and other stakeholders.

WATCH 'Profit's Not Always the Point', a TED Talk from Harish Manwani, Unilever, January 2014. Search for 'Harish Manwani' on the TED Talks website.

READ 'Why Companies Are Becoming B Corporations', an article in the *Harvard Business Review* by Suntae Kim and team exploring an element of the third sector shift. Search by the article title in Google.

READ this academic article, which focuses on NFPs: A. M. Bach-Mortensen and P. Montgomery (2018). 'What Are the Barriers and Facilitators for Third Sector Organizations (Non-Profits) to Evaluate Their Services? A Systematic Review', *Systematic Reviews* 7.

WATCH this TED Talk from Tolu Oyken: 'A For-Profit Mindset for Non-Profit Success', February 2023. Search for 'Tolu Oyken' on the TED Talks website.

READ *Too Big to Fail,* a book by Andrew Ross Sorkin, which has a movie of the same name, exploring the global financial crisis, what caused it, and the widespread implications.

CHAPTER THREE
Managing through Disruption

Sarah Birrell Ivory and Emma Macdonald

OPENING CASE STUDY HOW WWF CHANGED WHILE STAYING THE SAME

The World Wide Fund for Nature (WWF) was established in 1961 (then known as the World Wildlife Fund), and is globally recognized through its panda logo. Since its founding, the management of WWF have consistently responded to the changing world around them, while staying true to their mission to protect species at risk from human development.

In the first year, they focused on specific species: the Giant Grebes in Guatemala, Tule geese in Canada, and sea birds in Hawaii. However, they soon recognized the need to shift focus to research, and so contributed to the establishment of two organizations:

- The Charles Darwin Foundation in 1962 in the Galapagos Islands off the coast of Ecuador, focused on how to best protect species and entire ecosystems.
- The College of African Wildlife Management, Mweka in 1963 in Tanzania, focused on increasing the knowledge and skills of local communities in Africa dealing with the complex wildlife management across the continent.

Recognizing that the threat to species was often linked to habitat destruction, in the 1970s they began directly buying key parcels of land, including 37,000 acres adjacent to Kenya's Lake Nakuru, home to 30 bird species including a million flamingos.

They also worked with governments and other bodies to establish national parks and nature reserves in almost every continent globally.

In the 1980s, WWF Vice President, Dr Thomas E. Lovejoy, showed significant foresight in recognizing that crippling foreign debt in developing nations was contributing to a lack of attention to habitat and species protection. WWF proposed 'debt-for-nature' swaps, purchasing some of the nation's foreign debt at a discount, with the money used to finance local conservation efforts. The first debt-for-nature swap occurred in Ecuador in 1987, with such swaps having now occurred in countries in Africa, South America, Asia, and Europe, totalling over US$1 billion (Sheikh, 2010). This helped these nations by removing their reliance on foreign debt while supporting local communities to protect fragile ecosystems.

Frustrated by inaction on environmental crises including climate change, in 2007, the management of WWF established their now famous 'Earth Hour', asking everyone to switch off their lights for one hour. This has become one of the biggest annual grassroots events globally, succeeding in part because of their effective and innovative digital engagement strategy, using Twitter, Facebook, and Instagram, as well as Viber and other channels to increase public engagement and action (Gilliland, 2017).

3.1 **Introduction**

We are facing a world of uncertainty. Technology-driven disruption is radically changing entire sectors of the economy. Online technology enables the rapid spread of information via the 24-hour news cycle, which means that we hear in real-time about environmental disasters, conflict, war, and cultural and political trends. Global trends in inequality continue to rise, resulting in growing gaps between those with and those without access to resources, in areas such as wealth, technology, and social support (visit Inequality.org for details on these trends). Digital channels enable access to a wider world but are also a source of real or perceived threat to our personal safety and security. The ability for firms and governments to track individuals' online behaviour creates the potential for intrusion into our personal freedoms. Looming over all of these trends is the climate crisis and the destruction of nature and biodiversity. These diverse disruptions and their complex interactions will impact organizations and their managers for the coming decades; managers will undoubtedly be focused on managing disruption. We will explore some of these topics in this chapter.

What is less clear is the uniqueness of this situation. That is, our current times are often depicted as unusually disruptive. We perceive that we are facing higher than usual rates of change and uncertainty—a blip in a previously stable and certain history of humanity. This is probably because, unless you are a historian, it can be difficult to think further back than the past few decades, which have been relatively stable.

However, picture yourself as a UK-based manager in one of these time periods:

- Imagine it is the 1930s. Ahead of you is a world war that will cost over 70 million lives worldwide, in which most of your young male workforce will leave (many never to return), where the government may instruct your business to shift your manufacturing to items for the war effort, where your supply chain is severely disrupted and where any resources from outside the UK are cut-off completely, while your customers are consuming via ration books and are only able to buy essential products.

- Or imagine it is the 1960s. Your national competitors are moving their manufacturing operations offshore, making use of improved communications, global shipping, and access to developing economies which marks a dramatic increase in globalization. Globalization also sees you facing a set of new unknown competitors from abroad. Consumers are being offered lower-priced products than your own locally manufactured goods, and some of your local suppliers are going out of business because of these shifts.

- Or imagine it is the 1970s. You have developed a stable manufacturing business which has consistent and predictable costs. Then the 1973 oil crisis begins. Oil producers in the Middle East impose an embargo on other countries in response to their support of Israel in the Yom Kippur War. The price of oil per barrel quadruples (from US$3 to US$12 per barrel), leading to petrol rationing and long queues for fuel, while inflation (the increased cost of goods across the economy) hits a high of 24 per cent (Macalister, 2011). For comparison, inflation in the UK was around 1 per cent in 2020, around 3 per cent in 2021, and even in 2022—known for its high inflation—averaged 10 per cent (Statista, 2023). Food prices, already high due to global shortages, rise further. Trade unions begin demanding higher wages for their members given price rises. Consumers, tired of high prices and queueing for petrol, start a shift to smaller and more energy-efficient cars, contributing to the dominance of Japanese imports such as Toyota and Honda.

- Finally, imagine it is the 1980s. World wars, mass globalization, and energy crises feel like they are behind you. But in the background, a digital revolution has been brewing. The internet (which started as a research project in the 1960s by the US government) comes into existence on 1 January 1983, when the Transfer Control Protocol/Internetwork Protocol (TCP/IP) provides all computer networks with a standard way of communicating. It is then revolutionized in 1989 when Tim Berners-Lee invents the World Wide Web (www), allowing anyone to search these computer networks. In the 1990s, bulky computers are still firmly fixed on people's work and home desks. As a manager at this time, could you have foreseen that in a few short decades individuals all over the world would own multiple computers, including on their person (smart watch), in their pocket (smart phone), in their bag (tablet), and on their desk (computer), not to mention in their car, fridge, television, gaming consoles, and speakers?

The point is that managing *is* managing through disruption. The types of disruption may change, our ability to predict and prepare for them may vary, and the implications and impacts may be different. Managers in different countries may face different disruptions (consider the manager in the example above—how would their experience be different if they were a manager in Argentina, Nigeria, or Thailand?). Moreover, the losses and gains from disruptions are far from certain: some will be winners and others losers. However, many managerial roles *exist* because we need someone to make a decision in light of these disruptions and uncertainty. This entire text explores aspects of management which are inherently linked to disruption caused by technology, data, information, contexts, impacts, policy, human behaviour, or environmental phenomena. Your job as a student of management is to appreciate the likely disruptions that managers will face in the coming decades and beyond. However, you also need to be ready for those disruptions which we cannot predict or foresee. For instance, it is unlikely that students in recent decades were guided to think too deeply—if at all—about the disruptive impact of a global pandemic on management, and yet managers all over the world have had to rapidly respond to such a reality.

Is disruption good or bad? The answer, of course, is that it depends. It depends on the disruption, it depends on what is being disrupted, and it may depend on your perspective. While it is undoubtedly true that disruption leads to change—changed behaviours, actions, values, priorities, or power—it does not follow that change is bad. Some change should be celebrated, as previously marginalized communities are accepted into society, as polluting processes are changed, or as technologies provide transparency and accountability. How we choose to manage through disruptions and, indeed, contribute to them as managers, is determined by several factors: the type of organization that is affected; the industry or sector in which it operates; the culture and values of the organizational members; and the values, ethics, and priorities of the managers themselves.

The second half of this chapter is divided into three broad categories of disruption with examples within each: geopolitical, technological, and environmental. However, before we delve into these, let's explore two different approaches which help us to understand and encapsulate our world and the scale of the disruptions we face.

3.2 **Understanding disruption**

It is useful to have frameworks that help to describe the disruptions that organizations and their managers encounter, and to consider effective responses to them. One approach is related to the concept of the **VUCA world**, which has been extended to defining a **VUCA Prime manager**. Another viewpoint zooms into focus on the actual issues which managers face in a VUCA world and describes these as **wicked problems**.

3.2.1 **VUCA world**

University Professors Bennis and Nanus (1985) coined the phrase VUCA to describe the changing nature of the world. VUCA is an acronym for volatility, uncertainty, complexity, and ambiguity. These terms can be defined as follows:

- Volatility: Change is a constant and it happens quickly, but the nature, speed, volume, and magnitude of change are not predictable.

- Uncertainty: A lack of predictability of issues or events means past issues or events cannot be used as predictors for future outcomes, making forecasting difficult and the future uncertain.

- Complexity: Everything is related or interconnected, and actions we take can have unpredictable and unintended consequences for many other things.

- Ambiguity: Increased volatility, uncertainty, and complexity mean that the best solutions or reactions are unclear, while the meaning of events may also be obscure or vague.

The VUCA acronym has been used to describe the turbulent and disrupted world in which we live and work, and the idea has been embraced by those looking to define how managers should behave and what skills they require for a VUCA world.

3.2.2 **VUCA Prime manager**

The acronym VUCA provides a broad understanding of the internal and external conditions affecting organizations today. However, it can be quite an abstract concept when being used to understand management, especially in practice. We may live in a VUCA world, but what does that really mean, and what should a manager *do*? This question has been explored by renowned leadership academic Bob Johansen (2012), who argues that a VUCA world must be met by a VUCA manager. He provides an alternative VUCA acronym—changing the words associated with each letter—which he calls VUCA Prime:

- Meet Volatility with *Vision*: A clear vision, which succinctly describes the goals of the organization, is key in turbulent times to provide a stable point of reference. Irrespective of the VUCA context, vision is the element that should not need to change; it needs to be explicit and go to the heart of both the organization's purpose and the way it measures success.

- Meet Uncertainty with *Understanding*: Managers need to understand their key stakeholders, especially their employees. They need to deploy effective, continual, and consistent two-way communication which, in turn, helps employees understand the uncertainties management is facing. Combined with proactive collaboration and teamwork, a shared mindset is developed on the back of this mutual understanding.

- Meet Complexity with *Clarity*: A key skill is being able to cut through the chaos to see clearly the elements of the complex environment which are most relevant to the organization. Managers need to maintain a sharp focus on what matters to the organization, and must resist tangents, distractions, and never-ending alternatives. However, they should also appreciate that such focus needs to be reflective and self-critical to avoid stagnation.

- Meet Ambiguity with *Agility*: Agility is the ability to quickly and effectively implement solutions to challenges, when necessary. This is not just important in the moment of change, but also relates to how managers structure organizations and effectively develop a vision and shared mindset with their stakeholders, so that they are *able* to change (we will explore this more in Chapter 6).

Figure 3.1 summarizes the VUCA Prime model of management in a VUCA world.

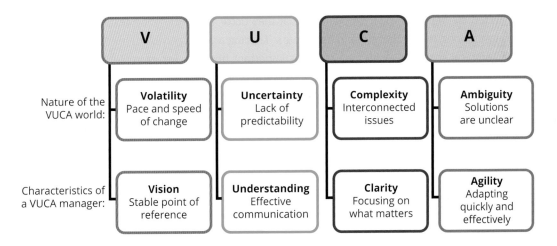

FIGURE 3.1 **The VUCA Prime model of management in a VUCA world.**

In sum, VUCA managers need to retain a consistent foresight about where they are going, while remaining flexible about how they are going to get there. However, this does not mean managers will perfectly understand the VUCA world. As Johansen (2012: 2) points out 'If you're not confused about current events you're not paying attention.'

3.2.3 **Wicked problems**

Wicked problems, introduced by Rittel and Webber (1973) and sometimes called 'global grand challenges', are those that are difficult or impossible to solve because of contradictory information, or changing requirements. Typically, there is no 'right or wrong' solution to a wicked problem, but only better and worse options, and no way to test potential solutions or engage in trial and error. Even 'solving' a wicked problem (to the extent that this is possible) may create or reveal other problems due to complex interdependencies. This means that wicked problems have no discernible stopping point or resolution: these problems are never solved definitively.

Poverty is often used as an example of a wicked problem as it is complex, multidimensional, unclear, and changeable.

Levin et al. (2012) expanded on the concept to suggest that **super wicked problems** have four additional characteristics: time is running out, there is no central authority, those seeking to solve the problem are also causing it, and policies fail to take sufficient account of the future. The climate crisis is often used as an example of a super wicked problem.

Wicked and super wicked problems describe many of the problems that managers face. Camillus (2008) argued that wicked management problems:

- involve many stakeholders with different values and priorities;

- have complex, tangled roots and causes;

- are difficult to comprehend, and change with every attempt to address them;

- have no precedent and are completely new; and

- have nothing to indicate the right answer to the problem.

A neglected element of wicked problems is that they occur in a societal context, involving established institutions, human beliefs, and behaviours. Tackling a wicked problem from the perspective of the technical challenge alone may miss this important obstacle. For example, a societal transition to renewable energy is increasingly not a technical problem: we have the renewable-generating technology and are solving the distribution challenges. The wicked challenge comes because the transition also requires policy and legal changes to be implemented (which require leadership from governments who may face political pressures), as well as behavioural and attitude changes (from consumers, organizations, and communities). Consider Imperial's VUCA challenges in Running case 3.1.

RUNNING CASE 3.1 MANAGING IMPERIAL IN A VUCA WORLD

Lucy shudders when she remembers the pandemic hitting the country soon after she joined the business as Commercial Director. This was before she was promoted to CEO, so she worked with her father to make decisions daily based on limited information and uncertainty about what the next few weeks would bring. There were decisions about staffing, operations, deliveries, cleaning protocols, and suppliers.

As a food company, Imperial was considered an essential service because people needed to keep eating. But given their main customers were restaurants, cafeterias, and university and school campuses, who had been shut down as a result of lockdowns, sales had fallen by 50 per cent. At the other end of the value chain, suppliers also found it difficult to fulfil Imperial's orders of raw materials, especially from overseas.

What really helped during that tough time was an encounter Lucy had with Jazz Jha, one of the food preparation team—or the 'pie-makers', as they liked to call themselves. Lucy was reviewing the cleaning protocols and safety arrangements for onsite staff with Jazz. Jazz mentioned from behind her mask that she 'wasn't sure who was left to buy their products'. Lucy shook her head.

'The thing is, people haven't disappeared, Jazz. They're just eating in a different way: from home. If anything, there will be a whole market of people who will want fine food, now they can't eat out. And they might not all want pies. We just need to work out how to reach them! And how to turn these supplies that we *can* get, the potatoes from the farm up the road, these olives from Italy, and these marinated chilli peppers from Mexico into a meal that people can heat up at home. If we can't do that—who can?'

'You are so right!' said Jazz, who immediately came up with a whole list of tasty food ideas she could create for customers to eat at home. Lucy said, jokingly, 'Have you got any other ideas hidden away?' Jazz replied, 'I have lots of ideas, Lucy. We all do. But nobody ever asks us.'

Lucy thought it over and then discussed her emerging thoughts with her father, Hugh Green, and her CFO brother, William. Hugh was initially sceptical. 'We're a purveyor of fine foods and ingredients to restaurants, Lucy, not a fast foods company. What will our business customers think of us?' But then William backed Lucy saying: 'If we don't do something fast, what they think will be irrelevant, because we won't exist anymore.'

The following week, after some creativity and hard work from the food prep team, stimulated by the enthusiasm of Jazz, Imperial began advertising a new approach to delivering their ingredients. They offered a 'Heat-at-Home' range, which comprised one-pot stews and soups, as well as meal packs including prime cuts of meat, par-cooked vegetables, and luxury sauces. A well-known local celebrity chef recorded a video of herself cooking an Imperial's Heat-at-Home meal, which gained invaluable coverage on social media.

Questions for reflection

1. Consider the four elements which comprise the VUCA acronym: volatile, uncertain, complex, and ambiguous. Write a sentence for each describing what Imperial faced in this Running Case insert.

2. How should Imperial's managers prioritize their tasks in the event of a crisis hitting the business? How might a VUCA Prime model of management have helped them at this time?

3. Using an example different to the pandemic, describe a wicked or super wicked problem which impacts Imperial. How should Imperial respond?

The remainder of this chapter will focus on disruptions that are taking place in a VUCA world, creating wicked problems that managers must face. We divide these into geopolitical, technological, and environmental disruptions (as depicted in Figure 3.2), and briefly explore a number of examples in each category. However, remember that different organizations, industries, and geographies will face their own unique circumstances, and current and past disruptions may not predict the future. These examples will help you imagine just some of the challenges of managing through disruption.

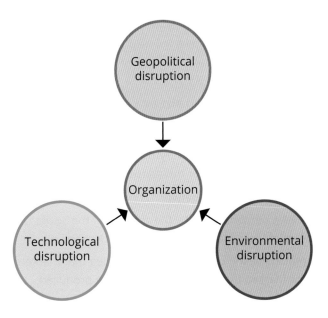

FIGURE 3.2 **Categories of disruption in a VUCA world.**

3

3.3 **Geopolitical disruption**

Geopolitics refers to the interactions between politics, geography, power, and economies which contribute to international treaties or disputes, trade agreements or barriers, cooperation or conflict. While the discussion of geopolitics is typically focused at nation-state or regional level, the potential for disruption to organizations and management, in particular, can be significant. Some organizations will be directly involved in geopolitical issues, including government departments, international bodies like the World Trade Organization, or charities specializing in conflict areas like Médecins Sans Frontières (Doctors Without Borders).

For a number of reasons (some of which we will explore in this section), geopolitical disruptions, at least up until 2022, were not considered as significant as environmental crises and technological disruptions. While this might be linked to the inherent seriousness of the climate crisis and the pervasiveness of technology, it is also possible that complacency emerged at the start of this century: the risk of war between nations becoming globally significant was severely underestimated. The Russian invasion of Ukraine in February 2022 shook many people out of that complacency, and international armed conflict between industrialized nations regained its position as a significant source of actual and potential disruption and uncertainty for many organizations.

Further, at a nation-state level, the polarization of societal viewpoints is impacting voting patterns and behaviours across the world, with more extremes of opinion that focus on differences, rather than a more conciliatory central position which focuses on commonalities. There is an increasing fragmentation of society linked to social media and other forms of online connection which allow individuals to find and connect with like-minded people. This polarization is linked to the declining quality, type, and amount of public discussion and debate, which Hoggan (2019) argues 'stall our ability to think collectively and solve the most dangerous problems that are stalking everyone on Earth'.

In this section, we will explore three geopolitical disruptions that impact managing organizations. We appreciate that there are whole courses, degree programmes, and, indeed, professions dedicated to the study of these. While we do not have room in this chapter to explore the topic in that level of detail, our examples will help you understand how this area relates to management at this stage of your studies.

3.3.1 **Globalization and deglobalization**

Much of the focus of the late twentieth century was on globalization. A consensus developed among leaders and decision-makers that everything and everyone was becoming more connected. There were a variety of reasons for this consensus:

- the increased movement of people between countries and cultures;
- political homogeneity, demonstrated by the collapse of the Soviet Union and the growing belief that all countries were moving towards liberal democracy;
- economic assumptions based on the fundamental idea that markets produce prosperity and, the bigger the market, the more prosperity will be produced;
- rapid economic growth in several countries, but especially in India and China, increasing the size of the available global workforce and allowing markets all around the world to source products at lower prices than they could previously;

- the last point bringing prosperity to many millions of these new workers, in turn creating new and very large consumer markets;

- the development of the internet, which created new global connections (such as between individuals, between companies, and between individuals and companies) and markets (arenas for the exchange of goods or services) often ignoring national borders; and

- the emergence of internationally-shared cultural interests, such as K-Pop or Premier League football.

These trends have not necessarily held, however. Many point to the global financial crisis of 2007–2008 as a turning point for globalization. From about the 1980s, computer technology accelerated and deepened the integration of international financial markets. This process was intensified by the rise of the internet, allowing money to move quickly across boundaries to support globalized commerce. This led to a 'financialization' of the world economy, where financial markets, financial institutions, and financial elites gained greater influence over economic policy and outcomes, and became intricately interconnected. As such, when an economic crisis hit just one economy, it had knock-on effects on many others, eventually causing the global financial crisis of 2007–2008, in which several global banks failed or had to be bailed out by national governments.

At the same time, other drivers of globalization began to falter and to be called into question. Politically, economic nationalism (where the nation-state promotes and preferences businesses within its borders and limits access to businesses from other countries) became the dominant way of thinking in the US, Russia, China, Brazil, and other countries. Foreign investment was increasingly challenged as suspicions emerged that companies might act in the interests of their home country, rather than the host economy. The UK left the European Union, an act described by the then Governor of the Bank of England as the first reversal of globalization (Carney, 2017).

Another factor that contributed to the trend towards *de*globalization was the Covid-19 pandemic, which made it more difficult for people to travel and for goods to be moved along

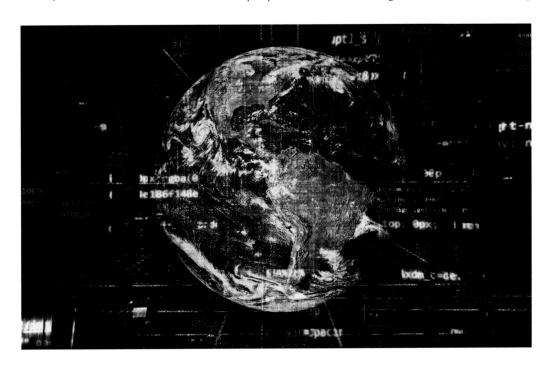

international supply chains. Delays in supply and related shortages of goods occurred in many countries. Many began to question whether they could continue to rely on extended supply chains when they could so easily be disrupted by pandemics or, increasingly, the climate crisis' contribution to increased instances of extreme weather. The 'splinternet' came into existence, as large economies such as China and Russia limited access to some international internet platforms or providers, leading to internet economies (sub-sectors of the economy driven by internet-based platforms or services) developing separately but in parallel, globally (Rajan, 2020).

While globalization has not stopped, there are now significant forces in play that seem likely to make its progress variable and uncertain. The vision held by some in the late twentieth century, of a world where every country sooner or later would be on course to join an open, globalized economy of interrelated markets and cultures, now seems unlikely to be realized in the near future, if ever. With the growth of economic nationalism, and the realization following the Covid-19 pandemic that globalized economic relationships can be fragile, the unpredictable nature of geopolitics becomes a major issue for managers in many different types of organizations. While organizations do not necessarily need to become political, some political awareness and understanding is likely to be an important part of a manager's skill set.

3.3.2 **Regional conflict, terrorism, and war**

Compared to earlier epochs, the period since the end of World War 2 in 1945 has been relatively peaceful. Although sometimes referred to as the 'Long Peace' (Gaddis, 1989), there have been wars going on throughout that time. Some are civil wars, where people of the same country fight against each other, and others have been international wars. Some have been about politics, particularly during the period known as the Cold War (1945–1991), when the world was divided, with some exceptions, between 'the West', which mostly consisted of countries with open, capitalist economies, and countries that had embraced versions of Communism, the largest being the USSR (Union of Soviet Socialist Republics) and the People's Republic of China.

This separation into two competing world blocs, one broadly based on the ideas of democracy and open markets, and the other on the ideas of Karl Marx, dominated geopolitics until 1991 with the collapse of the Soviet Union and the emergence of Russia as a post-Communist state. The post-Cold War period coincided with the rapid and historically unprecedented economic growth of China, led by Deng Xiaoping, who introduced market reforms and allowed Chinese manufacturers to export and become part of the phenomenon of globalization.

Further fragmentation of the competitive relationship, between the 'Capitalist West' and the 'Communist East', led to more regional conflicts, as countries began to pursue their own interests outside either of these blocs. This made the world more unpredictable. With globalization making it easier for people and ideas to travel, extremist political and religious ideas provoked outbreaks of violence and terrorism. For example, the terrorist attacks on the World Trade Center in New York in 2001 was used as justification, in turn, for the US-led invasion of Iraq, and led to a period of even more war and instability in an already fractious Middle East. In Spotlight 3.1 we explore the role of one significant global organization—the United Nations—in relation to avoiding or resolving such regional conflict, terrorism, and war.

Complicating the global landscape further, in more recent times we have seen technology creating new kinds of conflict and new weapons of war. The internet and computers are now part of

SPOTLIGHT 3.1 **THE UNITED NATIONS**

The United Nations was founded in 1945 immediately following World War 2. It comprises 193 member states and aims to bring nations together to discuss common problems and to find shared solutions that benefit all of humanity, with the ultimate aim of maintaining peace and stability globally. The UN was established in response to the devastating effects of the two world wars experienced in the twentieth century, as well as widespread and often violent decolonization as European nations stepped away from control of colonized countries that they had taken over during expansion in the previous centuries. The UN's existence was founded on the recognition that understanding and respect at a nation-state level may help to avoid similar future global violence and tragedy.

Geopolitically, it is possible to view the success of the United Nations broadly in relation to the relative global stability which has existed since its inception. We can see its influence in attempting to resolve such conflicts that do emerge, through, for example, functioning as a forum for ongoing dialogue, deploying international peace-keeping forces, and sanctions agreed by the UN's governing body, the Security Council.

Questions about its ongoing influence have emerged, however, due to the increased threat to global security from non-state actors (e.g. terrorist or guerrilla groups that are not part of official nation-state government institutions), over whom the UN has little power or influence, as such actors may not be linked in formal ways to the governance of the nation.

Moreover, questions have been raised over the ongoing governance of the UN, as the five permanent members of the Security Council have not changed since its inception in 1945: United States, France, United Kingdom, China, and Russia. Finally, the UN's legal arm, the International Court of Justice, has no formal legal power over nation-states but relies on nation-state respect for and acceptance of their jurisdiction. As the trends towards nation-state animosity and conflicts continue to grow, the ongoing convening power of the UN—that is, its ability to bring nations together into meetings and collaborative agreements—is in doubt. This has been highlighted by Russia, a permanent member of the UN Security Council, invading Ukraine in 2022, resulting in a case being brought before the UN's own International Court of Justice, relating to charges of genocide.

the essential infrastructure in every economy in the world. A society can be badly disrupted if this infrastructure is attacked or disabled. Such 'cyberattacks' are part of an array of weapons that are not military, in the traditional sense, but which can nevertheless harm countries. Another example is disinformation, which can be used to create misunderstanding and conflict where people depend on the internet and social media as a source of reliable information about the world. This can interfere with political processes such as elections, in turn contributing to political instability. Prior to the existence of the internet, wartime governments exerted effort on propaganda to maintain morale at home and to undermine opponents. Where the internet is easily accessible, information as well as disinformation and the spreading of false rumours can have a similar, arguably even more powerful and less detectable, effect on societies and opponents.

3.3.3 Resource geopolitics

There are many examples in history of war and political instability emerging from competition between nations and peoples over natural resources. For example, colonial wars were often fought so that the colonizing power could take over resources, or find new markets for its own

3

products. The British colonized India partly to take control of its natural resources, such as tea and precious metals, and partly in order to create demand for British cotton goods, and then to profit from their supply (Sanghera, 2021). These are two of the ways in which empires extract wealth from the countries they colonize.

Many resources can be extracted from nature and then monetized, such as precious metals, and oil. However, they are valuable only because there is demand for them in the world economy. While we often think of war as fought because of political ideology, beliefs, or national pride, economics can also be the motivation for fighting a war. An example is Iraq invading Kuwait in 1990 in order to take control of Kuwaiti oilfields. In that case, the Iraqi government believed it could cut oil production in Kuwait, thereby raising the price of oil in international markets, which would allow it to make more money from its own oil as well as from the Kuwaiti oil it had seized (Colgan, 2013). For such a plan to work, however, there has to be an international oil market with buyers that are prepared to buy from you, so that the value of the oil can be monetized and then used for other things. Oil is of relatively little value in itself; it is only when it can be turned into money, through buying and selling, that it becomes worth fighting a war over.

However, not all resources depend on international markets for their value. Many are valuable because they are fundamental to the sustenance of human life. Water, for drinking and irrigation, is an obvious example of such a resource, which we return to in Section 3.5.2. Others might include clean air and the materials to protect people from extremes of weather.

Other resources, while not necessary to keep people alive from day to day, are nonetheless essential to the functioning of the twenty-first-century economy. The world is now dependent on computers for the provision of many of the basic elements of human society, including health care and many forms of transport. They have become as much part of our social infrastructure as bridges and buildings. The rare metals needed to make a computer, such as gold and palladium, are found in only a few countries. As the data-driven economy grows, and becomes ever more complex, competition to control the materials necessary to make it work is likely to increase. One of the key roles of management is to ensure all resources necessary for their organization are available or to make decisions when it becomes apparent that availability may be an ongoing challenge.

The implications of geopolitical disruption for management are significant, and we will see this topic raised again throughout this text. Indeed, Chapter 4 is dedicated to the external environment of an organization, focusing on how it deals with such impacts. Chapter 5 moves on to explore strategy and planning in which geopolitical disruptions are likely to have a key influence. Supply chain and operations, explored in Chapter 12 is another notable touchpoint, in which geopolitics can have a significant disruptive impact on organizations.

3.4 **Technological disruption**

The rapid advance of technology in society that we are seeing today is often referred to as the fourth Industrial Revolution. An **Industrial Revolution** refers to a significant change in the means of production that powers economic activity. The first Industrial Revolution occurred in the mid-to-late eighteenth century when steam engines, often powered by coal, were invented

First Industrial Revolution— mid-late 18th Century	Second Industrial Revolution— late 19th Century
• Steam engines to mechanise production • Powered by coal	• Internal combustion engine, communication, and transport advances • Powered by oil and gas

Third Industrial Revolution— late 20th Century	Fourth Industrial Revolution— early 21st Century
• Digital technologies and computers • High levels of automation	• Internet enabling hardware, software and biology interconnection • Increase in AI and decrease in human intervention

FIGURE 3.3 **The four Industrial Revolutions.**

to power machines that mechanized production, as we discussed briefly in Chapter 2. The second Industrial Revolution, known as the technological revolution, followed in the late nineteenth century. It was largely powered by oil and gas, with the invention of the internal combustion engine used in trains, cars, and factories, as well as electricity becoming accessible across society, which contributed to mass production. Communication and transport were also revolutionized with the widespread establishment of railroad and telegraph networks. The third Industrial Revolution, known as the digital revolution, occurred in the late twentieth century, with the rise of digital communication technologies and computers, which saw unprecedented levels of connectivity and automation. Figure 3.3 provides a summary of this progression.

The ubiquity of the internet is now driving the fourth Industrial Revolution, with the combination of hardware, software, and even biology, driving machine-to-machine communications and the internet-of-things, often characterized by little or no human intervention. Technologies that will increasingly become mainstream include smart factories (in which devices, machinery, and production systems are connected and continuously collect and share data), artificial intelligence (AI), nanotechnology, 5G wireless technology, anthropomorphic (human-like) robots, 3D printing, and fully autonomous vehicles. From a management perspective, just one of these technologies could disrupt the business model of a traditional private sector organization (e.g. autonomous vehicles replacing taxi drivers), alter operational approaches for a third sector organization (e.g. 'care-bots' providing monitoring and companionship in care homes), or create significant policy and control challenges in public sector organizations (e.g. a national government's role in the ethics and responsibility of AI).

The reliance of organizations on technology makes it a significant potential disruptor in both positive and negative ways. We will now explore three elements of technological disruption that will have a significant impact on management and managing into the future.

3.4.1 **Online communication and communities**

Information and communications technology (ICT) typically refers to the internet, wireless networks, mobile phone networks, computers, software, video conferencing, social networking, and apps and services, which exist to enable users to access, retrieve, store, transmit, and manipulate information in digital form. ICT has transformed workplaces, education, policymaking, and community support services, to name just a few areas of impact. It has also contributed to increased transparency and accountability, as most areas of an organization's operations can be video recorded or photographed, and communicated almost instantly online. This ubiquity of ICT changes the way organizations function, the issues that require management, and the way that managers conduct themselves. More broadly, it changes the way in which society interacts, organizes, and learns.

A challenging consequence of the intersection of ICT with social trends is polarization of political and social views, because technology enables extreme niche online groups to spread misinformation, conspiracy theories, and distrust of authority. A backlash against science was particularly notable during the Covid-19 pandemic, where niche online groups spread concerns about Covid treatments and misinformation about vaccine side effects, leading to vaccine hesitancy. The World Health Organization (2021) warned that so-called 'post-truth' politics, enabled by the ubiquity of ICT, are 'amplifying hate speech; heightening the risk of conflict, violence and human right violations; and threatening long-term prospects for advancing democracy'. This is where we see the interconnection of disruptions due to technology, geopolitics, and society, and even the environment, as we see climate deniers joining these online groups.

More positively, ICT has contributed to making education more accessible and potentially less expensive. The internet has provided a relatively barrier-free mechanism to access customers online, which makes it possible to start and grow a business, enabling many people to become entrepreneurs. Access to information facilitated by ICT helps to ensure that people are aware of their rights, of agencies who can support them, and of options and opportunities they have to address issues or advance themselves, and can find online communities of those with similar interests, challenges, or conditions.

3.4.2 Cybersecurity

Increasingly, our physical and digital lives are almost entirely interconnected. This has implications for many things, including our physical and digital safety and security. Data, and particularly personal data, is a valuable commodity. For example, our personal data might be beneficial for public policy reasons to assist with community planning, or to identify and target specific members of the community for social or health campaigns. It might be useful for marketing or sales reasons, as businesses and other organizations attempt to better understand their customers in a context where they are less likely to ever meet their customers face-to-face, to assist with product or service design, or to simply target potential customers. Or personal data might be used for criminal reasons linked to hacking, identity theft, and cybercrime.

Cybersecurity, given the reliance most organizations place on technology and data, can be a significant source of technological disruption. Cyber threats include:

- cybercrime, involving single actors or groups attempting to achieve financial gain;
- cyberattacks, which include politically-motivated information gathering and data breaches; and
- cyberterrorism, which is intended to undermine entire technological systems (often ICT) to cause panic, fear, or social and political instability.

Some incidents that have had significant impacts on management and managers include denial of service attacks, where cybercriminals prevent computer systems from carrying out necessary functions, which may be combined with ransomware that requires a ransom to be paid for regaining access to the service. For these reasons, the role of Chief Technology Officer is increasingly an important position within large organizations, while management roles and functions including risk, human resources, and finance need to consider how to protect their organization from such threats, and be ready to act if a breach occurs.

3.4.3 Digital inequality

The World Economic Forum Global Risks Report (2022) includes digital inequality as a key global risk of the future. The digital divide, which results from differing access to technology and devices, has the potential to isolate, disadvantage, and ostracize entire communities. Many aspects of our lives are increasingly digitized, including how we do business, participate in education, and even act as a responsible citizen in relation to community engagement and voting. Indeed, anyone with a computing device and access to the internet can potentially set up a business in a day. This disadvantages individuals who lack reliable access to the internet, lack access to up-to-date technological devices, and lack the skills needed for rapidly accelerating technology change. Those lacking technology face significant disadvantages in accessing the services and resources they need to survive and thrive, and risk being left behind. Those who face such problems are often part of communities that already suffer disadvantages for a number of different reasons: geographic location and access to public infrastructure; poverty and financial uncertainty; or digital experience and acumen. The forced and rapid online shift linked to the Covid-19 pandemic makes this an even starker situation. For example, the Cambridge

Centre for Housing and Planning Research (2021) noted that online learning during pandemic lockdowns could result in children from financially disadvantaged households falling further behind in their schooling when compared to their peers from wealthier households, due to insufficient Wi-Fi access.

This digital shift includes different facets of disruption. For example, decisions and analysis which were previously conducted by humans—such as diagnosing health issues, choosing investments, assessing educational achievement, or even resolving legal disputes—are increasingly being undertaken by sophisticated algorithms applying machine learning to large datasets. Conducted effectively, some of these interventions can have a positive impact on society. However, they often require individuals and communities to have access to digital technology to benefit from these innovations. Also, there are many questions being raised about the ethical implications of such algorithms, and whether they perpetuate existing societal inequalities such as racism. Indeed, in 2021 Google's co-lead of their ethical artificial intelligence team, Timnit Gebru, was fired after she published a research paper that questioned the ethics of large language AI models because of their reliance on big data, which may in turn use skewed datasets that may deepen socio-economic and other biases (Simonite, 2021).

These issues become important to management and managing in different ways. While many organizations will find that technology provides opportunities to achieve their purpose, increase performance, improve efficiency, access new markets, communicate with their customers, or help their service-users, being aware of issues of digital inequality is essential. For example, while online banking may be a more efficient way of providing that service, there are many who still feel a sense of security from in-person banking and do not have access to digital options. Also, from a recruitment perspective potential job applicants from diverse backgrounds may not see online job advertisements or have access to a computer or the relevant skills to be able to apply.

In summary, technological disruption comprises issues as broad as online communication, cybersecurity, digital inequality, and many others. These impact managers in various ways, with both positive and negative potential implications.

3.4.4 Technology and the future of work

Technology has always disrupted long-held jobs, working patterns, and job categories, and therefore had much wider implications for the way in which society functions. In his groundbreaking book, *23 Things They Don't Tell You about Capitalism*, economist Ha-Joon Chang's (2010) 'Thing 4' stated that 'the washing machine has changed the world more than the internet has'. He argues that household technologies such as the washing machine caused significant social upheaval by changing the lives of women, disrupting entire job categories and indeed an entire gender. Prior to their invention, it was expected that women would stay home to cook, clean, and wash clothes: time-consuming manual tasks which allowed no spare time for women to enter the paid labour force. Wealthy families, of course, were able to employ people (often women) for these manual tasks. But when household technology was introduced, hours dedicated to such tasks were reduced from over 60 hours per week to under 10 hours per week. Women had time and energy to work, and those employed for these tasks—maids, cooks, and cleaners—saw whole categories of jobs lost. This new-found potential for women to work in the paid labour force meant that families had fewer children, had them later, and invested more in each child, especially female children. Additionally, women increased their bargaining positions and power within the household and in wider society (Chang, 2010).

Today, the World Economic Forum (WEF) 'Future of Jobs' report (2020: 3) warns that 'millions of individuals globally have lost their livelihoods and millions more are at risk from the global recession [period of economic decline], structural change to the economy and further automation'. The consequences of automation and technological disruption go beyond the mere *replacement* of jobs and job categories. There are also questions emerging about how such technology changes the experience and possibilities for work. Opportunities to work are often correlated with opportunities in life, which, in turn, are linked to social and global inequalities. That is, technology does not just change or replace the job of a human worker, it also impacts the meaning of work—what counts as work and what we do as part of that work—and, hence, the management of employees (employment relations) on a global scale.

Self-employment opportunities, including through the '**gig economy**'—a labour market that focuses on temporary, short-term contracting of individuals for very specific projects, whereby workers gain flexibility and independence, but lack job security and benefits—are often made possible because of the internet, advanced communications, smart phones, and app technology. This casualization of the workforce may work for some, especially those with specialized skills and greater bargaining power. However, it can also keep others in ongoing cycles of temporary work with the associated uncertainty, inconsistent income, and an inability to plan for the future, access facilities like home mortgages, or change their circumstances. It can deny them protections they are typically due under employment law, or a sense of community which comes from being part of an organization. As we will see throughout Part 3 of this text, technological disruptions have impacted managing people, and managing them well, in many ways. When automation changes how work is done, managers control the commitment to reskilling or reallocation of employees whose jobs have been lost. When an employee leaves the organization, managers decide whether to hire a direct replacement on a permanent basis or to outsource the work to a contractor.

3.5 **Environmental disruption**

All organizations are reliant on the natural environment to continue to operate. The environment provides humans with a vast array of resources including food to eat, timber to build homes and workplaces, water and waterways to drink from and to support many industrial processes, not to mention clean air to breathe. For many people the environment also represents a connection we have with the Earth, and a habitat for other species to live and thrive, which deserves our respect and protection irrespective of its actual contribution to human advancement. However, for some people, the natural environment represents a series of free and never-ending resources to be acquired, exploited, and often taken for granted. Indeed, the environment has been exploited throughout many centuries, including widespread deforestation and land-use change; species extinction due to hunting and poaching or habitat loss; biodiversity loss with habitats, plants, insects, and animals all disappearing; and the pollution of rivers, lakes, and oceans from effluent, pesticides, litter, and chemicals.

3

Murdock (2023: 715) contrasts industrial thinking (as demonstrated in the Industrial Revolutions depicted in Figure 3.3) with indigenous thinking originating from Indigenous peoples located in North America—specifically, the USA and Canada. She argues that 'Indigenous societies, governments, and political structures are all created and built in accordance with and respect for natural law.' By contrast, she suggests 'industrial thinking believes in the human species' dominion over nature', which has contributed to the degradation and destruction of nature. A key moment in questioning such industrial thinking in the field of management came with Rachel Carson's book, *Silent Spring*, published in 1962, as well as ongoing efforts by the United Nations Environment Programme (UNEP) and NGOs such as Greenpeace. Despite this, the natural environment is in its most dire state in history. Indeed, according to the WEF, environmental risks make up four of the five most likely global risks: extreme weather, climate action failure, human environmental damage, and biodiversity loss (World Economic Forum, 2022).

Here, we very briefly identify and explore three incredibly complex environmental disruptions which are already impacting, and will increasingly impact, management and managing across all types of organizations. As we explore these, it is worth considering the significant societal disruptions that such environmental disruptions contribute to: ultimately all of society, geopolitics, and technology is dependent on the environment.

3.5.1 The climate crisis

The climate crisis is the culmination of many environmental issues that have grown progressively over the past decades. It is likely that every single organization is already, or very soon will be, impacted by the disruption it causes. **Climate change** refers to changes in the global climate (long-term weather patterns) caused by the increasing average global temperatures, which are themselves caused by greenhouse gas (GHG) emissions. The scale of the current and expected impacts of climate change means that this phenomenon is increasingly being called the climate emergency or climate crisis.

Most emissions come from the burning of fossil fuels for electricity, heat, energy, and transport, as well as agricultural emissions from livestock and soils, and land-use change and forestry. Figure 3.4 depicts the *cumulative* CO_2 emissions by country from 1750 to 2021, excluding emissions from land-use change. It is important to note, however, that there is an ongoing debate about who should be responsible for GHG emissions. For example, while China's emissions are high and growing rapidly, a large proportion of these are linked to the manufacturing of products which are then exported and bought (often cheaply) by consumers in other countries.

The UN's Intergovernmental Panel on Climate Change (IPCC) researches and reports on the climate crisis culminating in an annual Conference of Parties (COP) in which delegates from countries around the world discuss action. Notable recent COPs include the Paris Agreement in 2015, where governments committed to attempting to limit the temperature increase to 1.5°C, and the Glasgow Climate Pact in 2021, which included important agreements to phase down the burning of coal and commit to climate finance for developing countries. The latter is intended to address issues of climate justice, given the climate crisis is impacting some of the world's poorest nations sooner and more deeply than richer developed nations who are responsible for a much greater proportion of CO_2 emissions and impacts.

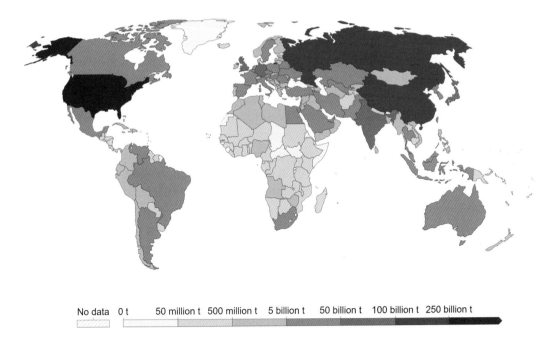

No data   0 t   50 million t   500 million t   5 billion t   50 billion t   100 billion t   250 billion t

FIGURE 3.4 **Cumulative CO$_2$ emissions by country from 1750 to 2021.** Credit: Hannah Ritchie, Max Roser, and Pablo Rosado (2020)—'CO$_2$ and Greenhouse Gas Emissions'. Published online at OurWorldIn-Data.org. Retrieved from: 'https://ourworldindata.org/co2-and-greenhouse-gas-emissions' [Online Resource]

It is widely accepted that we need to reduce GHG emissions rapidly, and reach Net Zero (where our only emissions are balanced by those we can remove from the atmosphere) by 2050 at the very latest, in order to avoid the catastrophic impacts of global temperatures exceeding an average increase of 2°C.

If we fail to achieve this, scientists predict that we will face an increase in:

- severe and debilitating heatwaves;

- heavy and unexpected rainfall leading to widespread flooding;

- droughts caused by little or no rainfall leading to famine;

- hot and dry weather contributing to extensive wildfires;

- the intensity of tropical cyclones making landfall and devastating entire coastal communities, as well as those further inland; and

- sea-level rise caused by the melting glaciers and ice sheets, as well as an expanding ocean as the water warms.

Even at just a 1.2°C warming, which we have already caused, we are seeing some of these impacts affecting communities and habitats, with the loss of lives, homes, and livelihoods now common in extreme weather events like floods, cyclones, wildfires, or storms.

The impacts of the climate crisis on management and managing are extensive. Risks associated with the crisis are typically divided into physical and transition risks. Physical risks are those caused by the impacts of the climate crisis itself—such as floods or wildfire—on an organization's offices, factories, employees, supply chains, consumers, or stakeholders.

3

Despite the severe impacts of physical risk, most organizations will see more significant impacts from transition risk. Transition risk refers to the fact that the economy and society are already and will continue to change in the coming years to attempt to address the climate crisis. We are seeing individual organizations choose to alter their operating model to either avoid physical risk or take advantage of opportunities. We are also seeing organizations forced into change because key partners—banks who provide finance, suppliers who provide key components, or even customers who buy products and services—place expectations or demands on them. Governments are increasingly mandating that organizations change through legislation.

Whatever the driver, various organizations in different industries will face diverse transition risks and timelines to address these. For example, fossil fuel companies are facing pressure from investors, governments, and customers to scale back high-emissions assets such as coal or gas-fired power stations, and invest in renewable and lower-emitting options such as wind, solar, and tidal technologies. Indeed, if government policies changed globally to meet the UN Paris Agreement's aims to limit the temperature increase to 1.5°C, it is estimated that two-thirds of the world's known fossil fuel reserves (e.g. coal and gas) would need to remain underground (Bank of England, 2019). Such a policy change would revalue the assets and therefore the share price of these companies significantly. That is, the potential financial impacts of the physical and transition climate risks are significant. Figure 3.5 provides a summary of these.

It is important to remember that the risk of not acting, and not acting collectively, far outweighs the risks, uncertainty, and disruption associated with transitioning to a lower emissions society. Failure to address the climate crisis will result in increased and often catastrophic physical risks to organizations, with the associated tragic impacts on lives lost, communities changed forever, destruction of nature, and entire regions which are no longer liveable. Such collective action requires all organizations, governments, and individuals to embrace the necessary transition risks and contribute to building a new, more sustainable, economy and society.

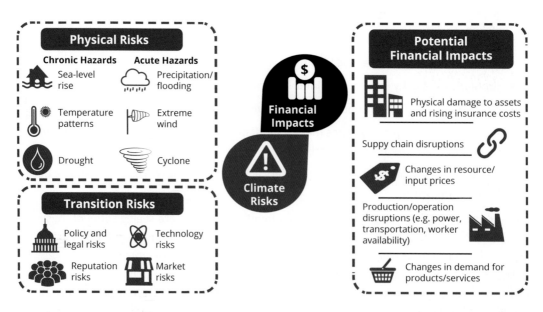

FIGURE 3.5 **Climate-related risks and financial impacts.** Credit: Copyright © United Nations Environment Programme, July 2019

3.5.2 **Water scarcity**

Another significant environmental disruption is linked to water. The availability of fresh and plentiful potable (drinking) water is key to human (and other species') survival. It is also a key input in many organizations, either directly or indirectly. For example, the food and beverage sector relies on water supplies for cleaning, cooking, and often as a direct ingredient in their products. Beverage producers are particularly aware of this. Global brewer SAB Miller partnered with WWF to analyse the water used in their products. The results estimated that it takes 45–155 litres of water to produce every 1 litre of beer, with the difference mostly linked to the water associated with irrigation needed to grow crops such as hops (SAB Miller & WWF, 2009). These production considerations make the availability of freshwater supplies a key issue for such organizations.

Despite its importance, many people take a limitless supply of clean, running water for granted. However, existing water supplies such as aquifers are being drained, and surface reservoirs and rivers are being impacted by the changing precipitation (rain) patterns caused by the climate crisis. More humans on Earth need more water to drink, and more food to eat—agriculture is a key industry for water consumption. Since the 1900s, freshwater use for agriculture, industry, and municipal use has increased six-fold (Ritchie & Roser, 2017). Currently, two-thirds of the global population—four billion people—face water scarcity at least one month per year. With the impacts of the climate crisis felt in the coming decades, this is projected to double (Munia et al., 2020).

In addition to availability for organizations, there are two significant factors to consider in relation to water scarcity. The first is that water is essential for human survival, but also for

3

human health and sanitation. Where fresh, clean drinking water is scarce, many are forced to use unclean supplies, spreading disease. The second is the potential for mass migration and conflict associated with water. As water availability decreases, people choose to migrate, looking for places to live which provide clean water, and safe and secure futures for their families (Nagabhatla et al., 2020). Often, this includes crossing borders, which is referred to as water migration. Additionally, it is expected that the water stress in many countries will contribute to existing political conflicts, or even create new conflicts. Three former UN secretary generals (Boutrous Boutrous-Ghali in 1985, Kofi Annan in 2001, and Ban Ki-moon in 2007) have warned that conflict and wars will be increasingly fought over water, not politics or land (Water Online, 2011).

3.5.3 Biodiversity loss

The final environmental disruption we will mention is biodiversity, and particularly the loss of key habitats and species. While there are many links to the climate crisis, there are some elements which are occurring because of more direct human intervention and destruction. Biodiversity refers to the diverse range of species (plant and animal) which coexist on Earth and have done so for millennia. We often refer to biodiversity more broadly as 'nature'. It is widely accepted that human intervention has seen the loss of significant and important habitats, as well as animal and insect species. The losses often lead to the erosion of 'ecosystem services', which are the beneficial contributions provided by such habitats and species. For example, mangrove forests often sit between land and the ocean, especially in tropical zones, and are one of the most biologically diverse ecosystems on Earth. Among the many other benefits of mangroves, they absorb up to four times more CO_2 from the atmosphere than a typical forest, and they protect coastal areas from erosion, not to mention providing food, shelter, and livelihoods to local communities. Some estimates suggest the 14 million hectares of mangroves worldwide are worth up to US$800 billion per year in the ecosystem services that they provide. Despite their environmental and ecosystem services value, mangroves are being cleared for urbanization; felled for logging, agriculture, and aquaculture (e.g. establishing rice paddies or shrimp farms); lost to the climate crisis due to changes in precipitation and ocean temperature needed to maintain them; or polluted to the point of degradation (IUCN Marine and Forest Programmes, 2018).

Bees and other pollinating insects offer another example of a common ecosystem service. Insects are essential pollinators of crops and wild plants. Many plants, including those that provide crops such as fruits, vegetables, textile-related fibres, and medicinal products, require insect pollination. Bees are the most common pollen carriers, estimated to be responsible for the pollination of one-third of our crops (Catarino et al., 2019). If bees become extinct, studies suggest we might lose all the plants that bees currently pollinate, as well as the animals which are sustained by those plants. One study of nature-based agriculture (as opposed to agriculture requiring chemical inputs), found that bee pollination outperforms pesticides for yield (amount of product grown in a specific area) and profitability (Catarino et al., 2019). Despite this, pesticides which are still legally used in many countries, are linked to widespread deaths of bees (Gill, 2021).

In summary, the climate crisis, water scarcity, and biodiversity loss are key disruptions to the environment which will impact organizations and management in many different ways. We will see this in more detail in Chapters 4 and 5. The days of managers being able to ignore nature and the environment are very much behind us. Indeed, many of the most successful organizations of the future are likely to be those who do not just manage the risks associated with environmental disruption, but whose purpose is to help either avoid such disruption or help humans to adapt to it. We continue to explore these themes in Running case 3.2.

RUNNING CASE 3.2 **IMPERIAL IS RESILIENT**

A year after the initial pandemic lockdown, Imperial's decision to deliver direct to customers has largely been a success. An online shop has been added to the website and a number of marketing campaigns have directed potential customers to the Heat-at-Home range of products. Marketing manager, Gita Patel, had been concerned that a key older age group might not be able to easily navigate the website. One of her team members had flippantly replied: 'Well, if they can't use a website, they just have to accept that they cannot access our products'—an opinion that Gita had found troubling. While she continued to think about that issue, in the immediate term she developed a campaign to demonstrate how meals could be bought and gifted to older and vulnerable relatives and friends, which became one of their main sales avenues.

When Lucy passed Jazz in the factory she thanked her for an inspiring chat a year ago and for her creativity in designing Heat-at-home menus which had inspired the business to pivot. 'Who knows what the next disruption will be though, Lucy?', says Jazz.

'That's so true,' Lucy replied. 'We need to be prepared.'

Lucy has been thinking about the question of Imperial's resilience for some time. The pivot to online sales direct to consumers has been a big change. William reports that 15 per cent of revenue is now coming via website orders. But what they don't know is how consistent that number will be. And just how secure is their website? The most popular 'Heat-at-Home' meal packs are reliant on specific ingredients but do they have a plan for disruptions to the supply? Do they need a plan? And what questions have they not even thought of yet?

Thinking of the many operational tasks she has to focus on, she wonders if she is spending enough time on the uncertain 'what-if' questions.

Questions for reflection

1. Should people who don't shop online miss out on products that are only sold via websites? Or should brands have multiple ways in which people can buy their products?

2. Does Lucy need to plan for a disruption to the supply of all of their ingredients? Some of their ingredients? Or is it impossible to plan for everything?

3. Could a 'pandemic-level' disruption ever occur again? Should an organization prepare for it? If yes, how? If no, why not?

3.6 **Organizations impacting the world**

This chapter has largely focused on how we can understand a disrupted world, through the notions of VUCA and wicked problems, as well as some of the disruptions in the world which are likely to impact organizations. However, it is interesting to also explore the reverse relationship by considering the impact that organizations can have on the world. That is, organizations can

3

contribute to these disruptions—and many more—in both positive and negative ways. While this will be a constant theme throughout Parts 2, 3, and 4 of this text, here we will introduce two concepts that are regularly used to explore such interactions: Corporate Social Responsibility (CSR) and sustainability.

Corporate Social Responsibility (CSR) was a label introduced by Howard Bowen (1953) to refer to the responsibilities businesses have for the world around them. This has also been called 'corporate responsibility' and the 'social contract' between businesses and society. It became particularly popular from the 1990s onwards, when many organizations—businesses in particular—produced CSR strategies and CSR reports to demonstrate the positive impact they have on the world. While admirable, many criticized these for being selective in what they chose to report.

In recent years, the related concept of 'sustainability' has become more prominent. The word originates from a 1987 report by the UN World Commission on Environment and Development (WCED) called *Our Common Future*, also known as the Brundtland report, named for the chair of the WCED, former Norwegian Prime Minister, Gro Bundtland. The aim of this report was to bring the development community (those addressing global poverty) together with the environment community (those addressing degradation and destruction of the natural world). The report defined 'sustainable development' as 'meeting the needs of the present without compromising the ability of future generations to meet their own needs' (Brundtland, 1987).

From these broad and complex origins, however, sustainability has often been simplified. Some people focus almost exclusively on sustainability from the perspective of the environment, ignoring any other aspects. Others adopt a broader perspective, but categorize issues into one of three elements: economic, environmental, and societal. These elements have undergone various iterations as depicted in Figure 3.6. Originally, they were presented as a Venn diagram with the 'sustainability sweet spot' at the intersection of all three. Increasing environmental crises have, however, emphasized the fact that both society and the economy are simply subsets of, and entirely located within, the environment. This idea led to an updated depiction which is often referred to as 'nested sustainability'.

A more recent approach sees sustainability as a lens through which to understand, interpret, and analyse all aspects of the organization. One of the reasons to move to the concept of a sustainability lens is the recognition that managers are likely to face many varied tensions

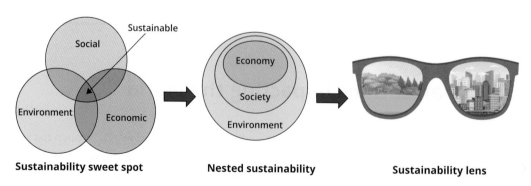

Sustainability sweet spot   Nested sustainability   Sustainability lens

FIGURE 3.6 **Perspectives on sustainability.**

and trade-offs between economic, environmental, and societal elements, and even within each element. As such, simplified depictions fail to account for these complexities. We will see these management challenges repeatedly throughout Parts 2, 3, and 4 of this text. You can learn more about these ideas from one of the authors of this text, Dr Sarah Ivory, in a blog post entitled *What Is Sustainability Anyway?* focused on teaching sustainability, or hear her talking about sustainability in the finance industry at the Global Ethical Finance conference. Find out how to access these talks in the 'Explore more' feature at the end of this chapter.

The United Nations attempted to build beyond the simplified three elements of sustainability by introducing the Sustainable Development Goals. These are the focus of Spotlight 3.2.

Drawing on the idea of nested sustainability at the level of the whole economy, Oxford economist Professor Kate Raworth (2017) developed the idea of Doughnut Economics,

SPOTLIGHT 3.2 SUSTAINABLE DEVELOPMENT GOALS

In 2016, the United Nations launched the 'Sustainable Development Goals', setting the ambitious target of meeting them by 2030. The 17 goals, listed here, have a total of 169 specific targets behind them and were described by the then UN Secretary-General Ban Ki-moon as 'a to-do list for people and planet, and a blueprint for success' (United Nations, 2015).

Goal 1: No poverty

Goal 2: Zero hunger (No hunger)

Goal 3: Good health and well-being

Goal 4: Quality education

Goal 5: Gender equality

Goal 6: Clean water and sanitation

Goal 7: Affordable and clean energy

Goal 8: Decent work and economic growth

Goal 9: Industry, innovation, and infrastructure

Goal 10: Reduced inequality

Goal 11: Sustainable cities and communities

Goal 12: Responsible consumption and production

Goal 13: Climate action

Goal 14: Life below water

Goal 15: Life on land

Goal 16: Peace, justice, and strong institutions

Goal 17: Partnership for the goals

While the SDGs have been influential in both the public and third sectors, what has been most interesting is the engagement with them by private sector businesses. The Global Reporting Initiative (GRI), an independent, international organization that helps organizations take responsibility for their global impacts, released a report in 2022 entitled *State of Progress: Business Contributions to the SDGs* (GRI, 2022). In it, they find that:

- 83 per cent of reporting companies state that they support the SDGs

- 69 per cent articulate which goals are most relevant to their business

- 61 per cent specify how their actions support the SDGs

However, the picture may not be as promising as it seems. In 2021, B Lab, the not-for-profit organization that manages B Corp accreditation (which we introduced in Spotlight 2.2), released their *SDG Insights Report 2021* (B Lab, 2021). In it, they conclude that in adopting the SDGs, businesses have largely focused on their own internal operations. B Lab calls for businesses 'to go beyond what are the easiest and simplest placed for them to make contributions' to, and to direct attention 'towards the most significant and impactful places they can contribute' (Joffre, 2021). That is, to focus on their supply chain, as well as the actions of their customers and clients.

3

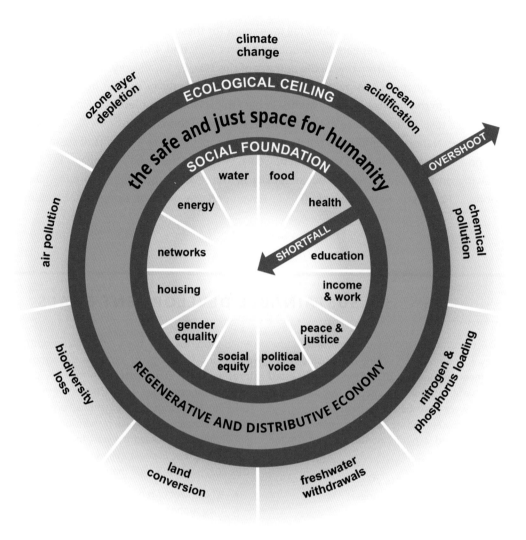

FIGURE 3.7 **Doughnut Economics.** Credit: Kate Raworth, *Doughnut Economics: Seven Ways to Think Like a 21st-Century Economist*, 2017, Chelsea Green Publishing

depicted in Figure 3.7. This reorients the whole economic system towards a regenerative and distributive economy which provides a safe and just space for humanity. This is particularly reacting to the contributions made by private sector businesses to both environmental and societal crises. Indeed, the private sector purpose-shift referenced in Section 2.6.3 is entwined with these ideas. The doughnut depicts an ecological ceiling—and the specific areas of over-shoot that need to be avoided, including issues identified in this chapter in relation to environmental disruption—climate change, biodiversity, and water. It also introduces the social foundation—and the factors which are required for a strong society, such as education, peace, food, and health. We come back to Professor Raworth's ideas in Chapter 4 and you can find resources from her in the 'Explore more' feature of that chapter.

3.7 **Conclusion**

In this chapter, we have argued that managing *is* managing through disruption, but that disruptions may be good or bad, depending on a number of different factors. We introduced the idea of a VUCA world, a VUCA manager, and wicked problems as a way of defining and understanding these disruptions. We divided our analysis into geopolitical, technological, and environmental categories and explored a number of disruptions in each. These disruptions are interconnected in many different ways, can be difficult to understand, are constantly changing, and do not come close to covering the full range of potential disruptions that organizations and managers face. As a student of management, therefore, the point is not to learn and be able to repeat the parameters of the disruptions covered here, but to use them as examples to develop your critical thinking skills to analyse how disruptions can impact organizations, and the implications for different responses from management. Also, we introduced the concepts of CSR and sustainability, which focus more on the impact of organizations on society. As we now turn to Parts 2, 3, and 4 of this text, we will see many of the tools, frameworks, and models we introduce are specifically designed to help with this process of thinking about disruption (existing or future), and deciding on action.

CHAPTER SUMMARY

○ Managing organizations always requires the consideration of different disruptions that can have positive or negative impacts, although these will vary based on factors such as the type of organization, geographic location, and level of preparedness.

○ The VUCA world is Volatile, Uncertain, Complex, and Ambiguous, and needs VUCA Prime managers who meet Volatility with Vision, Uncertainty with Understanding, Complexity with Clarity, and Ambiguity with Agility.

○ Wicked problems, like poverty, are difficult or impossible to solve because of contradictory information or changing requirements; have no 'right or wrong' solution but only better and worse options; and have no way to test potential solutions or engage in trial and error.

○ Additionally, in relation to Super Wicked problems, such as the climate crisis, time is running out, there is no central authority, those seeking to solve the problem are also causing it, and policies fail to take sufficient account of the future.

○ We can consider categorizing disruptions into geopolitical, technological, and environmental; however, we could also identify many other categories and there are significant linkages between all categories.

○ CSR and sustainability take the perspective of the impact of the organization on society, and attempt to both understand and report on these impacts, as well as improve them.

○ It is for these reasons, that many managers have wide-ranging knowledge and experience in many different areas, not just expertise in the study of 'management' alone.

3

CLOSING CASE REFLECTION

How WWF changed while staying the same

Reflecting on WWF in the opening case study, we can see how what appears to be a very focused environmental charity, has both dealt with and leveraged significant disruptions throughout its 60-year history. This includes pivoting away from stand-alone localized projects and to a wider focus on habitats, nature, and eventually the global climate crisis as key disruptors to their mission of protecting species. However, WWF has also proved adept at engaging with geopolitical disruption, developing innovative solutions such as debt swaps to support nations to achieve environmental missions, as well as increased financial resilience and independence. Technological disruption has proved a useful leverage point for reaching a global audience with their campaigns, such as the globally influential Earth Hour. Without the explosion of social media and smart phones, such reach would not have been possible.

REVIEW QUESTIONS

1. What does VUCA stand for? How might this idea impact your own career journey?

2. Which geopolitical, technological, and environmental disruptions do you think will be the most challenging for organizations to cope with in the next five years?

3. Should organizations ignore the geopolitical context in which they operate? Why? Why not?

4. Has the rapid advance of digital technology been a barrier or an enabler to effective organizational management? Explain your reasons.

5. Why should managers care about bees? Which organizations rely on them and why? Think broadly, beyond the obvious.

EXPLORE MORE

═ READ the book by Bob Johansen titled: *Leaders Make the Future: Ten New Leadership Skills for an Uncertain World*, which focuses on the VUCA world.

═ READ the article from global consulting firm McKinsey & Company by Patrick Finn, Mihir Mysore, and Ophelia Usher 'When Nothing Is Normal: Managing in Extreme Uncertainty' by googling the title.

⦿ WATCH the documentary about the climate crisis, entitled *2040*. Search for the title on streaming platforms in your location.

⦿ WATCH the fascinating Netflix documentary *Coded Bias*, which explores the biases in algorithms, following work done by MIT researcher Joy Buolamwini.

READ Karl Schwab's short essay from 2017 about the 'Fourth Industrial Revolution', by googling the author's name and essay title. If interested, read the book by the same name.

WATCH Dr Sarah Ivory, talking about sustainability in the finance industry at the Global Ethical Finance Conference in 2022. Search for 'Forgive Me Father, for I Have Measured' on YouTube.

READ a blog from the author of this text, Dr Sarah Ivory, exploring how we should approach teaching sustainability: 'What Is Sustainability Anyway?', 7 Apr. 2020, by googling the article title and author name.

3

PART ONE **CONTEXT**

**PART TWO
ORGANIZATION**

PART THREE **PEOPLE**

PART FOUR **VALUE CHAIN**

PART
TWO

Managing an Organization

CHAPTER FOUR
The External Environment

Simon Brooks and Sarah Birrell Ivory

OPENING CASE STUDY **EASY SOLAR'S WAY FORWARD**

Easy Solar was co-founded in 2016 by Alexandre Tourre and Nthabiseng Mosia. It is one of the fastest growing off-grid solar companies in Africa, having powered over 900,000 people in its home of Sierra Leone, and branching out more recently into neighbouring Liberia. It is a social enterprise that sells solar panels and other products, with a vision of making energy, financial services, and life-improving products affordable and accessible for all.

The co-founders of Easy Solar met at Columbia University, New York, where Mosia was studying energy in order to bring solutions to Africa, given her experience of blackouts while growing up. They undertook a survey of energy availability across Sierra Leone, finding 87 per cent of the population (6.5 million people) lacked access to a reliable electricity grid.

They identified the most significant challenges were in rural areas, with a distributed population, no large industry giving hope to future grid connection, and severe poverty making their attractiveness as paying customers limited.

Nevertheless, the co-founders creatively focused on the market potential—albeit not in a traditional way that looks at the disposable income of their customers. Instead, they developed a lease model for their products on a pay-as-you-go basis. Their packages comprise different-sized solar panels, inverters, and batteries across three ranges:

- the Basic Range for a small home ('power the essentials');
- the Enjoy Range for medium-sized homes, an office, or school without computers, and small health clinics ('power for peace of mind'); and
- the Comfort Range for large homes ('power your life'), offices, schools with computers, and medium-sized clinics and hospitals.

The electricity they produce is able to power lanterns, charge phones, and run appliances. However, the benefit to their customers goes beyond power. The contract customers have with Easy Solar provides them with financial visibility, often for the first time ever. This means that they are able to demonstrate they have an asset as well as a credit history, which can lead to other financial opportunities such as bank loans. It can also allow individuals to become more productive and generate income, either from the solar device itself or from the longer hours of light which they now enjoy.

On a bigger scale, it provides a potential model for developing nations to leapfrog the expensive and polluting fossil fuel-based economy, moving straight to clean, secure, and abundant renewable energy (easysolar.org).

4.1 **An introduction to Part 2**

In Part 1 of this text, we defined management and considered its different functions, processes, roles, and levels, as well as its purpose (Chapter 1). We considered different categories of organizations in which management takes place, including private, public, and third sectors, as well as the overlaps and shifts between these sectors (Chapter 2). Finally, we explored management through disruption characterized by a VUCA (Volatile, Uncertain, Complex, Ambiguous) world and wicked problems, manifesting as geopolitical, technological, and environmental disruptions (Chapter 3). We will now move on to explore the task of actually managing an organization. That is, we move from discussions about the *context* of management as a concept, as depicted in Figure 4.1, to focus in on the actual task of managing. We start with a focus on managing an *organization* broadly in this part of the text (Part 2), before exploring the specifics of managing people (Part 3) and managing through the value chain (Part 4).

The first step in managing an organization is recognizing the organizational environment, which can be understood as the set of circumstances that influence the organization. The word 'environment' here is the general use of this term (and not a specific reference to nature or ecosystems). This chapter starts by distinguishing between the internal and external environments of an organization. We then focus on the external environment and specific tools managers use to understand and analyse it. The next chapter will move to explore the internal environment.

4.2 **Distinguishing the internal and external environments**

We can divide the organizational environment into the internal environment and the external environment. While there are overlaps between these, in general, the external environment refers to aspects beyond the organization's direct control, while the internal environment focuses on aspects within the boundaries of the organization that are largely within its control.

The internal environment includes the organization's strategy, which is its overall objective and its approach to achieving this, and its culture, which encompasses the shared ways of thinking, feeling, and behaving. Analysing the internal environment in order to develop strategy and undertake planning will be explored in Chapter 5. Exploring organizational culture as well as undertaking change management of an organization will be the focus of Chapter 6. An organization's people are a significant part of its internal environment, which is the focus of the chapters in Part Three. The organization's value chain—from upstream suppliers through operations to marketing and sales, and the innovation and entrepreneurial processes associated with this—are the focus of the chapters in Part 4. These elements are all largely within the direct control (to varying degrees) of the organization.

In this chapter, we examine the external environment, which comprises elements that influence the organization, but which are largely beyond their direct control, including ecosystems and nature, societal trends, government at varying levels, suppliers, interest groups, and individuals such as clients or customers. To gain some perspective on these trends, we can divide

4

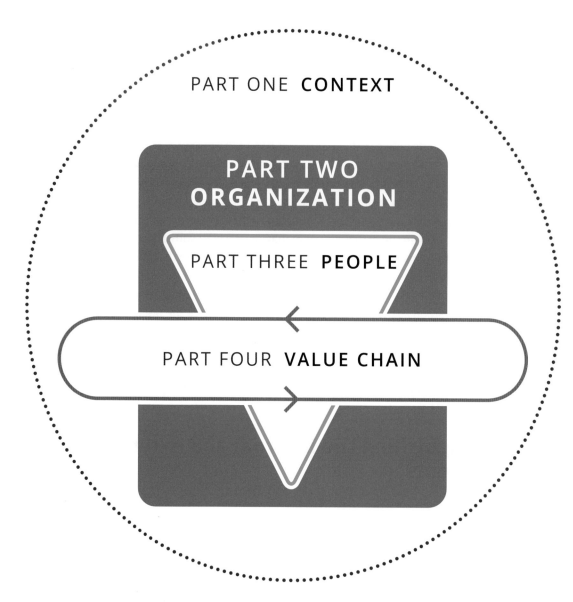

FIGURE 4.1 **Interrelated elements important in managing organizations.**

the external environment further into the organization's near environment and its broader, general environment.

When considering for-profit business in the private sector, the near environment is often termed the 'competitive environment'—that is, aspects that influence the competitiveness of the business. However, in order to be inclusive of many different types of organizations, we will refer to this near environment as the **micro-external environment**. This term describes aspects of the external environment that have an immediate, directly identifiable, and tangible impact on the organization's existence, purpose, or operations. The broader, more general environment in which the organization exists will be referred to as the **macro-external environment**. This comprises aspects of the external environment that

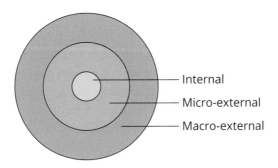

FIGURE 4.2 **The three aspects of the organizational environment.**

may not have an immediate, directly identifiable, or tangible impact on the organization's existence, purpose, or operations. This might include trends in changeable weather conditions, the political situation, or societal norms and expectations. Just because these factors do not have immediate, tangible impacts does not mean they can be ignored, as we will learn throughout this chapter.

Figure 4.2 depicts these three different aspects of the organizational environment: the internal environment, the micro-external (sometimes called competitive) environment, and the macro-external environment.

4.2.1 **Managerial view: Inside-out versus outside-in**

This distinction between internal and external environments extends to appreciating different perspectives or views from which managerial analysis and decisions are made.

The **inside-out resource-based view** (explored in detail in Section 5.2.1) sees organizational success as largely dependent on what and how many resources the organization has access to, and how managers best leverage and use those resources. Resources can include physical assets such as buildings, human beings such as employees, or less tangible things such as brand and reputation. That is, this view focuses on the organization's internal environment.

Conversely, the **outside-in market-based view** focuses on the external environment in which the organization operates. This view sees organizational success as largely dependent on being aligned with this external environment. Note that the word 'market' is used because these ideas have their origins in for-profit business linked to economic markets, but here we take it to mean micro- and macro-external environments for a diverse range of organizations, including those in the public and the third sector.

Consider a chef who aims to delight and satisfy her customers. She might decide what meal to serve by first looking internally to assess the finest ingredients she has access to and the best combinations of these, as well as the skills she and her team possess to create delicious flavours. Alternatively, she might start by looking outside the organization to analyse her customers' tastes, evaluate what will best satisfy them, and go in search of ingredients or improve her skills to achieve that. The former describes the inside-out resource-based view. The latter describes the outside-in market-based view. In all likelihood, she will combine aspects of both in order to produce meals to delight and satisfy her customers.

In Figure 4.2, we can visualize a manager who adopts an inside-out resource-based view as being more focused on the middle circle in order to achieve success, while a manager who adopts an outside-in market-based view would be more focused on the two outer circles and align the organization with these. In reality of course, as with our chef example, both are important. Taking too much of an outside-in view means managers can lose sight of what their organization is good at. However, taking too much of an inside-out view means managers fail to respond to changes in the external environment, which can become more acute in the VUCA world. We will return to the importance of balancing external and internal focus in Chapter 5 and introduce frameworks dedicated to helping with this.

Having distinguished between the internal and external environments, we will now focus on the two-way relationship between an organization and its external environment, before introducing tools and frameworks that will help us to analyse this environment. But first, let's see how these concepts play out for Imperial in our Running case 4.1.

RUNNING CASE 4.1 **INSIDE-OUT OR OUTSIDE-IN?**

Imperial's CEO, Lucy Green is feeling frustrated. Yesterday she had the monthly management meeting with CFO, William Green and Chairperson, Hugh Green. Things have been getting increasingly tense between Lucy and William. He keeps pointing out that profitability is deteriorating steadily. He believes they should put all their efforts into maintaining Imperial's reputation and increasing sales of products that they have always been known for and have expertise in. He has also started talking about needing to think about cutting costs and jobs. What concerned Lucy in this meeting was that her father Hugh had agreed strongly with William. 'It's all very well talking about new trends like microwaveable meals, Lucy. But in my view William's absolutely right: we should get back to what Imperial has always been good at, sell more traditional meat products, and start to look at cutting costs. I care about our people as much as you do, but we can't keep 100+ staff in the factory when our sales can barely pay for 75.' Lucy had left the meeting feeling undermined. She felt certain that going back to the past wasn't going to help Imperial manage its future. But what could she do about it?

Lucy meets with Marketing Manager, Gita Patel. 'The trouble is, Gita: they're right. We're making less

and less profit each month. Maybe we should just focus on what we've been good at in the past. But I think I'm right too! The world is changing. We need to get a better understanding of how, and then we need to change too!'

Gita reflects for a moment. 'You're right, Lucy. Let's collect some data and I'll conduct a proper analysis of what's happening outside Imperial. Then we'll be able to see much more clearly where we are.' Lucy agrees and asks Gita to set up an offsite staff-meeting to identify and plan for overall trends in society that are impacting Imperial, and that might impact the organization even more in the future.

Questions for reflection

1. Instinctively, do you side with William and Hugh—focusing on an inside-out resource-based view and emphasizing what the company has always been good at, or Lucy and Gita—focusing on an outside-in market view and what is happening outside Imperial? Reflect on why you have that instinct.

2. What 'overall trends in society' do you think might be raised when Imperial analyses its external environment?

4.3 **Influence on and of the external environment**

The external environment determines a range of factors in an organization, including:

- the resources and inputs it has access to,
- what outputs are expected from it,
- the regulations and laws it needs to follow,
- the social norms and ethical considerations it must conform to,
- the impact of nature and ecosystems on it, and ultimately
- its purpose for being.

After all, an organization is simply a grouping of people and their resources aimed at contributing to or influencing some aspect of the external environment. A vehicle manufacturer aims to contribute cars for consumers to buy or lease, while a public transport organization aims to contribute a system that provides transport services throughout a city, and a bicycle lobby group aims to influence individuals to cycle more, and demand governments provide better cycling infrastructure.

This conceptualization reveals something that seems obvious but has not always been acknowledged in studies of organizations: an organization's relationship with its external environment is two-way. That is, while we often focus on the influence *of* the external environment *on* the organization, the reverse situation also exists—that is, the influence *of* the organization *on* the external environment. This is known as the embedded perspective—where the organization is embedded in its environment, rather than separate from it. We will explore each of these dynamics in turn.

4.3.1 **Influence on the external environment**

Some organizations have a more significant impact on their external environment than others. This might be those who are larger, those who are more innovative, those who have this as a stated goal, or simply those in the right place at the right time. They can influence their micro- and macro-external environments in different ways, such as through lobbying governments directly, through decisions about industries they will support or those they will withdraw support from (for example the widespread divestment from fossil fuels), through the products or services they develop, or through the campaigns they run. We will explore a few examples here.

Organizations can influence their external environment via innovations in the products and services they develop. One example is Apple's iPhone innovation, which was the first 'smart phone' developed, and launched in 2007. Prior to this, mobile phones were largely only used to make and receive phone calls or send text messages and had limited connection to the internet. This product changed Apple's micro-external environment as mobile phone competitors raced to catch up and provide customers with alternative smart phones to rival Apple's product. However, it also changed the macro-external environment by contributing to technological developments, both in relation to the phone itself and the apps that could use that platform.

Additionally, the innovation of smart phones and the access to the internet in our pockets has created a number of impactful societal trends. Arguably, this has contributed to the explosion of social media use, requirements for firms to demonstrate transparency and accountability (whistle-blowing is more common with video or photographic material immediately uploaded to the internet as evidence of corporate wrongdoing), and political uprisings (as individuals are able to organize and circumnavigate security forces attempting to stop protests). The Arab Spring, a series of anti-government uprisings in the Arab world in 2010, was referred to by some as 'the first smartphone revolution', given the use of smart phones and social media apps to quickly rally supporters against the government (*Economic Times*, 2020).

Other organizations may have a more direct and explicitly-stated desire to influence their external environment: indeed, this may be their purpose. The UK-based charity Help for Heroes aims to bring attention to the impact of serving in the military on current members and recent veterans, drawing attention to, and receiving donations for, their needs. These actions have influenced UK society's view of what a military veteran actually is: previously thought of as old men who fought in World War 1 and 2, but now understood as younger members of all genders whose recent experiences in the military have been life-changing either physically, mentally, or psychologically. They use their platform to influence not only public perception, but also government policy and corporate support for pathways to healing, purpose, and satisfaction in veterans' post-military lives (helpforheroes.org.uk, 2022).

Whether it be Apple or Help for Heroes, or the hundreds of thousands of other organizations globally that influence their external environment, appreciating this two-way relationship is vital. It speaks directly to the issue of purpose, which we explored in Chapter 2. In particular, both public and third sector organizations are likely to link their purpose directly to improving an aspect of their external environment. However, the purpose shift relating to the private sector, which we discussed in Section 2.6.3, is amplifying the ways in which for-profit businesses also focus on positively impacting their external environment. Of course, it is also the case that private, public, and third sector organizations can have a negative or harmful impact on their external environment through their behaviour, lobbying, products, or services, either intentionally or as a by-product of their operations and choices. We will see examples of both positive and negative influences on the external environment throughout this text.

4.3.2 Influence of the external environment

A more common focus of management is the influence of the external environment on the organization. Indeed, making sense of the external organizational environment is one of the key tasks of management, and one of the key skills of a good manager. Recall Table 1.2 in Chapter 1 which outlined the 10 management roles: how many of these require managers to understand or react to the organization's external environment?

By conducting an analysis of the external environment, a manager can help to identify relevant opportunities and threats that the organization may face. However, doing so requires the categorization of the external environment into manageable parts for analysis. This is because the external environment is vast and complicated. Indeed, it could be said to include all of the economy, society, and the natural world, or at least significant parts of them. Moreover, as we learned in Chapter 3, the external environment is increasingly part of a VUCA world and so is constantly being disrupted by geopolitical, technological, and environmental factors. As such, understanding the external environment is not a one-off task to tick off on a manager's to-do list, but rather is an ongoing process.

Many tools and frameworks are available to assist managers with the process of understanding and analysing the influences of the external environment, and ultimately determining how to respond. These help managers make sense of the complexity of the environment by dividing it up into more manageable chunks that are easier to comprehend and analyse. However, it is important to remember three things:

- First, we are not claiming that the external environment naturally divides into (for example) six easy categories as we do with PESTEL analysis (Section 4.4); we are only suggesting that, at least initially, it helps our analysis to have some understandable groupings to use.

- Second, as we will discuss towards the end of this chapter, and depict visually at the start of Chapter 5, it is important to consider how analytical tools relate to each other and can be used in combination, as well as how they impact the organization we are managing or analysing.

- Third, we should always remember that the external environment and internal environment are complementary, and the boundaries between them blurred. As such, considering the external environment in isolation from the organization's internal environment may result in skewed analysis.

In this text, we will introduce and examine three different tools which are useful for managers attempting to analyse and understand the influence of the external environment on their

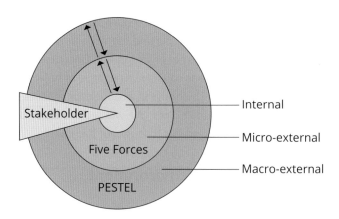

FIGURE 4.3 **Tools for analysing the external environment.**

organization. We will start with PESTEL analysis (Section 4.4), which maps to the macro-external environment of the organization. We will then introduce the Five Forces analysis (Section 4.5), which focuses on the micro-external environment of the organization. Finally, we will explore stakeholder analysis (Section 4.6) as our third tool. This tool extends through the micro- and macro-external environments as well as the internal environment, and so will provide a useful bridge into Chapter 5 which moves on to explore the internal environment.

Figure 4.3 depicts the three environments and the scope of the three different tools we will explore here. The arrows remind us that while the external environment influences the organization's internal environment, the reverse is also true.

4.4 **PESTEL analysis**

Managers need to be actively aware of and engaged in the macro-external environment of their organization. PESTEL analysis is a tool commonly used by managers to help track and make sense of the macro-external environment in a systematic way, and to identify trends that represent potential opportunities or threats to the organization and its activities. PESTEL is an acronym for the six categories that are most commonly included: Political, Economic, Sociocultural, Technological, Ecological, and Legal. Note that while we use 'Ecological' for the second 'E', this is sometimes called 'Environmental'. Irrespective of which word it used, this category refers specifically to nature and ecosystems. This same tool is sometimes taught with variations of the numbers of categories and/or the acronym—for example, STEEPL, PEST, or STEP (which excludes legal and ecological), or STEEP (where legal is combined into political). Figure 4.4 depicts these categories of a PESTEL analysis.

Note that a number of disruptions we explored in Chapter 3 are explicitly mentioned here or fit within one of the six categories. As such, a PESTEL analysis can be a key tool when managing through disruption in a VUCA world and facing wicked problems. However, that does not mean that every category is relevant for every organization: some organizations will focus more on some categories and less on others. We should not necessarily expect to find something important in all

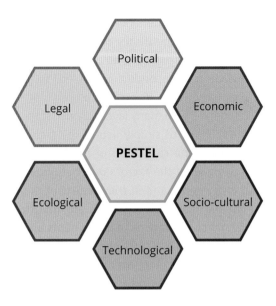

FIGURE 4.4 **PESTEL analysis.**

SPOTLIGHT 4.1 **TELEHEALTH IN AFRICA**

Health care organizations in Africa have traditionally focused on sociocultural elements of their external environment: the health care needed in different communities. As they are operating in areas with some of the lowest doctor–patient ratios globally, many organizations will have expanded their operations by leveraging political and economic trends: getting approval and often funding from different levels of governments, as well as understanding the role of economic upturns (and downturns) when identifying donors, funders, or patients' own abilities to contribute to costs. The ecological and technological factors in a PESTEL analysis were likely lower on their list of priorities, perhaps excepting location-specific floods, or improved transport for doctors to remote areas.

However, things have changed dramatically in the last decade across the entire continent. Ecological factors have become increasingly relevant with impacts of climate change felt both through increasing extreme weather and unprecedented disease spread as mosquitos and other insects follow the warmer weather (World Health Organization, 2022).

In addition, changes to the technological landscape have disrupted the entire industry, making digital health care a reality with improved access to the necessary hardware, internet connections, and software. One company based in Uganda has seen a 500 per cent increase in virtual consultations (Bloomberg, 2021). Meanwhile DabaDoc, a start-up founded in Morocco in 2014 by brother and sister team Zineb and Driss Drissi-Kaitouni, now connects thousands of doctors across Africa with millions of patients every year, largely using video and audio appointments. Additionally, they are partnering with governments and other private companies to transform health care delivery, and therefore health outcomes (World Economic Forum, 2022). This is an example of a purpose-driven business having significant impacts on its external environment.

six categories of PESTEL. However, by having the discipline to at least examine all six categories, we can identify those most important now, but can also uncover unexpected results, changes since our last analysis, or potential future issues. Spotlight 4.1 on Telehealth in Africa demonstrates this.

An effective PESTEL analysis should systematically examine different scales of the macro-environment. In other words, it should specifically consider local, national, and global factors that may influence the organization. For example, an aid organization based in Indonesia, with projects in Vietnam and Bangladesh, may conduct a detailed PESTEL analysis for all three nations. A business operating globally with a diversified portfolio of brands and products may have a more detailed PESTEL analysis with many layers divided by geography or product.

Many managers make the mistake of simply listing key factors in each of the six categories. While this is the first step, the real value of PESTEL comes with *analysis* of these factors. That is, not just knowing what the factors *are*, but understanding what this *means* for the organization—both in isolation, and in the context of the other categories, as well as the internal environment. This again demonstrates the importance of critical thinking in successful management. Managers need to make judgements about which factors are most relevant to their organization, why, and how they choose to respond. This also demonstrates the breadth of knowledge that the most effective managers either develop themselves or—especially in complex organizations—draw on from the teams they build around them. It shows why the best managers take an interest not only in studying management, but also in understanding elements of politics, economics, society, technology, the legal system, and ecology.

We will now briefly define and explain each category of the PESTEL analysis. Then we will explore how to undertake and use a PESTEL analysis as a key tool in understanding and managing an organization and its external environment.

4.4.1 **Political**

An organization is influenced, at least to some degree, by every political environment in which it and its key partners operate. This may include local, regional, and national governments, as well as the global political environment—for example, supranational organizations such as the United Nations (recall Spotlight 3.1). The political category is important because governments regulate certain industries, such as energy and electricity, financial services, and telecommunications. While this is an example of links between political and legal categories (see Section 4.4.6), not all politics is linked to actual legislation. The stability of political regimes and national governments may be a key factor influencing an organization's operations or future strategy. Moreover, this category of PESTEL may also include societal trends relating to politics, such as the increasing polarization of political views, or the growth of nationalism at the expense of regionalism or globalization, as we explored in Section 3.3 in relation to geopolitical disruption.

It is worth also considering the ways in which organizations may influence aspects of their political environment. Managers may provide information, advice, and guidance to policymakers (i.e. ministers and civil servants). Where this is used to contribute to fair and effective policy, this influence may be judged as good and useful. However, where lobbying, political donations, and other levers of influence are used to promote the organization's self-interest at the expense of others, this raises questions about what is acceptable, transparent, and appropriate political support, and what is inappropriate, corrupt, or unethical political influence.

4.4.2 **Economic**

The economy comprises the production, distribution, and consumption of goods and services. Managers of organizations across all sectors need to be aware of structural elements of the economy that influence how their organization functions, as well as trends that may impact their organization directly, or others in their value chain, such as their suppliers or customers. Economic factors that may influence organizations include changes in costs of inputs or production costs, exchange rate costs for foreign currency exchange, costs of capital (e.g. interest rates), or costs of staffing (e.g. wage costs). Overall economic trends, such as the recession following the global Covid-19 pandemic, may also contribute to reduced demand where consumer spending power or even just confidence is affected.

While the economy seems like a vast system that individual organizations could not possibly influence, we can see examples where this has happened. Indeed, the role of organizations like the World Trade Organization (WTO) is to ensure that economic trade flows as smoothly, predictably, and freely as possible around the globe. The global financial crisis of 2007–08 (which we referred to in Section 2.6.1) was caused in part by the banking industry failing to appropriately cost in the risk of the mortgage products they were offering. When declining housing prices caused these mortgages to fail, the impacts of decisions by managers in this industry were felt across the global economy (Sorkin, 2009).

The economic category of PESTEL is closely linked to the political and legal categories, given many laws are enacted to structure, support, and drive economic activity. However, increasingly, the links between economic and ecological categories are becoming more prominent as issues such as the climate crisis, water scarcity, and biodiversity loss (outlined in Section 3.5) impact the economic system. We also referenced this in Section 3.6 in relation to Oxford economist, Professor Kate Raworth and *Doughnut Economics* (2017). Raworth has stated that all economists should be required to study ecology, given the economy is simply a subset of, and completely reliant on, the ecological system (Future Startup, 2021). Links to Professor Raworth's work can be found in the 'Explore more' feature at the end of this chapter.

4.4.3 **Sociocultural**

The sociocultural category of a PESTEL analysis explores the general make-up and perspectives of human beings in a society. As with the political category, this category can be analysed at local, national, and global levels depending on which are more relevant to the organization. It comprises social values, attitudes, beliefs, norms, and knowledge, as well as population demographics, such as identifying an ageing population, and characteristics such as skills availability. For example, if an organization sells baby products in only one country, the demographic trend of a declining birth rate in that country should concern managers, who may need to offer alternative products to maintain sales or look for other countries with higher birth rates.

Social values, attitudes, beliefs, and norms change over time and such changes may impact organizations. In relation to the example above, if those baby products are ecologically damaging, and societal trends are increasingly turning away from such harmful impacts, the organization may need to consider innovating to meet the expectations of its customer base and society more broadly. This link to ecological concerns has contributed to a variety of sociocultural trends, such as ecotourism, the tiny house movement, exemplified in the Netflix series *Tiny House Nation*, which aims to decrease overall consumption, and the increasing adoption of plant-based diets such as vegetarianism and veganism.

Another significant societal trend relates to the increasingly important focus on equality, diversity, and inclusion in society, which will be a consistent theme in Part 3 of this text. This trend can drive expectations and behaviour of consumers, employees, investors, clients, and other stakeholders. For example, there is increased expectation that managers and board members will comprise more diverse characteristics.

It is often suggested that sociocultural trends are the most difficult to analyse because they are not easy to predict and measure. Moreover, they can sometimes appear to be quite niche and slow-growing, until a 'tipping point' is reached and seemingly overnight the external environment has shifted. For this reason, the sociocultural category of PESTEL needs careful monitoring.

4.4.4 **Technological**

The technological category comprises traditional infrastructure systems such as power and water supplies, as well as transport and ICT (information and communications technology) systems. In particular, ICT impacts almost every facet of society, including how we communicate, how we buy and sell goods and services, how we access and use information, and how information about us is collected and used. We explored a number of examples of technological disruption in Section 3.5.

It is important for a PESTEL analysis to focus on the *external* technological changes that could impact the organization positively or negatively (rather than focus on *internal* technological developments within the organization). External factors might include changes to power supply or internet infrastructure, or developments in machine learning, block-chain, or artificial intelligence.

4.4.5 **Ecological**

The ecological component (sometimes called 'Environment') comprises nature and ecosystems. These provide direct inputs for organizations, including resources such as trees for wood in furniture and buildings, plants and minerals for chemical compounds in pharmaceuticals, fossil fuels for power and energy, rocks and ore for concrete and steel, cotton and bamboo for textiles, and, of course, animals and crops for food and feed. Even organizations that do not directly use such inputs rely on clean air and water, and a stable climate, for their stakeholders—employees, partners, and customers—to live in, survive, and thrive.

However, as we identified in Section 3.5 on environmental disruption, many of our natural systems are in crisis. Because of this, every organization globally, out of necessity and/or responsibility, is having to seriously consider ecological factors in their PESTEL analysis.

The ecological system is the overarching system that supports all life on earth, and so links directly to all other categories of PESTEL. We already identified these links with the sociocultural category in Section 4.3.3 and the economic category in Section 4.4.2. However, there are also increasingly strong links to the other categories. Politics and politicians are focused on (or expected to focus on) addressing ecological crises (recall the role of the UN and nation-state in addressing the climate crisis in Spotlight 3.1). A growing trend has seen legal systems in various nations being used to punish governments and organizations who fail to act to stabilize ecological decline. Moreover, technology is a key driver of scalable innovations aimed at solving a number of ecological issues. For example, the purpose-driven business Space Intelligence combines satellite data analytics, AI, and forest ecology, to support nature-based climate solutions with projects in nations including Peru, Mozambique, and Cambodia (www.space-intelligence.com/).

4.4.6 Legal

All organizations are subject to the legal system of the countries in which they operate. This includes where they are physically located—with premises and staff—but it also includes the legal regime of countries of their key suppliers as well as their key markets. Labour, employment and trade union laws affect how organizations manage people (see Part 3), while product safety, testing, and intellectual property (IP) laws affect whether and under what conditions products may be developed, innovated, or sold (Part 4). Tax laws have implications for accounting practices, and each country has legislation on health and safety, environmental issues such as pollution, and data protection laws. Organizations need to understand not just what the laws currently are, but be aware of areas in which laws may be changing and be ready to respond accordingly. For example, in recent times we have seen a tightening of data protection laws in many countries.

The legal category of PESTEL is often also a reflection of the importance or treatment of the other categories. Governments decide which fundamental ideas or systems deserve legal treatment—such as the protection of human rights or the ecological system—and also use laws to shape the economy and subsequent economic activity. Legal systems also need to keep up with changes in other categories of PESTEL. For example, the increasing use of social media for bullying, political influence, misinformation, or invasion of privacy has required new laws, given the existing ones did not account for such a digital forum.

4.4.7 **Undertaking a PESTEL analysis**

As has become clear, a PESTEL analysis is not a static document or a one-off exercise, especially in a disrupted and disruptive world. Managing an organization means being constantly aware of the key factors in all categories of PESTEL. In large organizations in particular, this can be a complex task, which is why they may have a dedicated Chief Legal Officer, Chief Economist, or Chief Technology Officer.

Undertaking a PESTEL analysis comprises six steps which can be divided into three stages (see Mackay et al., 2020 for more detail). These are summarized in Figure 4.5 and then explained in greater detail.

Stage One: Preparation

1. Define Scope. The scope of the analysis might be geographic, but it could also include other scopes such as timescale. For example, if an organization's production, supply chain,

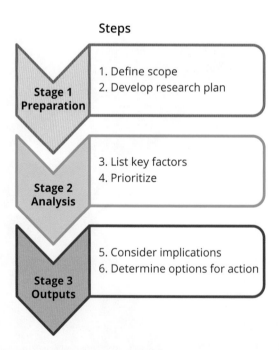

FIGURE 4.5 **Undertaking a PESTEL analysis.**

and customer base is only in the European Union, they can focus on political, legal, and sociocultural categories in that region alone. However, they may expand analysis to a global level in relation to economic and technological categories.

2. Develop Research Plan. Managers need to think carefully about what information and data they will need for the analysis and how they will collect it. This might include statistical evidence, market analysis, or trends and expert opinion. Sources might include reputable organizations' reports, industry or academic journals, publications of government bodies and trade associations, or the mainstream media. It is important to ensure that the source information is timely and rigorous.

Stage Two: Analysis

3. List Key Factors. The number of factors that should be listed in each PESTEL category depends on the type of organization, which categories are the most important, and the level of detail that will be useful. For example, a simple PESTEL analysis (which we will undertake here in the Running Case during this chapter), may include three to six factors for each category.

4. Prioritize. Prioritization of each factor focuses attention on those that are either most likely or most impactful. Managers need to actively consider the research that has been conducted to develop the list, and also engage in debate and discussion with those working on the PESTEL analysis as well as those who are able to provide useful input, which may include employees at all different levels in the organization.

Stage Three: Outputs

5. Consider Implications. Two further steps take this from a list to specific outputs which inform action. The first considers the implications of the factors you have identified within each category. While it is possible to equate each factor separately with one (or more) implication, often multiple factors will be interrelated. As such, a better approach is to depict the combined factors which point to one specific implication. It can be useful to consider implications across the short, medium, and long terms.

6. Determine Options for Action. The second output is to identify different possible actions, given the implications identified. Note that these are not recommendations, but rather a brainstorm of a number of potential ideas for actions, without (at this stage) feeling limited by direct consideration of the internal environment (like organizational strategy). Indeed, this output of PESTEL would then be used *to inform* other tools of the external and internal environment (such as the SWOT/TOWs analysis). This will be explained in greater detail in Chapter 5.

In summary, a PESTEL analysis is used to identify key factors that impact the organization, broken down into six different categories. Let's see Imperial Fine Foods undertake their own PESTEL analysis in our Running case 4.2.

RUNNING CASE 4.2 **PESTEL AT THE AWAY DAY**

Marketing Director, Gita Patel is looking around the large semi-circle of chairs at all those invited to contribute to what they have called the Imperial Away Day. Lucy, Hugh, and William are there, as well as COO Bob Smart, and John Brown, the Sales Manager. Food prep team member Jazz Jha is the youngest person in the room, invited by Lucy to contribute a new perspective. Lucy starts the morning by briefly summarizing the position of the business, its relationship to its external environment, and the need to understand the impact of trends that may shape Imperial's future success. Gita leads an exercise at the whiteboard to identify key trends. She applies the PESTEL concept which many of those present had never heard of, and asks them all to write down the key trends in each category. A number of attendees had arrived armed with data and evidence relating to different trends. Only an hour into the process, Gita is pleased to see a whiteboard including a comprehensive set of trends for each theme in the PESTEL:

Political

- Government is committed to reaching carbon-reduction targets, including methane from grazing cattle.
- Government is promoting campaigns to reduce obesity and increase healthy eating, so pies and other traditional foods may be targeted.
- Local education authorities throughout the country are boosting healthy eating and are planning changes to school campus catering.
- Government and major food companies are concerned about food security and food supply chains because of geopolitical and pandemic risks.

Economic

- Rising cost of living makes eating out less affordable which is likely to hurt our sales to restaurants and pubs.
- Rising cost of living could make it less attractive to eat meat and Imperial's other premium food and tea products.
- Rise in heavy-discount supermarkets and own-label products is reducing value of the Imperial Fine Foods brand and our ability to charge premium prices.
- Increasing energy prices and other input costs in our factory are hurting Imperial's profit margins.
- Skills shortages across our region lead to rising wages.

Sociocultural

- Current customer base average age is over 55 years, and our traditional products and branding appeal mainly to the older demographic.
- In general population, average meat consumption is reducing.
- Growing percentage of under-20s say they prefer vegan and vegetarian diets.
- High percentage of adults worried about impact of climate change and are making lifestyle changes.
- Many younger workers want to work in companies whose values they share.

Technological

- Plant-based meat substitutes (e.g. soya-based) now a viable alternative.
- Laboratory-grown meat being introduced into some markets.
- Some of Imperial's competitors have invested heavily in factory automation and are much more productive than we are.
- Food industry investing in online e-commerce platforms to meet big increase in online food-ordering rather than in-store buying.

Ecological

- The Carbon Trust is asking Imperial to start publishing the greenhouse gas emissions associated with different products and meals.
- Our diesel delivery trucks are being hit with emissions charges when we deliver into big cities which have low emissions zones, and more cities are planning emissions charges.
- Government is pushing for ban on single-use plastics as used for 'Heat-at-Home' range.
- Government and NGOs warning of risk to food supplies from climate change and biodiversity loss.

Legal

The lack of trends in the legal section concerns Gita but no one seems to have identified anything significant. 'I think that's natural,' says Lucy. 'We're not in a particularly controversial sector, and the existing laws that affect us—like food safety—are pretty well established.'

After a coffee break, Gita moves the task on to prioritization. 'We need an agreed priority listing within each category—for example, within Technological put the three trends in order of most significance for our future.' The rest of the morning sees a robust debate about the business, the world, and—interestingly—the reliability of data. However, Gita keeps the discussions on track and they end up with something they all agree on, to some degree at least.

Lucy is keen to move on to options for action given the prioritized themes, but Bob speaks out. 'Before we get to the actions, I think we need to understand a bit more about the commercial aspects of the external environment. We don't yet directly consider our suppliers in this list of trends.' John, the Sales Manager, agrees: 'It's great talking at a high level like this, but we need to think specifically and directly about our actual customers, who are becoming more and more demanding.'

'What we need,' says Jazz, who is studying Business at college in the evening, 'is a Five Forces analysis.'

Questions for reflection

1. Using the list of trends provided above, undertake Gita's task of prioritizing each trend within each PESTEL theme with 1 as most important. Then prioritize all the trends across the categories with 1 as most important.

2. The reliability of data was questioned by some of the Imperial team in relation to the trends. Which specific data would you question, and why? How could you determine whether the data is reliable? What if no reliable data exists?

4.5 **Five Forces analysis**

While a PESTEL analysis can be used to explore an organization's macro-external environment, managers also need to focus on the more direct external environment. We call this the micro-external environment, although for the private sector it is also often called the 'competitive' environment.

A useful model to understand the micro-external environment is Five Forces analysis (sometimes called 'Porter's five forces') developed by Michael Porter (1979). Porter's work comes from the field of strategic management, and so Five Forces analysis is focused on for-profit business organizations, aiming to identify the potential profitability of an industry or segment (which he called 'industry attractiveness'). As such, the language used is very oriented towards business. However, with some careful analysis the principles are applicable to all types of organizations, including those in the public and third sectors. First, we will examine Five Forces analysis as it was originally intended in a for-profit business context. We will then demonstrate its applicability to different types of organizations.

Taking a lead from the outside-in market-based view described in Section 4.2.1, Five Forces analysis is interested in the structure and dynamics of the market in which a business operates, as depicted in Figure 4.6. That is, it is focused on how the micro-external environment is constructed, who is in that environment, what power they have, and the forces that have the potential to change that micro-external environment. This tool enables businesses to understand their current position, and their pathway to continued profitability. For a non-business organization (or indeed a purpose-driven business), this can be thought of as their pathway to

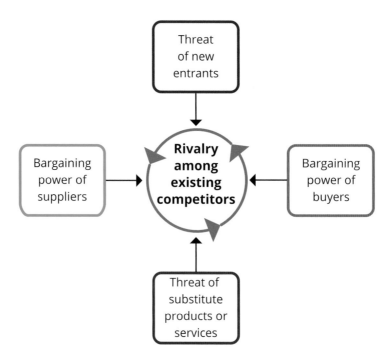

FIGURE 4.6 **Five Forces analysis.** Credit: Reprinted by permission of Harvard Business Review. Excerpt/Exhibit. From 'The Five Forces That Shape Industry Competition' by Michael E Porter. January 2008. Copyright ©2008 by Harvard Business Publishing; all rights reserved.

achieving their purpose. The first two forces focus on the power balance between the organization and its suppliers and buyers. The second two forces focus on the threat of new entrants or substitutes. The final force—industry rivalry—helps to determine which players in the industry appropriate (or 'win') that profit.

It is worth noting that some (although not Porter himself) add a sixth force—complementors. This is a product or service that complements another, meaning the availability of one can impact the other. For example, video game designers and distributors are complementors of gaming console hardware manufacturers. The market for the consoles is linked to the availability of games, even though the games designers are not suppliers, buyers, substitutes, new entrants, or part of the console market. While this can be significant in some product or service categories, we will focus on the Five Forces in the original model. We will explore each of these, before using examples to help with our understanding of how to apply this tool.

4.5.1 Bargaining power of suppliers

Most organizations are reliant on suppliers of inputs. This may include raw materials such as grain or cotton, mechanical components such as car parts, technologies such as computers or software, or educational resources such as textbooks. Inputs can also include services such as legal or accounting services. If there are many potential suppliers of an input for your organization, they have less power, as you can negotiate a better price or better terms. If the supplier does not meet your expectations, you can easily switch. If there are very few suppliers, they will have more power over your organization as you are reliant on them.

Consider supermarkets. In many countries, there are a small number of dominant large supermarket companies. As such, suppliers to these supermarkets, including farmers and food wholesalers, have comparatively less power, as they need the contracts with these large supermarkets in order for their goods (such as fruit and vegetables) to reach consumers.

4.5.2 Bargaining power of buyers

The 'buyers' in the Five Forces analysis refers to the clients or customers of a business. If there are many buyers of your product or service, each buyer has less power. If you have only one or two buyers, they have more power. Consider a business making components for large passenger aircraft. The buyers for these components might be limited to just two options globally: Boeing and Airbus. As such, these buyers have more control over the price and terms of supply contracts. A complicating factor is switching. If there are many buyers, they have low power. But, if they are easily able to switch, your business can lose them as a customer. If just one customer does this, it may not matter too much. But if many customers start switching—the collective impact can be significant. Consider now Spotlight 4.2, which considers the extremes of the balance between buyers and suppliers.

SPOTLIGHT 4.2 THE BALANCE BETWEEN BUYERS AND SUPPLIERS

While in most situations there are multiple buyers and multiple suppliers, situations do exist at the extreme. These have particular characteristics that require careful management (and in some cases, regulation).

A monopsony describes a situation where there are many suppliers and only one buyer. While this is an unusual situation, one example may be radio drama in the UK, where the BBC is the only station that still broadcasts performed radio drama. As such, while there are many potential suppliers of radio drama (production companies with script writers), there is only one buyer (the BBC).

The converse is a situation where there is only one supplier, but there are many buyers. This is known as a monopoly. A common example is an electrical transmission network which comprises the electrical poles and wires that deliver produced electricity (for example from wind farms or power plants) into people's homes. For example, in the UK the National Grid owns and runs the electrical transmission network. Because there are many buyers

of their service (electricity producers who want to deliver their electricity to consumers), National Grid has significant power and—theoretically—could set any price they choose: the buyers have no alternative power grid. However, to prevent the abuse of this power, as is the case in many industries with monopoly characteristics, the government intervene to regulate and set fair prices, ensuring access to this service. That is, the government limits the bargaining power of National Grid as a supplier.

Because of the power monopolies can have, some countries will not allow businesses to own and run vital infrastructure such as electricity transmission networks, but also railways, roads, or ports. Therefore, the governments will own and manage this infrastructure themselves. They may also restrict mergers of two competitors, if they feel the resulting merged business would have a monopoly of the market and result in less competition and so an unfair situation for consumers—that is, if the bargaining power of the merged company is too high, but buyers have no switching power.

4.5.3 **Threat of new entrants**

While most markets have existing players (which we will consider in Section 4.5.5 on internal rivalry), there is also the threat of new entrants who may join and disrupt the existing market. The likelihood of this is determined by a number of factors. If the market is highly profitable, there is more incentive for new entrants to join and attempt to win a share of those profits. However, whether they choose to, or are even able to do so, may be determined by the barriers of entry to that market—that is, the requirements and obstacles an organization would need to overcome to join the market.

For example, to join the market for webpage design, an organization only needs a business registration, a person who can design webpages, and the software necessary to do so. Conversely, to join the market for private surgical procedures, an organization would need the appropriate business registrations and approval of the medical board, premises with a fully fitted-out surgical suite, and trained staff who would, themselves, need approval from the health board of that area. Even higher barriers to entry exist in the pharmaceutical industry. Pharmaceutical companies first need to identify an effective drug that will actually work, and then show many rounds of clinical testing (i.e. testing for safety in humans), which is monitored by government agencies. Such research takes many years or decades, and requires a great deal of investment long before any potential profits are earned. This is why pharmaceutical companies have long pipelines of potential products, knowing that not all of them will reach the market.

In relation to the examples above, a web design company has a high threat of new entrants, a private surgical practice has a medium threat of new entrants, while a pharmaceutical company has a low threat of new entrants.

4.5.4 **Threat of substitutes**

The threat of substitutes refers to customers finding an alternative means of achieving their ultimate need or aim, but from a different market. For example, a consumer in Berlin may be looking to buy a spa day experience. The competitors (see Section 4.5.5 on internal rivalry) will be all those providers of spa days in Berlin and surrounding areas. But the threat of substitutes will comprise other ways in which the consumer might spend their money and achieve a similar aim. If the aim is relaxation, they may choose a yoga retreat instead. If the aim is a gift for a friend's birthday, the substitute may be something completely different, such as a gift hamper.

4.5.5 **Internal rivalry**

Internal rivalry reflects the direct competitors in the market who offer the same or a very similar good or service. If there are many competitors, this may affect the profitability of each. That said, provided there are enough customers or consumers, the number of competitors is not necessarily a determinant of profit.

It is also worth reflecting on the idea that the other four forces can impact upon the level of internal rivalry. For example, if potential entrants find a way of overcoming barriers to entry and manage to join the industry, then the level of internal rivalry will increase. Similarly, if there are fewer suppliers of a needed resource (perhaps because a major supplier goes out of business), the bargaining power of the remaining suppliers may increase, leading to greater internal rivalry as competitors compete not just for customers, but for suppliers.

Now that we have considered all of the Five Forces, we will apply them first to a for-profit business organization, as was the original intent of the tool. We will then apply them to a third sector charity. In both cases, as we will see, the information and analysis undertaken by managers provides a useful foundation for understanding the micro-external environment in which they operate.

4.5.6 Five Forces analysis: For-profit business organization

Consider *Pret a Manger*, the sandwich shop found in cities across the UK, which has expanded globally, including to France, India, Canada, and Hong Kong, as well as in many airport terminals.

- Bargaining power of suppliers: The main suppliers to *Pret a Manger* are wholesale food companies, who buy from farms or food producers, and sell to restaurants and cafés. While *Pret a Manger* may have some power given their size and bulk orders, there are only a limited number of suppliers (especially in some more remote areas) and, given many products are perishable (food that will spoil within a specific time frame), *Pret a Manger* have limited power in switching suppliers, certainly in the short term. As such, suppliers in this industry have relatively high bargaining power compared to *Pret a Manger*. That said, the larger that *Pret a Manger* grows, the more power they will have over their suppliers.

- Bargaining power of buyers: *Pret a Manger's* buyers are consumers who are walking up and down the high street. These individual buyers have very little power to influence the price or quality of the products *Pret a Manger* offers (their power is in choosing to buy from *Pret a Manger* at all). As such, the individual bargaining power of buyers in this context is relatively low.

- Threat of new entrants: There are very few barriers to entry to start a sandwich shop: it does not take a lot of investment, expertise, or time. As such, there is a high threat of new entrants for many *Pret a Manger* stores individually. However, the threat of a new entrant rivalling *Pret a Manger's* size and dominance in the market across the entire UK is less likely.

- Threat of substitutes: Nevertheless, there is the threat of substitutes. This may include consumers choosing not to buy lunch at all—but to bring it from home. However, there is also an interesting dynamic in this market. In the past, supermarkets would sell raw materials (bread, cheese) to consumers so they could make lunch at home. As such, supermarkets would be considered a substitute. However, given supermarkets increasingly have small stores in city centres offering pre-packed sandwiches, they have become a direct competitor (internal rivalry).

- Internal rivalry: There is strong internal rivalry between existing competitors in the high street sandwich shop market. This includes Subway, who focus on sandwiches, but also coffee shops that provide food options, such as Starbucks, Costa Coffee, and Caffè Nero, as well as fast food brands like McDonald's, and supermarkets with their pre-packaged sandwiches.

This example demonstrates the micro-external market in which a sandwich shop operates, and even at this level begins to demonstrate how different elements of each of the forces can change and thus need careful tracking. We can now similarly apply Five Forces analysis to understand the micro-external environment of a non-business organization.

4.5.7 Five Forces analysis: Not-for-profit charity organization

Consider a charity running a day centre for disabled adults to attend, enjoy activities, learn skills, and access the support and networks they need, which receives government funding as well as donations:

- Bargaining power of suppliers: Supplies may include food (for the provision of lunch), or craft materials for activities and skills training. The power of these suppliers is relatively high as there are many people to buy food and craft materials. However, suppliers may also include external training providers who are engaged to coach users on interviewing skills. These training providers may have a number of different alternative clients (in addition to the charity day centre) and so may have higher bargaining power. They may use this to negotiate a higher fee or better conditions. However, they may choose not to do so if their own purpose is to provide their services at a low fee so that users of this charity can benefit.

- Bargaining power of buyers: In a non-business context, the 'bargaining power of buyers' element needs some revision. The disabled adults are not buyers or customers in the traditional sense, as they do not pay for a product or service. However, we can call them service users of the day centre. Their bargaining power is very low because they have limited power to choose an alternative or alter the provision of the service. This is one of the key issues we identified in Section 2.5.3 relating to the public sector, but which also applies to the third sector.

- Threat of new entrants: The threat of new entrants exists if other day centres open in the same area. The limited government funding that already exists for such provision would be a barrier to a new entrant. However, it could also be that an existing facility, such as an aged care facility, decides to extend its offering to provide day centre services for disabled adults.

- Threat of substitutes: The threat of substitutes exists if alternatives exist for the service users. For example, if a social enterprise is established nearby that offers paid employment for those same people (perhaps using some of the skills they learned in the training at the day centre). This does not mean the day centre is annoyed—indeed, they are likely happy that their service users are moving to an alternative occupation that is now paid, as helping their clients to transition may be a key part of their organizational purpose. But it does have implications for their service offering, as they need to have enough service users to justify funding.

- Internal rivalry: The 'competition' from other existing day centres in the area reflects the internal rivalry in this example.

In summary, Five Forces analysis enables an organization to identify the key factors of the micro-external environment in which they operate, and in particular to focus on the different levels of power that exist in relation to different aspects. As depicted in particular with the arrows in Figure 4.3 the micro-external environment will be influenced by the PESTEL factors in the macro-external environment. This means that it can help managers if they have completed a PESTEL analysis before attempting the Five Forces analysis.

We will now see our managers at Imperial in the Running case 4.3 use a Five Forces analysis to understand their micro-external environment.

RUNNING CASE 4.3 **FOCUSING ON FORCES**

As Jazz explains Five Forces to her senior colleagues, the COO, Bob, and Sales Manager, John, become enthusiastic about the framework as a means of highlighting their own challenges. Gita, the Marketing Manager, is already familiar with the tool, and she sketches out the five components on one of the meeting room's whiteboards. 'Let's give it an initial run-through,' Lucy suggests. 'Why don't we start with the threat of substitutes? Let's go back to our PESTEL and see what the external trends tell us.'

As they go back and look again at the PESTEL analysis, the group acknowledges that some significant shifts are underway. Chairperson Hugh expresses scepticism about the statistic on under-20s making a permanent shift towards vegetarian and vegan food, but Gita shows the research data which evidences her point. The group also observes that the rising cost of living is making the purchase of meat less affordable for families, and that more people are determined to live in a healthier and environmentally friendly way.

'That doesn't automatically mean that the market for meat is going to disappear,' says John. 'I can't see how vegan stuff is going to replace people's interest in our meat pies. My team is out there selling them every day.' But he does find the trends captured by the group investigating 'Technology' (the T in PESTEL) are persuasive. Procurement team member, Maria Ortiz presents reports showing the quality of plant-based meat replacements is improving rapidly, to the point where national burger chains are now selling plant versions of their most famous products and supermarket freezer displays of plant-based products are getting bigger and bigger.

'So,' says Gita, as she begins to write in the Substitutes box on the whiteboard, 'we agree that plant-based alternatives are becoming a realistic substitute for Imperial pies specifically. But what other Substitutes do we think might affect our business?' Several in the group say that plant-based meat alternatives are the only reasonable substitute for meat pies that they can think of. But Gita reminds them that substitutes for related products and services count too: 'Think about the rising cost of living. Isn't it affordable food at home that becomes the substitute for Imperial pies in pubs and restaurants? And what about other demographics, like communities who don't think to eat pies at all, and prefer curries, or noodle dishes?'

As they work their way through the other four Forces, the group begins to realize how much is at stake. What some thought might have been a short meeting to decide how to sell more Imperial pies, now seems to be an inquest into every area of the company. And they are feeling increasingly uncomfortable the more they hear. COO Bob Smart, for example, has come to the meeting confident that his long-standing relationships with Imperial's meat and flour suppliers are still a major strength. But as they begin to explore the Bargaining Power of Suppliers, he realizes that there are multiple factors that are bringing rapid changes, from geopolitics to the fact that he doesn't know a single person in the plant-based alternatives industry. It is clear, Bob has to admit, that Imperial's suppliers suddenly seem to have a lot more bargaining power than they'd all thought.

Questions for reflection

1. The focus of this analysis has been on Imperial's pies. But what about some of Imperial's other products, for example fine-leaf tea. What value might conducting a Five Forces analysis have on understanding the contexts of these other markets?

2. Consider the recognition of 'plant-based' alternatives as a threat of substitutes. How could Imperial respond to this?

4.6 **Stakeholder analysis**

The third tool we will explore in this chapter is stakeholder analysis, which straddles both the macro- and micro-external environments, as well as the internal environment. As such, we explore stakeholder analysis here, as a bridge into Chapter 5.

4.6.1 **Understanding stakeholder analysis**

Stakeholder analysis is the process of identifying all of the people, groups, and organizations who impact or are impacted by the organization. It is an essential tool for managers of organizations across public, private, and third sectors, so that they have a clear understanding of who they rely upon, and who relies on them. We touched on stakeholders briefly in Section 2.3.3 as a key management challenge, outlining the stakeholders of an organization in **Figure 2.6**. To some degree, stakeholder analysis is a key factor in both PESTEL analysis and Five Forces analysis. In PESTEL, the overall factors and trends that influence an organization either originate from or may influence the set of relevant stakeholders. Five Forces analysis is, in essence, an in-depth analysis of direct stakeholders such as customers and suppliers and their power. However, we present stakeholder analysis here separately as it takes a broader and more holistic view.

The importance of stakeholders to an organization's purpose and ultimate success, especially in the long term, was the focus of R. Edward Freeman in his book, *Strategic Management: A Stakeholder Approach* (1984). He argued that **stakeholders** are any one group or individual who can affect or is affected by the achievement of the organization's purpose. Often, they have a vested interest in the organization—that is, their own interests and future are intertwined with that of the organization. They may be internal or external to the organization, and can be individuals, groups, or other organizations. Internal stakeholders include employees and managers. However, the range of external stakeholders is much wider. It includes suppliers (and the suppliers of suppliers all the way through the supply chain), consumers, and their families, shareholders and lenders (e.g. banks), and local communities or towns that rely on the organization for employment. More broadly, trade unions, trade associations, or governmental bodies may have a stake in the success of an organization.

An essential role of management is not only to know who their organization's stakeholders are, but to be able to prioritize them. Managers must determine which stakeholders need greater attention and involvement at different stages or for different decisions, in order for the organization to achieve its aims. In very large organizations external stakeholders, in particular, can dominate a CEO's time. A Chief Operating Officer of a large organization explained why he turned down the CEO role: 'I like working inside the firm, with my people, my teams, our processes, our buildings. Being CEO I'd spend most of my time dealing with external stakeholders—regulators, shareholders, consultants. I'm happier being inside and looking in, than being inside and looking out. That's the CEO's job' (personal communication).

There are many ways to categorize stakeholders—internal and external, narrow and wide, primary and secondary, active and passive, or voluntary and involuntary. Freeman (1984) himself referred to direct and indirect stakeholders. **Direct stakeholders** are those with their own voice to express their interest in the organization. That is, those who have a role in at least one of the Five Forces. **Indirect stakeholders** are likely to lack that direct 'voice' in the organization. This might be because they lack power (e.g. one individual consumer), they do not exist yet (e.g. future generations), they literally have no voice (e.g. nature and ecosystems), or they are remote from the organization (e.g. geographically). In relation to stakeholder analysis, this raises questions of interpretation—how do we interpret and so understand and analyse the interests of these stakeholders? Are environmental charities reliable conduits or communicators of the interests of nature and ecosystems? What are the needs of future generations, how does our organization impact those needs, and should we be responsible for them? These complexities can make it difficult to find appropriate spokespersons for these indirect stakeholders.

4.6.2 Stakeholder mapping

Stakeholder mapping is an exercise aimed at identifying an organization's stakeholders. However, in order to be useful to managers it needs to go beyond a listing exercise. Managers do not just need to know who their stakeholders *are*, they need to understand their perspectives, interests, and power in order to engage with them appropriately and effectively. Mendelow (1991) proposed a stakeholder power-interest matrix as a tool to effectively map stakeholders, which is reproduced in Figure 4.7.

The stakeholder power-interest matrix maps stakeholders based on their power, and their level of interest in the organization. It tells us that stakeholders who have high interest and high

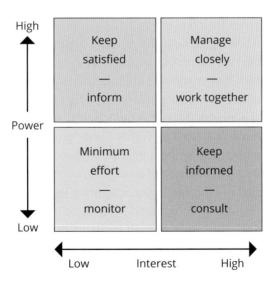

FIGURE 4.7 **Stakeholder power-interest matrix.** Credit: *Strategy: Theory, Practice, Implementation*, by David Mackay, Mikko Arevuo, and Maureen Meadows, Figure 4.5. Copyright ©2020 Oxford University Press.

power should be managed closely by the organization. Those with low interest but high power should be kept satisfied. Those with high interest but low power should be kept informed, while minimum effort is needed for stakeholders with low interest and low power.

While this mapping may be useful for categorization, it is worth noting that stakeholders may not all be the same. For example, while 'customers' are a group we might list on a stakeholder map, one group of customers may have power, while another group may not. In addition, a single customer of a large retailer might have almost no power, but a group of customers—perhaps a particular demographic group—might have more power if they come together with a complaint. Also, we may list the community as a stakeholder if, for example, we have a factory in a town. But the level of interests may vary between different members of the community. Additionally, even community members all grouped as having a 'high' level of interest may vary: one group may be highly interested in continued employment, and another group may be highly interested in the environmental impacts of the factory on the local river. Finally, a group, such as a local government, may change from having low interest to high interest based on a change in their leader, or a group such as a bank lender may change from low power to high power based on a change in their credit policy or the economy impacting the organization's financial position.

What this tells us is that this is a useful mapping and initial analysis tool. But to be effective, managers need to carefully consider the level of specificity (e.g. not just 'the community', but groups with different interests in the community), and actively evaluate their stakeholders interests and power on an ongoing basis, and especially in response to any changes in the external environment. That is, stakeholder analysis is a dynamic and active function aimed at making sense of an ever changing external (and in the case of employees—internal) environment. Moreover, individuals and groups can also influence each other in different ways, meaning that stakeholders can come together to try and acquire more power. For example, consider how unsatisfied customers or disgruntled employees might link with the media or politicians to get their voice heard and increase their power.

Finally, it is worth considering stakeholder analysis broadly, and the stakeholder power-interest matrix, in particular, with an ethical or moral lens. Just because a stakeholder has less power does that make them less important? This question is especially critical where interest is high: that is, they are affected by the organization in a significant way. Figure 4.7 tells us that low power + high interest = inform. But is that sufficient? If such a group is merely 'informed' (rather than the engagement suggested for higher power groups), could this lead them to organize and build their power, moving them into the higher power category? For example, if individual consumers are simply informed of an organization's plans, but have high interest in the product or service, they could come together to bring legal action or use social media to influence the organization's reputation or brand. They could impact stakeholders who *do* have more power over the organization, such as their investors or suppliers. This is an example of where a tool is *useful but not sufficient* in the exercise of management, and managers need to make judgement calls.

We will now see Imperial undertake a stakeholder mapping exercise in Running case 4.4 and, crucially, how they use this to change their attitude to a specific stakeholder group.

RUNNING CASE 4.4 **THINKING ABOUT STAKEHOLDERS**

CFO, William now speaks out. He admits the data is persuasive; they really might have to accept that some change is on the way. But he cautions against losing focus. 'Our concern should be the people who are our suppliers and customers now. All these other people we're talking about really don't have anything to do with us, do they?' COO, Bob and Chair, Hugh agree: if the company's decline is going to be reversed, what Imperial needs is more existing customers buying more pies—even if they include some meatless pies—and decent suppliers cutting their prices.

Lucy invites them to take a wider perspective. Current customers and suppliers are important, of course, she says, 'But there are so many other stakeholders in our business. We have to take them into account too.' Lucy and Gita explain the concept of stakeholders. But as Gita draws on the board a 2×2 matrix mapping power against interest, several members of the group begin talking among themselves. Jazz is in earnest conversation with a couple of her young colleagues. And when Lucy invites suggestions for stakeholder groups they should take into account, it's Jazz who speaks up first: 'Students and schoolchildren, everyone between 12 and 22,' she says. Chairperson, Hugh, is always keen to encourage their young staff members to speak up, but he looks sceptical: 'We're a BtoB business, so students and children have nothing to do with Imperial,' he says. Jazz responds bravely in front of all the senior people of her organization: 'Sorry Hugh, but we think they do. We've seen the data on people's changing eating habits.' She points to her other young colleagues. 'We may not represent every young person but of the three of us, none of our friends eat meat pies. Some of us don't eat meat at all. And we're the people who eat out in pubs or in university cafeterias.

Whether you like it or not, we're the people who will be eating Imperial's products in the future. And we won't be eating many meat pies.'

William is thoughtful. He is beginning to see that his scepticism about shifting Imperial's market focus to new groups of customers might be misplaced. He looks at the 2×2 matrix on the whiteboard. 'Are you suggesting, Gita and Jazz, that we might put younger stakeholders in the bottom-right box? That we should keep communicating with them through our marketing to show them we're aware of their interests?' Gita nods. 'And maybe more than that, William. If we want to stay a leading food-producer in the future, shouldn't we be consulting the future generation of consumers, to understand what they want from us, how they expect us to consider environmental matters, how important plant-based products are becoming in their diets?'

As they update the matrix, there is an excited burst of conversation in the room as the different staff members, from different departments, suddenly realize just how many stakeholders there are in Imperial's future . . . and just how few of them have been properly taken into account. Sue Smith, the Factory Manager, speaks up passionately to say that in her view, all of Imperial's employees, at all levels, should be considered stakeholders in the business too.

Questions for reflection

1. Using Figure 4.7, consider the different groups you would write in each of the four boxes.

2. Recall the comment about the group aged 12–22 years. Should they be in the bottom-right box, the bottom-left box, or not included at all? Why? Explain your reasoning.

4.7 **Conclusion**

Understanding the External Environment is fundamental to the management of all organizations. As we have seen, however, evaluating the external environment is not a one-off exercise, but rather an ongoing, dynamic and in some cases reactive process. Moreover, it is undertaken not by one manager in isolation, but with the collaboration of many different people across the organization. We have presented three different tools here to help with what can seem an overwhelming task of understanding and reacting to the external environment: PESTEL analysis, Five Forces analysis, and stakeholder analysis. Each analysis has different uses and strengths for managers attempting not only to understand the environment, the opportunities and threats represented by the trends identified, but also to make decisions based on factors in the external environment. However, as will be a theme throughout this text, the decisions managers make and the actions they take are rarely the 'right' or 'perfect' ones. Rather, managers need the skills and confidence to use the information and analysis provided by tools such as these to improve their critical thinking and, ultimately, their decisions and outcomes.

4

 ## CHAPTER SUMMARY

○ The external environmental comprises factors which the organization does not have direct control over, but boundaries between external and internal can be blurred.

○ An inside-out resource-based view focuses on the internal environment, while an outside-in market-based view focuses on the external environment. However, managers are likely to need to adopt both views to some degree.

○ A PESTEL analysis categorizes trends and influences from the macro-external environment into Political, Economic, Sociocultural, Technological, Ecological, and Legal.

○ A Five Forces analysis focuses on the organization's micro-external environment, sometimes called the 'competitive' environment, and comprises the power of buyers and suppliers, the threat of new entrants and substitutes, as well as internal rivalry. While it was developed for use in for-profit business organizations, it can be applied to other types of organizations.

○ Stakeholder analysis considers the people, groups, or organizations who have a direct or indirect interest (or 'stake') in the operations and success of the organization. They can be classified in the stakeholder power-interest matrix based on whether they have high or low power over, and high or low interest in, the organization.

 ## CLOSING CASE REFLECTION

Easy Solar's way forward

Easy Solar is an example of an organization acutely aware of the external environment in which they operate. Their PESTEL analysis of Sierra Leone, in particular, would include concerns such as political uncertainty in the country and economic hardships due to widespread poverty and lack of large-scale industry. However, their analysis supports the success of their business model also, with the technological advancements they are able to introduce to the country, a sociocultural context in which there is both great need and great willingness to embrace opportunities for development, and an ecological imperative to find an alternative to the fossil fuel grid. While their difficult competitive environment provides challenges for establishing a customer base who can afford their products, it also protects them from a threat of new entrants or substitutes, as well as internal rivalry of other solar firms.

Co-founders Tourre and Mosia won the 2019 Social Entrepreneurship Award from the World Economic Forum's Schwab Foundation. Their final words here demonstrate how they hope to impact their external environment across a continent where it is estimated that over 600 million people have no access to reliable electricity (Lecaros et al., 2019):

> When you talk about the impact, it is mostly psychological. Yes there are economic savings, yes there are the health benefits, but imagine just going home, like we all do, turn on the lights. It's really just about having a life where energy is in the background (World Economic Forum, 2019).

REVIEW QUESTIONS

1. Why do managers need to understand the external environment of their organizations, especially when planning for the future?

2. How might an evaluation of the macro-external environment differ between an international retailer like IKEA and a local hardware store?

3. In what ways does Five Forces analysis differ between a business and charity organization? Are some forces more likely to be important in one or the other?

4. Identify how categories of PESTEL analysis interact with the Five Forces.

5. Imagine you are a manager at Easy Solar (the focus of our Opening case study and Closing case reflection). Using Figure 4.7 conduct a stakeholder mapping exercise, populating each of the four quadrants.

EXPLORE MORE

— READ *Doughnut Economics*, by Professor Kate Raworth to understand how all of the aspects of an organization's external environment are reliant on nature and ecosystems, and what happens when the economic system is contributing to their destruction and decline.

● WATCH a Ted Talk by Professor Kate Raworth entitled 'A Healthy Economy Should Be Designed to Thrive, Not Grow', by searching for Kate Raworth on the TED Talks website.

● WATCH an interview with Michael E. Porter, Professor of Strategy at Harvard Business School, on the 'Five Forces' industry analysis. Search for Michael E. Porter on YouTube.

● WATCH an interesting panel discussion from 2015 exploring how board members and management cope with conflicting interests and expectations of stakeholders in a range of industries, hosted by Deloitte Canada. Search for 'Full panel discussion on understanding your stakeholders' on YouTube.

● WATCH Dame Vivian Hunt discuss the importance of and focus on stakeholders for businesses in this TED Talk on 'How Businesses Can Serve Everyone Not Just Shareholders', Oct 2020. Search for Vivian Hunt on the TED Talks website.

4

CHAPTER FIVE

The Internal Environment: Strategy and Planning

Simon Brooks and Sarah Birrell Ivory

OPENING CASE STUDY AMBER: POWERING A DIFFERENT WAY

Amber is an energy management and consultancy organization focused on working closely with clients to reduce energy consumption, control costs, and develop their strategies to work towards 'Net Zero'. They were founded in 2009 by the current CEO, and his values have underpinned the way the company has grown and developed since. They now employ 150 people.

Amber is a 'B Corp', which means that while they are a profit-seeking company, they are legally obliged to be accountable to all stakeholders in their strategy, as well as being committed to the highest standards of environmental and social performance. They seek to combine their strategy with a wider purpose.

The value that Amber add to their clients involves being able to offer a bundle of services. This includes consulting on carbon emissions, helping with regulatory compliance, and providing advice on their clients' 'Net Zero' greenhouse gas strategies, as well as sourcing renewable energy and electricity.

Amber base their success on a workforce with a diversity of skills, as well as their differentiated position as a 'B Corp'. They have recruited colleagues with experience in many of the sectors in which they operate, such as retail and property development, giving them capabilities and a brand that can be difficult for competitors to copy.

The way that Amber develops strategy and makes decisions has evolved as they have grown. The CEO is the main shareholder and exercises overall control, but decision-making is increasingly delegated throughout the firm.

Amber has a 10-year plan, matching that of the long-term view of the energy industry and markets. However, the company is very aware of the importance of remaining flexible in their shorter-term tactical decisions, to take advantage of opportunities and deal with challenges. For example, while decisions over which sectors and geographical areas they want to operate in are deliberate, the Covid-19 pandemic required a somewhat unexpected shift into commercial properties.

5.1 **Introduction**

In Chapter 4, we examined how we can analyse and evaluate the external environment of an organization. We defined the outside-in market-based managerial view as being largely focused on these external factors. In this chapter, we shift the focus towards elements of the organization itself: its internal environment.

This focus on the internal environment can be described as an inside-out resource-based view of the organization, which focuses on the resources, knowledge, and competences or capabilities of an organization. Of course, organizations need to monitor and be sensitive to both the internal and external environment. However, it is unrealistic for an organization to quickly shift direction because they identify an opportunity in the external environment if they have invested in existing resources, skills, and capabilities which do not support that shift.

We start this chapter by considering ways in which managers can understand and analyse the internal environment of their organization, focusing in particular on a resource and capability audit, the VRIO framework, and Value Chain analysis. We then look at how to integrate the external analysis from Chapter 4 with the internal analysis introduced in this chapter. Specifically, we introduce the related SWOT summary and TOWS framework, as well as the SAF framework as tools to help managers achieve this. Finally, we focus on two actions that result from this extended analysis: strategy and planning.

Given the complexity of these tools, frameworks, and actions, we present Figure 5.1 as a means to show the relationship between different elements. Organizations undertake external analysis (including PESTEL and Five Forces introduced in Chapter 4) as well as internal analysis (including resource and capability audit, VRIO, and Value Chain introduced shortly in this chapter). Stakeholder analysis is a tool that bridges the external and internal environment. The results of these analyses are integrated using a SWOT/TOWS framework or SAF framework. The result of this integration leads to the development of strategy and planning.

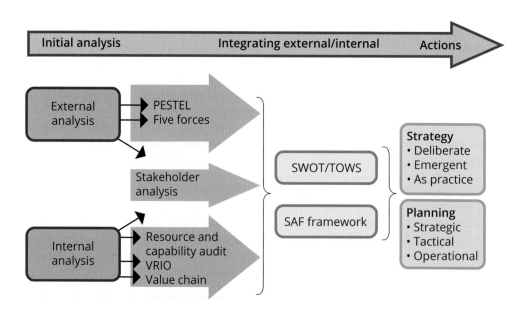

FIGURE 5.1 **Elements of external and internal analysis, and integration tools.**

5.2 **Internal analysis**

5.2.1 **Inside-out resource-based view**

In Chapter 4, we introduced the importance of analysing the macro- and micro-external environment of the organization. We described this as an outside-in market-based view in Section 4.2.1. Conversely, the inside-out resource-based view (RBV) focuses on the internal environment of the organization. It is focused on the resources and capabilities of the organization. Because this idea emerged in relation to for-profit business, the intent was to help managers gain competitive advantage by being distinctive and therefore making it difficult for competitors to acquire or copy. However, it is applicable to the public and third sectors where managers focus on achieving their purpose through value creation. To understand RBV and apply the tools presented in this text, it is important to be able to define and distinguish between resources and capabilities.

Resources refer to those things an organization possesses, or has access to, that they can use in their activities. This might include:

- human resources, such as employees or Board members,
- physical resources, such as buildings or computers,
- financial resources, such as money, and
- intangible resources, such as a strong brand.

Capabilities can be described as the organizational activities and knowledge necessary to effectively use the resources. This might include how research and development is managed, or how a computer system is used to monitor logistics and sales. In other words, capabilities are more likely to depend on the skills and knowledge of people in developing and managing systems and processes to ensure resources are employed effectively.

Not all resources and capabilities are equal. We can distinguish between threshold and distinctive resources and capabilities.

Threshold resources and capabilities are necessary for an organization to achieve and maintain a minimum performance level. These may be the resources required to 'cross the threshold' to operate in a market, industry, or area, such as legal or regulatory matters. For example, a charity will need to register with the charity regulator in the country in which it operates. However, they may also be linked to an operational matter. For example, if a vegetable grower and wholesaler wants to be considered a credible option as a supplier to a major supermarket chain, they need a reliable and consistent logistics capability.

Distinctive resources and capabilities are unique, or, at least, rare, and difficult for others to copy. They give the organization competitive advantage, or the ability to achieve their purpose through value creation. For example, the vegetable grower and wholesaler may satisfy the threshold conditions for reliable and consistent logistics, but may also have a distinctive capability in being the distributor of a range of high-quality organic vegetables, in addition to more common goods that all other wholesalers offer. The charity may have a celebrity spokesperson who only works with that charity, or may have a database of potential donors, and an innovative and effective process for targeting donation requests resulting in a high success rate. We will explore this concept in greater detail in Section 5.2.3 when we introduce the VRIO framework.

Now that we understand the inside-out RBV, we can introduce three tools which facilitate the analysis of the internal environment: a resource and capability audit, the VRIO framework, and Value Chain analysis.

5.2.2 Resource and capability audit

A key tool—and input into all of the other tools for internal analysis—is a **resource and capability audit**. This allows an organization to identify and categorize all of the resources and capabilities that comprise its internal environment. It is worth noting that the internal elements of the Stakeholder mapping tool (explored in Section 4.6.2) are likely to be useful here. Managers can choose how extensive their resource and capability audit should be. Mackay et al. (2020) suggest 12 different categories that would comprise a very thorough and in-depth audit: physical, natural, financial, informational, knowledge, reputational, cultural, organizational, managerial, skills, relational, and motivational. While this is useful for a complex audit, an approach with just four categories is more common for a simple audit: physical, human, financial, and intangible. These are depicted in Figure 5.2. For each of these categories, we should consider both resources and capabilities.

By way of example, Table 5.1 identifies the resources and capabilities of the hypothetical vegetable grower and wholesaler already referenced in this chapter. It is interesting to note that

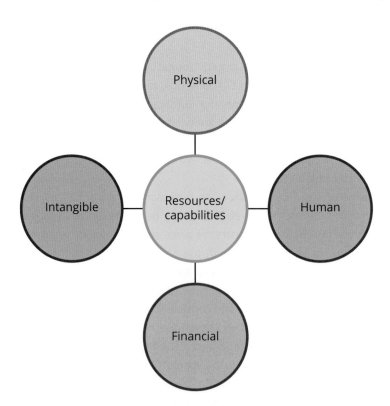

FIGURE 5.2 **Categories for a simple resource and capability audit.**

TABLE 5.1 **Resource and capability audit for vegetable grower and wholesaler**

Category	Resources	Capabilities
Physical	• Land and greenhouses • Sowing and harvesting equipment • Warehouses and cold storage	• Efficient processes for picking and packing produce • Knowledge of optimum storage conditions • Expertise in using equipment
Human	• Managers • Equipment operators and packers • Sales and marketing team	• Research skill in organic production • Continuous professional development for managers • Maintenance of effective sales relationships with key customers
Financial	• Strong balance sheet and cashflow • Overdraft facility at the bank	• Skills in cashflow management and strong financial controls • Good relations with bankers offering the ability to access debt if needed
Intangible	• Strategic partnership with logistics firm • Goodwill from key customers	• Maintaining relationship of trust and flexibility with key logistics partner • Regular meetings with customers and customer perceptions of supplier's ability to engage in transparent dialogue and customer-perceived reputation for reliability

many of the capabilities are based on relational or social practices, making it difficult for their competitors to identify, understand, or copy. This will become important as we consider the VRIO framework in Section 5.2.3.

5.2.3 **VRIO framework**

The VRIO framework, initially proposed by Jay Barney (1991), examines the resources and capabilities of the organization based on four factors: **Value**, **Rarity**, **Inimitability** (the quality of being impossible to copy), and **Organizational Support**. Using the resource and capability audit, managers can analyse and evaluate which of these resources and capabilities are likely to contribute to achieving the organizational purpose. For a for-profit business organization, the focus of this framework is on identifying contributors' competitive advantage. Each of the four elements of the VRIO framework is defined in Figure 5.3.

Depending on the depth of analysis being attempted, an organization may examine each of the resources and capabilities listed in their audit, or they may just choose specific elements for attention. However, it is important to note that this should not be considered a 'one-off' exercise: in a dynamic VUCA (volatile, uncertain, complex, ambiguous) world both the internal and external environments can alter the 'VRIO' status of different resources and capabilities dramatically and sometimes suddenly.

Using the resource and capability audit of the vegetable grower and wholesaler from Table 5.1, we can provide some illustrations of the VRIO analysis.

Examining the physical resources and capabilities of an organic food supplier, the quality of the supplier's farm location, including the soil, the climate, and the proximity to supply routes

VALUE

Does the resource or capability add value to the organization, either directly, through a key stakeholder, or by neutralizing a threat?

RARITY

Does the organization have unique or rare access to the resource or capability? Note that commonly available resources or capabilities may still be important to satisfy the 'threshold' requirements.

INIMITABILITY

Is the resource or capability difficult, impossible or costly for competitors to copy? This is more likely to apply to intangible resources and capabilities that are not obvious to the outside observer.

ORGANIZATIONAL SUPPORT

Do the organization's systems, structures, and processes ensure they are able to take advantage of the resources and capabilities they possess?

FIGURE 5.3 **VRIO framework.**

could be seen as valuable. These may also be very difficult to imitate, because the blend of soil quality, microclimate, and local geography may be unique. Combined with the physical equipment and the expertise needed to operate their farm, the supplier's location enables the organization to respond to changes in demand and maintain the product quality needed to add value to the ultimate customer for the goods.

The supplier's specialist equipment could be bought by competitors, so may not be necessarily rare or inimitable, but the interactions between the farming equipment, warehousing, ordering, delivery, and invoicing processes may form the elements of organizational support, which may allow more efficient and effective use of that equipment.

More typically, rarity and inimitability are related to less tangible resources and capabilities. For example, the innovative capacity of the organic food producer may have been built up over decades of continuous improvement and investment in training for staff. That is not to say these features are completely unique or impossible to imitate, but once behaviours and processes are embedded in the culture and history of an organization, they become very difficult for outsiders to understand and copy. Similarly, relationships with logistics partners, key customers, and bankers are built on trust and goodwill that take time to establish and are therefore not easy to copy, certainly for new entrants to an industry.

In summary, the VRIO analysis enables us to evaluate the resources and capabilities of an organization to arrive at an analysis of sources of sustained competitive advantage. We should recall, however, that while distinctive resources and capabilities may garner more attention, threshold resources and capabilities are crucial as the foundation of the organization's ability to function in their environment and therefore should not be ignored. Let us join Imperial as they attempt to apply these tools to their organization in Running case 5.1.

RUNNING CASE 5.1 **THINKING ABOUT RESOURCES**

Lucy feels Imperial's management team has made some progress since the company Away Day. Throughout the business, morale is up and staff have a strong sense of purpose. Factory Manager, Sue Smith gives the factory staff regular updates on the general situation and is getting some useful comments back from her workers. Marketing Manager, Gita Patel has asked young food prep operator, Jazz Jha to keep paying attention to the '12–22-year-old' stakeholder group, and together they review any relevant trends each month. Supply Chain Manager Declan O'Rourke and Buyer, Maria Ortiz have held meetings with possible suppliers of plant-based meat alternatives. Sales Manager, John Brown was concerned after the meeting about short-term sales potential, but has been surprised how positive his Sales Executive, Aidan Roberts has been about sales opportunities for meat alternatives.

Though she recognizes the need to remain agile, Lucy is reassured by the recent VRIO analysis they completed. Su-Li Chan, the HR Manager, had suggested that a review of Imperial's resources might highlight some capabilities—or weaknesses—they could be overlooking. Su-Li introduced the VRIO analysis, and then facilitated a meeting with the senior team—Lucy, Gita, William, and Bob—making sure that all the key areas of the business were represented. They began with an initial review of Imperial's resources.

After completing the initial audit of the Resources and Capabilities, they completed the VRIO review, to calibrate whether Imperial's capabilities offered them a competitive advantage. Bob had been working on a copy of the VRIO himself, and has started trying to fill it in.

Though Lucy and Bob feel optimistic about some parts of it, they are worried about some of the gaps

Category	Resources	Capabilities
Physical	Factory; production equipment; warehouse; cold storage; delivery trucks; packaging; office with IT equipment; website.	Certified to all relevant food-safety standards. High levels of production efficiency with modern IT systems. Efficient delivery systems. Branded packaging.
Human	Managers at all levels; production workers; warehouse workers; sales & purchasing staff; marketing team.	Skilled production workforce. Strong family commitment in top management. Low staff turnover. Effective customer & supplier relationships.
Financial	Strong balance sheet with no debt & good cash holdings; good payment performance and cashflow; bank overdraft facility.	Good management of payment. Good financial controls. Strict financial reporting. Long-term bank relationships.
Intangible	Well-respected brand. Long-established supplier and customer relationships. 'Spirit of community' within the business.	Able to collaborate with suppliers and customers on new ideas. Brand strength allows for new products and services to be added. Loyal staff want business to succeed.

(Continued)

	Physical	Human	Financial	Intangible
Value	Good factory & office facilities & equipment enable strong manufacturing capabilities.	Skill levels generally high. Management a good mix of experience and youth.	Positive financial position.	
Rarity	Location is great: close to staff residential areas & customers, but is easily accessible for logistics.	Low turnover. Imperial seen as good place to work, has won city's Employer of Year award.	No debt & cash holdings enable investment in ventures.	
Inimitability	High brand recognition in B2B markets of traditional products.			Family spirit in business; Green family's commitment.
Organizational Support	Strong HR team backing a capable management team.	All staff used to working together while complying with high legal standards.	Capable finance team with credibility in finance community.	Strong tacit knowledge in traditional areas of business and in external relations.

they see. As Bob says, it's one thing to consult new stakeholder groups and find possible market opportunities. And it's great to know that Imperial has some strong existing capabilities. But it's another thing completely to plan and execute the strategy required to deliver fundamental changes in a 90-year-old company whose brand is built on traditional foods.

Questions for reflection

1. What would you add in the missing boxes of Bob's VRIO framework?

2. Reflecting on the framework, what do you think are the gaps that Lucy and Bob are starting to see?

In our discussion of both the resource and capability audit and the VRIO framework, we have introduced the importance of linkages, relationships, and organizational systems. We develop these themes further as we turn to our final framework: Value Chain analysis.

5.2.4 Value Chain analysis

The Value Chain analysis tool was developed by Michael Porter (1985), who also developed Five Forces analysis (Section 4.5). It helps us identify all of the *activities* of an organization and analyse how they link together in the process of producing goods or providing a service. Understanding these activities, their linkages, and where the organization's resources and capabilities interact is useful for identifying the key activities and links that add value to the organization and its customers, enabling the organization to achieve its purpose. Note that this tool shares its name with Part 4 of this text—Managing through the Value Chain. This is because we will be exploring a number of these activities in much more detail in Part 4.

It is worth exploring the idea of 'value', which we can think of in different ways (and we have already explored some of these ideas in Section 1.5.1 in relation to management). We can think of it as the value to customers or service users from the goods or services that the organization provides. We can also consider value from the perspective of the organization. This might be financial value and its attempts to reduce costs or increase revenue in order to increase profits (or in the case of public and third sectors, 'financial surplus'). However, it can also be more in-tangible forms of value which the organization may be focused on, including social or environ-mental value. As with Five Forces, because this tool was introduced to help for-profit businesses increase profits, it may use language related to this context. However, it is a useful tool across all types of organizations.

The Value Chain analysis divides activities into primary and support activities. Primary activi-ties follow the traditional flow of a product manufacturer from inbound logistics, through oper-ations, outbound logistics and marketing and sales, and end with after-sales service. However, this view of activities may be modified for service-based businesses as well as non-business organizations. We demonstrate this in Table 5.2. Support activities comprise organizational

TABLE 5.2 **Value chain activities**

Activities	Product-based organization	Service-based or non-business organizations
Primary		
Inbound logistics	Activities linked to receiving and storing inputs for operations	Activities linked to receiving customer, client, or user requests and logging these appropriately
Operations	Activities whereby raw inputs are transformed into more valuable outputs	Activities whereby customer, client, or user requests are transformed into outputs or services
Outbound logistics	Activities linked to the collecting, storing, and distribution of operational outputs	Activities linked to communication to or delivery to customers, clients, or users
Marketing and sales	Activities aimed at ensuring customers become aware of and purchase operational outputs	Activities aimed at ensuring customers, clients, or users become aware of and purchase services
Services	Activities linked to after-sales, which aim to maintain or enhance the value of the operational outputs to customers	Activities linked to after-sales/use, which aim to maintain or enhance the value of the service to customers, clients, or users
Support		
Firm infrastructure	Activities linked to leading, governing, managing, and arranging the environment in which all other activities occur.	
Human resource management	Activities which organize human resources: hiring, firing, remunerating, developing, training, motivating	
Technology development	Activities to develop systems, products, technologies, and knowledge used by the organization	
Procurement	Activities purchasing or arranging inputs and resources to be used by the organization.	

infrastructure, human resource management, technology development, and procurement. A Value Chain analysis can occur across the entire organization. However, for a particularly large or complex organization, it can also occur based on a geographic (e.g. Fujitsu UK and Ireland) or brand/product scope (e.g. PepsiCo's 'Quaker Oats' brand).

While evaluating the distinct activities of the value chain is useful, the real benefit of Value Chain analysis is uncovering the ways in which the activities link together. However, one of the challenges with applying the Value Chain analysis is that attempting to map all the links can result in a complex and messy 'spider's web' of connections. The aim should be to understand the key 'value-adding' linkages in the organization. Spotlight 5.1 provides some examples of these linkages.

The wider value system

While Value Chain analysis often focuses on linkages inside an organization, it can also be extended to consider linkages outside the organization. This is an example of where a tool can bridge internal and external analysis. This is sometimes referred to as the wider value system, which includes external stakeholders such as suppliers. As such, once again stakeholder

5

SPOTLIGHT 5.1 LINKAGES IN THE VALUE CHAIN

Steve and Priya were friends, even though they worked in the same type of role for competitors. They both marketed financial products to independent financial advisers (IFAs). Their aim was to get the IFAs to recommend their own company's products to clients.

Steve worked for a company with a long history in the industry. It was known to have a traditional culture and to be quite risk-averse.

Priya worked for a company that was newer to the market, more willing to try different strategies and more agile.

Steve complimented Priya on her new company car and suggested that her company's success must be due to a well-rewarded sales force, backed up by a great marketing department. This part of their organization's activities was visible with the glossy presentations and the prestigious company cars. Priya thought for a moment and then replied that actually the source of their success was more likely to be in the human resources department. Steve was curious and Priya explained that while the sales and marketing activity of her company was good, the recruitment of staff was very rigorous, and the continuous professional development provided was

excellent. This meant that high-quality staff were recruited and retained, with their product knowledge and sales skills being constantly updated.

Priya remarked to Steve that he 'didn't have it so bad' in his own company, reminding him that he enjoyed the support of a responsive legal department. In fact, a recent opportunity for a large account had been a source of rivalry. Steve eventually won the business because his head office legal team had been able to offer quick and accurate tax advice to the potential client, who was grateful as he didn't have his own advisers. Priya's company used external legal advisers that were not accessible to the sales force.

Over the weekend, Steve felt he had learned some interesting things about the two companies. Firstly, the visible effectiveness of Priya's firm's sales and marketing activities was actually based on a less visible link with the support activity of the human resources department, which brought excellence into the business through careful recruitment and staff development. Secondly, his own recent success had been based on being able to access the expertise of his legal department, another important link, crucially, that was valued by the potential client.

mapping, explored in Section 4.6.2, can be a useful tool to contribute to Value Chain analysis. One key benefit of this wider view is that it can help managers determine whether activities should be internal (undertaken by the organization itself) or external (undertaken by a supplier or external provider). Such analysis may result in decisions to outsource some activities which the organization currently undertakes themselves, or bring other activities, which are provided by suppliers, in-house. Broadly speaking, if activities are not central to the organization, or are not adding significant value, and can be outsourced at lower cost and undertaken for the same quality, then this is a positive move, enabling the organization to focus on its own core activities that add value.

Consider our vegetable grower and wholesaler described in previous sections of this chapter. This organization might keep its logistics and delivery function internal to the organization while it remains small and deliveries happen locally. However, as it grows—and perhaps as a threshold capability to win a contract with a major supermarket—the organization may realize that this activity provides little added value and may choose to outsource to a dedicated logistics company. This would move the logistics function from being inside the organization's value chain to being part of the organization's wider value system. Conversely, while most electric car manufacturers currently source their batteries from specialist manufacturers, a number (such as Toyota and General Motors) are exploring investments in battery manufacture themselves. They are using joint ventures with manufacturers such as Panasonic, which may result in battery production being more closely integrated into the value chains of the car manufacturers. This is driven partly by the need to have more control over supply and the cost of shipping heavy batteries long distances from other suppliers.

To summarize, Value Chain analysis and understanding the wider value system has three specific benefits:

1. It develops our thinking beyond resources and capabilities to consider the activities undertaken by the organization and the linkages between activities that add value.

2. It helps identify activities which are either creating obstacles to value creation or those in which opportunities exist to improve value creation.

3. It allows the organization to consider which activities should be within its direct value chain, and which may be better happening in the wider value system. This can allow the organization to focus on its own value-adding activities.

This section has focused on the internal analysis of organizations, including a resource and capability audit, VRIO framework, and Value Chain analysis. While we now are likely to have a better understanding of the internal environment of the organization, the next step is to integrate the external analysis (covered in Chapter 4) and the internal analysis presented in this chapter. But first, let's see how Imperial engages with Value Chain analysis in Running case 5.2.

RUNNING CASE 5.2 THINKING ABOUT THE VALUE CHAIN

Now the VRIO analysis has been completed, Lucy arranges the next Away Day. This time, the agenda is focused on the approach to launching a new range of plant-based meals, developed from the successful Heat-at-Home range first offered during the pandemic. Imperial's Marketing and Sales teams have made great progress identifying market opportunities. Sue Smith in production has worked with their celebrity chef to set out some exciting recipes. But now they have to think about practicalities. So, for this next Away Day, Lucy wants to concentrate on conducting a Value Chain analysis.

As the group settles down in the meeting room, she reveals the model that they will use to help them think through Imperial's capabilities and state of readiness for the new range (see Figure 5.2).

She explains that they are going to address each of the key areas in Imperial's value chain, starting with its primary activities. They will then conduct

an initial evaluation of how good they are in each area. 'We know that we have resources that are rare and, in some cases, inimitable,' she tells everyone. A question comes from the back of the room 'Lucy, remind us what that means?' Lucy replies 'It means difficult for our competitors to copy. They're great assets to have. But now we need to assess whether we're capable of using them to take us in this new direction.'

The group splits up into different breakout rooms to address each of Imperial's primary activity areas and to rank their strengths relative to what everyone is expecting the plant-based range to require. First to present back to everyone is the group reviewing Inbound Logistics. Their findings are summarized in the table opposite.

The other working groups reveal their own findings and recommendations, and it is obvious that within its primary value-chain activities, Imperial has some real strengths. But other groups besides

Activity	Capability relative to current products	Capability relative to plant-based products	Requirement	Recommendation
Reception of inbound deliveries	**High**. Good space, loading ramps. Processes all good.	Also **high**.	No change.	Leave as-is.
Storage of fresh commodities	**High**. Have well-established meat cold stores.	**Low**. To be certified, vegan products need separate handling and storage.	Have to set up separate product-reception and cold-storage facilities.	1. Procure temporary cold stores. 2. Conduct study on adding permanent cold-store facilities.
Supplier delivery arrangements	**High**. We've been dealing with meat-delivery firms for years.	**Medium**. Our processes are good but we have no relationships with vegan product suppliers.	Establish logistical arrangements with vegan suppliers.	1. Set up individual meetings, show them our facilities, and understand their capabilities. 2. Check whether we can leverage existing relationships by using same delivery companies who know us from meat deliveries.

the one analysing Inbound Logistics have identified weaknesses too. It's clear there is still work to be done, and Lucy decides that they need a deeper consideration of Imperial's strengths and weaknesses, and of the threats it faces and the opportunities it could possibly exploit.

Questions for reflection

1. Choose another one of the primary or support activities listed in Figure 5.2. Develop your own table similar to the one completed by Inbound Logistics.

5.3 Integrating internal and external analysis

While Chapter 4 introduced tools for external analysis, and the start of this chapter introduced tools for internal analysis, there are also tools that have been developed to help managers integrate the analysis and results of these. This section will first explore the related SWOT summary and TOWS framework, before turning to the SAF framework.

5.3.1 SWOT summary and TOWS framework

The SWOT summary is a very widely used, and occasionally misused, tool in management. The acronym stands for Strengths, Weaknesses, Opportunities, and Threats, as depicted in Figure 5.4. The strengths and weaknesses are largely derived from our internal analysis of

FIGURE 5.4 **SWOT summary.**

resources, capabilities, and value-adding activities analysed in this chapter. The opportunities and threats are largely derived from the analysis of the macro- and micro-external environments, as covered in Chapter 4. As such, SWOT provides a mechanism to integrate information, data, and analysis collected from these other tools. This is why we term this the 'SWOT summary': to properly use a SWOT, we need to have undertaken a range of other analyses in order to say something meaningful about organizational strengths and weaknesses, together with the threats and opportunities they face. When employees are asked to simply 'do a SWOT analysis', and they start to list the first things that come to mind, we see this approach misused and the outcomes of limited use. We will now explore each of the four elements.

Strengths

Strengths might be distinctive resources and capabilities, but also any threshold resources and capabilities at which the organization excels, and which therefore offer it a strong foundation. Such resources might include relational resources identified from external value chain links as well.

Weaknesses

Weaknesses cover the resources and capabilities that the organizations lacks, or that fail to meet VRIO characteristics—especially in comparison to competitors or if these are important for their service users. They can also be limitations in the linkages in the organization's value chain activities or wider value system.

Opportunities

Opportunities comprise trends that enable the organization to achieve its purpose or create value. It might include markets that are underserved and so have an unmet demand, or a PESTEL trend that is contributing to an increased demand for the organization's product or service.

Threats (challenges)

The 'Threats' section is sometimes referred to as 'challenges', which is more applicable for public and third sector contexts. This comprises trends which might be a threat to demand for the organization's product or service, or which might create greater competition.

Whether a trend represents an opportunity or threat is not always obvious and needs careful analysis. For instance, changes in legislation might appear favourable to the organization, but if they reduce barriers to entry they may also raise the threat of new entrants to the market.

One of the most difficult aspects of undertaking a SWOT summary is deciding what *not* to include, as much as what to include. It is easy to become overwhelmed with the amount of information and to struggle with integrating information and prioritizing different factors. In line with the critical thinking lens of this text, it is important to understand that there is no 'right' SWOT summary. Each SWOT will vary based on the perspective of the person or team who is undertaking the exercise.

Using the TOWS framework

The real value of a SWOT summary is achieved when we extend it using the TOWS framework as depicted in Figure 5.5. This method overlays the strengths and weaknesses on one hand, with threats and opportunities on the other. This is based on the idea that organizations should match their internal strengths and weaknesses with the opportunities and threats they face in their external environment. The result is four categories labelled SO, WO, ST, and WT.

The TOWS framework is especially effective as a tool to prompt discussion among team members, to inspire ideas for actions, and to then categorize and organize these. It can also help to push a team beyond the obvious. Some organizations will insist on reaching a specific number of ideas in each quadrant not because the quantity is the aim, but because it forces people to move beyond the obvious and start thinking creatively, removing previously assumed limitations.

Earlier we used an example of a vegetable grower and wholesaler to help explain how we might think of resources and capabilities. Building on this, the TOWS example presented in Figure 5.6 shows how we can use our resource and capability audit as part of the analysis to

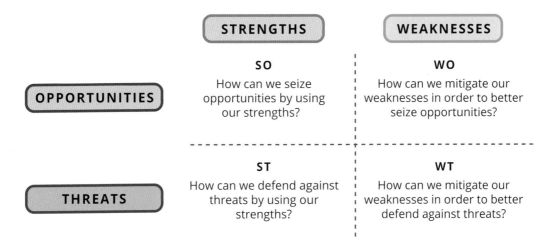

FIGURE 5.5 **TOWS framework.**

	STRENGTHS	WEAKNESSES
OPPORTUNITIES	**SO** *How can we seize opportunities by using our strengths?* An opportunity exists to supply a large chain of supermarkets, and the company can use its strength in consistently producing high quality organic food to add value to the supermarket.	**WO** *How can we mitigate our weaknesses in order to better seize opportunities?* The wholesaler lacks the scale and expertise to run its own delivery operation, so it could partner with a logistics specialist to transfer its goods to the supermarkets.
THREATS	**ST** *How can we defend against threats by using our strengths?* The increasing border controls after Brexit have threatened the company's ability to export to Europe. It can use its expertise and increasing focus on organic goods to develop markets in the UK, and its good relations with existing customers to expand further.	**WT** *How can we mitigate our weaknesses in order to better defend against threats?* The company can mitigate the current lack of scale by re-investing profits from new sales and using the overdraft facility to increase the size of the operation, perhaps through acquiring new land.

FIGURE 5.6 **Example TOWS framework for a vegetable grower and wholesaler.**

help this firm develop strategic options. Of course, to produce a TOWS analysis we must also undertake analysis of the external environment to generate a recognition of the opportunities and threats facing the firm. The resource and capability audit should also be subject to a VRIO analysis to understand the strengths and weaknesses as fully as possible.

The SWOT summary and TOWS framework provide one approach to integrating external and internal analysis. We will now explore a means of evaluating the options that might be generated by a TOWS framework—the SAF framework—before then turning to consider the resulting strategy and planning to which these tools all contribute.

5.3.2 **SAF framework**

The external analyses covered in Chapter 4, together with the internal analyses considered here in Chapter 5, allow us to undertake the SWOT summary and so complete the TOWS framework. Each quadrant of the TOWS framework depicted in Figure 5.5 will include a number of possible options, or courses of action, which the organization could pursue. These might include developing new services, expanding into new markets, employing new people, trying to diversify, or even simply doing nothing for the time being.

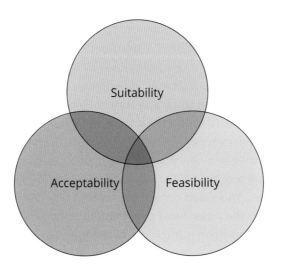

FIGURE 5.7 **SAF framework.**

Given the range of options, organizations will need to make decisions about which options to pursue. These decisions—especially if significant—are likely to be intertwined with the process of strategy-making and strategic decision-making, which we explore in detail in Section 5.4. However, it is worth briefly introducing one more tool which can be used in combination with the TOWS framework to evaluate the different options it generates.

The Suitability, Acceptability, and Feasibility (SAF) framework, developed by Johnson et al. (2011), uses these three criteria to help rank or filter strategic options. It also comprises a fourth criterion, Evaluation, to act as a summary check of all three main criteria. The SAF framework is depicted in Figure 5.7 as a Venn diagram. While the 'sweet spot' in the middle may be the ideal option, it is likely that the reality will see much more complex considerations, as we will explore. First, let's consider each of the three criteria.

Suitability

The suitability criteria ask whether a strategic option will help take advantage of opportunities identified in the external environment or help defend against challenges or threats the organization might face. This means the criteria draw on the external analyses like PESTEL and Five Forces. While this may seem obvious—an option that is not suitable probably should not have been listed in the TOWS framework—this extra check can be useful, and it is also possible that the SAF framework may be used on its own, and not following TOWS.

For example, a PESTEL analysis might show that a political decision has resulted in a new trade deal with another country. This means an option developing new markets might be a way of taking advantage of the opportunity of reduced trade barriers. The potential increased scale and turnover, combined with a firm's existing industry experience, might then act as a defence against new entrants coming into the industry, attracted by the improved trade terms. This option might therefore be considered suitable.

Arguably, the suitability analysis could also consider whether a proposed option will use an organization's strengths or minimize its weaknesses. However, the Feasibility criteria will draw on the internal analyses in more detail.

Acceptability

This criterion evaluates whether a proposed strategic option is acceptable to stakeholders. There are several ways of assessing acceptability depending on which stakeholders will be impacted by the strategic decision and what their expectations are. For this criterion, we return to our stakeholder analysis. This should tell us why stakeholders are interested in the organization and how much power they have to support or disrupt strategic decisions.

Acceptability for shareholders, for example, might relate to the financial rewards and risks of a particular option. Expanding into new markets might look suitable and may offer potentially high returns, but this could also be a high-risk option requiring investment, meaning reduced dividends for shareholders. This could reduce the acceptability of the option for this specific stakeholder. Employees on the other hand might find this option very acceptable since it involves little immediate risk for them but could provide opportunities for increased travel and promotion.

A key role of management is to both be aware of and manage these competing claims and assess the overall acceptability of the options being proposed.

Feasibility

Feasibility considers whether an organization has the strategic capabilities to pursue an option. Internal analyses of resources and capabilities using the VRIO framework and Value Chain analysis can provide useful information for the application of this criteria. The key factor is whether the organization has access to the necessary capabilities or can acquire them.

Earlier in Section 5.2.2 we introduced the idea of physical, human, financial, and intangible resources and capabilities. All of these can inform our feasibility deliberations, but the exact resources and capabilities needed will of course depend on the proposed option. For example, the organization seeking to expand into new markets may judge that they have the necessary skills in their human resources and are confident in the strength of their brand (intangible resource). However, the financial resources necessary to invest in advertising and creating new physical resources may not be available or easy to obtain, making this option unfeasible.

Evaluation

As we have seen in the example used to illustrate these criteria, it is important to undertake an overall evaluation of the strategic options available. Expanding into new markets may be highly suitable at first glance and may be acceptable to many stakeholders, but the option might not be feasible when the internal analysis is taken into account. The SAF framework is often used with a scoring system, as depicted in Table 5.3. Here we have adopted a scoring system on a scale from 1 to 5 with 5 being the highest score.

Using a scoring system allows us to filter and rank options, and provide an overall comparison. However, this should only be used as a summary. The scores should be supported by detailed consideration of each of the three criteria, and then the overall evaluation should take into account all three. It is possible to propose an option that may be very high scoring in two criteria but very low in the third. This might result in a good score (comparatively) but be a poor option to pursue. For example, if an option is very suitable and very feasible, but stakeholders simply won't accept it, managers should either look to changing their stakeholders or choosing an alternative option that is acceptable.

TABLE 5.3 **SAF framework evaluation table**

Options	Suitability	Acceptability	Feasibility	Totals
Expand the range of products for existing markets	5	5	4	14
Develop new markets	5	4	2	11
Withdraw from some markets	3	3	4	10
Diversify into a new industry through acquisition	2	2	1	5
Do nothing	2	2	5	9

We now turn in this chapter to understand both strategy and planning, which are actually key elements for consideration in a SAF framework.

5.4 **Strategy**

Strategy refers to the long-term direction or overriding objective of the organization linked to its purpose. As distinct from operations, strategy focuses not on what an organization does day-to-day, but where it aims to be in the long term and (broadly) how it aims to get there. Related to strategy is the concept of planning, which is the focus of Section 5.5 and involves the process for how an objective (such as a strategy—but it can also include other objectives) will be achieved with more detailed timelines, activities, and necessary resources. The aim of both external and internal analysis, as well as the tools which integrate these perspectives, is to inform the overall organizational strategy, and the specific plans needed to achieve it. A simple summary is that strategy is what the organization aims to do and planning shows how they will do it. While these ideas are often taken for granted as key roles of management, it is worth considering whether and why organizations *need* to develop strategy and engage in planning. Consider Spotlight 5.2, which explores these questions, before we move on to define different approaches to strategy.

5.4.1 **Deliberate vs emergent strategy**

Beyond the broad definition provided here, there is no consensus on what strategy actually *is*. The word, and the related word 'strategic', is sometimes used simply to make something sound significant, far-reaching, or future-focused: strategic direction, strategic leadership, or strategic resource, for example. Strategy is sometimes considered an input, sometimes an output, and sometimes a process. One way of thinking about strategy is to distinguish between deliberate strategy and emergent strategy.

Deliberate strategy refers to a top-down approach in which senior leadership and key organizational members match internal resources and capabilities to the external environment, and develop a specific strategy for a period of time (e.g. a five-year strategy), which is often communicated in a static document. This then gets revised when the original strategy comes to

SPOTLIGHT 5.2 **THE NEED FOR STRATEGY AND PLANNING**

Strategy and planning might feel inevitable when managing an organization. But are they needed? And why? Consider these three scenarios:

1. Imagine a barber based in Madrid, Spain, who is an owner-operator of his own barber shop. He offers a simple walk-in and wait service. If he has no plans to change the direction, size, or complexity of his business, and there are no significant threats in his external environment, he is unlikely to need a strategy. Moreover, other than ordering supplies so they don't run out, or putting up a sign announcing his holidays, he probably doesn't need to do much planning either.

2. Now imagine a charity based in a suburb of Nairobi, Kenya, which offers a much-needed service to elderly people helping them to engage in social activities. They estimate they could help three times more people if they expanded their offering and geographic reach throughout the entire city. They will need to develop an overall strategy to help them achieve this expansion, as well as more detailed plans for how to achieve it.

3. Finally, imagine a global energy organization, with operations and customers around the world. Even if they did not want to change, because of their reliance on fossil fuels they may be facing falling revenues as demand decreases, investors divest (sell shares) due to concerns about the climate crisis, and governments regulate more heavily. As such, they realize they need a new strategy. This might include a greater investment in renewable forms of energy, or diversifying to another industry entirely. Once they have formulated their strategy, they need to undertake detailed, complex, and extensive planning to work out how to achieve this.

Notice that we have mentioned change in the second and third examples. The Kenyan charity wants to help more people and will have to change to achieve this. The global energy company is being forced to change to address the factors that are making its current strategy increasingly risky. While change and change management are often closely linked to strategy and planning, we will focus on this topic in Chapter 6.

its completion (e.g. at the end of the five years). Deliberate strategy adopts a logical and rational approach, is developed in advance of implementation, and assumes a relatively stable and predictable external environment.

In contrast, **emergent strategy** is a pattern of successive actions or behaviours that are consistent over time, which may be informed by an overall direction. These actions or behaviours change as the organization learns from implementing the deliberate strategy and in response to the external environment. Emergent strategy accepts that it is actually impossible to separate the creation of strategy from the implementation of strategy, and acknowledges that the external environment is rarely stable or predictable. This has the advantage of being more flexible and allows for the organization to be more agile in adapting to a changing environment.

In reality, it is likely that most organizations will combine a deliberate and emergent strategy. The deliberate strategy we begin with will change as elements of emergent strategy come into play. The result will be the realized strategy. Indeed, this is recognized in the commonly-depicted image of strategy in Figure 5.8, which demonstrates how intended strategy becomes

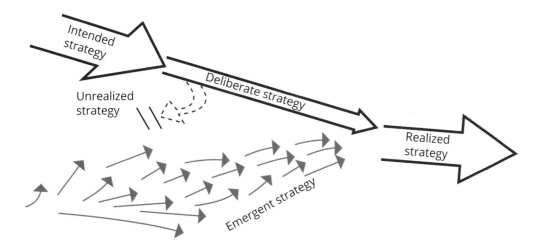

FIGURE 5.8 **Deliberate and Emergent Strategy.** Credit: Mintzberg, H., & Waters, J. A. (1985). 'Of Strategies, Deliberate and Emergent.' *Strategic Management Journal*, 6(3), 257–272. © John Wiley & Sons, Ltd

the realized strategy of the organization. Students interested in this—and the field of strategy more broadly—should read *Strategy Safari* by Henry Mintzberg et al. (2008) (whom you may recall from Chapter 1 of this text). The reference is in the 'Explore more' feature at the end of this chapter.

5.4.2 **Strategy-as-practice**

Considering these two different approaches to strategy begs the question of who actually 'does' strategy? Deliberate strategy may be seen as the domain of the most senior leaders, such as the CEO. However, emergent strategy comprises contributions of those implementing the deliberate strategy—and the variations they make to it along that journey. These ideas have come to be referred to as 'strategy-as-practice' (Whittington, 1996), paying attention to those involved in developing and implementing strategy and how they actually carry out that practice. This view acknowledges the importance of a range of people who contribute to the process of strategizing and the resulting strategy of the organization. Running case 5.3 considers Imperial's inner debate about which way to approach strategy.

5.4.3 **Strategic decision-making**

Ultimately, the aim of all of the internal and external analysis we have learned about in Chapter 4 and this chapter is to make decisions about strategy, which is often termed strategic decision-making. We have already made reference to this in Section 5.3.2 on the SAF framework. However, decision-making is a key role of management beyond just strategy. As such, the approaches presented in this section may equally be useful when making decisions about people, products, suppliers, or service delivery.

Decision-making is an area of management in which elements of science, art, and craft, which we identified in Section 1.2, are all apparent. Even decisions that are presented with 'scientific'

RUNNING CASE 5.3 DEVELOPING STRATEGY AT IMPERIAL

Lucy is still finding her job stressful, but she feels more in control than she did when she first started. Her second management meeting with Hugh and William progressed much more smoothly than the first one. Though they had started the first Away Day very sceptically, William's mood in particular had improved during the day, and Lucy senses she will have more of his support for the changes they all now acknowledge need to be made.

As they think about their next steps, Hugh tries to persuade Lucy to continue the annual strategic planning exercise he'd carried out every March, which resulted in a large formal document present-ed to the full Board of Directors. Lucy has always suspected that the document was then largely left in a drawer until it was dusted off to update it the following March. She says she is going to try for a more dynamic and ongoing strategy development

approach, given they are having to react to and anticipate so much that is new. This approach wor-ries Hugh: he's concerned that they are just making things up as they go, without formal structures and appropriate reflection.

Questions for reflection

1. What are the benefits of Hugh's way of ap-proaching strategy—with a formal process undertaken every March? What are the risks and costs of such an approach?

2. What are the benefits of Lucy's way of ap-proaching strategy—as an ongoing and con-tinuous process? What are the risks and costs of such an approach?

3. Which approach do you favour? Why?

---

evidence as entirely rational and logical may have been reached with elements of instinct, emotion, or bias, and so be related to art or craft. Indeed, sometimes these factors can act as a 'sense check', ensuring higher-quality decisions.

Typically, we can consider two different approaches to strategic decision-making (and decision-making more broadly): optimizing and satisficing. However, as with many aspects of this text, the intention is not to suggest that a specific approach is 'right' but rather to help us to think about different aspects of decision-making that managers are likely to face.

Optimizing decision-making

Optimizing decision-making typically requires an assumption that economists call *homo eco-nomicus* (which translates to 'economic man'), which assumes that humans make rational, self-interested decisions to achieve optimum outcomes. They do not make irrational decisions or altruistic decisions.

Based on this assumption, a six-step rational decision-making model can be followed, which aims to achieve an optimum outcome of the decision: that is the optimum strategy. While this model provides a good starting point to think about strategic decision-making, it is important to consider the limitations of each step, some of which are presented in Figure 5.9 (see Bazerman & Moore, 2008 for much more detail).

Limitations to optimizing decision-making include the politics of decision-making that may go beyond rationality and comprise interpersonal conflict driven by power relations or self-interest at different steps of the decision-making process. A further criticism of this approach is that it

1: Define the problem	2: Identify decision criteria
• May be difficult to do accurately. • Actual cause may be hidden.	• May be difficult to determine all appropriate decision criteria. • May be different views on which criteria should be included, and some politically inappropriate criteria may be included. • Some decision criteria may be opposed to others.

6: Compute the optimal decision	3: Weigh the criteria
• While a mathematical 'optimum' is possible, ultimately this reflects the judgements and assumptions that have gone into every step along the way.	• May be difficult to assess different criteria as they are measured in different ways. • May be different views on which criteria are more important. • May be political reasons for some criteria to be given greater importance.

5: Rate each alternative on each criterion	4: Generate alternatives
• Much judgement is needed to rate each alternative based on each criterion, impacting the 'rational' foundations of this model.	• Judgement is needed to determine how many alternatives to generate, as this could be an almost endless task. • The search for a perfect alternative (which is unlikely to exist) can delay any decision — often called 'paralysis by analysis'.

FIGURE 5.9 **Rational decision-making model.**

fails to consider that many decisions are time-pressured. The amount of time needed for an approach that considers all the steps may not correspond to the amount of time available.

With so much criticism, why present this optimizing approach to decision-making at all? We do so because this model is useful in providing some structure to what otherwise may be an entirely messy and convoluted process that decision-makers must tackle when trying to identify the optimal strategy.

Satisficing decision-making

An alternative approach draws on the work of March and Simon (1958). They argued that all human judgement is bounded or limited in its rationality. Because of this limitation, instead of looking to achieve an optimal solution, we look to 'satisfice' (that is combine 'satisfy' and 'suffice'). That is, to choose a solution that is 'good enough'. While this may sound pessimistic, the focus on satisficing can still be associated with a search for alternative strategies or options (and a dismissal of a number of unsatisfactory alternatives). However, that search ends once a satisfactory solution is found that will suffice, even though a more optimal solution may be found with further searching.

Importantly, the satisficing approach to strategic decision-making better reflects the reality of a VUCA world characterized by uncertainty. Moreover, it better reflects the 'human' element of decision-making. This is for two reasons. First, human judgement may be limited by information. Decision-makers may lack information that is needed to accurately define the problem, may have unclear decision criteria, and may lack information about the future that would be necessary for optimal decision-making. Second, human judgement may be limited by the individual themselves. Individuals are only able to hold a limited amount of information in their memory. They may also have limited intelligence or mental capacity for processing the information, or may have cognitive biases that affect either how the decision problem is perceived or their ability to accurately calculate the optimal choice. Later authors (Eisenhardt & Zbaracki, 1992) added politics and power as further limitations that can impact optimal decision-making, as the most powerful individual or collation of individuals may push their own preferences. This leads to a third approach to strategic decision-making: group decision-making.

Group decision-making

Much of the discussion here has assumed that strategic decisions are made by individuals: for example, the CEO. However, there are many instances in which groups work together to make many different types of decisions, including those about organizational strategy. For example, strategy is often developed and decided by a Board of Directors, or an 'ExCo': an Executive

Committee comprising all of the different 'Chiefs' (Chief Executive Officer, Chief Financial Officer, Chief Technology Officer, and Chief Sustainability Officer, etc.).

There are a number of advantages associated with group decision-making. A key advantage is that such groups can call on greater resources from the wider pool of knowledge and experience contributed by each group member. As well as the quantity of perspectives, a group can provide wider and more diverse perspectives. This is especially the case where groups are intentionally designed for diversity relating to gender, ethnicity, sexuality, function, or any other aspects. Moreover, the function and processes of group decision-making can foster interaction and interpersonal connections and discussions, leading to synergies and better thought-through analysis and outcomes. Finally, the group members involved in the decision-making are more likely to support the outcome, and are already informed not only of the decision but of the reasons leading up to it.

Nevertheless, there are some disadvantages which, if not managed, can impact the quality of group decision-making. It typically takes longer for groups to form, bond, discuss, and make decisions (which we explore in Chapter 8). Where time pressure exists, this factor can cause issues and may even lead to conflict if some individuals push their perspectives in light of the deadline. Too many compromises to meet everyone's success criteria and keep everyone 'on board' can ultimately lead to a strategy that does not actually work for anyone. Finally, groups can end up suffering from 'group think', where the hoped-for diversity of views and perspectives is lost, and groups advocate their decisions without recognizing the drawbacks.

Having explored strategy and strategic decision-making in particular, we now turn to consider planning: a more detailed process which is intended to actually achieve the strategy that has been decided. However, as we will see, and given our observations about emergent strategy, in reality planning and strategy are often intertwined.

5.5 Planning

While strategy has been introduced as the long-term objectives of the organization, **planning** is a process of determining exactly how an objective will be achieved. Planning can focus on steps necessary to achieve an entire organizational strategy, but also on a specific product launch, enacting a change in the supply chain, restructuring people and departments, among many other projects. A **plan** specifies what resources, activities, and processes are needed in what combination, in order to achieve an objective.

Planning is essential to many aspects of organizational life because it provides direction and focus, enables assessment and monitoring of predetermined objectives and performance, helps to minimize waste and inefficiency by coordinating responses, and ensures the organization looks to the future to achieve more, better, differently, or in different places.

However, there are disadvantages to planning. Planning takes significant time and effort, which needs to be diverted from the day-to-day operations of the organization. Once a strategy has been set and planning has commenced, individuals can become blind to the flaws in the strategy, and can rigidly focus on developing and then delivering the plan. As we outlined in Chapter 3, with the necessity of managing through disruption, a willingness and ability to change a plan when the context changes is essential. That said, constantly changing plans can lead to failure as well. As Henry Mintzberg (1994) said, 'Too much planning may lead to chaos, but so too would too little.'

While plans at different levels of organizational hierarchy are distinct, all plans need to specify three parameters: what has to be done, who will do it, and by when. However, for most plans, at least one, and possibly all three of these parameters will actually change once the plan is put into action. This does not mean that the plan was wrong or even that it was unnecessary. Plans are a blueprint and provide a guide for managers and decision-makers to work from when things change (which they inevitably do). As such, it is important to note that the process of planning is not static. One aspect of planning is anticipating future resources or actions that may be needed depending on how the original plan progresses, or what other factors may cause unforeseen impacts.

5.5.1 Levels of planning

Managers are almost always involved in planning, and many would argue that it is the need for planning that creates many managerial roles. While there are no definite rules, we can identify three different levels of planning that are typically developed by managers at different levels of the organization. Figure 5.10 maps these onto the three levels of management we identified in Section 1.9.

Strategic plan

The strategic plan is the overall plan for the organization and is akin to its strategy, as explored in Section 5.4. This is likely developed by senior management and signed off by the Board of Directors. It is important that all other types of plans are aligned with the strategic plan for the overall strategy of the organization to be achieved.

Tactical plan

A tactical plan (sometimes also called a functional plan) is the level below a strategic plan, and aims to translate this into a specific plan for each of the organization's key departments.

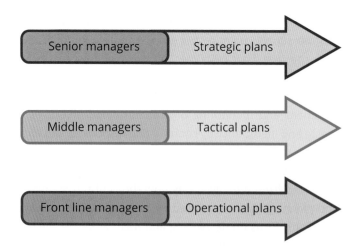

FIGURE 5.10 **Mapping levels of management and types of planning.**

As such, separate tactical plans might be prepared by the human resources department, procurement department, or finance department. Tactical plans are typically developed by middle managers or those responsible for a specific department or function. Tactical plans need to be aligned with the overall strategic plan as well as coordinated between departments, given they are dependent on each other for delivery. Gantt charts and PERT charts are two popular tools used to assist with this process, depicted in Figure 5.11:

- A Gantt chart is a tool that shows how all the different tactical plans are progressing. For this reason, it is useful when actually deploying a plan.

- A PERT chart (Program Evaluation and Review Technique) focuses on the dependencies between different elements. They can include completion points, also known as 'milestones',

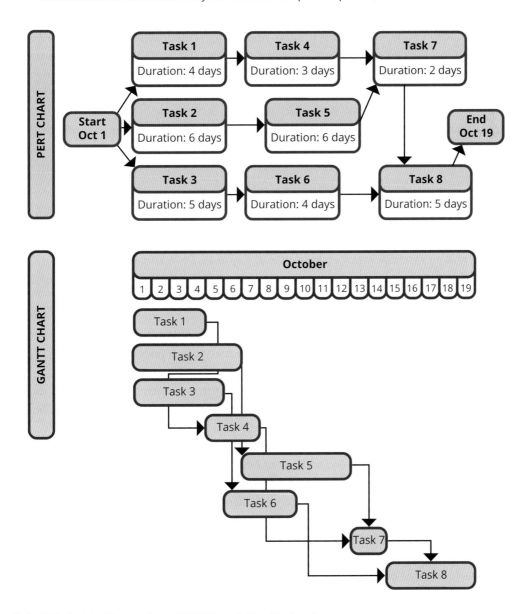

FIGURE 5.11 **Examples of PERT and Gantt charts.**

which determine whether the next element of the plan can commence. This means that the chart displays the 'critical path activities' for the project completion. If these critical path activities are delayed, this can impact the overall completion date. As such, this is very useful prior to implementation to determine which elements are critical, in particular to meeting deadlines.

Increasingly, simple apps or more complex computer programs are used by management to assist with planning using Gantt and PERT charts.

Operational plan

An **operational plan** (sometimes called an action plan) focuses on a very specific and relatively stand-alone goal, and is likely to be developed by front line managers directly involved in that particular function. Operational plans may be developed in response to a strategic change for the organization, but can also be for an ongoing objective. The human resources department may have developed an operational plan for the recruitment of an entirely new department to address an element of the strategic plan, but may also have an ongoing operational plan for the delivery of essential training to all staff, which they roll out over time.

Operational plans can be as simple as a list of required tasks, detailing the individual responsible, the resources they need to draw on, and the date by which it is needed. Required resources may include financial resources, human resources, or specific data such as customer insights.

5.5.2 Goal setting

Goal setting is an essential first step for a plan at any level. For a strategic plan, this might be akin to agreeing the purpose of the organization, as we discussed in Chapter 2. For tactical or operational plans, this is likely to be more specific and department-specific.

Goals are important for a number of reasons. Without a goal, it is impossible to assess when a plan is completed or whether it was successful. It can also be difficult to identify everything that needs to be achieved to complete the plan without a specific goal (indeed, even with a specific goal this can be difficult).

A popular conceptualization of goals is the SMART acronym, which provides criteria for assessing the quality of goals. They should be Specific, Measurable, Attainable, Rewarded, Timed, as outlined in Figure 5.12.

Goals can be focused on impact, production levels, financial outcomes, employee satisfaction, contribution to the community, addressing environmental issues: anything can be turned into a goal. Goals often equate to end points of operational plans but can also be milestones within tactical plans. That is, goals should be both aligned and cumulative from the level of the operational plan, through the tactical plan, and to eventually achieve the strategic plan.

In this section, we have introduced planning as a process of determining how an objective (such as the organization's strategy) will be achieved. It covers different levels of planning, as well as the importance of goals of each plan being carefully determined. Before turning to the conclusion of this chapter, let's see how Imperial puts the SMART acronym to use in developing goals in Running case 5.4.

SPECIFIC GOALS

- A specific goal should provide a clear and unambiguous statement as to what is aiming to be achieved.
- The opposite of this would be a vague goal that does not get to the point or could be interpreted in multiple ways.

MEASURABLE GOALS

- A measurable goal should have some mechanism for assessing the goal's achievement (or not).
- This may be quantitative (e.g. increase sales by 10%), or qualitative (e.g. improve customer satisfaction as evidenced through feedback surveys).
- Note that some goals may be very difficult or impossible to measure given the resources of the organization (e.g. reduce employee stress).

ATTAINABLE GOALS

- An attainable goal should be neither too easy, nor too unreasonably difficult.
- Setting easy goals can deter action or motivation.
- Setting unreasonably difficult goals that are unlikely to be achieved can impact people's willingness to even try.

REWARDED GOALS

- A rewarded goal should ensure that there is some benefit to the individual or team if it is achieved.
- While this can be monetary, it may also be effective if it is a reward of recognition, additional resources, or time off.

TIMED GOALS

- A timed goal should provide a specific and reasonable time frame necessary to achieve the goal.

FIGURE 5.12 **Defining SMART goals.**

RUNNING CASE 5.4 **SETTING SMART GOALS FOR IMPERIAL**

Lucy and the senior team have conducted two more analyses, first a SWOT based on the many details they have pulled together in their various reviews, and then a TOWS review, so they can see what needs to be done. As Lucy tells William, reminding themselves of Imperial's many strengths and opportunities is great. But it's now time for action.

(Continued)

5

Following the continuing feedback from Jazz and colleagues, who are monitoring the 12–22 stakeholder group and who have been keeping the Marketing Manager, Gita, updated, the team has met and decided that their first introduction of a plant-based food range should target younger age groups. Lucy has intentionally included all the key managers from each department, as well as colleagues from a diversity of ages and backgrounds, in the decision-making process. With such a diverse group sharing decades of experience between them, Lucy believes, Imperial should have a high degree of confidence in their strategy.

With a proposed launch date of 1 October, it is now time for everyone in the business to play their part in the plant-based food range. Lucy and the team believe they should adopt a SMART goal for the launch. 'Otherwise,' as Lucy says, 'We may lose focus.' Their initial SMART goal has been agreed by everyone:

- achieve £20,000 in sales across the UK of the new plant-based food range in Q4 (the fourth quarter, October–December), focused on sales to university and school catering departments (sales of their existing range to this sector for this period is typically worth £200,000).

With the SMART goal set, each department has its own plan, and everyone has goals to achieve. For the Sales Manager, John, and his sales team, the priorities are to visit every educational institution with details of Imperial's new products, and to gather information from their visits to feed back to the Marketing and Operations teams. Aidan Roberts, the Sales Executive, develops a list of weekly appointments, starting with those places that already have a good relationship with Imperial. Each week, he has to review his progress with John, and every two weeks there is a commercial meeting in which John's sales team and Gita's marketing team meet to discuss progress.

Questions for reflection

1. What would you expect to come up in a SWOT and TOWS analysis for Imperial?

2. What types of plans can you see described here? Are they mostly strategic, tactical, or operational? How does the type of plan which is needed change throughout the course of a project?

3. Evaluate Imperial's goal. Is it 'SMART' based on the definition provided in Figure 5.12?

5.6 Conclusion

In this chapter, we have focused on the internal analysis of an organization in relation to the RBV. We introduced three tools focused on helping managers with this: a resource and capability audit, the VRIO framework, and Value Chain analysis. Combining these with analysis of the external environment ensures managers develop a comprehensive and rounded perspective. Both the SWOT summary and related TOWS framework, as well as the SAF framework, are tools to help with this integrated analysis. Both strategy and planning follow on from these comprehensive analyses. The development of strategy—the overall objective of the organization and broadly how this will be achieved—should be approached from both a deliberate and emergent perspective: the former typically developed by senior managers, and the latter the result of strategy implementation and ongoing adjustment. Planning, at different levels, provides a more granular roadmap for what will be done, by whom, and by when. Taken together, Chapters 4 and 5 of this text provide guidance on managing an organization but starting with the foundations: understanding the external and internal environment in which it finds itself. This is a key role of management.

CHAPTER SUMMARY

○ The inside-out resource-based view of the organization focuses on identifying and evaluating its resources and capabilities.

○ Tools to help managers undertake this analysis include the resource and capability audit comprising physical, human, financial, and intangible categories, as well as the VRIO framework, which determines value, rarity, inimitability, and organizational support.

○ The Value Chain analysis, and wider value chain system, focus on the activities undertaken by the organization, and the linkages and relationships between these.

○ Integrating all of these internal analyses with the external analyses in Chapter 4 can be done using the SWOT summary and TOWS framework, which themselves can be then augmented by the SAF framework.

○ All of this analysis contributes to an aligned strategy for the organization, as well as detailed planning for how that strategy will be achieved.

5

CLOSING CASE REFLECTION

Amber: Powering a different way

Reflecting on the opening case of Amber, we can see evidence of their approach to strategy, and also ways in which some of the tools and frameworks introduced in this chapter might be applied.

Firstly, Amber has a blend of deliberate and emergent strategies. They have an overall 10-year plan, but they also take account of changes in their environment such as the Covid-19 pandemic. Amber has taken new opportunities in commercial property, resulting in an element of emergence in their strategy. This is also partly a 'resource-based' strategy since it is built on existing expertise and relationships.

Secondly, applying a VRIO analysis, it seems clear that Amber is differentiated based on a brand that is difficult to imitate, as well as the rarity of their status as a 'B Corp'. In addition, the expertise of the staff, together with the relationships established with clients, is a combination of human and intangible resources which is also difficult to copy. The range of services provided by Amber means they develop a deeper relationship with their clients, making them part of the 'value system' in which Amber is embedded.

Finally, tactical decision-making and planning are increasingly taken at different levels below the top team. This arguably helps with flexibility to respond to challenges and opportunities, as well as making use of the expertise of staff.

REVIEW QUESTIONS

1. Distinguish between threshold and distinctive resources and capabilities. Why are both important to organizational success?

2. Consider the primary and support activities in the Value Chain analysis. Draw a simple value chain for a business that bakes bread to sell to supermarkets.

3. Why might it be useful for managers to list many options in each of the TOWS framework quadrants?

4. Identify ways in which the global Covid-19 pandemic impacted managers' use of deliberate versus emergent approaches to strategy. What does this tell us about the relative importance of each of these approaches?

5. What are the three main levels of planning, and why are these key to organizational success?

5

EXPLORE MORE

— READ a book called *Strategy Safari*, which covers a wide approach to strategy by management guru Henry Mintzberg et al. (2008).

● WATCH the TED Talk by Martin Reeves about the challenges of both strategy and planning, and mistakes made by many organizations (in particular businesses) called 'Your Strategy Needs a Strategy'. Search for Martin Reeves on the TED Talks website.

— READ a blog by Ken Favaro from 18 June 2019, entitled 'Strategy Talk: How Strategy Differs for Nonprofits'. Search for the title on Google.

— READ Max Bazerman and Don Moore's 2008 book called *Judgment in Managerial Decision Making*, 7th ed., Wiley.

CHAPTER SIX

Organizational Culture and Change Management

Emily Yarrow and Sarah Birrell Ivory

OPENING CASE STUDY **HAIR CARE: BLENDING IN**

It is well reported that many mergers and acquisitions—where two companies join together or one acquires another—often fail. This is in part because of insurmountable corporate culture differences, characterized by different ways of working and management styles.

In 2001, Procter and Gamble (P&G) headed at the time by CEO, A. G. Lafley, acquired the haircare brand Clairol, increasing their share in the haircare market, which already included Head and Shoulders, Pantene, and Pert. The purchase brought with it many leading haircare products, including the well-known Herbal Essences and Aussie shampoo brands. It also brought many of Clairol's long-serving employees, including the CEO and several senior executives, who would be new to the P&G way of doing things.

P&G is known globally for having a very strong, North American corporate culture, with a long history and a core focus on the customer and continuous improvement. It is still one of the top firms for graduate recruitment and is a key target employer for Business School students.

Following the acquisition, P&G needed to ensure that Clairol was integrated effectively into their business. To do so, they focused on assimilating new employees to the culture of P&G, through a process of onboarding and educating them on the organization's heritage, strategy, values, and 'how things are done at P&G'. They focused in particular on managing this process at Clairol's European production site, where added national cultural differences and different ways of working could have proved challenging. They also changed some of their own ways. They adopted a more flexible 'matrix' structure of reporting (which Clairol employees were more used to) to help with the integration.

Ultimately, the acquisition was a success, in part because of P&G's ability to successfully integrate former Clairol employees into their corporate culture and the way things are done at P&G. This underlines the major importance of corporate culture on organizational success, both in the long and short term.

6.1 **Introduction**

In Chapter 1 we defined management as a social and operational process with the aim of bringing people and organizational resources together to get something done. So far, in Part 2 of this text, we have focused on analysing the external and internal environments, with a view to developing strategy and engaging in planning. The final chapter in Part 2 turns our focus to organizational culture and change management. Organizational culture is a general term (and often debated, as we will see) that encapsulates shared ways of thinking, feeling, and behaving, which exist within the internal environment of an organization. Change management is concerned with driving or delivering changes within an organization, and is a key role of management.

Both of these topics could have feasibly been discussed in Part 3 of this text on Managing People. After all, a large part of organizational culture and a significant factor in change management is the approach, attitude, management, and leveraging of employees and other people as we will see throughout this chapter. However, because organizational culture is such a significant part of the internal environment of the organization, and because it comprises factors beyond just the people, such as the layout of the office or the role of policies and procedures, it is well placed in Part 2. Moreover, change management is typically required because of the strategy and planning decisions of the external and internal analysis processes. As such, the second half of this chapter brings all of these ideas together to explore how change occurs (or is planned and managed, but fails to occur) within an organization.

6.2 **Understanding organizational culture**

Organizational culture is a term that encapsulates shared ways of thinking, feeling, being, and behaving within a particular organization, often referred to as 'the way things get done around here' (Deal & Kennedy, 1982). Beyond this general statement, definitions and conceptualizations of organizational culture vary greatly. Indeed, there is debate over whether culture can be defined at all and, even if it can, whether it can be changed or developed. Do we define culture as something the organization 'is', something the organization 'has', how the organization 'acts', or what the organization 'does'?

Edgar Schein's (1984: 3) definition is the most commonly used; he defined **organizational culture** as 'the pattern of basic assumptions that a given group has invented, discovered, or developed and therefore taught to new members as the correct way to perceive, think and feel in relation to problems'. We can describe a specific organization's culture (for example, 'Apple's culture'), or the culture of an organizational typology (for example, 'a work hard/play hard culture' which we define later in this chapter). Organizational culture is an intangible construct—this means that it is something that we cannot see, touch, or even perfectly define. Yet, we also know that it is something that can be incredibly powerful, such that it influences every aspect of the organization, including its strategy, processes, buildings, partners, and of course, employees (CIPD, 2022).

It is important to ask not just what organizational culture is, but what purpose it serves. An organizational culture provides a unifying point and shared meaning for employees and other stakeholders, providing them with a sense of identity and an understanding—perhaps consciously, but also sometimes subconsciously—of the fundamental rationale, ideology, or philosophy of the organization. Employees become part of that culture and also active contributors to it when they behave and continue to behave in ways that are aligned with the culture. However, they can also rebel against it, or, indeed, leave an organization because they are uncomfortable with, and even outwardly disagree with, its organizational culture.

We can understand this as the idea of **organizational fit**, which is how an individual's own values and beliefs fit with those of the organization. Organizational fit is often cited when individuals leave an organization, but it is also often and problematically discussed in recruitment and selection, whereby it can lead to discriminatory decision-making and contribute to inequality in an organization, such as gender inequality (Simpson, 2000).

Given the fact that organizational culture is a key element of the internal environment of an organization, it is unsurprising to see it feature in tools that adopt a resource-based view as outlined in Section 5.2.1. Indeed, culture was mentioned in relation to the VRIO framework in Section 5.2.3, with resources and capabilities becoming embedded in the culture of an organization and, therefore, more likely to be rare and difficult to imitate. This view presumes, of course, that the organizational culture we are referring to is positive and supportive of the organizational strategy and purpose, rather than destructive and an obstacle to it. One important aspect is acknowledging the 'toxic culture' of certain workplaces and organizations. Recent research of business organizations by Sull et al. (2022) found that a 'toxic corporate culture' was the strongest predictor of employees leaving their roles (and 10 times more important than compensation). They found that the leading elements contributing to a toxic culture included: failure to promote diversity, equity, and inclusion; workers feeling disrespected; and unethical behaviour. Read more about this research in the 'Explore more' feature at the end of this chapter. We will now look to break organizational culture down into its composite parts, exploring Schein's three levels of culture.

6.3 Schein's three levels of culture

Identifying organizational culture can be difficult. Edgar Schein presents organizational culture as a pyramid with three different levels, as depicted in Figure 6.1. Given the first level is the one that is most visible, many commentators have compared this to an iceberg, adapting the idea from Edward T. Hall's (1976) notion of the cultural iceberg. What we can see, touch, observe, and study is just 'the tip of the iceberg' in terms of organizational culture. This includes observable artefacts, like buildings, or dress code. It also may include some—but not all—espoused

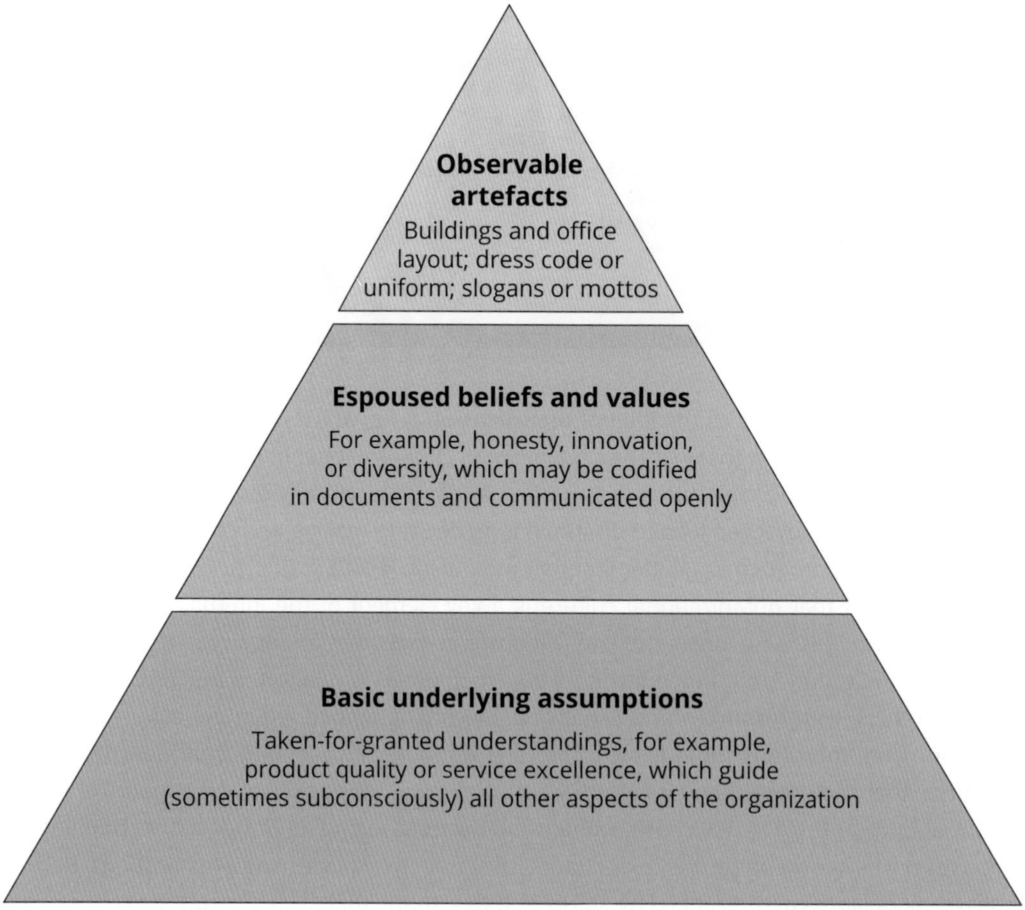

6

FIGURE 6.1 **Schein's three levels of culture (Adapted from Schein (2017)).**
Credit: © 1984 Massachusetts Institute of Technology. All rights reserved. Distributed by Tribune Content Agency

beliefs and values. Below the surface, there are elements of organizational culture that are more fundamental, intangible, entrenched, and often difficult to identify or interpret. While those aspects above the surface are the ones that are easiest to change, they have the least significance or effect on the organization. It is what is below the surface that matters most: the deeper the elements are, the greater the impact on the organization but also the harder they are to change.

Schein's three levels of an organizational culture are distinguished by how visible and observable they are, and how consciously aware group members are of the different elements.

- **Observable artefacts**: These can be easily seen, observed, experienced, and identified, and are typically highly tangible. However, it can still be difficult for outsiders to identify these, or appreciate their importance and role in culture.

- **Espoused beliefs and values**: 'Espoused' means beliefs and values employees *claim* to have (even if their behaviour suggests otherwise). These may be codified in mission statements, communicated to new staff during induction, and reinforced to the whole organization through training, meetings, strategy, and how things are done in the organization. While these are very important, they may sometimes reflect aspiration rather than reality.

- **Basic underlying assumptions**: These are deeply held beliefs by group members, but may be at a subconscious level. Indeed, they may be so innate to organizational members, particularly those who have been with the organization for a long time, that they may not even be explicitly understood and so not discussed (or discussable) or challenged.

Consider Spotlight 6.1, in which we discuss a very public commentary on organizational culture within the computer industry.

SPOTLIGHT 6.1 **MAC VERSUS PC CAMPAIGN**

The 'Get a Mac' campaign—often known as 'I'm a Mac/I'm a PC'—was a television campaign which ran from 2006 until 2009. Developed by Apple, it was focused on winning the home computing market, by presenting its Mac computer as an alternative to the dominant PC. While this was primarily a marketing campaign, it was also trying to depict the vastly different organizational cultures which each company held. The ads themselves depicted observable artefacts—style of dress, stance, style of speaking. You can watch some of these ads on YouTube and hear clear articulations of the espoused beliefs and values of Apple from actor Justin Long, who represented the Mac, as well as Apple's depiction of the beliefs and values of PC from the 'PC guy'. For example, in one advertisement the 'PC guy' has a devil on his shoulder saying 'you don't care about arts and crafts, you like work! "Fun"? We tried that once, it was nothing but pain and frustration.' The implication (remember: from Apple) is that the company has a boring organizational culture.

Whether these espoused beliefs and values are an accurate representation of the underlying assumptions of the actual company would be impossible to tell without inside knowledge or experience of each organization. However, the fact that such an 'organizational culture war' was played out so publicly, and was leveraged so obviously by Apple to distinguish themselves as new and different, demonstrates the importance of organizational culture.

6.3.1 **Tensions between different levels of culture**

Elements of culture above the surface are not possible without the underlying elements of organizational culture, many of which may not be visible. Ultimately, everything is influenced, driven by, or may fail because of the deepest levels of culture. This is what makes organizational culture so powerful, and difficulties understanding it so frustrating for those trying to transform or change an organization (as we will explore in the second half of this chapter). As stated by Schein (2004: 36):

> If one does not decipher the pattern of basic assumptions that may be operating, one will not know how to interpret the artefacts correctly, or how much credence to give to the articulated values. In other words, the essence of a culture lies in the pattern of basic underlying assumptions, and once one understands those one can easily understand the more surface levels and deal appropriately with them.

Given that it may be argued that we can only study the observable elements of culture—physical artefacts and espoused beliefs and values—we often need to use these to help identify an organization's basic underlying assumptions. Where there is consistency between the observed and underlying aspects, this may be easier. However, this can be difficult when an organization says one thing but acts in another way.

We can consider this issue and conflicts between espoused values and beliefs and what an organization actually does in relation to organizational purpose and, in particular, the shift to purpose-driven business organizations, which we discussed in Section 2.6.3. An organization may write a mission statement that focuses on the social purpose of the business, and the CEO may make speeches that emphasize this. These are observable artefacts—visible and tangible indicators of an organizational culture which prioritizes social outcomes. Indeed, management and employees may also openly articulate the fact that they prioritize social purpose and outcomes, and the organizational strategy may emphasize this. However, hidden well below the surface may be taken-for-granted assumptions that profit maximization still drives organizational decisions, irrespective of what is being said.

A similar issue may be seen with the equality, diversity, and inclusion (EDI) agenda, which we explore in detail throughout Part 3 of this text. For example, an organization may have events that support LGBTQA+ colleagues, a mentoring network to promote women's empowerment and success as well as reporting on the gender pay gap, and a carefully-planned office building layout and amenities to support employees who have physical disabilities or who are neurodiverse. All of these observable artefacts may point to an organizational culture that supports EDI. However, if there is no diversity training offered, no policies to require or support inclusion, and the espoused beliefs and values of the majority of management and employees are sceptical of—or indeed actively against—EDI as an important element of the organization, this would mean the observable artefacts were not actually consistent with the shared espoused beliefs and values, let alone the shared basic underlying assumptions.

In both of these examples, organizations can be accused of 'impact-washing', which we discussed in Section 2.6.3, where their stated commitments are not in line with their actual behaviours or cultures. However, while some tensions between the three levels of organizational culture are to be expected, these are not necessarily incompatible (Byrd & Sparkman, 2022). Indeed, one key role of management is to identify and understand these potential issues, and decide which need to be addressed. Let's look at contrasting organizational cultures in Running case 6.1.

RUNNING CASE 6.1 **AN EXPLORATORY VISIT**

Lucy is looking forward to today. This morning she is going with Bob Smart, COO and Declan O'Rourke, Supply Chain Manager, to visit NoBull, a plant-based food manufacturer whose products are getting rave reviews. They're all wondering whether NoBull might be a viable supplier of the plant-based ingredients they're looking for. As she goes down the panelled staircase outside her office, hung with the long, framed photographs of Imperial's entire workforce taken on the last working day before Christmas for the past 90 years, she wonders what she'll find at NoBull. Outside, Bob is waiting in his SUV in his director's parking space, and they drive away from the office building and head towards the motorway.

An hour later they arrive at a rather small industrial unit on a rural enterprise park. The company's logo features a smiling bovine giving a cheerful thumbs-up. They notice that there aren't many cars in the car park, and most of those that are there are plugged in. The bike racks, however, are full. Bob straightens his tie, Declan does the same, and they pick up their briefcases and head for the entrance door; next to it, a plaque proclaims that they are entering a carbon-neutral building. When they enter, there is no receptionist (unlike at Imperial, where

Daphne has been on the Reception desk since Lucy was a child), just a bell, which Bob pushes. Down the stairs comes a young man in jeans and scruffy trainers and a Daft Punk t-shirt, with his hair tied back. 'We're here to see the Managing Director, Marcus Truelove,' says Bob. 'That'll be me,' says the young man. 'Great to see you. Come and have a look round.' Bob looks disconcerted by Marcus's casual attitude, not to mention his appearance—proud of Imperial's high food safety and hygiene standards, he wonders what this visit is going to uncover.

Questions for reflection:

1. Based on what you have learned about NoBull so far, and considering Figure 6.1, what observable artefacts of organizational culture can you identify? What do these tell you about the organization's espoused values and beliefs, and basic underlying assumptions?

2. Using specific cues in this description, compare Imperial and NoBull's organizational culture.

3. What assumptions is Bob making about NoBull's attitude to food safety and hygiene? Are these valid? If yes, why? If no, why not?

6.4 **Perspectives on organizational culture**

Now that we understand what comprises organizational culture we can introduce different perspectives commonly used in studying management. However, while this can be helpful, it needs to be done responsibly and with contextual sensitivity and awareness (Johns, 2006). This is in part because, as we have discussed, it can be difficult to observe and understand the underlying assumptions that drive a culture, especially where this is inconsistent with observable artefacts.

However, there is another more complex reason which makes sensitivity important in relation to perspectives of organizational culture, especially where we attempt to categorize these. Even if we can identify an organization's culture, specific organizations rarely fit perfectly into neat categories. This can be because they display cultural characteristics of two or more categories, because they are made up of a number of subcultures (as we will see in Section 6.4.3), or because cultures rarely remain entirely static and change—albeit incrementally—over time (as we will see in Section 6.9).

In part, these issues may be linked to the concept of unifying force. This is an idea which contrasts 'tight' cultures and 'loose' cultures. A 'tight' culture is one that focuses on conformity and brings all employees together into one collective way of thinking and behaving, and so is internally consistent (everyone behaves similarly), widely shared, and explicit about what matters and how it expects people to behave. A 'loose' culture allows for, and even embraces, different ways of thinking and behaving among teams, departments, or subgroups within the organization. There are pros and cons to each end of this spectrum.

From the perspective of society, a tight or strong culture, in which everyone embraces shared assumptions, values, and thinking, says nothing of what these values actually are. At the extreme, a criminal gang or a terrorist organization may have a very tight organizational culture in which all members have shared ways of thinking and behaving.

However, from a management perspective there are issues here also. Tight cultures may prevent individuals from speaking up as a whistle-blower to point out inappropriate practices, if this is at odds with the focus on conformity. Sometimes, whistle-blowers can be ostracized and forced to leave the organization. Moreover, in an ever-changing world, managers are likely to want or need to introduce incremental or planned changes to their organization. A tight organizational culture can resist such change. Finally, a tight culture which values conformity may create obstacles to an EDI agenda which is focused on diversity—of backgrounds, life experiences, approaches, and perspectives. Such a culture may also stifle creativity more generally by limiting the acceptance of difference.

Because of these, and other issues, most organizations are likely to display elements of a 'loose' organizational culture. This comprises a less explicit organizational culture, and will likely comprise subgroup cultures. Moreover, from our perspective of studying management, it is also less amenable to simplistic categorization.

Nevertheless, in this section we first introduce two attempts at categorizing organizational culture, as a useful starting point on your journey studying management. We then explore subgroup culture and national culture as important aspects of management. However, throughout this topic in particular, it is essential to approach it with a critical thinking lens, an open mind, and a willingness to examine context.

6.4.1 Deal and Kennedy's organizational culture typology

Deal and Kennedy (1982) believed that organizational culture was inherently linked to the risk involved in making a poor decision, as well as the time that it took for the organization to find out whether the decision was the right one.

The first dimension focuses on the degree of risk associated with an organization's key activities. The success of one specific range of clothing at a retailer that stocks thousands of ranges is likely to pose a low risk to the organization. By comparison, a pharmaceutical company that needs to invest years in the success of a specific drug candidate is likely to classify such decisions as high risk. Many organizations 'spread' their risk across a number of brands, markets, or offerings, both in corporate for-profit organizations and in not-for-profit organizations. Examples could include Fentimans' lemonades entering new markets globally to spread the risk from the UK market alone, or the charity Oxfam, which formed a group of independent NGOs in 1995 to have more impact, as well as becoming the first UK charity to have an online shop in 2001.

TABLE 6.1 **The dimensions of risk and feedback in organizational culture**

Fast	**Work hard/play hard** • Fun-focused • Performance and action driven • Strong customer focus • Small risks • High energy level • Example—sales and manufacturing	**Tough-guy macho** • Quick decision-making • High risk—all or nothing • Highly driven people • Individualistic • Competitive—low teamwork • Example—stockbrokers, media, sports, and construction
Slow	**Process culture** • Bureaucratic—clear rules that must be followed • Highly regulated • Often need for precision • Status oriented • Takes years to discover if decision was correct • Example—government bureaucracies	**Bet-your-company culture** • Long-term outlook • High-risk and high-cost decisions but years before outcome is known • High planning, technical expertise, and diligence throughout • Examples—pharmaceutical firm devising a new drug, oil companies
	Low **Degree of risk** **High**	

Speed of feedback (vertical axis label)

Credit: *Corporate Cultures: The Rites and Rituals of Corporate Life* by Deal, T. and Kennedy, A., © 1982, Hachette Books Group

The second dimension is the feedback speed, referring to how long it takes for the organization to learn whether their actions and strategies are successful. An online fashion retailer will know immediately if a new design is attractive to customers based on early sales figures. Government departments or charities such as Care International that aim to address poverty, may have to wait years to see if their interventions are effective.

Bringing these two dimensions together provides a matrix and resulting typology with four different organizational cultures, which is summarized in Table 6.1.

Work hard/play hard

These cultures are likely to embrace elements of 'fun' and require high levels of energy and an upbeat, optimistic attitude to work and life. Employees take some small risks with decisions themselves but receive fast feedback on how they are performing. They often comprise teamwork and recognition of different individuals' contributions to the success of the organization. This traditionally includes sales organizations, but also increasingly technology companies.

Tough-guy macho

This an 'all-or-nothing' culture, which is attractive to highly driven individuals who embrace the possibility of being seen as a star. It is likely to contain individualists who thrive on risk and use fast feedback on the success of their decisions to adjust the strategies, behaviours, and style. As such, teamwork is unlikely to be highly valued, and turnover can be relatively high. This might include sports organizations, stockbrokers, or the advertising industry, for example.

Bet-your-company

These cultures comprise high-risk decisions with long-term consequences. Because of this, they typically require a lot of planning and analysis of the external environment. They are also likely to analyse the different potential outcomes of decisions, often leaning on expert reports or input, and due diligence. This might include pharmaceutical companies, as well as fossil fuels companies with their exploration strategies.

Process

These cultures are characterized by low risk and slow feedback. Often described as very bureaucratic, regulated, and focused on the formal status of individuals (sometimes based on longevity with the organization). This might include government agencies, particularly given the types of wicked problems that they attempt to address, in which feedback on success can be delayed for many years and can be unclear even then. Due to this lack of feedback on success, employees are likely to focus on excelling at how they do things, hence being known as a process culture.

It is important to remember that organizational culture is difficult to define and accurately identify in a simplistic typology. In particular, looking closely at the Deal and Kennedy typology we may see particular gaps for specific types of organizations. Spotlight 6.2 explores one of these. This suggests that, depending on the nature of what an organization does, it may be more helpful to think about the Competing Values Framework, introduced in Section 6.4.2.

6.4.2 Competing Values Framework

Cameron and Quinn (2011) developed a framework that compares organizational culture across two dimensions, shown in Figure 6.2. First, they contrast flexibility and discretion with stability and control. Second, they contrast internal focus and integration with external focus and differentiation. These parameters can be understood as follows:

- Flexibility and Discretion:

  organizations adopting a more flexible approach to how work is done, and where employees can use discretion in their decisions and acceptable behaviours.

- Stability and Control:

  organizations adopting a stable, consistent, and predictable approach to how work is done, and where there is centralized control over decisions and acceptable behaviours.

- Internal focus and Integration:

  organizations that look inwards to effectively integrate their own operations, resources, and people.

- External focus and Differentiation:

  organizations that look outwards to the needs and expectations of their customers and the market, and look to differentiate from their competitors.

The result of this matrix is a framework with four different types of organizational culture.

SPOTLIGHT 6.2 **PHILANTHROPIC CULTURE**

While Deal and Kennedy's typology has been popular, it is clear that it excludes a whole range of organizations, particularly those who are focused on a cause. This would probably include third sector organizations, but potentially also purpose-driven businesses. For example, not-for-profit organizations and charities may find it very difficult to recognize their place in this typology. This might be because they comprise a range of subcultures that are bound together loosely by shared values and beliefs about the cause for which the organization works. However, more recently, Dr Ruth Knight (2022) has proposed a new cultural typology which she calls 'philanthropic culture' characterized by 'decisions that are aligned with the organization's philanthropic goals to achieve their impact in the community' (Knight, 2021). As such, the organization's culture is shaped by the nature of its cause, but also encompasses belief in the organization's work and the appreciation of donors to the cause, who are also key stakeholders and custodians of the sustainability of the charity. You can read more about philanthropic culture in a blog from Dr Knight in the 'Explore more' feature at the end of the chapter.

6

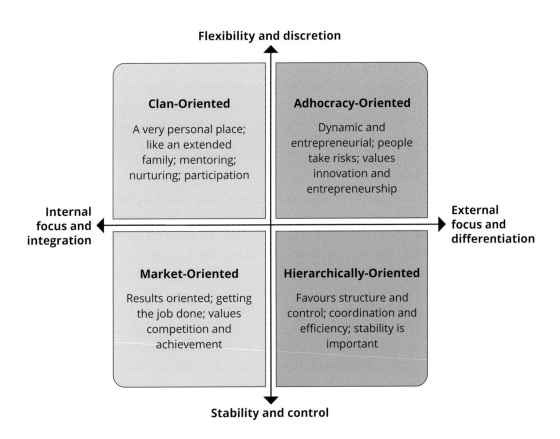

FIGURE 6.2 **Competing Values Framework.** Credit: *Diagnosing and Changing Organizational Culture Based on the Competing Values Framework*, Revised Edition, by Kim S. Cameron and Robert E. Quinn, Figure 3.3, page 50. © 2011 John Wiley & Sons, Ltd

Clan-oriented culture

Clan-oriented culture sees an organization behaving like a family (hence the name). It embraces flexibility and is internally-focused. There are commonly shared values, high loyalty, and cohesion. Employees are valued not just for their contribution to the organization, but in their own right, as diverse, unique individuals. The environment of a clan culture can be warm, safe, friendly, and trusting. An example may be a small, family-run business, where employees may also have several different roles, or organizations in the third sector which may have highly democratic decision-making processes.

Adhocracy-oriented culture

Adhocracy-oriented culture embraces a flexible approach but is more focused on the external environment. This is often seen in creative or technology-based organizations that thrive on idea transformation, and can be associated with entrepreneurs who are often driven by idea creation. Such cultures rarely have defined organizational charts, and focus on fast response to specific market gaps or immediate customer demands. As such, project teams are commonly temporary or specialized. There is an emphasis on individuality, creativity, and risk-taking in pursuit of a specific goal. An example may be found in organizations such as Google, Airbnb, or Apple, where organic idea creation is highly valued.

Market-oriented culture

Market-oriented culture focuses on the external market, but values stability and control, as well as efficiency and reducing costs. They push strong relationships with external stakeholders, especially customers and supply chain partners. They are often very results-driven, focused on their market position in comparison to competitors, growing and strengthening their customer base, and their profitability. An example may be found in organizations such as Amazon, or consumer goods companies such as Unilever.

Hierarchy-oriented culture

Hierarchy-oriented culture focuses on stability and control but looks inwards. This is often described as a bureaucratic culture and is traditionally seen in large, administration-heavy organizations, with clear hierarchies of management. They embrace standard operating procedures (SOPs), employee manuals and policies, and rules and regulations, and do not encourage individual discretion. An example may be found in the public sector or government, but can also be seen in very large businesses, such as car companies.

As with all typologies, it is not that one option is better or worse than another. Rather, we should focus on whether the culture of the organization fits with factors such as the context of the external environment, the industry or purpose, and the resources and capabilities of the organization. That is, it links to issues of the type of organization (Chapter 2), as well as external analysis of the environment (Chapter 4), and internal analysis of the organization (Chapter 5).

As we can see from the typologies presented here, they have the benefit of also providing insight into appropriate and acceptable ways of managing people. As such, they can be useful as regards change management (which we will review later in this chapter), and many aspects of Managing People, which is the focus of Part 3. Now that we have a better understanding of such typologies, consider how we might apply them to NoBull and Imperial in Running case 6.2.

RUNNING CASE 6.2 **POST-VISIT REFLECTIONS**

'Well, what do you both think?' asks Lucy, as Bob drives them out of NoBull's car park, accelerating past the other industrial units. Bob considers her question. He isn't used to senior businesspeople dressing like Marcus, and it had turned out that the rest of the staff were just as casual in their appearance. Declan speaks up from the back seat. 'I have to say I thought it was very good. I know he looked a bit casual, they all did. But did you notice how immaculate that laboratory was? All the kit was top of the range and brand new, and all the people looked like they knew what they were doing.' Bob then speaks up himself. Despite his initial discomfort, he surprises Lucy by agreeing that things at NoBull aren't quite what they first seem.

Bob had done some research in advance of the visit and discovered that Marcus and his three business partners all have PhDs in food science or biology. They have all also worked for famously demanding manufacturers with globally recognized safety standards. 'You could see it when we went through the working areas,' he says, 'Their standards are really high. And they all seem very committed—to quality, to safety, to the environment . . . to everything really.' When Lucy had remarked how many different backgrounds people seemed to come from, Marcus had told her that they tried to keep the entire company as diverse as possible, to make sure they were getting the best ideas from everywhere.

In their meeting, Declan asked Marcus if he could share any performance figures, and they had all been stunned when he sat them down in front of a giant screen and showed them real-time data-monitoring from every part of NoBull's operations. They were even more impressed to see the ongoing performance statistics from NoBull's relations with two notoriously demanding supermarket chains,

showing 100 per cent perfect delivery and quality performance. 'We really are here to change the world,' Marcus had told them brightly. 'But we know you've got to perform if you're going to make it happen.'

When Lucy had asked him to tell them something about the way NoBull is organized, Marcus had told them that they tried to minimize the bureaucracy and maintain an environment where people felt they could be entrepreneurial. 'The tricky bit is, though,' he'd said, 'knowing how to be entrepreneurial without taking any risks with food quality, because if anybody gets sick eating NoBull products, we're doomed.'

As they drive back to the city, Lucy reflects silently on the differences between Imperial and NoBull. She's always been proud of the family business. But she sees now that if Imperial is to remain successful they will have to find a way to react to feedback more quickly while thinking for the long term. She wonders how Marcus and his colleagues see themselves: NoBull had seemed like a place where the staff were having fun, but they were trying to make long-term changes to the food market, which must be a tough balancing act, she thinks.

Questions for reflection

1. How did some of the organizational culture cues (seen in Running case 6.1) lead Bob to make assumptions about other aspects of the organization? Did you make similar assumptions?

2. Where would you place NoBull and Imperial, based on what you know so far, on Deal and Kennedy's typology (Table 6.1) and the Competing Values Framework (Figure 6.2)? What more information do you need to make a better assessment? Can they be easily placed into one box?

6.4.3 Subgroup culture

As we discussed in the introduction to this section, it is possible that different groups within one organization develop their own distinct cultures. For instance, the IT department might have a culture that is distinctive from the finance team. This is not necessarily bad, as long as they are still able to work effectively together and are not in conflict with the central organizational culture, or with achieving the organizational purpose and goals. However, cultural differences can be difficult to manage, and can also lead to issues or conflict between different groups, which may end up affecting the organization. Nevertheless, Ogbonna and Harris (2002) argue that managers should only attempt to reconcile differences between subgroup cultures if these are impacting the central organizational culture. Where this is not the case, these should be both recognized and, indeed, celebrated.

For example, within a manufacturing business, the team in the factory may have a safety-first culture of worker protection and following rules and regulations given they operate dangerous machinery. However, the sales team may have a less rigid culture which focuses on customer relationships and the discretion of the sales staff. Management's role is to facilitate appropriate, diverging subgroup cultures, while also ensuring that groups can work together to achieve the purpose of the organization.

Diverging subgroup cultures are also common when two different organizations join together, in a merger or acquisition, as was demonstrated in the opening case in this chapter. When this happens, individuals within the same function may be put into one team, and may even be co-located in the same open-plan office. But this does not unify their culture. Each organization (and member of the organization) brings their own history, expectations, ways of doing things, and their own understanding of the culture. During mergers and acquisitions, organizational cultural assimilation is notoriously difficult to enact and achieve. Indeed, the process of the merger itself can impact the potential for such a cultural integration. Integrating this over time becomes a key role of change management, as we will explore in the second half of this chapter.

6.4.4 **National cultures**

The role and presence of national cultures in organizations is also very important to consider. While this is particularly relevant in global or multinational organizations, most organizations have employees, suppliers, clients, customers, or other stakeholders who span a range of national cultures. Research by Geert Hofstede on national culture, first published in 1980, is still widely used today, though also often critiqued. He framed national culture as having six key dimensions (adapted from Hofstede, 2022):

1) **Power distance**: the degree to which the less powerful members of a society accept and expect that power is distributed unequally—that is, how a society handles inequalities among people as well as how hierarchical a culture is.

2) **Individualism vs Collectivism**: whether a national culture is more individual-oriented, primarily taking care of themselves, versus collective-oriented and working together. This can be simplified to whether people in the society define themselves in terms of 'I' or 'we'.

3) **Masculinity vs Femininity**: while now outdated, within Hofstede's work the masculine-side refers to societal preferences for heroism, achievement, and rewards for success, whereas the feminine-side refers to higher levels of cooperation and consensus-oriented decision-making.

4) **Uncertainty avoidance**: focuses on the degree to which members of a society feel uncomfortable with uncertainty and ambiguity. It can be explored based on whether the society believes we should try to control the future or just let it happen.

5) **Long-term orientation vs Short-term orientation**: this refers to how change, traditions, and norms are perceived, as well as levels of appetite for planning for the future.

6) **Indulgence vs Restraint**: Indulgence reflects a society that values gratification of human impulses linked to enjoying life and having fun. Restraint reflects a society that suppresses gratification, regulating this through strict social norms.

Different national cultures can also be associated with different beliefs, religions, and ways of working and interacting. It is useful to consider which parts of your own national culture you bring to the workplace or university, and what role this plays in your thinking, how you see the world, and in turn, also how you perceive and interact with organizational culture.

While this is a popular approach to categorizing national cultures, it is important to remember that we should not generalize individuals and their culture/s, and that stereotyping can also lead to discrimination and inequality, as well as tensions between organizations, individuals, and various subgroups. There have been many academic critiques of Hofstede's work, which argue that such simplifications are potentially dangerous and damaging to our understanding of others. You can explore Hofstede's Country comparison tool, listed in the 'Explore more' feature at the end of the chapter and consider your own views on its accuracy, relevance, and usefulness.

The first half of this chapter has explored organizational culture, introducing different levels of culture, as well as perspectives and categories that have been proposed. We now turn to examine the process of change management within organizations.

6.5 **Understanding change management**

Change management is focused on driving or delivering both proactive and reactive changes within an organization. Often these are related to actual or expected changes or disruptions to the organization's internal or external environment. In Chapter 3 we explored some of these disruptions, classifying them as geopolitical, technological, and environmental. While some disruptions may be larger, more difficult to manage, and infrequent, others may be smaller and less difficult, but happen very regularly. Effective change management should help an organization not only to survive the disruption but also to respond appropriately and therefore flourish in the longer term.

Reactive change management happens when an unexpected change or disruption occurs. Many organizational responses to the Covid-19 pandemic required reactive change management, such as determining ways for employees to effectively work from home when lockdowns were announced for non-essential workers. Proactive change management happens when managers anticipate future disruptions and decide to act in anticipation. For example, many organizations are undertaking change management programmes in response to the climate crisis by reducing their greenhouse gas emissions.

Change management is often considered one of the most difficult processes to manage because it includes so many varying factors. The human elements need to be carefully and appropriately managed, in order to embrace enthusiasm and support for change, as well as overcoming inertia and resistance. This is especially difficult when the aim is ultimately to embed the changes in an organization's culture, which we will explore towards the end of the chapter.

While we will introduce different models for undertaking change management, it is important to remember that many of these present a tidy rational model with neat linear steps to manage change. In reality, organizational change is a complex, obscure, iterative process, comprising organizational power and politics, competing narratives and histories, and multiple agendas, aims, and goals, which are often not aligned (Applebaum et al., 2012). As such, more than almost any other role, change management comprises the science, art, and craft of management (discussed in Chapter 1).

6.6 Categorizing organizational change

Effective change management needs to consider the organizational change being managed, which we can categorize in two ways: the type of change, or the ambition of the change.

6.6.1 Type of organizational change

While there are many different types of organizational change, we can categorize four common ones—strategic, structural, technological/process, and human resource/people:

- Strategic change management focuses on changing the direction of the organization to better align with the aims, objectives, vision, and mission. In a business organization, this can often be linked to driving competitive advantage.

- Structural change management involves significant changes in the way in which the organization is organized, including its hierarchical structures, and the responsibilities of different teams, departments, or functions. The aims of such change may be to empower employees, recalibrate organizational control centrally or de-centrally, or respond to external forces that require increased efficiencies.

- Technological or process changes may be driven by the external or internal environment. Advances in technology may provide opportunities for innovation, cost savings, or process improvements. Process changes—how things are done—are most commonly driven by technology, or by legal or compliance requirements, for example in health and safety requirements.

- Human resources or people-centric changes focus on policies related to the management of employees, changes in recruitment and selection processes, increasing or decreasing the size of the workforce, training and development, or changes in roles and responsibilities.

6.6.2 Ambition of organizational change

Organizational change can also be categorized by the ambition of the change. This refers to its scale or intensity. Three categories of organizational change ambition are developmental, transitional, and transformational, which are depicted in Figure 6.3.

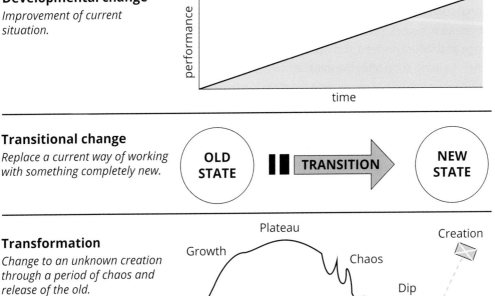

Developmental change
Improvement of current situation.

performance

time

Transitional change
Replace a current way of working with something completely new.

OLD STATE → TRANSITION → NEW STATE

Transformation
Change to an unknown creation through a period of chaos and release of the old.

Growth — Plateau — Chaos — Dip — Creation

6

FIGURE 6.3 **Ambition of organizational change.** Credit: 'How to put people at the heart of strategic transformation', from 'Strategic Transformation: Essential Insights for the 21st Century', by People Change, retrieved from consultancy.eu: https://www.consultancy.eu/news/5559/how-to-put-people-at-the-heart-of-strategic-transformation

Developmental change

Also referred to as incremental change, developmental change focuses on improving or building upon what an organization is already doing. A key example is total quality management (TQM) or 'Kaizen' translated as 'good change or improvement' and stems from Japanese manufacturing companies that became internationally renowned for ongoing process improvement, the reduction of waste, and incremental improvements in efficiency, which we explore in greater detail in Chapter 12.

Transitional change

With a strong process orientation, transitional change focuses on changing how things are done. It often requires employees to retrain or do something very differently from how they have been done in the past, which may result in higher levels of resistance to change. Mergers and acquisitions are common precursors to transitional change. This is because the new combined entity will need to integrate policies, technology platforms, and ways of doing things, not to mention developing a cohesive organizational culture, to effectively function.

Transformational change

The most ambitious form of change for an organization and its employees, transformational change, sees an organization's entire purpose, direction, or strategy change. It is likely to require changes to strategic, structural, technological, and human elements, including organizational culture. As such, it can take a very long time to be rolled out, let alone to be embedded and deemed 'successful'. Transformational change has the highest potential for resistance to change and failure. Indeed, it is not uncommon for those who decided on and implemented the change, to leave soon after the initial embedding, because the level of upheaval (often including redundancies) means they struggle to retain the trust and commitment of those who remain.

Having explored different aspects of organizational change, we will now move on to explore the change management process, as well as the barriers to change and ways in which managers can overcome them.

6.7 The change management process

In relation to change management, the role of a manager is to develop and lead a process that results in effective change. Understanding the external and internal drivers of that change is essential, as is determining the type and ambition of the organizational change. However, there are also tools that can help managers with the process of change management. We will explore three here. The first is a well-known, but widely debated Three-Phase Approach to change management often attributed to Kurt Lewin. The second is an Eight-Step Model of change management developed by John Kotter. Finally, the Kübler-Ross Change Curve focuses on the emotions felt by those involved in the change during these various stages.

6.7.1 Three-Phase Approach to change

The widely referenced Three-Phase Approach to change is attributed to Kurt Lewin, based on an article he wrote in 1947. However, it did not become popular in the field of management until the 1980s. Also, the approach, as it is commonly presented (including here in this text), bears little resemblance to what Lewin originally described.

Nevertheless, the approach is presented in so many texts, as part of management training, and in academic studies, as to have become ubiquitous and so is a helpful starting point for understanding change management. We present this Three-Phase Approach to change in Figure 6.4, but then use a critical thinking lens to reflect on some inconsistencies in, and criticisms of, this approach.

FIGURE 6.4 **Three-Phase Approach to change (originally attributed to Kurt Lewin, 1947).**

The three phases depicted in this approach to change management are unfreezing, changing, and refreezing.

Phase 1. Unfreezing is where the current situation is intentionally disrupted by managers of the organization to unsettle the equilibrium and prepare the organization for change. It is at this phase where the first signs of resistance to change, which we will explore in Section 6.8.1, may arise. The processes of communication and vision of what change may bring are very important at this stage to ensure buy-in, understanding, and, in the longer term, acceptance.

Phase 2. Changing is the process of enacting and implementing the change: a period of creating the new reality of the organization, and potentially adapting new practices, policies, and ways of doing things. This stage is potentially the most volatile, as the change becomes a daily reality. It is critical at this stage for there to be a shared understanding of the practical value of the change.

Phase 3. Refreezing occurs (theoretically) when the change is embedded, with new and different ways of working becoming the norm in the organization. This places the emphasis on the new status quo, how things are done now, and anchoring the changes into the organizational culture.

While there is beauty in such a simple model of change, there are a number of criticisms of this approach. The first is that the Three-Phase Approach includes an implicit assumption that there is a state of equilibrium and stability—that managers can 'unfreeze' this equilibrium, before implementing their change and then 'refreeze' into a new state of equilibrium. In most organizations, and in an increasingly disrupted world as outlined in Chapter 3, there is an ongoing state of flux and change. While it is true that some changes may be more significant and planned than others, the idea that there is a definable equilibrium is questionable. We must also ask whether 'refreezing' is wise (even if it is possible), given the need to be prepared for further disruptions expected in the future. Indeed, these ideas are explored in Patty McCord's book *Powerful* (2018), which explores her time at Netflix (listed in the 'Explore more' feature at the end of this chapter).

In addition to this, there is ongoing critique around the simplicity of the Three-Phase Approach, which many argue does not account for the 'messiness' and complexity of change and its successful implementation. Indeed, it offers very little detail on what actually happens in the all-important 'change' phase. Finally, and importantly, in his original article, Lewin didn't present this as the three-phase, linear format that is now attributed to him. Moreover, he wasn't proposing this as something to be proactively *used* by a manager, but rather reflecting on the different phases that we can see when looking back on change processes. While this does not preclude the approach from being used proactively, it does force us to question whether there is a rigorous basis for this as a proposed model of change. Those interested in these inconsistencies should refer to the Bridgman and Cummings book recommended in the 'Explore more' feature of Chapter 1.

6.7.2 Kotter's Eight-Step Model

Following on from this Three-Phase Approach, Kotter's Eight-Step Model focuses on the process of leading and managing change. The model outlines the success factors observed in hundreds of organizations attempting to enact change. While there have been several iterations of this model, the most recent was updated in 2014 (Kotter, 2014), with eight steps, as depicted in Figure 6.5.

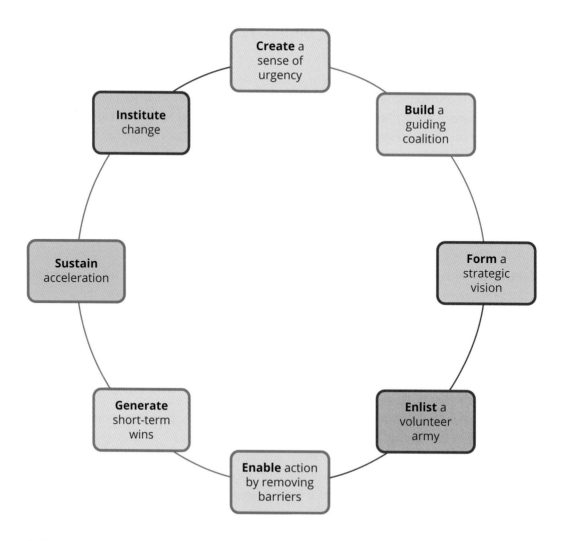

FIGURE 6.5 **Kotter's Eight-Step Model.** Credit: © Dr John Kotter, Kotter International Inc

This change model helps us to understand the different steps necessary for those respon-sible for leading and managing change. Of note is the fact that leading change is not a solitary task: it requires the engagement, involvement, and support of many others within the organiza-tion. We will now explore each of the eight steps.

Step 1. Create a sense of urgency

Focused on getting people within the organization to understand why the change is necessary. This may be achieved by issuing a bold statement that outlines the importance of change and its urgency. However, it is also likely to involve regular, consistent, and personal interactions directly with key people within the organization.

Step 2. Build a guiding coalition

Requires the leader to bring together an effective group of people to guide the changes, com-municate them throughout the organization, and coordinate and enact the activities associated with the change programme.

Step 3. Form a strategic vision and initiatives

Achieved with clear communication about what the changed organization will look like, what this will mean for employees, and why the planned change management process will ensure that future vision will become a reality. This step is integral to the success of change as it creates trust that managers and leaders not only have a vision of the future but have carefully developed a pathway to achieve it.

Step 4. Enlist a volunteer army

In big organizations particularly, large-scale change requires many people to feel engaged in the future vision and opportunity, in order to create a groundswell of support for the change. This ensures that the change is not seen as being imposed from above but is embraced by people at all levels.

Step 5. Enable action by removing barriers

Involves being able to both identify and then remove various barriers to change to ensure those within the organization have the freedom to work towards new goals and the vision of the proposed change. We will explore common barriers in Section 6.8.

Step 6. Generate short-term wins

As a way to track progress and keep people motivated to successfully enact the organizational change programme, small wins, milestones, and successes along the way need to be recognized and celebrated as steps towards the end goal.

Step 7. Sustain acceleration

For an organization to sustain success on the route of the change, leaders need to constantly promote the momentum and direction towards the new vision. Complacency in the change management process at any stage can lead to stagnation and, ultimately, failure.

Step 8. Institute change

This is linked to the integration of change into the everyday of the organization. It is essential to ensure new and different ways of working are constantly communicated and expected to replace old organizational habits, in order to ensure they are embedded effectively.

Kotter's Eight-Step Change Model is useful because it comprises very clear steps and places a strong emphasis on the importance of the engagement of employees in the change management process. This people-centric approach addresses one of the key barriers to the success of change programmes which we will explore in Section 6.8: human acceptance of change.

However, there are also some potential disadvantages to this model. The steps may require considerable time and resources to progress through, and there are still no guarantees that the proposed changes will be effective. Also, the model tends towards a traditional hierarchical organizational structure where senior leaders and managers have considerable control over their employees' roles and job design. This may not be as effective in an organization that is less hierarchical. It is also worth considering what happens to a planned organizational change if the key manager leaves during the process. How might their departure and absence affect the eight steps, and what additional challenges might face the new manager introduced in the middle of a change management process? Finally, note that in both the Three-Phase Approach and the Eight-Step Model, there is no reference to determining whether change is actually necessary or advisable for the organization. This is something which many organizations often fail to consider, particularly where managers may be promoted or rewarded for driving and enacting change/s which may be unnecessary. This may be linked to a 'pro-change' bias: an assumption that change is necessary, good, and constant. However, change fatigue, described by Abrahamson (2004) as 'repetitive change syndrome', can lead to a culture typified by change-related chaos, cynicism, and burnout.

6.7.3 **Kübler-Ross Change Curve**

The Kübler-Ross Change Curve (Kübler-Ross, 1969) is not a change management tool per se; rather it focuses on the emotions that people experience when faced with change. It was originally developed by Elisabeth Kübler-Ross in the 1960s to explain the grieving process, but was adapted into the Change Curve to explain change management in the 1980s. By focusing on the emotions employees work through, it can enable managers to better predict how morale, employee engagement and performance may be affected by the announcement and implementation of change. The Change Curve comprises three stages:

Stage 1. Shock and denial

The initial shock of an announcement change can lead to a slowdown in work and loss of productivity and/or engagement as employees try to make sense of the situation. This can be made worse by a lack of information and by people's fear of the unknown. Following shock, employees can experience denial, in part because they yearn for the certainty and stability of the status quo, or they feel threatened by the change. Managers may face employees or teams who consciously or subconsciously avoid information relating to the change, or convince themselves it will not affect them. Management should provide clear and direct communication regularly and consistently, reiterating both the reasons and plans for the change. They should also be patient and provide as much reassurance as possible.

Stage 2. Anger and depression

Anger often follows, as employees look for a scapegoat to blame—sometimes in the organization or management, but also possibly an external factor/s such as the economy. This is often associated with feelings of suspicion and scepticism. Morale and performance continue to fall as employees become resigned to the fact that change will happen. At this point, self-doubt and anxiety may be a significant issue. The resulting depression stage (note: not to be confused with clinically diagnosed depression as a mental health issue) can lead to periods of apathy, as well as fixation on small issues or problems in an attempt to obstruct the change. Management should acknowledge these are valid feelings and ensure individuals are aware that others feel similarly, to prevent isolation.

Stage 3. Acceptance and integration

The final stage sees more optimistic emotions emerging. Typically individuals accept that change is inevitable, and begin to work with the changes instead of against them. This may lead to feelings of excitement for new opportunities as well as relief that they have survived the process. When individuals reach integration they are firmly focused on the future, buoyed by hope and trust, and see the change as the new reality. Management should give people specific tasks to support the change, so they feel a sense of control and ownership over it, as well regular communication and praise of success in the process.

The Change Curve is a particularly useful tool for managers to identify and appreciate the journey that their employees or teams will go on. However, it is not prescriptive and does not explain everyone's experience. Moreover, there is no 'right' or 'wrong' journey: different individuals will reach different stages at different times (or indeed skip entire stages), and experience different emotions and reactions to these at different times.

Having explored different models of the change management process, we will now explore some of the barriers to change that an organization may face when trying to plan for and then enact change.

6.8 **Barriers to change**

Barriers to change are sometimes called 'change hurdles': things that an organization needs to overcome in order for change management to be successful. In this section, we explore the main types of barriers that organizations commonly face, and how these might be overcome. However, ultimately, it may be that an organization simply is not ready to, or is unable to, enact change because of one specific barrier, or a combination of several barriers.

Mosadeghrad and Anasarian (2014) identified five main types of change barriers. We will explore all five here, focusing in particular on the final 'human' barrier, often called 'resistance to change', and commonly considered one of the most significant contributors to failed change management within organizations.

Strategic barriers to change arise where there is a mismatch between the chosen strategy and the appropriate strategy. Consider Figure 5.1 in Chapter 5. Strategic barriers occur when the chosen organizational strategy is inconsistent with the results of the internal and external analysis. This might occur because of poor analysis, or because there is a political or self-interested reason for managers and leaders to choose a specific strategy irrespective of what the analysis tells them. For example, a manager might decide on a change management programme to compete with a rival firm, even though their own internal resources and capabilities would not support such a change.

Procedural barriers are related to the process of change and how things get done. Again considering Figure 5.1 in Chapter 5, this barrier is likely to be linked to a lack of appropriate planning, or a resource and capability audit that fails to identify a key gap. For example, the organization may lack people with the skills or abilities to implement change, but fail to appropriately plan to address this gap.

Contextual barriers are related to the context in which the organization exists. This category includes factors such as inappropriate organizational culture and difficulties in changing it, lack of innovation or problem-solving mindset among teams, and a lack of trust in senior management. External contextual factors such as socio-economic factors and stakeholder and shareholder requirements can also be barriers to change management programmes and are an important consideration (Johns, 2006).

Structural barriers are mostly related to organizational structure—either too hierarchical or too flat. However, they also include a lack of resources required for change management to be effective, such as physical assets, financial support, or information systems support, which can limit the monitoring and measurement of change initiatives.

Human Resource barriers include general issues such as lack of skills, training, and education; employee turnover; lack of management or employee commitment to the organization; and lack of motivation and satisfaction generally. They also include employee shortages or workload issues, inadequate empowerment of employees, and lack of recognition and rewards for success. In addition to these general human resource barriers to change, a more specific and significant issue is resistance to change, which we will explore in greater detail.

6.8.1 Resistance to change

Human resistance to change is one of the most significant factors leading to the failure of a change management process. Resistance to change is an unwillingness to change the status quo generally or to change something specific. Such resistance may be identified at the level of an individual, a specific group or team, a whole department, or an entire organization. Typically, the greater the group of resistors, the more difficult such resistance is to overcome, not only because it involves more people, but because it involves established group norms and cohesion. You can access recent TED Talks on resistance to change and some of the reasons for resistance in 'Explore more'.

At an individual level, resistance to change can exist because a person is fearful of the implications of the change for their security or their identity. They may see change as threatening the existence of their job or role, their ability to perform in a revised role, or their understanding of promotion pathways and prospects if they have such ambitions. Moreover, an individual's job is often an extension of their identity, including their values, beliefs, ideals, and self-worth. The prospect of an organizational change calling some of these into question may be enough for individuals to resist. For example, if a health organization begins a change management programme focused on changing processes to check-in, treat, and discharge patients more efficiently, some health care workers may resist if they are concerned it calls into question their fundamental belief that all patients should be treated with dignity, respect, and human kindness, rather than simply being processed through a system.

At an organizational level, resistance to change is sometimes referred to as organizational inertia, where there is widespread and deeply embedded resistance to changing the way things have always been done. Some types of organizations and industries have a reputation for resisting change more than others. For example, we explored some reasons why the public sector in general has a reputation for resisting change in Section 2.4. Large business organizations in established industries are also often known for being resistant to change, in part because they associate their success with 'how we have always done things'. These attitudes can make new entrants, who do not have such history, particularly able to leverage opportunities created by such inertia, as we have seen with new online-only banking organizations disrupting the consumer finance market and competing with existing large high-street banks.

Sometimes, resistance to change is used by managers as a catch-all and even accusatory reason for the failure of a change management initiative. No doubt it can be very frustrating when a planned change faces obstacles because all, some, or just one key individual resists such

change. While it is the case that well-meaning managers with well-designed and much-needed change initiatives may do all they can to argue their case and still fail to get buy-in and overcome resistance, it is also often true that resistance exists for very good reasons. Managers could and should use such resistance to better understand their organization, better align their change management plans, and better focus their persuasive efforts. For example, in the instances where trade unions are organized to protect workers' jobs, conditions, and wages, management wanting to undertake change have two options before them. They can ignore the union in the process of developing the change management plan, and then fight them on the aspects that they disagree with. Alternatively, they can involve unions in the process of developing the change management plan, which will help surface the factors that are of concern to workers in advance of introducing change. While both pathways have their pros and cons (and success is likely dependent on the ability of both parties to develop an effective working relationship), this demonstrates the ways in which the role of managers, especially in relation to change management, is complex, multifaceted, and rarely easy or politically neutral.

Finally, it is important to note that there are often precursors of resistance to change in organizational culture. We will explore that specific relationship in Section 6.9. However, first we will briefly explore how managers might attempt to overcome resistance to change.

6.8.2 Overcoming resistance to change

Resistance to change is a natural human response to the unfamiliar or unknown. However, existing academic and industry literature typically identifies three key recurring themes in advice for overcoming such resistance. The first focuses on understanding the root causes of the resistance. The second focuses on active communication from senior leadership, not only of why the change is necessary but also how it will be done and what it means for individuals. The third key theme focuses on communication throughout the organization in a way that aligns with the established norms and culture of the organization. The change management models we explored in Section 6.7 are all aimed at these challenges in overcoming resistance to change: the 'unfreeze' phase of the Three-Phase Approach and the early steps in Kotter's Eight-Step Model—creating a sense of urgency, building a coalition, and enlisting volunteers.

However, in his early writing, Kotter also provided a more specific model for overcoming resistance to change. While somewhat dated now, it is useful in providing a framework for understanding the different options that may be available for managers facing resistance. As we will see, however, some of these options are likely to be more acceptable and effective than others, depending on the organization, the organizational culture (and potentially national context and culture), and the attitude of the workforce. Kotter and Schlesinger (1979) presented six different ways for overcoming resistance to change, as shown in Figure 6.6. We will explore each of these in turn, including a reflection on what might affect the success of each in overcoming resistance to change. You can also discover more about resistance to change in the digital resources suggested in the 'Explore more' feature at the end of this chapter.

Although Figure 6.6 summarizes the main ways in which resistance to change may be overcome, it is important to remember that resistance to change will differ by context, nature of the change, and even at the individual level. As such, managers need to be not only aware of resistance to change but also understand the reasons behind it and actively listen to those whom the changes affect.

- Education and communication:

    Education about the change can help overcome misunderstandings and anxiety as to what will happen. For example, additional training may help in overcoming knowledge gaps not

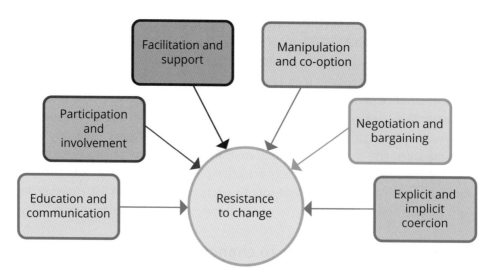

FIGURE 6.6 **Overcoming resistance to change.** Credit: Reprinted by permission of Harvard Business Review. Excerpt/Exhibit. From 'Choosing strategies for change' by John P. Kotter and Leonard A. Schlesinger. July–August 2008. Copyright © 2008 by Harvard Business Publishing; all rights reserved.

only about the change but also about new ways of working, such as the integration of a new IT system. Communication and listening are key to both fostering engagement and managerial understanding of the resistance to change.

- Participation and involvement:

  Involving people in discussions around the change can be helpful in breaking down resistance to change, and employee voice is also integral in keeping employees engaged. Many organizations hold forums or 'town hall meetings' to gain ideas from employees. Larger organizations may also bring in external change consultants to foster dialogue, transparency, and engagement.

- Facilitation and support:

  Facilitation and support focus on active and explicit offers of additional managerial support and mentoring, ensuring that employees do not feel forgotten, ignored, or uncertain of what to do during the process.

- Manipulation and co-option:

  This method involves not giving individuals full information about the actual change to avoid problems associated with their expected resistance. This approach may be adopted if there are elements of uncertainty or unknowns in the change process or if the manager aims to minimize the anxiety that may result from anticipated change. However, this approach may be contrary to the notion of participation and involvement. It may also be seen as unethical as well as risky if it engenders mistrust, leading to more problematic resistance later in the process.

- Negotiation and bargaining:

  This may involve incentivization for embracing the change, by offering financial incentives or rewards or building new goals and objectives into individuals' performance criteria. Where organizational restructuring is a part of change, financial incentives for some individuals to leave the organization, in the form of redundancy packages, may be offered.

- Explicit and implicit coercion:

  These approaches make very clear the negative consequences of not being on board with proposed changes. This may include direct or indirect threats, leading potentially to a culture of fear in an organization. This may be damaging to employee engagement, trust, and ultimately the success of the proposed changes, as well as contributing to further resistance or in the most severe instances, people leaving the organization.

It is important that managers consider not only which techniques are likely to suit specific situations, but also when to combine different techniques to the greatest effect, and how to engage employees in the process. It is also important to consider the unintended consequences of deploying specific techniques, in particular those which may involve the use of differing levels of power between employees and management, such as manipulation, negotiation, or coercion, which can potentially have a deeply detrimental effect on employees and their well-being. Let's check back in on Imperial and their attempts at change management in Running case 6.3.

RUNNING CASE 6.3 THE CHALLENGE OF LEADING CHANGE AT IMPERIAL

It's only a month into Quarter 4, and some people at Imperial are excited to find that they are already over halfway to their £20,000 revenue target for their new plant-based food range. COO, Bob was surprised to see just how quickly sales were building. He had been vocal about his concerns to Lucy in particular at the start of this process. Lucy hadn't dismissed his concerns, but—he now realized—had been very adept at managing him. She'd acknowledged the arguments that he and others were making, without ever actually agreeing with them, so he couldn't say that she had ignored him. As he looks back now, he can see how smart she has been. At their first Away Day, Lucy had managed to make it feel like Imperial's issues were very serious, providing comparative sales figures and other supporting data. Having all those different people, including young Jazz, in the meeting had been very clever, Bob now sees: Lucy and Gita had encouraged them all to bring their ideas, and had dismissed none of them. When Bob had complained that their PESTEL analysis ignored day-to-day business reality, Lucy had done another good job in initiating the Five Forces review and then following it up with the stakeholder review. Though he'd gone into those meetings feeling sceptical, he felt that everyone's views had been included and validated: Lucy had respected their different perspectives, but balanced them with other evidence and viewpoints.

Bob has to admit he is now feeling both more concerned, and more confident, than he was six months ago. Concerned because he now has a much better sense of the issues the business is facing, which he had been blind to before. Confident because he can see how Lucy has built a real coalition within the business, with people in all parts of Imperial now playing their own parts in delivering the change. Change is underway, and it's proving to be a success. That visit to NoBull had been a brilliant idea. Bob found himself completely out of his comfort zone when he first met NoBull's CEO, Marcus, but by the end of their visit, and after several subsequent meetings, he is a real admirer of the NoBull team and their products. He wonders now how Imperial can take the best of what they have learned from Marcus and from their own Away Day meetings over the past few months, and make Imperial as strong in the future as it always has been in the past.

Questions for reflection

1. Consider Kotter's Eight-Step Model in Figure 6.5. Which steps do you think Lucy has addressed? Provide examples of what she has done.

2. What barriers to change was Lucy facing when she first started to think about identifying and addressing the issues Imperial was facing?

3. What further actions should Bob and Lucy take to further embed change at Imperial?

6.9 Changing organizational culture

One particularly important and incredibly difficult challenge for change management relates to changing organizational culture. What do organizations do if their culture, or parts of their organizational culture, need to change? As we explored in the first half of this chapter, there is debate over the extent to which management can control or change culture. This is because culture is so diffused across the organization and within individuals. To the extent that culture change is possible, it is universally agreed that organizational culture changes incrementally. While actions to shape culture can have impact, the impacts can be difficult to predict and control. This is because managers control only what they do and say, and what they can ask employees to do; they cannot control what employees think or believe.

Senior leadership, in particular, play a key role when attempting to change organizational culture. While this is in part linked to their power and control, and ability to shape policy and strategy, there is also something much deeper, linked to their actions. This includes what they say, how they say it, how they behave, and what they do every day. Any signs of inconsistency with the stated or desired cultural changes from senior management will affect the success of these. Even seemingly insignificant factors can be very powerful, such as who is praised (and who is ignored) in meetings, who is given access to senior management (and who is denied access), and which issues management dedicate their time, effort, and attention to.

For example, a public speech from the CEO about prioritizing the local community, even if matched by a monetary donation, is likely to fail in shifting organizational culture in that direction unless it is accompanied by other fundamental signals and action from management. This might include the CEO establishing and leading a community engagement team, regularly meeting community members, and consistently communicating the importance of this underlying value, as well as actively listening to concerns of employees.

Edgar Schein, introduced in Section 6.3, describes these as embedding mechanisms. The primary embedding mechanisms for managers include:

- what they pay attention to, measure, and control on a regular basis;
- how they react to critical incidents and crises (and whether this is consistent with previous statements and behaviours);
- how they allocate resources (including financial resources, but also human resources and their own time);
- how they allocate rewards and status; and
- how they recruit, select, promote, retire, and terminate employees.

These are the factors that have the potential to contribute to the success of any change management programme, and to changing something as ingrained as organizational culture, in particular. Indeed, any similar large-scale transformational change requires the careful and dedicated attention to these embedding mechanisms.

6.10 **Conclusion**

This chapter has explored two aspects of the internal environment of the organization: their culture, and their approach to change management. Organizational culture can be observed to some extent, but also includes elements that are deeply embedded, even to the point of employees being unaware of, and yet deeply influenced by, different elements. This is one reason why change management, when it attempts significant changes including to the organizational culture, is so difficult. Change management itself is often presented as a neat and sequential process, but in reality is much more complex and messy. Nevertheless, it is a key role of almost all managers to some degree, in particular in the disrupted world that organizations continually face. Now, having reached the end of Part 2 of this text, we can see the way in which the external environment, internal environment, as well as organizational culture and change management all come together to help us to understand managing an organization. Yet we are missing a key factor in management, which we have briefly referenced throughout this part: that is the management of the people who form the organization. This is the focus of Part 3, Managing People, to which we now turn.

CHAPTER SUMMARY

○ Organizational culture encapsulates shared ways of thinking, feeling, being, and behaving within a particular organization, often referred to as 'the way things get done around here'.

○ Schein's pyramid comprises three levels of organizational culture: observable artefacts, espoused beliefs and values, and basic underlying assumptions.

○ Deal and Kennedy's typology of organizational culture comprises work hard/play hard, tough-guy macho, bet-your-company, and process, to which we can add philanthropic culture.

○ The Competing Values Framework includes clan-oriented, adhocracy, market-oriented, and hierarchy cultures.

○ Change management can be categorized at different levels (strategic, structural, technological/process, and human resource/people) or based on different ambitions (development, transitional, and transformational).

○ The Three-Phase Approach, Kotter's Eight-Step Model, and the Kübler-Ross Change Curve all offer tools to understand and guide the change process, although care should be taken with the extent to which these can depict what is a complex and often messy challenge.

○ Barriers to change include strategic, contextual, structural, and human, with this final one proving challenging, as humans can resist change for many reasons, which requires the careful attention of management.

CLOSING CASE REFLECTION

Hair care: Blending in

The case of P&G acquiring Clairol was an explicit example of the merging of two different corporate cultures. However, what is also interesting is that it is also an example of a change management challenge. We can imagine the task of the International Division was particularly important to overcome the resistance to change that would naturally arise from employees' reactions to a new owner with an entirely different culture. Looking more deeply into these emotions, we can imagine how the employees must have felt. Kübler-Ross' Change Curve suggests they may have felt shocked at news of the acquisition, but also denial that it would lead to any significant changes: after all, Clairol was a successful independent company—why would P&G risk the success that was in part due to their own culture. Once the International Division's plan for change became apparent, they may have felt anger and depression at their lost ways of working, because they were both comfortable and perhaps even linked to their less hierarchal national culture. Acceptance and integration would have come over time—and at different stages for different employees (or perhaps never for some). While the acquisition was a success, the road was likely very bumpy.

REVIEW QUESTIONS

1. How would you define organizational culture? Identify an organization with a noticeable culture.

2. Identify tangible elements of organizational culture, as well as less tangible elements. Which are more important?

3. How might organizational culture impact the organization? Its employees? Society?

4. Can change management be easily divided into specific steps? Why? Why not?

5. What are some of the key barriers to successful change management and what can managers do to overcome these?

EXPLORE MORE

▬ READ about how your own national culture is categorized and discussed in Hofstede's Country Comparison Tool. Does it mirror your own experience and perspective? You can find it by searching 'Hofstede country comparison' online.

▬ READ a blog by Dr Ruth Knight from 2021, about philanthropic culture: 'Is Building a Philanthropic Culture the Key to Your Success?' Search for the title online. (Retrieved 19 Jan. 2023).

▬ READ the article by Donald Sull, Charles Sull, and Ben Zweig, 'Toxic Culture is Driving the Great Resignation', published in *MIT Sloan Management Review*, 11 Jan. 2022.

◉ WATCH Manu Shahi's TED Talk from 2019: 'How Changing Your Mindset Can Help You Embrace Change'. Search for Manu Shahi on the TED Talks website.

))) LISTEN to the podcast on 'Embracing and Leading Organizational Change', CIPD, 6 July 2021. Search for the title on the CIPD website.

◉ WATCH international consulting firm Deloitte discuss 'Implementation Challenges: Change Management', 20 Sept. 2019. Search for the title of the video on YouTube.

◉ WATCH a TED Talk from Heather Stagl: 'How to Deal with Resistance to Change', TEDxGeogiaStateU, 30 June 2015. Search for Heather Stagl on the TED Talks website.

▬ READ a book by Patty McCord (2018), *Powerful: Building a Culture of Freedom and Responsibility*, which explores her time in various workplaces in Silicon Valley, culminating in her work at Netflix to create their unique and high-performing culture.

PART ONE **CONTEXT**

PART TWO **ORGANIZATION**

PART THREE
PEOPLE

PART FOUR **VALUE CHAIN**

PART
THREE

Managing People

CHAPTER SEVEN
Human Resource Management

Catherine Berrington and Emma Macdonald

OPENING CASE STUDY P&O FERRIES

On 17 March 2022, 800 employees were made redundant from P&O Ferries, a British shipping company that operates from the UK to Ireland, and to Continental Europe. P&O announced these job losses to staff without warning via a pre-recorded video, reportedly lasting less than three minutes (Topham, 2022). P&O had not issued prior notice or consultation, meaning the news of the redundancies came as a complete shock to employees. The case made front-page news across the UK as an example of brutal management, and inspired a letter of 'anger and disappointment' from the UK Government and Minister of Business (Department for Business, Energy & Industrial Strategy, 2022a).

The move by P&O was said to be a cost-saving one, with staff being replaced by agency workers. P&O claimed it was necessary for business survival. However, there was widespread condemnation of the treatment of loyal employees, whose lives were turned upside down overnight. While the realities of business mean that job cuts will sometimes be necessary, all attempts should be made to navigate these in the fairest and most ethical manner possible. The case of P&O showcases an extreme example of the challenges that human resource professionals face in balancing the economic interests of the organization while still having a responsibility to ensure legal and ethical decisions are made with regard to employees. Questions have since been raised as to how delivering the news of these redundancies in this way was approved by the organization and in particular, whether the human resources function supported this approach. The outrage resulting from P&O's actions highlights the importance of effective HRM processes. Public scandals can have a significant impact on the morale and satisfaction of remaining employees and irreparably damage an organization's reputation, affecting its ability to both recruit future employees and gain customer support.

7.1 **An introduction to Part 3**

Part 1 of this text focused on the context in which management happens, while Part 2 explored the organization itself (see Figure 7.1). While we acknowledged in Parts 1 and 2 that the topics of Context and Organization necessarily include the people who comprise the organization, in Part 3 we focus on the People element in detail.

A key activity of management is managing individual human beings and the various groupings of people that make up organizations—such as teams, functional departments, and working groups—as well as the overall organization and its culture. As individuals and groups of

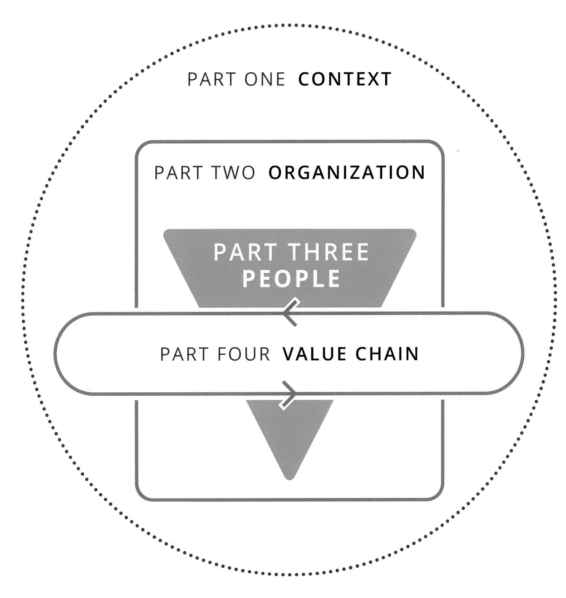

FIGURE 7.1 **Interrelated elements important in managing organizations.**

people undertake work in various forms to achieve organizational objectives, there is a need to coordinate and manage their activities.

Part 3 starts with an overview of the human resources function within an organization (Chapter 7), it then examines work and the nature of fair work (Chapter 8), then turns to organizational behaviour and teams (Chapter 9), before looking at the role of leadership and influence in organizations (Chapter 10).

7.2 What is Human Resource Management?

Mention the phrase Human Resource Management (HRM), and most people would immediately think of activities like the hiring and firing of employees. Although these activities are an important part of HRM and will be discussed later in this chapter, they do not account for the full range of activities and the complex nature of HRM. Before we discuss HRM, it is useful to first begin by defining the notion of **human resources** (HR). Boxall (2013) refers to these as the 'resources that are intrinsic to human beings', including people's knowledge, skills, abilities, experiences, or personality. By contrast, Wright et al. (1994: 301) take an organizational perspective, defining human resources as 'the pool of human capital under the firm's control in a direct employment relationship'. In this chapter, among other things, we will further explore how organizational versus employee perspectives of HR may differ.

There are various and often conflicting views of HRM and the role of the Human Resources Manager. Boxall and Purcell (2003) capture the underlying purpose of HRM in a definition that says HRM 'refers to the activities associated with the management of employment relationships in the firm'. By 'employment relationships', they mean the relationships between the **employer** and the **employee**. This is an intentionally broad definition because HRM often looks very different depending on the organization we view it in. Any organization will engage in at least some HRM activities, and HRM is needed whenever there are multiple people within any kind of organization, regardless of size. If an organization is very small, it may not have a named HR **functional department** or anyone working in it as an HR practitioner. This does not mean the organization is not conducting HRM activities; it simply means other managers are conducting these activities. Most larger organizations are likely to have an established HR function.

Since the 1980s, the discourse around HRM has given increased focus on the notion of Strategic HRM. Again, there is a lack of consensus on a definition of this concept, but there is a general understanding that Strategic HRM considers how HRM activities and practices contribute to organizational performance (Boxall & Purcell, 2000). Practitioner literature largely aligns with this, with the Chartered Institute of Personnel and Development (CIPD, 2021) defining strategic HRM as 'creating a coherent planned framework for employees to be hired, managed and developed in ways that supports an organization's long-term goals.' We discuss the link between HRM and organizational performance in more detail in Section 7.4.

Finally, it is important to be aware of critical perspectives of HRM, particularly as it concerns the **employment relationship**, and issues around power and control in this dynamic. Most people would agree that shareholders, CEOs, directors, and even managers, have significantly more power in the employment relationship than the average employee. Critical perspectives of HRM bring these power imbalances to the forefront and highlight how different HRM activities can be criticized because of this. Some examples of issues highlighted by critical HRM include:

- differences between high/low pay employees;
- gender and ethnicity pay gaps;
- critical perspectives on performance management relating to the control of employees through performance management tools;
- critical perspectives on employee voice mechanisms including how meaningful management-led voice initiatives really are; and
- management resistance to indirect forms of employee voice (such as trade unions).

Critical perspectives of HRM are important as, through this lens, we are also able to understand how HRM activities contribute to broader societal inequalities such as income inequality and discrimination. We will discuss some of these issues throughout the chapter.

7.2.1 Approaches to HRM

As noted, we can view HRM as being predominantly concerned with managing the employment relationship. Industrial sociologist Alan Fox popularized the idea of three key perspectives for understanding the notion of employment relationship: unitarist, pluralist, and radical (Geare et al., 2006). These three perspectives are not approaches to HR but are deeply rooted management views of the employment relationship. The unitarist perspective views the employment relationship as harmonious: the stakeholders—employer and employee—are aligned in their goals, and it is assumed that both have the same interests. The pluralist perspective perceives stakeholders as pursuing differing aims and objectives; conflict is, therefore, seen as a natural occurrence in organizations that needs to be managed through dialogue and compromise. The radical perspective differs in the sense that it understands the employment relationship as being exploitative in nature; it views employer and employee interests as being strongly opposed in all aspects. This perspective sees consistent employee resistance as imperative to push back on this exploitation. All three concepts have been widely discussed in the context of the HR function, with the unitarist view underpinning much of how HRM is conducted in the UK—that is, the predominant view is that organizations create and enact their HRM activities with the view that employer and employee interests are predominantly in alignment (Keegan & Francis, 2010).

Managing the employment relationship is complex, and organizations will approach this in different ways. Two contrasting approaches that are widely referred to within the management literature are 'hard HRM' and 'soft HRM'. The notion of hard and soft HRM originated in the USA but has since become commonplace in countries such as the UK (Gill, 1999; Truss et al., 1997). Hard and soft approaches to HR in organizations can be argued to place different focus on the two words 'human resource'. Hard HRM places significant emphasis on the 'resource' aspect and takes the perspective of 'humans as resources'. By viewing employees as resources, these humans are seen as an unavoidable cost of doing business. Organizations adopting this

Soft HRM	Hard HRM
• Focus on commitment • High trust in employees • Investment in the training and development of employees • Increased autonomy given to employees	• Focus on tight control • Low trust in employees • Focus on performance and results • Close supervision of employees

FIGURE 7.2 **Soft HRM versus Hard HRM.** Based on Truss et al. (1997)

style are often then concerned as to how best to maximize the return on this unavoidable cost. Coercion and control from managers are therefore a key part of the employment relationship from this approach. On the other hand, soft HRM places emphasis on the 'human' aspect of HR and views employees as 'resourceful humans'. Employees are therefore seen as valued assets to an organization and, as a result, more concern is given to the development and commitment of these employees, rather than treating them like any other resource. Figure 7.2 shows the characteristics of hard and soft HRM. All organizations take their own approach to HRM, but there is evidence that the hard HRM approach is more commonly seen in private sector organizations due to a greater focus on organizational performance and profits (Knies et al., 2022).

When considering these approaches to the employment relationship in practice, organizations often wish to portray that they adhere to a soft HRM approach. The rhetoric from organizations is often one that places value on its employees and sees them as their greatest asset. However, the reality of organizations is sometimes in conflict with this desired image, and many organizations adopt more of a hard HRM approach. Spotlight 7.1 compares how two organizations, John Lewis and Sports Direct, practise these different styles of HRM.

SPOTLIGHT 7.1 **SOFT VS HARD HRM**

Sports Direct and John Lewis provide good contrasting examples of soft and hard HRM. Sports Direct epitomizes many of the key characteristics of hard HRM. The organization adopts an approach of low wages, close monitoring of employees, and provides them little opportunity to voice any opinions or grievances (Goodley & Ashby, 2015). On the other hand, John Lewis is well known for its soft HRM approach, whereby it views employees as valuable assets to the organization (Inman, 2020). This soft HRM approach taken by John Lewis encourages employees to have a voice in the organization, referring to employees as 'partners', and having a profit-sharing scheme for employees at all levels (ICAEW Insights, 2023).

7.2.2 **Who does HRM?**

Now that we have learnt what HRM is and the ways in which it can be viewed in organizations, it is important to consider who actually conducts HRM activities. One way in which HRM differs from many other organizational functions is that the HR function can never take full claim to HRM activities. Line managers—those who are responsible for the day-to-day management of employees—are based in functions throughout the business (for example, the Marketing Manager might be **line manager** to the Marketing Assistant) and are a key part of conducting HRM in organizations, so even those outside of the HR function will find themselves needing to have a solid understanding of HRM.

While all organizations will have a slightly different structure to the HR function, one of the most common approaches is the '**Three-Legged Stool**' proposed by Ulrich (1995). The three 'legs' refer to the HR function being divided into:

- HR service centre
- HR centre of expertise
- HR business partners

The idea behind Ulrich's work is to create a close partnership between line management and HR, given that both need to work together to conduct HRM. In order to accomplish this, an HR service centre is to be used to conduct the bulk of transactional and administrative activities, and the centre of expertise is used as a hub of specialist HR knowledge. Ulrich places particular emphasis on the third 'leg', HR business partners. The business partnering role is often also referred to as an 'internal consultant', the basis being that an **HR business partner** is an internal adviser to line managers in a specific organizational department, team, or function (Ulrich, 1995). The introduction of the business partner role shifts the responsibility of carrying out certain activities, such as disciplinaries and performance management, to line managers, who will be supported and advised by their HR business partner (Pritchard, 2010). The idea is that this then allows HR business partners to become 'strategic partners' to the managers in organizations (Heizmann & Fox, 2019) and that it will free up time spent conducting transactional activities and allow HR to support line managers as masters of their own practice. It is also argued that this model means HR is able to shift towards being fully integrated within the business alongside line managers, and ensure HR practices are aligned with business goals (Boglind et al., 2011).

As noted, although the 'Three-Legged Stool' is just one way of structuring an HR function, it has been widely adopted and has become commonplace in the UK. For example, a study conducted by the CIPD reported that 40 per cent of the organizations surveyed stated they had adopted the business partnering model (CIPD, 2013).

Now that we have considered who does HRM and how in different organizations, let's examine HRM at Imperial, in Running case 7.1.

As this section reveals, HRM is a contested field that is filled with debates and controversies, and we can see evidence of this in the very different approaches organizations may take, such as soft and hard HRM. There are also differences in the ways in which HR functions may be

7

RUNNING CASE 7.1 **HRM AT IMPERIAL**

Su-Li Chan is 42 years old and has been Imperial's HR Manager for five years. She began her working life in the factory of another food-products company, starting straight from school on the production line. Over the next five years, Su-Li performed so well that she was offered successive promotions until she became a production team leader. At that point, she started a part-time Management degree leading to a CIPD qualification. Su-Li loves Imperial and admires the Green family's values, which have helped shape a very caring culture. But when she was working under Hugh's leadership she saw opportunities for change and is glad that Lucy is now in charge.

Imperial doesn't have a large HR department, so Su-Li thinks it's important to act as the personal HR adviser to the different line managers—those at the front line, those in middle management, and the senior managers themselves. This isn't always easy: Bob, the COO, has a somewhat old-school approach to discipline and hierarchy, but Su-Li has worked with him over the years to show him a different approach, which can get better results. Having come from a production background herself, she understands what needs to be done on the factory floor in order to continue Imperial's success, and she can be forceful when she needs to be, such as in one case where a worker on Bob's team had been very disruptive.

Recent years have been difficult for HR professionals in the industry. There have been challenges with recruitment and retention of staff. The pandemic required a rapid response from Su-Li's team to prioritize the health and welfare of all employees, especially those working in the factory who couldn't work from home. The worst part had been having to make people redundant when it was clear that Imperial couldn't retain all its staff. In those conversations some colleagues were in tears, some furious, one accusing her of forgetting where she had started and betraying the factory workforce.

Now that the pandemic is over, Su-Li's priority is to work with Lucy and Bob and their teams to ready the business for the next set of challenges: including social changes, becoming more sustainable, and introducing a new range of plant-based foods. To do that will require further recruitment and selection—and some rapid but thorough training. Some culture change work may also be required as Su-Li is concerned that not all employees realize the seriousness of keeping the plant-based and meat-based production lines completely separate. She heard reports of some factory staff moaning about vegans and is contemplating how to tackle this: whether to treat it as harmless banter or a more serious diversity issue. And she needs to do this while helping Lucy to maintain morale and ensure that, in these difficult times when talent is so hard to find, all the workers they want to keep are incentivized to remain. In periods like these, Su-Li feels under tremendous pressure. But she also derives great satisfaction from knowing how important the HR function is to Imperial, and how critical her knowledge and management skills are to everyone in the business.

Questions for reflection

1. Why is an HR Manager so important to a small company like Imperial?

2. Should Su-Li be concerned about factory staff criticizing 'woke vegans'? How would you act if you were in her shoes? What should she do?

3. In a change-management programme like the one Lucy is undertaking, what is the role of the HR Manager?

structured in organizations, with more than just HR practitioners involved in HRM activities, as line managers also play a key role. Yet despite these variations in how HRM is approached and carried out, there are core activities common to HRM across organizations, and we will now move on to explore these in the next section.

7.3 Core HRM Activities

Although HRM is a disputed topic and there is little consensus as to how to define the concept, there are a number of key activities that are typically associated with the HR function in organizations. Some of these key activities are recruitment and selection, training, reward, equality and diversity, and employee voice, summarized in Figure 7.3. In this section, we will consider each of these activities, alongside examples of what they may look like in organizations.

7.3.1 Recruitment

The activities of recruitment and selection, which are summarized in Figure 7.4, are important activities of HRM. Organizations need to ensure that they have the right skills, experience, and knowledge to achieve organizational objectives; recruitment and selection play an important role in making this happen. Given the value that the right employees can bring to an organization, it is important that the recruitment and selection process is effective. Effectiveness can mean a number of things, but most importantly the process needs to be:

- valid—the tools used in selection need to be a good indicator of future job performance;
- fair—the process must not disadvantage any social groups; and
- cost-effective.

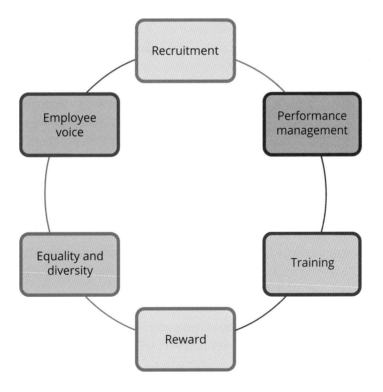

FIGURE 7.3 **Core HRM activities.**

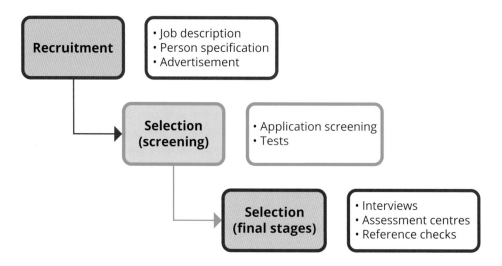

FIGURE 7.4 **Recruitment and selection (example activities).**

While often referred to simultaneously, recruitment and selection are distinct but interrelated concepts. Recruitment refers to the process by which an organization seeks prospective employees to fill a workforce gap. For each vacancy, a job description and person specification are usually created. The job description sets out the tasks and responsibilities associated with the role, and the person specification details the knowledge, skills, abilities, and experience that are required to do the job. Once these descriptions have been created, the organization will typically advertise a job vacancy. Advertisements can be via internal channels (within the organization) and external channels (outside of the organization), such as job boards. Word of mouth or 'grapevine recruitment' is also sometimes used, but it is important to note that this may introduce bias into the process and can lead to discrimination.

Once the recruitment process is complete, the organization will go through selection. Selection is a process that narrows down prospective employees (those who have responded to the recruitment process) until a final person (or persons) is chosen. Where there has been a large number of responses in the recruitment process, organizations will often undergo a phase of initial screening. During this stage, applications and CVs will usually be screened to remove any candidates that do not meet the minimum level required for the job. Online tests will sometimes also be used at this stage—these can be numerical, verbal, situational, or personality tests. Once the organization narrows down the pool of potential employees to a smaller number, other tools are often used to determine the final person or persons best suited to the role. These tools may be interviews, assessment centres, job simulation tests, and reference checks.

Psychometric and social exchange approaches to recruitment

The approach an organization takes to recruitment and selection will largely depend on the perspective it holds about the process. Two key perspectives are the **psychometric approach** and the social exchange approach. The psychometric approach is the traditional view and focuses on the idea of fit. Organizations that hold this perspective view recruitment and selection processes like a puzzle where they are trying to find the right piece to fit either with the organization or with the job role itself (Newell, 2005). This is often referred to as person-job fit or person-organization fit. As a result, job roles are narrowly defined so that the right person or persons can be found. In this approach, selection tools are used in a rigid way to identify the person that best fills a gap. By contrast, the social exchange perspective views recruitment and selection as a reciprocal process between potential candidates and the organization (Newell, 2005). The social exchange approach places emphasis on the potential candidate also learning about the organization to establish whether they see themselves working there. This 'socialization' process does not end when a candidate is selected but continues as the new recruit begins to work in the organization.

The psychometric perspective, which assumes that jobs and their accompanying criteria can be precisely defined, is the best-established view of recruitment and selection. However, in a fast-changing world, the social exchange view may be more beneficial (Searle & Al-Sharif, 2018) because selecting candidates from a narrow definition may be counterproductive when jobs and organizations are needing to adapt and change quicker than ever.

Automation in recruitment

In recent years, technological advancements have driven forward new tools for the recruitment and selection process. It is now becoming increasingly common for organizations to utilize some form of artificial intelligence in the recruitment and/or selection process (Jacobs, 2019). This can include using technology to support the recruitment stage by automatically scanning data on social media sites (e.g., LinkedIn) to identify potential candidates who can then be reached through targeted advertisements or emails (Black & van Esch, 2020). Technology is also often now used in the selection process including scanning CVs automatically, identifying similarities between candidates and existing top performers in the organization, and using AI interviews (whereby the candidates are presented questions via a robot rather than a real person) (Black & van Esch, 2020).

As automation becomes more commonplace in recruitment and selection, there are significant limitations to be considered. The multinational recruitment organization Randstad (2017) conducted a survey looking at the impact of automated recruitment and selection procedures in the Asia-Pacific region. The study found that many job seekers feel negatively towards automated processes, with 49 per cent of those surveyed in Singapore, Hong Kong, and Malaysia finding the experience frustrating and 49 per cent feeling that the experience has become more impersonal because of automation. The rise of automation in recruitment and selection also raises further concerns of discrimination and bias. As noted earlier, automation will often seek to identify candidates that have similarities to top performers in the organization. While this may seem beneficial, this does not encourage diversity and may even perpetuate existing discrimination. Automated tools are only as unbiased as those that have created them and the data from which they are making decisions. For example, if a company has historically failed to promote women into senior positions (either through intentional or unintentional bias and/or discrimination), this pattern may be inadvertently factored into any automated selection processes.

7.3.2 Performance management

Performance management is a broad term encompassing all elements around the efforts to ensure the work that employees do and the way they do it contributes to organizational goals (Beardwell & Thompson, 2014: 426). Performance can refer to skills, characteristics, and results;

consideration needs to be given to which aspects are important to 'manage'. While an organization's approach to performance management may be set within the HR function, it is typically the line managers across the various departments of the organization that manage the performance of their direct reports.

Two important and different concepts are: performance appraisal and performance management.

Performance appraisal

Performance appraisal is typically a description of how an employee has been performing over a set time frame and is a very common approach to managing employee performance. Traditional performance appraisals are held on an annual basis with a focus on assessment rather than improvement. This often involves the manager or the employee collecting information on the performance of the employee in advance and detailing this in an appraisal form/report (Wildman et al., 2011). The manager and employee will typically then meet to discuss the performance, address any concerns, and consider development opportunities. The details of the performance appraisal are then recorded and used as guidance for the rest of the year and for other HR activities such as whether the employee should be promoted, receive a pay increase, require more training, or be dismissed.

Performance management

Performance management typically refers to a more continuous process of measuring and developing the performance of employees with the aim of improvement. While performance appraisals remain a tool frequently used by organizations, in recent years there has been more of a shift away from the traditional annual appraisal towards ongoing performance management (Pulakos & O'Leary, 2011; Kellaway, 2015). The aim behind this is also to build an environment of trust between management and employees via a regular ongoing dialogue rather than a once-a-year examination.

As discussed earlier in the chapter, critical perspectives in HRM consider the impact of power dynamics between management and employees in organizations. One such area of scrutiny is the approach to performance management, as it has the potential to be a method for controlling employees (McKenna et al., 2011). These concerns are arguably more present with approaches to managing performance, where ideals of 'good performance' are narrowly defined (e.g. requirements to meet certain output or sales targets). If the outcomes of annual performance appraisals are used to determine other decisions such as pay, promotion, and termination, this may also be seen as a more coercive approach to the control of employees.

7.3.3 Training

Training is often considered in the context of ensuring a new employee has the appropriate knowledge, skills, and abilities to perform their job. However, while training new employees is important, training and development should be an ongoing process for employees regardless of their tenure. This is partly important to ensure employees are capable in their jobs. However, there are a number of other reasons why organizations need to have appropriate training and development activities in place. Firstly, organizations need to adapt quickly in a VUCA world (as outlined in

Chapter 3), and having a multi-skilled workforce allows for greater flexibility in how the workforce can respond. Secondly, highly trained employees may require less close supervision, allowing the organization to operate in a leaner way, with less management time required and fewer layers of management. Finally, an organization that invests in training and development will often benefit from increased loyalty and satisfaction from employees and higher workforce retention.

Training, learning, and development are interrelated but distinct terms that mean different things. Training refers to an activity that happens externally to the individual—that is, an organization 'delivers training' to an employee with the intention that this has a direct impact on what happens internally to that person (i.e. how the person thinks and feels). In contrast, the term 'learning' refers to a process that happens internally within the individual—that is, an employee may learn from something that is shown to them during training, which subsequently changes their perceptions, beliefs, and behaviours. Finally, development also refers to an internal process within an individual, but one which is focused on the long term and comes about as a result of learning. Due to the nature of learning and development being internal to the individual, the organization cannot guarantee that either of these will happen. The organization can, however, ensure its training is as effective as possible to increase the chances of learning and development taking place. So, for example, an employee might be sent on a university training course to learn a new skill, but their learning and future development will depend on how well they paid attention, internalized the lessons, and retained the messages from the training.

In practice, an organization will typically follow a cycle similar to the one depicted in Figure 7.5 when facilitating learning and development. First, the organization needs to ensure it has

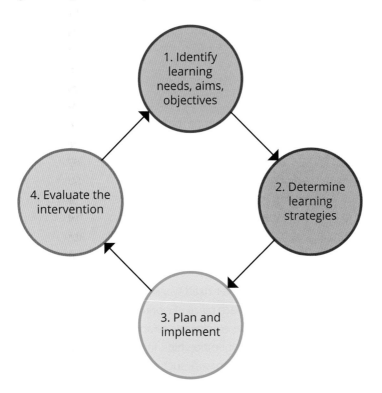

FIGURE 7.5 **Training and development needs analysis.** Credit: *Human Resource Management: A Contemporary Approach,* Beardwell, J. & Thompson, A, © 2017, Pearson Education UK

identified any gaps between the requirements (or future requirements) of a job and the abilities of those in the role. This is often done by conducting a learning needs analysis. The organization then aims to determine the best type of training and how to implement this. Training can be on or off the job. On the job training refers to activities that are conducted within the organization, such as observation, mentoring, rotating around different job roles, or online courses (known as e-learning). Off the job training is less common and refers to activities conducted outside of the organization, such as formal qualifications where lessons may take place at a college or university.

As noted in Figure 7.5, the final important aspect of training is to evaluate its effectiveness. Kirkpatrick (1996) suggests a Four-Level Model to evaluate training that has taken place:

- Level 1: Reaction—how has the learner responded to the training? Organizations can evaluate this using a survey immediately after the training.

- Level 2: Learning—what have participants learnt? Organizations can use short quizzes or tests to measure the change in participants' knowledge and skills.

- Level 3: Behaviour—has the participant's behaviour changed as a result of the training? Before/after workplace observations can be used to assess this level.

- Level 4: Results—has the training resulted in improved performance? This is often challenging for organizations to measure but might include higher productivity levels, employee morale, employee turnover (i.e. number of employees staying versus quitting), absenteeism, and customer satisfaction ratings.

Through the evaluation of training, organizations can understand whether changes need to be made to training processes and whether their training is producing a good return on the cost invested.

7.3.4 **Reward**

Pay and **rewards** are some of the most important aspects of the employment relationship and therefore an important activity for the HR function. For the individual employee, pay and rewards have significant implications for their quality of life. For the organization, pay and rewards are a significant cost. Because pay and rewards are a substantial cost, organizations want to ensure they are getting a good return on their investment. When pay and reward are discussed, we tend to think of the salary assigned to an employee. However, in practice, salary is often just one component of a larger collection of rewards available to employees. Total rewards can be segmented into two key areas: extrinsic rewards and intrinsic rewards.

Extrinsic rewards are tangible and typically split into pay and benefits. Pay is the salary an employee receives, whether this refers to their fixed wages or incentives such as commission, piece rate pay (when employees are paid for each piece of work/unit they produce), or bonuses. Benefits refer to tangible rewards outside of the employee's salary. These may include pension schemes and perks such as company cars or gym memberships. Intrinsic rewards refer to the intangible (i.e. non-physical) assets that can be gained from work such as status, work-life balance, and enjoyment.

Pay and reward may look quite different depending on the sector in which the organization is based. While most employees will receive a fixed wage, incentives related to performance may be more common within the private sector. Intrinsic rewards such as self-fulfilment are more commonly associated with the public and third sector, as there is a view that these employees are more likely to be passionate about the cause they are working for. Voluntary employees within the third sector will not receive a salary and will typically do this work for the intrinsic rewards they gain. However, voluntary employees may still receive benefits such as free food at events, company parties, and compensation for necessary travel.

When it comes to determining the level of pay an employee will receive, this can be calculated in a number of different ways. Most large organizations utilize 'pay scales' whereby individuals are assigned to a salary band. Such salary bands are typically benchmarked to the market rate (i.e. what other organizations in the same industry pay their employees in similar roles) and adjusted for inflation. As noted, pay can refer to both fixed pay but also incentives (also referred to as performance-related pay). Incentives are based on the *results* an employee creates at work rather than just their time at work. Different forms of incentives are common in different industries. For example, within the manufacturing industry, piece rate pay may be used based on how much an employee or team produces. Similarly, commission is common in some roles, where pay is linked to how many sales an employee or team make. The rationale behind incentives is that employees will work harder to attain higher pay (this is known as the incentive effect). It is also argued that lower-performing employees will leave the organization as they may be able to get higher fixed pay elsewhere, whereas high-performing employees will stay or join the organization due to the ability to achieve higher pay through incentives (this is known as the sorting effect) (Cadsby et al., 2007). However, it should be noted that there is limited evidence to show that performance-related pay increases employees' motivation, and, in some cases, it may have the opposite effect if performance targets are not clearly defined or realistic (Lewis, 1998; Lundstrom, 2012; Marsden & Richardson, 1994). We examine this issue further in Spotlight 7.2.

SPOTLIGHT 7.2 ORGANIZATIONAL CULTURE AND PERFORMANCE-RELATED PAY

There is limited evidence to suggest performance-related pay has resulted in improved motivation in UK organizations (CIPD, 2022a). So, are there other reasons why organizations may still implement the practice? One argument relates to the organizational culture. During the 1980s in the UK, the privatization of many state-owned companies took place, including what had previously been referred to as 'public utilities', including telecommunications, gas, electricity, water, and transport. As the transition from public to private status occurred, it was thought that the newly-privatized organizations required more commercial and profit-conscious cultures in order to attract and retain talent (CIPD, 2022a).

The introduction of performance-related pay was seen to align with this. For these organizations, the concern was less around whether performance-related pay improved individual motivation and more whether it helped to create a results and profit-focused culture. In the UK rail sector, there have been concerns that privatization has not led to the desired outcomes, as service quality for the passenger has declined. Avanti was recently criticized for paying shareholders £11.5m despite 'abysmal' service for rail users as the 'worst performing rail-operator' in the UK, cancelling one in three trains on its West Coast line (Ungoed-Thomas, 2022).

As mentioned in Section 7.2, the way in which organizations manage their people through their HRM practices has an impact on broader inequality issues in society. Reward is one area of HRM that organizations need to consider carefully in relation to this. In recent years, organizations have been increasingly held to account for disparities in pay between their lowest- and highest-paid employees and disparities between certain social groups, based on gender or ethnicity. In 2023, 'high pay day' was at 2 pm, Thursday, 5 January in the UK, representing the time and day when the median FTSE 100 CEO has already made as much money as the median UK worker will for the full year (High Pay Centre, 2023). The same issue is prevalent across many countries with the US, India, the UK, South Africa, and the Netherlands topping the list of countries with the most significant CEO-to-employee pay gaps (Statista, 2018). Organizations have a role and responsibility in the creation and perpetuation of this income inequality. The most senior executives in private companies often have complex pay plans (including a salary, bonuses, benefits, and shares in the company) making these hard to scrutinize. Legislation, such as the national minimum wage and CEO pay gap reporting, and initiatives such as the national living wage, are designed to try and curb these significant inequalities in relation to high and low pay. Pay can also further social inequalities in relation to the discrimination and disadvantage faced by certain groups. The following section on EDI refers to the gender pay gap in the UK, which organizations (with over 250 employees) are now required by law to disclose. Gender pay gaps are complex and caused by a variety of factors. However, organizations may contribute to these gaps through direct discrimination (setting different pay for male and female employees for the same work), allowing more favourable pay conditions to roles that are typically more male-dominated, or discriminating (directly or indirectly) during selection and promotion processes, resulting in women remaining in lower-paid positions.

7.3.5 Equality, diversity, and inclusion

Equality, Diversity, and Inclusion (EDI) (the 'E' is sometimes also 'equity') has become a focus for many workplaces. Indeed, it is a key issue for society, as we continue to confront the historical legacies of discrimination and oppression faced by many social groups, who in the past may have been victimized on the basis of personal characteristics such as race, gender, religion, and sexuality, among many others.

EDI issues are particularly important in managing the employment relationship, and they run through all HR activities, including recruitment and selection, training, reward, and employee voice. While these terms are often conflated, they do focus on different aspects. Equality is fundamentally concerned with the notion of 'fairness' and treating people the same. As such, organizations concerned with equality are likely to focus on reducing barriers to equal treatment of employees. Diversity, on the other hand, is focused on embracing and celebrating individual differences, rather than seeking to treat everyone as the same. Inclusion is an extension of diversity and equality; it refers to practices that ensure everyone feels included within a specific group or organization.

Despite increased societal awareness, many EDI issues still persist, which may result from **unconscious bias**. We can see examples of this when assumptions are made that the older, white male in a group of people must be 'the boss'. There is also evidence that companies adopting artificial intelligence algorithms to help the recruitment process and sift through job applicants' CVs have found unintended bias embedded in the technology: the CVs of earlier successful applicants that fed into the machine learning process correlated with male-biased characteristics (Dastin, 2018). These issues can be challenging for an HR manager to identify and manage.

The importance of EDI in organizations can be considered from two angles: the social justice perspective and the business case perspective. The case for social justice emphasizes that there is a moral obligation to treat employees with fairness and dignity. This is especially the case given that managers often have the power and influence—to some degree at least—to affect how employees think, feel, and behave within the organization. However, it is also a recognition that this power and influence extends outside the organization as well. Influencing how individual employees and the whole organization thinks, feels, and behaves—and recalling discussions on organizational culture in Chapter 6—means that managers have the potential to influence the values held by entire professions, communities, or broader society. We will explore these issues in Chapter 8.

However, not all organizations prioritize the social justice case, and therefore the business case for EDI is also important. This emphasizes the strategic or financial benefits organizations can gain to help them achieve their purpose. For example, embracing an EDI agenda may:

- allow the organization to recruit and select from a more diverse pool of candidates, thus enabling recruitment of the best employees from a wider selection of talented individuals;

- ensure diverse groups are engaged in problem solving, to leverage their differing perspectives and strengths, thus benefiting the organization with a wider range of rich and innovative ideas;

- help the organization to achieve public recognition and reputational advantages (of course, being mindful of potential ethical pitfalls that occur if an organization's 'acceptable' behaviours are inconsistent with its espoused beliefs and values); and

- ensure that diverse employees feel welcomed, accepted, and appreciated irrespective of, or even because of, their identity, who will in turn be more committed to the organization, work harder, and be less likely to leave.

EDI in organizations can be addressed from different angles, both outside the organization in the form of legislation, or inside the organization in the form of policies and practices. Different countries adopt different approaches to their equality legislation. For example, the European Union (EU) Charter of Fundamental Rights includes directives on discrimination and equal treatment. The UK's Equality Act 2010, prohibits discrimination based on a number of protected characteristics, including 'age, disability, gender reassignment, marriage and civil partnership, pregnancy and maternity, race, religion or belief, sex, and sexual orientation' (Equality and Human Rights Commission, 2010). The focus of this UK equality legislation is on ensuring certain social groups are not discriminated against—a type of legislation often referred to as the liberal approach to equal opportunities.

On the other hand, countries such as Norway and South Africa adopt what is often referred to as the 'radical approach' to equal opportunities and engage in positive discrimination. Positive discrimination in organizations refers to actively giving preference to certain social groups that have historically been under-represented and discriminated against. For example, in South Africa, there has been the introduction of 'Employment Equity Legislation' and the 'Black Economic Empowerment' initiative. These initiatives are largely focused on redressing the systemic discrimination and disadvantage faced by Black, Indian, Chinese, and multiracial groups during the Apartheid regime, which impacted the quality of life in South Africa from 1948 to the early 1990s.

South Africa's Employment Equity Legislation is designed to nudge organizations to have plans in place to improve the representation of women and non-white workers by requiring these plans to be made explicit and reported to the Department of Labour (Employment Equity Act, 1998).

Beyond legislation, organizations may also adopt various policies and practices in relation to EDI, such as training initiatives, and celebrating diversity through events and initiatives. In Spotlight 7.3, we uncover how Capgemini approaches EDI. However, while many companies

SPOTLIGHT 7.3 **CAPGEMINI**

Most organizations now recognize the importance of EDI. However, whether the organizational rhetoric actually matches the reality of their actions is another question. It is often argued (e.g. by the CIPD, 2022b) that a real commitment to EDI needs to come from the most senior levels of the organization. This is where Capgemini can be seen as a positive example. Capgemini is a technology services and consultancy organization that has won a number of EDI awards. While they have initiatives targeting a range of protected characteristics, one of their key focuses is ensuring the board of directors is involved. In the UK, the board sponsors the inclusion strategy, with each board member accountable for inclusion in their business area. Inclusion is also on the agenda for every board meeting, showing the organization's commitment to embedding inclusion throughout the organization. The list of protected characteristics, included in Capgemini's (2021) Code of Business Ethics, includes 'social, cultural, ethnic or national origins, religious or other beliefs, caste, gender identity/expression, marital status, pregnancy status, sexual orientation, disability, age, skin colour, race, parental status, political ideology, military/ veteran status, or trade-union activity'.

endeavour to engage more meaningfully with EDI policies and practices, the business case for EDI is not always simple to evidence. As discussed earlier in this section, the EDI business case relies on organizations recognizing and valuing the benefits, but these are not always tangible, may not be easy to identify, particularly in the short term, and may not always be prioritized in businesses during tough economic conditions.

This is one of the key reasons why Dickens (1999) argues that when it comes to tackling inequalities in the workplace, addressing the issue from multiple angles has the most effect, including legislation, democracy, and the business:

- Legal change: To fully address inequalities, legislation needs to be strengthened.
- Social democracy: Employee voice is vital for addressing inequalities. This includes the work of trade unions (discussed in greater detail in Section 7.3.6). Trade unions can ensure employees have information on their EDI rights, may bring EDI issues to the attention of management, and engage in political lobbying on EDI issues. The effectiveness of trade union EDI work is somewhat dependent on the strength of unions.
- Business case: The business case that the organization makes for investing in EDI initiatives cannot be neglected in effecting change.

Given the importance of EDI for the HR function, for managing people generally, for organizations more widely, and even for society, it is worth very briefly exploring just some of the specific EDI issues that exist in workplaces.

Gender

An ongoing focus of EDI relates to gender, and in particular equality for women. While the progress of women in the workforce over the past century might suggest that gender as a basis of discrimination has been largely addressed, there are enduring issues. The number of women in leadership posts is nowhere near the numbers of men in most industries, political circles, or international organizations. For example, the 2022 FTSE Women Leaders Review report stated that, as of January 2022, almost 40 per cent of UK FTSE 100 board positions were held by women, placing the UK second in international rankings for board representation. However, despite this level of board representation, only 1 in 3 leadership roles and around 25 per cent of all executive committee roles were held by women, with very few women in the CEO role (Department for Business, Energy & Industrial Strategy, 2022b). Those women who are in leadership posts are often held up as examples of what is possible, or even suggested as proof that the gender discrimination issues have been solved. However, statistics on the gender pay gap in the UK would suggest otherwise: in April 2021, the gender pay gap among full-time employees was 7.9 per cent (Office for National Statistics, 2021), with high-profile examples emerging in recent years, such as pay differences between presenters of different gender at the BBC (Waterson & Marsh, 2020). Gender discrimination also takes on added complexities when it intersects with gender identity, which we discuss in the next section.

LGBTQ+

Another EDI-related issue surrounds sexuality and gender identity. LGBTQ+ stands for lesbian, gay, bisexual, trans, queer (or questioning), and '+' for any other identity linked to gender or sexuality that may not fit within these categories. Workplace discrimination is an ongoing issue for individuals who identify as LGBTQ+; a report by Stonewall revealed that 18 per cent of respondents reported that they were 'discriminated against because of their sexual orientation and/or gender identity while trying to do a job' in Britain (Bachmann & Gooch, 2018). Discrimination in the workplace may occur either explicitly, through verbal harassment or exclusionary hiring practices, or implicitly, where such individuals feel unable to—or do not wish to—share their identity for fear of discrimination (Sears et al., 2021). Indeed, 18 per cent of LGBT people (the term used in the report) in Britain have experienced such negative behaviour from their colleagues in the workplace because of their identity (Bachmann & Gooch, 2018). In most (but not all) countries, discrimination against people in the workplace based on sexuality and gender identity is illegal. This has implications for an organization's HRM function, which needs to have policies in place to manage this. But beyond this, there is a welcome trend of organizations recognizing the value of diversity and working to ensure individuals feel accepted into the organization's community irrespective of such diversity.

Neurodiversity

Neurodiversity describes the differences in cognitive processes or brain functioning between individuals (CIPD, 2018: 8). In other words, it expresses 'the idea that people experience and interact with the world around them in many different ways; there is no one "right" way of thinking, learning, and behaving, and differences are not viewed as deficits' (Baumer & Frueh, 2021). While the word is broad in scope, it is now 'also being used to represent a fast-growing sub-category of organizational diversity and inclusion that seeks to embrace and maximise the talents of people who think differently' (CIPD, 2018, p.3). Part of these efforts include recognizing and valuing the benefits of the unique skills and different perspectives that people with specific diagnoses, such as ADHD, autism, dyslexia, dyspraxia, or dyscalculia can bring to an organization (Armstrong, 2015). Organizations are increasingly looking to improve neurodiversity in their workforce. In doing so, however, they may need to adjust management approaches, and the expectations and skill sets of managers to ensure such diversity is both celebrated and effectively integrated.

Race and ethnicity

Issues surrounding racial and ethnic discrimination are similarly challenging. For example, in the UK, while there has been progress in reducing employment and pay disparities among ethnic groups, there are still differences in employment rates that may be related to discrimination. The disparity is particularly noticeable in high-ranking positions: a report from the Commission on Race and Ethnic Disparities (2021) cited a 2020 study that discovered that only 4.7 per cent of the 'most powerful jobs' were held by ethnic minority individuals. The effects of discrimination are further amplified when an intersection occurs—that is, where an individual has more than one personal characteristic that can make them vulnerable to marginalization, so, for example, gender and race. The same report by the Commission noted that 'women in the Pakistani and Bangladeshi ethnic group . . . tend to have persistent disadvantages relative to white women in terms of both employment status and class position.' Consider the dilemma discussed by Lucy and Gita from Imperial Fine Foods in Running case 7.2.

RUNNING CASE 7.2 **WHAT'S IN A NAME?**

It is time for Marketing Manager, Gita Patel's weekly update meeting with CEO, Lucy. Gita joined the company first as a trainee and was Advertising and Communications Assistant for three years before the former CEO, Hugh, promoted her to Marketing Manager. Lucy and Gita get on well, although Gita was at first annoyed when Lucy returned from Africa and was given the title of Commercial Director, a role that hadn't existed until then. But over time she has come to respect Lucy's hard work and her personal values. Gita has had something on her mind for a while, and today she feels the need to initiate a difficult conversation with Lucy.

'Good weekend, Gita?', Lucy asks.

'It was great, thanks. I went to the Black Lives Matter event in the city centre. It was really interesting. They had great speakers. One theme was about the British Empire and how its success was tied up with the global slave trade.'

'That must have been fascinating.'

'It was. But, Lucy, it did prompt me to mention something that's been bothering me. Do you think it's still right for our company to be called Imperial? It sounds as though it's connected to the British Empire, and everyone is much more aware nowadays of the problems of colonialism.'

There is a long silence. Gita is starting to feel a little uncomfortable when Lucy speaks:

'Gita, you are so right about the name. If we were launching the business today, I wouldn't dream of naming my company Imperial. But it's now a well-established brand name. Everybody knows us.'

Gita's reply is immediate—Lucy sees that she has been thinking about this for a while. 'Have you ever wondered what it is like for someone like me—with my grandparents born in India—to work for a company with a name like Imperial? Do you ever wonder

if others like me feel the same? Don't we want to be recognized for the values we stand for today?'

Lucy considers this. Emotionally and morally, she totally understands Gita's point. Practically, the idea of such a significant change makes her anxious. Lucy tries to work out the priorities in her head. 'Would it really be right to change it now, given how difficult market conditions are? What if we lose our brand recognition and our customer base? I'm not sure a name change should be at the top of our list of priorities right now.'

'Lucy, with your approval, I'd like to start looking into the pros and cons for changing the brand. The world is changing, and we need to be open to the possibility. I think with the right communication to all of our stakeholders, we can continue to reassure them that we're a company they can trust now and in the future.'

As Gita leaves with an agreement to report back, Lucy reaches for the phone. She would like to update Su-Li on the conversation she has just had—as HR manager she may have a view on the extent to which this is a concern for other staff. But beyond that, she thinks she and Su-Li should be speaking about EDI more broadly and considering ways in which it is relevant to Imperial.

Questions for reflection

1. Do you think that a company's name reflects its values? Explain your answer.

2. Make a list of the positive and negative implications of not changing the company name, as well as of changing the company name. Which do you favour?

3. Do you think this is an HR issue? Do you think Su-Li will see this as an HR issue? Why? Why not?

7.3.6 **Employee voice**

As we mentioned in Section 7.3.5, employee voice is an important aspect of addressing equality and diversity issues. However, employee voice is also significant more broadly as an HRM activity (Dundon et al., 2004). There are a number of, sometimes conflicting, definitions for employee voice. Broadly speaking, employee voice refers to practices intended to give employees a say in the running of the organization. There are two main purposes of voice described in management literature, which are very similar to the purposes of equality and diversity. Firstly, the social justice perspective argues that voice is a fundamental human right and a means of employee self-determination. Secondly, the business case perspective argues that employee voice is a tool for increasing employee involvement, whereby employees share suggestions and ideas 'upwards' to improve the functioning of the organization (CIPD, 2022c). These views closely align with the prior discussion of the unitarist, pluralist, and radical perspectives of the employment relationship. The view that voice is a fundamental right (and a means of self-determination) is more in line with the pluralist and radical perspectives that see there being natural conflict in organizations between the employer and employee. On the other hand, the business case for employee voice aligns more with the unitarist perspective in that employer and employee are working towards the same interests, as such any voice mechanisms in place would benefit the organization.

In practice, organizations can conduct 'employee voice' activities in a direct or indirect way. Direct employee voice is sometimes called employee involvement, and refers to voice initiatives that happen inside of the organization. Indirect employee voice refers to initiatives that happen outside of the organization. Direct forms of voice are often initiated by management and are designed to provide workers with a space to express their views, interests, and complaints. As these forms of voice are initiated by management they can vary significantly in different organizations. Some forms of direct voice may allow employees an opportunity to have influence in certain aspects of the organization, whereas other forms of voice may only allow employees to express their views and opinions. Examples of direct employee voice include suggestion schemes, self-managed groups, complaints to line managers, and formal grievance procedures.

Indirect forms of voice are independent of the organization. Trade unions are one of the most common forms of indirect employee voice. Trade unions are organizations that comprise voluntary members of specific groups of workers, whether these be professional, sectorial, or regional. The trade union is responsible for organizing and representing employee views and interests. Trade unions will often negotiate with organizations over various working conditions, pay being one of the most commonly negotiated. This process of consultation and negotiation is referred to as collective bargaining. If a satisfactory agreement is not reached through negotiation, members of the trade union may vote for industrial action where they go on strike or only adhere to the minimum levels of effort required by their contract (called action short of strike). Industrial action is designed to be disruptive in order to pressure organizations to meet the interests of trade union members.

In recent years, industrial action has been seen around the world in response to various economic and social issues. The UK saw industrial action across several different sectors including health care, education, postal services, and railways in 2022 and 2023. While sectors do vary, a key factor in this industrial action has been the fact that salaries are not keeping up with the rising cost of living in the UK. Industrial action took place in France in 2023, due to the government's decision to increase the minimum retirement age. In 2022, nurses and midwives in Australia went on strike over pay and working conditions. Sri Lankan workers across health care, education, and railway sectors also engaged in industrial action over the cost of living and tax increases in 2023.

There are different approaches organizations can take regarding indirect voice and trade unions. Many organizations have a formal relationship with associated unions, referred to as trade union recognition. Having a formal recognition agreement does not mean that the organization automatically has a good relationship with that union, but refusal to recognize a union can lead to employee hostility, so a voluntary approach to recognition is often encouraged. Nevertheless, some organizations refuse to recognize unions. Amazon is a key example of an organization that openly opposes the unionization of its workforce. Amazon has stated that this is because the organization values having direct dialogue and relationship with its employees (i.e. direct forms of employee voice), rather than the indirect voice approach of trade unions (Lee, 2022). However, Amazon is also criticized for how it manages pay and working conditions, so the extent to which the organization meaningfully engages with direct forms of employee voice might be questioned. The organization's stance against unions might more realistically demonstrate a concern that increased collective power of employees might push up salaries, improve working conditions, and ultimately increase costs for the organization (Palmer, 2022).

In this section, we have covered key HRM activities that are conducted in organizations. While these may seem like distinct activities, in practice, the idea is that they should align with the aim of improving organizational performance. In Section 7.4, we will explore how this may be achieved.

7.4 HR strategy and organizational performance

So far, we have considered what HRM is, who conducts it, and how it is enacted in organizations through a range of different activities. However, the question remains as to why we actually need HRM, and how it can contribute to improved organizational performance.

Many organizations claim to understand the importance of HRM and regularly use the phrase 'people are our most important asset'. But what exactly do organizations mean by this and is it really the case? Part of this claim comes down to the inimitability of HR systems. This is what can give HR a degree of power in terms of being able to contribute towards organizational performance. Essentially, what inimitability means is that it is very difficult for other organizations to imitate HR practices that are in place and that work well. For people standing outside a successful organization, it can be very challenging to have a clear understanding of what it is that makes an organization's HR system work so well. Therefore, if organizations get it right, this can lead to the potential for sustained competitive advantage. In comparison, the technology that organizations have in place, or even arguably their marketing strategy (because it is so public), can be much easier to copy. To fully understand an HRM system, competitors would need to understand the culture in the organization, the power dynamics in place, and how employees feel about their organization. All of this makes HRM systems challenging to imitate and a potential source of competitive advantage.

7.4.1 High-commitment models of HRM

So, how do organizations get their HR systems 'right'? Over the past three decades, there has been extensive research exploring how HRM activities and the HR function influence wider business strategy and performance. There have been a number of frameworks and theories put forward in the academic literature, with one of the most well-known approaches being 'high-commitment models of HRM'. High-commitment models of HRM state that an organization's primary goals should be HR goals and that an organization's performance will improve if it achieves these HR goals. High-commitment HRM models are also largely underpinned by the idea that if employees are treated poorly, they are unlikely to go beyond the bare minimum of their contracts, whereas if the organization fosters a sense of loyalty and commitment from employees this will result in positive outcomes. The high-commitment model of HRM is closely aligned with the soft HRM approach discussed in Section 7.2.1. This high-commitment model of HRM is considered to be 'best practice'; in other words, it is seen as the best way to do HRM in order to see positive organizational outcomes.

So, what does this look like in practice? The influential work of Pfeffer (1998) is closely aligned with the high-commitment model. Pfeffer listed a series of 'best practice' HR practices for organizations to follow (this type of list is also referred to in the academic literature as 'high-performance work practices'). An important factor here is that these practices should be introduced as an integrated package, with practices aligning with each other, rather than as stand-alone initiatives (this is sometimes referred to as internal fit).

The list put forward by Pfeffer (1998) is:

- employment security;
- the selective hiring of new personnel;
- decentralized decision-making;
- high compensation contingent on organizational performance;
- extensive training;
- minimal status distinctions and barriers; and
- extensive sharing of financial and performance information throughout the organization.

However, we should be cautious about the idea that there is one best way to conduct HRM or that there are seven practices that will result in a more effective organization. If this were really the case, then all organizations would take a high-commitment approach to HRM or simply implement the list of high-performance work practices and automatically see improved organizational outcomes. In practice, it is a lot more complex than this 'best practice' view of HRM.

7.4.2 Situational contingency models of HRM

One of the key criticisms of the 'best practice' approaches is that they fail to take into account the context of the organization. Situational contingency models, or the 'best-fit' approach, address this weakness, arguing that HRM strategy should fit with the broader strategy of the organization (sometimes referred to as external fit). Schuler and Jackson (1987) put forward one of the best-known situational contingency models. They argue in the context of for-profit organizations, that organizations will ultimately need to adopt one of three main business strategies: either act in their market as a cost reducer, a quality enhancer, or an innovator. The idea behind the Schuler and Jackson model is that organizations will require different HRM practices and approaches, depending on the business strategy they are following. For example, a high-commitment style of HRM might be well-suited to an organization focused on quality or innovation. In contrast, organizations operating with a cost-reducer strategy will likely take a hard HRM approach and focus on reducing labour costs where possible (e.g. at the extreme, through zero-hour contracts and paying employees a minimum wage).

While the approach of considering the overall business strategy and the wider context seems to make a lot of sense, there has been extensive criticism of the situational contingency model (Ayman et al., 1995). The situational contingency model relies on the organization knowing exactly what its business strategy is and being able to clearly align business strategy with HR strategy. However, the challenge for many organizations is that their business strategies are not clearly articulated. Many organizations operate on a short-term basis and simply do not have a long-term business strategy for the HR strategy to align with. It can also often be challenging for organizations to understand the fit between HR strategy and wider business strategy until it has been tested in practice.

7.5 Conclusion

This chapter has explored the key debates, activities, and challenges in conducting HRM in organizations. It has emphasized that, although there are numerous ways in which HRM can be understood, the primary concern is how to manage people in the workplace. Activities such as recruitment and selection, performance management, training, EDI, and employee voice can all be approached in different ways and this may be dependent on factors such as organization size, industry, sector, and strategy. HR is an organizational function that often struggles to receive the same level of legitimacy and status as other organizational functions. This inevitably poses challenges for HR functions to enact the HRM strategies contributing to organizational performance that we discussed in Section 7.4. In many organizations, it remains the case that there is no HR person on the board of directors, meaning nobody at the most senior level is there to champion the HR strategy that should be adopted. As such, the ability of HRM to contribute to overall organizational performance may be limited to the extent to which the organization sees the HR function as a valued contributor in strategic decision-making.

CHAPTER SUMMARY

○ HRM comprises all the activities associated with managing employment relationships in an organization.

○ 'Hard HRM' emphasizes humans as resources akin to any other resource—that is, a cost of doing business that needs to be managed. 'Soft HRM' emphasizes the human as different to other resources—that is, people who should be developed and treated well.

○ Some of the key functions of HRM include undertaking recruitment and selection, developing and delivering training and performance management, determining rewards, and addressing EDI and employee voice.

○ Best practice approaches to HRM assume there is one best way of conducting HRM. The high-commitment model is a key example of this approach. The high-commitment model sees an organization's primary goals as HR goals and argues that an organization's performance will improve if it achieves these HR goals.

○ Best-fit approaches to HRM assume that context is important in determining how to conduct HRM. The situational contingency model is a key example of this approach and argues that HR strategy should fit with the broader strategy of the organization, which may differ depending on the sector and many different factors.

CLOSING CASE REFLECTION

P&O Ferries

It could be argued that P&O Ferries adopted a 'Hard HRM' approach to their staff. Employees were treated as any other cost and replaced with what managers believed was a better and cheaper alternative (i.e. agency staff). Little consideration appeared to have been shown for individual employees and their circumstances or future prospects. Managers of P&O Ferries appeared to eschew the high-commitment models of HRM which assume that the most important focus should be on employees as the conduit to organizational performance. However, if, as stated by P&O, the staff costs were prohibitive, the company might argue that they had no alternative option available. The case raised important questions about the laws surrounding HRM, as well as the ethics of extreme practices.

REVIEW QUESTIONS

1. Why might some organizations choose to adopt a hard HRM approach?

2. In what ways can performance-related pay produce positive outcomes for organizations? Why might it produce negative outcomes?

3. How would you use the business case for diversity to convince the leaders of an organization to improve its EDI practices?

4. Why does employee voice matter? Compare the advantages of direct forms of employee voice with indirect forms. Which is likely to be more successful in encouraging employee involvement?

5. Evaluate two models that explain the link between HR strategy and organizational performance (see Section 7.4). What are the strengths and limitations of each model?

EXPLORE MORE

○ WATCH this TEDx Talk by Mary Schaefer, which aligns with the points made in this chapter about soft HRM: 'Putting the Human Back into Human Resources'. Search for the title on YouTube.

)) LISTEN to this podcast produced by the CIPD, the professional body of HR: 'What Value Does HR Bring to Today's Organizations?' Search for the title on the CIPD website.

═ READ about the Harvard Implicit Association Test (IAT), which is a useful resource for identifying your own unconscious biases. Through becoming aware of your own unconscious biases, consideration can be given to how these may affect your interactions with others (both in a work context and more broadly). Google the test name to find it.

═ READ J. Beardwell and A. Thompson (2014). *Human Resource Management: A Contemporary Approach* (Madison, Pearson Education UK), which provides a more comprehensive discussion around some of the key aspects mentioned in this chapter.

═ READ the Chartered Institute of Personnel and Development website to understand more about the role of HR in organizations. Google 'CIPD' to find it.

CHAPTER EIGHT
Designing Work Well

Ishbel McWha-Hermann and Emma Macdonald

OPENING CASE STUDY **THE FOUR-DAY WORKING WEEK EXPERIMENT**

Game developer Hutch confirmed in December 2022 that it would permanently operate a four-day working week for its employees (Hutch, 2022) after taking part in a six-month experiment. The five-day working week, of 35–48 hours per week, has been the default model for full-time employment for over a century. But in a fast-changing world and with a greater understanding of the negative impacts of poor physical and mental health on employee well-being, many are questioning the value of the five-day working week.

In 2022, a group of 33 UK organizations with a combined employee pool of almost 1,000 individuals took part in an experiment to trial a transition to a four-day working week, supported by the not-for-profit organization, 4 Day Week Global Foundation (4dayweek.com), and the Wellbeing Research Centre at the University of Oxford. The pilot study attracted interested observers from across the globe, with the outcomes of the trial reported in media outlets across the world. Six months later, many participating organizations consider the trial to have been a success and intend to continue with the four-day model going forward (Simpson, 2022).

One such organization is games developer, Hutch, which trialled the new way of working in all three of its offices. Many organizations would hesitate to offer their employees reduced hours of work

for the same pay, with concerns particularly centred on productivity impacts. However, in a blog article following the trial, Hutch (2022) reported that it had measured organizational productivity throughout the six-month trial and found that it remained stable. Hutch considered employee outcomes to be as important as those for the organization. As proud winners of gamesindustry.biz 'Best Place to Work' award for three years in a row, Hutch was happy to observe improvements in employee metrics, including reduced turnover of staff (i.e. better retention of existing staff) and higher job offer acceptance rates (i.e. greater success in attracting new staff). CEO Shaun Rutland reported a change in how tasks were evaluated:

> The trial taught us a great deal about making the most of the time we have . . . A key learning from the trial is that productivity should not be valued by time spent on tasks, instead we needed to ensure that we were focused on outputs. The way we work and how we spend our time day to day has improved as a result, helped by our Hutchies feeling refreshed after a three-day weekend. There are challenges we will still need to resolve and better ways of working to be tested, but we're excited to put this into practice in the new year.
> *(Hutch, 2022)*

8.1 **Introduction**

In 2022, media articles reported on 'the great resignation', as unprecedented numbers of people in developed countries (see: **developed country**) quit their jobs and employers struggled to fill vacancies (Buckingham, 2022; WEF, 2022). Organizations started to consider the impact of these vacancies on achieving organizational objectives, and what they could do to retain staff. Forward-thinking employers reflected on how they could design work well, to attract and keep potential employees. But what do we mean when we talk about 'work'? According to the United Nations, an individual is defined as being involved in *work* if they are engaged in economic activities (UN, 2008, in International Labour Organisation (ILO), 2008) and according to the ILO, an individual is a *worker* if they are employed by an organization to carry out work, whether it is for a private, public, or third sector organization (ILO, 2008). There is an important distinction between *work* and *jobs*, whereby **work** is a broader concept than a **job**. Jobs include the specific **tasks** and duties an individual engages in to earn a living, while work extends this such that any type of physical or mental activity could be considered work. In this chapter, we want to emphasize the importance of a holistic approach to work, including, for example, non-traditional work such as informal work and the gig economy; hence, we focus on designing work and not designing jobs.

At the individual level, the way work is structured is important for how employees feel and perform at work. Organizations increasingly acknowledge this aspect, with examples such as Unilever's Compass for Sustainable Growth recognizing that 'people with purpose thrive' (Unilever, 2022a). At an organizational level, it is important to understand how to design work so that it supports organizational success. This means there are multiple levels that managers need to consider when structuring work; they need to design work that creates a sense of purpose for individuals (Buckingham, 2022), but which takes account of how teams fit together, how jobs and tasks are shared across organizational structures, and how these contribute to organizational performance. However, it is also important to consider not only the outcomes for individuals and organizations of designing work well, but for society more broadly. The benefits of good quality work that enables individuals to thrive will extend to their families and communities, and may even contribute to societal issues such as **poverty**, inequality, and climate change. Recognizing the importance of good quality work for individuals, organizations, and societies, the ILO provides a clear and explicit focus for decent work—a topic we will return to in Section 8.4—and goal number 8 of the UN Sustainable Development Goals aims to 'promote sustained, inclusive and sustainable economic growth, full and productive employment, and decent work for all'. Good quality employment that is secure and offers protection to employees, as well as decent and fair working conditions, forms the foundation for addressing global grand challenges such as poverty, inequality, and climate change.

That said, the current state of work is worrying. Even prior to the disruption caused by the Covid-19 pandemic, the ILO's statistics on the state of the global workforce painted a bleak picture. In 2019, it was estimated that 3.3 billion people employed globally had inadequate economic security, material well-being, and equality of opportunity. Though these people were in formal employment, the *quality* of the work offered by their employer was low. Additionally, 61 per cent of the global workforce was engaged in the **informal sector** (sometimes called insecure or precarious work) which is characterized by no formal employment contract and a lack of protection for workers. A report by the Infrastructure and Cities for Economic Development facility identified that informal working is very common and leaves employees vulnerable to low wages, long hours, and poor safety conditions (ICED, 2018).

We will start this chapter by considering the main issues facing managers and workplaces today, before shifting our focus later in the chapter to what it means to design work, and how to do it.

8.2 Issues facing the contemporary workplace

Contemporary workplaces must simultaneously navigate a number of internal and external pressures and other issues, some of which they have control over, but many over which they have limited or no control. It is important to think about these issues and to consider how they might impact the experiences that people have of work, and how organizations might need to shape their workplace in response. The World Economic Forum (WEF, 2022) identifies five challenges for work in the post-pandemic environment:

1. volatility in wages and the cost of living;
2. divergence in the demand for flexible working;
3. a 'silent pandemic' in well-being;
4. an erosion of equality, diversity, and inclusion (EDI) gains; and
5. the need for a reskilling revolution to prepare for technological change and the green transition.

In response to these challenges, the WEF provides a New Vision for Good Work as depicted in Figure 8.1, which comprises five specific objectives.

In the next few sections, we explore wide-ranging issues facing society which have relevance for management. These include managing people who are not necessarily employees, the challenge of precarious work, and the shift to online and hybrid working. Related to these issues is a growing trend for managers to take responsibility for the well-being of both directly employed people and people employed across the organization's supply network. We start by considering how self-employment has been changing the dynamic between employee and employer.

8.2.1 Self-employment

The composition of employer–employee relationships has changed over time so that more people are relying on informal self-employment or temporary employment, meaning they are working outside the standard organizational structures but are still an important focus for managers because their inclusion in teams has important implications for shaping organizational culture. For instance, many people in **creative industries**—such as journalists, copywriters, and designer—work in the 'gig' economy, where they are paid on a piecemeal (per unit output

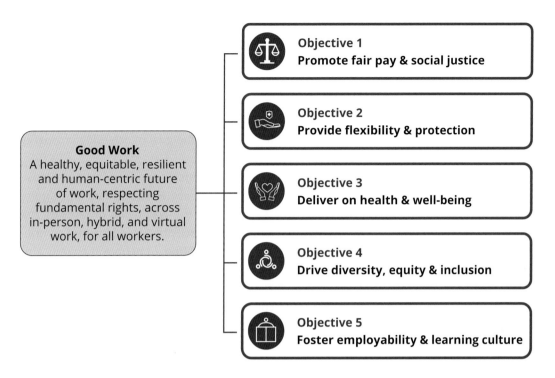

FIGURE 8.1   **WEF's New Vision for Good Work.** Credit: World Economic Forum

basis) or on a temporary basis (ILO, 2022). We explored this issue briefly in Section 3.4.4's discussion of technological disruption and the future of work, especially in relation to issues for the workers. However, it also has specific implications for designing work generally, and designing work well in particular. This is because these approaches to work remove the worker from the formal 'employee' role or organizational structure. This can impact the ongoing development of the worker (through training and developing professional relationships in the workplace) and lead to stand-alone or disjointed projects that struggle to fit within or contribute to the organization's overall purpose.

8.2.2 **In-work poverty**

It is not only self-employment and the gig economy that can contribute to an individual being in precarious work. **In-work poverty** occurs when a person has a job but does not earn enough to meet the cost of living (CIPD, 2022). Research by the Joseph Rowntree Foundation (2023) has found that in the UK, 7.9 million working-age adults are living in poverty, and two-thirds (68 per cent) of those live in a household where at least one adult is in work. Low-wage workers are often forced to take two jobs in order to make ends meet for themselves (and their families). The tiredness and exhaustion which results can lead to motivation and performance issues at work, as well as negatively impacting well-being more generally (Searle & McWha-Hermann, 2021). In-work poverty is therefore not only an individual issue but also one in which organizations play a key role through thinking about decent working conditions (see also Spotlight 8.2 on living wages later in the chapter). While this has been an issue for a long time, since the pandemic there have been noticeable increases in individuals in work experiencing poverty, even in comparatively wealthy countries like the UK. A report by the UN found that global monthly wages had fallen in real terms by almost one percentage point in 2022, as a result of the rising costs of essential goods and services, impacting poorer families especially hard. This marks the first instance of negative growth this century (UN News, 2022a). The ILO's Director-General warned that the consequences of pushing tens of millions of workers into poverty could 'fuel . . . social unrest across the world and undermine the goal of achieving prosperity and peace for all' (UN News, 2022a).

It is essential to address such underlying structural deficiencies and inequalities because without secure employment and fair wages, people cannot live well. This has flow-on impacts on physical and mental health, as well as impacting the well-being of families, the ability of parents to provide for their children, and their capacity to participate and contribute to their communities. Societies that experience large numbers of people in poverty also tend to experience higher levels of crime and social disruption. The UN reported that the least developed countries that were struggling with weak economic growth saw fewer job opportunities for young people, increases in child labour, and increases in child marriage (UN News, 2022b).

8.2.3 **Hybrid and remote working**

The shift to online work and the work-from-home culture—either temporarily, semi-permanently, part-time, or for some organizations and job roles, permanently—was a growing trend that accelerated rapidly during the Covid-19 pandemic. We identified this issue explicitly in the introduction to this section, when discussing the challenges to organizations identified by the WEF. While a Boston Consulting Group survey of employees reported that the future of work is likely to be hybrid, with individuals working through a blend of onsite and remote locations, the blurring of work–life boundaries and lack of social connectivity will be ongoing challenges (Dahik et al., 2020). Some organizations have reported difficulty in encouraging employees back into full-time, office-based work (Kislik, 2021). Others who have instituted permanent remote-working conditions have seen employees struggling with isolation and poor mental health (Kislik, 2021). Moreover, this shift has increasingly put the onus on employees to maintain their own working conditions, which has seen many people using not-fit-for-purpose home spaces, such as kitchens and living rooms, as workplaces.

Hybrid working can also worsen inequalities between those in differing socio-economic circumstances: it may be easier to work remotely if you have a dedicated office in your home. There are concerns in particular for the loss of a sense of community, connection, and belonging that employees derive from work, which is not easily replicated in remote-working conditions. It is particularly challenging at a time when many employees may look to their jobs as a source of social structure and relief from pressures at home, or anxiety about the future. Strategies to address this loss include online meeting and collaboration tools, virtual communities, providing incentives (or actually paying) for exercise equipment or gym memberships, or providing training in mindfulness and meditation. However, it is worth questioning the value of these later approaches. We will now consider these issues with a critical thinking lens to understand their complexity.

8.2.4 **Employee well-being**

While the last century saw an increasing focus on the physical health and safety of employees in the workplace, this century has seen an additional focus on mental health and well-being (Nielsen et al., 2017; Guest, 2017). This shift has significant implications for designing work well because it requires consideration of well-being as a key aspect of how people experience work, and something which organizations have a responsibility to consider. It is an important shift because it reflects a recognition that people are not machines that can be optimized, but rather complex emotional and creative beings that need to be supported in order to do their best work. It may also seem obvious that work that is boring, or where there is too much to do within the time allocated, will lead to workers feeling stressed, lacking motivation, or generally unhappy. When these experiences continue for sustained periods of time, they can have negative implications for employee well-being and performance, because bored employees lack engagement in their work, and stressed employees tend to make more mistakes (Schaufeli & Salanova, 2014). However, while this may seem obvious, responsibility for employee well-being is not universally accepted by all employers.

Discussions regarding employee well-being often focus on either the business case or the social case (as we saw in Chapter 7 in relation to EDI). The business case demonstrates how well-being initiatives in organizations lead to increased employee performance and in turn enhanced organizational outcomes (Bryson et al., 2017), often measured via profit, growth, or other types of organization-level outputs (for a recent review, see Peccei & Van De Voorde, 2019). The social case argues that it is the employer's duty of care for their employees to consider and enhance their well-being, and that it is in the interests of society overall. From this perspective, organizations therefore have a responsibility to address workplace experiences that have negative impacts on employee well-being.

Irrespective of business or social case, there is much debate about exactly how to improve employee well-being. Some initiatives focus on helping employees find balance between their work and non-work lives, offering opportunities to work flexibly, or rethinking the nature of work entirely, as demonstrated by the 4-Day Week movement profiled in the opening case study. At a more granular level, though, while an increased concern for well-being and mental health is a welcome trend, it raises many questions about what managers actually *do*. If we think back to Chapter 1 when we discussed this topic, we did not use the descriptions 'counsellors', 'support services', 'coaches', or 'therapists' to describe the roles and functions of managers. Yet managers are reporting that they are expected to fulfil such roles, as their employees struggle with the disruption and difficulties caused by the mental health and well-being issues, all the while feeling that they themselves or their dependants are suffering as well.

However, not all commentators are convinced by these seemingly supportive strategies. In their book, *The Wellness Syndrome*, Cederström and Spicer (2015) explore what they see as a darker side of this shift. They argue that an ever-present pressure to improve our wellness is in fact causing the reverse, as people feel judged for their choices and health in comparison to their colleagues. Even more insidious, they suggest, is that this has come at a time when workloads are increasing, wages are stagnating or decreasing, contracts and jobs are increasingly precarious, and individuals are facing personal and family pressures. As such, Cederström and

8

Spicer ask whether initiatives commonly pursued to support well-being and mental health—such as step counters, smart watches, and mindfulness—are simply outsourcing a problem that management themselves have created or contributed to through their decisions around increased workloads, decreased resources, pressure-filled work environments, and unrealistic expectations.

8.2.5 Supply chain impacts

Managers are increasingly focused not just on their own directly employed workforce employees, but on those within their supply chains also. Fair and ethical workplace practices are crucial for employee well-being and are linked with organizational effectiveness (as discussed in the previous section). The importance of fair and ethical practices across the whole supply chain therefore has upstream implications for organization effectiveness (in addition to the reputational implications). Furthermore, supply chains are a way for organizations to influence global challenges like poverty and inequality, particularly when these workers are in less developed countries. While we may assume that governments should be the key focal point for addressing poverty and inequality, organizations are also key actors in this space, given the decisions they make, which can affect the livelihoods of many of the world's most vulnerable workers. Unilever (2022b) estimates that in 2021 their supply chain included 54,000 suppliers in over 160 countries, these include multinational companies, start-ups, and small local producers. Unilever promotes a strong commitment to human rights across their supply chain, alongside a commitment to reducing environmental impact.

The WEF (2022) estimates that over 615 million people work in global supply chains, where working conditions often attract less scrutiny. In the past, companies may have viewed the working conditions of employees of their suppliers as outside their remit of concern. However, it is increasingly recognized that organizations cannot ignore their responsibility to understand the impacts of their behaviours on the other organizations with which they work. So, for example, when a company puts pressure on producer prices and delivery times, it needs to consider how this may negatively impact the employee health and well-being of those employed within that supply chain. Recent examples of these issues include the exposure of working conditions of workers in the fashion industry. An estimated 170 million children are engaged in child labour (UNICEF/ILO, 2015), which a report by UNICEF and *The Guardian* defined as 'work for which the child is either too young . . . or work which, because of its detrimental nature or conditions, is altogether considered unacceptable for children and is prohibited' (Moulds, 2015). Child labour is particularly problematic in the fast fashion industry because of the complexity of supply chains that make it hard for companies to control every stage of production, and therefore difficult for big brands and their customers to find out that it is occurring (Moulds, 2015). We will explore these issues again in Chapter 12, Operations and Supply Chain Management.

We have covered here a number of specific issues facing managers who are looking to design work well. We now turn to some more concrete elements of this topic, including organizational structure and work design. Before we do so, let's join Imperial and Lucy as they turn their mind to all the workers in their supply chain in Running case 8.1.

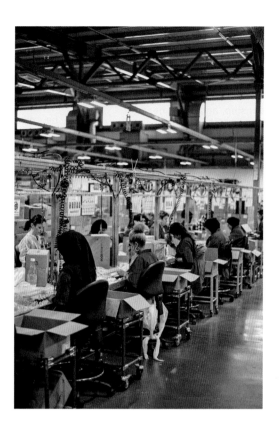

RUNNING CASE 8.1 **IMPERIAL'S TEA SUPPLY CHAIN**

While the plant-based food strategy is taking shape, Lucy is keen to turn her attention to the other side of Imperial's business—tea import and distribution. It was started by her great-grandfather and has been part of the company for over 80 years, 'since the days of Empire', as her grandfather used to proudly say—an expression Lucy recalls with some embarrassment.

Almost all of Imperial's tea comes from Kenya and the Indian state of Assam. Imperial's purchasing agents in each country have enjoyed comfortable relationships with the company for decades; the Kenya agent Mr Turner, for example, is an elderly British gentleman who was appointed by Lucy's grandfather decades ago and has been resident in Kenya ever since. Though Lucy's grandfather travelled to both countries often, Hugh was a much more occasional visitor, choosing to rely on the agents that his father had appointed. With all the

turmoil of the UK's Brexit, the global pandemic, and the handover of Managing Director responsibilities, in fact, it has been seven years since his last trip.

Conscious of the growing public appetite for premium teas, but just as conscious of Imperial's commitment to the UN's Sustainable Development Goals (SDGs), Lucy has decided it's time to pay a visit to the agents and their tea growers. She will go to Kenya first. When news spreads in the factory, there is a surprising level of interest in her trip: some younger staff members tell Lucy they hope Imperial's tea isn't produced by the workers featured in recent media reports about poor conditions on tea plantations supplying UK supermarkets. Lucy has heard about these reports from two of her cousins who are also shareholders; they were very concerned about what they'd seen on the news and relieved that Lucy is planning to visit their operations in Kenya.

(Continued)

Though Lucy is excited about the trip, making the arrangements has slightly unsettled her. In reply to her initial email, Imperial's Kenya agent, Mr Turner, had expressed enthusiasm about the chance to meet Lucy, talk about the continuation of their business relationship, and show her around the capital city, Nairobi. When she called to tell him that, rather than sightseeing, she intended to visit every tea plantation that supplies Imperial, she had sensed Mr Turner had become much more guarded. It had taken much longer than she had expected for him to send her a visit itinerary. Now the day for travel is here, and she boards the plane with a sense of excitement. It has been a while since she did in-country visits in her previous NGO role, and she is keen to get back to Kenya.

Questions for reflection

1. Why does a company's Managing Director need to be concerned about working conditions among its suppliers thousands of kilometres away?

2. If you were helping Lucy to prepare for her trip, what would you research, and why?

3. If Lucy had also asked your advice on whether she should go in person to Kenya or just have a video call with Mr Turner, what would you have said?

8.3 Organizational structure and work design

Structuring job tasks and designing work in a way that is fair and engaging enables employees to thrive and flourish. Work that is designed well encourages motivated and satisfied employees who are committed to their organization (Parker et al., 2017). This in turn means employees are more likely to engage in extra-role behaviours at work—that is, going above and beyond what is in their job description, helping others, and being more engaged in the success of the organization (Demerouti et al., 2015). In this section, we focus on two key aspects of designing work well. First, we offer an introduction to organizational structure and some of the ways this can vary. We then introduce the concept of work design and chart the academic theory around this concept, offering some ways to think about how to design work well. However, before we start, it is important for us to reflect on the scope of the existing research on workplaces and work design, in Spotlight 8.1.

8.3.1 Organizational structure

When we think of organizational structure, we commonly talk about how much hierarchy there is within a given organization, and how individual jobs relate to one another. Figure 8.2 depicts three common structures: tall, flat, and matrix. Historically, organizational structure was rigid, hierarchical, and vertically integrated (see: **vertically integrated organization**), with an emphasis on layers of hierarchy, wherein each lower level reports up to the next layer. These are often known as tall structures. Hierarchical structures are still common, particularly in large organizations where there is a clear chain of command and a need for oversight/guidance of employee tasks. Amazon is one organization that retains a hierarchical structure from parcel sorters and delivery drivers up to the CEO. Newer forms of organizational structure are flatter, meaning they have fewer layers of hierarchy. A flatter structure removes barriers to easy communication that may arise from formal hierarchical structures, preventing those lower in a 'chain of command' from speaking directly

SPOTLIGHT 8.1 **REFLECTING ON WEIRD WORKPLACES**

The vast majority of research on workplaces and work design is focused on higher-income contexts, such as in so-called developed countries. This reflects a broader bias within research on workplaces (and more generally), which has been criticized for being WEIRD (Western, Educated, Industrialized, Rich, Democratic) (Henrich et al., 2010). Research in WEIRD populations has been more commonplace because these populations are the easiest to access. Research findings tended to reflect these biases, so for a long time the research limitations were unnoticed. The danger with research concentrated on WEIRD populations is that many theories about key topics have developed based on limited understanding of large groups of people around the globe. For example, the entire field of work psychology has been criticized for largely ignoring the 61 per cent of workers in the informal sector (who are predominantly based in lower-income countries), and furthermore for assuming that all workers within the informal sector are low-skilled. In reality, there are highly skilled workers around the globe, such as pottery makers in India, who work in their homes in what is sometimes referred to as 'cottage industries' (Saxena, 2021).

Researchers are working to address this bias, and research is now expanding into new contexts (Duffy et al., 2020), recognizing the crucial need to understand the lived experiences of all people (not only the WEIRD ones). There are many people working hard to create an understanding of the global world of work that is relevant for everyone, but it is an immense task. As you go through your studies, take a critical thinking approach and keep in the back of your mind the questions about how theories and ideas might have evolved, and think about the context of their evolution—who has developed them and where have they been tested? Are they relevant for people from non-WEIRD backgrounds and contexts? Are there any underlying assumptions underpinning them which may not be universal?

upwards. The underlying notion of a flat organizational structure is reduced hierarchy to encourage full participation of all employees, allowing the flow of communication up and down and across the organization, and thus enabling an organization to be more creative, responsive, and flexible. Google is one well-known example of a flat organizational structure, where innovation and open communication and sharing are encouraged.

Both tall and flat structures can be organized around either functions or divisions. Functions include human resource management, finance, manufacturing, and marketing. Divisions are often based on different product types or brands, or geographies, or markets of operation. Sometimes these are combined into a matrix structure, where employees sit within both a function, such as marketing, as well as a division, such as consumer products. The employee would then have a manager in each. But as the nature of work has evolved, there has been a shift towards more boundary-less and networked organizations, populated with empowered employees.

8.3.2 **Work design**

Work design is a well-established area of research in psychology and management, which focuses on 'the content and organization of one's work tasks, activities, relationships, and responsibilities' (Parker, 2014). Originally, research in this area focused on understanding the

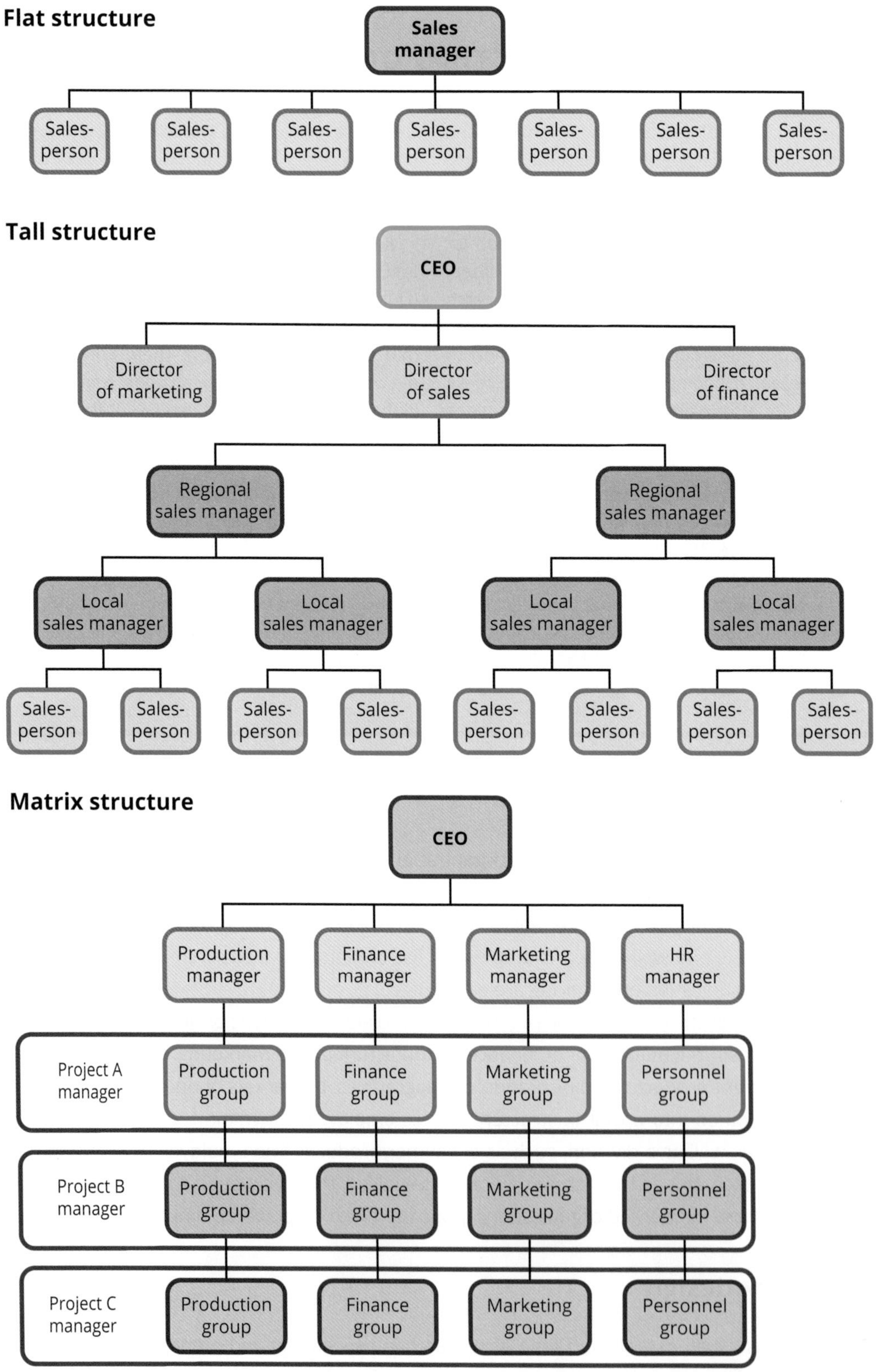

Flat structure

Tall structure

Matrix structure

FIGURE 8.2 **Examples of a tall, flat, and matrix organizational structure.**

content and organization of objective *tasks* required in jobs. However, it is increasingly recognized that work also includes activities beyond these specific tasks, for example spontaneous, emergent activities, as well as social activities. In other words, work is not only about what is done but also about the person doing it. Crucially, while job tasks are set by the organization, the work itself is often shaped by the employee. Though jobs are clearly defined by organizations through a job description, employees may naturally put more effort into the tasks they enjoy or find rewarding, than those they enjoy less. An example of this is *job crafting*, which is another (related) area of research that we will not go into here, but is an important process through which an employee creates meaning in their work and tries to shape their work to be more rewarding. Examining job tasks without considering the person within them, and their broader activities, relationships, and responsibilities, gives an incomplete picture of how to design work well.

Job Characteristics Model

The most influential model of work design is the Job Characteristics Model, developed by Hackman and Oldham in the 1970s (see Parker et al., 2017). The original model outlines a set of measurable job characteristics:

- skill variety,
- task identity,
- task significance,
- autonomy, and
- feedback from job.

These characteristics affect a set of work-related outcomes, including high motivation, satisfaction, and performance, and low absenteeism and turnover, through three psychological states: experienced meaningfulness of the work, experienced responsibility of the outcomes of the work, and knowledge of the actual results of the work activities. Figure 8.3 depicts this model.

This model has been critiqued and further developed over the years, and other models have developed alongside it. But what is important is that it began to tease out and identify key characteristics of jobs and directly link them to work outcomes.

SMART work design

While the Job Characteristics Model has been highly influential in the area of work design, its narrow focus on specific job tasks ignores the role the person plays in shaping their work. Contemporary models of work design take a broader approach (beyond tasks alone), as mentioned earlier. For example, Professor Adam Grant introduced the idea of relational work design (Grant, 2007), recognizing that work can motivate employees to engage in prosocial activities by connecting work activities with the experiences of the beneficiaries of that work, thereby enhancing the meaningfulness of the work they do.

A new framework called SMART Work Design (www.smartworkdesign.com.au) can be used to optimize job characteristics in order to enhance meaningfulness and motivation at work, and in doing so contribute to designing healthy and productive work, which enables employees

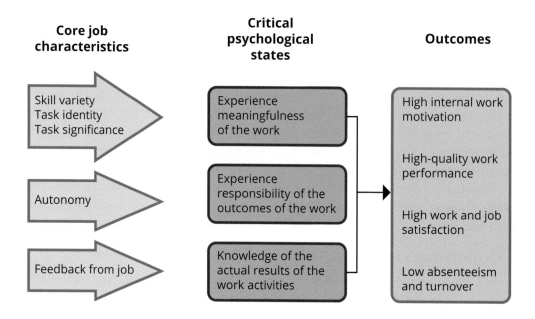

FIGURE 8.3 **Job characteristics model.** Credit: J. Richard Hackman, Greg R. Oldham, 'Motivation through the design of work: test of a theory', *Organizational Behavior and Human Performance*, Volume 16, Issue 2, 1976, Pages 250–279. Copyright © 1976. Published by Elsevier Inc.

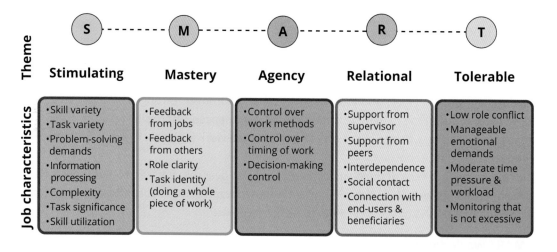

FIGURE 8.4 **SMART work design.** Credit: Professor Sharon Parker, Centre for Transformative Work Design

to thrive (see Figure 8.4). Developed by Professor Sharon Parker based on extensive empirical research (see Parker et al., 2017), this framework identifies five areas of work characteristics that are important for positive outcomes:

1. **S**timulating—work should include tasks that are varied, interesting, and meaningful.

2. **M**astery—the importance of understanding what your role is, if you are doing well in that role, and how your role fits with others.

3. **A**gency—having control over the methods and timing of job tasks, and the autonomy to make decisions about it. Agency also includes being consulted for feedback and input on organizational decisions and changes.

4. **R**elational—reflecting the social nature of work, and the need for connection and support from others. This includes having support from peers, supervisors, and other team members, as well as appreciating how your work impacts the lives of end-users and beneficiaries.

5. **T**olerable—it is important that work is not overly demanding or overwhelming, e.g. in terms of working hours, reasonable monitoring, and appropriate performance expectations.

This very practical framework can be a helpful tool for working with employees to optimize their work. For example, it can be used in a joint review between managers and employees about current work, and to identify how the role can be improved by adding, removing, or changing their current tasks or responsibilities.

This section started by focusing on fairly functional questions about the structure of organizations and tasks within job roles. We then moved on to some more normative questions about how work *should* be designed by considering SMART work design. We continue that theme in Sections 8.4 and 8.5, which focus on the related concepts of decent work—which considers the minimum standards that should be expected of work—and organizational justice—which provides insight into employee perceptions within the workplace.

8.4 **Decent work**

The idea of **decent work** is a simple yet helpful approach developed by the ILO for teasing out the different objective components of work, and what minimum standards are needed to make work of good quality. Decent work is a broad concept that encompasses job quality but other aspects as well. The ILO, a United Nations agency that focuses on social and economic justice, particularly as it relates to work and the workplace, provides this definition:

> decent work sums up the **aspirations** of people in their working lives. It involves opportunities for work that is **productive** and delivers a **fair income**, **security** in the workplace and **social protection** for families, **better prospects** for personal development and social integration, **freedom** for people to express their concerns, organize and participate in the decisions that affect their lives and **equality** of opportunity and treatment for all women and men. *(Emphasis added)*

The ILO contributes to the UN's SDG8: 'Decent Work', with a remit to promote decent work around the globe. According to its comprehensive definition, decent work includes a number of important components, which we have emphasized in bold in the quote. The idea of decent work recognizes that people have different aspirations for work, and that people should be free to fulfil those aspirations, rather than feel trapped in a particular job because of a lack of social mobility or lack of equal opportunity. It highlights the importance of feeling productive at work—that what an employee is doing has meaning and is contributing to something bigger. Decent work also requires that basic conditions such as income, security, and social protection are met. Income must be fair, but work should also offer security—people should know in advance what hours they will work and therefore what income they will receive, and should receive sufficient notice if their role is terminated. It should also offer social protection in case of injury or other threats to well-being at work. Decent work is more than a means to an end; it offers people the opportunity for their personal development. It also enables people to be involved in their community, and to speak up about (and participate in decisions related to) issues that are important to them without fear of adverse impact on their job. Finally, it supports both equality of opportunity *and* treatment, meaning that everyone should have access to the same opportunities at work, and should receive the same outcomes also.

Decent work is about creating work that is satisfying and which provides fair and decent working conditions. Since the concept was introduced by the ILO in 1999 there has been increasing attention from academics to understand precisely what aspects of work can be considered and improved. Though the ILO's description sounds positive, it lacks clear and specific information about what exactly can be measured in order to evaluate whether or not work is decent.

Psychology Professor Ryan Duffy has written extensively on this topic. With his colleagues (Duffy et al., 2016), he defined decent work as consisting of five factors:

1. physical and interpersonally safe working conditions (e.g. absence of physical, mental, or emotional abuse);

2. hours that allow for free time and adequate rest;

3. organizational values that complement family and social values;

4. adequate compensation; and

5. access to adequate health care.

This list is helpful because it draws out five key practical components of work that make it decent, and which can be clearly measured. The concept of decent work has gained traction because it addresses the fact that many workers around the globe do not have adequate choice about the type of work they do, and indeed the quality of that work. This is true in lower-income and developing countries and also in higher-income and developed countries. The increasing prevalence of short-term and insecure job contracts (including zero-hours contracts), such as those common in the gig economy, highlight the importance of thinking about decent work.

An influential academic theory developed by Professor David Blustein (2013) offers a philosophical perspective on the importance of decent work. Developed further in *The Psychology of Working Theory* (Duffy et al., 2016) the authors argue that being in work helps to fulfil the human needs of:

1. basic survival,

2. connection with others, and

3. self-determination.

Self-determination describes the ability of an individual to decide their own future. The opposite of self-determination is feeling trapped in an uncontrollable present, living day-to-day. Experiencing self-determination impacts a person's ability to decide how they want to shape their own future and is important for providing a sense of meaning, for creating self-identity, and for offering a sense of accomplishment and dignity. Blustein (2013) argues these human needs can be met, through decent work, thus enabling people to move beyond surviving, to thriving.

In fact, Blustein's theory argues that decent work is a human right but that there can be structural and individual characteristics that will predict if and when an individual experiences decent work. Structural characteristics are aspects of the context or environment that restrict one's access to decent work—for example, the economic situation in which one lives, and/or experiences of marginalization. Individual characteristics are specific to individual employees themselves, including motivation for working, social support, or personality characteristics, which influence access to decent work.

By understanding the components of decent work, organizations can aim to design work that is decent and that takes account of broader societal, economic, and political structures. This approach shifts the responsibility away from the individual to the company, to ensure that decent work is attained.

Key to achieving decent work are organizational policies and practices, and in particular HR policies and practices. The way employees are treated and the basic structures within which they work must align with the components of decent work. As well as focusing on working conditions, an emphasis on designing decent work also gives consideration to organizational values, compensation, rest time, and employee health (Duffy et al., 2016). Within this design activity, it is important to set minimum standards for organizational policies—for example, a minimum wage versus a living wage. Consider Spotlight 8.2, which examines the living wage as an element of decent work and which links to Section 8.2.2 on in-work poverty.

SPOTLIGHT 8.2 **THE LIVING WAGE**

One important component of decent work is the concept of 'adequate compensation' (Duffy et al., 2016), or a decent and fair wage. Here there is an important distinction to be made between a minimum wage and a living wage. A minimum wage is the lowest wage that can be legally paid and is calculated based on what is affordable for the company to pay employees. A living wage, however, focuses on the life of the employee and considers what is needed for the person to maintain their living conditions. It aims to go beyond just subsistence, where an employee is living from pay packet to pay packet. A living wage is calculated based on cost of living, by considering the cost of purchasing a standard basket of goods for a standard family. It is voluntary for organizations, whereas a minimum wage is legally mandated.

A living wage is important for three reasons (Searle & McWha-Hermann, 2021). Firstly, due to being based on regular estimates of cost of living,

it enables employees and their families to have sufficient income for a good quality of life. This means low-wage workers can work fair hours (rather than having to take multiple jobs to make ends meet), which enables them time to rest and recover from work, bringing positive implications for well-being. Where well-being is enhanced, this is positive for organizations too because employees are less likely to take periods of absence and are more likely to be engaged at work.

Secondly, a living wage enables employees to make choices about their lives. No longer trapped in a cycle of low wages and scrambling to make ends meet, a living wage provides space for self-improvement, or for spending time with family. By enabling working parents to spend better quality time with their children, a decent wage contributes to lower levels of stress in the home, with important implications for child development.

(Continued)

Finally, where low wages have negative implications for well-being and health, another benefit of a decent wage is that it reduces societal costs related to health and social care. Academic research (Searle & McWha-Hermann, 2021) has found important benefits for cardiovascular health, including life expectancy, as well as for mental health and depression. These health and well-being issues have considerable societal costs which are reduced through paying a decent wage.

8.5 Organizational justice

The concept of decent work introduced in this section provides an overview of the components of work and where minimum standards can be set and maintained. We can examine these components for a given job and make a judgement about whether work is decent or not, and on that basis we can identify which parts of a job need to be improved. However, while these components of decent work are crucial for employee well-being, and are in fact a fundamental human right, they are necessary but not sufficient for employee thriving. Subjective considerations of fairness at work are also important. There are also subjective components of work that can impact how employees feel about their work. Here, we focus on **organizational justice**, a well-established framework, which highlights why it is important to consider how procedures, outcomes, and interactions at work are perceived by employees. Where these are perceived to be unfair there can be negative implications for organizations.

For example, imagine that you have taken a part-time job waiting tables in a café to supplement your income during your university studies—many of you reading this text may already be supplementing your income in this way. You accept the job pays minimum wage without questioning it, assuming this is normal. Imagine how you would feel if, once you started the job, you discovered that the same job at a similar restaurant a few doors down the road from yours pays 15 per cent more. Same job, similar organization, but very different pay. Objectively, your job meets the conditions of decent work, but, subjectively, you feel it is not fair that you earn so much less for doing the same work. How would you react to this? You would probably put in a bit less effort at work, perhaps take slightly longer breaks than you should, or move a bit more slowly to serve customers. In other words, your motivation and engagement might be reduced, as well as your performance. This, in turn, might impact the performance of the restaurant—they might get slightly less positive reviews (e.g. 'service was slow'), meaning customers are less likely to return or to recommend the restaurant to their friends. So, what we can learn from this example is that it is not enough for your job to be 'decent', it also needs to be fair.

You would be hard-pressed to find someone who does not agree that feeling treated fairly is important, but the concept itself can be slippery to define and apply in practice because it is so subjective in nature. What one person feels is fair or unfair might vary significantly from someone else. This is why it is important for managers and decision-makers to understand the different facets of fairness and how they play a role in good quality work.

The theory of Organizational Justice is a well-established framework (Colquitt et al., 2001; Greenberg, 1990) for thinking about what fairness means within the workplace, and in particular for considering employee perceptions of fairness. There are three main facets commonly discussed in the organizational justice literature:

- *Distributive justice*: focuses on fair distribution of outcomes, including resources such as pay, or access to opportunities such as training. Fair distributive justice does not mean equal distribution, but tends to be calculated based on comparison of one's own skills and contributions with someone else's.
- *Procedural justice*: considers the fairness of processes and procedures within the organization. Where distributive justice is about the outcome of the decision, procedural justice is about the fairness of the process that has led to the decision of how outcomes are distributed and to whom they are offered.
- *Interactional justice*: relates to the interactions one has at work. This includes *interpersonal* aspects, which are connected to how management or those in positions of authority treat those at lower levels, such as treating employees with respect. It also includes *informational* aspects, which concern the information provided to employees about the processes and outcomes within the organization. This can include transparency of processes, as well as the amount and accuracy of the information.

All three facets of organizational justice should be considered together as they do not happen in isolation from one another (depicted in Figure 8.5). It is important to note that perceived unfairness in one area might trigger increased sensitivity to unfairness in the others. Conversely, something an employee might find unfair could be justified through another facet of organizational justice such that it helps to reduce the negative consequence for the employee. For instance, in the example about how waiting staff are paid in the two restaurants, if you were told (interactional justice) that your salary, though lower than at the other restaurant (distributive injustice) was linked with the profit of the restaurant, and would increase in line with the restaurant's profits, you may feel better about the situation. You may feel motivated to work harder in

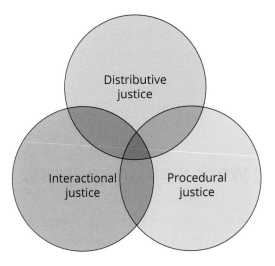

FIGURE 8.5 **Three facets of organizational justice.**

order to help enhance the organization's profits because you are now aware that this is directly linked to your own pay (procedural justice).

It is important that employees feel they are fairly treated across the outcomes, procedures, and interactions that occur in the workplace. While pay is an easy example to give, there are many everyday examples beyond pay, such as praise received for work well done, or opportunities to have ideas heard in meetings. Researchers are still trying to understand the extent to which perceptions of fairness impact employees at work. There are also important connections with other topics of research, such as power and identity, which, in turn, link with the equality, diversity, and inclusion (EDI) of employee groups. What is clear, however, is that numerous studies have identified organizational justice as important for influencing how committed employees feel towards their employer organization, their satisfaction at work, and, also their plans to look for a new job (also called turnover intention).

So, organizational justice is multifaceted. It is not only about the outcomes of decisions, but the process through which decisions are made, and how those decisions are communicated by those in leadership positions and through organizational communication channels. These decisions can be about significant topics like pay, promotions, and training opportunities, but also more subtle issues, like who is granted time to speak (airtime) in meetings. When feelings of injustice are triggered for employees, whichever facet of justice they may relate to, they tend to spell bad news for the organization. This bad news is what academic researchers call *counterproductive work behaviours*. For example, perceptions of injustice can lead to employees withdrawing at work, sometimes calling in sick or showing up late, or even more subtly through working more slowly or not offering to help a colleague who needs it. Counterproductive work behaviours can be even more serious. They can include theft, such as taking items of stationery home for personal use without permission, or sabotage, such as leaking ideas to competitors.

Managers need to be aware of the various facets of perceived organizational justice, and consider fairness implications within all their decision-making. To do this, it is important to obtain feedback from employees on important decisions, particularly in relation to policy decisions. Employee voice, outlined in Chapter 7, is an important mechanism to gauge potential breaches of organizational justice, which may lead to feelings of injustice among employees. Also consider who is getting access to opportunities, and whether there is a good range of people taking up opportunities. Where there is a lack of variety in who takes up opportunities, this might indicate procedural injustice. To avoid this, managers need to ensure that all employees are treated consistently and have access to the same information. Transparency is crucial for fairness.

Let's return to see the outcome of Lucy's visit to Kenya to understand Imperial's tea business in Running case 8.2.

8.6 Designing work well, in context

The extent to which it is possible to apply these concepts that are so important to designing work will depend on the context in which the work is occurring. For example, in higher-income contexts where basic social protection, decent pay, and good working conditions are standard, a more nuanced approach to justice and SMART work design may be an appropriate starting

RUNNING CASE 8.2 **ALARMING DISCOVERIES IN KENYA**

Lucy's visit to Kenya is now at an end. She realizes all too clearly that her long-held assumption was wrong: little of the tea that Imperial buys is produced by workers whose employment reflects Imperial's values. Before she visited the tea plantations, she'd thought that if any tea workers were being exploited, it was only by large corporate buyers. But having seen for herself the working conditions of Imperial's own growers—and having threatened angrily to terminate her company's agreement with Mr Turner—she sees the reality of the situation. She is ashamed to acknowledge that the workers helping Imperial to be profitable do not enjoy the decent work required by SDG 8; in fact their working and living conditions do not meet several of the SDGs.

After telling Mr Turner what changes she expects to see, Lucy takes action. Before she leaves Nairobi, she and Mr Turner meet the local manager of the Ethical Tea Partnership (ETP), Ms Chebat. Lucy commits Imperial to the ETP's aim of 'a thriving tea industry that is socially just and environmentally sustainable' and agrees to participate in its efforts to improve sustainability and, in particular, the welfare of plantation workers. She also takes Mr Turner to meet Mr Kipsang, the Kenya manager of the Fairtrade certification body, and commits Imperial to increasing its purchase price, on the understanding that the 'labour content' of the tea they import now includes a living wage for all plantation workers associated with its production (Fairtrade Foundation, 2022). She ensures the changes she wants to see are included in a new contract with Mr Turner, which she and he sign before she leaves. Though she has been greatly disturbed by some of what she has seen during her visit, Lucy feels that she has at least put Imperial back onto the right path in its Kenyan tea business.

As she is travelling home from the airport, however, Hugh forwards an email he has received from his cousin Charles, who owns 10 per cent of

(*Continued*)

Imperial's shares. In it, Charles has written: 'I cannot see what possible value there is in Lucy going to Kenya. If she wants to holiday in exotic locations, then she should do so at her own expense and not our company's. As I have said before, Lucy's ONLY responsibility is to maximize Imperial's profitability and look after the interests of its shareholders'.

Stung by this unfair criticism, still mulling over all that she has seen during her trip, and now absolutely certain of what must be done in the future, Lucy responds with an email to Hugh and Charles: 'Visiting our suppliers in Kenya and Assam is absolutely my responsibility. Perhaps some people do not understand the long-term value of sustainable business, but other stakeholders do and are asking us to confirm that we act responsibly in ensuring appropriate working conditions for all workers on whom this company depends. Without losing sight of generating profits, Imperial will be paying closer attention to the welfare of all workers involved in making this a great company, whether they work directly for us or for our suppliers.' After emailing Charles, Lucy briefly contemplates her next trip, to Assam. Then she starts another email, to Imperial's Marketing Manager, Gita Patel, headed 'Changes in our Tea business'.

Questions for reflection

1. How would you evaluate Lucy's actions in Kenya?

2. What is the value of aligning Imperial with organizations like the ETP and Fairtrade? Who benefits from Lucy's decision to do so?

3. If you were asked to draft Lucy's email to Gita, what changes would you advise making to Imperial's tea business? Why?

---

point. In other contexts, such as in lower-income contexts, or in work that is characterized by insecurity, more basic considerations of decent work might be the starting point. It is rarely so simple that only one of these concepts is appropriate within an organization. For example, within a **multinational organization**, where operations occur across different, nations, a different approach may be needed in each location. It may be difficult to incorporate consistent minimum standards across different social, economic, cultural, and even legal systems.

One example of an organization trying to manage the fairness of the total reward package offered to all staff is the international NGO, Water For People, which calculates the monetary equivalence of the benefits for staff across different locations, enabling the organization to take into account the different contexts in which staff are working. Furthermore, where operations are not multinational it is important to look beyond full-time contracted employees, to consider the organization's outsourced workers—for example, the cleaning staff and security staff—as well as looking within the supply chain, to understand the quality of work of employees within it, such as those working abroad in factories subcontracted to supply parts for a product in development.

It is critically important to consider cultural preferences for fairness which will influence how initiatives are received by employees from different cultural backgrounds. These act in addition to individual differences around fairness preferences. For example, in more collectivistic versus individualistic societies, team-based versus individually focused incentives may be preferred. These variations make it even more important to ensure there are employee voice mechanisms built into work design processes and strategies, and to constantly question the assumptions underpinning the way work is designed. Processes must be adapted for different contexts—for example, multinational organizations need to ensure decisions are not made at HQ and imposed in subsidiaries/country offices. In Spotlight 8.1 we talked about the WEIRD focus of existing research on workplaces and the impact this can have on our knowledge about designing work well for populations of the workforce that have historically been excluded. At all stages, managers should think critically about the approach being taken and be sure to seek divergent perspectives as much as possible.

8.7 **Conclusion**

In this chapter, we have focused primarily on the micro components of how to design work well, and we have emphasized its value for employees and their organizations. We explored concepts including SMART work design, decent work, and organizational justice. The impact of designing work well cannot be understated. Beyond just individuals and organizations, well-designed work contributes to addressing global grand challenges such as poverty, inequality, and even climate change by providing individuals with the stability and future vision to act. Work that is decent and fair enables individuals to thrive and flourish, improving their situation and that of their families, pulling themselves and their communities out of poverty. When people are in secure employment, they are able to challenge structures that keep them in poverty and advocate for addressing deeper inequality within communities. It also enables them to look up from day-to-day efforts of survival beyond just making ends meet and feeding their family, to working towards shared goals such as caring for the planet and addressing climate change. Through focusing on decent and fair work, organizations and managers have a key role to play in creating a fairer, more sustainable future.

CHAPTER SUMMARY

- ○ Designing work well is important at an individual level as it affects how employees feel and perform at work, as well as at a societal level as it collectively affects families, local communities, and societal issues such as poverty, inequality, and even climate change.

- ○ Contemporary issues facing management related to designing work well include self-employment, in-work poverty, hybrid and remote working, employee well-being, and supply chain impacts.

- ○ Organizational structure typically focuses on how much hierarchy there is within a given organization, and is often simplified to tall, flat, or matrix structures.

- ○ Work design comprises the tasks, activities, relationships, and responsibilities within one's job, with SMART work design focused on enhancing meaningfulness and motivation at work.

- ○ Decent work focuses on creating work that is satisfying and which provides fair and decent working conditions.

- ○ Organizational justice comprises distributive, procedural, and interactional justice.

CLOSING CASE REFLECTION

The four-day working week experiment

Hutch's decision to operate a permanent four-day week demonstrates a number of elements of work design linked to employees. The 4DayWeek organization found that most of the organizations who participated in their experiment to trial a transition to a four-day working week saw improvements in employee well-being (4dayweek.com). Though it is not easy to shape an organization's activities to fit into four instead of five days, improved productivity could be achieved through not accepting the status quo and applying deeper scrutiny to tasks and ways of working. Reducing the number and length of mandatory meetings was one way of improving the effective use of employee working time, without requiring employees to speed up their work rate to retain pre-trial levels of output. Following the success of the trial, the 4DayWeek organization continues to campaign for widespread change so that more organizations and employees can achieve improved well-being from 32-hour working weeks bookended by three-day weekends.

REVIEW QUESTIONS

1. Critically assess the importance of designing work well for employees and organizations. Ensure you differentiate between the business case and social case in your answer.

2. Discuss the concept of decent work and how managers can use this to improve the quality of work for employees.

3. Reflect on the importance of the different components of organizational justice. How do they link to one another?

4. How does SMART work design complement the concepts of decent work and organizational justice?

5. In what ways might the activities of organizations and managers influence global grand challenges such as poverty and inequality? Provide examples.

EXPLORE MORE

- WATCH an animation about the living wage on YouTube, by searching for 'EAWOP living wage'.

- READ about SMART work design in practice from the Centre For Transformative Work Design. Search 'SMART work design' in Google and hit the first result.

- READ the pages on the microsite authored by *The Guardian* and UNICEF to understand the scale of the problem of child labour in the fashion supply chain, in particular linked to the fast fashion industry. Search for 'Child labour in the fashion supply chain'.

≡ READ about the history of decent work on the ILO's website, including how it relates to other global initiatives such as the United Nations Agenda for Sustainable Development.

≡ READ about the topics of this chapter on the EAWOP impact incubator site, and play *Superbmarket*, the serious educational game designed to experience how decisions in the workplace (such as wage levels) impact employee well-being. Google 'EAWOP impact incubator decent work'.

◉ WATCH the videos of workers' experiences of living in poverty, and read the resources to understand the link between well-designed work and poverty, on the CIPD website. Google 'CIPD tackling in-work poverty'.

8

CHAPTER NINE

Organizational Behaviour and Teams

Thomas Calvard, Sarah Birrell Ivory, and Emma Macdonald

OPENING CASE STUDY **TEAM-BUILDING AT EMIRATES**

Emirates Airlines, one of the world's largest airlines, is consistently placed at the top of the airline industry rankings for customer satisfaction (SkyTrax, 2022). Like all passenger airlines, Emirates operates in the services sector with a value proposition to customers that includes not just safe transportation of passengers and luggage from departure point to destination, but an enjoyable travelling experience. Providing smartly fitted-out planes is important for inflight comfort, but another key component of the customer experience is passenger interaction with Emirates cabin crew and ground staff throughout the journey. For a manager of any service business that relies on people to deliver the experience, one of the greatest challenges is providing a consistent quality of service. This is because your human service providers—your team members—are not machines. People are infinitely variable in how they perceive and respond to the world around them, and this variability is amplified in an international organization like Emirates, which recruits staff from 130 nationalities.

Striving for consistent delivery of a great customer experience from a large and diverse workforce means that Emirates invests heavily in recruitment, training, and team-building. All new cabin crew undergo two months of training at Emirates' headquarters in Dubai, which includes simulators to prepare teams for a range of emergencies such as an on-board fire or delivering a baby (Stoddard, 2019). Crew members are trained how to recognize security threats and how to assist travellers with hidden disabilities such as autism (Future Travel Experience, 2023). They are also trained how to provide food service in a confined space, including silver service, and how to present themselves, including image training from cosmetics company, Dior (Loh, 2021). Crew members speak more than 60 languages and use this knowledge to **mentor** each other in learning language phrases and understanding cultural norms and traditions (Stoddard, 2019). Emirates' investment in training and team-building appears to pay off in a number of ways: high levels of customer satisfaction; a valuation as a top five most valuable airline brand (Brand Finance, 2022); and a Glassdoor.com (2023) employee rating of 4.1 out of 5.

9.1 **Introduction**

Organizational behaviour (OB) is an area of study focused on helping managers with the task of managing individuals and teams. This is not easy because human beings are variable, and each individual sees and responds to the world around them in different ways. The models and frameworks in OB draw on psychology and other social sciences to address this problem and help leaders to understand and manage the human beings that make up organizations. These frameworks seek to understand how people think, feel, and behave at work; how they interact and maintain relationships with each other; and, how they perform tasks and take up roles in the organization.

OB models pay attention to **personality** traits, knowledge, skills, and abilities. They seek to understand how management can influence people's levels of **motivation**, what motivates them, as well as the ways they perceive and interpret their jobs, their managers, and the wider organization. As such, OB is relevant in any situation where understanding human behaviour might help people to work, coordinate, and organize more effectively.

Teams—a subset of OB—focuses on how individuals work together. Although people have cooperated socially for much of human history, systematic management research and practice focused on teams has only evolved in the last century. This knowledge has been built up from the field of social psychology and its study of individuals and their relationships, to gradually encompass entire teams and even dynamic networks and systems involving many teams. While great progress has been made in learning about teams, there are still changing conditions and forms of work, organizations, and management that make observation and new discoveries around teams important and exciting.

This chapter starts with a focus on individuals, exploring theories that have been developed and deployed to manage them more effectively towards an organizational goal. It then turns to examine individuals working together—that is, in teams.

9.2 **Organizational behaviour**

Organizational behaviour is interested in how individuals bring their personalities, mindsets, and backgrounds to an organization, and the implications of this in how they are managed both individually and in teams. Management and OB are linked by questions about whether or not individuals can be managed effectively and, if so, how best to do so. This is a difficult task because human behaviour is often unpredictable and because there is a range of ways people can organize themselves individually and in groups, to work towards specific goals.

There is great variation in how people think, act, and feel in different types of work and varying organizational environments. This is where the word 'context' becomes important for OB. Contextualization has been the ongoing focus of work by Canadian OB researcher, Professor Gary Johns (2006, 2017, 2018). Johns argues that understanding the context of OB is a little like being a journalist, and requires asking the 'who', 'what', 'when', 'where', and 'why' questions. The answers to these questions provide insightful stories that explain people's experiences in organizations across different situations and conditions. Focusing on these contextual details means paying attention to the psychology of tasks, social relationships, and properties of the physical environment.

Social and psychological models are often used to track and explain the informal, emergent, spontaneous, and diverse qualities of how people think, feel, and act in situations involving work and team **coordination**. Many theories and models of OB have been developed around such topics to try to predict why people in organizations behave in the ways they do, under different conditions and through different processes. Some of these theories will continue to be revised and updated as the world around us changes, as the ways we work together continue to evolve due, for example, to opportunities afforded by changing communications and technology, and as more data and evidence are gathered and reviewed. Some theories may also be overtaken or replaced by new generations of theories, in trying to explain changing forms of organization and behaviour. However, while work environments may evolve, many of the underlying principles of deep human behaviour in organizations will remain relatively stable.

One of the key theories of OB is related to individual motivation: that is, understanding and attempting to change, leverage, or respond to what motivates individuals in relation to their work. We will now explore this topic with reference to key theories in this area.

9.2.1 Individual motivation

The topic of motivation has been the focus of much attention in OB. Motivation is a complex concept, which has generated many different theories and models to account for the many reasons why people may feel more or less motivated at work, with clear implications for their performance and well-being. We can think of motivation in terms of three main elements: (1) intensity—how hard we try and how much effort we are motivated to put into something; (2) direction—the goal we are motivated to try to work towards; and (3) persistence—for how long we are motivated to keep trying to do something (Kanfer, 1992) (Figure 9.1).

Many different sources can trigger motivation. We can frame human motivation in terms of survival—that is, behaviour shaped by basic and fundamental human needs, such as hunger, shelter, need for rest, and so on. We can also think of sources of motivation in terms of opposing

Intensity   Direction

Persistence

FIGURE 9.1 **Three elements of motivation.**

forces—incentives or rewards that might pull us towards doing something, and punishments or deterrents that might push us away from something and into doing something else. A relevant analogy is the 'carrot and stick': the carrot (incentive) is dangled in front of a horse meaning it chooses to move in that direction, while the stick (deterrent) is used to smack the horse if it stops or is moving in the wrong direction.

A further distinction is that of extrinsic and intrinsic motivation. *Ex*trinsic motivation is *external* to us, such as being motivated to do something at work to earn rewards (e.g. pay and bonuses) and avoid punishments (e.g. being disciplined, demoted, or dismissed). *In*trinsic motivation is *internal* to ourselves, such as being motivated to do something because it is meaningful, purposeful, and rewarding for internal, personal reasons (e.g. enjoyment, desire to learn, and feelings of pride, confidence, or achievement).

The American psychologist Frederick Herzberg developed a motivation theory based on this extrinsic–intrinsic distinction, often referred to as the 'two-factor' or 'motivation-hygiene' theory of motivation (Sachau, 2007). Motivation factors are concerned with the intrinsic value and satisfaction gained directly from the job itself (e.g. sense of achievement, personal growth, responsibility). In the absence of motivation factors, we may be less likely to see improved motivation, greater job satisfaction, and improved organizational performance. In contrast, hygiene factors tend to be less directly job-related and more extrinsic (e.g. pay and conditions). Surprisingly, perhaps, receiving more pay may be important for preventing dissatisfaction at work, but does not necessarily provide positive motivation.

It is interesting to consider the link between an individual's motivation and the management style of their manager. Managers' beliefs and assumptions about what motivates their employees are likely to give rise to different management styles. Another psychologist, Douglas McGregor, was interested in this link. He termed managers who believed their staff to be extrinsically motivated 'Theory X' managers, and those who believed their staff to be intrinsically motivated 'Theory Y' managers (McGregor, 1960). Figure 9.2 depicts the assumptions attributed to Theory X versus Theory Y managers. It may be useful to consider these assumptions and reflect on managers you have experienced yourself or witnessed in workplaces or television programmes.

While this depiction provides a simple distinction, in reality it is more complicated than choosing either X or Y as a management style. Again, we can consider contextualization: depending on the context of the individual or team being managed, the complexity of tasks, the different parts of the organization involved—and many other factors—X or Y may be more appropriate. Nevertheless, the trend towards more independent working, as well as issues of well-being, means that there is a continued emphasis on the importance of intrinsic aspects, with the assumption that most people will have a greater sense of motivation when they have a sense of purpose and connection to something bigger than themselves, of improvement and mastery, and of freedom and choice. As such, Theory Y is a popular positive idea for managing people so they are motivated to reach their full potential.

While motivation as a field of study is now over a hundred years old, there is still much to understand in OB and management about how intrinsic and extrinsic factors combine and unfold differently for different individuals working with different resources and in different jobs, environments, and cultures (Kanfer et al., 2017). We now turn our attention to a topic that comprises and impacts aspects of motivation as well as other key issues that impact managing people within an organization—that is, individuals working together in teams.

Theory X	Theory Y
• People dislike working • People avoid responsibility • People are lazy and self-interested • People are money motivated • People have little ambition • People require supervision • Rewards and punishments are needed to motivate people	• People have intrinsic interest in work • People seek responsibility • People are collaborative and want to contribute • People are motivated by more than money • People enjoy creatively solving problems and reaching goals • People can work well without supervision • Self-development opportunities are needed to motivate people

FIGURE 9.2 **McGregor's Theory X and Theory Y assumptions about staff motivation.**
Figure based on: McGregor, D. (1960), 'Theory X and Theory Y'. In Pugh, D. S. (Ed.), *Organization Theory: Selected Readings*, 2007, Penguin

9.3 **Focus on teams**

From the middle of the twentieth century, work relationships, groups, and teams started to be given serious attention in management as a creative and productive force. A key moment in the history of teams was the Hawthorne Studies (1924–32) (Hassard, 2012). This was a series of experiments carried out by Elton Mayo and a Harvard-based group of researchers with workers at a factory making telecommunications equipment, outside Chicago, USA. The aim of the experiments was to investigate the effects that changing certain aspects of the work—lighting, layout, pay—had on **productivity**. However, it became apparent to the researchers that productivity was more impacted by a range of other social influences, including the effect of being observed at work, receiving feedback, peer pressure, and choosing members of a team to work with.

These studies were linked to the shift away from the 'scientific management' approach of measuring and controlling the work of individuals, and towards the 'human relations' approach of taking a more active interest in nurturing positive social bonds and participation among workers (see a critical discussion of this shift in Section 1.8). However, it is important to recognize that the history and context of the Hawthorne Studies are much more complicated, controversial, and open to different interpretations than a simple shift or sudden discovery of social and human relations in the workplace (Hassard, 2012). Undoubtedly, many people were aware of social influences on work before the studies took place. To what extent more 'human' and less 'scientific' workplaces have been achieved or are always effective can also be questioned. Nevertheless, the Hawthorne Studies represent a powerful origin story that continues to be told in almost all OB textbooks to date. The 'human relations' emphasis remains an important core characteristic of OB as a field, and part of an explanation for the general rise in popularity of more formal team-working arrangements in organizations since the second half of the twentieth century.

A crucial part of OB is understanding how individuals work with or alongside others. We typically call such groups of individuals 'teams'. Being a member of a team and interacting with other team members, is almost taken for granted in most modern organizations. Teams are building blocks of organizations and represent an important focal point for management and leadership. Teams may also comprise members from different organizations working towards a common or shared goal or purpose.

Teams can vary greatly in size (i.e. number of members), how informal or formal they are, how they are led and managed, and their purpose for being. Within an organization's boundary, teams may comprise well-established functions and departments, or may be set up to work on special projects, develop innovative products and services, conduct research, plan strategies, build relationships, or try to bring about changes in the organization.

Moreover, there has been increasing attention on multi-team systems (MTSs) which can be described as 'teams of teams' often, but not always, from different organizations. While each team may have its own within-team goal, they may also be interdependent with other teams and share a cross-team goal. For example, a team of police officers, a team of firefighters, and a team of paramedics, may join to form an MTS with the goal of ensuring public safety. This might be an ongoing relationship, comprising meetings, planning, and shared information and tasks. Or it might occur in a time-sensitive situation when they are responding to an emergency, such as a road traffic accident or extreme weather incident, and need to rely on each other in order to coordinate their response and achieve their common goal.

While research into MTSs between different organizations is growing, knowledge and theories that focus on teams within organizations also apply to teams that form between organizations. As such, for the rest of this chapter, we will focus on such within-organization teams.

9.4 Understanding teamwork

There is no 'one-size-fits-all' or 'how-to' guide for forming, structuring, developing, or managing a team to ensure effectiveness. This is because there are many different contextual factors that impact team-working environments, and in particular because teams comprise humans themselves who defy perfect predictability or modelling. As such, the study of teams requires frameworks that reflect this complexity, and embrace the uncertainty of human behaviour and of human social interactions.

Teamwork always comprises **interdependence**. Interdependence occurs when more than one individual is involved in achieving a specific task or project—that is, each individual is dependent on others. This is the case regardless of whether the task is to build a wall, to sell a product, or to undertake surgery. However, for teamwork to be effective, managers need to understand the different types of interdependence and manage accordingly. We can identify three different approaches to teamwork which vary based on the type of interdependence: pool, sequence, and reciprocal approaches.

Teamwork adopts a *pool* approach when individuals are required to complete highly similar tasks in parallel, with a focus on consistent standards and efficiency. For example, a team of bricklayers may work side-by-side to each build a section of the same wall within a specific time frame.

Alternatively, teamwork may use a *sequence* approach, when there is a flow of information or materials from one individual to the next, which needs to be completed in a specific order. As such, the output from one individual's task becomes an input to the next individual's task, and so on, until the final task has been completed. For example, a customer in a car showroom may be passed from one team member to the next—from a receptionist to a sales representative, to a contracts and finance person, and finally to after-sales support—to complete the task of buying a car.

Finally, teamwork adopts a *reciprocal* approach, when individuals need to pass their work back and forth between members of the team, with constant and ongoing feedback and communication on different aspects of the delivery. For example, a surgical team often works in this way as anaesthetists, surgeons, nurses, and others pass information and equipment back and forth, mutually adjusting how they work in response to each other, checking and communicating issues, errors, problems and solutions, to complete the task of successful surgery.

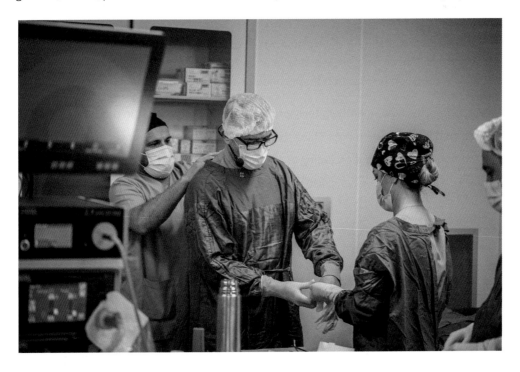

The ubiquity of technology in our working lives is increasingly impacting all of these ap-proaches. For example, some organizations have a 24-hour work cycle globally, where team members in one time zone pass the work on at the end of their working day to team members in a different time zone in order for the work to continue. This may comprise either a sequence or a reciprocal approach, depending on whether the work is then passed back. Also, innovations such as Google Docs have emerged to facilitate ease of reciprocal teamwork for those who are working from different physical locations and/or asynchronously (that is, not necessarily at the same moment in time).

Another approach to classifying teamwork is to typify important characteristics of the team along three different continuums (Hollenbeck et al., 2012). Teams vary in their *skill differentiation*—from everyone doing similar work through to every single team member having unique skills. Teams vary in their *authority differentiation*—from having one powerful leader with ultimate authority through to having complete democracy across all members and no leaders at all. Finally, teams vary in their *temporal stability*—from working together on a short, one-time basis through to teams that may work together for 10 years or more.

Irrespective of whether the interdependence is pool, sequence, or reciprocal, or where the team sits on the skill differentiation, authority differentiation, and temporal stability contin-uums, a key factor in their success lies in the effectiveness of coordination. We will examine this now.

9.4.1 The importance of coordination in teamwork

Many different factors will determine if teamwork will be successful. A key role of management is understanding these factors and ensuring that teams are formed, structured, supported, and managed with the greatest chance of success. One such determinant of the success of team-work is the activity of coordination.

Coordination is the process of interaction which occurs between individuals who have inter-dependent tasks: that is, who are working in a team. Okhuysen & Bechky (2009) suggest that successful coordination is reliant on three conditions (Figure 9.3) for team members:

1. Accountability: team members taking responsibility for their part in the task;

2. Predictability: team members doing the work when they are supposed to do it; and

3. Common understanding: including team members' knowledge of the whole task and their agreement as to how the work is to be done and the roles of team members within that process.

Common understanding is particularly important in situations of uncertainty, because this will increase the need to adjust or vary the work. This is linked to another concept known as social or team cognition (Mohammed et al., 2021). This refers to the way in which team members think, perceive, expect, and pay attention to each other's actions in the ongoing flow of their work and in unfolding situations. When team members do not develop a sense of team

Common understanding

Predictability

Accountability

FIGURE 9.3 **Three conditions for successful team coordination.**

cognition, they will be unable to form a coherent understanding or common frame of reference for their work and how best to accomplish it.

The three conditions of successful coordination—accountability, predictability, and common understanding—are achieved when both managers and team members themselves ensure that specific coordination mechanisms are both in place and functioning effectively. These co-ordination mechanisms include routines, meetings, plans, and schedules.

Where coordination is strong and accepted by all individuals, this should contribute to **cooperation** within the team, and see members helping each other on the path to achieving goals for mutual benefit. However, most individuals are likely to have competing motivations, and many organizations may also have multiple expectations and goals. This can result in both

competition and conflict within teams, and between different teams within organizations. While some forms of competition and conflict may stimulate achievement and productivity of a team, more personal conflicts and competition between individuals on the same team, or teams within the same organization, can harm cooperation and undermine achievement of the team's or organization's overall goals.

Conflict and competition within teams can be linked to situations where subgroups or factions emerge within teams because of actual or perceived imbalances of status, resources, or power. This is particularly concerning for team effectiveness and identity, and for issues of diversity and inclusion. This might include situations where subgroups emerge because of common characteristics and a common sense of being different and so marginalized. Examples include physical location (a small part of the team in a different office or city), gender, race, or many other factors. One of the key roles of managers, and a key function of Human Resources as depicted in Chapter 7, is to avoid or resolve such situations.

9.4.2 **The pitfalls of teams**

While teams are often lauded as effective or even enjoyable ways of working, it is important to remember that individuals and teams can, and probably should, always be analysed *critically*. This is because it is not uncommon for managers to overestimate the value and influence of teams. In reality, there are many ways teams can be dysfunctional, costly, and under-delivering or failing to meet their objectives. Self-interested, individual motives may be detrimental to the optimal performance of a team. In these cases, the success of the team will not be greater, and may even be considerably less, than the sum of the individual parts that make it up.

Managers may have idealistic expectations of teams as 'self-managing' collections of people destined to work well together and produce great results with little effort or oversight. Again, the reality in organizations is that there is just as likely to be disagreement and confusion, including about team membership (who gets to be on a team or not) and the role of multiple teams (how many teams the same person is on, etc.). Furthermore, the power and control dynamics around teams can lead to intense pressures from leaders and peers to be a 'team player', potentially requiring individuals to conform to norms that may not recognize their diversity or that may just be unhealthy for all individuals. We therefore need to keep in mind both the pros and cons of teams and remember that while team structures can be very productive, they can have potential downsides, including the extra time required (e.g. for team meetings, communication time, and relationship-building effort) and the psychological costs of team membership (e.g. pressure that individuals feel to conform and the sense of not fitting in that may affect some team participants). These realities may lead people to reject teams or feel deeply dissatisfied with their functioning and performance.

Increasingly, we are seeing organizations and managers looking to reduce the uncertainty around human behaviour generally, and team contributions specifically, in order to improve team functioning and organizational performance. For example, organizations are employing digital tools such as wearable sensors, eye movement tracking, and analysis of an individual's contributions in team meetings, to assess and potentially 'rate' their effectiveness as team members (Pentland, 2013). This kind of technological monitoring poses a number of concerns. The first is the extent to which such quantified analysis is useful in understanding something as complex as team interactions, team cognition, and ultimately effectiveness. The second is an ethical concern about the degree to which an organization has the right to monitor a human being's behaviour as if they were a machine. A third concern is whether it is appropriate for an organization to infiltrate an individual's non-work life and collect data on them. An example of the latter is a common technique used to inspire team identity and cohesion by creating a 'fun' competition between teams such as a Step Challenge, where members are encouraged, or sometimes required, to wear step counters, and their daily contribution to the team's overall step count is monitored and reported. The 'fun' can become insidious if team members with specific characteristics, such as disability, are marginalized or excluded.

We have now explored what teams are and identified fundamental aspects of teamwork including interdependence and coordination, as well as pointed out the potential pitfalls of teamwork. We now turn to the process of forming and developing teams, which is a key activity of management. But first, let's check in with Imperial in Running case 9.1, to see what challenges they face when implementing teamwork.

RUNNING CASE 9.1 **TEAM TROUBLE**

Sue Smith, Imperial's Factory Manager is reflecting on the first few weeks of Imperial's vegan foods project. Lucy seems pleased with the progress of the team responsible for creating the first products to be tested in the market. But Sue recalls some of the challenging moments they've had since Imperial's last Away Day strategy meeting (see Running case 5.2). First, Lucy had to overcome plenty of initial scepticism. But her combination of tact and determined energy had persuaded COO, Bob Smart and other doubters that launching plant-based foods in the education sector was worthwhile. People had been happy with Lucy's suggestion that they set up a Product Design project team of experienced staff with a very wide remit. Their responsibility would be first to select the new products to be developed, then to determine everything from sourcing raw materials to making changes in the food preparation and packing areas, then marketing the products and winning sales.

Lucy initially asked Bob Smart to lead the Product Design team because of his extensive experience in the industry and to ensure his buy-in to the project. Bob had thought that the best way to make progress would be to bring the company's senior managers into the project, so the first two names on his list were Sue Smith and Supply Chain Manager, Declan O'Rourke. Then he added Michael Evans, the Bakery Supervisor, and John Brown, the Sales Manager. The team's first meeting after its formation hadn't achieved much. Sue had pointed out that they lacked the awareness of the products that would appeal to the targeted customer group of young people in schools and colleges. Michael had let it be known that he didn't think much of this plant-based foods idea anyway and couldn't see why they were bothering. John had complained that he was already struggling to hit his sales targets and couldn't spare the time for lots of meetings. The team's second meeting was a stormy affair: though they were friendly enough as colleagues, they found themselves snapping at each other, and unable to agree on what they needed to do. Sue had suggested one idea, but Michael had reacted scornfully and been supported by John, making Sue feel as though she wasn't going to get far working with these two. Bob had looked like someone whose doubts about vegan products were being proved right after all.

A couple of days later, Sue Smith is telling Lucy about her frustrations with the Product Design working group. Lucy is concerned that this team seems not to be working out too well and she remembers that much of the energy in the strategy Away Day meetings came from the younger staff members and

(Continued)

Gita. Might it be better, Lucy wonders, to abandon the hierarchy and reconsider the scope of the team's work? Lucy realizes the team will achieve nothing unless its members feel a sense of psychological safety that will encourage open contributions. She also realizes its scope is far too ambitious.

Lucy deals tactfully with Bob Smart, saying: 'Why don't we see what happens if we get some different members of staff involved in thinking about the product design? Let's have some subgroups instead of your current team being responsible for

everything. We should think of you, Sue, and I being like a steering committee but sharing out the responsibilities to smaller groups who can get things done more easily.'

Questions for reflection

1. Why do you think Imperial's first Product Design team was not a success?

2. To what extent was the work of the team well coordinated (consider Figure 9.3)?

9.5 Team formation

Given the ubiquity of teams in organizations, a key role of management relates to making decisions about team formation. However, the first question should always be whether a team is needed. While this may seem like an obvious question, with the increasing popularity of teams in organizations managers may automatically look to set up a team to complete a task or project which may be better allocated to individuals working independently.

Managers need to think carefully about whether a team structure is necessary or useful. Can and should individuals be joined up together to cooperatively share their efforts and complete bigger tasks more effectively? Given many aspects of organizational life are still structured around individuals—including job descriptions, task allocation, pay and rewards, mentoring, and line management—setting up a team can result in potential misalignment with some of these other factors, which needs to be carefully and proactively managed.

Teams may be newly formed entirely of new members, roles, and goals. However, commonly teams will be formed (or re-formed) from an existing group or out of a different project. As such, while we discuss a number of best practices relating to team formation in this section, more commonly managers will be constrained by factors which they have limited influence over. This might be the availability of specific skills, the existing organization culture, or deep-seated (positive or negative) relationships that have already formed between team members.

9.5.1 Assigning team roles

Having decided that a team structure is appropriate, an important consideration in team formation is assigning team roles and allocating individuals to fulfil those roles. One way to achieve this is for potential team members to complete a tool called a 'team role inventory' where individuals rate themselves—and sometimes each other in the case of 360-degree feedback—on behavioural styles, personality characteristics, strengths, and preferences. The resulting data can be used to decide on the composition and size of the team, to identify which potential team members would suit particular roles, or even to anticipate whether the individuals would be compatible in a team at all.

The inventory tools typically include around 10 roles, each with a name reflecting the value that a team member in that role would contribute to the team (e.g. 'coordinator', 'monitor', or 'shaper'). Figure 9.4 shows an example of a popular inventory. The set of roles is typically subdivided to cover different areas of management and skills within the team, as well as different responsibilities for social relationships, tasks, and information. Some team role inventories might focus more on differences between roles in relation to thinking, feeling, acting, leading, or evaluating.

Team role inventories have been subjected to criticism in recent decades because the roles they suggest are not always helpful in practice. There are also concerns about whether data generated can reliably distinguish team members, predict their actual behaviours, or help determine optimal team sizes and configurations. Given the amount of uncertainty, disruption, and change that is common in many work contexts, it is likely that roles will need to at least adjust, and often change entirely, to cope with these situations. For example, someone might join

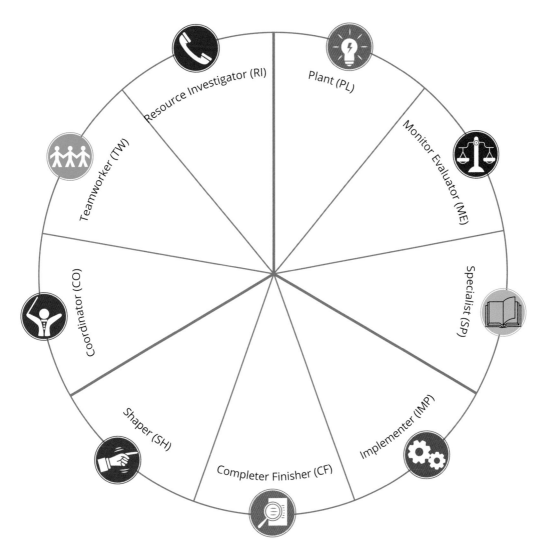

FIGURE 9.4 **Team role inventory example—the Belbin Team.** Credit: Belbin and Culture Report (2018). Belbin Ltd 2023. All rights reserved.

a team in a monitoring role, but if the coordinator leaves may be asked to step up to this challenge. Assigning team roles may ensure some baseline level of coordination and proficiency, but if they are too limiting or fixed, they risk failing to take into account that team members may need to be adaptable and change their roles, and may need to be proactive in developing new approaches.

Nevertheless, inventories remain a popular tool, and at the very least can help team members get to know each other by prompting a conversation about how they might best structure to work effectively.

A related, but alternative view of teams is to focus on the ties and relationships between members rather than the characteristics of the members themselves. This involves treating the team as a social network of individuals including leaders, followers, experts, friends, enemies, loners, or 'brokers' (bridges between otherwise disconnected people), among many other 'relational' possibilities. Individuals may relate to other team members in multiple ways. For example, a team member may have a relationship with another member which comprises mentor, expert, as well as friend. Or they may have a **mentor–mentee** relationship with one team member, but a leader–follower relationship with another. Such complexity requires individuals to be able to respond to different demands and obligations from different people at different times on a highly personalized basis.

9.5.2 Socialization

As part of team formation, it may be helpful for new team members to receive some form of socialization. Just as a new employee might receive an induction introducing them to a new job and organization, new team members might also need to learn about how to be a proficient team member in terms of the norms (expected behaviours), beliefs, and values inherent to a particular team. There may be some preparatory training, but also specific rituals to acknowledge the change to the team, such as a welcome party or meeting to facilitate introductions.

Specific documents can be useful as a form of socialization. If most or all of the team members are new, or their work is changing or being relaunched in some way, a Team Charter may be developed to reinforce team formation and focus on socialization. A Team Charter documents the team's focus, purpose, direction, goals, and members' roles and responsibilities, and is typically developed with contributions from all team members. Similarly, if the team is working on a particular project, they may develop a brief summary of the most important information regarding the work the team has been formed to do. This is useful as it ensures all team members understand and support all aspects of the work. It can also be used within the team for communication, guidance, and reminders of the team's priorities. Additionally, it has external uses: to help other leaders and the rest of the organization understand what the team has been set up to do, how it does it, who is in it, and what it looks like.

9.5.3 Diversity

Team formation also needs to consider the diversity of team members. This has become increasingly important in recent years, as the moral imperative for diversity has gained acceptance, and also because the benefits of diversity to team success are increasingly apparent.

There are many different types of diversity that can exist between team members: attitudes, values, and experience; status, resources, and seniority; as well as age, gender, race, and other individual characteristics. Some forms of diversity may be immediately visible on the surface of the team, other differences more deeply concealed and only revealed as team members spend time together and get to know one another. Some forms of diversity might be considered directly relevant to the tasks and work of the team, such as expertise and experience, while other forms might be less relevant on the surface, but also important to team outcomes, such as gender and race.

The benefits of diversity may not be immediately apparent or easily accessed. For example, a team comprising members with very similar backgrounds, values, attitudes, and even gender and race might be easier to manage towards agreement. Conversely, a team with diverse members who all hold different views may have a bumpier road in terms of agreement of task aims, approaches, and processes. However, the team of similar individuals may not have the benefit of different views, expertise, perspectives, and creativity that a diverse team is able to consider.

Achieving the benefits of team diversity therefore requires careful development and management. Moreover, potential negative impacts of diversity need to be identified early and addressed proactively. There are a number of approaches to managing diversity, which will be appropriate in different circumstances. In some situations simply acknowledging the diversity that exists is effective, so long as there is general equality and inclusion. Other teams may benefit from openly discussing the diversity that exists in order to ensure it does not become hidden or ignored. Others may choose to celebrate that diversity as a key to the strength and success of the team and their aims.

Where diversity is not effectively celebrated, developed, or managed, issues can occur which can be detrimental to the team, and the individuals within it. For example, power may concentrate in a subset of the team that all hold a characteristic in common, such as gender or race, marginalizing those in the team who are different. This can occur when people form a 'team within a team', comprising those who have something in common and excluding others. While negatively impacting the individuals excluded, it also limits the teams' ability to access their talents, skills, and motivation.

A key role of the human resources function within organizations (explored in Chapter 7) is to prevent problems arising from diversity in teams, and address and solve issues when they do occur. For example, the rise in cross-cultural teams has been driven by the number of global organizations and more recently by the rise of virtual teams facilitated by technology. When cross-cultural teams are formed, their line managers and team members may be given training to understand cultural compatibility or clashes, and differences in communication, humour, working style, values, and world views. The human resources function is a key player in managing this.

9.5.4 Virtual teams

Although virtual teams have been used in organizations for many years, the Covid-19 pandemic has amplified the prevalence of virtual teamwork, as an inevitable result of increased home, remote, and hybrid working. Virtual teams are typically defined by members who work together using digital tools, and have two or more members distributed across time and geography.

This often includes team members in different countries or regions, and different geographical time zones.

While issues with virtual teams mirror those of other teams, other challenges are also unique to this type of team. One issue relates to how effectively technological media and tools support communication and coordination across time and distance. These virtual conditions can create particular issues with leadership, trust, relationship-building, knowledge sharing, and general awareness and understanding of context. This is because team members are not working together physically at the same location and lack face-to-face cues and the potential richness of immediate, synchronized, in-person interactions. However, virtual teams are likely to remain necessary and indeed popular given that they enable flexibility, global reach, and diversity, and can incorporate more sophisticated digital forms of technologically-supported collaboration.

9.6 Team development

Following team formation, we should consider the importance of team development, including how a team manages its activities, relationships, and results on an ongoing basis. This is important because it can help to explain or predict team outcomes and a team's overall effectiveness in relation to its wider environment.

9.6.1 Stage models

Team development is often explored using stage models, which depict specific stages that a team goes through. These models can be useful because they help teams understand which stage of development they are currently in, and if stuck, which potential team-building and leadership tactics might help them move from one specific stage to the next. However, as with many management models, they can never reflect the true reality of how teams develop, or the way in which they cycle through different stages.

One of the most well-known and long-standing models of team development is by the American psychologist Bruce Tuckman (from 1965 onwards), who identified a sequence of five stages of team development (Figure 9.5):

- *Forming*—team members get to know each other, define rules and boundaries.
- *Storming*—team members attempt to explore conflict and resolve differences.
- *Norming*—team members' cooperation and commitment to team goals grows.
- *Performing*—team members make decisions and achieve common goals.
- *Adjourning (or mourning)*—team members complete task, break up, redeploy.

Tuckman's stage model treats team development as a sequence of steps. This offers a simple and helpful way of thinking about managing the team. Moreover, it can be useful to identify how teams can move on to a later stage of development. For example, to move from *storming* to *norming*, a team may need to use some careful conflict management strategies, and to find ways for team members to voice and resolve differences, help each other, and build trust.

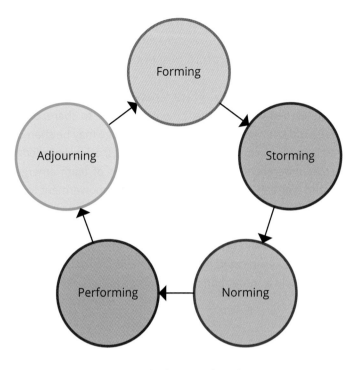

FIGURE 9.5 **Tuckman's stage model of team development.**

However, models such as Tuckman's have been criticized for implying that there is a relatively steady and continuous process by which teams develop. Others, such as Professor Connie Gersick, have suggested that in reality, teams develop following more sudden or profound one-off events (Gersick, 1988). That is, the steady state of equilibrium is 'punctuated' or disrupted suddenly, causing the team to develop in quite a new form or direction. Examples of this type of team development might include a significant change in leadership, the introduction of innovative new ways of working or organizational processes, or the need to survive and learn from a crisis.

9.6.2 **Team processes and emergent states**

Both Tuckman's model and the critique of it are addressed in an approach to team development defined in terms of *team processes*. This comprises all interactions and activities that help convert inputs of a team into outputs, and describes how they interact and behave over time. From this perspective, teams divide time through cycles of accomplishing their work versus changing the direction of their work. Under this approach, most processes can be classified and measured in terms of whether the interactions or activities in question help teams to (1) coordinate actions; (2) plan strategies or goals; or (3) manage the emotions, motivations, and conflicts affecting the interpersonal relationships of team members (Marks et al., 2001).

While team processes describe what a team does and how its members act over time, conversely *team emergent states* describe how teams think, feel, and are motivated together over time. Although team processes and emergent states may overlap, distinguishing between them can help us understand what is going on in a team. For example, a team may be lacking in confidence (emergent state), and therefore not set ambitious goals or deal with conflicts head-on (processes), which in turn may drive confidence down further (emergent state again).

Much of the focus on emergent states in team development is cognitive (i.e. about mental processes), and so concerned with how team members come to share, distribute, and represent thoughts, beliefs, and knowledge. While some knowledge may be shared across the entire team, allowing members to reach common understandings, other knowledge may be distributed differently across different team members. Examples of team emergent states include cohesion (bonding and wanting to stick together), trust, empowerment, commitment, or engagement. One recent concept within team emergent states is psychological safety, which is explored in Spotlight 9.1. Team emergent states are inherently difficult to identify because they are less easy to observe than team processes. However, this does not make them less important to team development. As indicated by the label, these shared states of mind can 'emerge' in teams such that the whole is more than the sum of the parts.

SPOTLIGHT 9.1 **PSYCHOLOGICAL SAFETY**

A team emergent state construct that has become particularly influential in explaining OB over the last 20 years is psychological safety. It was initially talked about in the 1960s as a state where people feel secure taking risks, changing their behaviour in response to challenges, and overcoming uncertainty and anxiety to achieve greater learning and innovation. It was then largely forgotten until it attracted renewed interest in the 1990s around how to engage employees and encourage them to express themselves when performing roles.

The work of Harvard Business School Professor Amy C. Edmondson has been particularly significant in re-establishing the importance of psychological safety in relation to teams, leadership, and organizational learning and innovation. Her studies of various types of teams, such as those working in product development, innovation, and health care contexts, have explored psychological safety as a shared belief that a team is a safe space in which individuals are able to take interpersonal risks. Research has shown psychological safety to be a key link in supporting higher levels of team learning and performance, particularly through behaviours

involving mutual respect for discussing differences, mistakes, and unconventional ideas (Edmondson & Lei, 2014). Two important conditions for improving psychological safety are: (1) non-defensive team leader coaching and a supportive team context for providing information and (2) resources and rewards.

Psychological safety is not the only state needed for high levels of team performance, but it removes important obstacles that can stop people from speaking up to address crises and suggest innovations. There are many ways for leaders, teams, and cultures to promote psychological safety in terms of humble, proactive, inquiring, and participative forms of organizational behaviour. However, it can take time, effort, and practice to demonstrate these complex social skills and create an atmosphere of trust, accountability, and initiative between people at work. Knowing that speaking up will not lead to excessive fear or blame in organizations is a compelling state of mind, although questions remain about how to recreate and sustain it in changing working conditions, such as virtual meetings and hybrid workplaces.

9.6.3 Conflict resolution

For teams to develop successfully, they need to determine ways of constructively and efficiently dealing with conflict resolution. Most teams will at times inevitably experience conflicts between members. These might concern tasks, relationships, or processes. If managed poorly, these conflicts will negatively impact team functioning and performance. Teams can respond to conflict in many different ways—simply trying to avoid it, putting issues to a vote, or improvising compromises. However, the best teams tend to anticipate conflict and discuss it openly and early, making plans to share and assign work appropriately and fairly, and focusing on the content and reasons behind conflicts, rather than the personalities involved. This manages and resolves conflict in ways that minimize its negative effects.

Let's return to Imperial in Running case 9.2, to see how they have responded to the challenges their team faced in Running case 9.1.

RUNNING CASE 9.2 **THE DREAM TEAM IN ACTION**

It has been a week since Lucy's meetings with Sue and Bob. The new approach to product design is already proving effective. A new subgroup has been formed with a very tight remit: to decide upon and create the first plant-based dish to be trialled. This gives members a sharper sense of purpose, and the composition and atmosphere of the team are very different from the original Product Design team. Sue has been appointed as the team leader, and Gita is the only other senior manager in it. There is also Piotr Grzybowski, the international buyer from the Purchasing Department, and three members from the food preparation team: Jazz, Bella, and a new part-time worker, Dylan. Bob was hesitant about including Dylan, until HR Manager Su-Li Chan pointed out that he was about to complete his BSc in Food Science, writing his dissertation on plant-based nutrition.

It's clear to Sue by the end of this first meeting that this team—who have decided to call themselves the Dream Team—will do well. At Gita's suggestion, they have agreed on a team charter, setting out their aims and the way they intend to work together. Sue's agenda was quickly agreed upon by all, with some good additional ideas coming from Bella, and worked through with a sense of commitment. The food production team are positive and energetic, and Sue has quickly realized that Dylan really knows his stuff. In fact, she has allowed him to take the lead in most of the conversation: Piotr, Bella, and Jazz clearly respect his expertise, and Dylan has been very skilled at identifying key issues to address and then stepping back to allow everyone else to contribute their ideas.

Based on Gita's initial market research, the team has agreed that the first product to be trialled will be a jackfruit and lentil pie. They have brainstormed an ingredient list, as well as the next steps to developing the dish. Sue has delegated the different tasks that they have all identified: Piotr is going to look at sourcing the ingredients, like lentils from France or Spain; Jazz and Bella are going to trial cooking the dish with either vegan cheese or non-dairy béchamel sauce; Dylan is going to produce a nutritional analysis; and Gita will consider branding and sustainable packaging. Everyone is buzzing and looking forward to reporting on their progress at next week's meeting.

Questions for reflection

1. How do you view the composition of the Dream Team? What general conclusions can be drawn from the team's structure that can be applied to other teams?

2. Consider psychological safety (Spotlight 9.1) and compare the experiences of the Dream Team and the original Product Design team (refer back to Running case 9.1). What do you see?

3. How do you evaluate Sue's conduct as the team's leader? Why was Sue chosen over Bob? Over Gita?

In the preceding sections we have explored both team formation and team development. The appropriate management of these functions is likely to contribute to the effectiveness of a team. However, we can also explore team effectiveness as an issue in its own right, which we turn to now.

9.7 Team effectiveness

Team effectiveness is achieved by both elements of team formation and team development, but can also be considered as a topic on its own. Many systematic team effectiveness models exist and continue to be proposed and refined. They represent efforts to gather together the most important factors for explaining whether a team will perform to the highest level or not. Core elements of models to predict highly effective teams often include: a compelling direction, a strong structure, a supportive context, a shared **mindset**, and some form of expert coaching. According to these models, a team will then be effective in the sense that it produces outputs perceived positively by others (e.g. customers), a sense of good dynamics through collaborative abilities, and individual development where team members improve their own knowledge, skills, and abilities.

   More recent team effectiveness models refer to a bigger picture of teamwork as an IPO (input-process-outcome) system (Figure 9.6). *Inputs* concern types of starting condition that allow or constrain team member interactions. These in turn drive *processes*, which concern how team members interact to accomplish tasks. Finally, *outcomes* are the results, and by-products of

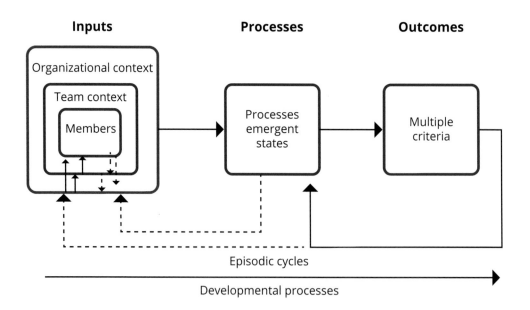

FIGURE 9.6 **Example input-process-outcome framework of team effectiveness.**
Credit: Mathieu, J., Maynard, M. T., Rapp, T., & Gilson, L. (2008). 'Team Effectiveness 1997–2007: A Review of Recent Advancements and a Glimpse into the Future'. *Journal of Management*, 34(3), 410–476. https://doi .org/10.1177/0149206308316061. Reprinted by Permission of SAGE Publications

teamwork that are valued by one or more audiences or stakeholder groups, which might in-clude team members or others beyond the team.

However, it is important to remember that these are just models of effective teamwork. As such they are always imperfect representations of the real world to some degree. Team effectiveness models have been criticized as tending to reduce teamwork to a few static ge-neric areas and generate long lists of necessary conditions that start to look repetitive and idealistic. Further, it is not always clear how to put team effectiveness models into practice in specific organizational contexts, which are often more uncertain, diverse, and complex in reality.

Nevertheless, team effectiveness frameworks are increasingly recognizing that teams com-prise many dynamically interacting parts. This is perhaps why highly effective teams or col-laborative relationships can sometimes seem like they have secret or mysterious ingredients; to understand them better we have to engage more systematically with some of the complex details driving that success. For example, the famous English rock band The Beatles worked as a team of four to write and record some of their most sophisticated songs in the second half of the 1960s. Analysis of The Beatles in terms of team effectiveness uncovers a surprising range of diverse and subtle insights into their success. Such insights include the psychologi-cal make-up of the team members and their unique roles; a shared willingness to take risks in discovering new sources of inspiration; taking leadership help and advice from outsiders; and freedom in how members accomplish ambitious work they all feel passionate about (The Economist, 2021).

To sustain high levels of performance, teams need sources of leadership (e.g. vision, support), ways to manage their performance (e.g. incentives, feedback), ways to manage people (e.g. delegation, skill/workload capacities), and values to emphasize from a wider organizational culture (e.g. well-being, innovation). However, 'effectiveness' also depends on the context and aims of the team. For example, for teams more concerned with creativity, innovation, and change, a diverse set of driven, innovative team members able to work through conflict and use norms and rewards for delivering innovative changes may be most important. In other settings, teams might be in conflict with senior management over their working conditions and need industrial relations support, be concerned with policies that select, reward, and assess members based on customer service targets, or other technical and cultural variations of team effectiveness supports.

It can also be worthwhile considering factors that lead to team *ineffectiveness*. Just because we can identify factors which contribute to an effective team does not mean that most teams are effective in practice. Any of the components in a team effectiveness framework can potentially be deficient or dysfunctional. Ineffectiveness could be due to some input, process, or output being out of alignment with the task and organization. A team might be confused about, in tension with, or liable to reject some aspect of its design or environment. There could be problems with people not putting in enough effort on behalf of the team (so-called 'social loafing'), ineffective coordination or communication, or ineffective leadership.

Diagnosing the exact issue or problem within a team requires careful observation, analysis and thinking how and where specific components might be absent or inconsistent, or might be undermining team performance, collaborative interactions, or the contributions and needs of individual members. Furthermore, understanding issues with a team's effectiveness will likely involve looking beyond the team itself and into the wider organizational environment of structure, culture, politics, information, and resources. For example, a team may be subject to wider managerial forces of hierarchical control, non-cooperative behaviours, inconsistent policies and practices, and other individual and organizational concerns that interfere with and act as obstacles to team effectiveness.

9.8 **Conclusion**

In this chapter, we have considered the overarching issue of managing people in relation to both OB, which considers what influences an individual's motivation and attitudes to their role, manager, and organization, as well as teams, which focuses on individuals working together towards a specific aim. The discussion about teams considered questions of team formation, development, and effectiveness. Managing people—as individuals and in teams—is a key role that most managers will have to take on at some point in their career. It can prove to be one of the most difficult tasks given the uncertainties involved. As such, becoming an effective manager is likely to require careful consideration of how best to motivate individuals, and to structure and develop teams.

CHAPTER SUMMARY

○ OB models seek to understand people's motivations and perceptions, and how management can influence these.

○ Teams are a subset of OB. They represent a creative and productive force.

○ Teamwork always involves interdependence and requires coordination of team members via accountability, predictability, and a common understanding.

○ Team formation involves assigning team roles, socialization, and ensuring diversity.

○ Team effectiveness comes from a shared mindset and values, a strong structure, a supportive context, and expert coaching.

CLOSING CASE REFLECTION

Team-building at Emirates

When a plane is in the air, the aircraft and its passengers are completely dependent on cabin crew for their needs. Without access to outside support, the crew must be well-trained and prepared for any eventuality including emergencies. Working in a confined space, over long periods of time, and with hundreds of lives dependent on them, Emirates team members require a strong shared vision and coordination skills so that they can carry out scheduled tasks including serving meals while being prepared to respond to issues as they arise. Emirates invests heavily in selecting motivated individuals and training them as part of effective teams, including an intensive two-month training programme for new recruits to learn skills and to understand the vision of the Emirates Experience.

REVIEW QUESTIONS

1. How are the concepts of organizational behaviour and teams related to each other?

2. How can managers use an awareness of different approaches to individual motivation in managing their team members?

3. Explain the importance of team roles, socialization, and diversity in team formation.

4. Apply Tuckman's model of team development (see Section 9.6.1) to a product development team or a medical emergency team. Reflect on the usefulness of the model and consider any ways in which it may not reflect reality.

5. Are teams always the most effective structure to complete tasks or projects? Explain using examples of teams that are effective or ineffective in practice.

EXPLORE MORE

READ M. Haas and M. Mortensen (2016). 'The Secrets of Great Teamwork', *Harvard Business Review*, 94(6): 70–76.

READ D. Rock and H. Grant (2016). 'Why Diverse Teams Are Smarter', *Harvard Business Review*, 4 November 2016.

WATCH Amy Edmondson's TED Talk on Psychological Safety. Search 'Building a Psychologically Safe Workplace' on YouTube.

LISTEN to 'The Surprising Truth about Motivation with Daniel Pink' (2019), on the Mindvalley Podcast.

9

CHAPTER TEN
Leading and Influencing

Sarah Woolley and Emma Macdonald

OPENING CASE STUDY LEADERSHIP IN THE NATIONAL HEALTH SERVICE

Health care systems are essential but provided in very different ways around the world, with national health care systems based on various mixes of publicly- versus commercially-funded services. The UK's National Health Service (NHS) is a publicly-funded health care service designed to provide population-based health care services, free at the point of need. Regardless of their source of funding, all health service organizations experience the challenge of dealing with multiple stakeholder interests in complex ecosystems.

Leaders in this sector may come from a wide variety of backgrounds, including medicine, nursing, science, or management, and may lead organizations (for example, hospitals or community care networks), departments (e.g. radiology and diagnostics department; trauma care department), or specialist teams (e.g. midwifery team). These leaders face the twin challenges of driving change initiatives that accommodate high quality individualized patient care but at the same time manage population-level cost control. To further add to the challenge, leaders in this sector respond simultaneously to frequently conflicting demands of clinical professionals, administrators, regulators, and patient groups. Both the variety and volume of stakeholders and interests can place strain on managers, and, to further complicate matters, some of these stakeholder groups are very powerful. Two such powerful stakeholder groups are the British Medical Association and the Royal College of Nursing, the UK's professional bodies for doctors and nurses, respectively. These professional bodies have high levels of expertise and are well respected by government and society. There are many other influential stakeholder groups and collectively these influential stakeholders can make the work of health care leaders challenging on issues where they have strong viewpoints.

One analysis of multiple programmes in the UK's NHS (Dixon-Woods et al., 2012) identified a list of 10 challenges that needed overcoming for a change programme to succeed:

1. convince people there's a problem;
2. then convince people there's a solution;
3. collect data and monitor, which the study found 'always takes more time and energy than anticipated';
4. if employees are fatigued from many prior change programmes, avoid claiming big project goals and talking up the intended 'transformation';
5. understand the organization's current goals and pressures on employees;

(Continued)

6. tribalism within professions can affect motivation, so make sure key groups are represented, such as surgeons, specialist doctors, and nurse groups;

7. getting the right approach to leadership may require adopting 'quieter' leadership, oriented towards inclusion, explanation, and gentle persuasion;

8. motivation may need to be incentivized ('carrots') but also penalties ('sticks') may be required (the analogy of carrots and sticks was described when discussing the topic of Motivation in Chapter 8);

9. sustainability of initiatives needs to be considered to ensure implemented actions will continue once the change management project ends; and

10. vigilance will need to be applied to pick up on potential side effects of change, i.e. where solving one problem creates a different problem.

Leaders in the health care sector are therefore required to consider the interests of multiple stakeholder groups in their day-to-day work. Increasingly, leaders in this sector adopt participative leadership practices, which include involving multiple managerial levels and professions in service delivery and change processes. These more consultative approaches can make implementing organizational goals cumbersome because they require the involvement of a wider range of people in decision-making. They may also slow change efforts as managers attempt to accommodate multiple demands from different stakeholder groups.

10.1 Introduction

Leadership and influence are key dimensions of management, across all types of organizations including business, politics, public service, not-for-profit, and social enterprises. However, leadership is a highly contested and controversial concept, which can be defined in multiple ways, including as a position, a personal characteristic, an outcome, or a process (Grint, 2010). Leadership is by its nature a complex, **multidimensional** activity, which is shaped according to various individual and social factors. We draw on an early definition that describes leadership as a process or act of influencing the activities of a group (or organization) towards goal setting and goal achievement (Stogdill, 1950).

There is an ongoing debate about the distinction between leadership and management. Some define these as two distinct domains of practice, undertaken by different people and roles. For example, Kotter (1990) views managers as handling complexity through planning staffing and control while leaders galvanize change by setting direction, aligning people, and solving problems. Grint (2010) distinguishes between managers as those who deal with tame problems and leaders who solve wicked problems. However, we take the view that managing and leading are mutually entwined activities that need practising by the same people at different times (Mintzberg, 2009).

To understand the concept of influence, we draw on the work of Reuben and Gigliotti (2016), who view it as a social, interactive, communicative process occurring between group and organizational members. Influence considered in this way involves the intentional verbal acts that leaders, followers, and group members might use to influence each other. It may also include non-verbal communication modes such as gestures and body language (e.g. a smile or a frown to encourage or discourage someone from participating), material artefacts like clothing or electronic devices, and symbolic means including desk position, staff awards, and ceremonies. The dynamics of influence between organizational members may also involve unplanned and accidental events and occur through both formal and informal role-based behaviours. For example, you might bump into your CEO in the lift and have an opportunity to shape their views on an issue in a way that your position within the organizational hierarchy would not usually allow you to do.

Whenever we use the term leadership, we also need to consider the idea of followership—that is, the process by which individuals or groups accept the influence of others to accomplish a common goal (Northouse, 2021). Different theories of leadership treat leader–follower relations differently. As we will see later in this chapter, traditional perspectives are leader-centric (Bass, 2008) with followers viewed as recipients of the leader's influence, while more recent perspectives emphasize followers as active 'constructors' of leaders and leadership (Meindl et al., 1985).

In this chapter, we consider some of the critical debates and tensions relating to leadership and influence. We structure the chapter around four particular perspectives: trait-based leadership; behaviour-based leadership; context-based leadership; and collective leadership. These perspectives define leadership in different ways, making particular assumptions about the purpose of leadership, the way managers enact leadership roles, and how they leverage influence as part of this. As we discuss each of these leadership theories, we consider how leadership is defined, the implications for how leadership is practised, and the limitations of understanding leadership from each of these perspectives. We finally discuss examples of influence without leadership.

10.2 Trait-based leadership

Trait-based theories are some of the earliest approaches to understanding leadership, emerging at the beginning of the twentieth century. Sometimes referred to as 'great man theories', these theories focus on the specific individual attributes, qualities, and **characteristics** that differentiate leaders from their followers. Specifically, they consider how well-known political, social, and military figures were able to reach leadership positions, having substantial power to influence and direct the lives and activities of others. Leadership understood in this way emphasizes it as something that involves inherent, unique, and special qualities—that is, it embodies the view that leaders are born, rather than made, irrespective of the type of people they lead or the specific situations they find themselves in. As such, these theories are very different to other theories of leadership because they focus solely on the leader, rather than considering the needs of followers or the context in which leaders operate.

There was significant interest in studying and classifying leadership **traits** during the first part of the twentieth century. An early contribution to this area came from Ralph Stogdill (1948), who conducted a review of all of the research that sought to identify leadership traits. He found that individuals who occupied leadership roles could be differentiated from followers according to eight traits: intelligence, alertness, insight, responsibility, initiative, persistence, self-confidence, and sociability. Consider, for example, the case of Harriet Tubman, described in Spotlight 10.1.

SPOTLIGHT 10.1 **HARRIET TUBMAN (1822–1913)**

Harriet Tubman was an American abolitionist and social activist who was born into slavery in Dorchester County, Maryland, USA. In 1949, she escaped to freedom in Philadelphia and from this point on, she led numerous missions to rescue family members from slavery, as well as guiding other slaves to freedom in the North. Harriet not only freed slaves but also actively participated in the American Civil War, initially working for the Union Army as a cook and nurse and then becoming an armed scout and spy. She became the first woman to lead an armed expedition during the war, leading 150 African-American soldiers of the Second Carolina Infantry to rescue, and transporting more than 750 former slaves in what became known as the Combahee River Raid. Later in life, she also played a key role in supporting the women's suffrage movement, campaigning for women's right to vote in the USA.

Harriet Tubman exhibited many of the traits that early researchers of leadership tended to associate with leaders. Not only did she show great courage and undertake many heroic acts, she also demonstrated the self-confidence to challenge the established social order at the time and took responsibility for overseeing multiple humanitarian missions (National Women's History Museum, 2016).

Harriet Tubman, 1895. Source: Public Domain/ Horatio Seymour Squyer, 1848 – 18 Dec 1905

Interest in trait-based leadership waned in the mid-twentieth century because of the increasing number of attributes that were found to be associated with leadership, and the difficulty with identifying a consistent set of leadership traits. However, more recently, there has been a resurgence of interest in this approach with research evaluating the link between the 'big five' personality traits (Goldberg, 1990), shown in Figure 10.1, and leadership (Judge et al., 2002). Four of these personality traits have been found to relate to leadership effectiveness, with extraversion being the most important, followed by conscientiousness and openness, in combination with low neuroticism (Judge et al., 2002).

At the same time, there has also been particular interest across academic and practitioner communities in two leadership qualities: charisma and emotional intelligence. Leaders with charisma are described as transformational. They have an exceptional ability to inspire and motivate others to perform, beyond expectation (Burns, 1978). These leaders encourage their followers to identify with their personal mission and feel better about their participation. Research on charismatic leadership has been found to be positively associated with leadership effectiveness and organizational outcomes (Avolio et al., 2009; Judge & Piccolo, 2004).

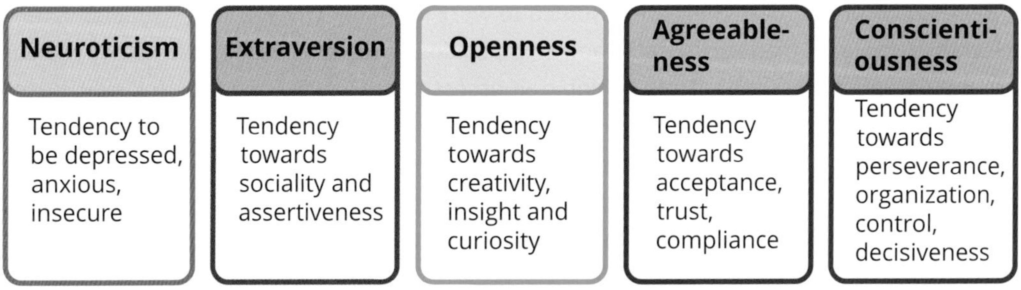

Neuroticism	Extraversion	Openness	Agreeable-ness	Conscienti-ousness
Tendency to be depressed, anxious, insecure	Tendency towards sociality and assertiveness	Tendency towards creativity, insight and curiosity	Tendency towards acceptance, trust, compliance	Tendency towards perseverance, organization, control, decisiveness

FIGURE 10.1 **Summary of the 'Big Five' personality traits (Goldberg, 1990).**

Nevertheless, charismatic leadership is also seen as having a dark side. One study found transformational leaders had higher rates of employee sickness absence in their teams (Nielsen & Daniels, 2016), while others have found that individuals rated as high on charisma are not always rated as effective by others (Vergauwe et al., 2018).

Emotional intelligence is the ability to carry out accurate reasoning about emotions and use emotions and emotional knowledge to enhance thinking (Mayer et al., 2008). Daniel Goleman (1998) has popularized this idea and developed leadership capabilities linked to this concept (Goleman, 1998). This has five specific components as outlined in Figure 10.2. Goleman (1998) emphasizes that leaders with well-developed emotional intelligence are better equipped to meet collective goals. Moreover, he suggests that while this is something that individuals are born with to varying degrees, people can strengthen their skills in this area through practice and feedback from colleagues.

10.2.1 The role of influence in trait-based leadership

Trait-based theories focus on the individual attributes of the leader and are silent on the relational and contextual aspects of leadership. The assumption is an individual's inherent dispositional leadership qualities are what makes them a leader, and that they use these traits to influence more junior employees to achieve organizational goals. As such, influence over others is automatically assumed, as long as leaders exhibit the right set of leadership traits.

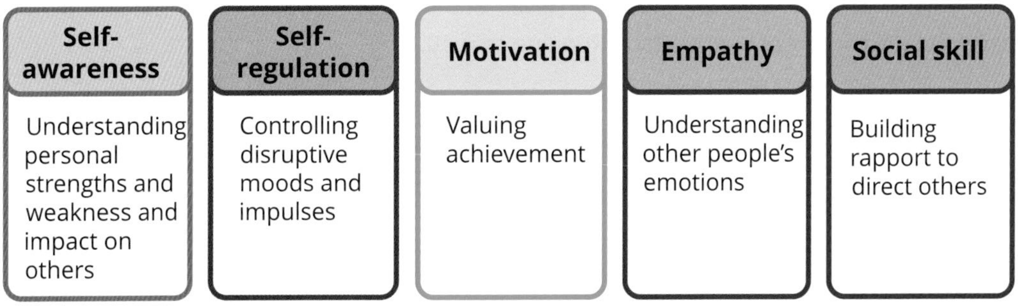

Self-awareness	Self-regulation	Motivation	Empathy	Social skill
Understanding personal strengths and weakness and impact on others	Controlling disruptive moods and impulses	Valuing achievement	Understanding other people's emotions	Building rapport to direct others

FIGURE 10.2 **Leadership characteristics linked to emotional intelligence.** Credit: Reprinted by permission of Harvard Business Review. Excerpt/Exhibit. From 'What makes a leader' by Daniel Goleman, 76 (6), 1998. Copyright ©1998 by Harvard Business Publishing; all rights reserved.

Because of this, organizations are assumed to work more effectively if they can identify and select the people for managerial and leadership positions who have the 'right' traits. By seeking out and selecting these individuals—using trait assessments initially and then focusing development and training programmes on these individuals—organizations can improve their influence and effectiveness. In this perspective of leadership, no consideration of the situation that the leader finds themselves in is included, and therefore there is no consideration of the leader's ability to increase their influence by changing aspects of the situation, or the situation followers find themselves in.

10.2.2 Criticisms of trait-based leadership perspectives

Trait-based theories have been criticized in three ways. The first category of criticism is linked to the traits themselves. While a wide range of traits have been identified, most are largely generic, subjective, and may mean different things to different people. For example, what do the traits of openness, agreeableness, or insight really mean? For this reason, there are questions about the usefulness of identifying these traits and the extent to which such traits can be properly validated through research studies that attempt to measure traits and evaluate their connection to effective leadership.

The second category of criticism points out the failure to notice the effect of situation on leadership. This criticism argues that trait theories ignore the fact that effective leadership traits need to be relevant to the situation in which the leader operates. Leadership traits also need to be appropriate given the relationship between the leader and group members, while also taking into account team characteristics and organizational culture. For example, think back to Deal and Kennedy's typology of organizational culture in Chapter 6. Some leadership traits may be effective in a 'work hard/play hard' culture, but those same traits may be ineffective in a process culture.

The final category of criticism is linked to the fact that trait-based theories focus on identifying so-called leadership traits in individuals, without considering the impact of these traits on leadership outcomes, effects on group members, work efforts, productivity, or employee well-being. In other words, trait theories are leader-centric and do not really consider the impact of leadership traits on either followers or the wider organizational activities they may be involved in leading. For example, these traits may end up having negative impacts on followers, as we saw earlier with the leaders who show high levels of the charisma trait. Let's consider Imperial's leaders in the context of their traits, in Running case 10.1.

RUNNING CASE 10.1 **IMPERIAL'S LEADERS AND THEIR TRAITS**

Anyone walking up the wood-panelled stairs at Imperial Fine Foods gets a very clear impression of the company's history over almost a century. There are the annual Christmas photographs of all staff and workers, the framed customer testimonials, and the awards for outstanding products won at leading culinary championships. As you enter the boardroom, you also get a very clear impression of Imperial's three previous generations of leaders: Edward Green, the company's founder, his son James, and his grandson Hugh who each looks out at visitors from his own oil portrait. In the words of Hugh's cousin Charles, on his last visit for a shareholders' meeting, 'They all *look* like leaders, the sort of people who are born to be in charge.'

If he were asked to explain himself, Charles would have no trouble describing what being a leader should mean. In his day, leaders were male and had 'recognizable' leader-like traits; self-confident men with presence, able to dominate a situation. Though he finds much to disappoint him in his cousin Hugh's chairmanship of the business ('He has become far too soft in his old age'), Charles would acknowledge that Hugh has always looked and acted like a leader himself: he is tall and invariably wears a dark, pinstriped suit and tie; he is intelligent, assertive, and is always ready to take charge of any meeting. Though he is less formal than his father James, and though Imperial's staff are friendly towards Hugh and he towards them, there was never much doubt throughout most of his tenure at the head of Imperial that it was Hugh's place to decide, and his employees' place to follow his decisions.

From Charles's perspective, Hugh's son William would have been a far better choice than Lucy to become the fourth CEO of the business. William looks, and in Charles's view acts, much more like a leader than his sister: he too is tall and properly dressed; he is not prone to chat; and he is inclined to think of task first and people second. Charles applauds this approach; the company should be focused on getting the job done and maximizing its profits. As CEO, Lucy should stop wasting her time consulting everyone and just tell them what needs to be done. He has noticed that Lucy is prone to casual conversations with even the most junior employees. And that is before she starts talking about her values which he sees as an indulgent distraction. He is still digesting the contents of Lucy's stinging email in response to his criticism of her trip to Imperial's tea suppliers in Kenya.

Questions for reflection

1. How do you view the trait theory of leadership as seen by Charles? How far do you agree that some people are just 'born leaders'?

2. What are some of the obstacles faced by women like Lucy as they begin to assume leadership responsibility in organizations previously dominated by men?

3. From the perspective of Imperial's staff, how would you view the merits of William and Lucy as leaders?

10.3 Behaviour-based leadership

Behaviour-based leadership theories focus on what leaders do in relation to two types of leadership behaviour: task activities and relationship activities. These theories emerged during the 1950s in response to difficulties in identifying a consistent set of traits that could be associated with leaders. Researchers at Ohio State University and Michigan University began two large studies to investigate leader behaviour. Although they used different approaches, both research groups generated similar results.

The Ohio-based studies defined leadership behaviour as requiring two elements. The first was consideration and the second was initiating structure (Stogdill & Coons, 1951). The Michigan studies labelled these employee-centred behaviour and job-centred behaviour (Katz et al., 1950). These are depicted and described in Figure 10.3.

Considerate leaders are interested in employees and are relationship-oriented, encouraging participation in decision-making, and supporting **subordinates** with personal issues. Leaders who initiate structure are task- and job-centred, focusing on assigning work, task structuring, making expectations clear, and expecting subordinates to follow instructions. Consideration and

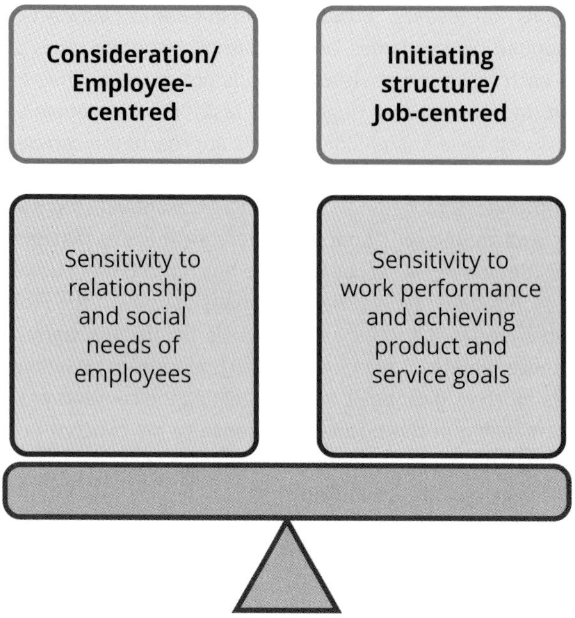

FIGURE 10.3 **Leadership behaviour elements (based on Stogdill & Coons, 1951).**

initiating structure are considered to be separate behaviour patterns and leaders may emphasize one or both, to varying degrees. Neither is 'right' or 'wrong' and each has strengths. Where leaders emphasize considerate behaviour, job satisfaction is likely to be higher, with lower complaints and turnover. In contrast, when leaders focus on initiating structure, task performance is higher.

More recently, researchers have drawn on this approach to develop the Integrated Model of Leadership Behaviour (IMoLB), which reflects more modern conceptions of organizations and demands on leaders (Behrendt et al., 2017) (Figure 10.4). The IMoLB sets out a wider range of task and relational activities for leaders than prior behaviour-based models. Here, task-oriented behaviours focus on organizational change demands by envisioning change and innovation, and encouraging learning. Relations-oriented behaviours focus on influencing followers to meet external demands through networking, monitoring, and mobilizing resources.

10.3.1 The role of influence in behaviour-based leadership

Behaviour-based leadership broadens our understanding of leadership beyond individual leader traits to consider what leaders do, how they act in different situations and the impact they have on followers. While the assumptions remain that leadership is a mechanism for influencing subordinates to achieve collective goals, these models recognize that leaders might not always be effective at influencing others. Leaders need to behave in particular ways to gain influence over others by attending to tasks, relations, or both. Leaders are therefore assumed to have flexibility and the capacity to develop and adapt their style to accommodate organizational goals and employee needs. From this perspective, whenever leadership occurs, leaders need to adopt a dual focus on task-oriented goal attainment and relations-oriented care for employees, for influence to be achieved.

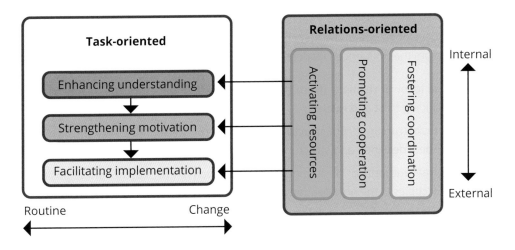

FIGURE 10.4 **The Integrative Model of Leadership Behaviour.** Credit: Peter Behrendt, Sandra Matz, Anja S. Göritz, 'An integrative model of leadership behavior', The Leadership Quarterly, Volume 28, Issue 1, Pages 229–244. 2017, with permission from Elsevier.

10.3.2 Criticisms of behaviour-based leadership perspectives

While behaviour-based perspectives offer a broader conception of leadership relative to trait-based theories, they still have a number of limitations. The first category of criticism focuses on outcomes. Studies have not clearly shown how leader behaviours influence performance outcomes such as employee morale, job satisfaction, or productivity (Yukl, 2003). Additionally, much of the research is based on follower perceptions of leader behaviour, which may differ from leader behaviour in practice (Dinh et al., 2014). The second category relates to the appropriate integration of these behaviours. Although the models suggest leaders need to adopt a high level of concern for both employees and tasks, this approach has been unable to identify a universal style of leadership that is effective in doing so. The final criticism is that these models do not take account of the different operating conditions (e.g. industry, level of leadership, existing relations between leaders and followers) that leaders need to work within. For example, leading groups in technical tasks associated with engineering industries like the aviation and automotive sectors is very different to leading people in hospitality and health industries where the emphasis is on customer care and people-oriented tasks. Behaviour-based models do not acknowledge these contextual differences or offer any suggestions about how leadership should adapt to various situations.

10.4 Context-based leadership

Context-based theories of leadership move away from idealized leadership traits or behaviours. They assume that leaders need to behave differently according to the situation they find themselves in. This group of theories is also referred to as contingency theories of leadership because the most appropriate and effective behaviours will be contingent on the context. Fred Fiedler (1967) developed one of the first contingency models of leadership and his studies identified three factors that influenced leadership effectiveness:

- leader and follower relations (from good to moderate to poor), i.e. the quality of relationships, including trust and respect;

- follower task structure (from structured to unstructured), i.e. the clarity with which tasks are described, designed and structured; and

- leader formal authority or positional power (from high to low), i.e. the formal position that a leader occupies in the organization and their ability to reward and punish colleagues and subordinates.

He found that these factors gave rise to three typical sets of contexts—which he called 'conditions'—that affect which leadership styles are effective under these different situations (Figure 10.5).

Situational Leadership Theory is another popular approach (Hersey & Blanchard, 1988), which focuses on the behaviours leaders need to use to influence followers. These behaviours can be either directive or supportive. Directive behaviours help individuals and groups meet goals by giving direction, goal setting, defining roles, evaluating performance, and setting timescales. Supportive behaviours focus on listening, facilitating, and showing emotional and social support for followers, helping them to feel comfortable with their roles, activities, and tasks. Leaders can express these two styles to varying degrees. The situational leadership model depicts four leadership styles based on the extent to which leaders exhibit directive and supportive behaviours—summarized in Figure 10.6. These are Directing, Coaching, Supporting, and Delegating leadership styles. The idea is that leaders need to modify their leadership style

	Condition 1 Highly structured task High position power Good relationships	**Condition 2** Unstructured task Low position power Moderately good relationships	**Condition 3** Unstructured task Low position power Poor relationships
Leadership styles	Task-orientated leaders get better results Focus is on setting targets and monitoring progress	Relationship-orientated leaders get better results Focus is on leveraging relationships to exert influence	Task-orientated leaders get better results Focus is on structuring situation, reducing uncertainty, and ignoring resistance

FIGURE 10.5 **Fiedler's (1967) conditions and styles of leadership.** Credit: *Organizational Behaviour*, Buchanan, D. A. and Huczynski, A. A, © 2019, Pearson Education UK

according to the situation they are operating in—that is, the task or goal they are working on and the needs of the followers or group members they are working with. In other words, some tasks and team members may suit a more coaching style, while other tasks may be better suited to a more directive style. Equally, some team members may prefer to be left alone to work on tasks and work best when led with a delegating style. Contrastingly, other team members may prefer lots of interaction and input to decision-making about tasks and would be better suited to a supportive leadership style.

10.4.1 The role of influence in context-based leadership perspectives

Context-based theories of leadership build on behavioural theories but extend these by taking account of the different situations leaders need to operate in. They recognize that there is no ideal leadership behaviour for all situations and that the most effective leadership depends on the context. As with the other theories we considered earlier, contingency theories continue to assume that leadership is a mechanism for influencing subordinates to achieve particular organizational goals. However, these theories differ in emphasizing that leadership effectiveness is

Style 1-Directing	Style 2-Coaching	Style 3-Supporting	Style 4-Delegating
High directive behaviour Low supportive behaviour	High directive behaviour High supportive behaviour	Low directive behaviour High supportive behaviour	Low directive behaviour Low supportive behaviour
Leader focuses on communicating goal achievement; gives instructions about what and how goals are met, and supervises closely.	Leader focuses on communicating goal achievement and meeting followers' social/emotional needs. Focus is on giving encouragement and getting follower input but leader still decides what and how goals are achieved.	Leader focuses on using supportive behaviours to bring out followers' skills to accomplish goals; involves giving praise, listening, asking for input, and giving feedback. Control of day-to-day decisions given to followers but leader facilitates problem solving.	Leader focuses on facilitating followers' confidence and motivation in achieving the goal. Leader gives less goal input and social support and does not participate in planning or control details of goal. Focus is on letting followers take responsibility for getting job done in their way.

FIGURE 10.6 **Situational Leadership Theory (based on Hersey & Blanchard, 1988).**

determined by the extent to which leaders can balance and flexibly adapt their style to accommodate varying organizational conditions. A second way they differ is that they place much more emphasis on follower characteristics and the relationships between leaders and followers. As part of this, they draw leaders' attention to influencing and appealing to followers through more considerate, participative styles of leadership, rather than relying on directive behaviours associated with positions of formal authority, linked to traditional bureaucratic forms of organization.

10.4.2 Criticisms of context-based leadership perspectives

There are several criticisms associated with contingency theories of leadership. The first category of criticism is linked to evidence. There have been very few studies which test these models, in order to show that there is, in fact, evidence of the impact of context-based leadership on leadership effectiveness and outcomes. For example, despite its popularity, there has been extensive criticism of the situational leadership model (depicted in Figure 10.6) because of the limited testing of the model, meaning questions remain about its validity as a way to categorize and measure leadership activities (Graeff, 1997). The second category of criticism is related to the fact that these models assume that leaders can diagnose the situation they are operating in and adapt their style accordingly. There is ongoing debate about the extent to which leaders can actually do this effectively, given the vagueness of many of the situational variables. There is also debate about the extent to which leaders can adapt or change their style. While some researchers assume leaders are inherently adaptable (Goleman, 1995), others suggest that leaders are limited in their capacity to do this and really need to change their organizational context in order to fit their style (Fiedler, 1967; Mintzberg, 2009). The final category of criticism turns to the followers. While these models do consider follower relations and motivations, they still adopt a leader-centric perspective—that is, it is the behaviours of the leaders that are deemed necessary to influence and motivate followers. This may result in dependence on leaders, and prevent or ignore the autonomy and independence of the follower, in achieving their goals.

10.5 Collective leadership models

The leadership theories we have outlined in this chapter so far consider leadership to be an individual phenomenon—that is, about the characteristics of the individual leader. The family of leadership theories we now review takes a different direction. These theories view leadership as a collective activity, which is shared across groups and teams, operating across multiple levels and organizational boundaries. There is increased interest in these forms of leadership coinciding with global changes in working patterns connected with the emergence of flatter, less hierarchical organizational structures (see: **Flat structure**, **Hierarchical structure**), team-based approaches, and increasing reliance on highly skilled knowledge work and **inter-organizational** collaboration. While we label this perspective collective leadership, it has also been termed shared, pooled, distributed, and relational leadership (for more detail on these we recommend students read Ospina et al., 2020). In this section, we explore two forms of collective leadership: shared leadership and distributed leadership, starting with shared leadership.

10.5.1 **Shared leadership**

Shared leadership is defined as 'a dynamic, interactive influence process among individuals in groups for which the objective is to lead one another to the achievement of group or organizational goals or both. This influence process often involves peer, or lateral, influence and at other times involves upward or downward hierarchical influence' (Pearce & Conger, 2003: 1). From this perspective, different team members may take on different leadership roles at different times. Moreover, this may be both an emergent (i.e. not defined in advance) and dynamic (i.e. constantly changing) phenomenon, which may vary depending on the team's inputs, processes, and outputs. Because of this, this view of leadership shifts it from a one-directional influence that originates from a (typically senior) individual over others, and instead views leadership as occurring from a more reciprocal pattern of influence between members, reinforcing and developing relationships. A further dimension of the shared leadership perspective is recognition that group members can play different roles based on their expertise or the different tasks they are collectively participating in. Proponents of shared leadership have suggested it is most appropriate in situations where there is issue urgency; high task interdependence and complexity; and a need for employee commitment and creativity (Pearce, 2004).

While this form of collective leadership emphasizes the sharing of leadership activities, it is built on two key underlying assumptions:

- participants need motivating and
- participants need to actively engage in self-leadership.

Because participants need motivating, this approach continues to involve active management to bring about the conditions to enable shared leadership. Thus, although those in formal positions of 'leadership' might adopt different roles from a traditional leadership perspective, they still play a role in motivating and empowering other leaders/followers to participate in leadership. The aim of those in senior positions in the hierarchy is to encourage self-leadership among employees. Self-leadership is 'a process through which people influence themselves to achieve the self-direction and self-motivation needed to perform' (Houghton et al., 2003: 126). Self-leadership of individuals helps groups to collectively perform and act more independently by ensuring each individual takes responsibility for goals, progress monitoring, and decision-making.

10.5.2 Distributed leadership

Distributed leadership theories focus on the configuration of collective leadership across multiple levels within the organization and between different organizations. The term has been used to describe the status given to individuals and groups working in concert to influence each other in undertaking workplace-related activities (Gronn, 2002). As such, while traditional 'focused leadership' emphasizes the status and roles of individual leaders in authority positions, whose primary focus is on influencing subordinates, 'distributed leadership' is dispersed among many individuals and does not emphasize the work of particular individuals or categories of people. All organizational members, whether in formal management or leadership roles or not, are viewed as potential leaders, who are capable of influencing each other as they conduct leadership activities. Of note, the concept of followership is de-emphasized, and leadership is seen as a continual process of negotiation between multiple leaders (Miller, 1998).

Central to effective distributed leadership is the importance of 'concertive action', which comprises three elements (Figure 10.7):

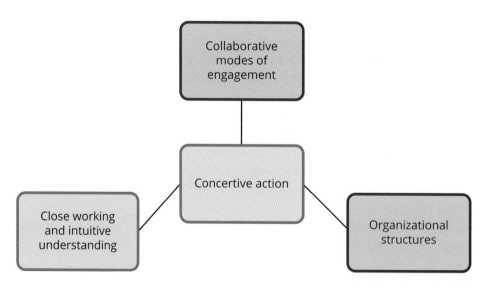

FIGURE 10.7 **The three elements of concertive action (based on Gronn, 2002).**

- The first element is **collaborative modes** of engagement, which reflects the notion that leadership occurs through interactions involving multiple individuals, rather than through the actions of a single heroic leader. The notion of leadership therefore becomes extended across multiple organizational situations, involving different levels of management and business units and may involve leaders working across different organizations.

- The second element comprises the **close working** and intuitive understandings that develop, which enable shared roles and co-leadership. For example, different leaders might balance each other's skills gaps (such as an engineer and architect working on a building), or have overlapping responsibilities (such as two members of a medical team—surgeon and anaesthetist—being responsible for the health of a patient undergoing an operation).

- Finally, it is important to consider the specific **organizational structures** that ensure the distributed leadership is effective. Under traditional models of leadership, a single leader may bear full responsibility for all actions taken; however, a distributed leadership model involving multiple leaders, increases the complexity of decision-making and responsibility. This requires the development of mechanisms that help determine responsibilities and pathways for resolving problems. These might include taskforces, committee meetings, organizational architectures, governance frameworks, and/or policies and procedures. These elements of concertive action enable leaders to 'synchronise their actions by having regard to their own plans, those of their peers, and their sense of unit membership' (Gronn, 2002: 431).

The effectiveness of distributed leadership has been researched. Buchanan et al. (2007) investigated the successful establishment of a regional health care network. They found it worked well because multiple managers collaborated around a unified goal of service improvement, and they were able to effectively hand over leadership to each other at appropriate times throughout the project. In a different context, Davis & Eisenhardt (2011) researched innovative technology projects and found that 'rotating leadership' between firms gave them access to complementary capabilities, diverse skill sets, and a broader pool of ideas.

10.5.3 The role of influence in collective leadership perspectives

As we have seen, traditional models of leadership emphasize individual leaders' characteristics or behaviours as mechanisms to influence followers, typically by directing, motivating, and inspiring them to pursue particular goals. However, collective leadership theories challenge this view, emphasizing leadership as potentially involving many people and extending leadership roles beyond those of formal positions. In contrast to the other theories, they de-emphasize one-directional leader–follower influence, with some variants rejecting the category of 'follower' altogether. With collective leadership, all leaders involved in working on a particular goal, mutually and reciprocally influence each other in the pursuit of that goal, co-constructing the work of leadership together. However, it is important to note that the decision to engage in collective leadership models is typically still within the control of those higher up in the organization. As such, they may still have control over who is able to engage in collective leadership—and so achieve influence. This hierarchical approach may be at odds with the emphasis of collective leadership on more democratic values within leadership processes and the ongoing interaction of participants involved in leadership activities.

10.5.4 Criticisms of collective leadership perspectives

There are a number of criticisms of collective leadership relating to power dynamics, the challenge of agreeing common goals, and the practical issues of coordination across multiple leaders.

The first category centres on issues of power. Formal organizational structures mean employees have varying levels of authority—and therefore power and influence—over each other, according to the role positions they occupy within the organizational hierarchy. However, collective leadership theories do not take account of these power and influence imbalances or the associated power dynamics. They tend to assume it is possible for leaders to operate in an egalitarian mode. Where collective leadership approaches need to be managed and planned, individuals at lower hierarchical levels or those operating outside of the organization entirely, may end up simply following the dictates of those in more senior roles. If this is the case, how is collective leadership any different from traditional views of leadership?

The second category of criticism relates to the fact that collective leadership approaches implicitly assume that leaders naturally converge on common goals and directions. That is, it pays little attention to notions of conflict, resistance, and competition within leader collectives, despite this being a well-recognized phenomenon within and between organizations. This raises a question about the extent to which leader collectives can mutually agree and work collaboratively on shared goals.

Finally, criticism has emerged following studies that demonstrate that collective leadership arrangements can be problematic in practice. For example, they do not always lead to more democratic forms of participation, they can lead to problems with accountability where one person is required to take responsibility for the work of the entire team despite having not led all aspects, and can be challenging with regards simple logistical issues like coordinating across multiple actors, times, and locations.

We can see some of these issues at play in the UN, which we discuss in Spotlight 10.2.

SPOTLIGHT 10.2 **COLLECTIVE LEADERSHIP: CLIMATE CHANGE AND THE UNITED NATIONS**

In 1994, the United Nations (UN) formally established the Framework Convention on Climate Change, which sets out an aim to prevent 'dangerous' human interference with the climate system (United Nations, n.d.). The framework was ratified (signed) by 198 countries. Signatories are expected to regularly report on progress with climate change policies and measures. Over the last 30 years, there have been a series of meetings led by different signatories, to track progress, reconfirm commitments, and periodically agree more specific targets to cut greenhouse emissions. One such meeting in Paris in 2015 resulted in 196 countries agreeing to limit global warming below an average of 2°C, with an ideal target of below 1.5°C. Global emissions need to be halved by 50 per cent by 2030 for the world to meet the 1.5°C goal. The UN recognized that the world is currently well off course to meet this goal.

The issue of climate change and the UN's efforts to galvanize climate action globally provides a good example of the challenges organizations face in implementing distributed leadership processes. Taking action to limit climate change is extraordinarily complex and requires leadership that involves multiple stakeholders, from commercial, regulatory, political, and activist sectors, as well as needing international input. Traditional forms of leadership are not sufficient to drive these kinds of collective, complex goals, where leaders have to collaborate across organizational boundaries, and in this case, international boundaries. If we refer back to Gronn's (2002) ideas about distributed leadership, we can see the three elements of concertive action in play.

Firstly, the UN provides structuring mechanisms through various legally binding agreements, regulatory processes, and progress reviews to track progress in meeting goals. Secondly, these structuring mechanisms support collaborative modes of engagement by extending goals and responsibilities across multiple countries, who in turn need

to operationalize this through local policies and measures that are applied to their citizens and businesses. Thirdly, both industrialized and developing countries have to participate in close working arrangements through sharing responsibilities (e.g. reporting on progress with meeting climate goals) and supporting each other with meeting goals (e.g. industrialized countries may give assistance to developing countries to support meeting climate goals and addressing impacts).

However, we can also see evidence of the challenges of distributed leadership, particularly around aligning collective goals. The UN, as well as many academics and activist groups, have expressed frustration with the lack of progress in meeting climate change goals. At times, individual countries choose to prioritize home goals, rather than collective international climate change goals. For example, under Donald Trump's administration, the USA withdrew from the Paris Agreement and some oil-producing countries have not ratified the agreement (e.g. Iran and Libya). Linked to this, there are no sanctions to punish countries that don't honour their commitments.

Now that we have discussed some of the different styles of leadership, let's return to Imperial in Running case 10.2, and assess Lucy's approach.

RUNNING CASE 10.2 **LEADERSHIP FOR THE PRESENT AND FUTURE**

Hugh Green knows that traditional thinking about leadership, as embraced by his cousin Charles, has had to change. Some of the recognized leadership traits are of course still important—who would want a leader who is not hard-working or intelligent? But as he realized some time ago—and Charles has not yet understood—the world of work has changed greatly since Hugh first became CEO. Employees have a choice of places to work, and they expect to be part of a diverse workforce that reflects the world they have grown up in. They do not see themselves as followers, to be told where to go and what to think: they expect to be involved, and for the company's senior management to respect them

and their wider contribution. While Hugh is proud of how he led Imperial, he knew a different approach was needed to take Imperial forward into the future.

It was no accident that Hugh had wanted Lucy to replace him as CEO instead of her brother, William. It was evident very soon after she joined how employees at all levels responded to her, but also how curious she was to understand the whole business landscape, see into the future, and consider carefully everyone's opinions and views. She recognizes the potential in everyone, and has created a feeling that they all need to take some leadership responsibility—that taking the business forward must be a collective endeavour. But Hugh knows too that she
(Continued)

is determined and will not be put off doing the right thing—as Charles learnt when using his position as a shareholder to question her motives in going to Kenya.

During the strategy Away Day meetings, Lucy pushed everyone forward with the goal of reviving Imperial's flagging product sales, patiently coaching meeting participants to contribute their ideas and encouraging everyone to get involved. When it came to finding product-development solutions, Lucy had not insisted on directing everything herself but had delegated team-leader responsibility to Bob and then, once it was clear that the situation with his product-design team wasn't working out, to Sue.

Questions for reflection

1. How do you view Lucy's belief that leadership must be a collective endeavour?

2. What are the advantages of having an inclusive leadership style? What are the disadvantages?

3. Should employees be expected to adapt to a new CEO's leadership style? Or should a new CEO ensure their leadership style suits existing employees?

10.6 Ethics, responsibility, and leadership

Ethics is concerned with the kinds of values and morals that an individual or a society finds acceptable. The ethics of leadership has growing prominence in research (Lemoine et al., 2019; Treviño & Brown, 2014) and is developing as a key area of concern for leadership practice. This has been driven by numerous high-profile corporate scandals and the evolving global challenges connected to climate change and social inequality. Leaders and their organizations are increasingly expected to take on a corporate social responsibility agenda (Waldman, 2014) and respond to broader societal and environmental issues by building sustainable organizations that contribute to wider society and the communities they are situated within (Lemoine et al., 2019; Waldman, 2014). Equally, from an internal organizational perspective, leaders need to consider their moral responsibilities towards followers (Treviño & Brown, 2014).

Again, the leadership literature varies in the way leadership ethics are dealt with. Traditional approaches view leadership as a neutral process that is not guided by values (England & Lee, 1974; Thompson, 1956), while newer perspectives explicitly set out moral responsibilities for leaders to do what is right for the common good of their followers and society, more generally, as outlined in research that focuses on servant leadership (Liden et al., 2014), authentic leadership (Gardner et al., 2011), and ethical leadership (Brown & Treviño, 2006). These theories suggest leaders need to be aware that many of the activities they participate in will involve ethical issues, either explicitly or implicitly, and that the judgements and choices they make as part of their leadership activity are guided by their own ethical values and frameworks.

From a leadership perspective, ethics focuses on the virtuousness of leadership behaviours (Northouse, 2021). Ethical leaders have moral characteristics such as being caring, honest, trustworthy, and fair, which they communicate and role model to other colleagues (Brown & Treviño, 2006). Ciulla (2001), however, suggests that to develop moral character and virtue, leaders need to follow the advice of ancient philosophers like Aristotle, Plato, Confucius, and Buddha. This involves a broader range of moral attributes including altruism, prudence, temperance, justice, fortitude, wisdom, holiness, courage, and righteousness. This requires leaders to understand themselves and their values and engage in reflective and effortful practice (Ciulla, 2001).

As suggested above, ethical leadership is closely connected with the idea of responsibility and encourages leaders to move beyond thinking about business and management purely in economic and financial terms, where organizational goals are focused on maximizing shareholder value. By thinking about the responsibilities and ethics of leadership in a broader sense (Maak & Pless, 2006), leaders can orientate organizational and team goals towards the full breadth of the stakeholders they interact with, orientating their organizational purpose towards the common good (Maak & Pless, 2006). Being a responsible and ethical leader entails adopting an inclusive, egalitarian approach, such that the core leadership task is to 'weave a web of inclusion where leaders engage themselves among equals' (Maak & Pless, 2006: 104). In practice, this means taking account of their responsibilities to all stakeholders, internal and external to the organization. This involves a complex set of leadership activities, including: integrating people from different cultures to work together effectively; caring for the well-being of different constituencies (e.g. indigenous people in the countries where a company produces); understanding the interests, needs, and values of different groups and facilitating dialogue among them; simultaneously mobilizing and aligning the energy of different people to achieve common objectives, and supporting the realization of a common vision (Maak & Pless, 2006: 104).

This growing emphasis on embracing ethical and responsible leadership in business presents a particular challenge as regards the traditional theories of leadership discussed earlier in this chapter (i.e. trait-based, behavioural, and situational leadership theories). These more traditional perspectives are increasingly recognized as emerging from a western cultural context that is based on notions of individualism, masculinity, and hierarchy (Iszatt-White & Saunders, 2017). Researchers taking a more critical approach to studying leadership have highlighted the way these kinds of hidden assumptions about leadership practices and preferences have impacted the diversity of leadership in terms of gender, ethnicity, and disability. For example, women and members of black and ethnic minority groups face a 'leadership labyrinth' (Eagly & Carli, 2007; Wyatt & Silvester, 2015) of challenges and barriers that they need to navigate to achieve leadership positions. Taking an ethical and responsible approach to leadership involves opening up our thinking about what it means to be a leader, critically engaging with different approaches to leading and being aware of the positive and negative impacts of different leadership practices on the full range of stakeholders a leader works with. Consider Spotlight 10.3 on Nelson Mandela, in this context.

SPOTLIGHT 10.3 AN ETHICAL AND RESPONSIBLE LEADER: NELSON MANDELA

Nelson Mandela (1918–2013) was a South African lawyer and political activist who fought to end apartheid (i.e. the South African system of segregation and discrimination of black people that existed between 1948 and 1991). In the early 1950s, he established South Africa's first black-owned law firm with Oliver Tambo. He also became a leading member of the African National Congress (ANC) party, which mounted legal challenges and civil disobedience campaigns against apartheid laws. His political

(Continued)

activism made him a target for the authorities. In 1956, he and his supporters, including men and women of all races, were tried for treason, although subsequently acquitted. In 1960, police killed 69 unarmed people during one of many civil protests against apartheid. This led to increasing tensions across the South African population, between the ANC and the ruling authorities, culminating in the banning of the ANC in South Africa. In 1962, through the course of his activism, Mandela, along with other activists was tried and found guilty of state sabotage and sentenced to life imprisonment. During his famous speech from the dock, he set out his democratic principles:

> I have fought against white domination, and I have fought against black domination. I have cherished the ideal of a democratic and free society in which all persons live together in harmony and with equal opportunities. It is an ideal which I hope to live for and to achieve. But if needs be, it is an ideal for which I am prepared to die. (Nelson Mandela Foundation).

He was incarcerated until 1990, when South Africa's governing administration legalized the ANC. Following his release, Mandela, as the newly appointed leader of the ANC, began intensive negotiations with President F. W. De Klerk to end white minority rule. In May 1994, he was inaugurated as South Africa's first democratically elected president. Mandela went on to share the Nobel Peace Prize with De Klerk for his work in ending apartheid and overseeing a peaceful transition to non-racial democracy. As president, he established a Truth and Reconciliation Commission, which investigated human rights violations under apartheid. He also introduced housing, education, and economic development designed to improve living standards for Black South Africans, as well as other minority ethnic groups in South Africa who were not white.

Throughout his life, we can see that Nelson Mandela embodied a virtuous approach to his leadership in the struggle to end apartheid in South Africa. He demonstrated the values of altruism and justice by working towards improving the living standards for all South Africans and showed great courage in challenging the established authorities, as well as enduring personal hardship to realize his longer-term goals. In gaining international support for his cause, he showed an inclusive approach to mobilizing wider stakeholders. He also showed an inclusive approach when he engaged in active negotiation with South African authorities during the country's transition out of apartheid, even though they were his former jailers. Under his leadership, South Africa was able to transition to a more democratic society.

(Source: Nelson Mandela Foundation)

10.7 Influence without leadership

A further noteworthy aspect of leadership and influence is the rising impact of citizen influencers in society. Social media allow a single person to reach out to others across the world via media channels (of which there are now hundreds in existence, in addition to the well-known giants of Snapchat, Instagram, TikTok, WeChat, and Facebook). As social animals, human beings have always influenced each other, particularly those who are most proximate. However, social media have enabled a small proportion of people to have a much larger than average impact on others, such that they become known as opinion leaders through having a significant influence on attitudes and decision-making of a large network of followers (Casaló et al., 2020).

Social media influencers achieve this influence through one or more of the following characteristics: they are an active member of an online community; they participate with high frequency and make substantial contributions; they are perceived as an expert in a particular area; their online contributions are perceived as original, authentic, and trustworthy. As a result, they come to be seen as a model for others (Casaló et al., 2020). One of the most famous citizen influencers in recent times is teenage climate activist, Greta Thunberg, whose Fridays For Future movement is reported to have inspired strike action by more than 1.5 million young people in 125 countries (Maven Road, 2019). Organizations recognize the value of influencers for communicating their key brand messages to their audiences. Influencer marketing spend by brands reached US$21 billion in 2023 (Influencer Marketing Hub, 2023). In paying an influencer to promote their brand messages, companies seek to leverage the influencers' follower networks, personal positioning, communication content, and follower trust (Leung et al., 2022). We will discuss the activities of marketing further in Chapter 11.

10.8 Conclusion

In this chapter, we have explored the concepts of leadership and influence within organizations. We did so through the lens of four perspectives on leadership: trait-based, behavioural, context-based, and collective leadership. No one perspective provides an absolute understanding of leadership. However, each provides a useful lens to help us appreciate the different elements that contribute to the complex activities involved in leading. The first three adopt a traditional view where leadership is viewed as a more individualized phenomenon, closely connected to formal roles and influencing followers (often subordinates in the organizational hierarchy) to achieve organizational goals and performance. Collective leadership theories take a different position on leadership, emphasizing the collective, social, and interactive dimensions, while de-emphasizing followership and formal organization. Influence from a collective leadership perspective is more oriented to collaboration and reciprocal re-enforcing of relationships that support participants in contributing to shared goals, often across multiple organizational settings.

CHAPTER SUMMARY

- Leadership can be defined in multiple ways, including as a position, a personal characteristic, an outcome, or a process.
- We can define trait-based, behaviour-based, and context-based theories of leadership, each of which has its strengths and weaknesses.
- Collective models of leadership can be understood as shared (where different team members may take on different leadership roles at different times) and distributed (which focus on leadership across multiple levels within the organization and between different organizations).
- There is increasing attention on ethics and responsibility in leadership, driven by high-profile corporate scandals and evolving global challenges such as climate change and social inequality.
- Influence is a social, interactive, communicative process occurring between group and organizational members. Influence does not need to be linked to formal leadership.

CLOSING CASE REFLECTION

Leadership in a complex ecosystem: The UK's National Health Service

Managing complex services in the UK's NHS requires the adoption of multiple approaches to leadership. Leaders may use task-oriented approaches to set goals that support staff with meeting individualized care, while also controlling high levels of demand and the overall costs of services at population level. At the same time, leaders need to seek to maximize the involvement and expertise of different professional employees. For example, it is particularly important that professional experts like doctors and nurses participate in decision-making about how service goals are achieved. Typically, the medical experts will have more knowledge about patient services than administrators and general managers. This means leaders in the health service seeking to maintain and improve the quality of health service provision and patient outcomes will aim to complement traditional leadership activities with more distributed leadership arrangements to encourage and support the involvement of professionals in the operational oversight of health care services on a daily basis.

REVIEW QUESTIONS

1. 'Leaders are born, not made'. Discuss this quote in relation to trait-based and behaviour-based leadership models.

2. Which models of leadership discussed in this chapter would work best in the following situations and why?

   a. Leading a well-established family business during a crisis such as a pandemic or heatwave.

   b. Setting up an innovative global business with virtual offices and organization members physically dispersed across several time zones.

   c. Responding with agility to a competitor introducing a new product that threatens to take an entire segment of your customers.

3. To what extent do you think leadership is an individual activity or can it be accomplished collectively? Justify your answer.

4. Consider a foodbank reliant on community members to provide their time and labour voluntarily. How should the three elements of concertive action be used by the foodbank's leaders to run the organization effectively?

5. Are leaders always able to act ethically? Why or why not?

EXPLORE MORE

▬ READ this book, which provides more depth on the leadership theories discussed in this chapter: M. Iszatt-White and C. Saunders (2017). *Leadership*. Oxford: Oxford University Press.

))) LISTEN to a podcast from the London School of Economics, LSE IQ series, in which leadership academics discuss 'What Makes a Great Leader?', drawing on their many years studying leadership in business, the health sector, military, and many other contexts. Google the title and 'LSE' to find the episode.

◉ WATCH 'Ethical Leadership, Part 1: Perilous at the Top' to learn more about ethical leadership and why it is important. Recorded by the Centre for Leadership and Ethics at the University of Texas at Austin. Search for the video on YouTube.

◉ WATCH Professor Nicola Pless discuss responsible leadership, climate change, and its impact on business on YouTube. Search for 'zoom Pless 1 GRLI RL'.

◉ ADDITIONALLY, watch Professor Pless' responsible leadership dialogues with business leaders on her YouTube channel: @plessresponsibleleadership7414.

◉ WATCH Professor Alice Eagly discussing the 'labyrinth of leadership' and the challenges women face in navigating their careers and leading. Search for 'Short Takes: Alice Eagly' on YouTube.

PART ONE **CONTEXT**

PART TWO **ORGANIZATION**

PART THREE **PEOPLE**

PART FOUR **VALUE CHAIN**

PART
FOUR

Managing through the Value Chain

CHAPTER ELEVEN
Marketing

Farah Arkadan and Emma Macdonald

OPENING CASE STUDY BURBERRY'S CUSTOMER EXPERIENCE: BRIDGING PHYSICAL AND DIGITAL WORLDS

Burberry, headquartered in London, is one of the world's most valuable luxury fashion brands (Figure 11.1) (Sabanoglu, 2022). It is known for its pioneering experimentation with digital and social media brand touchpoints to enhance its customer's shopping experience. Within the luxury industry, Burberry has been an early adopter of digital tools to enrich the customer experience. It was one of the first fashion brands to adopt Facebook (Bloomberg, 2019) and more recently, the first luxury brand to broadcast its runway show live on the video streaming service, Twitch (Burberry Group Plc, 2020a).

Burberry's Julie Brown observed that 'social media and store experiences are important sources of inspiration for luxury consumers, and the customer journey between these touchpoints is becoming increasingly fluid' (Bloomberg, 2019). Customers familiar with Burberry's website were accustomed to quick service and instant access to product information and brand content. In 2012, the organization unveiled a new retail store which translated its website experience into a bricks-and-mortar store so that shoppers could enjoy the same convenience physically through utilizing in-store technology (Cartner-Morely, 2012).

When launching its new puffer jacket collection in 2019, Burberry introduced an online game called B Bounce where players competed for prizes like custom-made GIFs and virtual Burberry puffer jackets edited onto a digital picture of their choice. First prize was a real jacket from the new collection (Burberry Group Plc, 2019).

In 2020, Burberry incorporated video-game culture into its in-store experience in its Shenzhen store in China (Williams, 2020). Customers could use a dedicated app as a digital companion with QR codes on all products which, when scanned, provided product storytelling. The app was gamified so that the more customers used it, the richer their in-store experience became through unlocking exclusive experiences, such as a store tour, and treats from the store's café (Burberry Group Plc, 2020b).

In 2022, Burberry launched a collaboration with the popular video game, Minecraft (Burberry Group Plc, 2022). This involved firstly, an in-game Burberry adventure and virtual Burberry outfit skins for dressing video game characters, and secondly, a limited-edition physical collection of sweatshirts, hoodies, hats, and scarves. In 2023, Burberry provided virtual handbags in the online game platform, Roblox (Figure 11.2).

Burberry's use of in-store experiences that mimic the information-rich experience of a website, and more recently, their use of gaming platforms and gamified in-store experiences demonstrate how a brand that traditionally operates in the physical world may combine physical, digital, and social platforms to enhance the appeal of their offerings to customers.

FIGURE 11.1 **Burberry luxury fashion brand.** Image: Burberryplc.com (2023)

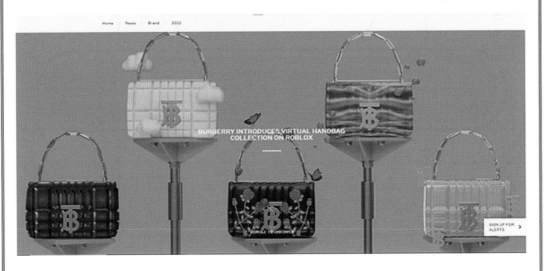

FIGURE 11.2 **Burberry virtual handbags in online game platform, Roblox.** Image: Burberryplc.com (2023)

11.1 **An introduction to Part 4**

Part 1 of this text focused on the context in which management happens, while Part 2 explored the organization itself (see Figure 11.3). In Part 3 we then focused on the people who comprise the organization. In the final part of this text, Part 4, we explore three different elements of an organization that are linked to the value chain.

We have explored the idea of the value chain a number of times throughout this text, most notably in Section 5.2.4. Value Chain analysis focuses on the functions of the organization which ensure stakeholders upstream (like suppliers) and downstream (like customers) are effectively integrated into the organization's activities. The Value Chain also comprises the managerial

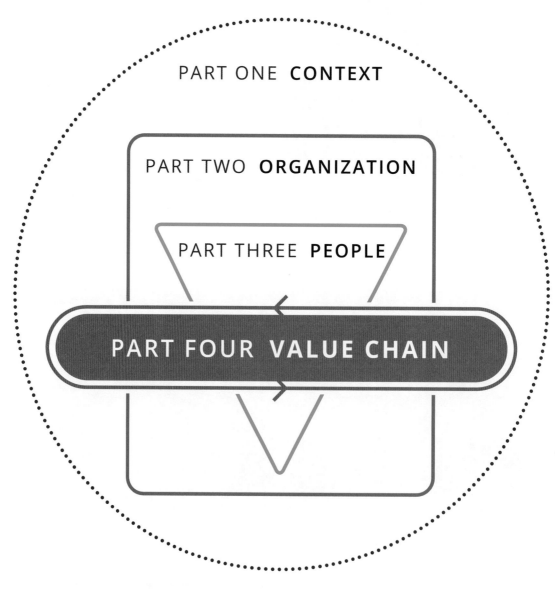

FIGURE 11.3 **Interrelated elements important in managing organizations.**

activities of organizing and decision-making, with a focus on creating value for specific stakeholders. It is with these ideas in mind that we group these final three chapters in Part 4: Marketing (Chapter 11), Operations and Supply Chain (Chapter 12), and finally Entrepreneurship and Innovation (Chapter 13).

11.2 Why marketing?

When we seek to identify the causes of the world's wicked problems such as poverty, inequality, climate change, and biodiversity loss, marketing is often pointed to as a major culprit. Marketing is seen as responsible for encouraging people to desire what they do not need, consume more than is sustainable, and waste resources in ways that cause damage to the planet. This perspective is in some ways valid as marketing encompasses the organizational activities that include the creation and distribution of products to marketplaces of buyers and users, as well as communication about these products to encourage people to develop an awareness of and preferences for them (which we will explore further in this chapter).

However, it may be surprising to realize that marketing activity is not exclusively the domain of for-profit consumer brands, such as chocolate bars or fashion labels. Almost every organization has a marketing function, including goods manufacturers but also producers of intangible services, third sector organizations such as charities, and public sector organizations such as government departments. The existence of marketing activity and functions in such a variety of organizations demonstrates a wider range of uses than is often recognized. This includes the use of marketing as a tool to encourage adoption of new ways of behaving, such as within the markets for electric vehicles and car-sharing systems, but also in its role in creating awareness of how people can protect their health, for instance through government campaigns in the media to encourage participation in flu and Covid-19 vaccination programmes.

Marketing is defined by the American Marketing Association as: 'the activity, set of institutions, and processes for creating, communicating, delivering, and exchanging offerings that have value for customers, clients, partners, and society at large' (AMA, 2017). As the AMA's definition suggests, while organizations concern themselves with a wide range of important **stakeholder** groups, including employees, government, communities, partners, regulators, and shareholders (as discussed in Chapter 2), the main stakeholder of interest to the marketing function is the **customer**. Customers are varied and may number in the millions. This makes the organization's interactions with its customers and potential customers a continual challenge. We will talk more about how organizations manage the way they engage with customers in this chapter.

In order to support the organization in making the best strategic and **tactical decisions** about customers, marketers undertake three sets of activities, which we will discuss in this chapter:

1. **Segmentation** is a tool that helps marketers understand the potential groups of customers within a marketplace, while **Targeting** is a tool that enables the organization to select and focus on meeting the needs of subsets of these customer groups. Segmentation and targeting ensure the organization can deploy its resources effectively.

11

2. ***Customer insight*** processes provide the organization with an understanding of customer needs. Customer insight is gathered through activities like listening to customers' complaints, tracking customer satisfaction, and conducting market research.

3. Customer insight then feeds into the creation of **value propositions** to address the identified needs. Customer value propositions may comprise physical goods or intangible services. When creating a value proposition, marketers will coordinate a bundle of organizational activities. These activities are known as the ***marketing mix***, or more specifically, the 4Ps. The marketing mix includes detailed decisions around product or service characteristics, price, how the value proposition will reach the customer, and how we will communicate with our customer. We will discuss the elements of marketing mix later in this chapter.

Defining who the customer actually *is* can depend on the nature of the organization and the form of its value propositions. Because of this, the terms used to describe the customer may vary by organization and industry sector. For instance, some organizations plan their marketing activity around customers (those who pay for the organization's value propositions), consumers or users (those who make use of the organization's value propositions), members (those who participate with the organization in its activities), or audiences (those who enjoy an organization's largely experiential value propositions). Sometimes the same person represents multiple roles or sometimes different individuals play separate roles. Figure 11.4 demonstrates examples of this.

In the case of the language tutoring services in Figure 11.4, the fact that the customer and consumer are different is very relevant for the marketing function. This is because the tutoring service provider would need to *create, communicate, deliver, and exchange* (following the AMA

Customer and consumer are the same   Example: train travel

- I buy my train ticket: **customer**
- I use the train service: **consumer**

Customer and consumer are different   Example: language tutor

- Parent pays for language tutoring service: **customer**
- Child attends language tutorials: **consumer**

Customer and consumer are different   Example: office furniture

- An organization's Procurement Officer purchases office furniture for staff to use: **customer**
- Employee uses office furniture while at the business premises: **consumer**

FIGURE 11.4 **Distinguishing between customer and consumer.**

definition of marketing discussed above) the language learning experience (which is the *offering* they provide) so that it leads to value for both the parent (the customer) and the child (the consumer). Likewise in the case of the business customer buying office furniture for use by the organization's employees.

As we can see, there is a range of activities undertaken by the marketing function. Moreover, many of these activities give rise to potential ethical questions and dilemmas. These include the potential for stereotyping and exclusion in the processes of segmentation and targeting, issues of privacy and intrusive customer tracking in customer insight gathering, wasteful and unsustainable value propositions in the development of products, and potentially harmful messaging in marketing communications, particularly when they address audiences considered vulnerable such as children. Marketing activities may also be considered harmful if they appear to contain poorly evidenced claims about sustainability that are confusing for the customer and may be referred to as greenwashing. The application and usefulness of tools of marketing as well as some important ethical considerations will be discussed throughout this chapter.

11.3 Segmentation and targeting

Let's say you launched a new business to produce bicycles. What kinds of bicycles would you sell and who would they be for? Cycle manufacturer, Brompton Bicycles identified an opportunity to create collapsible bicycles for city office workers (see Spotlight 11.1). Now imagine if you launched a business to manufacture and sell footwear. What kinds of shoes might you produce, and for whom? Should you produce shoes for adults or children? Gendered or gender-neutral styles? Shoes for people whose objective in owning shoes is playing a particular sport, wearing them in a business context, protecting their feet in a high-risk situation, such as on a construction site, enjoying leisure time at the beach, or dressing up for special occasions? What form of footwear products should you produce to address the needs of these customers: runners, sandals, steal-capped boots, or high heels? With what kinds of materials: cloth, plastic, rubber, animal leather, vegan leather, or straw?

Once you start considering the possibilities of products matched to customer needs, the potential opportunities might seem endless. However, your new venture—like every venture—will face resource constraints that restrict the range of possible footwear types you can simultaneously and successfully produce and sell. You're not likely to have the capacity to perfectly address the needs of every type of potential customer, especially because in addition to their varying functional needs for footwear, your potential customers will also differ in their preferences in terms of styles that they like, where and how they like to shop, how much they are able or willing to pay, and where and how they typically learn about new products.

So, what do you do? Most organizations, even larger ones, find that it is essential to spend time trying to understand the needs of their potential customers before they begin a design process. They do this by listening to customers, perhaps by conducting customer research through qualitative and quantitative methods, such as interviews and surveys (see Section 11.4). The data that they gather from these research methods is known as customer insight. Customer insight helps organizations design their value propositions. It also helps organizations to identify groups

11

SPOTLIGHT 11.1 **BROMPTON BICYCLES**

Brompton Bicycles is widely regarded as a UK manufacturing success story (Butler-Adams & Davies, 2022) with worldwide sales rising by a third to 93,000 bicycles by March 2022 (Telling, 2023). The Brompton Bicycle has a unique collapsible design including small wheels, that allows it to be conveniently folded and carried onto public transport, stored under the desk at work or in a city apartment, and then quickly reassembled for use. It is designed for city commuters combining different forms of active transport and surged in popularity during the Covid-19 pandemic.

Founded in London, the Brompton brand name is well known in the UK and is expanding worldwide, particularly into German cities which have higher proportions of cyclists than the UK. Despite the company's success in generating attention and sales, CEO Will Butler-Adams is quoted as saying Brompton's philosophy is that: 'we're not big fans of marketing' (Dugdale, 2010). This claim leads to questions about how a small British brand has become well known and successful on the global stage despite its anti-marketing stance.

If we dig a little deeper into the activities of Brompton, comparing these with the AMA definition of marketing outlined in Section 11.2, we find a company that in many ways is an exemplar of good marketing. Brompton has a strong engineering culture which drives its focus on innovative product design and this same focus ensures its output of quality products. However, it is a design and production focus that is centred around the needs of customers, with the aim of enhancing the feasibility of cycling for the city commuter. This means Brompton produces bicycles that are sturdy and adaptable, thus creating value for the commuter customer. Furthermore, encouraging people to get out of their cars has the larger scale impact of reducing inner-city pollution, which has benefits for not just commuters but for society at large (again, we can compare this outcome with the AMA definition of marketing).

Brompton does not spend on broadcast media such as television advertising, hence the basis for the 'no marketing' claim. However, the company is a very effective user of non-mass forms of marketing communications which they use to build awareness, preference, and connection with their existing and prospective customers:

- Social media: On their socials (brand-owned social media channels), Brompton is active in encouraging interaction and dialogue with

← **Tweet**

Brompton Bicycle ✓
@BromptonBicycle   ···

What's your next addition to your Brompton? Let us know what you have your eyes on •• #Brompton

11:00 am · 18 Feb 2023 · **11.2K** Views

2 Retweets   **1** Quote Tweet   **66** Likes

Imran Khan @imranjk16 · 18 Feb   ···
Replying to @BromptonBicycle
New pedals and a brooks saddle for sure :)
♡   ⟲   ♡   ᵢₗᵢ 158   ⬆

Sonny Bennett @SonnyLBennett · 23h   ···
Replying to @BromptonBicycle
The new bell you have on the Barbour edition and the little triangle bag from the chpr4
But you probably won't release them to existing owners
♡   ⟲   ♡ 1   ᵢₗᵢ 176   ⬆

Chella ní Dhubhagáin @ChellaDug · 22h   ···
Replying to @BromptonBicycle
Just bought the vincita nash rack bag. I'm not allowing myself to spend any more money on stuff for the Brompton.
♡   ⟲   ♡   ᵢₗᵢ 169   ⬆

(Accessed 19 Feb. 2023)

FIGURE 11.5 **@BromptonBicycle on Twitter.**

11

Instagram

Q Search

germanroamers ✓ [Follow]

1,880 posts   434k followers   14 following

German Roamers
Consortium of photographers //
Creating Collectively //
Germany and Worldwide.
#weroamgermany #weroamabroad
germanroamers.com

ZDF Beitrag

UP NORTH

Why Brompton? What advantage do you see?

The bike offers an incredible amount of flexibility and mobility, especially in the city. It's the ideal companion when I'm out and about. I've developed a much closer bond with my Brompton than I would with a regular bike because I can take it with me everywhere. For me personally, a Brompton opens up a lot of new possibilities and makes everyday life as a photographer a lot easier. On my Brommie I can get from one spot to the next really fast.

FIGURE 11.6 **Brompton and social media influencers, German Roamers.**

The Brompton World Championship is our flagship Brompton only racing event. With qualifying heats held in 15 countries and a final in the UK. The event has been running for 11 years and is held in cities around the world.

Buy hospitality area tickets here.

[View all races]

A mixture of orienteering and cycling, teams taking part in a Brompton Urban Challenge complete challenges and follow clues around a city.

[View all urban challenges]

(Accessed 2020)

FIGURE 11.7 **Brompton events.**

their customers and fans. For instance, in Figure 11.5, @BromptonBicycle asks their Twitter followers: 'What's your next addition to your Brompton?', and fans respond by mentioning their desire for a new bell, pedals, and various branded saddle bags they would like to buy. An unpopular brand that does not deliver value for its customers could not expect such a positive and engaged response.

• Influencers: Brompton also aligns with social media influencers, such as a recent linkup with @GermanRoamers (Figure 11.6), a 'community of outdoor loving photographers' with more than 400,000 Instagram followers who rode Bromptons from Munich to Austria, demonstrating their use outside urban areas (Brompton, 2021).

• Events: Brompton holds fun events for customers and fans such as the 'Brompton Urban Challenge' (Figure 11.7) where teams riding bicycles follow trails of clues around a city. These events are effective in building connections and a sense of community between the brand and its customer base.

(Continued)

- Brand partnerships: Brompton also has a continual programme of partnerships with brands that share a similar ethos, including saddle bags designed by Barbour, the British countrywear brand, and special edition Liberty print bags. These partnerships reinforce the Brompton brand image of 'British quality'. The brand's line-up of brand collaborations and linkups with influencers create ongoing excitement for the brand's community of fans.

of customers who will *most* appreciate the benefits of their value propositions. This process of understanding the marketplace of potential customers and their needs, and then using the data gathered to form clusters of groups with similar needs, is called segmentation. Each of these customer clusters is called a sub-market or a market segment. Having segmented a market, and profiled the segments in terms of their needs, organizations will typically identify particular segments as 'targets'. As such, segmentation and targeting go hand-in-hand in the typical marketing planning process depicted in Figure 11.8.

11.3.1 Effective use of segmentation as a tool

For a segmentation analysis to be useful to the organization, it needs to identify customer segments that are accessible to the organization. This means that the organization needs a clear understanding of the communications and delivery channels preferred by people in this customer segment. For instance, a furniture manufacturer might identify an attractive segment of customers a few hundred miles away, but delivery costs for heavy furniture items will make that segment inaccessible by the company. Furthermore, each segment needs to have distinctive sets of needs and be large enough to justify the creation of separate product or service offers.

For example, Fitness First gyms conducted a segmentation analysis that identified six customer segments, shown in Figure 11.9. Each segment differed in their confidence in using the gym, their interest in receiving coaching, the classes they preferred to attend, and their hours of usage. The segmentation analysis allowed the gym chain to be more effective in addressing the needs of customers by providing varying offerings to each segment. This also meant they

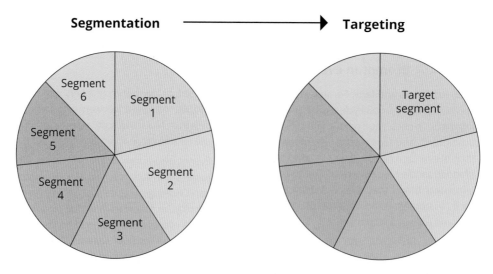

FIGURE 11.8 **Market segmentation and targeting.**

Segment name	The Confidence seekers	The Learners	The Neutrals	The Free Spirits	The Achievers	The Focused
Service needs	"Support me"			"Inspire me"		
Gym-confidence	Low	Low	Moderate	Moderate	High	High
Desire to set goals	Moderate	High	Moderate	Low	High	Low
Motivation	Appearance	Appearance	Balanced	Well-being	Well-being	Appearance
Belief	"Hold my hand and don't let go"	"I'm willing but need help"	"The gym's not really my thing"	"Fitness should be fun"	"Set me a challenge"	"Leave me to it"

Low confidence ←————————→ High confidence

FIGURE 11.9 **Segmentation analysis for Fitness First gyms.** Credit: © Fitness First Ltd

were more efficient in not wasting resources on features that customers in some segments did not appreciate. For example, the least confident segment expressed a strong desire for support captured in the expression 'hold my hand' and were positive about coaching support, whereas the most confident segment had an attitude of 'leave me to it' finding offers of help redundant and possibly even a negative.

As shown in the Fitness First example in Figure 11.9, segmentation is a useful practical tool for organizations to manage when they have large numbers of existing or potential customers whose varying needs they aim to best satisfy while also managing the organization's objectives and resources. Let's see how Imperial approached their first attempts at segmentation in Running case 11.1.

11.3.2 Responsible segmentation

The use of segmentation is not without its potential risks, particularly around issues of diversity and exclusion. By assigning customers into segments, and then designing the organizational response to those segments, organizations need to ensure they do not unintentionally cause harm

RUNNING CASE 11.1 **IMPERIAL INVESTIGATES A NEW CUSTOMER SEGMENT**

Following the Away Day meeting, in which the Imperial team brainstormed options for plant-based foods, Gita Patel, Imperial's Marketing Manager conducted some important initial research into customer preferences. Knowing that Jazz Jha, from the food prep team, and Saffron Walden, her own Marketing Assistant, were already adopting plant-based food alternatives into their diets, Gita worked with them to design a simple customer survey aimed at under-25-year-olds. Gita made sure the survey met the principles of the Market Research Society's code of conduct so that information was transparent to participants about the use of the data. The team promoted the survey via their social media accounts and asked their friends to fill it in and pass it on. Using this snowball technique, they received close to 1,000 responses, which Gita considered to be a very good response. More impressively, they discovered that parents and older relatives had also filled out the survey, so they now had a good sense of the interest in plant-based and vegan foods across all age ranges in the sample.

Armed with this information, Gita worked with Saffron to segment the potential market through the creation of multiple customer segments that have different customer journeys. They'd all enjoyed thinking up the names of the segment personas, settling on 'Green Fiends', 'Flexi Explorers', and 'Traditional Carnivores'. This also focused on the significance of each segment to their business and reminded them that they could not afford to ignore the needs of current customers. If they were to go ahead with a plant-based food range, they realized that it would have to be carefully marketed in a way that wouldn't detract from the positive perceptions of Imperial's brand held by existing customers. Acknowledging the diversity of their future consumer base would be critical: as Gita put it, 'Whether they're steak pies or jackfruit pies, customers are buying Imperial pies, and people have got to believe they're the best they can buy and that we're genuinely supportive of their tastes.'

Questions for reflection

1. Segmenting the customer base into three segments of customers will make Imperial's marketing activity more efficient, but what risks might be associated with viewing a diversity of customers in this way?

2. If you were a marketing consultant, how would you advise Imperial to successfully provide products for two very different customer segments, Traditional Carnivores and the Green Fiends?

to individuals by over-generalizing and stereotyping. So, for example, an organization that applies segmentation based on whether an individual is a member of the Millennial generation (born 1981–1996), might decide to fully replace live human customer service agents with AI chatbots for services aimed at this age group, on the assumption that 'everyone' in this age range prefers online social engagement. However, just because people share a demographic characteristic does not mean that they are identical; there is always variation in any demographic group. For instance, within this one age range there will be people with specific accessibility requirements, those who lack access to or skills in using technology, those with literacy or language challenges, or those with differing preferences. Many people with these characteristics—even if they are millennials—might require or value the support of a human rather than a bot, for at least part of their customer journey.

11

This issue of exclusion is directly regulated by government bodies in industries that are deemed essential to people's lives and livelihoods. We explore one example in Spotlight 11.2, focusing on the UK's financial sector **regulator**, which is responsible for addressing issues of exclusion in financial services. However, most industry sectors are not subject to specific regulation, and so it is up to the organization itself to ensure that their market segmentation and targeting activities do not inadvertently exclude and harm groups or individuals in society. This puts an onus on those responsible for customer data management, customer operations, and marketing to ensure that they use customer data and the tools of segmentation and targeting appropriately and carefully. With the increasing use of artificial intelligence, machine learning, and algorithms in the provision of customer service and support, there is some evidence of bias in the way these systems treat customers (Chandy et al., 2021). Organizations—as well as governments and regulators—will need to continue monitoring these technologies very closely as these machine-driven technologies continue to evolve and proliferate over the coming years and play an ever-increasing part in how customers are understood and how organizations interact with them.

SPOTLIGHT 11.2 **THE FINANCIAL CONDUCT AUTHORITY**

In services considered essential, such as energy, telecommunications, and banking, government regulators, such as Ofgem, Ofcom, and the Financial Conduct Authority (FCA), respectively, provide regulations to protect consumers. Regulations from the FCA require banks and insurers to be aware of and pre-empt issues created by variations in customer needs, which might lead to individuals being excluded or vulnerable with regard to financial services (FCA, 2018). For example, the FCA conducted a multi-agency study on sources of exclusion in the UK banking market called 'Mind the Gap' (Rowe et al., 2015) and found that almost any consumer may struggle at times with:

1. the processes of banking such as application forms and eligibility;

2. understanding and navigating a confusing marketplace of banking and insurance products; and

3. issues related to digital or physical barriers to services.

The FCA found that consumers may be vulnerable to financial exclusion due to a number of circumstances that might affect any one of us at different times in our lives: job loss, relationship breakdown, illness, or bereavement. These factors are in addition to low income, financial illiteracy, lack of confidence with technology, lack of access to technology, as well as disability.

Instances of consumer exclusion uncovered in their research included:

- an elderly couple living in a rural location who were unable to access banking services locally and were therefore resorting to doorstep lenders despite being aware they were paying too much for these loans;

- cancer survivors wanting to get away on holiday who were unable to access travel insurance; and

- foreign entrepreneurs trying to set up in the UK who were unable to meet prohibitive ID requirements to set up a banking account.

In the banking sector, banks are as free to apply segmentation models in their marketing activities as any organization might in any sector. However, as a regulated sector, they are required to apply segmentation not just to identify the most profitable customers, but also to identify and protect consumers deemed vulnerable or at risk of exclusion.

11

11.4 Customer insight and customer needs

In Section 4.5 we considered Five Forces analysis, which examines the relative power of key entities within an industry. The marketing function focuses mostly on just one of these, the customer. In doing so, it puts a customer lens on all of the activities of the organization, looking at organizational activities from an outside-in perspective to understand how they will be perceived by customers. To ensure they understand customer perceptions and needs, marketers gather customer insight. This customer insight enables the organization to design and deliver appealing value propositions with the intention of creating value for the customer.

Customer insight might take several forms and is collected for many different purposes in the marketing planning activities of the organization. Three uses of customer insight are:

- auditing the marketplace of customers at an aggregate level to identify customer segments with differing needs;
- seeking depth of insight into customer needs to create or improve the value propositions that address these needs; and
- tracking customer feedback across the customer journey to ensure that promised value is delivered to customers as intended via the organization's activities.

We will now explore these three examples in greater detail.

11.4.1 Auditing the marketplace of customers

Understanding the external environment was previously discussed in Section 4.3 when we discussed PESTEL and identifying trends in the marketplace of customers is part of this external analysis. Auditing the marketplace of customers is typically done by gathering demographic data about the number of customers or prospective customers that exist, with the aim of establishing the total market opportunity. An organization may use government statistics from census data, for example, to determine the demographic breakdown of the customer base, such as the numbers of people in each gender and age group. The organization may match this demographic data with sources of behavioural data, such as information collated in its own customer relationship management (CRM) systems about customer responses to the firm's communication messages and previous purchasing behaviour. For instance, in Figure 11.9, we saw how Fitness First used data about how often their existing customers visit the gym to help identify six different customer segments with different patterns of usage of gym facilities (i.e. differing behaviours) and therefore different needs for value propositions. They then used this insight to put together different packages for customers that fall into those six different groups. These packages are known as value propositions and are delivered via varying marketing mixes (see Section 11.6).

11.4.2 Understanding customer needs

Seeking depth of insight into customer needs is often achieved through qualitative research, which is defined by the Market Research Society as 'an unstructured research approach with a small number of carefully selected individuals used to produce non-quantifiable insights into behaviour, motivations and attitudes' (Market Research Society, no date). Examples of qualitative research include:

- one-on-one interviews with customers to discuss a new product or service prototype;
- a focus group with around six to eight existing customers to understand their experience of using an existing product or service; and
- asking a group of families to complete an online daily consumption diary, listing all of their experiences in a particular category, such as food consumption or television viewing.

The aim of qualitative research is *understanding* rather than quantification, so it is important to listen to the words that customers use. Paying careful attention to the way that customers express their views and emotions will help an organization to design and deliver optimal value propositions that meet customers' needs and that differentiate the organization from its competitors.

11.4.3 Tracking customer insight

Tracking customers across the customer journey (see Section 11.4.4 and Figure 11.9) might include asking customers to complete a brief customer satisfaction question (e.g. 'On a scale of 1 to 5, how satisfied are you with your experience with us today?') at key points in the purchase and usage journey. This provides a brief read on how the organization is creating value for the customer at different stages and may flag up issues that need further investigation. Another popular customer metric is Net Promoter Score (NPS) which asks 'On a scale from 1 to 10, how likely are you to recommend us?' As customers value the views of other customers when making choices, NPS has been shown to be correlated with customer acquisition and further sales (Baehre et al., 2022).

As market contexts are continually changing, customer-focused organizations will typically have a **strategy** for:

- collecting customer insights on a regular or continuous basis;
- combining different customer insight sources and triangulating learnings from them to verify conclusions; and
- ensuring that these insights are shared around the organization in order to keep everyone in it focused on customer needs and on delivering customer value.

11.4.4 The customer decision journey

As described above, one of the jobs of marketing is to understand customer needs and perceptions of value. This helps the organization design appropriate value propositions that will meet customer needs. The second main activity of marketing is to understand the customer decision journey, and to manage the interactions of the organization and its brands along the stages of this customer journey. There are occasions where customers decide to purchase and then instantly make that purchase, such as repeat-buying a favourite cosmetic on Amazon.com, or an impulse buy of sweets at the cash register. However, in many purchase decisions, customers go through a series of steps that are often described in five stages: need recognition, information

11

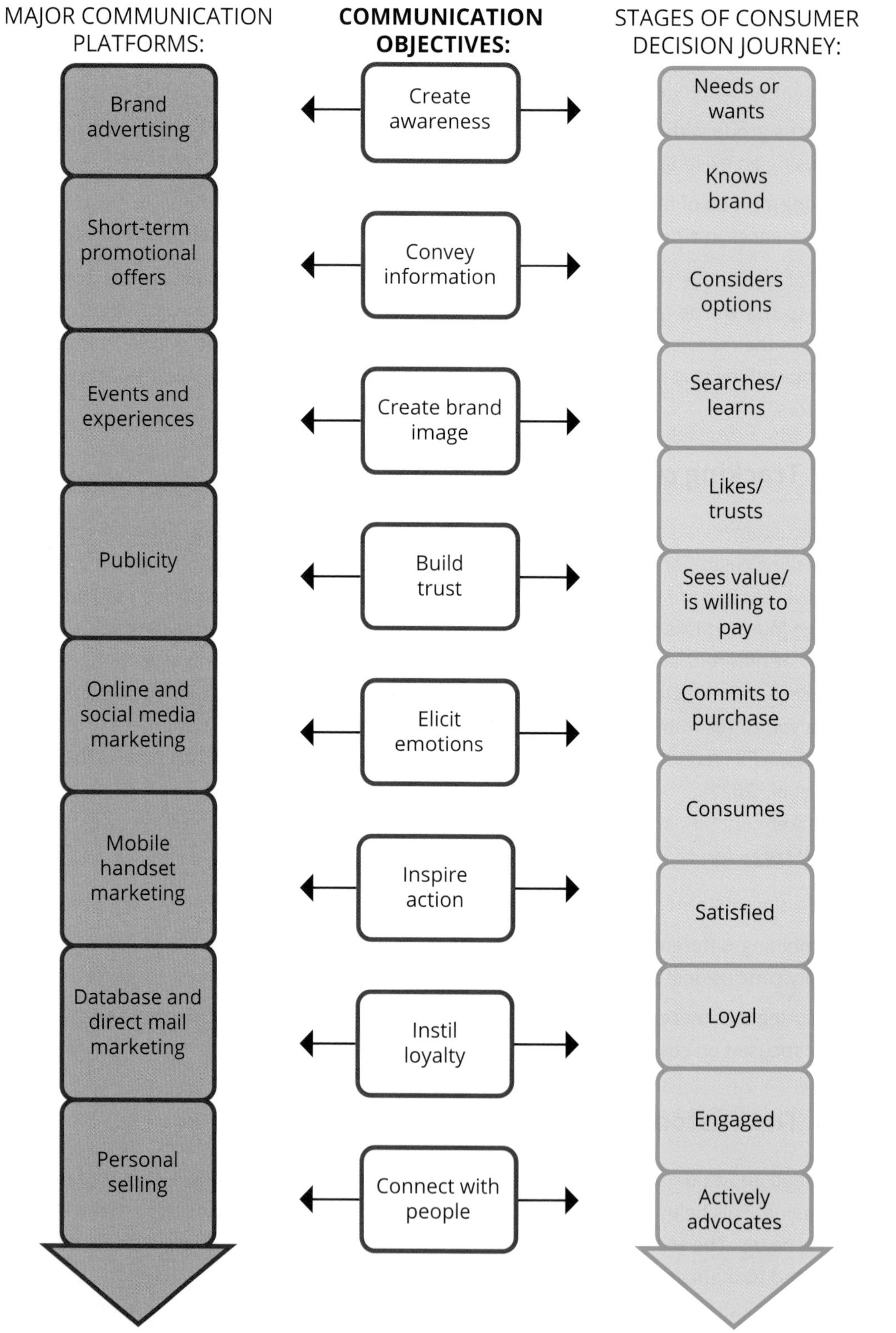

MAJOR COMMUNICATION PLATFORMS:

- Brand advertising
- Short-term promotional offers
- Events and experiences
- Publicity
- Online and social media marketing
- Mobile handset marketing
- Database and direct mail marketing
- Personal selling

COMMUNICATION OBJECTIVES:

- Create awareness
- Convey information
- Create brand image
- Build trust
- Elicit emotions
- Inspire action
- Instil loyalty
- Connect with people

STAGES OF CONSUMER DECISION JOURNEY:

- Needs or wants
- Knows brand
- Considers options
- Searches/ learns
- Likes/ trusts
- Sees value/ is willing to pay
- Commits to purchase
- Consumes
- Satisfied
- Loyal
- Engaged
- Actively advocates

FIGURE 11.10 **Major communication platforms matched to the consumer decision journey.** Credit: Batra, R., & Keller, K. L. (2016). 'Integrating Marketing Communications: New Findings, New Lessons, and New Ideas'. *Journal of Marketing*, 80(6), 122–145. © 2016, SAGE Publications.

search, evaluation of alternatives, purchase, and experience. This five-stage model assumes that decision-making is neatly linear—which of course, in reality it seldom is. However, this framework helps organizations recognize the need to plan their interactions with customers so that they are ready to respond to each of these stages of the journey to ensure that customers feel supported and informed enough to shift to the next stage. An updated view of the customer decision journey is shown in Figure 11.10.

Traditionally the organization's interaction with a customer across the stages of the decision journey would be managed by a human sales force, with experienced sales managers having skills to interpret customer needs, recognize moments when additional information might be useful, and know the right moment to close the deal on a sale. The same kind of expertise might be applied by skilled fundraisers seeking donations for a charity.

Increasingly, these interactions take place entirely in the online world, without any human-to-human live contact. This means that the possibility of customers becoming lost along their journey increases. Organizations keep track of customer progress along the online customer journey via data tracking, which is logged into the organization's CRM system. Organizations devise content marketing strategies to sit alongside their CRM systems as they attempt to track and influence the consumer decision journey online. Content marketing is defined as 'a technique of creating and distributing valuable, relevant and consistent content to attract and acquire a clearly defined audience—with the objective of driving profitable customer action' (ama.org). Figure 11.10 shows how and for what purposes different communications media might be deployed at different stages of the customer decision journey (Batra and Keller, 2016).

At some points across this customer journey, such as where the objective is to inspire action, the marketing function may hand over the custodianship of the customer journey to the operations function in the business. For instance, in the case of the coffee shop, the marketing function may create awareness, provide information about opening times, and publicize its new Summer tasting menu to be launched at an in-store event. The operations function may then pick up the task of taking table bookings, managing day-to-day customer interactions and complaints, and collating data about customer behaviour.

Next, we discuss two main ways that marketing supports the success of the organization.

11.5 Marketing objectives

Marketing is both a strategic and a tactical organizational activity. As we have already seen, marketers apply a number of tools to help their organization make strategic decisions about *which customers* they wish to address with *which products*. Having identified target customers, organizations then use marketing to implement a variety of activities and tactics to reach these customers. In for-profit business organizations, marketing objectives include acquiring and retaining customers in order to generate sales leading to revenue and profits.

Acquisition of customers is particularly a driver when a market is new, growing, and/or competitive, such as the recently emerged market for electric scooter sharing services. The Boston Consulting Group reported (Schellong et al., 2019) that since the e-scooter sharing market was first launched by US-based company Bird in 2017, a dozen further e-scooter start-ups had entered the market. Each of these dozen start-ups is attracted to the market's growth potential

11

and the ability to attract investment, but in order to be successful they need to win—or ac-quire—customers. The rewards for successful players will be substantial. The report predicts the market will grow to US$40 billion by 2025.

Retention of customers is a motive for organizations in established, mature markets where there is less market growth, which means that there are fewer customers around who have never purchased in that product category. The smart phone handset market is an example of such a market with 93 per cent of UK adults and 99 per cent of 18–24-year-olds owning a hand-set in 2022 according to Statista (Laricchia, 2022). This compels organizations to try to retain the customers they already have by providing differentiated offerings based on better customer service or locking customers into a community or ecosystem.

In third sector organizations, marketing objectives will be less about revenue and instead focus on the achievement of a purpose-driven mission, such as addressing homelessness (Hab-itat for Humanity), poverty in children (UNICEF), or endangered species (World Wide Fund for Nature). Some examples of third sector organizations and their marketing objectives are illus-trated below:

- **Acquiring and retaining members:** The nature charity, Royal Society for the Protection of Birds (RSPB) aims to encourage families to purchase subscriptions which provide them with free entry to the RSPB nature reserves and a quarterly magazine. Funds from sub-scriptions contribute to the charity's activities, which include protecting habitats as well as researching and saving bird populations.

- **Encouraging donations:** The anti-poverty charity, Red Nose Day uses televised fund-raising campaigns to encourage people to donate money to the charity which it can use to deploy in its anti-poverty programmes.

- **Connecting with beneficiaries:** Many charities will identify specific groups of people in society they deem as their beneficiaries. They will use marketing to create awareness among, and connect with, these beneficiary groups who need their help. The children's charity, Childline provides a phone line, online chat facility, email address, and British Sign Language service (for those who are deaf) (Figure 11.11). Key marketing objectives are to let beneficiaries (in this case, children under 19 years) know about the Childline contact details, guide them to help that is available to them, and encourage them to contact Child-line when in need. Childline also provides helpful videos on its website and YouTube site (Figure 11.12).

So far, we have followed the process of determining where opportunities exist in a market-place (through the process of market segmentation), identifying preferred groups of customers (through the process of targeting), defining the value propositions we are going to offer these target customers (based on customer insight), and then determining whether our marketing objectives should be focused on acquisition or retention of customers. The next step is to deter-mine *how* the organization is going to present itself to their chosen customers. A key framework for marketing implementation is the idea of the marketing mix. This involves putting a customer lens on a whole bundle of activities within the organization to form a value proposition that, from a customer point of view, feels integrated, feels relevant, and is attractive to purchase, use, or support. We will explore the concept of the marketing mix in the next section.

FIGURE 11.11 Childline's website provides multiple ways for under 19-year-olds in the UK to contact them and find advice.

FIGURE 11.12 Childline's YouTube channel has videos aimed at 13–18-year-olds.

11.6 Marketing implementation

Marketers make tactical decisions about how to best address the needs of selected target customer groups while achieving the goals of the organization. The tactical decisions of marketing include the elements of the marketing mix, also known as The Four Ps: product, price, place, and promotion (Figure 11.13). These decisions are, of course, not made in isolation from the rest of the organization. In fact, many of these activities are not necessarily owned by the organization's marketing department. This will become clear as we explore each of these areas of decision-making.

11.6.1 Marketing mix: Product

Product decisions include product features, design, sizes, packaging, range, brand name, service, and warranties. Many of these decisions are owned or contributed to by other departments in the business including Research & Development, Brand and Product Management, Operations, and Finance and Legal.

11

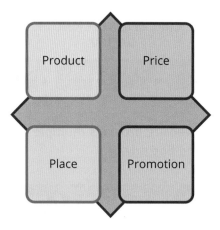

FIGURE 11.13 **Marketing mix: The Four Ps.**

A product may be a physical good, such as the Brompton Bicycles described in Spotlight 11.1, or an intangible service, such as Childline discussed in Section 11.5. We will discuss the extra challenges of marketing services in Section 11.6.6.

Product decisions include the brand. A **brand** is 'a name, term, design, symbol or any other feature that identifies one seller's goods or service as distinct from those of other sellers' (ama.org, n.d.). Over time, brand touchpoints (i.e. points of interaction with the customer) build up bundles of associations in the minds of customers. The sense of familiarity from a known brand helps reduce risk for customers when making a choice within a product category. An important component here is a brand's mental availability: that is a brand that a customer remembers when they are considering a product category (Romaniuk & Sharp, 2021). Mental availability is associated with a brand's increased likelihood to be purchased and so is often a key objective of a brand's marketing communications (discussed in Section 11.6.4).

Over time, brands develop a perceived brand personality in the minds of the customer base. This means that if asked in an interview or survey, most customers could describe the brands they know in human personality terms, such as exciting, sensible, or rugged. Recall Spotlight 6.1 relating to the 'Get a Mac' campaign which was comparing the Apple brand with the PC brand. A key challenge for brand managers is that they do not directly control how the customer base views brand personality. Sometimes there may be a mismatch between the organization's intended brand positioning and the way it is perceived in the minds of customers, in which case, the brand has a perceptual challenge. For example, in the Australian car market, Volvo cars had a perceptual challenge in that consumers perceived the brand's messages about being 'safer to drive' as meaning that it is a car brand for poor drivers. As a result, a stigma had formed in the Australian marketplace around owning a Volvo which impacted their sales (Drive.com.au, 2016). It took many years of different marketing campaigns to change this perception. Volvo's electric vehicle launch in 2022 appeared to finally break this curse with the brand achieving record sales (Volvocars.com, 2023).

11.6.2 Marketing mix: Price

Price decisions include choosing the listed retail price, discount prices, payment period, refunds, credit terms, and provision of payment technologies, such as apps that allow customers to track and split payments. Many of these decisions are owned or contributed to by other departments including Finance, Legal, Operations, Sales, or Channels, the latter being a catchall term for the departments that are responsible for the distribution of the organization's products or services to the customer including via the organization's shops, websites, and retailer partners.

Organizations that provide services, such as hotel rooms, airline seats, and concert tickets, have always applied variable pricing as a way to manage demand. This is because, unlike a manufacturer of shoes who can store unsold stock to be sold another day, the provider of hotel services cannot sell an unused hotel room from the night before as that opportunity has now been lost forever. Thanks to computing power and artificial intelligence, organizations across more industry sectors now apply variable pricing (Walker, 2017). In some cases, this may see some segments of customers paying higher prices than other customers for the same value proposition. One report found that people booking services via the internet on their Apple devices (mobile handsets and laptops) might pay up to 30 per cent more than users of other branded devices (Walker, 2017). This is because when customers book online, their device communicates a unique IP address which includes information about the device type. Apple users are generally known to belong to wealthier segments of the customer base, so the seller's AI systems nudge these shoppers to more expensive options than if they were booking via a device with a different operating system.

UK consumer champion, Which? recently identified that supermarkets were unintentionally penalizing low-income families who live without a car in inner-city locations. This is because the supermarkets' smaller city stores charge higher prices for basic goods such as vegetables and bread, and fail to stock the range of affordable budget brands found in their larger out-of-town stores which are accessible only by car (Simmonds, 2022). Which? campaigned to shift these practices as part of its focus on fairness during the UK's cost of living crisis.

11.6.3 Marketing mix: Place

The 'Place' element of the marketing mix, often referred to as Distribution, encompasses all the decisions to ensure its value propositions are available to customers at the right place and time. This includes distribution channels, defined as 'the paths travelled by a product from the manufacturer—through any middlemen—to the end user' (Marketing Accountability Standards Board). These decisions include whether the organization makes its products available via bricks-and-mortar stores or via an e-commerce website, or both. This is known as the offline–online channel decision. Other place decisions include whether the organization should own and manage retail outlets or arrange partnerships with other organizations that have specialist retail expertise. Fashion brand Zara, for example, typically sells its Zara-branded clothing in its Zara-branded retail outlets or via its own branded website. Many other fashion brands choose

11

to manufacture their products but then distribute them via retail outlets and websites owned by other organizations, referred to as channel partners, such as:

- the bricks-and-mortar outlets and websites of department stores, such as Macy's in the USA or John Lewis in the UK;
- the bricks-and-mortar outlets and websites of specialist stores, such as French sports retailer, Decathlon or German shoe retailer, Deichmann; and
- the websites and apps of online-only retailers, Amazon and Alibaba, and JD.com which mostly operates in China (Kharpal, 2021).

For instance, in the case of Brompton Bicycles (Spotlight 11.1), the company might decide to provide bicycles via a website, Brompton-branded stores that they own, or other retailers' stores. In fact, Brompton uses all three of these channels. Many Place decisions are contributed to or owned by Operations, Customer Service, or Sales departments. In the case of digital value propositions, such as the games provided by Nintendo, the Information Systems department and Website Manager will play a key role in Place decisions.

Technology is changing the way that companies manage the Place element of their marketing mix. For example, the prevalence and consumer take-up of online and mobile phone banking has meant that mainstream banks have closed many of their face-to-face bank branches over the last decade. (See Spotlight 11.2 for implications of this change for some banking customers.) Online shopping has seen many bricks-and-mortar retail outlets close down. The use of new delivery tech for the 'last mile' is rapidly changing with delivery bots already operating in many cities in the UK, USA, and Asia (Figure 11.14). Drone technology is likewise being used to deliver food to sites across the world. Other tech likely to impact the Place element in the coming years includes self-driving vehicles and augmented and virtual reality. For example, the latter will help customers to 'try on' shoes and clothes without having to physically touch an item prior to purchase, thus saving millions in postage costs for returned items.

FIGURE 11.14 **Starship bots delivering groceries and takeaway foods to the home.** Credit: Shutterstock

11.6.4 **Marketing mix: Promotion**

The 'Promotion' element of the marketing mix includes all decisions about communications that an organization makes to let target customers know about the organization, including its brands and value propositions. Many of the organization's communications decisions are contributed to or owned by other departments including Strategy, Public Relations, Brand Management, Product Management, Sales, Customer Service, Information Systems, or Delivery.

Table 11.1 outlines some of the communication tools that an organization might consider using to reach out to potential and existing customers.

TABLE 11.1 **Marketing communications activities**

Activity	Example
Brands and brand advertising	Creating a message (such as a 30-second television ad or an online ad that shows during search or on a website) to promote the brand's name and logo, without any promotion of the actual product. The aim with brand-building messages is to encourage customers to notice and retain information about the brand so that it becomes top-of-mind when making future consumption decisions.
Short-term promotional offers	Offering a time-limited offer (such as a price discount) to encourage customers to buy immediately.
Events and experiences	Earth Day is an event-based climate change campaign that successfully engages a billion people around the world each year on 22 April.
Publicity	Sharing a press release with news about the company and its products/services or conducting an activity to attract the attention of the media, influencers, and customers.
Website and app marketing	Using a pop-up message to appear on a website or mobile app encouraging customers to buy an additional product or service.
Social media communities	Ensuring the organization has a presence within online groups of customers or potential customers. The organization appoints a social media manager (or team) to represent the organization and join online conversations in an authentic way.
Database and direct mail marketing	Using information that the organization has collated about an existing customer or a potential new customer (known as a 'lead') to individualize a letter that is sent either by physical mail, email, or other digital channel.
Personal selling	Employing a salesperson to meet with the customer physically or online with the intention of promoting and selling products or services.
Influencer marketing	Influencer marketing is like a celebrity endorsement of the brand, although not all influencers are famous celebrities. Many influencers are everyday people who have managed to build a following on a social channel. Typically 1,000-plus followers is a minimum but many influencers have many thousands of followers. A brand will work with the influencer to get brand and product messages out to the people who follow the influencer on a social channel, such as Instagram. We discuss the reasons why an influencer shapes the opinions of others in Section 10.7.

Marketing communications encompasses many activities with many choices to be made about format and channels of communication. For this reason, it is a resource-intensive activity. Organizations need to be very clear about when and why they want to interact with customers. The communications tools all have different strengths and may be better suited to different stages of the customer decision journey, as discussed in Section 11.4.4.

Marketing communications is an area of the business that can keep employees very busy and can rack up costs without necessarily being able to quantify the benefit. Overall, there are two main objectives of marketing communications: to drive sales today and to build brand associations for the future. In the 'Explore more' feature at the end of this chapter, we have included a reference to a presentation by Les Binet called 'The Short of It'. His analysis, based on many years of the Advertising Effectiveness Awards, discusses the trade-offs between short-term and long-term objectives of marketing communications.

11.6.5 An integrated value proposition

The marketing function of the organization coordinates a range of organizational activities with the aim of integrating them around the customer so that—from a customer viewpoint, at least—the branded offering to the customer appears joined-up, consistent, and holistic rather than a disconnected set of decisions from siloed organizational departments.

As already discussed, the marketing department itself does not necessarily own all the activities of the marketing mix. However, what the marketing function does do is put a customer lens on all of these decisions to ensure that what is presented to the customer appears coordinated and integrated, makes sense to the customer as a single integrated proposition, and creates value for the customer in a way that they find appealing and would be prepared to pay for (or support, in the case of third sector organizations).

So, for example, if you were to launch the shoe business discussed at the start of this chapter, and your aim was to create an impression of youthful sportiness, then you would want to ensure that the styling and features of your shoes (product), the payment terms (price), the stores you sell them in (place), and your sales people and your website (promotion) all reflect this intended messaging, as perceived by the customer.

11.6.6 The extended marketing mix: 8Ps

When a value proposition includes a high degree of intangibility, such as legal advice, banking, or transport services, then the marketing mix may encompass a further few elements. This extended view of the marketing mix is shown in Figure 11.15.

- **Physical evidence:** If a value proposition involves a high degree of intangibility, such as legal advice, then the provider may seek to provide sources of physical evidence of the organization's existence and quality. For example, if you pay a lawyer for advice, you may receive some spoken words and perhaps a legal document that is printed on paper, but mostly what you receive is not tangible because you are paying for the expertise of the lawyer and the reassurance provided by their expert advice. The challenge with an intangible value proposition is that the customer may find it difficult to judge its value and to

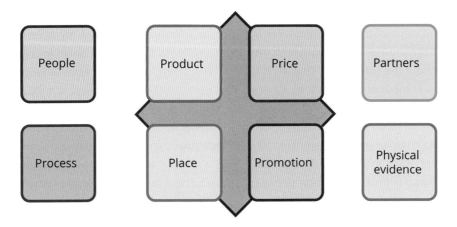

FIGURE 11.15 **The extended marketing mix: The eight Ps.**

assess whether they have received a good level of experience. Providers of an intangible service like legal advice might therefore seek to pay attention to aspects of the value proposition that are physical as signals to the customer of quality. For example, a legal practice may be located in an office building in an upmarket business location and its staff may dress professionally and be trained to behave in certain ways when meeting with clients. Likewise, banks traditionally were located in buildings with solid pillars and marble floors as indicators of security and stability, and airlines have staff wearing crisp uniforms as a message of professional competence. When you collect your car after it has been for a maintenance visit with a car mechanic for the day, you might find a card or a note in the vehicle when you collect it, plus it may have been cleaned and some car fragrance may have been sprayed. These are all tangible signs that your car has been attended to even though the treatment to your car may not be visible.

- **People:** If your organization provides value propositions that have a high dependence on people delivering them, then there may be an important People element to your marketing mix. In a hair salon, stylists engage physically with clients, spending a minimum of 30 minutes—but sometimes hours—in close proximity of the customer, touching their body (their hair and scalp). For this reason, the manager of a hair salon will expend effort in training apprentices with skills of hair-cutting but also in standards of customer service. Similarly, recall Emirates' investment in people in Chapter 9 Opening Case.

- **Process:** If your organization provides a process, such as the Eurostar company that provides train services to move customers efficiently between cities in Europe and the UK, then a key aspect of the marketing mix will focus on managing the customer through the process and on the experience of the customer in that process. Eurostar provides instructions to customers about arriving at the departure gate on time as follows: 'IMPORTANT: Please come to the station early and not just before the ticket gates close. This will ensure that you have enough time to go through all checks before your train departs' (Eurostar.com). By helping their customers manage their own time planning more effectively, Eurostar is likewise better able to ensure they can create the service experience they have promised.

11

- **Partners:** Organizations may also align with partners as another way to boost the perceived value of the proposition. For instance, in a famous example of 'ingredient marketing' from the 1990s, microprocessor manufacturer, Intel began a campaign to tell consumers about the 'Intel Inside' their PCs. Up until that point, consumers were largely unaware of the components within their devices. Intel agreed with their partners, the PC manufacturers that an 'Intel Inside' sticker should go onto the outside of the PC as this would be beneficial to both parties, especially when Intel accompanied this strategy with a mass media communications campaign to raise awareness among everyday consumers of the quality of the Intel brand. The campaign was a success and today, devices continue to be produced with an Intel sticker telling consumers about the non-visible components inside.

11.7 Sustainable customer behaviour

We explored a number of environmental disruptions in Section 3.5, including the climate crisis, water scarcity, and biodiversity loss. Organizations are increasingly aware that, even if they are attempting to reduce the impact of their own operations, the impact of their products and services can be much more significant. In relation to GHG emissions, this is known as 'Scope 3 emissions'. As described by the World Resources Institute (Bhatia et al., 2011), Scope 1 covers emissions directly from the organization and Scope 2 includes emissions from the electricity and energy the organization uses. However, Scope 3 emissions comprise the GHG emissions from both upstream (e.g. supply chain) and downstream activities (e.g. customer/consumer use) (see Figure 11.16).

As such, increasingly marketers are focused on Scope 3, linked to their customer's behaviour. This might include travel agents aware of the emissions associated with air travel of the flights they sell, or vehicle manufacturers aware of the emissions from customers driving the cars they have bought. Organizations with a large customer base in particular, may recognize not just a sense of responsibility for the behaviour of their customers but also, because of the sheer number of customers they have (which may number in the millions), the substantial opportunities for dramatically changing human impact on the environment if they can change behaviour of a significant portion of their customer base. Forward-thinking organizations also recognize the potential to develop new value propositions that will have a win-win of creating profits and reducing the organization's environmental impacts. But what are the mechanisms available to an organization to encourage consumers to behave more sustainably?

In a recent review of marketing and behavioural science tools, White et al. (2019) identified that there are barriers to consumers adopting sustainable behaviours, often because the more sustainable choice incurs extra cost or inconvenience to the customer, or because it is new it creates uncertainty, or simply because habit and inertia make adopting a new behaviour less likely. Achieving shifts in customer behaviour requires organizations to design value propositions and communications very consciously in order to reduce inertia that may hold back changes in customer behaviour. White et al. identified five broad categories of psychological factors that organizations could use to achieve desired shifts in consumer

11

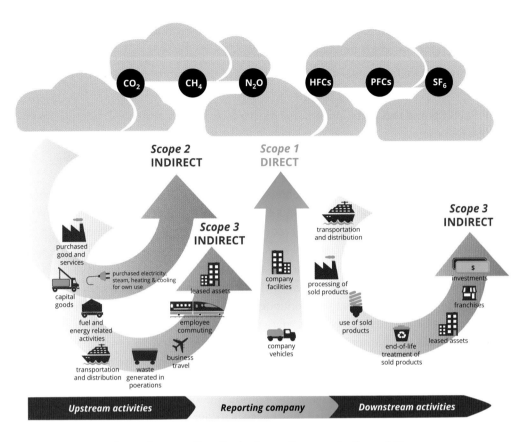

FIGURE 11.16 **Greenhouse Gas Emissions: Scopes 1, 2, and 3.** Credit: World Resources Institute: www.wri.org

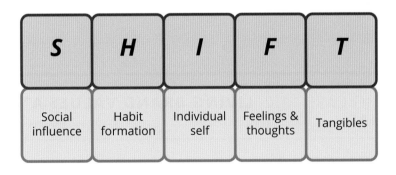

FIGURE 11.17 **SHIFT-ing consumers to more sustainable behaviour (based on White et al., 2019).**

behaviour towards pro-environmental behaviour, which they referred to using the acronym SHIFT (Figure 11.17):

- **S: Social influence:** People's behaviour is often influenced by what they think other people consider to be acceptable behaviour and whether they believe other people will see them and judge them during the consumption process. Organizations need to understand whose opinions people are likely to pay attention to when making consumption decisions.

- **H: Habit formation:** Consider what aspects of the individual's behaviour are linked to existing habits or which could become habits.

- **I: Individual self:** Consider the characteristics of the customer who will be enacting the behaviour.

- **F: Feelings and thoughts:** Understand the person's feelings and thoughts associated with that behaviour.

- **T: Tangibility:** Consider the degree of certainty and clarity around the behaviour.

White et al. found that sustainability options often require greater effort from the customer, and that often a combination of two or more of these tools is needed to achieve a shift. For example, up to 80 per cent of the energy required for washing a load of laundry might come from heating the water (White et al., 2019). With awareness of this issue, two of the world's biggest laundry detergent players, Unilever and Procter & Gamble have developed value propositions of clothes detergents that work effectively in cold water. However, having developed these cold-water products there continue to be barriers to adoption. The first barrier is that consumers believe that hot water is more effective than cold at removing stains; this is a 'F: feelings & thoughts' barrier according to the SHIFT framework. To overcome this barrier, and shift such thoughts, the brand needs to provide information about cold-water detergents, perhaps encouraging trial through samples. But a second strategy will also be required, so the message might focus on the interests of the individual 'I: Individual Self', promoting that cold washes do not require as much waiting time because the water does not need heating up, and that cold washing does not wear clothes out as quickly and thus make clothes last longer. The focus on changing consumer thoughts plus appealing to self-interests in this case may achieve the desired shift in behaviour. Let's see how Imperial is thinking about customer behaviour in Running case 11.2.

RUNNING CASE 11.2 **LIVING BRAND VALUES AT IMPERIAL**

As the members of the 'Dream Team' concentrate on their separate tasks, Marketing Manager, Gita, continues to focus on branding and packaging. She is enthusiastic that Imperial is bringing the UN's Sustainable Development Goals (see Spotlight 3.2) into its own objectives and is excited about introducing a plant-based range to demonstrate Imperial's active commitment to sustainability. Like many businesses, Imperial has selected a subset of the UN's SDGs for special focus and Gita is delighted that Lucy is so determined to ensure Imperial 'lives its values'. In Gita's view, this is demonstrated by

the actions arising following Lucy's recent trip to Kenya where she sought to review Imperial's tea supply chain.

On her office wall, Gita has set out the four SDGs chosen by Imperial. Next to each, she has written statements showing how Imperial's current and planned work will demonstrate its commitment to these important goals. From now on, she plans to highlight Imperial's sustainability commitments in its branding and communications activity:

- **SDG 8: Decent Work:** Imperial purchases its tea and other foodstuffs only from producers

11

who guarantee decent work at a fair wage in safe conditions.

- **SDG 11: Reducing Inequalities:** Imperial insists on equality of treatment and opportunity for all its stakeholders. Our strength is in our diversity, which is valued and maintained throughout our business.

- **SDG 12: Responsible Consumption and Production:** Imperial's meats are sourced only from low-intensity, low-carbon, environmentally-friendly farms. All our other ingredients are produced sustainably. Our plant-based foods reflect our commitment to increasing dietary choices for our consumers and to further reducing our carbon footprint.

- **SDG 13: Climate Action:** As well as ensuring our ingredients are sustainable and health-enhancing, we minimize the environmental impact of all our operations.

There is one thing Gita has been struggling with, though. As she contemplates the next stages of her branding strategy, she reflects on the conversation she and Lucy had months ago (see Running case 7.2). Is Imperial really an appropriate name for a diverse and ethical company in the 2020s? Gita is still uncomfortable with the idea that people might associate her workplace with a colonial past. But as a marketer, she is also uneasy about throwing away brand value built up over decades, especially now her own marketing activity is showing the world that as well as selling products of outstanding quality, Imperial Fine Foods is sustainable, diverse, and inclusive. When she looks up the definition of imperial in her dictionary, she wonders whether people will remember that the term also refers to 'a commercial product of special size or quality' (Oxford English Dictionary): isn't this what they're producing?

She keeps this positive message in mind in this week's weekly meeting with Saffron Walden, her Marketing Assistant, to discuss their social-media strategy. Saffron has been working on how they're going to manage to appeal to 'Green Fiends' without putting off the 'Traditional Carnivores', and vice versa. She has found a vegan influencer, @plantbasedstudent, who she thinks could play an important part in helping them establish a presence in the student foods market. However, she thinks that @plantbasedstudent may have concerns about being connected with Imperial's traditional products. Gita acknowledges the concern, but tells Saffron, 'We have to find a balance. It might be tricky as we're getting started. But the fact is our business depends on meat-eaters and flexitarians and will continue to do so. We have to make sure that our Instagram and Facebook posts make everyone, whatever they eat, associate Imperial with quality.'

Questions for reflection

1. Should Imperial change its name? What would it gain? What would it lose?

2. Draw a customer journey map for each of the three personas identified by Gita and the Dream Team. What do you find? How do the customer journeys you have outlined affect the conduct of Imperial's operations and marketing?

11.8 Avoiding greenwashing

While organizations increasingly seek to minimize the impact of their operations on the environment and to shift their customers towards more sustainable behaviours, they may find themselves at increased risk of greenwashing. Network for Business Sustainability defines greenwashing as: 'Creating falsely positive views of an organization's environmental performance. Simply stated: Organizations say that they are acting more sustainably than they really are. There's a range from slight exaggeration to full untruth. Greenwashing can be either intentional or unintentional' (Nemes et al., 2022a).

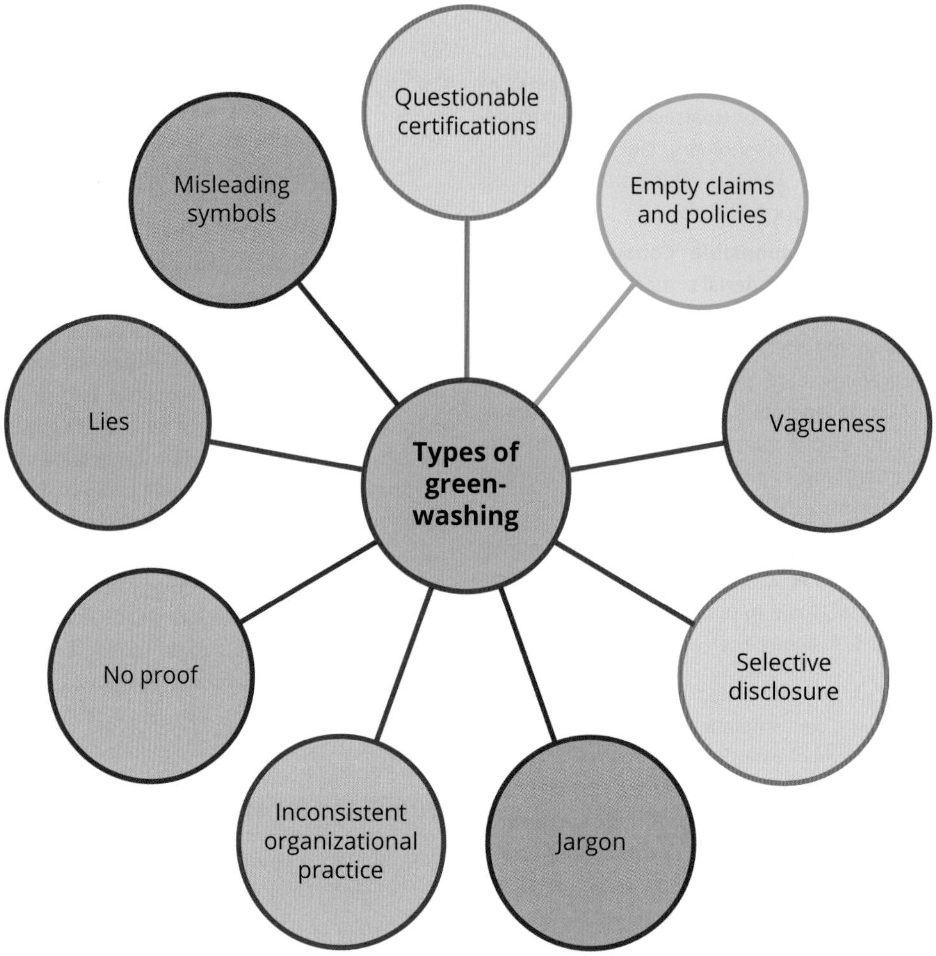

FIGURE 11.18 **Types of greenwashing.** Network for Business; Nemes, N.; Scanlan, S. J.; Smith, P.; Smith, T.; Aronczyk, M.; Hill, S.; Lewis, S. L.; Montgomery, A. W.; Tubiello, F. N.; Stabinsky, D. 'An Integrated Framework to Assess Greenwashing'. *Sustainability* (2022b), 14, 4431. https://doi.org/10.3390/su14084431

Greenwashing is a significant problem. A European Commission (2021) study of websites found that almost half lacked evidence for their claims. Greenwashing can occur when an organization makes claims about their products, such as 'conscious', or 'sustainable', or through the use of colours such as green, or images such as waterfalls, which give similarly vague messages. However, there are many other forms of greenwashing, illustrated in Figure 11.18

Nemes et al. (2022b) provide recommendations for how organizations can avoid unintentional greenwashing, summarized in Table 11.2.

An important reflection from the Network for Business Sustainability (2022) analysis is that organizations should: 'spend more on achieving [a sustainability] goal than on marketing it'.

11

TABLE 11.2 **How to avoid greenwashing**

Type of greenwashing	Examples
Vague claims	Avoid unclear terms such as 'green', or 'eco-friendly'. Provide evidence for claims, ideally from an independent source. State whether claims refer to part or all of the product.
Misleading symbols	Consider visuals and images in their entirety and ensure that they do not exaggerate claims.
Jargon	Use language customers can understand.
Selective disclosure	Assess sustainability impact across all stages of a product's life including production and end-of-life disposal. Be transparent about performance including negative impacts. Transparency builds trust.
Inconsistent organizational practice	Ensure that environmental claims reflect a sustainability focus across the entire organization, including products, operations, and vision.
Dubious certifications	Only use certifications verified by an independent body.

Credit: Network for Business Sustainability; Nemes, N.; Scanlan, S.J.; Smith, P.; Smith, T.; Aronczyk, M.; Hill, S.; Lewis, S.L.; Montgomery, A.W.; Tubiello, F.N.; Stabinsky, D. 'An Integrated Framework to Assess Greenwashing'. *Sustainability* 2022b, 14, 4431. https://doi.org/10.3390/su14084431

11.9 **Conclusion**

Marketing has relevance for almost every type of organization, regardless of whether it is private, public, or third sector. Marketing puts a customer lens and an outside-in focus on all of the activities of the organization. One of the main tasks of marketing is to identify customer groups with similar clusters of needs by conducting a segmentation of the marketplace. From this segmentation analysis, an organization can identify segments of customers that it may choose to target. Marketing helps to gain a depth in understanding of the **target market** and their needs by gathering customer insight. Once we understand the needs of our target customers and are sure about our marketing objectives, then the marketing function coordinates the value propositions that are offered to these customers. The value proposition is implemented by integrating a bundle of organizational decisions that include product features, brand and brand image, price, distribution, and communications. Customer decision-making often involves a number of steps in what is described as a customer journey. The marketing function will coordinate the steps in this journey by developing appropriate communications messages at relevant stages. There is increasing focus on how organizations can influence customer behaviour towards being more sustainable, though of course this creates a tension for the marketing function, which has traditionally been tasked with helping the organization encourage its customers to purchase and consume products. However, the tools of marketing can be used very effectively to address the sustainability challenge as marketing's expertise is in understanding people, their motivations, and levers for nudging customer behaviour.

11

CHAPTER SUMMARY

- Marketing is the function that focuses on the customer and their needs.
- It shapes and creates value to satisfy customer needs by gathering customer insight and using that to coordinate value propositions.
- Value propositions are implemented via the marketing mix, or the 4 Ps: product, price, place, and promotion.
- Marketing coordinates the organization's interactions with the customer across the customer decision journey.
- Customer behaviour is a significant contributor to the organization's environmental impact and organizations are increasingly considering how they can use the tools of marketing to shape more sustainable customer and consumer behaviour.

CLOSING CASE REFLECTION

Burberry's customer experience: Bridging physical and digital worlds

Burberry, the UK's largest luxury retailer by sales (Paton, 2018), works hard to ensure its brand attracts new customers and retains existing customers. It pays careful attention to all elements of the marketing mix, including creating appealing products, using communication via paid advertising and social media that reinforces its heritage as a quality British brand, and designing retail and website facilities that create exciting experiences for customers. Burberry targets younger luxury consumers through the brand's use of in-store and online gamification of the customer experience and via partnerships with brands such as Minecraft. A recent campaign providing virtual handbags in partnership with Roblox again demonstrates how the brand is positioned at the forefront of retail trends. Burberry is not without its critics, however, particularly following recent admissions that it regularly burnt excess stock as a way of maintaining exclusivity and preventing the erosion of its high-end prices (Paton, 2018). Having been called out on this behaviour, Burberry promised it would cease this practice and announced a partnership with the Royal College of Arts to develop sustainable materials for fashion (Paton, 2018).

REVIEW QUESTIONS

1. Why do organizations use market segmentation? Explain a scenario where an organization gets into an ethical dilemma when applying segmentation.
2. You have decided to launch a business to produce and sell shoes. Look back to the discussion in Section 11.3 and select your customer segment. Now apply the elements of the marketing mix to make decisions about the product, price, place, and promotion of your value proposition to match the needs of your selected customer segment.

3. How do organizations effectively use market research to better understand their customers? Discuss ethical considerations in gathering and using market research to influence the customer decision journey.

4. What are the opportunities and challenges for marketing that arise from technological advancements and the changing digital media landscape?

5. How can organizations drive favourable attitudes and behaviours towards sustainable consumption choices? Should they?

EXPLORE MORE

READ information that scrutinizes the fashion industry in the Good On You app, which aims to address SDG12 Sustainable Consumption and Production in the fashion industry. It gives clothing companies an ethical rating based on labour impact, environmental impact, and animal welfare to help shoppers make more informed purchases online or in-store.

READ about some of the recent rulings on the front page of the Advertising Standards Authority website, which aims to hold advertisers to account. These may include influencers who have not identified a social media post as an advertising communication.

READ up more on types of influencers and how companies use influencer marketing to shape people's attitudes and consumption behaviours at Influencer Marketing Hub.

READ 'Retail Dive' which provides short articles on news and trends shaping the retail sector. Identify examples of customer insight and how they are feeding into the creation or modification of retailer value propositions. Google 'retail dive' to find the site.

WATCH Les Binet talk about the two key activities of marketing communications: sales activation and brand building. Search for 'The Short of It' on YouTube.

11

CHAPTER TWELVE

Operations and Supply Chain Management

Anthony Alexander and Emma Macdonald

OPENING CASE STUDY **KILO SALES**

Kilo Sales are exciting events where bargain shoppers may find clothing very cheaply in a one-day pop-up sale. Vintage Superstore Cornwall (VSC) is a provider of Kilo Sales events in cities around the UK. The company sources excess clothing stock by acquiring reject and surplus stock very cheaply from manufacturers and retailers, supplemented by second-hand vintage and retro clothing. It also repairs and upcycles damaged branded goods into unique 'handmade' clothing items.

Unlike clothes that shoppers purchase via online or physical retailers, Kilo Sales clothes are not individually priced but are sold on a simple per-weight basis. For example, at the February 2023 Kilo Sale held at the Kia Oval Cricket Ground in London, clothes were priced at £5 per kilo. The sale included 2,500 pairs of trousers and shorts from brands Carhartt and Dickies; 5,000 pairs of jeans from Levi, Wrangler, and Lee; and 10 tonnes of clothing items including t-shirts, hoodies, coats, jackets, skirts, and more.

The VSC operations team manages the sourcing and logistics of stock, the set-up of temporary pop-up events in cities across the UK, and the crowds of shoppers that turn up for each event. The simplicity of the pricing model means that there is no need to put price labels on any stock. The low prices help to manage customer expectations and there are no promises about specific brands, sizes, types, and volumes of stock that will be offered.

The operations team manages the experience of customers who attend the Kilo Sale. The events attract a large crowd of shoppers queueing to enter to find the best bargains. Once the doors to the venue open, the rate at which the queue of people can enter depends on the speed by which they can be processed through the arrival gate. VSC opts not to charge for entry, though some of their competitors do charge an admission fee. Instead, VSC manages the crowd by requiring attendees to pre-book their attendance. This lets the company predict and control numbers. Throughout the day, additional stock is brought out on racks and in bins to ensure that the event is attractive for later attendees as well as the early queuers.

VSC's suppliers are major brands seeking cost-effective disposal for their stock that is unsold or that has been damaged during manufacture or transit. VSC can take very large volumes of clothing, which makes it a desirable option for manufacturers facing the problem of how to dispose of a big batch of unwanted clothing. It also helps to meet consumer demand for more affordable clothing and to avoid the environmental impacts of wastage. The success of the Kilo Sale model has seen it become a regular event in cities across the UK, promising the thrill of the hunt to bargain shoppers and reducing wastefulness in the clothing industry.

12.1 **Introduction**

Operations management and **supply chain** management happen everywhere, every day, but if done well, we do not even notice them. Operations management focuses on the activities that an organization undertakes internally, in order to meet its strategic goals. Supply chain management sources and coordinates all of the external inputs the organization needs in order to operate. All managers are responsible for operations in some form or other, although some organizations will have a specific department whose primary focus is on operations management. Operations management originated in manufacturing organizations where the objective was to ensure the greatest efficiency in the production of **physical goods**. However, many of the concepts developed for operations management in manufacturing are relevant for organizations in service industries, digitized and automated organizations, and non-business organizations.

All organizations from the private, public, and third sector, can be understood via operations and supply chain management ideas. For some this is relatively simple—the supply chain of a café includes inputs such as coffee beans and various types of milk (dairy, almond, and soya), while operations management focuses on how these ingredients are transformed into lattes and iced coffees, and delivered to customers. However, many organizations have incredibly complex supply chains—often better described as supply networks, as we will discover—as well as sophisticated operations management that makes use of digital management systems and AI decision-making. The online retailer Amazon is an example of an organization with a complex supply chain of literally millions of suppliers and warehouses that use innovative technology solutions to achieve the most efficient operations possible. Meanwhile, large charities have similar complexity in supply chains and operations. The International Federation of Red Cross and Red Crescent Societies is a group of not-for-profit organizations that must source and transport needed supplies all over the world and often, when responding to natural disasters, with very little notice. They must also coordinate operations for the distribution of such supplies, often in chaotic and uncertain situations where communities have been displaced by floods, earthquakes, or conflict.

The functions of operations and supply chain management may be undertaken by people with titles such as operations manager or supply chain manager, but may also include those with titles such as production manager, logistics manager, sourcing manager, **procurement** manager, facilities director, or factory manager. In small organizations, the activities of operations and supply chain may be undertaken by people without any specific reference to these activities in their titles at all. Moreover, sustainability and ethics are an increasing concern of both operations management and supply chain. This is because operations are often a source of both environmental and societal direct impacts of the organization, while supply chains can be sources of instances of poor practices, such as modern slavery. As such, sustainability managers are likely to be very engaged in elements of operations and supply chain.

An essential element of operations and supply chain management is for managers to determine what sits where. That is, what elements should be part of your organization's specific operations, and what should be outsourced to your supply chain. We addressed this question briefly in Section 5.2.4, which explored the value chain. This chapter looks in more detail at the activities of operations and supply chain, as well as at the linkages between these roles and other parts of the organization, including marketing, human resources, and strategy.

In relation to strategy, while operations management is typically focused on *delivering* strategy, it can also have a role in *developing* strategy. If we consider the Resource-Based View of strategy introduced in Chapter 5, the operations manager often has deep knowledge of both the resources and capabilities that form the organization's strengths. This is also true for not-for-profit organizations, where the organization's strategic objectives may be delivering social outcomes rather than economic ones. We will consider the strategic role of this function in Section 12.6. First, though, we will examine the role of operations management as a set of processes (Section 12.2), before looking in more detail at capacity management within those processes (Section 12.3). We will then turn to focus on supply chain management (Section 12.4), as well as the importance of ongoing process improvement (Section 12.5). By the end of this chapter, you should see the world around you differently—from whether and how you queue for your morning coffee, to what goes on in airport security halls—and appreciate how operations and supply chain management have played a role in your experience.

12.2 Operations as process

Operations management deals with processes. A **process** is defined as something that has an input, and then a transformation of that input to produce an output, as depicted in Figure 12.1. Inputs comprise resources that flow through the organization. These resources can take either physical form (a raw material like bread or a car component) or can be in the form of data (customer information). The transformation of these inputs is the processes—or the series of micro-operations shown in Figure 12.1—that operations management designs, enacts, controls, measures, analyses, and redesigns for improvements. Operations managers analyse how long each process takes, how effectively resources flow through chains of processes, and whether there are times when the operation is sitting idle and waiting for work, or is overloaded and cannot complete the work that needs to be done fast enough. Products moving along a **factory** assembly line as the next parts are added, queues of people in a coffee shop, and hospital waiting times are all issues that concern operations management.

The notion of resources transformed through a process can be applied to almost any type of organization. Spotlight 12.1 provides examples of operations management in a number of different contexts.

Given the importance of processes to operations, it is important to be able to analyse their characteristics. We can do this using the 4V framework captured in Figure 12.2, which comprises volume, variety, variation, and visibility (Slack et al., 2013). These characteristics include:

- Volume: amount of output able to be produced by a process.
- Variety: number of different activities in a process.
- Variation: changes in demand for outputs from a process.
- Visibility: degree to which processes can be observed by customers.

12

Feedback

Flour
Water
Salt
Yeast
Olive oil

Inputs → Transformation process → Outputs → Bread

Macro operation

Can be broken down into:

Mixing
Micro operation 1

Proving
Micro operation 2

Baking
Micro operation 3

FIGURE 12.1 **Resource transformation process when making bread.**

SPOTLIGHT 12.1 OPERATIONS MANAGEMENT EXAMPLES

Café

Inputs: customers, coffee beans, tea leaves, milk (dairy, oat, almond, etc.), bread, sandwich fillings, etc.

Transformation: roasting coffee beans, brewing coffee, making tea, making sandwiches, customers ordering and paying, serving customers.

Outputs: coffee, tea, sandwiches, satisfied customers.

Doctor's general practice surgery

Inputs: patients, carers, medical equipment, IT systems, pharmaceuticals.

Transformation: appointment bookings process, surgery welcome, patient queueing, consultations, diagnoses, treatments, prescribing.

Outputs: patient reassured, patient with treatment plan, prescription, referral to further services.

Airline

Inputs: aircraft, airports, fuel, pilots, stewards, airport security teams, cleaners, baggage handlers, passengers, baggage.

Transformation: booking process, passengers safely onboarded to their seats, the right luggage uploaded to the hold, people and luggage moved to their destination, people and luggage offloaded, cleaning and refuelling.

Outputs: passengers safely arrived with their baggage where and when promised, aircraft clean and fuelled for next journey.

Humanitarian logistics following a natural disaster or conflict

Inputs: Medical supplies, blankets, waterproof shelters, emergency food and water, portable heating systems.

Transformation: pop-up command centre established near site of disaster, delivery

(Continued)

12

methods including trucks and volunteers sourced, varying needs of community assessed and prioritized, supplies of emergency materials matched with needs, logistics planned and executed.

Outputs: emergency supplies packages loaded onto a cargo plane from humanitarian logistics centre, supplies unloaded near site of natural disaster, supplies reach people most in need, disaster victims given immediate relief.

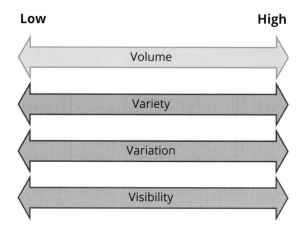

FIGURE 12.2 **4V framework: Characteristics of processes.**

As shown in the figure, each of these characteristics ranges on continuums from low to high. For example, a process might produce low or high volumes of output. Understanding this is essential in the design and analysis of operations. Operations managers pay attention to how these characteristics of processes are related to each other and also to relevant links between these characteristics of operations management and other elements of management, including:

- human resource management—how we determine job characteristics of employees
- marketing—how we measure the quality of customer service
- the external environment—the impact of issues external to the organization
- strategy—the alignment between the mission and strategy of the organization and resourcing and capabilities of the operations function

We next examine each of the 4Vs in greater detail.

12.2.1 **Volume and variety**

The first two characteristics of processes that comprise the 4V framework are closely tied together: volume and variety. Volume refers to the amount of output able to be produced by the process. Variety is the number of different activities in a process.

Processes typically focus on either one or the other of these characteristics: not both together. A process that can do a wide *variety* of different activities is typically not able to produce a high *volume* of output. High *volume* is best achieved when the process has a limited *variety* of activities (sometimes just one) done in a repetitive manner.

An early example of this observation was made famous by seventeenth-century economist Adam Smith, who noted the activities taking place in a pin factory and specifically the processes required to make a simple metal pin. He observed that this process required taking a rod of metal, cutting it, sharpening one end, flattening the other end, and polishing it up, with the final output of a pin. Smith identified 18 different activities involved in the traditional production method with just one worker carrying out all of the activities in a specific sequence to complete one pin, before starting the process again to produce the next pin. This one worker had a wide *variety* of tasks, which limited the *volume* of outputs that could be produced.

Smith proposed that if workers were each given a limited variety of activities—that is, if they specialized in just one part of the process—then several people working together could achieve a higher volume of output. He reported that by reducing the activities for each worker through specialization—often referred to as a 'division of labour'—10 people working together in sequence could produce 48,000 pins per day.

In the UK, we can see Adam Smith on the £20 note, along with a visual depiction of his pin factory example. This is because these ideas formed the basis of efficiency in operations management, which contributed to the significant growth of the UK economy during the Industrial Revolution (consider the discussion relating to management and efficiency in Section 1.5.2). Henry Ford used these ideas as the foundation for his approach to factory production lines to achieve mass production of cars. Prior to Ford's innovation of the production line, the first cars were built by hand, with a small team building the whole car. The cars produced in this way were expensive and affordable only by the very wealthy. Ford divided the entire process of car manufacture into specific activities. Individual workers would complete a limited number of activities in a repetitive manner before passing the product to the next worker in a line of production. This led to a much higher volume of output, resulting in economies of scale, defined as cost advantages resulting from efficiencies that can be obtained due to the scale of production. This reduction in costs allowed cars produced in Ford's factories to be priced within a range that was accessible to many more people. Ford's production line represents an example of how 'high-volume–low-variety' processes came to define operations management in the age of mass production.

In other sectors, 'low-volume–high-variety' processes play a role, particularly in service sector organizations. For example, specialist service providers such as management consultancy companies that provide advice on business strategy to CEOs and Boards of Directors comprise expert practitioners who possess a wide range of skills and perform a wide variety of activities that they dedicate to a specific client.

One example we can use to contrast 'high-volume–low-variety' with 'low-volume–high-variety' approaches is the food industry. In a five-star restaurant, a kitchen is designed for a chef to undertake many different activities to cook an entire meal, and the chef may change the offering from one day to the next. This is a low-volume (few customers) and high-variety (varying menus) approach. In contrast, a fast-food chain kitchen is designed so that each worker undertakes a limited number of activities to produce a high volume of very similar meals at a low cost. This is a high-volume (many customers) and low-variety (standard menu) approach.

12.2.2 **Variation (in supply or demand)**

Variation (sometimes called 'variability'), relates to the level of changes in **demand** for outputs from a process. This is a central idea of capacity management, which we will explore in Section 12.3. Much of operations management is focused on this characteristic. If variation is low it means that the demand for the output of the process is unchanging and consistent. For example, manufacturers might expect staple consumer goods such as milk, flour, bread, pasta, and toilet paper to experience low variation in demand. This makes the job of an operations manager easier, as it means that processes of production and distribution can be predicted and designed to be as efficient as possible. However, during the Covid-19 pandemic we saw how even these generally low variability categories can be disrupted, with supplies of toilet paper and flour in particular running low, as producers and suppliers were not prepared for the sudden switch to large numbers of people requiring toilet paper at home instead of in office buildings, and flour for home cooking instead of out-of-home eating at cafeterias and restaurants. See a *Financial Times* short video on toilet paper shortages and a TED Talk on flour shortages in the 'Explore more' section at the end of this chapter.

Variation in demand can sometimes be predictable. The demand for ice cream will predictably be higher in the summer than in the winter. There can also be a degree of unpredictability about the amount. For instance, a sports streaming service knows that there will be higher demand for subscriptions during major sporting events, but the level of that demand will be unpredictable, perhaps depending on which teams do well and make it into the finals. Variation can also be wholly unpredictable. This might include the impact of demand due to a natural disaster, an unexpected political event such as strike action, or a sudden public health emergency such as the Covid-19 pandemic.

12.2.3 **Visibility**

The final characteristic is visibility, which is concerned with the degree to which processes can be observed by customers. A process that is in front of a customer or client has high visibility, while one that takes place in a 'back-office' setting—a remote factory facility, or buried in a digital process—has low visibility. In high-visibility contexts such as retail, catering, health care, public transport, or any similar public-facing organizations, the operations department needs to consider the perceptions of the customer. This links operations to the functions of marketing and branding. If the processes designed by the operations manager perform better than expected, the customer is likely to be happy. If these processes do not perform as well as expected, or fail entirely, customers are likely to be unhappy. However, it may not necessarily be the 'fault' of the operations function. If the marketing and branding function over-promise, customers may develop unrealistic expectations that the organization's operations were never designed to meet. We will also return to this idea in Section 12.4.3 when we discuss sustainable and ethical supply chain management. For instance, we consider the impact of technology, such as cameras on smart phones, which enable the exposure of an organization's previously 'hidden' processes, and their impacts on making visible organizational practices, such as treatment of workers in factories, or the environmental impacts of mining and farming processes.

Thinking carefully about these characteristics shows that the design of *processes* to produce a product or service is as important as the design of the product or service itself. That is, the role of operations management is essential in achieving the aims of the organization, and in particular in achieving them efficiently and effectively. Let's revisit Imperial and Operations Manager Bob's focus on processes in Running case 12.1.

RUNNING CASE 12.1 **AN OPERATIONS REVIEW AT IMPERIAL**

As Lucy enters COO Bob Smart's office for their operations review, she's pleased to see he has the four Sustainable Development Goals that Imperial is focusing on pasted on his office wall, just like Marketing Manager, Gita has in her office. Bob is action-oriented so his charts are succinct and contain some sharp reminders for himself and his team:

SDG 8: Decent Work. Sort out the suppliers! No child labour! No unfair conditions! 100 per cent safety record in Imperial factory!

SDG 11: Reducing Inequalities. As above—supply chain!

SDG 12: Responsible Consumption and Production. Need supplier audits to check sustainable production! Sustainable packaging! Cut waste!

SDG 13: Climate Action. Install solar panels on roof of factory! Cut energy waste! Vehicles!

Although Bob rather enjoys his reputation as the grumpy old man of Imperial, Lucy has come to

appreciate that he is much more receptive to new ideas than people might think. His reaction on their first visit to NoBull had really taken her by surprise, and she has since been impressed by his interest in NoBull's production practices, especially in relation to automation (see Running case 6.1).

Bob and Sue Smith, the factory manager, have been reviewing operations throughout the factory to see where there are opportunities for process improvements. Their logistics manager, Harbin Singh, had long complained that the loading of the company's vehicles took too long and wasn't efficient, meaning the trucks had to do more trips than needed. Bob and Sue decided to implement a trial of loading optimization software designed to ensure vehicles do not run at less than full capacity. Results were impressive and the software was soon permanently installed. As a result, fuel use by the trucks has reduced by 5 per cent and overall reduced the fleet's carbon impact.

Now Bob is telling Lucy about a new investment he's contemplating following his latest chat with

(Continued)

12

Marcus: a CPS. 'What on earth is a CPS?' asks Lucy. 'A Cyber Physical System,' Bob replies, 'A set of scanners that will check for the safety of all our food to make sure there's no contamination in it. That protects us against any risk of causing sickness or having to recall products. Marcus from NoBull also says we can use it to guarantee vegan consumers that all our plant-based products are 100 per cent meat-free, because we monitor our production areas digitally.'

Bob goes on to say that he is currently wondering how to cut their production waste from the factory but can't bring himself to follow Marcus's suggestion to feed food scraps to insects to make protein. 'Who'd want to eat that stuff?' he asks Lucy. 'Having said that, there's quite an interest in making insect protein from food waste, so I'll keep an eye on developments.'

Questions for reflection

1. How important for Imperial's development is Bob's positive attitude towards technology?

2. How should business leaders like Lucy ensure that their company's technical capabilities are being developed in step with other changes in their company?

3. In this period of rapid technological change, the so-called Industry 4.0 era, what should come first at companies like Imperial, developing new product and marketing ideas, or investing in the latest technology?

12.3 Capacity management

Good operations management goes largely unnoticed. If you leave a coffee shop having not had to queue and being served exactly the drink that you wanted, have you ever silently thanked the operations manager? Probably not! However, when there is a disruption in operations, such as if the coffee shop has to close because of a machinery breakdown or a major disruption in the supply of coffee, it can be very noticeable and costly for the organization. Moreover, given the reliance of operations management on resources and demand, sometimes there is very little a good operations manager can do to solve the problems: rather they need to simply manage as best as they can. In health care facilities across Europe, post-pandemic spikes in demand for delayed health care appointments, and an under-supply of nurses and other specialist staff as many leave the industry, have stretched health care systems, leading to significant waiting times which operations managers in hospitals have struggled to address (World Health Organization, 2022).

This mismatch between supply and demand is a common issue in operations management and is referred to as capacity management. **Capacity management** involves the activities associated with predicting the expected demand for your organization's product or service, both in total and at specific times, and ensuring that the supply is sufficient, timely, and of sufficient quality to meet that demand. **Queueing Theory** is one element of this, also known as Little's Law, named after MIT professor John Little (Little, 2011). It states that the time taken to process each unit (the cycle time), multiplied by the total number of units waiting in a queue (the work in process) equals the total amount of time it will take for a new unit entering the queue to get through the whole system (the **throughput time**):

$$\text{Cycle Time} \times \text{Work in Process} = \text{Throughput Time}$$

Figure 12.3 depicts throughput time in a café context. If you are thinking of joining a queue to order coffee and you see it takes on average 30 seconds to take each customer's order and

12

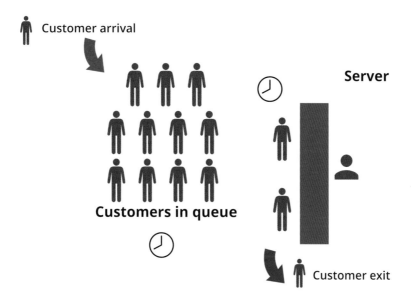

FIGURE 12.3 **Queueing theory in a café.**

make their coffee (cycle time), and there are 11 people in the queue including you (work in process), then you can expect to wait five-and-a-half minutes (330 seconds) for your coffee (throughput time). You might choose to go elsewhere or come back later.

Of course, operations management gets much more complex than this in practice as the simplified equations need to expand to take into account:

- expected downtime (the server takes a break);
- unexpected downtime (a coffee machine breaks);
- expected variables, such as different average times for making tea versus coffee and the expected ratio of each drink that is typically ordered, and at what times of the day; and
- unexpected variables, such as a particularly hot day that increases the orders for cold drinks.

Spotlight 12.2 provides an example of queueing theory in a context with which you may be familiar: airport security halls.

Queueing theory is reliant on matching supply with demand. We will now briefly explore the challenges of demand forecasting and supply flexibility, before introducing three approaches to capacity management.

12.3.1 **Forecasting demand**

Forecasting demand is a key challenge for operations management. It is also a task that requires input from several different departments, including marketing, sales, customer service, and strategy. Given there is often a delay for organizations in adding resources to increase supply, managers rely on demand forecasts to determine how much to invest in advance, to increase capacity.

SPOTLIGHT 12.2 **THE CASE OF AIRPORTS: QUEUEING THEORY IN ACTION**

Queueing theory is particularly visible in airports. Every person getting on a plane has to be processed through security scanning. Security halls are often very large and carefully designed to manage the queue build-up. Specific channels in the security area are roped to manage the order and pathway of people as they enter the hall, leading to spaces at the baggage screening counter to deposit bags, and multiple identical body scanners for people to walk through. The time taken per person is relatively similar, unless the security scan has difficulty viewing the item or if it flags a potential prohibited item.

Knowing the average time needed for one person to complete the process, and the total number of people in the hall at any time, we can calculate how long a passenger should expect to wait to get through security and proceed to catch a flight. When the process breaks down and the queue builds up, the time taken can be longer than the customer had planned for. This might occur if a scanner is not working, if there are not enough security officers, if multiple flights have unexpectedly had their departure times amended, or if a higher-than-expected number of passengers have potentially prohibited items flagged which require further investigation.

Issues with capacity management can be very visible both from over- and under-capacity. The airline industry experienced a huge fall in demand during 2020 due to the pandemic. To adjust for this and survive financially, airports made large numbers of staff redundant and so reduced their capacity. However, when demand for air travel returned once populations were vaccinated and travel was allowed, there was a mismatch between demand and supply. Airports struggled to re-employ security staff and baggage handlers, and airlines struggled to recruit pilots and cabin crew (Airports Council International, 2022). This led to significant queues, and harried operations managers trying to reduce waiting time, despite not having sufficient resources to address the issue.

Paparacy/Shutterstock

Managers often turn to 'predict-and-provide' models to forecast demand and therefore determine how much they should supply. This sees managers analyse past behaviour and predict a trend for future demand, using techniques such as:

- time-series analysis: looking at how a set of data points change over regular intervals;

- moving averages: taking the average in each of a series of time periods and seeing how that changes; and

- sophisticated data analytics using machine learning algorithms that sift through large amounts of sales data in combination with external data sources. These algorithms are statistical techniques that use artificial intelligence software to spot patterns in data.

Retailers, for instance, will use forecasting models to determine when the weather will improve in spring. They can then plan and order from their manufacturers to have products such as garden furniture delivered to their stores and promoted through marketing communications media as customers begin to look to the summer ahead.

If the demand forecast is too low (i.e. demand was higher than expected), then potential sales are lost, either because the products were not available or there weren't enough people providing the organization's service. On the other hand, if the demand forecast is too high (i.e. demand was lower than expected), then the organization is left with unsold products or idle service staff. In the case of goods retailers in particular, given the high costs of storage, organizations may try to sell excess stock at a reduced price. Discount sales are thus a frequent phenomenon resulting from a mismatch between supply and demand forecasting. The phenomenon is especially noticeable in clothing retail, where changes in fashions combined with seasonality-driven changes in demand over spring, summer, autumn, and winter, can mean high levels of unsold stock needing to be discounted. Business models such as the Kilo Sales described in our opening case study have emerged to take advantage of this. Another related phenomenon is the rise of event days such as Black Friday and Cyber Monday. Held in November, in line with the US Thanksgiving holiday, these events allow retailers to clear stock through discounts ahead of the main Christmas shopping period. Immediately after Christmas of course come the December–January sales with the same aim. Similar significant events around the world include Singles Day in China (on 11 November, i.e. 11/11), and Diwali in India, when a peak volume of purchases are made. All are examples of retailers' attempts to shift excess inventory as a result of predict-and-provide demand forecasting.

12.3.2 **Supply flexibility**

Understanding the total number of units that an operation can process is a key concern of capacity management. This is related to supply. Some organizations have a fixed supply; there are a fixed number of tables in a restaurant, shelves in a store, containers on a cargo ship, seats in a cinema, or beds in a hospital. This supply limitation puts a constraint on the maximum throughput. In organizations such as these, managers can attempt to achieve some flexibility in supply to meet demand, especially at peak periods. For example, a restaurant may add extra outside seating when the weather allows, a hospital may move patients to rehabilitation wards to free up high-care beds, or a store may add specific displays for peak shopping periods such as Easter or Father's Day. However, often supply constraints are hampered not by space, but by staffing.

12

For instance, *The Caterer*, a UK hospitality industry publication, reported that 1 in 9 hospitality jobs were vacant at the end of 2022 (Price, 2022). Following the pandemic, the hospitality industry found the supply of workers significantly constrained because many hospitality workers who were laid off during lockdowns have since moved into other industry sectors.

12.3.3 Approaches to capacity management

There are three common approaches to capacity management: level capacity, chase capacity, and demand management. The first two approaches focus on altering supply with a given forecast and actual demand (as well as other factors), while the final approach attempts to alter demand. These approaches are depicted in Figure 12.4. We will explore each in turn.

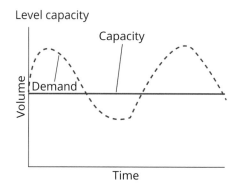

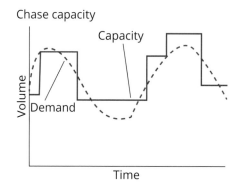

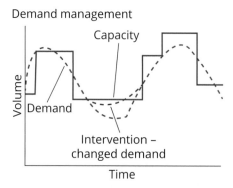

FIGURE 12.4 **Level capacity, chase capacity, and demand management.**

Level capacity

A key decision point in the process of capacity management involves determining how much supply or capacity an operation should be designed to achieve. This is typically linked to minimum levels of fixed demand that the organization is confident will exist. In a cinema, that decision might be based on the physical space available when designing or refurbishing the building. For an online service, it might be the size of computing power needed to service the expected demand. In a manufacturing facility, it might be the number of machines that should be installed to achieve a specific daily output of gadgets. This is known as 'level capacity' and it is fixed over time, irrespective of fluctuations in demand. These decisions are often linked to strategic goals related to the ambition of the organization, or finance decisions about what the organization can afford to invest in.

Chase capacity

In many situations, however, demand is not fixed or certain. Being able to respond rapidly to fluctuations in demand allows the organization to meet its customers' or users' needs. This is known as 'chase capacity'. An organization can meet temporary or unexpected spikes in demand in a number of ways. If a movie is nominated for an award, a cinema might add more screenings and bring in extra staffing, to meet the increased demand. An online service might rent additional computer server space on a temporary basis, or a manufacturer might outsource some of its production to another facility.

If the level capacity is set below actual demand, and added capacity is still not sufficient, then the full demand cannot be met. In many processes, having demand in excess of the ability to supply it can mean queues of people, or items, waiting to be processed, or stock outs with empty shelves meaning lost sales and unhappy customers.

Demand management

A third approach to capacity is termed 'demand management'. Rather than seeking to alter capacity, this approach focuses on shifting the demand to when capacity is available. There are a number of techniques organizations use to achieve this. A bar might advertise a 'happy hour' between 5 pm and 6 pm, or run a student night on Mondays. The offer of cheaper drinks is used to increase demand when there is unused capacity (i.e. when the bar is typically quiet). A hotel that is usually full during weekends and holidays might offer discounts for midweek events such as business conferences or fan conventions, to ensure available facilities are used. Where successful, temporary demand management approaches can even lead to significant changes in the strategy or focus of an organization. Ski resorts facing low occupancy in summer months and looking to increase demand tapped into alternative outdoor pursuits, including the increased interest in mountain biking (Robbins, 2023). Today, globally, many ski resorts convert chair lifts in summer to carry mountain bikes and their riders up the mountain to the start of designated bike tracks. In the USA, legislation issued by Congress (2011) now allows national parks to provide summer facilities that include zip lines and mountain bike trails but, in a move to prevent overdevelopment, explicitly excludes 'tennis courts, water slides, swimming pools, golf courses and amusement parks'. What started as attempts to increase demand to address unused capacity has become a significant strategic focus and revenue stream. Indeed, with the climate crisis making snowfall less predictable, some resorts see this summer business model as their main focus in the future.

Capacity management is one of those ideas that is hugely influential on how the world around us works, even if we aren't aware of it as a concept. We have all stood in a queue or walked past a shop with a large sales rack. Having an awareness of the discipline of operations management helps us to look behind the scenes and understand why these activities occur, have an understanding of who is analysing these organizational processes, why they are making decisions to manage these issues in the future, and why such things can go wrong.

12.4 Supply chain management

While operations management typically focuses on activities taking place within an organization, supply chain management has its focus outside the organization, sourcing the inputs required by the operations function. Within an organization, managers running their operations have a significant degree of direct control over what happens. However, beyond the organizational boundaries managers have less direct control. Nevertheless, most organizations are directly reliant on their supply chain to achieve their aims—be that of producing a good or providing a service. A hospital cannot function without the provision of surgical instruments, pharmaceutical drugs, clean laundry, and even food. So while managing a supply chain effectively is essential, supply chain management needs to rely on methods other than direct control, in order to ensure the organization is able to achieve its aims.

Supply chain management might comprise a simple arrangement with a supplier, or a more complex and formal process requiring detailed contracts for the provision of a good or service. One example of the latter is the process of *competitive tendering* that occurs where an organization invites potential suppliers to prepare a formal offer of products or services, in order to select preferred suppliers. Arranging the tendering process and related schedules of activity, setting desired *service-levels*, and negotiating final agreements (including price) are all part of supply chain management. This will likely result in a *service-level agreement* that confirms the specification of the goods or services, the price and payment terms, the timing and logistics of delivery, and the level of customer support that the organization should expect from the supplier. These tasks are often undertaken by people with job titles such as purchaser, procurement manager, or sourcing director.

Supply chain management and operations management are tightly intertwined, as can be demonstrated in the case of an organization like Boeing, which operates factories to manufacture aircraft. Consider the depiction of the components required to build a Boeing Dreamliner in Figure 12.5. All of the components produced by Boeing can be considered internal to the organization (and so the responsibility of operations management), including the final construction of the aircraft. Components produced by other organizations are the responsibility of the supply chain function. However, in reality, the reliance of Boeing on its many suppliers (including from its own internal departments) for the timely delivery of quality components to specification makes this distinction largely irrelevant. Operations and supply chain are tightly interlinked.

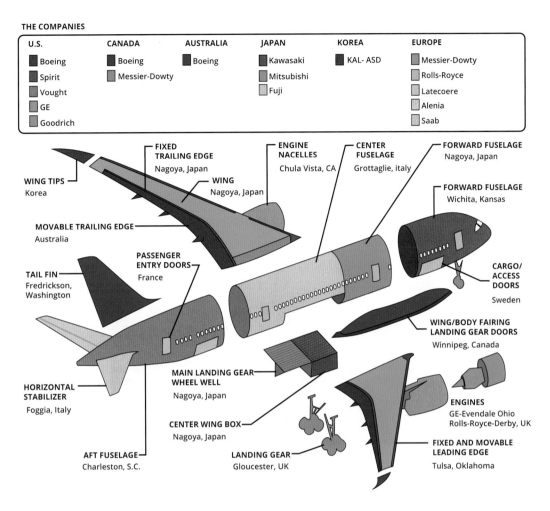

THE COMPANIES

U.S.	CANADA	AUSTRALIA	JAPAN	KOREA	EUROPE
Boeing	Boeing	Boeing	Kawasaki	KAL- ASD	Messier-Dowty
Spirit	Messier-Dowty		Mitsubishi		Rolls-Royce
Vought			Fuji		Latecoere
GE					Alenia
Goodrich					Saab

WING TIPS
Korea

FIXED TRAILING EDGE
Nagoya, Japan

WING
Nagoya, Japan

ENGINE NACELLES
Chula Vista, CA

CENTER FUSELAGE
Grottaglie, italy

FORWARD FUSELAGE
Nagoya, Japan

FORWARD FUSELAGE
Wichita, Kansas

MOVABLE TRAILING EDGE
Australia

TAIL FIN
Fredrickson, Washington

PASSENGER ENTRY DOORS
France

CARGO/ ACCESS DOORS
Sweden

WING/BODY FAIRING LANDING GEAR DOORS
Winnipeg, Canada

HORIZONTAL STABILIZER
Foggia, Italy

MAIN LANDING GEAR WHEEL WELL
Nagoya, Japan

CENTER WING BOX
Nagoya, Japan

ENGINES
GE-Evendale Ohio
Rolls-Royce-Derby, UK

AFT FUSELAGE
Charleston, S.C.

LANDING GEAR
Gloucester, UK

FIXED AND MOVABLE LEADING EDGE
Tulsa, Oklahoma

FIGURE 12.5 **Suppliers that provided inputs to the Boeing Dreamliner.** Credit: Kotha, S. and Srikanth, K. (2013), 'Managing A Global Partnership Model'. *Global Strategy Journal*, 3: 41–66. https://doi.org/10.1111/j.2042-5805.2012.01050.x

12.4.1 **Supply chain versus supply network**

A traditional view of the supply chain depicts it as a one-way rigid linear flow of materials or components into your organization. From this perspective, your supply chain represents a cost to your organization that you aim to minimize—for example, by negotiating reductions in the price of components from your suppliers, or by ensuring payment terms are favourable to your systems, irrespective of the impact on your suppliers' reliance on payment.

A different approach is increasingly popular, with a focus not on the supply chains, but on the **supply network** (Knipscheer et al., 2022). This approach recognizes that supply increasingly needs to be flexible, agile, and resilient, that there is a significant inter-reliance on a number of different suppliers, and that healthy and respectful relationships with suppliers can be

12

a strength to enable an organization to achieve its overall aims (Braziotis et al., 2013). As such, increasingly organizations are looking to 'invest' in their supply networks—both literally and figuratively—in order to ensure strong, reliable, and responsive suppliers, rather than just the lowest cost provider at one point in time. This makes the role of a supply chain manager much more focused on understanding the resources, capabilities, and strengths of supply chain partners, and on maintaining strong relationships that focus on mutual respect and all parties achieving their organizational aims.

Globalization in particular (Section 3.3.1) has had a significant impact on supply chain management, contributing to the increased complexity and global reach of supply chains. Good supply chain managers, especially of large global organizations, are well versed in the potential geopolitical, technological, and environmental disruptions outlined in Chapter 3, as well as the organization's external environment explored in Chapter 4. Global supply networks can be complex and it is not unusual for organizations to struggle to identify all of the different suppliers in their own supply network, because it can be difficult to identify your supplier's suppliers, and so on. This has become a high-profile issue for many organizations that are striving to demonstrate their sustainability credentials and provide transparency about their sustainable and ethical supply chain management practices, which we will explore in Section 12.4.3.

12.4.2 **Make-or-buy decisions**

As outlined in the introduction, a key interaction between operations and supply chain management is to determine what elements of your organization's operations should be kept in-house, and what should be outsourced to suppliers. Moreover, continually asking this question is important. This is often described as a 'make-or-buy' decision. The key determinants of such decisions are whether the activity is of strategic importance to the organization, whether it is linked to something the organization has specialized knowledge in, and whether it adds value.

12

If yes, then it should be retained within the organizational boundaries. If no, and especially where a suitable supplier can be found, it can make sense to outsource this activity or function, so that it becomes part of your supply network. A brand-driven company such as Apple sees 'value-add' in product design, branding, marketing, and holding the customer relationship. Thus for strategic reasons it retains these operations in-house, under the direct control of the Apple organization. The aspects of its operations that are considered less core are the manufacturing and assembly stages of production. Apple outsources these processes to Foxconn, one of the world's largest technology manufacturers and the top assembler of Apple's iPhones (Moorhead, 2019).

Given the complexity of supply networks, as well as the increasing disruptions in many areas of the world in which organizations operate, make-or-buy decisions are not necessarily straightforward. Importantly, there are costs or risks associated with outsourcing elements of operations to your supply chain. Some of these costs and risks are relatively visible and can form part of the initial outsourcing decision. This might include the costs of setting up outsourced production or the risks of relying on a supplier whom you have no direct control over. However, other costs and risks might be hidden, unexpected, or emerge only over time. Recent disruptions include increased costs in global transport networks arising from the global pandemic, labour disputes in ports, and a container ship running aground and blocking the Suez Canal. Dubbed the 'boat that broke the world' (Christian, 2021), the massive *Evergreen* container ship became wedged in a narrow part of the Suez Canal for six days in 2021, blocking passage for 300 other container ships and causing a backlog in global supply chains for months afterwards (Stevens, 2021).

As well as potential disruptions, an organization's brand and reputation often become associated with that of its suppliers, which can be a risk, as we will see in Section 12.4.3 in relation to ethics in the supply chain. The decision also requires careful consideration of the strategic focus of the organization. Many European fashion brands have chosen to 'offshore' the manufacture of their garments destined for their European markets to cheaper suppliers in Asia. However, more recently following disruptions in the global supply networks and the desire to be agile and sustainable, a number of brands including Benetton and Zara have made decisions to 'onshore' production back to Europe (Logistics Asia, 2021). Despite costs saved on transport, this still increases overall costs of production, given higher wages and costs in Europe. So why did they do it? They realized that wastage was one of their organization's greatest costs. Having their production facilities close enabled them to respond very quickly to consumer demand, resulting in fewer unwanted (and so unsold) garments.

12.4.3 Sustainable and ethical supply chain management

There is increasing external and internal scrutiny of organizations in relation to the sustainability and ethics of their supply chains. Across a range of social and environmental issues, legislation has been developed that requires organizations to acknowledge responsibility for their supply chains. Examples of issues addressed by this legislation include the minerals sold to fund armed conflict in Central Africa (the USA's 2010 Dodd-Frank Act) and the import of commodities associated with deforestation (the UK's 2021 Environment Act). It is not

12

uncommon for such legislation to be removed or weakened following lobbying by businesses or industry groups.

The drive for increased scrutiny from regulators and requirements for supply chain transparency is mirrored in the consumer space, where sustainable and ethical supply chains are increasingly expected and rewarded with sales and brand loyalty. However, it is not easy for a consumer to evaluate a supply chain. The complexity of supply networks means that the phone or clothes you buy today are likely to have travelled further than you have in the last year. Given the impact of international transport on greenhouse gas emissions, this aspect of operations is being more actively challenged. The shipping industry, which carries 90 per cent of the world's traded goods, is innovating away from heavy fuel oil and marine diesel oil, towards ships powered by renewable energy technologies (IRENA, 2021).

Ethics in the supply chain has focused on the prevalence of modern slavery, as well as preventable disasters. One example can be seen in the textiles industry in Bangladesh, which grew rapidly due to the removal of trade barriers, as well as the country's location on shipping routes, and very low wages. The expansion of this industry has undoubtedly provided many workers, particularly women, with jobs from which they can provide for their families. However, the Bangladeshi textiles industry will long be associated with the Rana Plaza disaster that occurred in April 2013. A residential building had been converted for use as a textile factory to meet significant international demand. However, the facility was built without proper permission on unstable land (Al-Mahmood & Wright, 2013) and health and safety measures were severely lacking. Severe cracks appeared in the building on 23 April, leading to the evacuation of the building. Despite this, workers were ordered to return to work the following day (Thapa, 2018). The building collapsed just before 9 am the following morning, killing more than 1,134 workers (Safi & Rushe, 2018).

This Rana Plaza incident shone a light not only on the conditions of workers in the supply chain of international clothing brands, but also asked who, ultimately, is responsible for such conditions. A number of high street brands did not even realize this factory was involved in making their products, given the complexity of supply networks. Often such disasters result not from a lack of rules being in place but from the rules being ignored, making it difficult for buyers to know the reality of what is happening in their supply chain. Many measures have been developed to try to improve supply chain transparency, largely including audit-based certification, where inspectors visit plants to check compliance. Such visits can still be misled by auditors being shown around the best factory available, while much of the work has been further subcontracted to worse locations without the buyer's knowledge (Huq et al., 2014).

The rise in public concern for sustainability, including human rights and environmental protection, suggests that the issues will continue to be prominent. We are also seeing digital tools increasingly used to improve monitoring in ways that help deliver compliance to laws or agreements, and transparency when supply chains fail to meet expectations. If we refer back to the 4V framework in Section 12.2, this is a situation where there is increasing visibility of processes that were previously hidden from customers. Let's return to Imperial in Running case 12.2, and recall the work they have been doing on supply chain management—as well as on their own operations.

RUNNING CASE 12.2 SUSTAINABLE PROCUREMENT AT IMPERIAL

Since Lucy's trip to see the Kenyan tea producers, the Purchasing Team have been reviewing Imperial's contracts with other suppliers. Declan O'Rourke, the Supply Chain Manager who went with Lucy and Bob on their first visit to NoBull, is a member of the Chartered Institute of Purchasing and Supply, and at his suggestion Imperial's buyers, Maria Ortiz and Piotr Grzybowski, have undertaken some sustainable procurement training. As well as looking out for any unethical employment practices on suppliers' sites, Maria and Piotr are focusing on opportunities to cut down waste. One example of this is insisting that their suppliers use renewable packaging, as well as ensuring that everything they buy is produced in an ethical and environmentally friendly way.

Declan has had some tense conversations with Bob and William in the past about rising input prices. He has been keen to persuade them that Imperial needs to look at the true cost of what it buys—and to remember its carbon footprint.

In reviewing Imperial's Operations department, CEO Lucy is pleased with the progress they have been making. Declan is identifying opportunities to improve supply chain performance. Sue Smith, the factory manager, is very efficient, coming up with ideas for operating the factory in a more sustainable

fashion. But Lucy suspects there is more to be done. Gita reminds Lucy and the other managers regularly that Imperial cannot just say it is sustainable in its marketing materials as it might be guilty of greenwashing (see Section 11.8). To be authentic and sustainable, this needs to be the focus in everything they do. Lucy discusses this with Bob Smart, COO. 'I get that, Lucy,' says Bob, 'but I'm running out of ideas. I'm 100 per cent up for being as sustainable as possible, but to be honest, I don't know how to get there.' 'What we need, I think,' Lucy replies, 'is some help for you. What do you think about us hiring a full-time Sustainability Manager for Imperial?'

Questions for reflection

1. Why is sustainable and ethical procurement so important? Are Declan and his team doing the right things?

2. What do you think Declan means when he talks about focusing on the cost of supplies rather than on their price?

3. How should the various departments and managers at Imperial work together to create a message about the company's sustainability practices to its stakeholders?

12.5 Process improvement

Given the importance of processes in both operations and supply chain management, a key focus of managers is on process improvement. This area has been significantly shaped over the past 50 years by developments that started in Japan and extended across the world. We will explore some of the ideas that now form the foundations both of operations and supply chain management, and how to achieve improvements in these functions.

12.5.1 Lean production and the Five Whys

American industrialist, Henry Ford's mastery of mass production in the early 1900s laid the ground for a whole consumer economy of mass production that accelerated significantly from the 1950s. From the 1970s, post-war Japan became a leading manufacturer of consumer goods such as cameras, motorbikes, and cars, that were both cheaper and of high quality. The Japanese producers improved upon mass production ideas with a distinctive approach that saw them rapidly outcompete manufacturing in the West. Understanding how this came about was the subject of a major international research programme, described in the book *The Machine That Changed the World*, by Womack et al. (2007).

The comparison between western and Japanese production approaches found a key difference in philosophy. Rather than thinking in terms of 'mass production', the Japanese had developed what came to be called 'lean production'. **Lean production** is an approach to operations and supply chains that focuses on cutting out waste while ensuring quality. This discovery inspired a wave of business improvement programmes throughout the 1980s and 1990s, with management consultancies advising on business process re-engineering.

Lean production has its origins in the work of Japanese car manufacturer, Toyota. Toyota's founder, Sakichi Toyoda, had originally focused on producing machines for the textile industry. Toyoda's techniques in the operation of weaving machines included designing the machines to automatically stop if there was a problem. Toyoda's son Kiichiro Toyoda continued the work of his father by transferring the quality-focused approaches learnt in the textiles sector to the production processes of car manufacturing. These innovations reduced the potential for the manufacturing process to produce work that would later be rejected as defective.

A key component of this lean approach was the Five Whys approach, which sees managers and workers interrogate a problem by asking 'why' in order to trace the nature of an issue back to its root cause (or causes) (Figure 12.6). This ensures workers focus on fixing the ultimate problem so that it does not reoccur in the future (ASQ, 2015). Applying the Five Whys approach, the worker and manager will initially state a problem and then keep asking why, until they arrive at a statement that can be acted upon—and in turn, a lesson that can be learnt. A worker might say: 'This tool does not seem to be performing correctly'. The manager would then ask: 'Why do you think that is?', and the response might be 'The pressure in the pneumatics seems to be off'. The manager would then ask: 'Why do you think that is?' and the answer might be: 'There's a problem with the air pipe'. Then: 'Why is there a problem with the pipe?' and response: 'I think the valve might be blocked'. The manager then would say: 'So go and investigate and find out if that is correct and if so, then why is it blocked', and so on.

12.5.2 The 'Toyota Way' and the seven sources of waste

The success of the Toyota company's approach to improving processes became known as 'the Toyota Production System' or the 'Toyota Way'. Toyota engineer Taiichi Ohno further refined this system by identifying different sources of waste. Waste is defined as any process that does not add value. The seven sources of waste are:

1. Material waiting in a queue (a delay).

2. Overproduction (producing more than needed leading to unsold units).

3. Unnecessary over-processing (adding cost without increasing value).

4. Transportation (moving things around more than necessary costing both fuel and worker time).

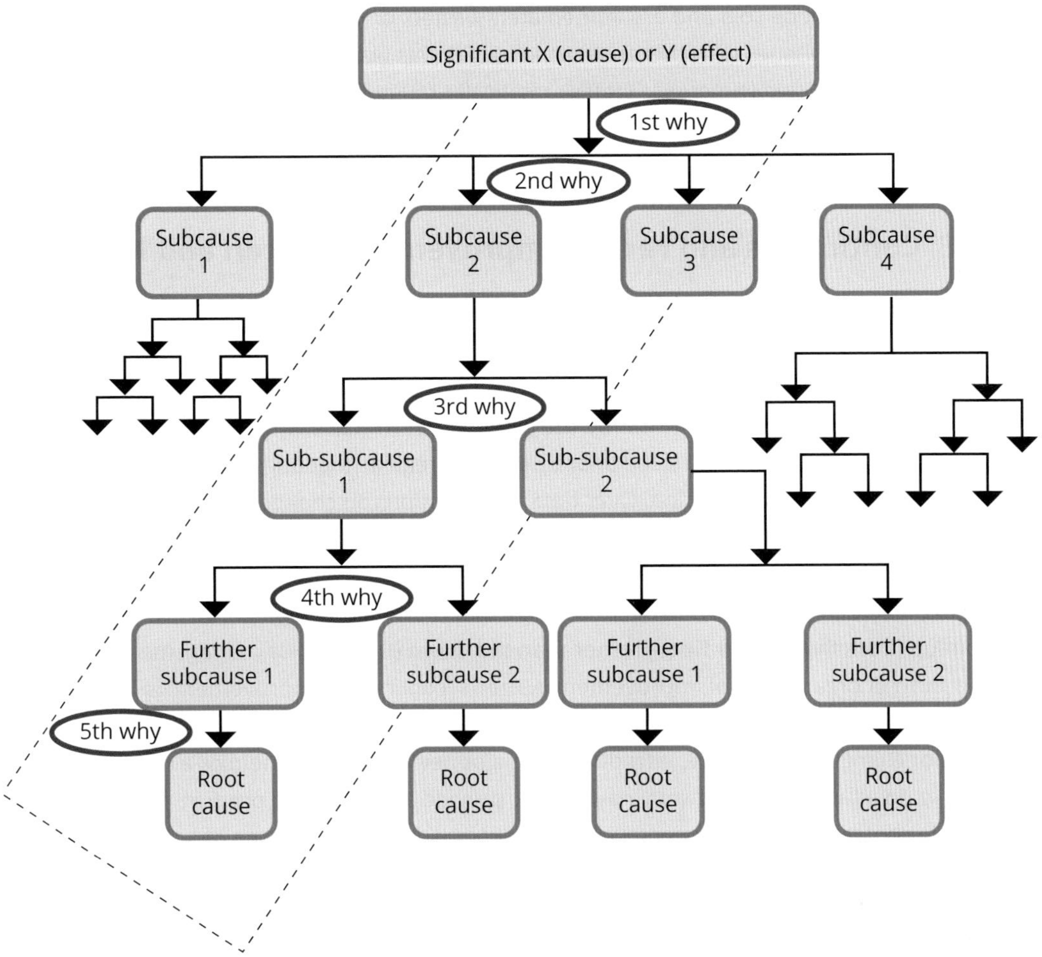

FIGURE 12.6 **The Five Whys Process.** Credit: 'Best Of Back To Basics: The Art Of Root Cause Analysis: Five Whys Analysis To Ask The Right Questions At The Right Time' Publication: *Quality Progress*, Date: January 2016, Volume 49 Issue 1, pp. 48   Author(s): A, Vidyasagar. Reprinted with permission from Quality Progress © 2016 ASQ, www.asq.org All rights reserved. No further distribution allowed without permission.

5. Inventory (storing products before they are needed incurring real estate costs).

6. Time and energy to move items out of storage and on to point of sale.

7. Defects (material produced incorrectly, and so needing to be rejected).

Typically, reducing the seven wastes requires redesigning processes. This is best achieved by enlisting all members of the workforce to take responsibility for their part of the production line. Under the Toyota Way, any individual worker seeing something not as it should be can call to stop the line, and then go through a 'Five Why' investigation. This empowers individual factory workers to bring an entire car production line to a halt.

Though this approach leads to disruption in the short term, in the long term it is far more cost-effective to bring a production line to a halt than it is to produce parts that are incorrect

12

and so either cannot be sold and are immediately wasted, or later need correcting or replacing. While Toyota faced issues with this approach in 2009, this was linked not to the Toyota Way itself, but to their decision to increase staff dramatically, but failure to train them effectively in the philosophy. This demonstrates the link between the operations function and the HRM function explored in Chapter 7, and in particular the importance of training.

12.5.3 Continuous and radical improvement: Kaizen and kaikaku

Part of the philosophy underpinning the Toyota Way is that things are best when they flow consistently and evenly. When many small problems are being corrected all the time then the operations become faster, more reliable, and more cost-effective. The act of continuous improvement in the operations' processes is known by the Japanese word 'kaizen'. It is common for workers' ideas for kaizen improvements to be shared through regular meetings, allowing best practice to spread through the organization. Over time an operation can change and look very different. Because it is the workers themselves who are involved in leading the practice of kaizen, it is better informed by the deep understanding of the production process and more readily adopted. As such, the kaizen approach has the advantage that it is more responsive to live issues and is bottom-up (from the **factory floor**) rather than top-down (from senior management).

As a form of organizational improvement, kaizen's 'continuous improvement' is incremental. Sometimes more radical change is needed, and here the term 'kaikaku' is used to refer to sudden, major change. For example, introducing a major new form of technology, a new type of machinery to do a task in a significantly new way or provide a new type of product, or a new digital system. In contrast to the incremental change of kaizen, the major change of kaikaku was especially relevant in the 1980s and 1990s as firms moved from traditional, paper-based administration to digitalization using desktop computer systems, such as the Microsoft operating system.

12.5.4 A pull-through approach and 'just-in-time' delivery

The shift from 'mass production' to 'lean production' involved a significant change to operations and supply chains. However, a further development followed. For Toyota especially, the potential for overproduction as a source of waste required a shift away from the conventional predict-and-provide model of manufacturing. Rather than a 'push-out' model, in which a certain number of cars were produced from the factory running at a given capacity, Toyota reversed the entire customer process. This 'pull-through' approach meant that required goods were produced only when demanded by a customer. Placing an order for a new Toyota would trigger the order to build, rather than the build being based on a forecast of what expected customer demand was going to be (and then either under-producing and losing a sale, or overproducing and being left with unsold stock).

The pull, rather than push, approach was also linked to managing the supply chain and to Toyota's desire to avoid excess transport and waiting for components. As such, Toyota would insist that its suppliers relocate their facilities to be near Toyota's plant as a condition of winning a supply contract. Through this approach Toyota brought its supply chain closer in what was called a 'keiretsu', meaning network. This allowed for more frequent and smaller deliveries of components as and when the Toyota factory needed them, in an approach known as a 'just-in-time' logistics system. This approach minimizes transport and storage costs, and again prevents the oversupply of a component which may then end up wasted if not needed.

12.5.5 **Systems resilience**

The success of lean production and just-in-time approaches inevitably meant it was copied by other organizations. Toshiba and Nissan were among the first to adopt Toyota's methods, but by the end of the 1990s, just-in-time in particular had become widespread across the world. However, though leading to process improvements, just-in-time logistics were found to have the downside of being vulnerable to major disruptions. The failure of a specific component to be delivered exactly when it was needed, would result in the entire production process being halted. Disruptions were caused by unexpected events such as volcano eruptions, port closures due to strikes, or major pandemics. Proponents of the lean just-in-time approach found that in circumstances of potential disruption, systems resilience is important: having some spare stocks available in warehouses was useful. But once conditions returned to a more stable situation, and an even flow to production, then lean philosophy became the optimal approach again. A dynamic interplay is thus ongoing between the supremely efficient lean production method and more resilient systems that have built-in surpluses (i.e. spare stock in warehouse) and redundancy (i.e. ability to fill in gaps in production due to unexpected disruptions to regular flow of activity).

Before we move on to look at the relationship between operations and strategy, let's see what improvements the new Sustainability Manager has in store for Imperial in Running case 12.3.

RUNNING CASE 12.3 **THE WAY FORWARD FOR IMPERIAL**

Today Lucy, William, and Bob are sitting down for the first-ever monthly review with Imperial's new Sustainability Manager, Madeleine Hannah. They have all been impressed by Madeleine in her first month. She spent the first week sitting down with each manager and interrogating them on all aspects of their work. Then she toured the factory, taking several days, identifying machinery, checking the lighting, noting down operating times and power usage, as well as shift patterns and hourly work. Next, she went through all the logistics and warehousing with Harbin Singh, the Logistics Supervisor, checking the truck fleet, adding mileage and fuel-use data to a huge spreadsheet that was growing bigger daily. Finally, she conducted a review of all Imperial's waste, in the office and throughout the factory, of food and hazardous products, recording any recycling that was taking place. Now she is going to explain what she's discovered.

'Hi Lucy, hi Bob, hello William. Thank you very much for all your support this month. It's been really interesting, and everybody has been very welcoming. I'm impressed with the culture here. But we have quite a few things to do, and I'd like to make some proposals to you.' Madeleine puts a presentation up on the screen and begins. She reminds them of the meaning of Scopes 1, 2, and 3, and proposes one or two initial actions to address each:

Scope 1: all Imperial's small vans should be switched to electric as soon as possible to reduce fuel consumption, with charging points installed in the yard. They should also install a heat-recovery system in the factory; they can use the heat produced by their food-refrigeration machinery to heat the building.

Scope 2: all Imperial's electricity is to be zero carbon as soon as possible. All factory lights should

(*Continued*)

be changed to LEDs, all suitable roofs should have solar panels installed, and all staff should undergo energy efficiency training.

Scope 3: all Imperial's water consumption must be monitored and reduced. A waste-management plan is to be implemented right away, not just sending food waste from the factory to composting, but also ensuring food isn't wasted at the point of sale.

Finally, Madeleine runs through the approaches they should be considering for procurement and factory operations. Bob is delighted to hear that Declan O'Rourke, Supply Chain Manager, and his staff have many of them covered already. He now sees why Madeleine asked about shifts: the more efficient they can make production, the fewer people they need to employ on overtime and in the evenings, meaning they don't waste time or wages, and don't waste power running lights and machines unnecessarily.

'If you're all happy with these suggestions,' Madeleine says, 'I'll put all the data and estimated costs and payback calculations together and send them to you. And then I'll start to work on Imperial's sustainability roadmap to 2030.' Lucy is delighted with this plan, knowing how much Gita will love being able to talk about their 2030 roadmap in her marketing communications.

Questions for reflection

1. What should go into Imperial's sustainability roadmap to 2030?

2. Whose responsibility is sustainability within a company?

3. What feedback would you give Lucy on her performance during her first year in charge at Imperial Fine Foods? If she asked you for advice, what would you say her top priorities should be next year?

12.6 The relationship between operations and strategy

As we explored in Chapter 5, one approach to developing the strategy of an organization is the Resource Based View (RBV). This considers what resources and capabilities the organization excels at, and uses this to determine the best overall strategy. While strategy is typically the focus of the CEO or a strategy function, it is likely elements of operations will be relevant. As such, operations managers may contribute to important strategy discussions and decisions.

Typically, however, the role of operations is simply to design processes so that the organization can meet its strategic objectives. That is, to deliver strategy, not to design strategy. We can observe this by contrasting hotel brands that have different strategies. One hotel brand may have a strategy focused on low prices and basic services. Aligning operations processes to this strategy might include automated check-in, minimum standard breakfasts, standardized fit-out, and few additional services. Hotel locations are likely to be in areas of high demand such as by airports or train stations, where people are in transit and staying for one night, or in 'city-break' destinations where people might go for a fun weekend, wanting cheap, reliable accommodation, and where the city will provide services in terms of bars, restaurants, and entertainment.

By contrast, another hotel brand might have a strategy focused on personalized experiences at a higher price point. From an operations perspective, they will focus on high levels of customer engagement and service, high-quality furnishings that impress with their luxuriousness, and a range of on-site facilities such as a pool, health spa, golf course, or business facilities. These

12

hotels might be located in appealing natural environments where the views make the hotel a destination in its own right.

From these examples, you can see there is a connection between strategy and the way different operational decisions are prioritized. However, the relationship between operations and strategy is often more complex. Operational capability, including supply chain management, can be fundamental to the strategic success or failure of an organization. One prominent example occurred when a lightning strike caused a fire in the manufacturing plant of a company that made the microelectronic chip component of mobile handsets (Figure 12.7) (Sheffi & Rice, 2005). The chip is an essential component that controls the functionality of the entire handset and only a small number of manufacturers exist (Dolcourt, 2019). The unexpected fire caused smoke damage to batches of chips awaiting shipment to mobile phone companies, Nokia and Ericsson. Nokia responded rapidly to the loss, securing new supplies from alternative manufacturers. It took Ericsson weeks to realize the seriousness of the impact on their operations. By then Nokia had secured all the alternative supplies available. Ericsson missed the crucial autumn product launch for new mobile handsets and was knocked out of the market as a result (Sheffi & Rice, 2005).

It is also the case that activities at the frontline of the organization—on the factory floor or directly with customers—can provide insights that contribute to a strategic change in the organization. An example of this occurred with the accidental innovation of a mildly adhesive glue in 1968 by a research and development scientist at 3M, Spencer Silver, who had been trying to make a strong adhesive. After seeking applications for his weak glue, the light bulb moment happened five years later when a fellow 3M colleague, Arthur Fry needed a way to attach temporary notes to his songbook during choir rehearsals. The two teamed up and pitched the idea of what was to become the ubiquitous Post-It note (National Inventors Hall of Fame blog, n.d.). This innovation did not result from customers demanding it, or even the strategy or marketing department identifying it as an opportunity, but rather from an operational error and a future-thinking employee.

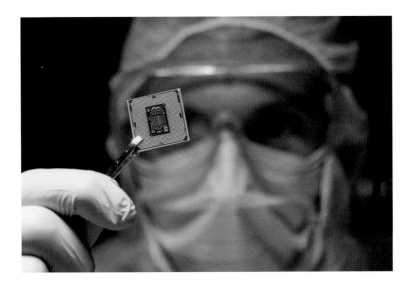

FIGURE 12.7 **The tiny microelectronic chip powering your mobile handset.** Credit: Gorodenkoff/iStock

12

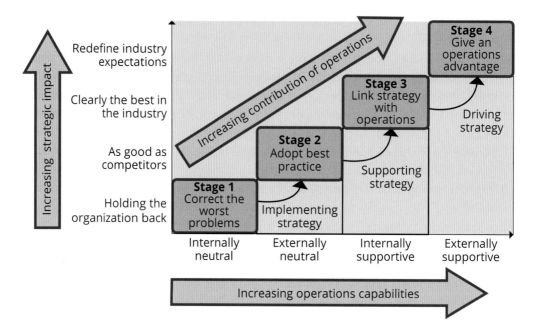

FIGURE 12.8 **Hayes and Wheelwright 4-Stage model of operations contribution.**
Credit: *Operations Management*, Slack, N. and Brandon-Jones, A., and Johnson, R. © 2013, Pearson Education UK

In relation to the link between operations and strategy, Hayes and Wheelwright (1985) developed a four-stage model, shown in Figure 12.8, after observing that the way many US organizations managed their factories was affecting their ability to compete globally. This is presented as a progression of the increasing contribution of operations to the strategic success of the organization. In Stage 1, the organization's operations prevent it from achieving its strategic goals. The priority for action at this stage is to start to correct the worst problems. The second stage is where the organization starts to adopt best practice with the aim of becoming as good as its competitors. The third stage sees operations and strategy become strongly linked, allowing the firm to differentiate itself towards becoming the best in its industry. Finally, in the fourth stage, the organization's operations allow it to redefine industry expectations and its operations capabilities lead to strategy. Very few organizations actually operate at Stage 4.

12.7 **Conclusion**

Operations management focuses on how inputs are transformed into outputs through processes, with the aim of achieving organizational strategy. Supply chain management ensures that inputs are available to the organization in the right quantity, to the right quality, and at the right time, in order for operations to proceed. When working well, the operations and supply chain management activities of an organization tend not to be noticed. These activities hum along in the background keeping the organization operating smoothly, thereby ensuring it can deliver goods and services as promised to customers, and likewise ensuring the organization can achieve its objectives, whether these are profit goals or broader mission-based social or environmental goals. The activities of operations management or supply chain become noticeable to members of the broader population when they are disrupted, either through poor planning or through unforeseen external events such as the Covid-19 pandemic, a container ship running aground, civil unrest, or wars. Then we become aware of how much of our daily lives depends on these activities.

In this chapter, we have covered some of the fundamental concepts of effective operations management, including the notions of processes and process management, the challenges and methods of capacity management, and approaches to process improvement. We also introduced supply chains and supply networks, the make-or-buy decision, and the important implications of supply chain management for an organization's approach to sustainability and ethics. The future of operations and supply chain management will see a continuing shift towards digital data management and automation, such as already seen in advanced predictive analytics to reduce supply chain disruptions, and the increasing role of the fourth industrial age (explored in Section 3.4).

Operations management is also central in transitioning existing company practices to more environmentally or socially sustainable alternatives. At a societal level, operations management can harness technology to meet new demands, such as the high volumes of clean energy needed to run digital services and bring power to around 700 million people in the world currently without access to electricity (IEA, 2022). Technology that improves supply chain traceability will also be significant in addressing issues such as modern slavery and deforestation.

 CHAPTER SUMMARY

○ Operations management focuses on the processes of the organization, and can be described using the four Vs: volume, variety, variation, and visibility.

○ Capacity management involves forecasting and three main concepts are: level capacity, chase capacity, and demand management.

○ An organization's view of its supply chain is increasingly focusing on responsibility for ethical and environmental implications. Legal regulations in various countries have introduced due diligence obligations to increase awareness of sustainability issues associated with the operations of international suppliers.

○ Process improvement is a constant concern for management. Pioneering work by Toyota led to companies around the world embracing 'lean management', including the associated notions of Seven Types of Waste, kaizen (continuous

12

improvement), and kaikaku (radical improvement) becoming embedded in industry practices.

○ The role of operations management and supply chain management in shaping the well-being and future of society was made evident by the disruption to these activities during the pandemic. Technology will bring many opportunities for improvements in the efficiency and quality of operations and supply chains and, with commitment from organizational leaders, will play a key role in enabling organizations to drive their sustainability impacts.

CLOSING CASE REFLECTION

Kilo Sales

The way in which the Kilo Sales model finds value from what would have been waste is similar to lean thinking, but unlike lean, this is not a pull supply chain, but push from unsold or damaged stock. Under a truly lean system, damaged and unsold stock would be avoided. Viewed using the 4Vs framework, the flow of material as outputs from factories and warehouses, through to inputs in the operations of the sale, sees the Kilo Sales model accommodate variability of specific stock via a low variety sales process (by weight not individual item) allowing for a high volume of throughput and economies of scale.

REVIEW QUESTIONS

1. Give an example of a product or service that has high annual variation in demand. To what extent is this variation predictable or unpredictable?

2. What factors might influence the level of capacity of an operation? What would happen if demand exceeded the level of capacity that the operation could supply?

3. Why are 'supply chains' increasingly referred to as 'supply networks'?

4. Why might the supply chain manager increasingly work closely with the sustainability manager? Give examples of specific projects they might work on together.

5. Think about what you have done today. How might an organization's operations function have affected your experience with an organization e.g. catching the bus, buying food, etc?

12

EXPLORE MORE

- WATCH a video which explores 'How a Boeing 787 Dreamliner Is Built', recorded at the Boeing South Carolina factory. Search the video title on YouTube.

- READ blogs about operations management from the Production and Operations Management Society or the European Operations Management Association, by Googling the names of the organizations.

- WATCH the *Financial Times* video 'What Toilet Paper Shortages Tell Us about Supply Chains', which explains why during the pandemic there was no toilet paper on supermarket shelves but plenty sitting unused in office buildings. Google the video title to find it.

- WATCH Sasha Duchnowski's TEDxTalk, 'Where Did All the Flour Go? Supply Chains and Covid'. Search the title on YouTube.

- WATCH the BBC's short film about the challenges of capacity management: 'American Giant: The Problems of Being an Overnight Success' 10 Mar. 2013. Google the title to find the film.

- WATCH Bloomberg's video about 'How Toyota Changed the Way We Make Things', which provides a short overview of how Toyota pioneered the concept of lean production and how it went on to influence process improvement around the world. Search the title on YouTube.

12

CHAPTER THIRTEEN

Entrepreneurship and Innovation

Alexander Glosenberg and Emma Macdonald

OPENING CASE STUDY **WINNOW INNOVATING TO PREVENT FOOD WASTE**

Marc Zornes graduated from Washington University in 2004 with a degree in Entrepreneurship and Computer Science. After graduating, he worked for a food distribution company, eventually becoming CEO. He also volunteered in Guatemala and worked for the not-for-profit US Green Building Council (USGBC), which promotes sustainable building construction. Later, he returned to university to study for an MBA, which allowed him to gain a job in the London office of global consultancy, McKinsey. While working there, Zornes reported: 'I had the chance to work on a report that explored the biggest opportunities to save natural resources like, food, land, water, energy, and minerals. Finding out food waste was one of the biggest global opportunities to save resources truly inspired me to build my own business to address this issue' (Plotkin, 2018).

Viewing the challenge of global food waste as an opportunity, Marc founded Winnow, with the aim of creating a measurement solution for commercial kitchens. Up to 20 per cent of all food purchased in kitchens in hotels, casinos, retailers, health care providers, caterers, and cruise ships is thrown away, leading to lost profits and wasted resources. Winnow's easy-to-install technology comprises a touchscreen located above the kitchen waste bin. The screen enables kitchen employees to conveniently record types of food being discarded as they are dropped into the bin. A set of scales beneath the bin weighs the waste as it enters the bin. The data collected by the Winnow solution provides daily and weekly analytics to the commercial kitchen's managers and chefs, helping them to run the kitchen cost-effectively and to provide a better meal selection to satisfy their diners. Winnow's solution is now used in kitchens across the globe, saving millions of meals each year from going in the trash (Ellen Macarthur Foundation, n.d.).

13.1 **Introduction**

Organizations need to be adaptive in a constantly changing world in order to survive and thrive. We explored some of the **disruptions** they face in Chapters 3, 4, and 5, and went on to introduce a number of tools that managers use to help them interpret the changes they observe in their external environment, and then exploit opportunities and minimize threats. Two related concepts that help an organization to be adaptable in a changing environment are entrepreneurship and innovation.

While entrepreneurship means many things to many people, a widely recognized view focuses on the discovery, evaluation, and pursuit of profitable opportunities (Shane & Venkataraman, 2000). Despite the mention of 'profit' in this definition, entrepreneurship can also be motivated by non-economic goals and may occur in contexts where organizations such as charities or government organizations seek to pursue an opportunity for the sake of solving a societal or environmental objective rather than an economic profit goal. Beyond the definition offered above, Johnson (2001: 138) observes that entrepreneurship:

- is a creative act whereby something is built or created that did not exist previously;
- invariably involves a degree of risk because of the 'newness' and differentness that makes it difficult to calculate value; and
- results in creation of value for the individual, community, or society.

Mintzberg identifies entrepreneurship as one of the activities of management (discussed in Section 1.8). People who identify opportunities, and start and lead entrepreneurial organizations, are often known as entrepreneurs. Because many new enterprises start out as small organizations with limited resources and few employees, the concepts of entrepreneur and entrepreneurship are often associated with small organizations. However, these notions do not necessarily overlap; entrepreneurship and innovation can create opportunities for larger organizations. Innovation that takes place inside larger or more well-established organizations is often described as intrapreneurship. Moreover, not every small enterprise founder is entrepreneurial. For instance, an entrepreneur typically focuses on building something that is new and different. However, some business founders may be mostly focused on creating an income stream for themselves—for example, by signing up to be a franchisee of an existing business, such as a Subway store or an existing cleaning franchise. In this way, they are signing up to an existing business model which they will need to follow but they are not focusing as much on creativity.

The notion of innovation is often associated with new products or services. But innovation can also include new processes (e.g., new ways of making existing products, new methods of delivering products or services, or new forms of organization) and new ways of relating to customers (e.g. using new skills or selling existing products/services to new markets).

Innovation can come in many forms, and we can understand these forms as existing along two dimensions. The first dimension describes whether or not an innovation is very different than before—with innovation existing on a continuum ranging from incremental to radical, as shown in Figure 13.1. So, for instance **incremental innovation** may involve making small improvements to

13

an existing product, such as slight increases in the computing power of a computer, or a detergent manufacturer reducing the scoop size needed to wash a standard load of clothes—with the aim of improving the brand's environmental impact and credentials. **Radical innovation** is not incremental in nature, instead it breaks dramatically from what has happened before—this is sometimes referred to as '0 to 1' innovation to indicate something entirely new (Thiel & Masters, 2014). Perhaps one of the greatest examples of radical innovation was the building of the world's first computer by Alan Turing (Watson, 2012). Other radical innovations create unique combinations of several pre-existing innovations—for example, the Apple iPhone was innovative in its combination of several already existing technologies—combining aspects of a phone with a computer and using existing technologies like touchscreens and integrated cameras (Lyytinen, 2017).

Innovation can also be understood in terms of the extent to which it is disruptive. While common parlance views disruptive innovation as any innovation that rapidly displaces pre-existing forms of a product or service in ways that lead to the demise of certain competitors (for example, Netflix replacing Blockbuster by offering a DVD home-delivery service), the concept of disruptive innovation is more nuanced (Christensen et al., 2018). Disruptive innovations when first introduced are often *worse* in comparison to pre-existing products/services according to many if not most customers. Because of this inferior performance, these innovations are often only successfully pursued by small and new companies that focus on selling those products/services to specific markets—with larger and more well-established companies shying away from the innovation due to lower profit margins and/or a lack of appeal to their existing customers.

One example of a potentially disruptive innovation is the electric car (see Christensen, 2016); when it was introduced in the modern era by well-established car makers like General Motors in the 1970s, the electric car was inferior to cars run by combustion engines according to well-established metrics such as speed and range (the distance a car can be driven on a single charge; US Department of Energy, 2014). However, in the second and third decades of the twenty-first century, the electric car has seen rapid growth—owing in part to greater performance through enhanced ranges and speeds offered by newer and smaller companies like Tesla that concentrated on the technology (International Energy Agency, 2022). If this trend continues, the electric car would be an excellent example of a disruptive innovation (Christensen, 2016). As we will see in Section 13.2.2, an important task for many entrepreneurs is helping larger or more well-established companies to be able to respond effectively to disruptive innovation.

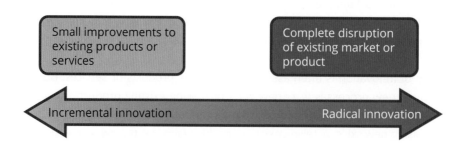

FIGURE 13.1 **The continuum of innovation ranging from incremental to radical.**

13

Successful innovations arise when people are willing to pay money for something they perceive as being of value to them, with examples including:

- A tangible product like an electrically-powered motorized scooter, a product category which we identified in Chapter 11 as growing in popularity. Innovations may also target consumers with limited purchasing power, such as in India where Pepsi's research identified that teenage girls suffered from iron deficiency. In response, Pepsi successfully launched a range of biscuits, fortified with iron, called Lehar Iron Chusti, aimed at this demographic (Simanis & Duke, 2014).

- A product-service solution such as Invisalign for teeth alignment includes both the clear plastic braces (a tangible product) and the 3-D scanning and fitting processes (a service).

- Creating a new marketplace and new processes, as seen in the way that Airbnb created a platform enabling everyday people to promote and rent out the unused space in their homes to leisure and business travellers.

This chapter focuses on the potential for entrepreneurship to be a positive source of change in the world. Accordingly, we highlight entrepreneurs not just creating value, but those creating *sustainable* value. What makes the creation of value sustainable? It's a matter of whether a new or novel way of putting together resources negatively or positively affects people and the environment—especially in the longer term. A new product, such as a more addictive cigarette, or energy from a new coal-fired power plant might be very profitable for the entrepreneur, and it might create value for customers in the short term (the rush of nicotine or energy to light a home) but we could question whether the creation of this sort of value is sustainable. A new product, such as AFRIpads reusable sanitary pads for girls in sub-Saharan Africa, which is affordable, produces less waste, and prevents girls from having to miss days of school when they are menstruating, is an example of a sustainable value proposition (Sanusi, 2022). If the new product or service damages communities and/or biodiversity (e.g. by causing higher rates of cancer or by polluting the environment), then the creation of this sort of value, with this combination of resources, is not sustainable because it undermines the company's customers and the world they live in. However, if the creation of value has an overall positive impact on not just those who purchase it or those who sell it, but on the Earth and those who live on it, then it is sustainable. AFRIPads reusable sanitary pads make it more feasible for girls to attend school and complete their education. The United Nation's Sustainable Development Goal SDG4 'Quality Education' has a key target of equal access to primary level education yet estimates that 15 million girls (and 10 million boys) are not currently in primary level education.

In the next section, we will discuss three different types of entrepreneurship and their roles in society by exploring examples of real-life entrepreneurs. Following that, we will consider entrepreneurship as a process with a special focus on how entrepreneurs come up with entrepreneurial ideas, and how they bring those ideas into reality via a process of experimentation. Finally, we will consider entrepreneurship as a mindset and will suggest ways to practise developing an entrepreneurial mindset.

13.2 **Types of entrepreneurship**

When you hear the word entrepreneurship you probably think of certain types of people and scenarios—perhaps you think of a small team of computer coders trying to launch their tech start-up or a hardworking couple working to open a new type of restaurant they always dreamed of starting. Yet entrepreneurship happens in many contexts—not just in small or new enterprises.

In the Spotlight sections in this chapter, we will hear the stories of entrepreneurs involved in, respectively, new venture creation, intrapraneurship, and sustainable entrepreneurship.

13.2.1 **New venture creation**

A venture is a start-up enterprise that is formed with the expectation and plan of financial gain (in the case of a for-profit organization) or social or environmental impact (in the case of a sustainable enterprise). In Spotlight 13.1 we meet an entrepreneur who has created a new venture.

Starting up a new organization, as in Spotlight 13.1, is the quintessential example of entrepreneurship (Block et al., 2017). Depending on which nation you consider, the percentage of adults who are starting or running a new business can range anywhere from 42 per cent in the Dominican Republic to 2 per cent in Poland (Global Entrepreneurship Monitor, 2022). Often, new

SPOTLIGHT 13.1 **STU LANDESBERG AND THE START OF GROVE COLLABORATIVE**

In 2012, Stuart (Stu) Landesberg had reached a point in his working life where he was dissatisfied with his job. Looking for a change, he identified a potentially profitable opportunity: he noticed that people were buying home cleaning and personal care products in big stores but not enjoying the process. Stu thought the shopping experience could be made easier and friendlier through personalized direct online shopping and shipping, so he started experimenting. He mocked up a Power-Point demo imitating a simple website where the customer could choose from a wide assortment of homecare goods. He would sit in coffee shops and offer randomly-selected patrons gift cards in exchange for their feedback on the website. Through listening to people he learnt customer preferences and he began to see that people val-ued non-toxic and environmentally-friendly products but were put off by the prospect of paying a higher price for them. Stu subsequently founded a company—which would eventually become Grove Collaborative—that provided an easy, friendly, and environmentally responsible way of purchasing homecare products (Tuchmann, 2022). Stu then worked to grow this new venture as a way to make money, engage in an exciting and meaningful form of work, and fulfil his passion to help the environment. Nearly 10 years after its founding, Grove Collaborative has grown beyond the typical size of a small business to employ over 1,500 employees generating over $US250 million in revenue. Stu subsequently led the company in going public so that it is no longer owned by a small number of people, but a large number of investors.

13

and/or small organizations play a critical role in the economy. In the UK, small enterprises are defined as comprising 0–49 employees and medium-sized enterprises comprise 50–249 employees. In combination, the 5.5 million SME (small-medium enterprise) organizations account for 61 per cent of UK employment in 2022 (DBEIS, 2022). 'Micro' enterprises involve less than 10 employees (Dewaelheyns & van Hulle, 2008) and account for 95 per cent of all businesses in the UK (DBEIS, 2022).

Smaller enterprises may have greater flexibility than larger ones because there are fewer decision-makers (potentially only one!) which means employees may be able to adjust strategy quickly. Recently-founded small enterprises may be forward-thinking because they have probably been started in response to some external reality spotted by the entrepreneur. Because the opportunity was recently spotted, the enterprise's ways of operating are just forming and can often easily be changed. This combination of flexibility and forward-thinking may enable smaller enterprises to develop novel products/services, processes, and/or ways of relating to customers more effectively than larger or older enterprises.

According to one of the largest surveys of entrepreneurs around the world, the Global Entrepreneurship Monitor (2020, 2022), motivations for starting an enterprise vary considerably across countries of the world. Some small enterprises are established in response to a specific opportunity; like Stu Landesberg's enterprise in Spotlight 13.1. Individuals who start such enterprises are called 'opportunity' entrepreneurs. Other enterprises are established because the entrepreneur has no better option for work; such individuals are known as 'necessity' entrepreneurs. Typically, there are higher percentages of necessity entrepreneurs in lower-income economies (Global Entrepreneurship Monitor Wiki). However, there are many motivations to start an enterprise, including the desire to make a great deal of wealth, a greater sense of autonomy, variety in one's working life, a desire to make a positive impact on the world (altruism), and intellectual stimulation (Wasserman, 2008). For example, many people start a business because it supports the sort of life they want to live—helping them to focus on what they love (e.g. an animal lover starting a pet-grooming business) and to be able to be their own boss. Thus, entrepreneurship can be viewed as a career choice for many people—and some entrepreneurs, known as 'serial' entrepreneurs, start new enterprises again and again.

The pattern of different motivations among entrepreneurs around the world helps to highlight that new venture creation occurs in many ways for different people from different circumstances. For those individuals with relatively few resources or forms of support, it might be more difficult to start highly innovative enterprises—and such individuals might tend to copy or imitate nearby enterprises (Dencker et al., 2021). This is in part because starting nearly any organization, especially a highly innovative one, is made easier by access to money and other resources, such as social connections and education. Those without easy access to money to start a business, including personal home equity loans, credit cards, loans from a bank, and loans from family or friends, might be particularly disadvantaged. If access to these forms of money is unequally distributed in society, then it is not surprising that we see different rates of new venture creation among certain groups (Marks, 2021). Nevertheless, especially in lower-income communities and economies, entrepreneurs often play a critical role in supporting the welfare of their families and communities (United Nations Development Programme, 2014, 2015).

13

13.2.2 **Intrapreneurship**

Entrepreneurs are not limited to starting or running small or new enterprises; they include people employed in larger and more established organizations. Individuals involved in such innovation can be referred to as *intra*preneurs (indicating that they are engaging in entrepreneurship *inside* a company; Antoncic & Hisrich, 2003) or as corporate entrepreneurs (indicating that innovation happens inside of larger and well-established corporations). 'Intrapreneur' is not usually a job title; instead, those who are intrapreneurs may have a variety of roles at various levels of the organizational hierarchy, such as chief innovation officer, project manager, or research and development specialist. Danielle Jezienicki, the Director of Sustainability at Grove Collaborative (Spotlight 13.2), is an example of an intrapreneur, as she has helped to drive innovation in the company by working with others to make many of Grove's products free of plastic.

Intrapreneurs are important in larger or well-established companies because as organizations grow, they may lose the ability to be innovative. In part, this is a natural part of growth because small and new ventures may have the advantage of less **bureaucracy** and greater flexibility to focus on an external opportunity. Long-established and larger ventures can become inflexible, focused on self-management, and stuck in certain ways of doing things instead of being focused on external opportunities and experimentation.

However, losing an innovation focus does not have to happen as a new company grows. As discussed by Christensen (2016; Christensen & Overdorf, 2000), to really break away from what has been traditionally done, often to embrace the sort of disruptive innovation described

SPOTLIGHT 13.2 **DANIELLE JEZIENICKI JOINS GROVE COLLABORATIVE TO INNOVATE FOR THE ENVIRONMENT**

Grove Collaborative (see Spotlight 13.1) had already grown beyond being a small start-up business when Danielle Jezienicki joined in 2019 as Director of Sustainability. Danielle was hired to help lead the company away from using plastics in its products, towards more environmentally-friendly materials. To do this, Danielle would need to be an innovator inside a larger organization. Establishing a team of employees, Danielle initially led a programme to categorize how much plastic was in use in all products sold by the company. She then worked with people in various roles across the organization to develop creative solutions for how they might go 'plastic-free'. While many employees at Grove believed deeply in a plastic-free future, such change was not easy because it meant questioning and changing the way that Grove did things and, perhaps, asking the organizations they partnered with to make similar changes. Danielle worked with Grove's suppliers and other companies that sold products on the company's website to see how they might find replacements for plastic components. Danielle recognized that some changes might affect the performance of Grove's products which would worry Grove's customers, and if this reduced sales then it would worry investors. Danielle therefore needed to balance driving the vision for a plastic-free company within the organization with striving to innovate Grove's products and effectively communicating this vision to key stakeholders outside the organization. It was challenging but Danielle knew that these changes would eventually lead to a stronger company and a healthier planet.

13

above, organizations might need to form an independent team (or even a spin-off business) to identify, evaluate, and then exploit opportunities that are different from those being pursued in the rest of the organization. Sometimes these teams are given special powers, such as being able to operate independently and to control their own budgets, and sometimes they even operate in secret. Such teams are often called 'skunk works' teams, in honour of a famous team that was responsible for innovative aircraft designs at the company Lockheed Martin during World War 2 (Garrison, 2010). Regardless of what sort of teams they are in, intrapreneurs meet unique challenges—like finding ways around established procedures, changing a company's culture to better embrace change, and working to ensure that usually well-intentioned members of the rest of the organization do not stop the pursuit of promising new opportunities that might threaten the status quo.

13.2.3 Sustainable entrepreneurship

We mentioned in Section 13.1 that entrepreneurship has unique potential to be a source of positive change in the world. In a sense, many entrepreneurs help the world by delivering value to customers; but some entrepreneurs seek to have impact on a broader scale through the creation of an enterprise that addresses the world's wicked problems (described in Section 3.2.3), such as poverty, inequality, hunger, global warming, and deforestation. These enterprise founders are known as 'sustainable' entrepreneurs (Stubbs, 2017; sometimes also called social entrepreneurs) because they seek to solve social and/or environmental problems. Such entrepreneurs have similarities to other players in society who are trying to address wicked challenges, including voluntary community groups, local governments, intergovernmental organizations (such as the UN), and charities. Critically, however, sustainable entrepreneurs are different because they deliberately seek to use the power of profitable opportunities to address social/environmental issues. Rochelle Webb, with her enterprise, Optimist Made (Spotlight 13.3) is an example of a sustainable entrepreneur. Such organizations are often known as social enterprises or sustainable enterprises, which we refer to in Section 2.6.3 when we explored the private sector's purpose shift.

Another example of a sustainable enterprise is the Nobel Peace Prize-winning Grameen Bank founded in 1976. Founder, Muhammad Yunus had a vision to establish a financial institution that would provide support for people living in poverty by means of loans on easy terms. Banks are traditionally unwilling to lend money to people unable to provide some form of security, which means that those with the fewest assets are infrequently able to get loans—even small ones. This holds them back from investing in themselves, their families, or their businesses. Grameen Bank, on the other hand, works on the assumption that even people living in poverty can manage their own financial affairs given suitable conditions, and makes small loans on relatively beneficial terms. Grameen Bank utilizes an innovative approach to providing these 'microcredit' loans by organizing those receiving loans into self-help groups so that if one person struggles to make a repayment, another can step in to support them. When Grameen Bank won the Nobel Peace Prize in 2006, they had already issued loans to more than seven million borrowers. The average amount borrowed was US$100. The repayment percentage was very high and over 95 per cent of the loans went to women or groups of women (NobelPrize.org, 2006).

SPOTLIGHT 13.3 **OPTIMIST MADE: ROCHELLE WEBB**

In her time working as a corporate-marketing executive manager for multiple international corporations, Rochelle Webb travelled extensively and met many local fashion entrepreneurs across the world who were trying to break through to larger markets. She observed that entrepreneurs starting out in lower-income communities would frequently have great products but lack the resources to connect to customers located in higher-income communities, who would appreciate the products they had to offer. Rochelle saw the opportunity to help these fashion entrepreneurs connect to a wider marketplace of customers. She launched Optimist Made combining her interest in fashion and skills in marketing into the creation of an online marketplace promoting fashion accessories from up-and-coming designers from under-represented backgrounds. The Optimist Made platform connects buyers and sellers but, in addition, helps entrepreneurs to build their brand by prominently profiling them on the website as 'muses'. Rochelle also supports entrepreneurs with market-

ing skills development to help them develop their own competency to grow their enterprises and win more customers in new markets.

Optimist Made is not a charitable organization. It is a sustainable enterprise that combines profit objectives with social objectives; this means it seeks to balance gaining profits while also supporting the success of entrepreneurs from less advantaged backgrounds. A win-win-win is achieved when:

- customers are able to find exciting, unusual items via the Optimist Made website;

- new entrepreneurs are able to create a name for themselves and generate profits from reaching wider audiences; and

- Optimist Made achieves its profit objectives by providing a platform for fashion buyers and sellers AND achieves its social purpose objectives by giving a lift to enterprises of entrepreneurs who might not otherwise have opportunities to reach such wide audiences.

It is useful to compare the nature of a sustainable enterprise with a charity. We explored charities in Section 2.5.2 as part of the third sector. A charity is typically understood as an organization that organizes voluntary donations for a particular cause—for example, to help disaster survivors or save an endangered species. Sometimes, charities are referred to as not-for-profit organizations, non-profit, or non-governmental organizations, as we learnt in Section 2.2.3. While charities sometimes provide a small token, such as a pin badge (Marie Curie Foundation) or a newsletter (*The Big Issue*), in exchange for the money they receive, the exchange of goods/ services for money is typically not the principal focus of a charity. In contrast, a sustainable enterprise has a similar focus on solving social/environmental problems, but it does so by focusing on selling products/services. Thus, Optimist Made is a sustainable (social) enterprise because it works to help empower entrepreneurs from disadvantaged backgrounds, and Grameen Bank is a social enterprise because it earns interest on the loans it makes.

A distinction also exists between sustainable entrepreneurship and corporate social responsibility (CSR). As we discussed in Chapter 3, CSR is whenever an organization attempts to address a social/environmental problem in a way that is not directly tied to it earning a profit. Typically, such efforts are only tangentially connected to the main focus of an organization— that is, to the products/services that it sells. For example, if a computer software company gives its employees a day off to help plant trees in a local forest, the CSR reforestation effort is not closely connected to the company's profitability as a seller of software. A social or sustainable

13

enterprise, by contrast, integrates the earning of a profit with the way in which it tackles a social/environmental problem. When Optimist Made makes a sale on its global marketplace, it makes a little profit but also directly benefits an entrepreneur from a less advantaged background—closely aligning its profitability with its positive social impact. It is important to note that to help support their prioritization of both social/environmental value and profit, many social enterprises take on a unique legal format known as a benefit corporation—the focus of Spotlight 2.2.

Combining profit goals with social or environmental goals has at least three important advantages in solving wicked problems. First, sustainable enterprises do not rely on the unpredictable nature of donations from individuals and organizations—but instead on the interests of their customers. This reliance sometimes allows sustainable enterprises to grow, or scale, more quickly than they might be able to do relying only on donations. Second, sustainable enterprises are typically highly responsive to the people they are trying to help; if the products/services offered are not selling well, this is an indication that the enterprise needs to adjust its approach. In charities and with CSR efforts, such quick and clear feedback may be missing—allowing well-intentioned efforts to sometimes be either ineffective or even harmful. Third, sustainable enterprises often involve the communities and ecosystems in the process of solving the social or environmental problem. Such involvement is a critical component of empowerment—that is, of beneficiaries being and feeling able to help themselves. For example, while Optimist Made could donate a portion of the money it earns to entrepreneurs, this might not leave them empowered if the company ever stopped those payments. However, by instead helping entrepreneurs to develop their own skill sets and build their brands, those entrepreneurs are more likely to prosper independently of the help provided. Importantly, this is not to say that charities, not-for-profit organizations, non-governmental organizations, or CSR initiatives are necessarily less effective at solving social or environmental problems, but instead they go about it in a different manner.

Having reviewed three forms of entrepreneurship, we next look at the practice of being an entrepreneur and the stages involved in the innovation process. First, let's return to Imperial to see how they are approaching entrepreneurship, in Running case 13.1.

RUNNING CASE 13.1 NEW ENTREPRENEURIAL MINDSET IN AN OLD BUSINESS

During Imperial's first visit to NoBull, Lucy was impressed by the entrepreneurial spirit of the company, personified in CEO Marcus Truelove's enthusiasm and energy. She has spent quite a bit of time with Marcus since that first meeting, and her positive impression of him as an entrepreneur with a mission to make a difference through his and his company's work hasn't diminished. She admires the way that Marcus and the NoBull staff are constantly talking to each other, enhanced by a scheme that allows workers to take time each week to develop new innovations and propose them to the company. In fact, Marcus says, three of the company's top-five products came from staff ideas, and the staff members involved receive a profit share that incentivizes them to keep innovating.

From the outside, Imperial Fine Foods must seem to most people to be the antithesis of the sort of entrepreneurial business that NoBull exemplifies. The traditional brick building, the photographs on the

(Continued)

staircase, Hugh in his suit and tie—all of these things seem a million miles away from the ponytailed Marcus and his partners in their start-up. But Lucy realizes that Imperial has actually embodied a different kind of entrepreneurship that is just as valid. Over the years her father and grandfather have stuck by their values, refused to sell the business to corporate buyers, and fought doggedly for what they believe in. The company—she realizes now she is in the driving seat herself—has only managed to keep up with its competitors over recent years because of Hugh's willingness to try new things. New machines have been evaluated and installed, processes have been adapted, and unexplored market opportunities have been pursued. Since she took over as CEO, though, she has realized that changes aren't happening as quickly as needed. Recovering from the pandemic and recent political upheavals are not excuses for complacency; with the rapidly emerging changes in their traditional markets, Imperial is now at real risk of being left behind.

For this reason, she is pleased and excited by some of the recent developments in the firm. Marcus reminded her in one of their meetings that being entrepreneurial is all about discovering, evaluating, and pursuing opportunities. As she looks around her now, she sees the changes that have been evolving since Imperial's Away Day meetings. The traditional Imperial approach had been challenged in a very direct way by Jazz and those who had spoken up for the changes in food consumption which some older members of staff had seemed unaware of, or at least unwilling to acknowledge. Their discovery of the potential threat to Imperial's traditional business—and more importantly the potential opportunity to revitalize the company—has been persuasively communicated over succeeding weeks and gradually accepted by almost everyone in the company. Since then, Gita Patel, leading the Imperial marketing team, has done great work in running a customer survey and establishing customer journeys for the potential new consumers of their plant-based food products. The company really is, Lucy feels, proposing a solution to a problem that none of its leadership team had been willing to confront until now: tastes are changing, commitment to the environment is increasing, and health-consciousness is rising.

13.3 The role of innovation in entrepreneurship

People involved in entrepreneurship—including those starting new ventures, intrapreneurs, and sustainable entrepreneurs—have one thing in common. They all engage in a similar process of innovation that relates to discovering, evaluating, and pursuing profitable opportunities. These three stages of innovation serve as the organizing framework for this section; they further break down into smaller stages, as visually depicted in Figure 13.2.

The stages in Figure 13.2 emphasize that successful entrepreneurs are action-oriented—that is, they are constantly discovering, acting, learning, and adapting (Frese, 2009). This entrepreneurial process progresses as follows:

1. It starts with *discovering opportunities*—that is, developing new or novel ideas as a result of scanning the environment, or gathering and appreciating resources available.

2. The process then moves to *evaluating opportunities* by considering which ideas are most promising and identifying the critical assumptions that make an idea workable.

3. Finally, the process moves to *pursuing opportunities* by setting goals, acting and testing the assumptions in those goals, and then seeking feedback on progress towards the goals.

4. The cycle then starts over again when the entrepreneur learns from *feedback and adapts*—resulting in new ideas.

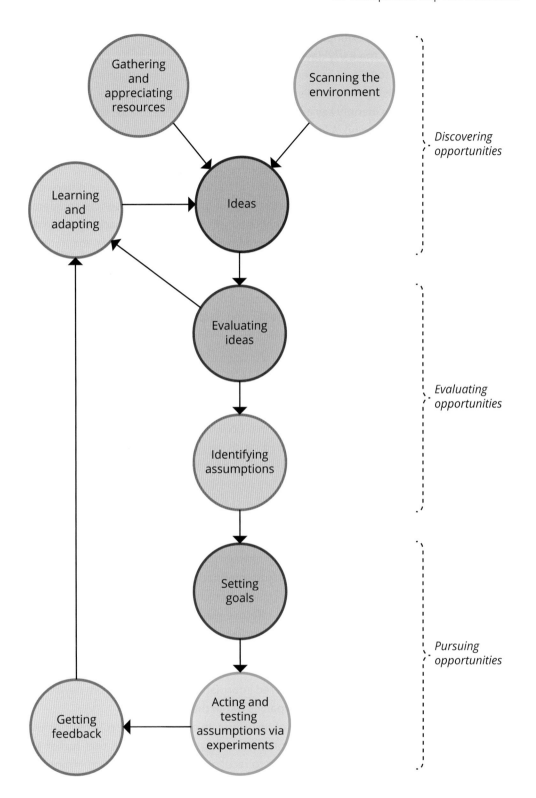

FIGURE 13.2 **The entrepreneurial process of innovation.** Credit: Michael Frese (2009), 'Towards a Psychology of Entrepreneurship: An Action Theory Perspective', in *Foundations and Trends® in Entrepreneurship*: Vol. 5: No. 6, pp 437–496.

We next consider a real-life example of the entrepreneurial process in Figure 13.2. Let's return to Stu Landesberg in the early days of Grove Collaborative (Spotlight 13.1). Stu's idea for a website for buying personal and homecare products resulted from him actively scanning the environment for a promising venture (discovering an opportunity). Before acting on the opportunity, Stu worked hard to identify key assumptions that would have to hold true for his idea to work (evaluating an opportunity). A key assumption was that customers would like the process of shopping on the website but like any good entrepreneur, Stu knew that his enthusiasm for his idea might not translate into reality, so he began acting in small ways by conducting experiments to test his ideas (pursuing an opportunity). In particular, through testing different website design mock-ups with customers he discovered that they wanted household and personal care products that were non-toxic and environmentally-friendly. This feedback led Stu to adapt his original business idea to focus more on environmental sustainability. This adaptation and learning then led to new ideas for how Stu could grow his business and the process of discovery, evaluation, and acting started over again.

While this might seem like an obvious and simple process for creating anything new, each of these stages can actually be quite involved, messy, and uncertain. Let's now consider the stages in the entrepreneurial process in greater depth.

13.3.1 Discovering opportunities

Entrepreneurial processes start with one thing—the discovery of opportunities—primarily by generating new ideas. These can be big ideas that occur only once in a long while—for example, an idea for starting a new venture that will satisfy an unmet customer demand, or a new direction to take an existing enterprise in. Ideas can also be small-scale—for example, an idea for how to run the organization a little better. But where do all these ideas come from? In short, there are two sources: scanning the environment and prior learning.

Scanning the environment involves being aware of what is going on in the world, in your nation, in your local community, in scientific disciplines/with new technologies, and within various markets and industries. There is a variety of ways in which entrepreneurs scan their environment. This includes gathering second-hand information, which is information collected and processed by others, and first-hand information, which is gathered and processed by the entrepreneur themselves. We consider some effective ways to scan the environment in Table 13.1, including methods that you might not be familiar with, like visiting conferences and informational interviews. In the case of Stu Landesberg, he had scanned the environment by being aware of which companies were offering home and personal care products and how those companies tended to sell their products. Stu gathered information second-hand from news sources and first-hand by speaking to people in companies within the industry.

Prior learning is another valuable source of new ideas. In a review of the role of prior knowledge on entrepreneurial effectiveness, Shepherd and Patzelt (2018) found that higher levels of education facilitate an entrepreneur's ability to recognize opportunities. Furthermore, prior knowledge of a specific industry or organization 'connects the known with the unknown' to better facilitate opportunity recognition (Shepherd & Patzelt, 2018: 38). Prior learning can also include unexpected events—indeed, accidents or unexpected outcomes of an **experiment** are often important sources of learning. Prior to joining Grove Collaborative, Danielle Jezienicki

13

TABLE 13.1 **Examples of approaches to scanning the environment**

Approach	Source of information	How it is helpful	Examples
Reading, watching, and listening to business- and entrepreneurially-related news sources, websites, and podcasts	Second-hand	Keeping track of changes and potential opportunities, in various markets and industries	*Wall Street Journal* *Financial Times* TechCrunch *The Economist*
Reading and listening to a wide variety of niche news sources, blogs, podcasts, and magazines	Second-hand	Being aware of new technologies and new trends that might not have obvious connections to enterprise opportunities	BBC Science Focus *Scientific American* Pew Research Centre *Psychology Today*
Private sources of information about markets, industries, companies, and economies	Second-hand	A large industry exists to collect information on markets, industries, and companies and much of this information is not otherwise easily obtainable	Bloomberg Professional Services PrivCo Nielsen
Internships and jobs—working for a company for a short or long period of time	First-hand	Immersing yourself in an environment is an excellent way to learn about an industry; an internship or job in a company that you are interested in can give an excellent grounding and be the source of ideas	Paid or unpaid (where legal and ethical) internships or jobs with start-up or established companies in industries you're curious about
Informational interviews—approaching someone (usually via email/social media) and asking to interview them about their work and life	First-hand	So much knowledge about how companies and industries operate is not formally written down but exists inside the heads of experts and leaders in that industry	Find someone who is doing something interesting—or is in a position that you would love to be in; send them a message/email telling them you admire them and would like to chat about their work/lives
Speaking with strangers in different walks of life	First-hand	The ability to understand and empathize with the perspective of others is often at the heart of being able to identify opportunities to make customers' lives better	Have a conversation with someone about their life and problems—be sure it is safe and in public—and consider giving a small token in appreciation of their time (e.g. a cup of coffee)

(Spotlight 13.2) worked at kitchenware manufacturer, Williams Sonoma, helping to make their products more environmentally sustainable. Based on that experience, Danielle knew that to be successful in realizing Grove Collaborative's 'plastic-free' mission she would need to spend a lot of time working closely with her suppliers. The importance of prior knowledge to new idea generation is one reason why many successful entrepreneurs start organizations or new projects

13

in industries in which they have already worked. The broader experiences of the entrepreneur, and their team, are another critical source of prior learning.

While environment scanning and prior learning are important sources of new ideas for entrepreneurs, Sarasvathy's (2001) Theory of Effectuation (where effectuation means making something happen) emphasizes that not all entrepreneurial ideas are based upon deliberate searching and abstract reasoning. Instead, entrepreneurs often come up with ideas based upon existing resources: either their personal resources—such as skills, special knowledge, natural talents, and passions—or the external resources available to them, to form an idea and drive it forward. (Resources were previously discussed in Section 5.2.1.) The resources an entrepreneur has at their disposal are wide and varied, and may include:

- financial resources, including your own money and money you can get from others;
- social connections, like family, friends, and acquaintances;
- physical space available to you, such as a garage; and
- your geographic location—for example, working in a technology innovation hub, living in a large, vibrant city, or near a beautiful pristine wilderness.

An example of an idea resulting from effectuation is Rochelle Webb's (Spotlight 13.3) idea for Optimist Made. Rochelle did not engage in an abstract process of planning and goal setting to form the idea of her company but rather combined some of her existing resources. In particular, she started a company that utilized her long track-record and expertise in marketing, and contacts met through the course of her travels.

Entrepreneurs need to always be thinking about building resources—through, for example, networking, learning new skills, and doing favours for others. If you have an entrepreneurial mindset (to be discussed in Section 13.4), you may recognize that even if you cannot see a clear reason right now for meeting new people, learning a new skill, or building social capital (i.e. a rich social network that can help advance your goals), you might be able to draw upon these resources in the future and they might lead to innovative enterprise ideas.

13.3.2 **Evaluating opportunities**

An important part of the entrepreneurial process is evaluating opportunities. Evaluation means making judgements regarding which of many ideas is the best one. To accomplish this, entrepreneurs often use a set of criteria to judge whether any given idea is worth pursuing. While there are many criteria, a useful shorthand is to ask yourself whether the idea is:

1. a **solution** to a problem that someone actually has?
2. **superior** to existing alternatives?
3. **sensible** to undertake with your existing or available resources?
4. a financially **sustainable** solution to undertake in the longer term?

Each of these questions deals with important aspects of a business model—that is, a plan to turn an idea into a working business process—that can be represented in a visual sense. We will briefly discuss each of the four 'S' criteria—solution, superior, sensible, and sustainable, found in Figure 13.3—in greater depth in the following sections.

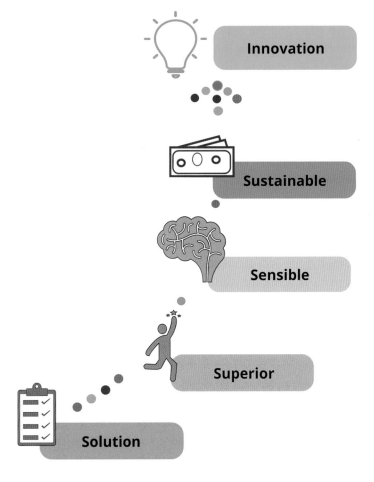

FIGURE 13.3 **The four 'S' criteria for evaluation.**

Solution to a problem

The most important question an entrepreneur must ask when evaluating a new venture idea is whether it is a solution to a real problem. The world is littered with failed attempts at bringing ideas into reality, which, despite being interesting, do not pass this basic test. Solving a problem for someone is the quintessential way of creating value and an essential component of entrepreneurship. The only way to evaluate whether an idea for a new product/service, a revised process, or a new way of relating to customers, will actually solve a problem is to have a deep understanding of the lives and goals of whoever would benefit from your idea. To accomplish this, an entrepreneur needs to spend meaningful time understanding the world from other people's perspectives, by developing empathy for them.

Empathy is the ability to understand and share the feelings and perspectives of others. How do you know when you've developed empathy with someone? You'll know when you can provide a long and specific list of examples of what their goals in life are, what obstacles they have in meeting those goals, and examples of what makes them happy. Many things on this list might only tangentially relate to your idea, but that's okay: to create real value in someone's life you have to understand them as a whole person. For example, if you have an idea for a new type of ice cream shop that will appeal to elderly people, you need to understand more about them than just their preferences in relation to desserts. What are their dietary goals and restrictions? What are their social goals and the realities that get in the way of those goals? How do they prefer to move around town and what mobility limitations might they have? Having a deep understanding of these issues might be crucial in creating an ice cream business that really gives value to elderly people.

How do you develop empathy? There are multiple ways, but a few promising ones include:

- conducting interviews by sitting down with someone for a long and deep conversation;
- spending time with people—for example, through sharing a meal and helping them throughout their day;
- spending time in the places that they spend time in, perhaps frequenting the organizations they frequent; and
- going through experiences that they go through and seeing what it's like to navigate the world in the way they do—for example, if your customer is a wheelchair user, then find out what is it like to move about the world in a wheelchair.

Superiority to existing alternatives

Once an entrepreneur is reasonably convinced that their idea would be a solution to a real problem, the second step is a comparison of their idea to existing alternatives. A key question here is whether or not the idea would, in the mind of the customer, be meaningfully superior to what already exists. It is tempting for someone with an idea to immediately conclude, yes, my idea is better! However, just because your idea is different to existing alternatives, it does not mean that it will be sufficiently superior to convince someone to purchase your new product, service, or process, rather than what they are already familiar with. To determine your idea's superiority, you need to return to the list of the goals of the people you are trying to help and honestly ask yourself, would my idea really create value for the customer in relation to these goals? If the answer is not a definitive yes, you might need to think harder about your idea. If your answer is no, you don't necessarily need to throw the idea away entirely, but it will need to change and evolve.

For example, returning to our idea of an ice cream shop for the elderly, you might propose to have a lot of parking and an easily accessible wheelchair ramp for those customers who might find this accessibility useful. However, is it really going to be easier for an elderly person with mobility issues to drive to your shop than having their ice cream delivered to them at home? If not, your idea might not be superior to existing ice cream delivery services.

Another trap many entrepreneurs fall into when evaluating the superiority of their idea is to think that their idea is so new and different that it doesn't have competitors. This is almost never the case. For example, let's consider an innovative ice cream shop for the summer months that is as cold inside the shop as a freezer—allowing customers to quickly cool off. Even if there are no ice cream shops around like this, there might be very different options for customers to cool off quickly, including free alternatives. Thus your 'competitors' might include standing in front of one's own air conditioner at home on a hot day, going to an ice-skating rink, or simply going to the local pool. Customers derive the same value (cooling off quickly) from these alternatives even though they do not superficially resemble your ice cream shop idea.

Sensible for the entrepreneur to undertake

Once you have settled on an idea that is a solution to a real problem, and is superior to existing alternatives, your job is to determine whether your idea is sensible for you, or the team you are hoping to put together, to make into a reality. That does not mean that you immediately will have all the necessary resources, nor be an expert in all activities required to make your new venture idea a success. Instead, it means that you need a sensible plan to acquire those resources and to find the people, or develop the skills, to be able to undertake key activities.

One way of testing whether your idea is sensible is to begin to list out all of the resources, other people/companies you need to work with, and activities required for the idea to become a reality. If you find yourself struggling to know what is required, then almost certainly you need to do more research to be able to determine whether you could undertake it. An entrepreneur is almost never able to assemble all the necessary resources and partners to undertake a business right away, but it is necessary to have a *sensible* plan about how to acquire those resources and partners and how to successfully undertake the critical activities that make a business a success. When considering the sensibility of an idea, you still need to keep in mind the issue of superiority. Ask yourself not just whether you can do it, but also do you have a plan to be able to undertake this business in a way that is better than your competitors. If the answer is no, you might need to adjust your business idea by solving a slightly different problem.

Sustainability in the longer term

Finally, if you have an idea that's a superior and sensible solution to a problem, your last step is to ensure that your idea is financially sustainable in the longer term. Doing so will require you to engage with questions of entrepreneurial accounting and finance. While a deep exploration of these issues is outside the scope of this chapter, consideration of the financial sustainability (also referred to as financial viability) of a new venture idea requires at least three general considerations.

13

The first element is costs, which are divided into fixed and variable. Fixed costs include everything in an organization that needs to be purchased or paid for—irrespective of the number of products/services made or sold to customers. This includes:

- general and administrative costs, such as salaries for accountants, information technology used by the organization, and rent of an office or shop space;

- marketing costs, such as the money it takes to post ads; and

- research and development costs, such as costs involved in developing or professionalizing your product/service.

For the case of an ice cream shop, the rent for the shop, the number of ads one places in the newspaper or online, and the money you spend experimenting to develop new ice cream flavours would all be fixed costs because they are relatively independent of how much ice cream you sell.

Variable costs are those things that you need to spend money on that are directly tied to the production/delivery of one additional unit of a product/service. For example, if you are running an ice cream shop, your costs for cones and napkins are variable costs because they all go up if you sell an additional ice cream cone.

Second, you need to consider types of revenue. Revenue refers to the income you generate from sales. Any given idea needs to generate revenue, but it is possible to generate multiple types of revenue in one idea. In our example of the ice cream shop for the elderly, the most obvious revenue source would be selling ice cream to in-store customers. However, additional sources of revenue might include ice cream delivery to homes and the selling of branded merchandise to those customers who love your shop. Each of these activities—ice cream sold in-store, ice cream delivery, and branded merchandise—can be considered a different 'revenue stream'.

Finally, there is the element of revenue over time. You need to consider how much revenue you can reasonably expect to generate across a period of time into the future. For each revenue stream, you will need to estimate—usually within the next three to five years—how much of a given product/service you can reasonably expect to sell. Estimating this number will require you to make realistic assumptions based on

- technical capacity, e.g. how much ice cream can you produce per day;

- likely demand, e.g. how many people are likely to come into your shop on a given day; and/or

- prior examples of similar enterprises, e.g. how much revenue do similar ice cream shops make?

Estimating answers to all three of these financial considerations allows an entrepreneur to complete what is known as a break-even analysis—a projection of when it is that your total costs (fixed and variable) will be exceeded by the revenue that you have generated. If there's no clear way for you to break-even in a reasonable time frame (often within the first three to five years, but sometimes much longer into the future), then your organization might not be financially sustainable.

13

13.3.3 **Pursuing opportunities**

The next step in the entrepreneurial process is pursuing opportunities—put simply: acting. Because entrepreneurs operate in complex, changing, and uncertain situations, the success of those actions is unknown. Consequently, successful entrepreneurs often find ways to avoid large investments of resources (money, time, supplies, energy, etc.) when pursuing opportunities by conducting small experiments. Experiments are important not because they will always work out the way the entrepreneur thinks, but because they will hardly ever work out the way the entrepreneur thinks! Yet, when an experiment 'fails' the entrepreneur has an opportunity to gather information about why the experiment failed and then learn and adapt to be more successful the second time around. Such learning and adaptation will lead to new ideas about what to do next (e.g. to offer a different product or to approach customers in new ways), which will lead to a new goal, and the cycle will begin again.

Conducting experiments

What exactly is an experiment in an entrepreneurial context? When we hear the word 'experiment' we probably picture a scientist in a lab coat—but in reality, entrepreneurs also often conduct experiments. Experiments are tests of an assumption or set of assumptions. In an entrepreneurial context, a key assumption is whether or not potential customers will like a product or service enough to buy it. For example, Stu Landesberg learnt about the appeal of his website and its offerings by experimenting with varying mock-ups of the website for his business idea prior to launch. There are at least three factors that make an experiment useful for an entrepreneur: structure, selection, and skin.

Structure: An experiment needs to be conducted in a structured manner. To be able to gain accurate insight from your experiment, you need to isolate what aspect your potential customers are reacting to. For example, if they are reacting to how you presented a product/service (e.g. if you greet customers with a smile one time and with a frown the next), their reactions might not tell you as much about the potential appeal of the product/service as they do about your approach and friendliness.

Interacting with potential customers is key to entrepreneurship.

Selection: An experiment needs to pay close attention to who is being selected to participate. Experiments are most useful when the participants are similar to your likely potential customers. For example, if you conduct experiments only with young college students, but your target customers are mature adults then you may find students unrepresentative.

Skin: An experiment needs to generate valuable feedback from potential customers. When you're willing to contribute something valuable to an effort, it is often said that you have 'skin in the game'. What are valuable sources of feedback? They are usually time, reputation, and money. Thus, if you show or tell a customer about your new product or service, and then just ask their opinion of it, they are not giving you a valuable resource. Any positive feedback, if it is simply an opinion, might be due more to politeness than actual interest. However, if a customer after seeing a preview of your product or service is willing to give you money for a pre-order, spend a meaningful amount of time providing information about why they like your product, and/or are willing to put their reputation at risk by liking your social media page for the product/service, then you are more likely to be detecting actual interest.

Minimum viable product

Within the world of entrepreneurship, there is a special form of experiment known as a minimum viable product (MVP). According to the 'lean start-up' method advocated by Eric Ries (2011), an MVP is a way for an entrepreneur to build a product or process to a just-sufficient standard that allows them to measure the results of introducing the idea in some way to the real world. This is usually done by introducing the MVP to potential customers.

Importantly, MVPs are different from prototypes. Prototypes are also early versions of a product or service, but they tend to emphasize physical or superficial similarity to the final product or service (e.g. looking a lot like it). By contrast, MVPs emphasize functional similarity to the final product by imitating the customer experience of using the product. This is a critical distinction because a lot of time and money can be wasted by focusing on physical or superficial similarity. However, for an experiment, it is functional similarity that matters because we are interested in customers' reactions to the underlying value they are receiving. Thus, Stu did not need to spend time making a perfect website (indeed it was just a PowerPoint presentation); his MVP aimed to explore whether certain online offerings would be appealing enough to customers for them to make purchases. This is a key assumption that needs to be tested for Stu's idea to work. Learn more about the lean start-up method by watching a YouTube video with Eric Ries (see 'Explore more') or reading his book (listed in the chapter reference list).

As we have seen in this section, the road to successful innovation and entrepreneurship is not necessarily straightforward, often involving phases of discovery, evaluation, and pursuit of opportunities. Many people would be put off by the challenges involved at each stage. This is why entrepreneurship often requires a certain mindset, which we will explore further below.

13.3.4 Open innovation

So far, our discussion may have implied that innovation is largely an individual or organizational activity. Under this assumption, an entrepreneur or an organization that develops a new idea will focus on commercializing it for the direct benefit of the organization and its customers. This may mean they are protective of the idea that they have developed and may categorize the

13

idea as intellectual property (IP) which they seek to protect by law. Intellectual property refers to 'creations of the mind, such as inventions; literary and artistic works; designs; and symbols, names and images used in commerce' (World Intellectual Property Organization (WIPO, n.d.)). IP may be protected by legal frameworks such as patents, copyrights, and trademarks. IP ensures that people or organizations can 'earn recognition or financial benefit from what they invent or create' (WIPO).

However, a related notion in innovation, particularly as it pertains to addressing wicked challenges such as poverty or climate change, is open innovation. Open innovation was popularized in the early 2000s by Chesborough (2003), who describes it as: 'conceptually, a more distributed, more participatory, more decentralized approach to innovation, based on the observed fact that useful knowledge today is widely distributed, and no company, no matter how capable or how big, could innovate effectively on its own' (Chesborough, 2011).

Open innovation involves an entrepreneur or organization willingly collaborating and sharing with other players, even those who may be direct competitors. There are two facets to open innovation—outside-in and inside-out. The 'outside-in' aspect of open innovation allows external ideas and technologies to be brought into the firm's own innovation process. The 'inside-out' aspect allows unused and under-utilized ideas and technologies in the firm to be shared outside the organization's boundaries to be incorporated into others' innovation processes.

An example of successful use of open innovation is Mozilla, which uses open-source software development to create its Firefox web browser. Firefox has been developed by Mozilla's worldwide community of coders, which includes both volunteers and paid employees. People are motivated to volunteer with Mozilla because it is a great learning experience, they get to be a part of a community and are able to take part in Mozilla events (Morikawa, 2016).

Collaborators in open innovation can come from a variety of contexts including entrepreneurial start-ups and businesses that are scaling up in size, but also not-for-profit organizations. Partners in an open innovation project may come from similar business sectors, and may even be competitors, or they may come from multiple non-related sectors. Organizations may attempt to tap into the creativity of everyday citizens through online challenges, contests, and hackathons, which provide fresh perspectives and diverse skills. Furthermore, while opening up the innovation process externally, organizations may likewise seek ways to open up innovation internally too, enabling anyone within the organization to be a part of the innovation cycle (WIPO, n.d.).

13.4 Entrepreneurship as a mindset

While we can view entrepreneurship as a set of processes, we can also think of it as a mindset, or a set of beliefs and attitudes. As Kuratko et al. (2021) describe, mindsets are complex. A mindset involves not only how one thinks, such as believing that certain things are possible or that certain things are good or bad, but also how one feels, like feeling good about doing a certain activity and feeling confident about accomplishing a task. Moreover, because a mindset shapes how one thinks and feels, it also influences how one acts on a day-to-day basis. What, then, is an *entrepreneurial* mindset? Let's first give some examples of what an entrepreneurial mindset might look like.

In terms of thinking, someone with an entrepreneurial mindset is frequently thinking about possible new profitable opportunities: new products or services, new ways of doing things, and new ways of relating to customers. In terms of feelings, someone with an entrepreneurial mindset feels a sense of confidence that through hard work and trial and error, they can succeed; put another way, they feel good about the process of being an entrepreneur. Critically, someone with an entrepreneurial mindset does not just think and feel in these ways but also acts. An entrepreneur will develop small habits like learning about new things, pursuing ideas sooner than others, and networking with others.

To better understand what a mindset might look like more broadly, let's engage with two important questions. First, what characteristics do many successful entrepreneurs hold in their entrepreneurial mindsets? Second, what happens if you find that you often do not have an entrepreneurial mindset? Are you destined not to be an entrepreneur? Is it possible to improve your mindset?

To answer these questions, we can look to research conducted by Campos et al. (2017) who tried to improve the performance of entrepreneurs using two different training techniques. The first technique was a traditional approach to entrepreneurial education where entrepreneurs were exposed to information about traditional topics like accounting, financial planning, and marketing. The second technique focused more on developing an entrepreneurial mindset by encouraging entrepreneurs to emphasize and practise three types of behaviour: proactiveness, innovativeness, and resilience. Campos et al. (2017) observed a positive effect on the profits of organizations that were given the entrepreneurial mindset method of training relative to those trained in the traditional approach. The entrepreneurial mindset approach led to, on average, a 30 per cent increase in profits in the 2.5 years following the training. Interestingly, the entrepreneurial mindset approach helped to boost profits for businesses that were already quite profitable and those businesses that were not as profitable. Importantly, this study did not indicate that the traditional method of training is not useful—indeed, it is possible the best method of training entrepreneurs combines both the traditional and entrepreneurial mindset methods. Nevertheless, it did provide some evidence that the entrepreneurial mindset is something that can be improved.

 Now that we have established the entrepreneurial mindset as something that can be worked on, let's consider the traits that research has linked with successful entrepreneurs and provide some opportunities for you to enhance your own entrepreneurial mindset. Critically, while these are relatively simple concepts to learn, perfecting them takes repeated practice. Building an entrepreneurial mindset is a bit like going to the gym—it's not enough to learn how to lift a dumbbell, you have to practise lifting the dumbbell and increasing the weight to derive benefit. Building an entrepreneurial mindset is really a form of mental exercise!

13.4.1 **Proactivity**

Proactivity is acting early to take control of a situation and focusing on future potential (Bindl & Parker, 2011). For an entrepreneur, being proactive is often the difference between launching a new product or service before others, or failing to get it off the ground because competitors beat you to the opportunity. Being proactive is also the difference between planning ahead and acting on your own timeline versus following the leader and having to react to the behaviour of others. In one's personal life, proactivity is working on a task in advance of an important deadline versus having to rush to finish right before the deadline. Proactivity is also believing that through initiative and hard work, you can influence your chances of succeeding, versus believing that your fate is already determined. How does someone develop a more proactive mindset? One of the most important ways is to become skilled at setting and working towards goals for the future. One type of exercise is to practise forming effective goals that are SMART: specific, measurable, ambitious, realistic, and time-bound (as introduced in Section 5.5.2). Declaring goals in this format helps you to work more effectively towards achieving them. Goals that are specific and measurable are ones where you can clearly determine whether you were successful or failed at your goal. Ambitious and realistic goals are those that are difficult to achieve but not impossible. Finally, time-bound goals have a specific date when the goal needs to be achieved. Structuring your goals will help you to act and work more effectively towards actually achieving them.

13.4.2 **Innovativeness**

Innovativeness is inventing something new or novel. This might be a novel type of product or service, novel processes such as a new way to make or deliver an existing product/service, or a novel way of relating with customers, such as a new type of customer service. For an entrepreneur, innovativeness is essential as it allows even a small enterprise to offer something superior to existing alternatives that are already offered, often by larger and more well-resourced organizations. Being innovative is the difference between having to compete for the same customers against an already established business, or instead, offering a new product to an untapped or underserved group of customers. Finally, being innovative is the difference between getting customers to notice and love the distinctiveness of your company, and having them view you as just another company no different than your competitors. How does someone have a more innovative mindset? One of the best ways to do this is to practise a three-step exercise to come up with innovative/creative ideas:

1. Identify 10 assumptions regarding a product/service category.
2. Question what assumptions are necessary/true and/or create random combinations.
3. Suspend judgement and find some potential in the ideas you have.

In this exercise, you will learn that innovation often occurs when you are able to break from your assumptions and resist shutting down ideas that seem bizarre, silly, or impossible. You can help to break from your assumptions through the random combination of words or pictures— but it is up to you to be brave enough to consider ideas that others might ridicule. In almost any bizarre, silly, or seemingly impossible idea, there is likely a grain of creative potential; part of being creative is asking 'what if' instead of criticizing an idea too early.

We can also see what innovativeness looks like in Imperial in Running case 13.2.

13

RUNNING CASE 13.2 FACING CHANGE HEAD-ON WITH AN ENTREPRENEURIAL MINDSET

Though Lucy is pleased with the entrepreneurial 'can-do' attitude that is now present in many parts of the business, she feels much more needs to happen. Her brother, William as CFO has been broadly supportive of the changes, though his original complaints are still, Lucy has to admit, valid: if they want to pay the wages and the rapidly increasing other bills ('Our energy costs are literally going through the roof, Lucy: every time we switch the heating on in the factory, I can see a fortune disappearing into thin air!', he said recently), these new ideas have to pay, and pretty quickly. At the same time, Lucy believes, this different world requires more than just a positive payback calculation: growth in these new markets will only come if Imperial communicates its values and starts to make a difference in the lives of its future customers.

It's with these considerations in mind that Lucy is intrigued by a proposal made by Sara Mbese, the Customer Service Centre Supervisor. Sara's team manages the day-to-day communications with Imperial's customers. Sara has pointed out to Lucy and marketing manager, Gita that if they want the vegan foods to be a success, they will have to think about communicating not just with their long-standing customers—the food suppliers, retailers, and catering groups—but now that they offer direct-to-consumer products, with their new consumers.

They already know that there is a lot of change happening in dietary preferences and strong interest in understanding the ingredients of food products. This is one of the reasons that Saffron Walden, Imperial's social media lead has recommended they collaborate with social media influencer @plantbasedstudent.

In the past, customers seem to have accepted and understood traditional food products, so Saffron seldom received social media enquiries from consumers. However, those wanting to try plant-based foods using alternative proteins are behaving differently. They're more inquisitive about the origin of foods and more values-driven. If the vegan lasagne, for example, is going to be a success, there will need to be a whole lot more information available about it than they've ever had to provide for a traditional lasagne.

Sara in the customer service centre is therefore proposing that they address these new customer needs (and take care of their current staff shortage) by starting a chatbot, which they're calling the Food Imp. She, Gita, and other staff have got together and developed some initial scripts, and Weijing Liu, the IT manager, has already started talking to contacts in the university's Computer Science faculty who are specialists in AI. The Food Imp will go onto the Imperial website and will become a source of knowledge for any consumer interested in plant-based food consumption and in nutritional health generally. As a result, Imperial will be seen, they hope, as an innovator and a source of reassuring expertise. Lucy is intrigued by the plan and has asked Sara and Weijing to set up a trial. William, who was sceptical when he heard about the idea ('I hate those chatbox things, Lucy!'), has become much more enthusiastic as Lucy points out the potential to increase sales without increasing staff numbers. He is going to work with the customer service team and the IT team to calculate the investment required.

Lucy is now seeing more of this intrapreneurial spirit among the staff. Bella and Dylan from the food prep team have been to see her recently to propose a new service that will show the world how socially committed Imperial is. 'We hate the idea that some of our food products go to waste every day while people are going hungry in the city,' they'd said. 'We'd like to cut down food waste by tracking expiring food at the customers' sites, collecting it instead of them throwing it away, and taking it to food banks, community fridges, and homeless shelters.' Lucy thinks this sounds appealing in principle, but complicated in practice. So, she has asked them to work with Harbin Singh, Imperial's Logistics Supervisor: if they can persuade him, she says, she will think about letting them implement the idea themselves. She's looking forward to hearing the results and to talking these through with Operations Director, Bob in their next Operations meeting. And she knows many more ideas will need to follow: the world is changing constantly, so Imperial will need to innovate constantly if it's going to remain relevant.

As she cycles home that evening, Lucy looks back on her first year in charge. There's lots to do, from sustainability planning to expanding the vegan products business to making a final decision on the company's name. But there's also so much to be proud of, and so much to look forward to. Next year, she's sure, will be a great one for Imperial Fine Foods.

Questions for reflection

1. What types of entrepreneurial activity are possible in emerging markets like plant-based foods?

2. What are the biggest challenges companies like Imperial face in acting entrepreneurially?

3. If you were setting up a plant-based foods company, how would you use your entrepreneurial skills to win business from companies like Imperial?

13.4.3 Resilience

Resilience is being able to bounce back when setbacks happen, such as when your idea is dismissed, or your new business does not succeed. It is also about being able to avoid, adapt to, and/or change situations where setbacks are likely to happen. There is oftentimes a belief that entrepreneurs are big risk-takers. Entrepreneurs are proactive and do things differently than others. Being proactive and innovative inherently involves risk because when you do something first or new, it of course might not work out. In this sense, entrepreneurs are risk-takers. Yet, entrepreneurs often use a variety of methods to reduce the chance of something going wrong. For an entrepreneur, being resilient may be the difference between meeting a barrier and giving up on their idea, or finding a way to overcome that barrier and succeed in the future. Being resilient is also the difference between being able to learn from and adapt to likely setbacks, rather than repeatedly encountering the same problem.

How does someone have a more resilient mindset? One of the best ways to do this is to bootstrap—to creatively appreciate and use resources already available to you instead of paying money for something. The term originally refers to the strap attached to a boot, which enables you to pull it on with no assistance from others, or from other tools. For example, instead of an entrepreneur buying a new piece of machinery to create a product or service, might it be possible for them to share that machinery with another organization? By conserving money, an entrepreneur is able to preserve their options because cash allows entrepreneurs flexibility. If the entrepreneur encounters a difficult situation like an economic downturn or an unexpected failure of key machinery, this extra cash will be critical in helping the business bounce back from this difficulty. To assist you in the exercise of bootstrapping, all you need to do is remember several key principles represented by the acronym STRAP: sharing resources, trading resources, reusing or repurposing resources, adjusting the timing of resource movement, and partnering to better utilize resources.

13.4.4 Resiliently innovative and proactive

A highly entrepreneurial mindset is not just characterized by resilience, innovativeness, or proactiveness—but instead by all three. In other words, highly successful entrepreneurs think about ways to be resiliently innovative and proactive—see Figure 13.4. What does a combination

13

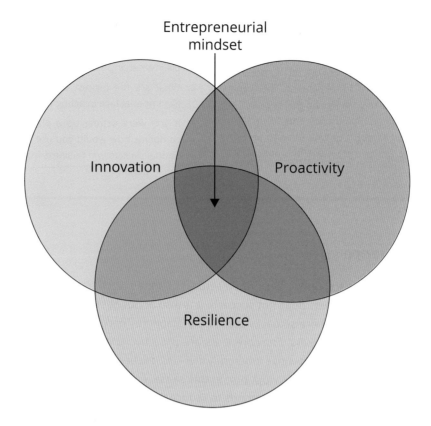

FIGURE 13.4 **The entrepreneurial mindset.**

of these three concepts look like? When you are resiliently innovative and proactive you tend to grow in your capabilities as a person and to focus on always growing your organization to be better. That is, at the core of an entrepreneurial mindset is a focus on a growth mindset—a belief that your abilities can be developed through hard work, trial and error, and feedback (Dweck, 2006). This is in contrast to a fixed mindset where you believe that your own abilities are stable and cannot change. As you might guess, because of the importance of learning and adaptation in the entrepreneurial process, having a growth mindset as an entrepreneur is critical.

You see an emphasis on growth in all three of the entrepreneurs we have featured in the chapter Spotlights:

- Stu Landesberg started out not focusing his company on environmental sustainability, but grew this expertise in response to early customer feedback;
- Danielle Jezienicki approached the challenge of eliminating plastic from hundreds of products by believing in her ability to bring together a team to change the practices within an established large organization; and
- Rochelle Webb believed she could improve the success of under-represented entrepreneurs and acted on that belief.

Each one of these behaviours indicates a strong growth mindset centred around the self-belief by the entrepreneur that they can be resiliently innovative and proactive.

13.5 **Conclusion**

Entrepreneurship and innovation are related concepts which focus on creating and implementing something new. While this can happen in the case of a new venture—focused on either profit, a social/environmental issue, or a combination of these—these ideas are also applicable to a wide range of situations including in large organizations where innovation is often called 'intrapreneurship'. The examples of Stu Landesberg starting Grove Collaborative, Danielle Jezienicki helping to change the course of a larger company, and Rochelle Webb starting an enterprise to tackle a social problem, show that entrepreneurship can take many forms. In essence, entrepreneurship is the discovery, evaluation, and pursuit of opportunities which add value. Entrepreneurship is both a manageable process characterized by experimentation with novel ideas and a mindset characterized by proactivity, innovativeness, and resilience. Critically, this means that being a successful entrepreneur embracing innovation is something attainable to anyone who is seriously interested in the process of growing yourself and an organization, to create added value in the world.

CHAPTER SUMMARY

○ Entrepreneurship involves identifying an opportunity to build or create something new which, in turn, results in value creation for an individual, community, or society.

○ Innovation broadly refers to something 'new' being introduced (a product/service, process, etc.) which can be defined on a continuum from incremental to radical.

○ Broadly, three types of entrepreneurship exist: new venture creation where a new enterprise is established; intrapreneurship where innovation takes place within large or established organizations; and sustainable entrepreneurship where rather than just a profit motive, the focus is on solving a societal or environmental problem.

○ Entrepreneurship can be considered a process which comprises three stages: discovering, evaluating, and pursuing opportunities.

○ Entrepreneurship can also be considered a mindset which emphasizes proactivity, innovativeness, and resilience.

CLOSING CASE REFLECTION

Winnow innovating to prevent food waste

Winnow founder, Marc Zornes adopted an entrepreneurial mindset to develop and launch a new venture that would address the sustainability challenge of food waste in corporate kitchens. While the rest of the world views food waste as an intractable problem, Zornes identified it as 'one of the three biggest global OPPORTUNITIES to save resources' (Plotkin, 2018). Zornes was explicitly aware of seeking to reassemble resources in an innovative new solution and

13

proactively sought ways to meet this opportunity, recognizing that 'if I could prevent food waste, then I could save a business money [and] if I could save the business money and have them pay me a lower amount than what they saved, then I would have a business model' (Plotkin, 2018). Since its launch in 2014, Winnow—now operating in 45 countries—reports that it has saved 36.5 million meals from the trash. In 2017, Winnow's ability to achieve a balance between economic profit as well as social and environmental outcomes helped the organization achieve the coveted B Corp Certification (Benefit Corporation, n.d.) (featured in Spotlight 2.2).

REVIEW QUESTIONS

1. Give an example of an incremental innovation and a radical innovation. What makes them incremental or radical? Which category of innovation is more important for society?

2. Give examples of the behaviours of the entrepreneurs profiled in this chapter that demonstrate their innovativeness. Why do you say so?

3. Which of the Four S evaluation criteria do you think would be most difficult for an entrepreneur to answer? Why? In what ways might this depend on the type of enterprise?

4. How have you employed an entrepreneurial mindset when solving a problem? Can you identify ways you might improve your approach?

5. To what extent do social and environmental problems benefit from the attention of entrepreneurs? Why do you think this is?

EXPLORE MORE

● WATCH 'How Grove CEO Stuart Landesberg Finally Scored a "Yes" after 75 Rejected Pitches', by Inc. Search for the title on YouTube.

● WATCH 'Eric Ries: Building a Startup for Long Term Success' by J. P. Morgan. Search for the title on YouTube.

● WATCH an overview of the business model canvas—what parallels and differences do you see with the 4S idea evaluation framework? Search YouTube for 'Business Model Canvas Explained'.

≡ READ 'Why Design Thinking Works: It Addresses the Biases and Behaviors That Hamper Innovation' by Jeanne Liedtka, *Harvard Business Review*, September–October 2018. What parallels and differences does it hold from the entrepreneurial process?

≡ EXPLORE some of the world's most promising sustainable entrepreneurs by searching for companies that have earned certification on the B Corps website.

≡ READ Carol S. Dweck's book, *Mindset—Updated Edition: Changing the Way You Think to Fulfill Your Potential*, Little, Brown Book Group, 2017.

13

GLOSSARY

Basic underlying assumptions Deeply held beliefs by group members, but may be at a subconscious level and so not discussed (or discussable).

Brand A name, term, design, symbol, or any other feature that identifies one seller's goods or service as distinct from those of other sellers'.

Budgeting A process of estimating expected income and expenses, often to determine the financial implications and viability of plans.

Bureaucracy A complex organization that has multilayered systems and processes. The systems and processes may slow the organization's decision-making but help to maintain uniformity and control.

Business An organization engaged in some form of trade: the production, distribution, and sale of goods or services for profit.

Capabilities The organizational activities and knowledge necessary to effectively use resources, which are likely to depend on the skills and knowledge of people in developing and managing systems and processes.

Capacity management The act of ensuring a business maximizes its potential activities and production output—at all times, under all conditions.

Change management Driving or delivering both proactive and reactive changes within an organization.

Characteristics (of a person) The qualities or features that belong to that person and make them recognizable.

Climate change Changes in the global climate (long-term weather patterns) caused by the increasing average global temperatures, which are themselves caused by greenhouse gas (GHG) emissions.

Consumer An individual who uses a product, service, or experience.

Contextual barriers Barriers related to the context in which the organization exists, such as inappropriate organizational culture and difficulties in changing it, or lack of innovation or problem-solving mindset among teams.

Cooperation The process of working together to achieve the same end.

Coordination The process of interaction which occurs between individuals who have interdependent tasks.

Corporate Social Responsibility (CSR) The responsibilities businesses have for the world around them.

Creative industries A range of economic activities that have creativity at their centre, including fashion, crafts, visual arts, music, publishing, TV, radio, and film.

Critical thinking A cognitive process of actively and carefully evaluating the reasoning and evidence behind knowledge and arguments, and developing defensible knowledge and arguments ourselves.

Culture Shared ways of thinking, feeling, and behaving.

Customer An individual, household, or organization that pays for a product, service, or experience.

Decent work Work that respects fundamental human rights, protects health, safety, and the environment in the workplace and provides a living wage.

Decision-making The process of making choices, individually or with a group of people.

Deliberate strategy A top-down approach in which senior leadership and key organizational members develop a specific strategy for a period of time, which is often communicated in a static document.

Demand Market demand refers to the willingness and ability of all consumers in a market to purchase a given good.

Developed country A country with sustained economic growth, security, high per capita income, and advanced technological infrastructure.

Digital The part of the organization responsible for all technological aspects likely to include hardware and software, as well as data storage and security.

Direct stakeholders Stakeholders with their own voice and access to be able to express their interest in the organization.

Disruptions Changes to an existing industry or market due (usually) to technological change.

Distinctive resources and capabilities Resources and capabilities which are unique, or at least rare, and difficult for others to copy, giving the organization competitive advantage, or the ability to achieve their purpose through value creation.

Ecosystem A business ecosystem is the network of organizations—including suppliers, distributors, customers, competitors, government agencies, and so on—involved in the delivery of a specific product or service.

Emergent strategy A pattern of successive actions or behaviours that are consistent over time, which may be informed by an overall direction or deliberate strategy, but is more flexible and adaptive.

Employee An individual that an organization hires to do a particular job.

Employer A person or company that provides a job paying wages or a salary to one or more people.

Employment relationship The legal link between employers and employees which exists when a person performs work or services in return for payment.

Equality, diversity, and inclusion (EDI) EDI focuses on creating working environments where every individual can feel safe, have a sense of belonging, and can achieve their full potential. Breaking these terms down further: equality is about ensuring equality of access, treatment, outcomes, and impact in both employment and service delivery; diversity recognizes that everyone is different in a variety of visible and non-visible ways, respecting and celebrating those differences; inclusion is the practice of including people in a way that is fair for all and empowering each person to be themselves and thrive at work. (Adapted from CIPD (2022) Factsheet.)

Espoused beliefs and values Beliefs and values employees *claim* to have (even if their behaviour suggests otherwise).

Experiment A procedure carried out to support or refute a hypothesis, or determine the efficacy or likelihood of something previously untried.

External environment Comprises elements that influence the organization, but which are largely beyond their direct control, including ecosystems and nature, societal trends, government at varying levels, suppliers, interest groups, and individuals such as clients or customers.

Externality An indirect cost or benefit incurred by a third party due to the actions of another.

Factory floor The people in a factory who make the products rather than its office workers or managers, or the place in a factory where the products are made.

Factory A building or group of buildings where goods are manufactured or assembled chiefly by machine.

Finance The part of the organization responsible for the monetary inflow and outflow in the organization, as well as debt and borrowing, and reporting on these aspects.

Flat structure An organizational structure with only a few layers of management.

Functional department A section of an organization that is in charge of specific activities within the organization—for example, the human resources department, the marketing department, the IT department.

Geopolitics Interactions between politics, geography, power, and economies which contribute to international treaties or disputes, trade agreements or barriers, cooperation or conflict.

Gig economy A labour market that focuses on temporary, short-term contracting of individuals for very specific projects, whereby workers gain flexibility and independence, but lack job security and benefits.

Governance The system by which an organization is controlled and held to account for the actions and decisions of management.

Hierarchical structure An organizational structure, resembling a pyramid, that follows a chain of command from top executives to regular employees.

HR business partner An internal role in an organization that sits within the HR department; the HR business partner helps to advise line managers across the organization in their role of managing employees.

Human resource barriers Barriers such as lack of skills, training and education, employee turnover, lack of management or employee commitment to the organization as well as lack of motivation and satisfaction generally.

Human resources (HR) This term is often used to refer to the pool of human capital under the firm's control. The term human resources may also be used to refer to the intrinsic resources of people (such as knowledge, skills, and abilities).

Human resources The part of the organization focused on all aspects of employees including recruitment, training, and performance monitoring.

Impact-washing A form of greenwashing in which organizations make commitments to a purpose shift, but whose actions do not reflect such commitment.

Incremental innovation Making a series of small improvements or upgrades to an company's existing product, service, process, or method.

Indirect stakeholders Stakeholders who lack their own voice or access in the organization because they lack power, are remote from the organization, do not exist yet (e.g. future generations), or literally have no voice (e.g. nature and ecosystems).

Industrial revolution A period characterized by significant changes in the means of production that powers economic activity.

Informal sector The part of any economy that is neither taxed nor monitored by any form of government.

Information and communications technology (ICT) The internet, wireless networks, mobile phone networks, computers, software, video conferencing, social networking, and apps and services, which exist to enable users to access, retrieve, store, transmit, and manipulate information in digital form.

Inimitability The quality of a resource or capability that makes it difficult, if not impossible, to copy.

Inside-out resource-based view Sees organizational success as largely dependent on what and how many resources the organization has access to, and how managers best leverage and use those resources.

Interdependence The dependence of two or more people on each other.

Internal environment Comprises elements within the organization's direct influence including its strategy and culture.

Inter-organizational Occurring between or involving two or more organizations.

In-work poverty Occurs when the total net income of a household, where at least one working-age adult is employed, is insufficient to meet the household's needs (St Vincent de Paul Society).

Job The specific tasks and duties an individual engages in to earn a living.

Lean production an approach to operations and supply chains that focuses on cutting out waste while ensuring quality.

Liability The extent to which an individual person who owns part of a business can be held legally responsible for it, including in relation to its debts.

Limited company An ownership structure whereby the business issues a certain number of shares, which are bought by individuals or other companies, who become shareholders.

Limited liability The owner (or owners) cannot be held personally responsible for the business (including for its debts).

Line manager An employee who directly manages other employees and day-to-day operations while reporting to a higher-ranking manager.

Macro-external environment Aspects of the external environment that may not have an immediate, directly identifiable, or tangible impact on the organization's existence, purpose, or operations.

Management A social and operational process with the aim of bringing people and other resources together in order to get something done.

Marketing The part of the organization focused on customers and responsible for the design, development, promotion, and sale of goods and services.

Mentee A person who is advised, trained, or counselled by a mentor.

Mentor Someone who teaches or gives help and advice to a less experienced, often younger colleague.

Micro-external environment Aspects of the external environment that have an immediate, directly identifiable, and tangible impact on the organization's existence, purpose, or operations.

Mindset A mental attitude or inclination.

Monitoring The process of observing, recording, or detecting what has occurred in the organization.

Motivating The process of providing others with a motive, cause, or reason to act.

Motivation The impetus that gives purpose or direction to human behaviour at a conscious or unconscious level. It results in a desire to change either the self or the environment.

Multidimensional Having many different parts or aspects.

Multinational organization Any corporation that is registered and operates in more than one country at a time; generally the organization has headquarters in one country and operates wholly or partially owned subsidiaries in other countries.

Non- departmental public body A type of organization established by a government for the delivery of a service, but not directly run by government within their departments.

Observable artefacts Things in an organization that are easily seen, observed, experienced, identified, and are typically highly tangible.

Operational plan Focuses on a very specific and relatively stand-alone goal, and is likely to be developed by front-line managers directly involved in that particular function.

Operations The part of the organization responsible for the production of goods and/or the delivery of services.

Operations management The activities and processes that an organization engages in to convert materials into finished products or services, in order to keep the organization running and earning money.

Organizing The process of coordinating resources, activities, and tasks in order to implement the strategy and plans.

Organizational culture The pattern of basic assumptions that an organization has invented, discovered, or developed and therefore taught to new members as the correct way to think, feel, and behave.

Organizational environment The set of circumstances that influence the organization.

Organizational fit How an individual's own values and beliefs fit with those of the organization.

Organizational justice The extent to which employees perceive workplace procedures, interactions, and outcomes to be fair.

Organizational support Systems, structures, and processes which ensure employees are able to take advantage of the resources and capabilities they possess.

Organizations A collective of people, working together, with a particular purpose, typically comprising structures, hierarchies, legal contracts, employees, strategies, and plans.

Outside-in market-based view Sees organizational success as largely dependent on it being aligned with the external environment in which it operates.

Partnership An ownership structure whereby a business is co-owned by a group of at least two individuals.

Personality Enduring characteristics and behaviours that comprise a person's unique approach to life, including traits, interests, drives, values, abilities, and emotional patterns.

Physical goods Goods that you can touch and feel, such as a piece of furniture or a computer, as opposed to intangible goods such as software or legal advice.

Plan Specifies what resources, activities, and processes are needed in what combination, in order to achieve an objective.

Planning A process of determining and documenting how a strategy or objective can be achieved.

Poverty Not having enough material resources to meet basic needs once the cost of living is taken into account (St Vincent de Paul Society).

Private sector Comprises organizations engaged in some form of trade: the production, distribution, and sale of goods or services for profit—often referred to as businesses.

Procedural barriers Barriers that are related to the process of change and how things get done.

Process A series of actions or steps taken in order to achieve a particular end.

Procurement Obtaining or purchasing goods or services, typically for business purposes.

Productivity A measure of how efficiently a person completes a task.

Profit The difference between how much is earned in a trade as compared to how much the trade costs the seller.

Psychometric approach An approach focused on finding the applicant that best 'fits' the role/organization. The approach assumes jobs can be clearly defined and will often apply testing, measurement, and assessment techniques from the field of psychology to identify the most suitable candidate.

Public enterprise A type of organization created and funded by national governments to oversee certain aspects of the economy or society, but run independently from government.

Public goods Includes goods or services that benefit all members of society, usually provided without cost for users.

Public sector Comprises organizations that are typically wholly or largely owned (and often run) by government.

Queueing theory Also known as Little's Law, states that the time taken to process each unit (the cycle time), multiplied by the total number of units waiting in a queue (the work in process) equals the total amount of time it will take for a new unit entering the queue to get through the whole system (the **throughput time**).

Radical innovation Creating an entirely new product, service, process, or method that breaks dramatically from what has happened before.

Rarity The quality of a resource or capability being unique or rare.

Regulator An organization appointed by national or regional government to set standards for an area of society's activity such as banking or industry practices.

Reporting Providing typically written accounts of what has occurred in the organization in relation to outputs, outcomes, and performance, as well as the implications of these.

Resource and capability audit A tool which allows an organization to identify and categorize all of the resources and capabilities that comprise its internal environment.

Resources Things an organization possesses, or has access to, that they can use in their activities, which might be human, physical, financial, or intangible.

Retailer A company that buys products from a manufacturer or wholesaler and sells them to end users or customers.

Rewards Rewards are an important component of the employment relationship between employer and employee. They comprise extrinsic rewards, such as pay, and intrinsic rewards, such as status and enjoyment.

Segmentation Dividing a market of existing and potential customers into subgroups of customers based on shared characteristics.

Shareholder A shareholder can be a person, company, or organization that holds shares in a given company.

Sole trader An ownership structure whereby a business is owned by one person.

Stakeholder analysis The process of identifying all of the people, groups, and organizations who impact or are impacted by the organization.

Stakeholders Any one group or individual who can affect or is affected by the achievement of the organization's purpose.

Strategic barriers Barriers that arise where there is a mismatch between an organization's chosen strategy and the appropriate strategy.

Strategic plan Overall plan for the organization and is akin to its strategy.

Strategy An organization's long-term direction or overriding objective linked to its purpose.

Structural barriers Barriers related to organizational structure—either too hierarchical or too flat—but may also include a lack of resources required for the change to be effective.

Subordinates People under the authority or control of another within an organizational structure.

Super wicked problems Wicked problems that have further complexity as time is running out, there is no central authority, those seeking to solve the problem are also causing it, and policies fail to take sufficient account of the future.

Supply chain A logistics system that consists of facilities that convert raw materials into finished products and distribute them to end consumers or end customers.

Supply network A supply network is a cluster of suppliers that assist a business in adding value for customers by manufacturing and delivering products.

Tactical decisions Short-term, specific actions that a company takes to achieve its strategic goals.

Tactical plan The level below a strategic plan, and aims to translate the strategic plan into a specific plan for each of the organization's key departments

Target market A subset of the market identified by the organization through the process of market segmentation. A group of customers or consumers with shared characteristics identified as a potential target for the organization's products or services.

Tasks Activities that need to be done as part of a person's job.

Third sector Comprises organizations with some form of social or environmental mission, which are neither private nor public sector, and sometimes referred to as the voluntary or civic sector.

Three-legged stool An approach that links line managers with the HR department to effectively manage the human resources in the organization.

Threshold resources and capabilities Resources and capabilities necessary for an organization to achieve and maintain a minimum performance level.

Throughput time The amount of time that it takes to run a process in its entirety from start to finish.

Traits Aspects of an individual's personality often measured on a scale, such as degree of extraversion or introversion.

Unconscious bias Occurs when people make judgements or decisions on the basis of prior experience, personal deep-seated thought patterns, assumptions or interpretations, and are not aware that they are doing it.

Unlimited liability The owner (or owners) can be held personally responsible for the business (including for its debts).

Value proposition A concise statement of the benefits that a company is delivering to customers who buy its products or services.

Value The relative worth of something which is often, but not always, linked to economic worth, or, in relation to the VRIO framework specifically, the quality of a resource or capability being valuable to the organization either directly or indirectly.

Vertically integrated organization One in which key stages of the supply chain are maintained 'in-house' directly by the organization rather than outsourced to partner organizations, with a key advantage being greater control over every stage of the supply chain.

VUCA Prime manager An acronym developed to outline how a manager should respond to a VUCA world, comprising vision, understanding, clarity, and agility.

VUCA world Acronym that describes the changing nature of the world comprising volatility, uncertainty, complexity, and ambiguity.

Wicked problems Difficult or impossible to solve problems due to contradictory information or changing requirements, which often lack 'right or wrong' solutions, and where solutions create or reveal other problems.

Work Activity involving mental or physical effort in order to accomplish or produce something.

REFERENCES

Chapter 1

Brech, E. F. L. (1957). *Organization: The Framework of Management*. London: Longman.

Bridgman, T., and Cummings, S. (2021). *A Very Short, Fairly Interesting and Reasonably Cheap Book about Management Theory*. London: Sage.

Crane, A., LeBaron, G., Phung, K., Behbahani, L., and Allain, J. (2021). 'Confronting the Business Models of Modern Slavery', *Journal of Management Inquiry*. Feb. doi:10.1177/1056492621994904

Cummings, S., and Bridgman, T. (2021). *The Past, Present and Future of Sustainable Management: From the Conservation Movement to Climate Change*. Cham: Palgrave Pivot.

Cummings, S., Bridgman, T., Hassard, J., and Rowlinson, M. (2017). *A New History of Management*. Cambridge: Cambridge University Press.

Drucker, P. F. (1954). *The Practice of Management*. New York: Harper & Row.

Graham, P. (1995). *Mary Parker Follett: Prophet of Management*. Boston: Harvard Business School Press.

How, W.-C. (2003). *Sun Zi Art of War*. Pearson Education Asia.

Ivory, S. B. (2021). *Becoming a Critical Thinker: For Your University Studies and Beyond*. Oxford: Oxford University Press.

Johnson, A. (2023). *Indra Nooyi*, https://www.womenshistory.org/education-resources/biographies/indra-nooyi (accessed 17 Mar. 2023).

Kollewe, J. (2021). 'Covid-19 vaccines: The Contracts, Prices and Profits', *The Guardian*, 12 Aug., https://www.theguardian.com/world/2021/aug/11/covid-19-vaccines-the-contracts-prices-and-profits (accessed 4 Sept. 2023).

Koontz, H., and O'Donnell, C. (1984). *Management*, 8th ed. USA: McGraw-Hill.

Larcker, D. F., and Tayan, B. (2020). 'Diversity in the C-Suite: The Dismal State of Diversity among Fortune 100 Senior Executives', *Stanford Closer Look Series*, 1 Apr., https://www.gsb.stanford.edu/sites/default/files/publication-pdf/cgri-closer-look-82-diversity-among-f100.pdf (accessed 4 Sept. 2023).

Mackay, B., Arevuo, M., Mackay, D., and Meadows, M. (2020). *Strategy: Theory, Practice, Implementation*. Oxford: Oxford University Press.

Mintzberg, H. (1973). *The Nature of Managerial Work*. New York: Harper and Row.

Nooyi, I. (2021). *My Life in Full: Work Family, and our Future*. London: Piatkus.

Office for National Statistics. (2023). 'Private Sector Employment as % of Total Employment; UK; HC; SA; Percentage', https://www.ons.gov.uk/employmentandlabourmarket/peopleinwork/employmentandemployeetypes/timeseries/g9c2/lms (accessed 14 Mar. 2023).

Tsoukas, H. (1994). 'What Is Management? An Outline of a Metatheory', *British Journal of Management*, 5(4): 289–301.

Chapter 2

Almquist, R., Grossi, G., van Helden, G. J., and Reichard, C. (2013). 'Public Sector Governance and Accountability', *Critical Perspectives on Accounting*, 24(7–8): 479–487.

B Lab. (2023). 'About B Lab', https://www.bcorporation.net/en-us/movement/about-b-lab/ (accessed 22 May 2023).

Battilana, J., and Dorado, S. (2010). 'Building Sustainable Hybrid Organizations: The Case of Commercial Microfinance Organizations', *Academy of Management Journal*, 53(6): 1419–1440.

Business Roundtable. (2019). 'Business Roundtable Redefines the Purpose of a Corporate to Promote "An Economy That Serves All Americans"', https://www.businessroundtable.org/business-roundtable-redefines-the-purpose-of-a-corporation-to-promote-an-economy-that-serves-all-americans (accessed 21 Apr. 2023).

CompaniesMarketCap. (2023). 'Companies Ranked by Number of Employees', https://companiesmarketcap.com/largest-companies-by-number-of-employees/ (accessed 14 Mar. 2023).

Flynn, N. (2016). *Public Sector Management*. London: Sage.

Gillespie, A. (2019). *Foundations of Economics*. Fifth Edition. Oxford University Press.

Hudson, M., and Rogan, L. (2009). *Managing without Profit: Leadership, Management & Governance of Third-Sector Organisations in Australia*. University of New South Wales Press.

Kim, S., and Schifeling, T. (2016). 'Varied Incumbent Behaviors and Mobilization for New Organizational

Forms: The Rise of Triple-Bottom Line Business amid Both Corporate Social Responsibility and Irresponsibility', https://papers.ssrn.com/sol3/papers.cfm?abstract_id=2794335 (accessed 4 Sept. 2023).

Kim, S., Karlesky, M. J., Myers, C. G., and Schifeling, T. (2016). 'Why Companies Are Becoming B Corporations' *Harvard Business Review*, 17 June.

Lapsley, I. (2009). 'New Public Management: The Cruellest Invention of the Human Spirit?' *Abacus*, 45(1): 1–21.

Marquis, C. (2021). 'Building a Purpose-Driven Movement: Brazil-Based Steel Company Looks to Scale Positive Impact through Supply Chain', *Forbes*, 5 Aug., https://www.forbes.com/sites/christopher marquis/2021/08/05/building-a-purpose-driven-movement-brazil-based-steel-company-looks-to-scale-positive-impact-through-supply-chain/ (accessed 14 Mar. 2023).

NCVO. (2021). *UK Civil Society Almanac 2021*, https://beta.ncvo.org.uk/ncvo-publications/uk-civil-society-almanac-2021/ (accessed 6 Apr. 2023).

Osborne, S. P. (2010). 'Introduction: The (New) Public Governance: A Suitable Case for Treatment?', in S. P. Osborne (ed.), *The New Public Governance? Emerging Perspectives on the Theory and Practice of Public Governance*. London: Routledge.

Remember Singapore. (2014). 'SCDF Heritage Gallery—Singapore's Firefighting History', https://remembersingapore.org/2014/08/22/singapore-firefighting-history/ (accessed 17 Mar. 2023).

Rumpff, L., Wintle, B., Woinarski, J., et al. (2023). '200 Experts Dissected the Black Summer Bushfires in Unprecedented Detail. Here Are 6 Lessons to Heed', https://www.preventionweb.net/news/200-experts-dissected-black-summer-bushfires-unprecedented-detail-here-are-6-lessons-heed#:~:text=The%20Black%20Summer%20bushfires%20of,vulnerable%20species%20were%20worst%20affected (accessed 17 Mar. 2023).

Simwa, A. (2019). 'History of Fire Service in Nigeria', https://www.legit.ng/1216919-history-fire-service-nigeria.html (accessed 17 Mar. 2023).

Statista. (2022a). 'The 100 largest companies in the world ranked by revenue in 2022', https://www.statista.com/statistics/263265/top-companies-in-the-world-by-revenue/#:~:text=Walmart%20was%20also%20the%20largest,million%20all%20over%20the%20world.&text=The%20concept%20of%20revenue%20itself,from%20one%20company%20to%20another (accessed 14 Mar. 2023).

Statista. (2022b). 'The 100 largest companies in the world by market capitalization in 2022',

https://www.statista.com/statistics/263264/top-companies-in-the-world-by-market-capitalization/ (accessed 14 Mar. 2023).

Stout, L. (2012). *The Shareholder Value Myth: How Putting Shareholders First Harms Investors, Corporations, and the Public*. San Francisco: Berrett-Koehler Publications.

Chapter 3

Bank of England. (2019). 'Climate Change: What Are the Risks to Financial Stability?', https://www.bankofengland.co.uk/knowledgebank/climate-change-what-are-the-risks-to-financial-stability (accessed 8 Sept. 2023).

Bennis, W., and Nanus, B. (1985). *Leaders: The Strategies for Taking Charge*. New York: Harper Row.

B Lab. (2021). 'SDG Insights Report', Sept., https://www.bcorporation.net/en-us/sdgs/17-days-17-goals (accessed 25 Apr. 2023).

Bowen, H. R. (1953). *Social Responsibility of the Businessman*. New York: Harper & Row.

Brundtland, G. H. (1987). *Our Common Future: Report of the World Commission on Environment and Development*. United Nations, Geneva, http://www.un-documents.net/ocf-ov.htm (accessed 26 Apr. 2023).

Cambridge Centre for Housing and Planning Research. (2021). '"Pay the Wi-Fi or Feed the Children": Coronavirus Has Intensified the UK's Digital Divide', *University of Cambridge*, https://www.cam.ac.uk/stories/digitaldivide (accessed 8 Sept. 2023).

Camillus, J. C. (2008). 'Strategy as a Wicked Problem', *Harvard Business Review*, May, https://hbr.org/2008/05/strategy-as-a-wicked-problem (accessed 8 Sept. 2023).

Carney, M. (2017). '[De]Globalisation and Inflation' [Speech], 2017 IMF Michel Camdessus Central Banking Lecture, p.17, 18 Sept., https://www.bankofengland.co.uk/speech/2017/de-globalisation-and-inflation (accessed 8 Sept. 2023).

Catarino, R., Bretagnolle, V., Perrot, T., Vialloux, F., and Gaba, S. (2019). 'Bee Pollination Outperforms Pesticides for Oilseed Crop Production and Profitability', *Proceedings of the Royal Society B: Biological Sciences*, 286(1912). https://doi.org/10.1098/rspb.2019.1550

Chang, Ha-Joon. (2010). *23 Things They Don't Tell You about Capitalism*. Penguin.

Colgan, J. D. (2013). 'Fueling the Fire: Pathways from Oil to War', *International Security*, 38(2): 147–180, http://www.jstor.org/stable/24480933

Gaddis, J. L. (1989). *The Long Peace: Inquiries into the History of the Cold War*. Oxford: Oxford University Press.

Gilliland, N. (2017). 'A Closer Look at WWF's Social Strategy', https://econsultancy.com/a-closer-look-at-wwf-s-social-strategy/ (accessed 17 Mar. 2023).

Gill, V. (2021). 'Farm Pesticides Killing More Bees—Study', *BBC News*, 5 Aug., https://www.bbc.co.uk/news/science-environment-58089545

GRI (Global Reporting Initiative). (2022). 'State of Progress: Business Contributions to the SDGs', https://www.globalreporting.org/media/ab5lun0h/stg-gri-report-final.pdf (accessed 25 Apr. 2023).

Hoggan, J. (2019). *I'm Right and You're an Idiot*. British Columbia: New Society Publishers.

IUCN Marine and Forest Programmes. (2018). 'Mangroves against the Storm', https://social.shorthand.com/IUCN_forests/nCec1jyqvn/mangroves-against-the-storm (accessed 8 Sept. 2023).

Joffre, L. (2021). 'Efforts of SDG-Focused Companies Slammed in New Report', Pioneer Post, 3 Sept., https://www.pioneerspost.com/news-views/20210903/efforts-of-sdg-focused-companies-slammed-new-report (accessed 25 Apr. 2023).

Johansen, R. (2012). *Ten New Leadership Skills for an Uncertain World*. 2nd ed. San Francisco: Berrett-Koehler Publishers.

Levin, K., Cashore, B., Bernstein, S., and Auld, G. (2012). 'Overcoming the Tragedy of Super Wicked Problems: Constraining Our Future Selves to Ameliorate Global Climate Change', *Policy Sciences*, 45(2): 123–152.

Macalister, T. (2011). 'Background: What Caused the 1970s Oil Price Shock?' *The Guardian*, 3 Mar., https://www.theguardian.com/environment/2011/mar/03/1970s-oil-price-shock (accessed 8 Sept. 2023).

Munia, H. A., Guillaume, J. H. A., Wada, Y., Veldkamp, T., Virkki, V., and Kummu, M. (2020). 'Future Transboundary Water Stress and Its Drivers under Climate Change: A global study', *Earth's Future*, 8, e2019EF001321, https://doi.org/10.1029/2019EF001321

Murdock, E. G. (2023). 'Indigenous Ecologies', in M. Ramgotra and S. Choat (eds), *Rethinking Political Thinkers*. Oxford: Oxford University Press, 713–730.

Nagabhatla, N., Pouramin, P., Brahmbhatt, R., Fioret, C., Glickman, T., Newbold, K. B., and Smakhtin, V. (2020). 'Water and Migration: A Global Overview'. *UNU-INWEH Report Series, 10*. United Nations University Institute for Water, Environment and Health, Hamilton, Canada, https://www.researchgate.net/profile/Nidhi-Nagabhatla/publication/341323257_Water_and_Migration_A_Global_Overview/links/5ebac41da6fdcc90d66f2753/Water-and-Migration-A-Global-Overview.pdf (accessed 8 Sept. 2023).

Rajan, A. (2020). 'No Such Thing as the Internet', https://www.bbc.co.uk/news/entertainment-arts-54514574 (accessed 28 Apr. 2023).

Raworth, K. (2017). *Doughnut Economics: Seven Ways to Think Like a 21st-Century Economist*. London: Random House.

Ritchie, H., and Roser, M. (2017). *Water Use and Stress*. Our World in Data, https://ourworldindata.org/water-use-stress (accessed 8 Sept. 2023).

Rittel, H. W. J., and Webber, M. M. (1973). 'Dilemmas in a General Theory of Planning', *Policy Sciences*, 4(2): 155–169.

SAB Miller and WWF. (2009). 'Water Footprinting: Identifying and Addressing Water Risks in the Value Chain', https://wwfint.awsassets.panda.org/downloads/sabmiller_water_footprinting_report_final_.pdf (accessed 29 Apr. 2023).

Sanghera, S. (2021). *Empireland*. London: Penguin Books.

Sheikh, P. A. (2010). 'Debt-for-Nature Initiatives and the Tropical Forest Conservation Act: Status and Implementation', Congressional Research Service, https://www.cbd.int/financial/debtnature/g-inventory2010.pdf (accessed 17 Mar. 2023).

Simonite, T. (2021). 'What Really Happened When Google Ousted Timnit Gebru', *Wired*, 8 June, https://www.wired.com/story/google-timnit-gebru-ai-what-really-happened/ (accessed 8 Sept. 2023).

Statista. (2023). 'Inflation rate for the Consumer Price Index (CPI) in the United Kingdom from January 1989 to March 2023', https://www.statista.com/statistics/306648/inflation-rate-consumer-price-index-cpi-united-kingdom-uk/#:~:text=The%20UK%20inflation%20rate%20was,11.1%20percent%20in%20October%202022 (accessed 21 Apr. 2023).

United Nations. (2015). 'Sustainable Development Goals Kick Off with Start of New Year', https://www.un.org/sustainabledevelopment/blog/2015/12/sustainable-development-goals-kick-off-with-start-of-new-year/ (accessed 25 Apr. 2023).

Water online. (2011). 'Former National Leaders: Water a Global Security Issue', 21 March, https://www.wateronline.com/doc/water-a-global-security-issue-0001 (accessed 8 Sept. 2023).

World Economic Forum. (2022). 'Global Risks Report 2022', https://www.weforum.org/reports/global-risks-report-2022/ (accessed 8 Sept. 2023).

World Health Organization. (2021). 'Managing the COVID-19 Infodemic: Promoting Healthy Behaviours and Mitigating the Harm from Misinformation and Disinformation', https://www.who.int/news/item/23-09-2020-managing-the-covid-19-infodemic-promoting-healthy-behaviours-and-mitigating-the-harm-from-misinformation-and-disinformation (accessed 8 Sept. 2023).

Chapter 4

Bloomberg. (2021). 'Covid-Induced Telehealth Boom in East Africa Is Picking Up Pace', 20 Aug., https://www.bloomberg.com/news/articles/2021-08-20/covid-induced-telehealth-boom-in-east-africa-is-picking-up-pace (accessed 8 Sept. 2023).

Economic Times. (2020). *Arab Spring: The first smartphone revolution*, 30 Nov., https://economictimes.indiatimes.com/news/international/saudi-arabia/arab-spring-the-first-smartphone-revolution/articleshow/79487524.cms?from=mdr (accessed 17 Mar. 2023).

Freeman, R.E. (1984). *Strategic Management: A Stakeholder Approach*. Harpercollins College.

Future Startup. (2021). 'OCF Conversation #01: Rethinking Economics For The 21st Century with Kate Raworth' [podcast] OCF Conversation with Shamir Shehab, 20 Sept., https://futurestartup.com/2021/09/20/ocf-conversation-01-rethinking-economics-for-the-21st-century-with-kate-raworth/ (accessed 27 Sept. 2022).

Helpforheroes.org.uk. (2022). 'About Us', https://www.helpforheroes.org.uk/about-us/ (accessed 8 Sept. 2023).

Lecaros, S. S., Ireri, B., Mentis, D., and Kaldjian, E. (2019). 'For the Millions of East Africans Who Need Electricity Most, Data Shows Renewable Energy Is a Viable—and Affordable—Solution', https://www.wri.org/insights/millions-east-africans-who-need-electricity-most-data-shows-renewable-energy-viable-and (accessed 8 Sept. 2023).

Mackay, B., Arevuo, M., Mackay, D., and Meadows, M. (2020). *Strategy: Theory, Practice, Implementation*. Oxford: Oxford University Press.

Mendelow, A. L. (1991). 'Environmental Scanning: The Impact of the Stakeholder Concept'. Proceedings From the *Second International Conference on Information Systems*, 407–418. Cambridge, MA.

Porter, M. E. (1979). 'How Competitive Forces Shape Strategy', *Harvard Business Review*, 57: 137–145.

Raworth, K. (2017). *Doughnut Economics: Seven Ways to Think Like a 21st-Century Economist*. London: Random House.

Sorkin, A. R. (2009). *Too Big to Fail: The Inside Story of How Wall Street and Washington Fought to Save the Financial System—and Themselves*. New York: Viking.

World Economic Forum. (2019). 'Bring the power of solar to Sierra Leone: | Ways to Change the World,' *YouTube*, 16 Dec., https://www.youtube.com/watch?v=auzkln9MMjk (accessed 20 Nov. 2023).

World Economic Forum. (2022). 'DabaDoc', https://www.weforum.org/organizations/dabadoc (accessed 8 Sept. 2023).

World Health Organization. (2022). 'Africa Faces Rising Climate-Linked Health Emergencies', 6 Apr., https://reliefweb.int/report/world/africa-faces-rising-climate-linked-health-emergencies (accessed 8 Sept. 2023).

Chapter 5

Barney, J. (1991). 'Firm Resources and Sustained Competitive Advantage', *Journal of Management*, 17(1): 99–120.

Bazerman, M., and Moore, D. (2008). *Judgment in Managerial Decision Making*, 7th ed. New York: Wiley.

Eisenhardt, K. M., and Zbaracki, M. J. (1992). 'Strategic Decision Making', *Strategic Management Journal*, Winter: 17–37.

Johnson, G., Whittington, R., and Scholes, K. (2011). *Exploring Strategy*. Harlow: Prentice Hall.

Mackay, B., Arevuo, M., Mackay, D., and Meadows, M. (2020). *Strategy: Theory, Practice, Implementation*. Oxford: Oxford University Press.

March, J. G., and Simon, H. A. (1958). *Organizations*. New York: Wiley.

Mintzberg, H. (1994). *The Rise and Fall of Strategic Planning*. New York City: Simon and Schuster.

Mintzberg, H., Ahlstrand, B., and Lampel, J. (2008). *Strategy Safari: The Complete Guide Through the Wilds of Strategic Management*. FT Publishing International.

Mintzberg, H., and Waters J. A. (1985). 'Of Strategies, Deliberate and Emergent', *Strategic Management Journal*, 6(3): 258.

Porter, M. E. (1985). *Competitive Advantage*. New York: Free Press.

Whittington, R. (1996). 'Strategy as Practice', *Long Range Planning*, 29(5): 731–735.

Chapter 6

Abrahamson, E. (2004). *Change without Pain: How Managers Can Overcome Initiative Overload, Organizational Chaos, and Employee Burnout*. Boston: Harvard Business Review Press.

Appelbaum, S. H., Habashy, S., Malo, J. L., and Shafiq, H. (2012). 'Back to the Future: Revisiting Kotter's 1996 Change Model', *Journal of Management Development*, 31(8): 764–782.

Bridgman, T., and Cummings, S. (2021). *A Very Short, Fairly Interesting and Reasonably Cheap Book about Management Theory*. London: Sage.

Byrd, M. Y., and Sparkman, T. E. (2022). 'Reconciling the Business Case and the Social Justice Case for Diversity: A Model of Human Relations', *Human Resource Development Review*, 21(1): 75–100.

Cameron, K. S., and Quinn, R. E. (2011). *Diagnosing and Changing Organizational Culture Based on the Competing Values Framework*, 3rd ed. San Francisco: Jossey-Bass.

CIPD (2022). 'Organisational Climate and culture', https://www.cipd.co.uk/knowledge/culture/working-environment/organisation-culture-change-factsheet#gref (accessed 8 Sept. 2023).

Consultancy EU (2021). 'How to put people at the heart of strategic transformation', https://www.consultancy.eu/news/5559/how-to-put-people-at-the-heart-of-strategic-transformation (accessed 18 Jan. 2023).

Deal, T. E., and Kennedy, A. A. (1982). *Corporate Cultures: The Rites and Rituals of Corporate Life*. Harmondsworth: Penguin Books.

Hall, E. T. (1976). *Beyond Culture*. Anchor.

Hofstede, G. (2022). 'Dimensions of National Culture', https://hi.hofstede-insights.com/national-culture (accessed 16 Jan. 2023).

Johns, G. (2006). 'The Essential Impact of Context on Organizational Behaviour', *Academy of Management Review*, 31(2): 386–408.

Knight, R. (2022). 'Measuring Nonprofit Organisational Culture: Key Issues and Insights', in C. Newton and R. Knight (eds), *Handbook of Research Methods for Organisational Culture*, 230–243. Cheltenham: Edward Elgar.

Knight, R. (2021). 'Is Building a Philanthropic Culture the Key to Your Success?', https://blogs.qut.edu.au/qutex/2021/02/08/is-building-a-philanthropic-culture-the-key-to-your-2021-success/ (accessed 19 Jan. 2023).

Kotter, J. P. (2014). *Accelerate: Building Strategic Agility for a Faster-Moving World*. Harvard Business Press Books.

Kotter, J. P., and Schlesinger, L. A. (1979). 'Choosing Strategies for Change', *Harvard Business Review*, 57(2): 106–114.

Kübler-Ross, E. (1969). *On Death and Dying*. New York: Macmillan.

Lewin, K. (1947). 'Field Theory in Social Science', *Human Relations*, 1(1): 5–41.

McCord, P. (2018). *Powerful: Building a Culture of Freedom and Responsibility*. Silicon Guild.

Mosadeghrad, A. M., and Ansarian, M. (2014). 'Why Do Organisational Change Programmes Fail?', *International Journal of Strategic Change Management*, 5(3): 189–218.

Ogbonna, E., and Harris, L. (2002). 'Organizational Culture: A Ten Year, Two-phase Study of Change in the UK Food Retailing Sector', *Journal of Management Studies*, 39(5): 673–706.

Schein, E. H. (1984). 'Coming to a New Awareness of Organizational Culture', *Sloan Management Review*, Winter: 3–14.

Schein, E. H. (2004). *Organizational Culture and Leadership*. 3rd ed. Hoboken, NJ: Wiley.

Schein, E. H. (2017). *Organizational Culture and Leadership*. 5th ed. Hoboken, NJ: Wiley.

Simpson, R. (2000). 'Gender Mix and Organisational Fit: How Gender Imbalance at Different Levels of the Organisation Impacts on Women Managers', *Women in Management Review*, 15(1): 5–18.

Sull, D., Sull, C., and Zweig, B. (2022). 'Toxic Culture Is Driving the Great Resignation', *MIT Sloan Management Review*, 11 Jan., https://sloanreview.mit.edu/article/toxic-culture-is-driving-the-great-resignation/

Chapter 7

Armstrong, T. (2015). 'The Myth of the Normal Brain: Embracing Neurodiversity', *AMA Journal of Ethics*, 17(4): 348–352. doi: 10.1001/journalofethics.2015.17.4.msoc1-1504.

Ayman, R., Chemers, M. M., and Fiedler, F. (1995). 'The Contingency Model of Leadership Effectiveness: Its Levels of Analysis'. *Leadership Quarterly*, 6(2): 147–167.

Bachmann, C. L., and Gooch, B. (2018). 'LGBT in Britain: Work Report', Stonewall, https://www.stonewall.org.uk/system/files/lgbt_in_britain_work_report.pdf (accessed 8 Sept. 2023).

Baumer, N., and Frueh, J. (2021). 'What Is Neurodiversity?', Harvard Health Publishing, https://www.health.harvard.edu/blog/what-is-neurodiversity-202111232645 (accessed 8 Sept. 2023).

Beardwell, J., and Thompson, A. (2014). *Human Resource Management: A Contemporary Approach*. Madison: Pearson Education UK.

Black, J. S., and Van Esch, P. (2020). 'AI-Enabled Recruiting: What Is It and How Should a Manager Use It?', *Business Horizons*, 63: 215–226.

Boglind, A., Hällstén, F., and Thilander, P. (2011). 'HR Transformation and Shared Services: Adoption and Adaptation in Swedish Organizations', *Personnel Review*, 40(5): 570–588.

Boxall, P. (2013). 'Mutuality in the Management of Human Resources: Assessing the Quality of Alignment in Employment Relationships: Mutuality in the Management of Human Resources', *Human Resource Management Journal*, 23(1): 3–17.

Boxall, P., and Purcell, J. (2000). 'Strategic Human Resource Management: Where Have We Come From and Where Should We Be Going?', *International Journal of Management Reviews*, 2(2): 183–203.

Boxall, P., and Purcell, J. (2003). *Strategy and Human Resource Management*. United Kingdom: Bloomsbury Academic.

Cadsby, C. B., Song, F., and Tapon, F. (2007). 'Sorting and Incentive Effects of Pay for Performance: An Experimental Investigation', *Academy of Management Journal*, 50: 387–405.

Capgemini. (2021). 'Code of Business Ethics', https://www.capgemini.com/wp-content/uploads/2021/12/Capgemini-CBE_2021_English-v3.2.pdf (accessed 30 Nov. 2022).

CIPD. (2013). 'HR Outlook—Views of Our Profession', https://www.cipd.org/globalassets/media/knowledge/the-people-profession/latest-updates/hr-outlook_2012-13-winter-profession-views_tcm18-11011.pdf (accessed 8 Sept. 2023).

CIPD. (2018). 'Moving Towards a New Framework for the Relationship Between Employers and Workers', https://www.cipd.co.uk/knowledge/strategy/governance/framework-employers-workers#gref (accessed 8 Sept. 2023).

CIPD. (2021). 'Strategic Human Resource Management', https://www.cipd.co.uk/knowledge/strategy/hr/strategic-hrm-factsheet#6744 (accessed 8 Sept. 2023).

CIPD. (2022a). 'Performance-related Pay: Fact Sheet', https://www.cipd.co.uk/knowledge/fundamentals/people/pay/performance-factsheet#gref (accessed 12 Jan. 2023).

CIPD. (2022b). 'Equality, Diversity and Inclusion (EDI) in the Workplace', 1 Nov. 2022, https://www.cipd.co.uk/knowledge/fundamentals/relations/diversity/factsheet#6430 (accessed 12 Jan. 2023).

CIPD. (2022c). 'Employee Voice: Fact Sheet', https://www.cipd.co.uk/knowledge/fundamentals/relations/communication/voice-factsheet (accessed 8 Sept. 2023).

Commission on Race and Ethnic Disparities. (2021). *Employment, Fairness at Work, and Enterprise*. UK Government, https://www.gov.uk/government/publications/the-report-of-the-commission-on-race-and-ethnic-disparities/employment-fairness-at-work-and-enterprise (accessed 8 Sept. 2023).

Dastin, J. (2018). 'Amazon Scraps Secret AI Recruiting Tool That Showed Bias against Women', Reuters, https://www.reuters.com/article/us-amazon-com-jobs-automation-insight-idUSKCN1MK08G (accessed 8 Sept. 2023).

Department for Business, Energy & Industrial Strategy. (2022). Letter to Peter Hebblethwaite, CEO, P&O Ferries, 18 Mar. 2022, https://assets.publishing.service.gov.uk/government/uploads/system/uploads/attachment_data/file/1061915/Letter_from_Rt_Hon_Kwasi_Kwarteng_MP_and_Paul_Scully_MP.pdf (accessed 23 Jan. 2023).

Dickens, L. (1999). 'Beyond the Business Case: A Three-Pronged Approach to Equality Action', *Human Resource Management Journal*, 9(1): 9–19.

Dundon, T., Wilkinson, A., Marchington, M., and Ackers, P. (2004). 'The Meanings and Purpose of Employee Voice', *International Journal of Human Resource Management*, 15(6): 1149–1170.

Employment Equity Act. (1998). https://www.gov.za/documents/employment-equity-act (accessed 8 Sept. 2023).

Equality and Human Rights Commission. (2010). https://www.equalityhumanrights.com/en/equality-act/protected-characteristics (accessed 5 June 2023).

Geare, A., Edgar, F., and McAndrew, I. (2006). 'Employment Relationships: Ideology and HRM Practice', *International Journal of Human Resource Management*, 17(7): 1190–1208.

Gill, C. (1999). *Use of Hard and Soft Models of HRM to Illustrate the Gap between Rhetoric and Reality in Workforce Management*. RMIT Working Paper Series, WP 99/13.

Goodley, S., and Ashby, J. (2015). 'Revealed: How Sports Direct Effectively Pays Below Minimum Wage', *The Guardian*, 9 Dec. 2015, https://www.theguardian.com/business/2015/dec/09/how-sports-direct-effectively-pays-below-minimum-wage-pay (accessed 12 Jan. 2023).

Heizmann, H., and Fox, S. (2019). 'O Partner, Where Art Thou? A Critical Discursive Analysis of HR Managers' Struggle for Legitimacy', *International Journal of Human Resource Management*, 30(13): 2026–2048.

High Pay Centre. (2023). 'High Pay Hour', https://highpaycentre.org/high-pay-hour-how-quickly-ceos-earn-the-uk-median-wage/ (accessed 8 Sept. 2023).

ICAEW Insights. (2023). 'John Lewis Review Prompts Employee Ownership Debate', Institute of Chartered Accountants in England and Wales, 6 Apr. 2023, https://www.icaew.com/insights/viewpoints-on-the-news/2023/apr-2023/john-lewis-review-prompts-employee-ownership-debate (accessed 5 June 2023).

Inman, P. (2020). 'When Staff Run the Show: The True Benefits of Employee Ownership', *The Guardian*, 29 Feb. 2020, https://www.theguardian.com/business/2020/feb/29/benefits-of-employee-ownership-john-lewis-richer-sounds (accessed 12 Jan. 2023)

Jacobs, E. (2019). 'How Artificial Intelligence Helps Companies Recruit Talented Staff', *Financial Times*, https://www.ft.com/content/2731709c-3043-11e9-8744-e7016697f225 (accessed 8 Sept. 2023).

Keegan, A., and Francis, H. (2010). 'Practitioner Talk: The Changing Textscape of HRM and Emergence of HR Business Partnership', *International Journal of Human Resource Management*, 21(6): 873–898.

Kellaway, L. (2015). 'A Blast of Common Sense Frees Staff from Appraisals', *Financial Times*, https://www.ft.com/content/8e3ae550-3166-11e5-8873-775ba7c2ea3d (accessed 8 Sept. 2023).

Kirkpatrick, D. (1996). 'Great Ideas Revisited', *Training & Development*, 50(1): 54–60.

Knies, E., Borst, R. T., Leisink, P., and Farndale, E. (2022). 'The Distinctiveness of Public Sector HRM: A Four-Wave Trend Analysis', *Human Resource Management Journal*, 32(4): 799–825.

Lee, D. (2022). 'Amazon Workers in Staten Island Vote to Form First US Union', *Financial Times*, https://www.ft.com/content/7c9fe555-6ac7-47ff-bff2-877a43b0b871 (accessed 8 Sept. 2023).

Lewis, P. (1998). 'Managing Performance Related Pay Based on Evidence from the Financial Services Sector', *Human Resource Management Journal*, 8(2): 66–77.

Lundstrom, U. (2012). 'Teachers' Perceptions of Individual Performance-Related Pay in Practice: A Picture of a Counterproductive Pay System', *Educational Management Administration and Leadership*, 40(3): 376–391.

Marsden, D., and Richardson, R. (1994). 'Performance Pay? The Effects of Merit Pay on Motivation in the Public Services', *British Journal of Industrial Relations*, 32(2): 243–261.

McKenna, S., Richardson, J., and Manroop, L. (2011). 'Alternative Paradigms and the Study and Practice of Performance Management and Evaluation', *Human Resource Management Review*, 21(2): 148–157.

Newell, S. (2005). 'Recruitment and Selection', in *Managing Human Resources: Personnel Management in Transition*, 115–147. Malden, MA [u.a]: Blackwell.

Office for National Statistics. (2021). 'Gender Pay Gap in the UK: 2021', https://www.ons.gov.uk/employmentandlabourmarket/peopleinwork/earningsandworkinghours/bulletins/genderpaygapintheuk/2021 (accessed 8 Sept. 2023).

Palmer, A. (2022). 'Morgan Stanley Explains How Unions Could Affect Amazon's Bottom Line', CNBC, https://www.cnbc.com/2022/04/04/morgan-stanley-explains-how-unions-could-impact-amazons-bottom-line.html (accessed 8 Sept. 2023).

Pfeffer, J. (1998). *The Human Equation: Building Profits by Putting People First*. Harvard Business Press.

Pritchard, K. (2010). 'Becoming an HR Strategic Partner: Tales of Transition', *Human Resource Management Journal*, 20(2): 175–188.

Pulakos, E. D., and O'Leary, R. S. (2011). 'Why Is Performance Management Broken?', *Industrial and Organizational Psychology*, 4(2): 146–164.

Randstad. (2017). 'Job Seekers in Singapore, Hong Kong and Malaysia Frustrated with Overly-Automated Recruitment Process', https://www.randstad.com.sg/about-us/press-releases/job-seekers-in-singapore-hong-kong-and-malaysia-frustrated-with-overly-automated-recruitment-process/ (accessed 8 Sept. 2023).

Schuler, R. S., and Jackson, S. E. (1987). 'Linking Competitive Strategies with Human Resource Management Practices', *Academy of Management Perspectives*, 1(3): 207–219.

Searle, R. H., and Al-Sharif, R. (2018). 'Recruitment and Selection', in D. G. Collings, D. T. Wood, and L. T. Szamosi (eds), *Human Resources Management: A Critical Approach*, 215–237. 2nd ed. Abingdon, Oxon; New York, NY: Routledge.

Sears, B., Mallory, C., Flores, A. R., and Conron, K. J. (2021). *LGBT People's Experiences of Workplace Discrimination and Harassment*. UCLA School of Law Williams Institute, https://williamsinstitute.law.ucla.edu/publications/lgbt-workplace-discrimination/ (accessed 8 Sept. 2023).

Statista. (2018). 'Ratio between CEO and average worker pay in 2018, by country', https://www.statista.com/statistics/424159/pay-gap-between-ceos-and-average-workers-in-world-by-country/ (accessed 31 Aug. 2023).

Topham, G. (2022). 'P&O Ferries Sacks All 800 Crew Members across Entire Fleet', *The Guardian*, 17 Mar. 2022, https://www.theguardian.com/uk-news/2022/mar/17/po-ferries-halts-sailings-before-major-announcement (accessed 12 Jan. 2023)

Truss, C., Gratton, L., Hope-Hailey, V., McGovern, P., and Stiles, P. (1997). 'Soft and Hard Models of

Human Resource Management: A Reappraisal', *Journal of Management Studies*, 34(1): 53–73.

Ulrich, D. (1995). 'Shared Services: From Vogue to Value', *People and Strategy*, 18(3): 12.

Ungoed-Thomas, J. (2022). 'Avanti Paid Shareholders £11.5m Despite "Abysmal" Service for Rail Users', *The Observer*, 21 Aug. 2022, https://www.theguardian.com/uk-news/2022/aug/21/avanti-paid-shareholders-115m-despite-abysmal-service-for-rail-users (accessed 30 Nov. 2022).

Waterson, J., and Marsh, S. (2020). 'BBC Facing Huge Bill for Equal Pay Cases after Samira Ahmed Verdict', *The Guardian*, 10 January, https://www.theguardian.com/media/2020/jan/10/samira-ahmed-wins-equal-pay-claim-against-bbc (accessed 31 Aug. 2023).

Wildman, J. L., Bedwell, W. L., Salas, E., and Smith-Jentsch, K. A. (2011). 'Performance Measurement at Work: A Multilevel Perspective', in S. Zedeck (ed.), *APA Handbook of Industrial and Organizational Psychology, Vol. 1. Building and Developing the Organization*, 303–341.

Wright, P. M., McMahan, G. C., and McWilliams, A. (1994). 'Human Resources and Sustained Competitive Advantage: A Resource-Based Perspective', *International Journal of Human Resource Management*, 5(2): 301–326.

Chapter 8

Blustein, D. (2013). *The Psychology of Working: A New Perspective for Career Development, Counseling, and Public Policy*. New York. Routledge.

Bryson, A., Forth, J., and Stokes, L. (2017). 'Does Employees' Subjective Well-Being Affect Workplace Performance?' *Human Relations*, 70(8): 1017–1037.

Buckingham, M. (2022). 'Designing Work That People Love', *Harvard Business Review*, May–June, https://hbr.org/2022/05/designing-work-that-people-love (accessed 28 Dec. 2022).

Carzo, R. Jr., and Yanouzas, J. N. (1969). 'Effects of Flat and Tall Organization Structure', *Administrative Science Quarterly*, June: 178–191.

Cederström, C., and Spicer, A. (2015). *The Wellness Syndrome*. Cambridge: Polity Press.

CIPD (Chartered Institute of Personnel and Development). (2022). 'What Is In-Work Poverty?', https://www.cipd.co.uk/knowledge/culture/well-being/employee-financial-well-being/in-work-poverty/introduction#gref (accessed 4 Jan. 2023).

Colquitt, J. A., Conlon, D. E., Wesson, M. J., Porter, C. O., and Ng, K. Y. (2001). 'Justice at the Millennium: A Meta-Analytic Review of 25 Years of Organizational Justice Research', *Journal of Applied Psychology*, 86(3): 425.

Dahik, A., Lovich, D., Kreafle, C., Bailey, A., Kilmann, J., Kennedy, D., Roongta, P., Schuler, F., Tomlin, L., and Wenstrup, J. (2020). 'What 12,000 Employees Have to Say about the Future of Remote Work'. Boston Consulting Group, http://www.g20ys.org/upload/auto/7139c0b4e3d35d31fe4c92c7347aec3422b64164.pdf (accessed 4 Jan. 2023).

Demerouti, E., Bakker, A. B., and Gevers, J. M. (2015). 'Job Crafting and Extra-Role Behavior: The Role of Work Engagement and Flourishing', *Journal of Vocational Behavior*, 91: 87–96.

Duffy, R. D., Blustein, D., Diemer, M., and Autin, K. (2016). 'The Psychology of Working Theory', *Journal of Counseling Psychology*, 63(2): 127–148.

Duffy, R. D., Blustein, D. L., Allan, B. A., Diemer, M. A., and Cinamon, R. G. (2020). 'Introduction to the Special Issue: A Cross-Cultural Exploration of Decent Work', *Journal of Vocational Behavior*, 116 (Part A), Article 103351.

Ethical Tea Partnership, 'Strategy 2030' (n.d.), https://ethicalteapartnership.org/strategy2030/ (accessed 12 Sept. 2023).

Fairtrade Foundation. (2022). Fintea Growers Co-operative Union Ltd, Kenya, https://www.fairtrade.org.uk/farmers-and-workers/tea/fintea-growers-co-operative-union-ltd-kenya/ (accessed 5 Jan. 2023).

Grant, A. M. (2007). 'Relational Job Design and the Motivation to Make a Prosocial Difference', *Academy of Management Review*, 32(2): 393–417.

Greenberg, J. (1990). 'Organizational Justice: Yesterday, Today, and Tomorrow', *Journal of Management*, 16(2): 399–432.

Guest, D. E. (2017). 'Human Resource Management and Employee Well-Being: Towards a New Analytic Framework', *Human Resource Management Journal*, 27(1): 22–38.

Henrich, J., Heine, S. J., and Norenzayan, A. (2010). 'Beyond WEIRD: Towards a Broad-Based Behavioral Science', *Behavioral and Brain Sciences*, 33(2–3): 111.

Hutch. (2022). 'Hutch 4 day week confirmed!', Hutch blog, 14 Dec. 2022, https://www.hutch.io/blog/company/hutch-4-day-week-update/ (accessed 30 Dec. 2022).

Infrastructure and Cities for Economic Development (ICED). (2018). 'Construction Sector Employment in Low Income Countries', 5 Jan. 2018, http://icedfacility.org/wp-content/uploads/2018/08/Report_Construction-Sector-Employment-in-LICs_Final.pdf (accessed 4 Jan. 2023).

International Labour Organization (ILO). (2008). *Gender, Employment and the Informal Economy: Glossary of Terms*. Geneva: International Labour Office, www.ilo.org

International Labour Organization. (2022). *World Employment and Social Outlook Trends 2022*. Geneva: International Labour Office, www.ilo.org

Joseph Rowntree Foundation. (2023). 'UK Poverty 2023: The Essential Guide To Understanding Poverty in the UK', https://www.jrf.org.uk/sites/default/files/jrf/uk_poverty_2023_-_the_essential_guide_to_understanding_poverty_in_the_uk_0_0.pdf (accessed 8 Sept. 2023).

Kislik, L. (2021). 'What to Do If Your Team Doesn't Want to Go Back to the Office', *Harvard Business Review*, 18 Jan. 2021, https://hbr.org/2021/01/what-to-do-if-your-team-doesnt-want-to-go-back-to-the-office (accessed 4 Jan. 2023).

Morgeson, F. P., and Humphrey, S. E. (2006). 'The Work Design Questionnaire (WQD): Developing and Validating a Comprehensive Measure for Assessing Job Design and the Nature of Work', *Journal of Applied Psychology*, 91(6): 1321–1339.

Moulds, J. (2015). 'Child Labour in the Fashion Supply Chain', https://labs.theguardian.com/unicef-child-labour/ (accessed 2 Jan. 2023).

Nielsen, K., Nielsen, M. B., Ogbonnaya, C., Känsälä, M., Saari, E., and Isaksson, K. (2017). 'Workplace Resources to Improve Both Employee Well-Being and Performance: A Systematic Review and Meta-Analysis', *Work & Stress*, 31(2): 101–120.

Parker, S. K. (2014). 'Beyond Motivation: Job and Work Design for Development, Health, Ambidexterity, and More', *Annual Review of Psychology*, 65: 661–691.

Parker, S. K., Morgeson, F., and Johns, G. (2017). '100 Years of Work Design Research: Looking Back and Looking Forward', *Journal of Applied Psychology*, 102(3): 403– 420.

Peccei, R., and Van De Voorde, K. (2019). 'Human Resource Management–Well-Being–Performance Research Revisited: Past, Present, and Future', *Human Resource Management Journal*, 29(4): 539–563.

Saxena, M. (2021). 'Cultural Skills as Drivers of Decency in Decent Work: An Investigation of Skilled Workers in the Informal Economy', *European Journal of Work and Organizational Psychology*, 30(6): 824–836.

Schaufeli, W., and Salanova, M. (2014). 'Burnout, Boredom and Engagement at the Workplace', in Maria C. W. Peeters, Jan de Jonge, and Toon W. Taris (eds), *An Introduction to Contemporary Work Psychology*, 293–320. Wiley Blackwell: Chichester.

Searle, R. H., and McWha-Hermann, I. (2021). 'Money's Too Tight (to Mention): A Review and Psychological Synthesis of Living Wage Research', *European Journal of Work and Organizational Psychology*, 30(3): 428–443.

Simpson, E. (2022). 'Four-Day Week Trial Ends and Some Firms Make It Permanent', BBC News Online, 6 Dec., https://www.bbc.co.uk/news/business-63808326 (accessed 1 Sept. 2023).

UN News. (2022a). 'Rising Inflation, Falling Wages Threaten Increased Poverty and Unrest: ILO', 30 Nov. 2022, https://news.un.org/en/story/2022/11/1131197 (accessed 10 Jan. 2023).

UN News. (2022b). 'Convergence of Conflicts, COVID and Climate Crises, Jeopardize Global Goals', 7 July 2022, https://news.un.org/en/story/2022/07/1122112 (accessed 10 Jan. 2023).

UNICEF/ILO. (2021). 'Child Labour: Global Estimates 2020, Trends and the Road Forward', https://data.unicef.org/resources/child-labour-2020-global-estimates-trends-and-the-road-forward/ (accessed 1 Sept. 2023).

Unilever. (2022a). Compass for Sustainable Growth, unilever.com, https://www.unilever.com/files/8f9a3825-2101-411f-9a31-7e6f176393a4/the-unilever-compass.pdf (accessed 8 Sept. 2023).

Unilever. (2022b). Unilever's supply chain, https://www.unilever.com/files/d3f86865-f6e2-4ab3-872c-bf395d1ef781/Unilever-Supply-Chain-Overview-Spend%20Analysis-May-2022.pdf (accessed 1 Sept. 2023).

United Nations, Sustainable Development Goals, Goal 8: Decent Work and Economic Growth, https://sdgs.un.org/goals/goal8 (accessed 8 Jan. 2023).

World Economic Forum (WEF). (2022). *The good work framework: A new business agenda for the future of work*. Geneva: World Economic Forum.

Chapter 9

Belbin. (2018). 'Belbin and Culture Report', https://www.belbin.com/media/1935/belbin-white-paper-culture-and-belbin-team-roles.pdf (accessed 8 Sept. 2023).

Brand Finance. (2022). 'Airlines 50 2022', https://brandirectory.com/rankings/airlines/ (accessed 8 Sept. 2023).

Economist, The. (2021). 'The Beatles and the Art of Teamwork', 18 Dec., https://www.economist.com/business/2021/12/18/the-beatles-and-the-art-of-teamwork (accessed 8 Sept. 2023).

Edmondson, A. C., and Lei, Z. (2014). 'Psychological Safety: The History, Renaissance, and Future of an Interpersonal Construct', *Annual Review of Organizational Psychology and Organizational Behavior*, 1(1): 23–43.

Future Travel Experience (2023). 'Emirates Cabin Crew and Ground Staff Complete Training to Assist Travellers with Hidden Disabilities, April 2023', https://www.futuretravelexperience.com/2023/04/emirates-cabin-crew-and-ground-staff-complete-training-to-assist-travellers-with-hidden-disabilities/ (accessed 8 Sept. 2023).

Gersick, C. J. (1988). 'Time and Transition in Work Teams: Toward a New Model of Group Development', *Academy of Management Journal*, 31(1): 9–41.

Glassdoor.com (2023). https://www.glassdoor.com/about/ (accessed 12 Sept. 2023)

Hassard, J. S. (2012). 'Rethinking the Hawthorne Studies: The Western Electric Research in Its Social, Political and Historical Context', *Human Relations*, 65(11): 1431–1461.

Hollenbeck, J. R., Beersma, B., and Schouten, M. E. (2012). 'Beyond Team Types and Taxonomies: A Dimensional Scaling Conceptualization for Team Description', *Academy of Management Review*, 37(1): 82–106.

Johns, G. (2006). 'The Essential Impact of Context on Organizational Behavior', *Academy of Management Review*, 31(2): 386–408.

Johns, G. (2017). 'Incorporating Context in Organizational Research', *Academy of Management Review*, 42(4): 577–595.

Johns, G. (2018). 'Advances in the Treatment of Context in Organizational Research', *Annual Review of Organizational Psychology and Organizational Behavior*, 5: 21–46.

Kanfer, R. (1992). 'Work Motivation: New Directions in Theory and Research', in C. L. Cooper and I. T. Robertson (eds), *International Review of Industrial and Organizational Psychology*, Vol. 7, 1–53. Chichester, England: Wiley.

Kanfer, R., Frese, M., and Johnson, R. E. (2017). 'Motivation Related to Work: A Century of Progress', *Journal of Applied Psychology*, 102(3): 338–355.

Loh, C. (2021). 'What Goes into Training Emirates' Cabin Crew?', SimpleFlying.com (accessed 10 Apr. 2021).

Marks, M. A., Mathieu, J. E., and Zaccaro, S. J. (2001). 'A Temporally Based Framework and Taxonomy of Team Processes', *Academy of Management Review*, 26(3): 356–376.

Mathieu, J., Maynard, M. T., Rapp, T., and Gilson, L. (2008). 'Team Effectiveness 1997–2007: A Review of Recent Advancements and a Glimpse into the Future', *Journal of Management*, 34(3): 410–476.

McGregor, D. (1960). 'Theory X and Theory Y', *Organization Theory*, 358(374): 5.

Mohammed, S., Rico, R., and Alipour, K. K. (2021). 'Team Cognition at a Crossroad: Toward Conceptual Integration and Network Configurations', *Academy of Management Annals*, 15(2): 455–501.

Okhuysen, G. A., and Bechky, B. A. (2009). 'Coordination in Organizations: An Integrative Perspective', *Academy of Management Annals*, 3(1): 463–502.

Pentland, A. S. (2013). 'The Data-Driven Society', *Scientific American*, 309(4): 78–83.

Sachau, D. A. (2007). 'Resurrecting the Motivation-Hygiene Theory: Herzberg and the Positive Psychology Movement', *Human Resource Development Review*, 6(4): 377–393.

SkyTrax. (2022). 'World Airline Awards', https://www.worldairlineawards.com/worlds-top-10-airlines-2022/ (accessed 8 Sept. 2023).

Stoddard, T. (2019). 'What It Takes to Train the Prestigious Emirates Cabin Crew', https://www.forbes.com/sites/taylorboozan/2019/04/30/what-it-takes-to-train-for-the-prestigious-emirates-cabin-crew/, 30 Apr. (accessed 8 Sept. 2023).

Chapter 10

Avolio, B. J., Walumbwa, F.O., and Weber, T. J. (2009). 'Leadership: Current Theories, Research, and Future Directions', *Annual Review of Psychology*, 60(1): 421–449.

Bass, B. M. (2008). *The Bass Handbook of Leadership*, 4th ed. New York: Free Press.

Behrendt, P., Matz S., and Göritz, S. A. (2017). 'An Integrative Model of Leadership Behavior', *Leadership Quarterly*, 28(1): 229–244.

Brown, M. E., and Treviño, L. K. (2006). 'Ethical Leadership: A Review and Future Directions', *Leadership Quarterly*, 17(6): 595–616.

Buchanan, D. A., Addicott, R., Fitzgerald, L., Ferlie, E., and Baeza, J. I. (2007). 'Nobody in Charge: Distributed Change Agency in Healthcare', *Human Relations*, 60(7): 1065–1090.

Burns, J. M. (1978). *Leadership*. New York, NY: Harper and Row.

Casaló, L. V., Flavián, C., and Ibáñez-Sánchez, S. (2020). 'Influencers on Instagram: Antecedents and Consequences of Opinion Leadership', *Journal of Business Research*, 117: 510–519.

Ciulla, J. (2001). 'Carving Leaders from the Warped Wood of Humanity', *Canadian Journal of Administrative Sciences*, 18(4): 313–319.

Davis, J. P., and Eisenhardt, K. M. (2011). 'Rotating Leadership and Collaborative Innovation: Recombination Processes in Symbiotic

Relationships', *Administrative Science Quarterly*, 56(2): 159–201.

Dinh, J. E., Lord, R. G., Gardner, W. L., Meuser, J. D., Liden, R.C., and Hu, J. (2014). 'Leadership Theory and Research in the New Millennium: Current Theoretical Trends and Changing Perspectives', *Leadership Quarterly*, 25(1): 36–62.

Dixon-Woods, M., McNicol, S., and Martin, G. (2012). 'Ten Challenges in Improving Quality in Healthcare: Lessons from the Health Foundation's Programme Evaluations and Relevant Literature', *BMJ Quality & Safety*, 21: 876–884.

Eagly, A., and Carli, L. (2007). 'Women and the Labyrinth of Leadership', *Harvard Business Review*, 85(9): 63–71.

England, G. W., and Lee, R. (1974). 'The Relationship between Managerial Values and Managerial Success in the United States, Japan, India, and Australia', *Journal of Applied Psychology*, 59(4): 411–419.

Fiedler, F. E. (1967). *A Theory of Leadership Effectiveness*. New York: McGraw Hill.

Gardner, W. L., Cogliser, C. C., Davis, K. M., and Dickens, M. P. (2011). 'Authentic Leadership: A Review of the Literature and Research Agenda', *Leadership Quarterly*, 22(6): 1120–1145.

Goldberg, L. R. (1990). 'An Alternative "Description of Personality": The Big Five Factor Structure', *Journal of Personality and Social Psychology*, 59: 1216–1229.

Goleman, D. (1995). *Emotional Intelligence*. New York, NY: Bantam.

Goleman, D. (1998). 'What Makes a Leader?', *Harvard Business Review*, 76(6): 93–102.

Graeff, C. L. (1997). 'Evolution of Situational Leadership Theory: A Critical Review', *Leadership Quarterly*, 8(2): 153–170.

Grint, K. (2010). *Leadership: A Very Short Introduction*. Oxford, UK: Oxford University Press.

Gronn, P. (2002). 'Distributed Leadership as a Unit of Analysis', *Leadership Quarterly*, 13(4): 423–451.

Hersey, P., and Blanchard, K. H. (1988). *Management of Organizational Behaviour: Utilizing Human Resources*. Englewood Cliffs, NJ: Prentice-Hall International.

Houghton, J. D., Neck, C. P., and Manz, C. C. (2003). 'Self-Leadership and Superleadership: The Heart and Art of Creating Shared Leadership in Teams', in C. L. Pearce and J. A. Conger (eds), *Shared Leadership: Reframing the Hows and Whys of Leadership*, 123–140. Thousand Oaks, CA: Sage Publications.

Influencer Marketing Hub. (2023). 'Influencer Marketing Benchmark Report: 2023', Influencer Marketing Hub, https://influencermarketinghub.com/influencer-marketing-benchmark-report/ (accessed 12 Sept. 2023).

Iszatt-White, M., and Saunders, C. (2017). *Leadership*. Oxford: Oxford University Press.

Judge, T. A., Bono, J., Ilies, R., and Gerhardt, M. W. (2002). 'Personality and Leadership. A Qualitative and Quantitative Review', *Journal of Applied Psychology*, 87: 765–780.

Judge, T. A., and Piccolo, R. F. (2004). 'Transformational and Transactional Leadership: A Meta-Analytic Test of Their Relative Validity', *Journal of Applied Psychology*, 89: 755–768.

Katz, D., Maccoby, N., and Morse, N. C (1950). *Productivity, Supervision, and Morale in an Office Situation*. Ann Arbor, MI: University of Michigan, Institute for Social Research.

Kotter, J. P. (1990). *A Force for Change: How Leadership Differs from Management*. New York: Free Press.

Leung, F. F., Gu, F. F., and Palmatier, R. W. (2022). 'Online Influencer Marketing', *Journal of the Academy of Marketing Science*, 50: 226–251.

Liden, R. C., Wayne, S., Liao, C., and Meuser, J. (2014). 'Servant Leadership and Serving Culture: Influence on Individual and Unit Performance', *Academy of Management Journal*, 57(5): 1434–1452.

Lemoine, G. J., Hartnell, C. A., and Leroy, H. (2019). 'Taking Stock of Moral Approaches to Leadership: An Integrative Review of Ethical, Authentic, and Servant Leadership', *Academy of Management Annals*, 13(1): 148–187.

Maak, T., and Pless, N. (2006). 'Responsible Leadership in a Stakeholder Society. A Relational Approach', *Journal of Business Ethics*, 66: 99–115.

Maven Road. (2019). 'Fridays for Future: The Social Media Impact of Greta Thunberg', Medium.com, 10 Sept, https://medium.com/@mavenmkt/fridays-for-future-the-social-media-impact-of-greta-thunberg-c8523d3313f8 (accessed 13 Sept. 2023).

Mayer, J. D., Roberts, R. D., and Barsade, S. G. (2008). 'Human Abilities: Emotional Intelligence', *Annual Review of Psychology*, 59: 507–536.

Meindl, J. R., Ehrlich, S. B., and Dukerich, J. M. (1985). 'The Romance of Leadership', *Administrative Science Quarterly*, 30: 78–102.

Miller, E. J. (1998). 'The Leader with the Vision: Is Time Running Out?', in E. B. Klein, F. Gabelnick, and P. Herr (eds), *The Psychodynamics of Leadership*, 3–25. Madison, CT: Psychosocial Press.

Mintzberg, H. (2009). *Managing*. Harlow, Essex: Financial Times Prentice Hall.

National Women's History Museum. (2016). 'Harriet Tubman', https://www.womenshistory.org/exhibits/harriet-tubman (accessed 2 June 2023).

Nelson Mandela Foundation. 'Biography of Nelson Mandela', https://www.nelsonmandela.org/content/page/biography (accessed 20 Mar. 2023).

Nielsen, K., and Daniels, K. (2016). 'The Relationship between Transformational Leadership and Follower Sickness Absence: The Role of Presenteeism', *Work and Stress*, 30(2): 193–208.

Northouse, P. (2021). *Leadership: Theory and Practice*. London: Sage.

Ospina, S. M., Foldy, E. G., Fairhurst, G. T., and Jackson, B. (2020). 'Collective Dimensions of Leadership: Connecting Theory and Method', *Human Relations*, 73(4): 441–463.

Pearce, C. L. (2004). 'The Future of Leadership: Combining Vertical and Shared Leadership to Transform Knowledge Work', *Academy of Management Executive*, 18(1): 47–59.

Pearce C. L., and Conger, J. A. (2003) *Shared Leadership: Reframing the Hows and Whys of Leadership*. Thousand Oaks, CA: Sage.

Ruben, B. D., & Gigliotti, R. A. (2016). 'Leadership as social influence: An expanded view of leadership communication theory and practice', *Journal of Leadership & Organizational Studies*, 23(4): 467–479.

Stogdill, R. M. (1948). 'Personal Factors Associated with Leadership', *Journal of Psychology*, 25: 35–71.

Stogdill, R. M. (1950). 'Leadership, Membership and Organization', *Psychological Bulletin*, 47(1): 1–14.

Stogdill, R. M., and Coons, A. E. eds. (1951). *Leader Behaviour: Its Description and Measurement*. Research Monograph, 88. Columbus, OH: Ohio State University Bureau of Research.

Thompson, J. D. (1956). 'On Building an Administrative Science', *Administrative Science Quarterly*, 1(1): 102–111.

Treviño, L. K., and Brown, M. E. (2014). 'Ethical Leadership', in D. V. Day (ed.), *The Oxford Handbook of Leadership and Organizations*, 524–538. Oxford: Oxford University Press.

United Nations. 'What Is the United Nations Framework Convention on Climate Change?', https://unfccc.int/process-and-meetings/what-is-the-united-nations-framework-convention-on-climate-change (accessed 28 Dec. 2022).

Vergauwe, J., Wille, B., Hofmans, J., Kaiser, R. B., and De Fruyt, F. G. (2018). 'The Double Edged Sword of Leader Charisma: Understanding the Curvilinear Relationship between Charismatic Personality and Leader Effectiveness', *Journal of Personality and Social Psychology*, 114(1): 110–130.

Waldman, D. (2014). 'Bridging the Domains of Leadership and Corporate Social Responsibility', in D. V. Day (ed.), *The Oxford Handbook of Leadership and Organizations*, 539–555. Oxford: Oxford University Press.

Wyatt, M., and Silvester, J. (2015). 'Reflections on the Labyrinth: Investigating Black and Ethnic Minority Leaders' Career Experiences', *Human Relations*, 658(8): 1243–1269.

Yukl, G. (2003). *Leadership in Organization*. 8th ed. Boston, MA: Pearson.

Chapter 11

American Marketing Association (ama.org). (2017). 'Definition of Marketing', https://www.ama.org/the-definition-of-marketing-what-is-marketing/ (accessed 2 Nov. 2022).

American Marketing Association (ama.org). (n.d.). 'Branding', https://www.ama.org/topics/branding/ (accessed 3 Mar. 2023).

American Marketing Association (ama.org). (n.d.). Content Marketing, https://www.ama.org/topics/content-marketing/ (accessed 3 Mar. 2023).

Baehre, S., O'Dwyer, M., O'Malley, L., and Lee, N. (2022). 'The Use of Net Promoter Score (NPS) to Predict Sales Growth: Insights from an Empirical Investigation', *Journal of the Academy of Marketing Science*, 50: 67–84.

Batra, R., and Keller, K. L. (2016). 'Integrating Marketing Communications: New Findings, New Lessons, and New Ideas', *Journal of Marketing*, 80(6): 122–145.

Bhatia, P., Cummis, C., Rich, D., Draucker, L., Lahdm H, and Brown, A. (2011). 'Greenhouse Gas Protocol Corporate Value Chain (Scope 3) Accounting and Reporting Standard', World Resources Institute (WRI), https://ghgprotocol.org/standards/scope-3-standard (accessed 26 Feb. 2023).

Bloomberg. (2019). 'Burberry Teams with Chinese Internet Giant Tencent as Sales Fall in Hong Kong', *Business of Fashion*, 14 Nov., https://www.businessoffashion.com/articles/luxury/burberry-teams-with-chinese-internet-giant-tencent-as-sales-fall-in-hong-kong/ (accessed 1 Mar. 2023).

Brompton. (2021). 'German Roamers x Brompton', https://www.brompton.com/news/posts/2021/german-roamers-x-brompton (accessed 23 Feb. 2023).

Burberry Group Plc. (2019). 'Race to the Moon with Burberry's First Online Game B Bounce', https://www.burberryplc.com/en/news/corporate/2019/race-to-the-moon-with-burberry-s-first-online-game-b-bounce.html (accessed 1 Mar. 2023).

Burberry Group Plc. (2020a). 'Burberry Is First Luxury Brand to Partner with Twitch to Livestream Its Fashion Show', https://www.burberryplc.com/en/news/corporate/2020/burberry-is-first-luxury-brand-to-partner-with-twitch-to-livestr.html (accessed 1 Mar. 2023).

Burberry Group Plc. (2020b). 'Burberry Debuts Luxury's First Social Retail Store in Shenzhen, China, Powered by Tencent Technology', https://www.burberryplc.com/en/company/social-retail.html (accessed 1 Mar. 2023).

Burberry Group Plc. (2022). 'Burberry launch bespoke in-game adventure and special collection in partnership with Minecraft', https://www.burberryplc.com/en/news/brand/2022/burberry-launch-bespoke-in-game-adventure-and-special-collection.html (accessed 1 Mar. 2023).

Butler-Adams, W., and Davies, D. (2022). *The Brompton: Engineering for Change*. London: Profile Books.

Cartner-Morely, J. (2012). 'Burberry Designs Flagship London Shop to Resemble Its Website', *The Guardian*, 12 Sept., https://www.theguardian.com/fashion/2012/sep/12/burberry-london-shop-website (accessed 1 Mar. 2023).

Chandy, R. K., Johar, G. V., Moorman, C., and Roberts, J. H. (2021). 'Better Marketing for a Better World', *Journal of Marketing*, 85(3): 1–9.

Drive.com.au (2016). 'Volvo Battle Gets Bloody', 3 Oct., https://www.drive.com.au/news/volvo-battle-gets-bloody-20030918-13k8r/ (accessed 3 Mar. 2023).

Dugdale, A. (2010). 'Interview: Will Butler-Adams, CEO of Brompton Bikes, Fast Company', 7 Feb., https://www.fastcompany.com/1665793/interview-will-butler-adams-ceo-brompton-bikes (accessed 1 Feb. 2023).

European Commission. (2021). 'Press Release: Screening of Websites for "Greenwashing": Half of Green Claims Lack Evidence', https://ec.europa.eu/commission/presscorner/detail/en/ip_21_269 (accessed 8 Sept. 2023).

FCA. (2018). 'FCA Mission: Approach to Consumers', Financial Conduct Authority, https://www.fca.org.uk/publication/corporate/approach-to-consumers.pdf (accessed 8 Sept. 2023).

Kharpal, A. (2021). 'JD.com Plans to Boost Overseas Investment as China's E-Commerce Giants Look to Challenge Amazon', CNBC.com, https://www.cnbc.com/2021/11/11/china-jdcom-plans-to-boost-investment-overseas-in-challenge-to-amazon.html (accessed 10 Nov. 2021).

Laricchia, F. (2022). 'Smartphone Ownership in the United Kingdom 2021–2022, by Age', Statista, https://www.statista.com/statistics/300402/smartphone-usage-in-the-uk-by-age/ (accessed 18 Oct. 2022).

Marketing Accountability Standards Board. (n.d.). The Universal Marketing Dictionary, https://marketing-dictionary.org (accessed 9 Mar. 2023).

Market Research Society (MRS). Market Research Glossary, https://www.mrs.org.uk/glossary (accessed 3 Mar. 2023).

Nemes, N., Fischhoff, M., and Litchfield, A. (2022a). 'How to Avoid Greenwashing, Network for Business Sustainability', 28 Sept., https://nbs.net/how-to-avoid-greenwashing/ (accessed 8 Sept. 2023).

Nemes, N., Scanlan, S. J., Smith, P., Smith, T., Aronczyk, M., Hill, S., Lewis, S. L., Montgomery, A. W., Tubiello, F. N., and Stabinsky, D. (2022b). 'An Integrated Framework to Assess Greenwashing', *Sustainability*, 14(8): 4431. doi:10.3390/su14084431

Network for Business Sustainability. (2022). '10 Kinds of Greenwashing and How to Avoid Them', https://nbs.net/wp-content/uploads/2022/09/10-Kinds-of-Greenwashing-And-How-to-Avoid-Them-3.pdf (accessed 8 Sept. 2023).

Oxford University Press. 'imperial, adj. and n.', https://www.oed.com/dictionary/imperial_adj?tab=meaning_and_use#847392 (accessed 4 Mar. 2023).

Paton, E. (2018). 'Burberry to Stop Burning Clothing and Other Goods It Can't Sell', *New York Times*, 6 Sept. 2018, https://www.nytimes.com/2018/09/06/business/burberry-burning-unsold-stock.html (accessed 2 Mar. 2023).

Romaniuk, J., and Sharp, B. (2021). *How Brands Grow: Part 2*. Oxford: Oxford University Press.

Rowe, B., De Ionno, D., Peters, D., and Wright, H. (2015). 'Mind the Gap: Consumer Research Exploring Experiences of Financial Exclusion across the UK', Financial Conduct Authority, https://www.fca.org.uk/publication/research/mind-the-gap.pdf (accessed 8 Sept. 2023).

Sabanoglu, T. (2022). 'Burberry: Statistics and Facts', Statista.com, 22 Sept., https://www.statista.com/topics/3458/burberry/#topicOverview (accessed 10 Sept. 2023).

Schellong, D., Sadek, P., Schaetzberger, C., and Barrack, T. (2019). 'The Promise and Pitfalls of E-Scooter Sharing', Boston Consulting Group, 16 May, https://www.bcg.com/publications/2019/

promise-pitfalls-e-scooter-sharing (accessed 10 Sept. 2023).

Simmonds, E. (2022). 'Which? Launches Cost of Living Campaign', Which?, 29 Sept. 2022, https://www.which.co.uk/news/article/which-launches-cost-of-living-campaign-azHEi8p965DF (accessed 26 Feb. 23).

Telling, O. (2023). 'Brompton's Profits Plunge as Inflation and Supply Chain Pressures Take Toll', *Financial Times*, 6 Jan. 2023.

Volvocars.com. (2023). 'Volvo Australia Breaks Sales Record', 15 Jan. 2023, https://www.volvocars.com/au/news/corporate-and-culture/2023-jan-volvo-australia-breaks-sales-record/ (accessed 3 Mar. 2023).

Walker, T. (2017). 'How Much? . . . The Rise of Dynamic and Personalised Pricing', *The Guardian*, 20 Nov.

White, K., Habib, R., and Hardisty, D. J. (2019). 'How to SHIFT Consumer Behaviors to be More Sustainable: A Literature Review and Guiding Framework', *Journal of Marketing*, 83(3): 22–49.

Williams, R. (2020). 'With Brand at Crossroads, Burberry's CEO Bets Big on China's Young Money', *Business of Fashion*, 31 July, https://www.businessoffashion.com/articles/luxury/burberry-wechat-tencent-china-shenzen/ (accessed 1 Mar. 2023).

Chapter 12

Airports Council International (ACI). (2022). 'The Impact of COVID-19 on Airports—and the Path to Recovery', 28 June 2022, https://aci.aero/2022/06/28/the-impact-of-covid-19-on-airportsand-the-path-to-recovery/ (accessed 11 Mar. 2023).

Al-Mahmood, S. Z., and Wright, T. (2013). 'Collapsed Factory Was Built Without Permit', *Wall Street Journal*, 25 Apr.

ASQ. (2015). 'Back to Basics: Why Ask Why?', American Society for Quality, May 2015, https://asq.org/quality-progress/articles/back-to-basics-why-ask-why?id=cb41e942ccba45cfa8cd06380331dde7 (accessed 4 Mar. 23).

Braziotis, C., Bourlakis, M., Rogers, H., and Tannock, J. (2013). 'Supply Chains and Supply Networks: Distinctions and Overlaps', *Supply Chain Management*, 18(6): 644–652.

Christian, A. (2021). 'The Untold Story of the Big Boat That Broke the World', WIRED, 22 June 2021, https://www.wired.co.uk/article/ever-given-global-supply-chain (accessed 11 Mar. 2023).

Congress. (2011). 'Ski Area Recreational Opportunity Enhancement Act of 2011', Public Law 125 Stat./538, https://www.congress.gov/112/plaws/publ46/PLAW-112publ46.pdf (accessed 12 Mar. 2023).

Dolcourt, J. (2019)., 'Why You Should Thank Your Phone's Most Undersung Feature: Its Processor', CNET, 22 Dec.

Hayes, R. H., and Wheelwright, S. C. (1985). *Restoring our Competitive Edge: Competing through Manufacturing*. New York, NY: Wiley.

Huq, F. A., Stevenson, M., and Zorzini, M. (2014). 'Social Sustainability in Developing Country Suppliers: An Exploratory Study in the Ready Made Garments Industry of Bangladesh', *International Journal of Operations & Production Management*, 34(5): 610–638.

IEA. (2022). 'For the First Time in Decades, the Number of People without Access to Electricity Is Set to Increase in 2022', International Energy Agency, 3 Nov., https://www.iea.org/commentaries/for-the-first-time-in-decades-the-number-of-people-without-access-to-electricity-is-set-to-increase-in-2022 (accessed 8 May 2023).

IRENA. (2021). 'A Pathway to Decarbonise the Shipping Sector', Oct., https://www.irena.org/Publications/2021/Oct/A-Pathway-to-Decarbonise-the-Shipping-Sector-by-2050 (accessed 8 Sept. 2023).

Knipscheer, L., Feenstra, S., and Sprenkels, B. (2022). 'From Supply Chains to Supply Networks', Deloitte, https://www2.deloitte.com/nl/nl/pages/enterprise-technology-and-performance/articles/from-supply-chain-to-a-supply-networks.html (accessed 11 Mar. 2023).

Kotha, S., and Srikanth, H. (2013). 'Managing a Global Partnership Model: Lessons from the Boeing 787 "Dreamliner" Programme', *Global Strategy Journal*, 3: 41–66. doi:10.1111/j.2042-5805.2012.01050

Little, J. C. D. (2011). 'OR FORUM: Little's Law as Viewed on Its 50th Anniversary', *Operations Research*, 59(3): 536–549.

Logistics Asia. (2021). 'Large Fashion Brands Are Shifting Production Away from Asia', 10 Nov. 2021, https://logistics.asia/large-fashion-brands-are-shifting-production-away-from-asia/ (accessed 11 Mar. 2023).

Moorhead, P. (2019). 'Who Are Apple's iPhone Contract Manufacturers', Forbes.com, 1 Apr. 2019, https://www.forbes.com/sites/patrickmoorhead/2019/04/13/who-are-apples-iphone-contract-manufacturers/?sh=43d256d24e6d (accessed 12 Sept. 2023).

National Inventors Hall of Fame (n.d.). 'The Invention of the Post-it® Note', https://www.invent.org/blog/trends-stem/who-invented-post-it-notes (accessed 12 Mar. 2023).

Price, K. (2022). 'One in Nine Hospitality Jobs Still Vacant as Staffing Crisis Continues', *The Caterer*, 22 Nov., https://www.thecaterer.com/news/one-nine-hospitality-jobs-still-vacant-staffing-crisis-cga-october-2022 (accessed 8 Sept. 2023).

Robbins, T. (2023). 'The Death—and Rebirth—of the Ski Resort', *Financial Times*, 10 Feb., https://www.ft.com/content/e595227f-7f57-4501-97d4-627647b06384 (accessed 12 Mar. 2023).

Safi, M., and Rushe, D. (2018). 'Rana Plaza, Five Years On: Safety of Workers Hangs in Balance in Bangladesh', *The Guardian*, https://www.theguardian.com/global-development/2018/apr/24/bangladeshi-police-target-garment-workers-union-rana-plaza-five-years-on (accessed 12 Mar. 2023).

Sheffi, Y., and Rice Jr, J. B. (2005). 'A Supply Chain View of the Resilient Enterprise', *MIT Sloan Management Review*, 47(1): 41.

Slack, N., and Brandon-Jones, A. (2019) *Essentials of Operations Management*, 2nd ed. Harlow: Pearson.

Stevens, P. (2021). 'The Ship That Blocked the Suez Canal May Be Free, But Experts Warn the Supply Chain Impact Could Last Months', CNBC, 29 Mar. 2021, https://www.cnbc.com/2021/03/29/suez-canal-is-moving-but-the-supply-chain-impact-could-last-months.html (accessed 11 Mar. 2023).

Thapa, T. (2018). 'Remember Rana Plaza: Bangladesh's Garment Workers Still Need Better Protection', Human Rights Watch, 24 Apr. 2018, https://www.hrw.org/news/2018/04/24/remember-rana-plaza (accessed 12 Mar. 2023).

Womack, J. P., Jones, D. T., and Roos, D. (2007). *The Machine That Changed the World: The Story of Lean Production—Toyota's Secret Weapon in the Global Car Wars That Is Now Revolutionizing World Industry*. New York: Simon and Schuster.

World Health Organization. (2022). 'COVID-19 Has Caused Major Disruptions and Backlogs in Health Care, New WHO Study Finds', https://www.who.int/europe/news/item/20-07-2022-covid-19-has-caused-major-disruptions-and-backlogs-in-health-care--new-who-study-finds (accessed 11 Mar. 2022).

Chapter 13

Antoncic, B., and Hisrich, R. D. (2003). 'Clarifying the intrapreneurship concept', *Journal of Small Business and Enterprise Development*, 10(1): 7–24.

Benefit Corporation. (n.d.). Winnow, https://www.bcorporation.net/en-us/find-a-b-corp/company/winnow (accessed 31 Jan. 2023).

Bindl, U. K., and Parker, S. K. (2011). 'Proactive Work Behavior: Forward-Thinking and Change-Oriented Action in Organizations', in *APA Handbook of Industrial and Organizational Psychology, Vol 2: Selecting and Developing Members for the Organization*, 567–598. American Psychological Association.

Block, J. H., Fisch, C. O., and Van Praag, M. (2017). 'The Schumpeterian Entrepreneur: A Review of the Empirical Evidence on the Antecedents, Behaviour and Consequences of Innovative Entrepreneurship', *Industry and Innovation*, 24(1): 61–95.

Campos, F., Frese, M., Goldstein, M., Iacovone, L., Johnson, H. C., McKenzie, D., and Mensmann, M. (2017). 'Teaching Personal Initiative Beats Traditional Training in Boosting Small Business in West Africa', *Science*, 357(6357): 1287–1290.

Chesborough, H. (2003). *Open Innovation: The New Imperative for Creating and Profiting from Technology*, Harvard Business School Press.

Chesborough, H. (2011). 'Everything You Need to Know about Open Innovation', *Forbes*, 21 Mar., https://www.forbes.com/sites/henrychesbrough/2011/03/21/everything-you-need-to-know-about-open-innovation/?sh=2a5d877d75f4 (accessed 8 Sept. 2023).

Christensen, C. M. (2016). *The Innovator's Dilemma: When New Technologies Cause Great Firms to Fail*. Harvard Business Publishing.

Christensen, C. M., McDonald, R., Altman, E. J., and Palmer, J. E. (2018). 'Disruptive Innovation: An Intellectual History and Directions for Future Research', *Journal of Management Studies*, 55(7): 1043–1078.

Christensen, C. M., and Overdorf, M. (2000). 'Meeting the Challenge of Disruptive Change', *Harvard Business Review*, 78(2): 66–76.

Dencker, J. C., Bacq, S., Gruber, M., and Haas, M. (2021). 'Reconceptualizing Necessity Entrepreneurship: A Contextualized Framework of Entrepreneurial Processes under the Condition of Basic Needs', *Academy of Management Review*, 46(1): 60–79.

Dewaelheyns, N., and Van Hulle, C. (2008). 'Legal Reform and Aggregate Small and Micro Business Bankruptcy Rates: Evidence from the 1997 Belgian Bankruptcy Code', *Small Business Economics*, 31(4): 409–424.

DBEIS (Department for Business, Energy and Industrial Strategy). (2022). 'Business Population Estimates for the UK and Regions 2022', Gov.uk, United Kingdom, 6 Oct., https://www.gov.uk/government/statistics/business-population-estimates-2022/

business-population-estimates-for-the-uk-and-regions-2022-statistical-release-html#what-you-need-to-know-about-these-statistics (accessed 1 Feb. 2023).

Dweck, C. (2006). *Mindset: The New Psychology of Success*. New York: Random House.

Ellen Macarthur Foundation. (n.d.). 'Reducing Food Waste, Increasing Profits: Winnow', https://ellenmacarthurfoundation.org/circular-examples/winnow (accessed 31 Jan. 2023).

Frese, M. (2009). 'Toward a Psychology of Entrepreneurship: An Action Theory Perspective', *Foundations and Trends in Entrepreneurship*, 5(6): 437–496.

Garrison, P. (2010). 'Head Skunk', *Air & Space*, https://www.smithsonianmag.com/air-space-magazine/head-skunk-5960121/ (accessed 8 Sept. 2023). Retrieved from www.airspacemag.com/

Global Entrepreneurship Monitor. (2020). 'Global Entrepreneurship Monitor: 2019/2020 Global Report', https://www.gemconsortium.org/report/gem-2019-2020-global-report (accessed 8 Sept. 2023).

Global Entrepreneurship Monitor. (2022). 'Global Entrepreneurship Monitor: 2021/2022 Global Report', https://www.gemconsortium.org/file/open?fileId=50900 (accessed 12 Sep 2023).

Global Entrepreneurship Monitor. Wiki, gemconsortium.org/wiki/1177

International Energy Agency. (2022). 'World Energy Outlook 2022', www.iea.org

Johnson, D. (2001). 'What Is Innovation and Entrepreneurship? Lessons for Larger Organisations', *Industrial and Commercial Training*, 33(4): 135–140.

Kuratko, D. F., Fisher, G., and Audretsch, D. B. (2021). 'Unraveling the Entrepreneurial Mindset', *Small Business Economics*, 57(4): 1681–1691.

Lyytinen, K. (June 29, 2017). 'Understanding the Real Innovation behind the iPhone', *Scientific American*, 29 June, https://www.scientificamerican.com/article/understanding-the-real-innovation-behind-the-iphone/ (accessed 12 Sept. 2023).

Marks, G. (2021). 'Enterpreneurs are Great, But Its Mom and Dad Who Gave Them Their Start', *The Guardian*, 31 Jan. 2021.

Morikawa, M. (2016). '16 Examples of Open Innovation—What Can We Learn from Them?', Viima.com, 20 Nov. 2016, https://www.viima.com/blog/16-examples-of-open-innovation-what-can-we-learn-from-them (accessed 8 Sept. 2023).

NobelPrize.org (2006). 'Grameen Bank—Facts', https://www.nobelprize.org/prizes/peace/2006/grameen/facts/ (accessed 26 Apr. 2023).

Plotkin, J. (2018). 'Office of Sustainability', Washington University in St Louis, https://sustainability.wustl.edu/alumni-series-marc-zornes/ (accessed 31 Jan. 2023).

Ries, E. (2011). *The Lean Start-Up: How Today's Entrepreneurs Use Continuous Innovation to Create Radically Successful Businesses*. New York: Crown Business Publishing.

Sarasvathy, S. D. (2001). 'Causation and Effectuation: Toward a Theoretical Shift from Economic Inevitability to Entrepreneurial Contingency', *Academy of Management Review*, 26(2): 243–263.

Sanusi, T. (2022). '6 Organisations Fighting to Help Women & Girls in Africa Have Better Periods', Global Citizen, https://www.globalcitizen.org/en/content/organisations-menstrual-health-periods-africa/ (accessed 9 Feb. 2023).

Shane, S., and Venkataraman, S. (2000). 'The Promise of Entrepreneurship as a Field of Research', *Academy of Management Review*, 25(1): 217–226.

Shepherd, D. A., and Patzelt, H. (2018). 'Prior Knowledge and Entrepreneurial Cognition', in *Enterpreneurial Cognition*. Cham: Palgrave Macmillan.

Simanis, E., and Duke, D. (2014). 'Profits at the Bottom of the Pyramid', *Harvard Business Review*, 92(10): 87–93.

Stubbs, W. (2017). 'Sustainable Entrepreneurship and B Corps', *Business Strategy and the Environment*, 26(3): 331–344.

Thiel, P., and Masters, B. (2014). *Zero to One: Notes on Startups, or How to Build the Future*. New York: Crown Business Publishing.

Tuchmann, R. (2022). 'How Success Happened for Stuart Landesberg, Co-Founder and CEO Of Grove Collaborative', Entrepreneur.com, 21 Mar., https://www.entrepreneur.com/leadership/how-success-happened-for-stuart-landesberg-co-founder-and/419624 (accessed 8 Sept. 2023).

United Nations Development Programme. (2014). 'Barriers and Opportunities at the Base of the Pyramid'. Retrieved from www.undp.org

United Nations Development Programme. (2015). 'Human Development Report 2015: Work for human development'. Retrieved from www.undp.org

US Department of Energy. (2014). 'History of the Electric Car'. Retrieved from www.energy.gov

Wasserman, N. (2008). *The Founder's Dilemma: Anticipating and Avoiding the Pitfalls That Can Sink a Start-Up*. Princeton University Press.

Watson, I. (2012). 'How Alan Turing Invented the Computer Age'. *Scientific American*, 26 Apr., https://

blogs.scientificamerican.com/guest-blog/how-alan-turing-invented-the-computer-age/ (accessed 12 Sept. 2023).

Watson, R., Wilson, H. N., and Macdonald, E. K. (2020). 'Business-Nonprofit Engagement in Sustainability-Oriented Innovation: What Works for Whom and Why?', *Journal of Business Research*, 119: 87–98.

World Intellectual Property Organization (WIPO). (n.d.). 'What Is intellectual property?', www.wipo.int, https://www.wipo.int/about-ip/en/#:~:text=Intellectual%20property%20(IP)%20refers%20to,and%20images%20used%20in%20commerce (accessed 12 Sept. 2023).

INDEX

Note: The following abbreviations have been used: - *b* = box; *f* = figures; *t* = table